THE COMPANION TO
WINE

Edited By
Frank Prial

with Rosemary George *and* Michael Edwards

Prentice Hall General Reference
NEW YORK   LONDON   TORONTO   SYDNEY   TOKYO   SINGAPORE

ACKNOWLEDGEMENTS

The publishers wish to thank Michael Aaron, Ron Batori, Janet Bacon, Christian de Bily, Pierre Bouard, Val Brown, Christopher Burr, Guy Burrier, Anthony Byrne, Roland de Calonne, Richard Cramp, Frances Delamain, Tim Dennison, Chris Donlay, Pierre-Jacques Druet, Barbara Edelman, Collette Faller, Pierre Ferraud, Blossom Flowers, Patricia Ford, Helen Gallo, David Gold, Martine Greslon, Anthony Hanson, Michael Hasslacher, Paul Hewitt, Bernard Hine, Honora Horan, Trevor Hughes, Pasquale Iocca, Katherine James, Christian Koehly, Jennifer Lambe, Michel Laroche, Olivier Leflaive, Antonio Lopez, Antony Mallaby, Catherine Manac'h, Jean-Bernard and Lynn Marchive, Ian McKerrica, Jeremy Platt, Rupert Ponsonby, Franco Rossi, Nicolas and Florence Rossignol, David Russell, Roger Seale, Melissa Sere, Dr. Alex Schaeffer, Nicholas Strachan, Lucia Suray, Richard Tanner, Gilles Vinet, Michael Yurch.

Special thanks goes to Bill Buckner for the special photography for The Color of Wine section, to David Langlands for his work on the Directory and for his careful checking of the text, to Riedel Crystal, to Nancy Rugus and Fiona Morrison Conover of Seagram Chateau and Estate Wines Co. and to The Wine Institute of California.

PHOTO CREDITS

Antinori (Stern Communications), 128, 139, 243 Ainsworth, Jim, 187; Austrian Wine Mktg. Service, 182, 183; Bollinger, 250, 345; Bonny Doon Vineyards, 17 bottom; Bridgeman Art Library, 1 (courtesy, British Library, London) Callaway Vineyards, 15 top; Cambria Vineyard, 12, 21 bottom; Campbell, Bob, 2-3; Chateau Carras, 192; C.I.V.A., 32(b), 102 (© P. Bonard); C.I.V.B., 30(b) (© Cronenberger photo), 30(c) (© Cronenberger photo), 32(d); Columbia Winery, Washington State, 30 (a); Comtesse de Vogüé, 298; Cousiño-Macul, 219; De Loaoh Vineyards, 22, 206; Diamond Creek Vineyards, 205; Domecq Estates, 16 bottom (photo by Studio Jean-Paul); Duboeuf, 87; Ealey, Cato, 147; Edwards, Michael, 68, 73 left, 73 right, 95, 97, 100; Equation, 65; Ferrand, Pierre, 67, 88, 98 top; Fall Creek Vineyards, 18 top, 217; Fetzer Winery, 15 bottom (© George Rose), 20, 24 bottom (© George Rose), 195; Food and Wine From France, 16 top, 42, 84, 109, 112, 117; The Forbes Magazine Collection, New York 196 top; Fulham Priory, 169; George, Rosemary, 126; German Wine Information Bureau, 25; German Wine Institute, 178; Gillette, Richard, 18-19; Grulich-Jones, Alice, 190; Heublein Fine Wine Group, 4, 8, 198 top, 198 bottom, 199, 247, 283; Hiram-Walker Allied Vintners (HK) Ltd., 12 bottom, 31 (d); Italian Trade Commission, 133; Jefford, Andrew, 165; Klein; Constantia, 236; Kobrand, NY 30(d) (Courtesy Louis Jadot); Llano Estacado Winery, 24 top, 27 bottom; Mayson, Richard, 17 top, 161, 168; Mirabel Books Ltd., 35, 36, 37, 38; Palace Brands Company, 12 bottom, 69 bottom right, 131, 135, 141, 144, 173; Palmer Vineyard, 216; Parzych, C., 81 bottom, 308; Penfold's Winery, 12 top, 223, 227; Portugese Trade Commission, N.Y, 64 (© Pascale Iocca); Prial, Frank, 346; Price, Janet, 29, 30(e), 31(a), 31(b), 31(e), 32(a), 32(c), 32(e), 32 (f), 60, 61, 63, 70, 81 top, 82, 89; Rhone-Alpes Agro-Alimentaire, 124 (© L. Frappat); Riedel's, 386; Rose, Anthony, 45, 47, 50, 52 top, 129, 151, 156; Schieffelin and Somerset Co., 21 top; Ste. Chapelle Vineyard, 212; © Saur/Visun, 10, 106; Seagram Chateau & Estate Wines Company, 5, 14 top, 44, 46, 51, 52 center, 55 top, 69 left, 160, 175; Sebastiani Vineyards, 201; Southeby's, 354; Stag's Leap Vineyard, 204; Stellenbosch Farmer's Winery, 238; Sterling Vineyards, 28 top (Faith Echtermeyer photo), 28 bottom, 39, 202; Swiss Wine Information Council, 14 bottom, 184; Taittinger, 98 bottom, 99; The Taylor Wine Co., 214; Thorn, John, 353, 355; Turner, John and Cynthia, 343; Wine Institute of California, 194 center, 200; Wine Magazine, 19 top, 23, 26, 53, 55 bottom, 57, 58, 59, 77, 78, 80, 85, 91, 92, 94, 111, 113, 121, 123, 137, 142, 145, 174, 221, 222, 224, 228, 232; Wines of Spain, 149, 153, 158; The Wine Society, 289, 291; Domaine Zind-Humbrecht, 11 top, 11 center right, 11 bottom right, 11 left, 13 bottom

Prentice Hall General Reference
15 Columbus Circle
New York, New York 10023

Copyright © 1992 by Mirabel Books Ltd.
Copyright © 1992 by Mirabel Books Ltd. Original Maps

All rights reserved,
including the right of reproduction
in whole or in part in any form.

Published simultaneously in Great Britain by W.H. Smith Ltd.
and in France by Editions Atlas

PRENTICE HALL and colophon are registered trademarks of
Simon & Schuster Inc.

Library of Congress Cataloguing-in-Publication Data

The Companion to Wine/edited by Frank Prial with
Rosemary George and Michael Edwards.

New York: Prentice Hall General Reference. 1992.
Includes index.
ISBN 0-13-155854-4
1. Wine and wine making.
I. Prial, Frank J. II. George, Rosemary, 1950- III. Edwards, Michael.
TP548.C65 1992
663 .2-dc20   92-11935
                     CIP

Conceived by Mirabel Books Ltd. Box 1214, London SW6 7ES
Photo research by Brenda Nicholls
Jacket design by Michael J. Freeland
Book design by The R & B Partnership
General editing/copyediting by Margaret Rand
Manufactured in Spain by Heraclio Fournier, S.A.

10 9 8 7 6 5 4 3 2 1

First Edition

Contents

7

Foreword

The human approach to the culture of wine is entirely different from the academic and analytical approach so prevalent today — where the emphasis is almost exclusively on oenology and viticulture.

Most of my 90 years have been devoted to grapes and wine — I can't live without them. But throughout my long career, I have always tried to be much deeper in my approach to wine, to go beyond looking at a product in a bottle, trying instead to see wine in a greater context of love and friendship.

The history of wine in America is the history of the efforts of many: the legion of men and women who have brought wine to the high level of quality we enjoy today. I have seen many developments in my 60 years in the wine industry — the selection of microclimates for the planting of grapes, the cold fermentation of white wine, the control of malolactic fermentation in red wines and many, many others.

But with all the technological advances in wine, we must never lose sight of the human aspect. What I enjoy in this all-encompassing but eminently readable book is the balance it achieves between the practical and the humanistic dimensions of wine. *The Companion to Wine,* just as I have always tried to do, celebrates the human aspect of wine, seeing it as a symbol of civilisation — simple, moral civilisation.

What I often find lacking in modern society, particularly in its attitude towards life's more mundane pleasures, is simplicity, the European approach, for example, to taking wine with food, to seeing these two things as an uncomplicated celebration of life. It's not just by accident that there is a strong bond between wine and religion, where it symbolizes a rejuvenation of the feelings of the heart.

The Companion to Wine expresses my deep personal belief in the historical value of wine as an expression of nature. It is not another book by critics, it is a book by people who know and love wine. It is a book that celebrates wine, hence a book that celebrates life.

André Tchelistcheff

How to Use the Book

One of the central assumptions behind the concept and organization of this book was that a team of internationally known contributors, expert in their particular field, could provide a more authoritative guide to wine in all its aspects than a single writer, however eminent. It was also felt that the authority of the book could be further enhanced by contributions both from working wine writers and from those experts actually involved in the production, selling and recommending of wine as their professional calling. Both categories of expert make up the team writing this book, providing sometimes different, but always complementary viewpoints.

The content and structure of most of the chapters in the book should be self-evident, but certain chapters require explanation.

In the section entitled The Wine Regions of the World, the organization is by country. The geographical coverage is as broad as possible, reflecting the growing interest in and importance of the wines of the New World besides those of traditional production areas in Europe. The defining characteristics, the style and significance of winemaking, recommendations of particular wines and growers and an indication of future trends are all explained and discussed. For more information on wines, growers and grape types the reader should refer to the directory located on pages 241-336.

Grower's Views

For every wine region, one or more Grower's Views are included. These "views" are a unique feature of this book — the first time that the opinions of the people actually producing wine have been articulated. The "views" are intended to supplement the main text, providing a personal, local viewpoint.

Wine Labels

How to read a wine label in the principal wine regions is explained in "The Appreciation of Wine" chapter on pages 33-34. In addition among the illustrations for each wine region are included selections of representative labels with a commentary explaining their significance. In this way, it is hoped that readers will understand much more about wine labels than can be gleaned from most wine books, where the labels are often just decorative.

Maps

Every wine-producing area is illustrated by specially commissioned maps, highlighting points of wine interest — vineyards, certain châteaux or wineries — particularly those mentioned in the main text and geographical features such as principal rivers relevant to the production of wine. These maps are not intended to provide a complete topography of any of the regions described. However, they should provide sufficient information to assist the reader, whether he or she is a visitor to the region or simply an armchair enthusiast.

Measurements

Throughout the book, both metric and Imperial measurements are provided and we have used the following conversion for hectares to acres: 1 hectare = approximately 2.47 acres.

Spirits

There is some discussion of spirits in the book. Only grape and fruit-based spirits are mentioned.

Wine Classification Systems

There are references to the wine classification systems used in wine regions of the world both in the main text, the directory and the appendices. This information was as accurate as could be at the time the book went to press. However, in certain regions, such as Italy and Eastern Europe, the data is changing.

Directory

Alphabetically organized, this section provides a selective gazeteer of wines, technical wine terms, grape types and certain wine growers throughout the world. The wine profiles in the directory, nominated by the expert contributors, supplement and expand on wines described in the main text and are intended to provide a guide to the character and quality of certain wines the reader may encounter and about which he or she would like to know more. There is no attempt to be comprehensive in the number of wines chosen. The selection of wines is based on what is considered to be of interest and importance and represents a good cross-section of wines of the world.

As for the technical terms and entries on grape varieties, the intention here is to provide as wide a coverage as is possible.

The profiles of a selected group of growers are based on a personal choice of people who are currently considered to be wine makers of importance and promise.

The Quality of Wine
by Olivier Humbrecht, M.W.

Wine is a natural product and winemaking, in its most simplified form, is essentially a straight – forward process. A vine will grow by itself in most terrains; crush the grapes and the yeasts already present on the outside of the skins will get to work on the juice. The total process needs minimal intervention, provided that the drinker is not too demanding.

For centuries, though, people have looked for quality, and both growing vines and making wines have long been highly skilled tasks. Modern science has made them more specialized than ever, and with a greater understanding of both viticulture and vinification, the average quality of wine in the shops has never been better. But to make it better, one must start at the very beginning, with the *terroir*. This can be defined as the combination of soil, climate and aspect affecting any given vineyard.

In the New World regions of California, Australia, New Zealand and South Africa, scientists have long stressed the importance of climate, rather than soil, in the making of wine; in Europe the reverse has been the case. This difference of approach reflects differing natural conditions in vineyards around the world. In France, for example, as much as half the rainfall occurs during the growing season but it is usually spread evenly throughout the season. In Australia, by contrast, rainfall during the all-important spring and summer months is often inadequate to nourish the vine, leading to a lack of moisture, producing grapes that are low in acid and chemically out of balance. This preoccupation with the climatic challenges leads winemakers in the New World to downplay the importance of soil as a factor in the quality of wine. But during the 1980s, growers, notably in California, came to understand that soil really does matter. "Wine begins in the vineyard" became the slogan of the decade, which is another way of saying that it is essential to grow the right sort of grape in the right sort of soil.

Soil

All soil is a mixture of minerals and organic matter, and the particles that form soil are of different sizes. The largest are the stones and small gravel; fine sand is smaller; silt is composed of particles that are smaller still, and clay has the smallest particles of all: if the particles are less than .000002 millimeters in diameter the soil will be clay. The higher the clay content of a soil the richer it will be; soil composed of a high percentage of bigger particles will be described as poor, and will have better drainage.

The size of the particles determines the texture of the soil; what is described as the structure of the soil is the molecular structure. Looked at through a microscope, the compounds that make up soil have different structures, and each is formed in its own particular way, like crystals or snowflakes.

How water behaves in soil is also part of the story, since the smaller the particles in the soil, the more it will retain water — but at the same time, the more difficult it will be for a vine to find and use that water. Soil with a lot of very small particles in it — clay — absorbs the water and keeps it, like a sponge. Conversely, stony soil drains faster, but any water that is left is more easily available to plants. Granite or volcanic soils, both high in stones and sand, enable plant roots to reach quickly what water there is; clay may contain more water, but the roots may not be able to reach it.

BELOW: A vineyard in the foothills of the Vosges, a wine region with some of the oldest soil in Europe. It is similar in its constituents of granite and volcanic rock to the soil of the wine regions of California and Oregon.

Then there is the climate of the soil. The growth of leaves and shoots is related to the temperature of the roots, not the air temperature, so a soil that is able to warm up quickly offers the vine a better chance of growth than a cold soil. And the coarser the texture of the soil, the warmer it will be.

This is again to do with drainage. Cold soils are those that retain water, so that the warm air cannot penetrate. Vineyards with cold soils, like the clay/limestone of Burgundy, warm up very slowly compared to the granite of Beaujolais or the gravel of Bordeaux. Cold, rich, heavy soils therefore tend to be late ripening sites, whereas warm, poor, gravelly soils are early-ripening.

In all these respects, the grape should suit the soil. Cabernet Sauvignon, for example, does not ripen well in the Loire Valley, but does so very successfully in Bordeaux, California and Australia. It likes regions that have a lot of sunshine but are not too hot, and it needs a poor, gravelly soil. Pinot Noir is the opposite: it is a much earlier-ripening grape that can be planted in quite cool climates like those of Burgundy and Alsace, Germany, Oregon, New Zealand and the cooler parts of South Africa. It likes slightly richer soils like limestone that retain more water and are a little cooler.

The pH, too, is a vital indicator when it comes to picking a grape variety for a particular soil. The pH scale is a measure of acidity and alkalinity, with readings below seven descending to increasing levels of acidity, and readings above seven rising to ever higher levels of alkalinity. Alkaline soils, generally speaking, are young soils, those which were at one stage covered by sea. As the land rose and the sea receded, the shells of molluscs and crustaceans and the skeletons of fish were left behind; and all contain calcium, which is the essential constituent of alkaline soils.

These soils are widespread in Europe. But the New World tends to have very old soils — Australia, for example, is a very old continent. The soils there

LEFT: Clay/limestone, a cold soil, is the principal soil of Burgundy.

LEFT: Gravel soil particularly suits the Cabernet Sauvignon grape, notably in Bordeaux, Australia and California.

LEFT: Granite soil showing the shells of molluscs and crustaceans.

have very little calcium and are more or less neutral, with a pH of around seven.

Soils with a pH of above seven are calcareous, or limestone/chalk soils. They are often planted with Pinot Noir, Chardonnay, Gewürztraminer, Pinot Gris and Pinot Blanc — the sort of grapes often found in northern Europe. Merlot, too, is grown on the limestone chalk St. Emilion plateau; Champagne is chalk and the *tuffe* soil of Chinon and Bourgueil in the Loire Valley, ideal for Cabernet Franc, is also chalky. Elsewhere in Touraine, on more acidic soils, Gamay is grown.

Some of the oldest soils in Europe are in Alsace, in the foothills of the Vosges mountains. There are granite and volcanic rocks here, similar to those in California and Oregon. South Australia's Coonawarra region has its famous *terra rossa* soil, a very old laterite soil that is essentially clay compressed until it resembles red brick. (Coonawarra is a good example of a New World wine region that is distinguished from its surroundings principally by its soil.) Old rocky soils usually have a low pH, and granite, especially, can be acidic. Delicate Riesling from Alsace and Viognier from the northern Rhône are examples, but granite is also ideal for great Syrah, robust and long lived, from the slopes of Hermitage and Côte Rôtie.

LEFT: The famous *terra rossa* soil of Coonawarra wine district in south Australia. This old laterite soil is clay compressed to such a degree that it assumes this brick red color.

The youngest soils of all are often alluvial, like the gravel soils of Bordeaux. In Bordeaux, though, the soil is very deep, so Cabernet Sauvignon and Cabernet Franc both flourish. But the soils of California's Napa Valley, also a mixture of gravel and alluvial deposits, are much older and more acid than those of Bordeaux.

Italy's Barolo region gives a graphic example of the effect of soil on the quality of wine. The soil in Barolo is tremendously rich clay, and quite young. The climate of the region is warm and sunny, and the Nebbiolo is an early-ripening grape here. In Alsace or Champagne it would not succeed, but here the soil retains a lot of water and thus enables the vine to withstand drought. The wines, as a result, are well balanced, because although planted in a hot southern country, the high altitude and cold soil enable them to retain good acidity — a good example of juggling grape variety, soil and climate to produce the whole.

Cold soils produce more acidic wines because it is heat that burns up acidity; a cold soil can thus compensate for a hot sun. Contrarily, a very poor soil with a low pH will produce less acidic wines because more acidity will be burnt off. The rockier the slopes, the greater the reduction in acidity — a factor which helps enormously the wines of northern areas like Germany, Canada or the Finger Lakes of the U.S.A.

Friuli in Italy offers very different opportunities to the winegrower. Here it is possible to cultivate just about any grape variety from Cabernet for red to Tocai for whites. The reason is that the land for the most part is flat and the soil is young, gravelly silt from the mountains, rich with good drainage.

In Spain, climate and altitude combine to produce the best wines. In France, some of the best vineyards are at sea level; in Spain they might be 200 or 300 meters/650 to or 980 feet above, or even more in the case of Rioja.

In China the loess soil is the key. The People's Republic is still a beginner in the winegrowing stakes, but all its vineyards are planted on loess, the same

ABOVE: Alluvial soil under the Cambria vineyard in the Santa Maria Valley, California. The soil here tends to be older and more acidic than the alluvial soil of Bordeaux.

RIGHT: The vineyards in Friuli, in the northeast of Italy, whose soil and terrain enable a wide range of grapes to be cultivated.

soil as is found on the plains of Alsace. Composed of windblown soil from mountains or high plateaux, it is found, in China, on the terraces bordering the main rivers like the Huang Ho and the Yangtse Kiang, all of which are being studied by the vineyard planners. It is rich, humid soil with a lot of clay and a lot of organic matter, and should prove suitable for many grape varieties; the climate will be the determining factor in deciding what to plant.

The climate is usually the crucial factor, too, when the soil is straightforwardly gravelly. This is perhaps why climate is given the greatest importance in California. For example, it was the climate that led Pinot Noir to be planted in cool Carneros rather than in torrid Calistoga, where Syrah, Merlot and Cabernet do well. The soil is suitable for most varieties; and it is fair to say that 99 percent of vineyards in Australia, California and Oregon rely mostly on their aspect, climate and rainfall pattern for their quality.

In Europe, as we have seen, soil is the more vital factor. There are no major climatic differences, for example, between St. Emilion and Pauillac, but the soil is certainly different. Or between St. Emilion and Pomerol: the soil in one is suitable for Merlot, and that in the other for Cabernet Franc, but they are only a few miles apart. Condrieu and Côte Rôtie are another example; or Puligny Montrachet and Volnay. In the former the vineyards are mostly Chardonnay, on rocky soil that stresses the fertile Chardonnay vine; in the latter they are Pinot Noir, on richer soil better suited to this fertile grape variety.

The actual mineral content of a soil is less important in deciding on a grape variety, because mineral deficiencies can be corrected, but subsoils are certainly important. The further the vine has to put down roots in order to find nutrients, the better the wine is likely to be, and the less in quantity. In a very rich topsoil the vine will not need to work this hard, and the yields are likely to be higher, and the quality poorer, as a result. Too much irrigation can produce the same result.

Left: A cut in the soil in a vineyard in Alsace showing the roots of the vine pushing deep into the soil. The deeper the roots go the better the quality of wine tends to be.

Before deciding on the ideal combination of vine variety and rootstock for a particular vineyard, the grower must know his soil. Previous experience of that vineyard is obviously invaluable, but a soil analysis will reveal still more.

With samples taken at different depths, a precise soil analysis will indicate the texture of the soil, the pH, the chlorosis indicator, the amount of organic matter present and the other elements and compounds available to the vine.

There is no perfect result. The optimum balance (because excess can be as dangerous to the vine as deficiency) will vary from one soil to another, and will depend on the weather, and what levels of yield the grower wants.

Minerals and organic fertilizers can then be added to the soil as needed.

BELOW: A vineyard in Germany being fertilized using modern equipment.

RIGHT: At an altitude of 1200 meters these terraced vineyards in the Valais in Switzerland are among the highest in Europe. Mountains can provide a complicating factor in the classification of vineyards into climatic zones.

Climate

If the soil is vital for the development of the vine, it is climate that has more to do with the ripening of the grapes. However perfect the soil, grapes will not ripen everywhere: there are latitudes beyond which *Vitis vinifera* grapes cannot ripen.

In cool climates the temperature of the soil and its ability to retain the heat of the sun are crucial. The darker the soil and the rockier the vineyard, the warmer the soil will be, which obviously helps the vine. The roots will grow better in warm soil, and in some areas this is just as important as having the right concentration of minerals in the soil; in Alsace, for example, the quality of the wine depends very largely on the heat retention of the soil.

Classifying vineyards into neat climatic zones is tempting, but it is a complex task. It involves much more than simply recording sunshine, wind, cloud, rainfall and its rate of evaporation. Factors like mountains can complicate the classification of a region. An elevation of 1,000 meters/3,300 feet is equivalent to 1,000 meters/1,100 yards along a meridian, in climate terms, and a rise in altitude of 100 meters/330 feet will reduce the average temperature by .5°C/1°F.

Differences in climate caused by such factors are best looked at in terms of the macro-, meso- and microclimates. The macroclimate is the climate of quite a large area; if the terrain varies very much — is very hilly, for example — then information about the macroclimate must necessarily be imprecise. For example, to say that the average day temperature in the Adelaide region of South Australia is 25°C/77°F means little in itself, since on the slopes it may be 21°C/70°F, and 29°C/84°F on the valley floor. It is more of use to look at the mesoclimate, which is the climate of a much smaller area — a specific vineyard, perhaps, or any parcel of land of similar contours and aspect, up to about 50 hectares/124 acres in size. Much more detailed information can be gained here. The microclimate is smaller still. It may apply to an area of 100 square meters/120 square yards, or even less; it may even refer to the differing conditions experienced by a grape close to the soil, compared to those found higher up the same vine; it allows for minute detail.

In temperate regions the mesoclimate can change quite drastically within small areas. Differences of slope, orientation, exposure to sun and wind and susceptibility to frost may vary considerably between one part of a hillside and another, and will explain, at least in part, why some are planted with vines while others are not.

The amount and intensity of sunshine is obviously crucial in viticulture, and is influenced by such factors as cloud cover, altitude and the angle of the sun. Long hours of sunshine, in places like Canada, Oregon, Washington State, northern France, Germany and Tasmania can also make up for its lesser intensity.

Climate also affects the complex process of photosynthesis, by which the plant absorbs and uses energy. Leaves at the center of a dense canopy will receive too little sunlight for efficient photosynthesis, so in cool climates vines are trained to expose their leaves to the sun, and pruned in summer to prevent leaves throwing other leaves into shade. The

ABOVE: The Rainbow Gap in southern California provides a unique and dramatic microclimate favoring the vineyards of Callaway and eleven other producers in the immediate area. As the desert air warms up behind the mountain range, cool air is created that pulls through the Gap off the ocean 23 miles away and creates at night a cooling effect on the vines.

LEFT: Good irrigation is an important factor in successful wine production in this hot region of central California.

RIGHT: Heaters are used in these vineyards in Burgundy to protect the vines from frost.

BELOW: Grapes ready to be picked for Eiswein. The grapes are pressed before they thaw to produce a wine that is a particular speciality of some German and Austrian wine growers.

temperature and the availability of water also affect photosynthesis, and the balance between them determines the level of activity of the vine. Thus in drought conditions, even though there is plenty of sunshine, the grapes will not ripen properly. Irrigate those same drought-ridden grapes and they will ripen, though intense heat may mean that in spite of high sugar levels, they lack aroma. Conditions of this sort, as well as those of soil, play a part in the choice of rootstock and grape variety to be planted in a specific site.

Only extremes of heat and cold can prevent the cultivation of *Vitis vinifera*. In more normal conditions it is always possible to find a variety that will cope with the soil and climate, though freezing conditions, generally below -20°C/-4°F in winter and -2° or -3°C/28° or 27°F in spring, will always present a serious threat. Some areas, where heavy, cold air can be trapped between hills, are particularly susceptible to frost damage: Chablis and the floor of the Napa Valley are examples. There are various methods that growers can use to protect their vines against frosts, which do most damage in the spring after the sap has begun to rise: wind machines, burning charcoal to produce smoke, or spraying vines with water to give a protective coating of ice to the buds to shield them against still lower temperatures, are all commonly used. Helicopters, too, have been tried, with the idea of creating air movement, but the results have not always been successful. And of course these methods rely on growers being able to predict sudden falls in temperature. Fall frosts, too, can damage the vines, and reduce the quality of wine if the grapes should freeze. In eastern Washington State, for example, frosts of -20°C/-4°F are not uncommon in October — conditions that would be welcomed in Germany and elsewhere by producers of Eiswein. For Eiswein, grapes are picked while still frozen, often at dawn, and are pressed before they thaw. The non-water components of the grapes, the sugars and acids, do not freeze as easily as water and thus emerge from the press in a very concentrated form.

If there are minimum temperatures that the vine can survive, there are also minimum temperatures below which the vine will not grow and develop. These minimum temperatures vary according to the grape variety, with the hardy Riesling and Gewürztraminer needing at least 8°C/46°F, the Merlot 10°C/50°F and the Ugni Blanc 11°C/52°F. For convenience, a minimum of 10°C/50°F is assumed to be necessary for all vine types. The total number of hours during the growing season when the temperature rises above this minimum is the heat summation of an area. Totting up the heat summation of a region gives a good idea of its viticultural potential, and allows useful comparisons to be made with other parts of the world, though as we have already seen, soil affects the equation differently in Europe and the New World.

Under the degree day system of Professor Winkler of the University of California, Davis, California is divided into five regions, with 1 being the coolest and 5 the hottest. When confined to California the calculation is both simple and accurate, but if applied to the wider world it shows certain inadequacies. No account is taken of variations in daylight hours and the differing dates of harvesting dictated by prevailing temperatures, for example. Nevertheless, the following comparisons can be interesting:

Region 1: Anderson Valley and Bay Area, California; Oregon; Geisenheim; Geneva; Burgundy; Alsace; Vienna; Bordeaux; Coonawarra, Australia.

Region 2: Napa, Sonoma and Santa Barbara, California; Washington State; Odessa; Budapest; Santiago, Chile.

Region 3: Calistoga, California; Montpellier; Milan.

Region 4: Sacramento, California; Venice; Cape Province, South Africa.

Region 5: Fresno and Modesto, California; Sicily; Algeria.

At first sight these groupings may seem improbable, but it is instructive to look at the degree-day values on their own. In Region 1, for example, Geisenheim stands at 995, Newberg, Oregon at 1,050, Coonawarra at 1,205 and Bordeaux at 1,328. Other systems exist which incorporate the duration of daylight and rainfall.

The more, and the hotter the sunshine, the greater the sugar levels in grapes. Acids, too, are affected by temperature: malic acid tends to fall in high temperatures, while tartaric acid remains stable. In very hot areas vines can be trained to protect the grapes from too much heat; this way they avoid both sunburn and too much loss of acidity. The phenolic components of the grape are also sensitive to temperature, and in very cool or very hot climates it is difficult to obtain grapes of the ideal color. Some varieties, like Cabernet Sauvignon, seem to be less affected by such considerations. It is more difficult to quantify the effects of heat on the flavor of a wine, but it does seem that aroma is reduced by very hot sunshine. Aromatic varieties like Riesling, Pinot Noir, Sauvignon Blanc and Gewürztraminer tend to be planted in cooler areas where they will not be affected in this way.

The Vine

The grape vine is a member of the *Ampelidaceae* botanical family which includes such plants as Virginia Creeper. Yet only the genus *Vitis* and the species *vinifera* produce consistently fine wines of interest to the consumer. According to Pascal Ribéreau-Gayon, the thousands of varieties included in *Vitis vinifera*, the classic European vine, have been reduced to 250, of which about 100 are economically viable. For all practical purposes, the truly great wines of the world are made from a much more limited range of noble grape varieties. The outstanding ones are Cabernet Sauvignon, Pinot Noir, Chardonnay and Riesling, with Syrah, Nebbiolo, Sémillon and Sauvignon Blanc all internationally important.

The conditions of soil and climate and the treatment of the vine are crucial factors in the quality of wine. The vine's yield can be significantly increased by fertilizers, the choice of rootstocks and clones, and the method of pruning. But great wine cannot be made from a vine grown in unsuitable conditions.

The biological cycle of the vine is similar in essence throughout the world, although its place in the calendar is dictated by climatic variations in areas where there are extremes of temperature. Thus in the northeast United States, with long and severe winters, the vine will produce its new growth rather later than in milder zones and its grapes often have difficulty in ripening fully at harvest time. Another example is the Mosel-Saar-Ruwer region of northern Germany. There the best wines are made from grapes left on the vine until late October and early November in order that the grapes may gain extra sugar.

The strains of *Vitis vinifera* are almost infinitely adaptable, but regardless of the nature of the individual vine, great wine can only be made where its grapes are able to ripen fully. This is illustrated in the Burgundy region of France, where in Chablis, despite the coldness of the winter and the ever-present danger of spring frost, the Chardonnay grape is able to produce some of the greatest white wines in the world.

The cycle of the vine in a Chablis vineyard: The first shoots in Chablis appear on the vine around the 15 April, and statistically there's always a risk of

ABOVE: In Portugal, Vinho Verde grapes are trained to grow on trellises in order that the leaves of the plant can protect the grapes from the heat.

BELOW: Young and experimental vines being cultivated in the greenhouse at Bonny Doon Vineyards in California, a producer known for its unusual grape varieties.

ABOVE: The new tender arm growths of the vines are tied to trellises with wire to train their growth and to protect them from wind damage at Fall Creek Vineyards in Texas.

Ripeness and Acidity

In the northerly wine-producing areas of France — Burgundy and the Central Loire are good examples — there is reckoned to be a 100-day period between the flowering of the vine and the harvest. There is much less variation in the cycle of the vine elsewhere in the world than one might think. Take Chardonnay.

In a hot area, like the Central Valley of California or the Robertson district of South Africa, the Chardonnay's cycle may be reduced to eighty-two or eighty-three days but not fewer, while in cold regions like Chablis and Champagne, the cycle won't be longer than 102 or 103 days — the cycle is consistent and there is little regional variation. The main difference is that in northern regions, in a cold year the grapes will be short of sugar, and the vine will not have had enough sunshine. Conversely in hot areas the problem is an almost total lack of acidity. Australian, and Californian wines may have just as great an imbalance, but it's an entirely opposite one.

A couple of years ago, a merchant and grower in Burgundy was shocked and horrified when he compared notes with an Australian enologist. The Australian told him that he harvested at night and only at night because by day it was far too hot, and he obtained acidity of the order of just 2 grams of acidity per liter in his Chardonnay. Compare this with the ideal 3.8 - 4.2 grams recommended for a good Chablis. The Burgundian, a widely travelled and open-minded man, was of the opinion that his Australian colleague could only make decent Chardonnay by adding tartaric acid; he would have no problem with the sugar content as the wine would have at least 12.5 percent alcohol for sure, but effectively no acidity at all.

Above 20°C/68°F malic acid will diminish, and above 30°C/86°F tartaric acid will decline. In hot regions like Australia's Hunter Valley or part of South Africa's Cape, where a vine is exposed to temperatures as high as 35°C/95°F, malic acid will be eliminated entirely and tartaric acid mostly disappear. Thus the harvested Chardonnay grape may be quite lacking in acidity.

frost then, for five or six nights on average: the more advanced the new growth, the greater the risk of damage. The frost-risk period lasts until about 15 May; by that date, the risk is 90 percent eliminated. In the critical period 15 April to 15 May, Michel Laroche of Domaine Laroche says that he never leaves Chablis.

What work is going on at this time? By 15 May, the shoots will be as long as 20-25 centimeters/8-9 inches. In the less protected parcels, vines are attached to wires to make the branches grow vertically. The heavy work in the vineyard is from 15 May to 15 August. The main preoccupation is the training of the vine to confine and control its growth. One can almost see the vine growing in June and July; if left to itself it will grow as long as 3 or 4 meters/10 or 11.5 feet in two months, which means there's nonstop work throughout the summer to restrict this very abundant growth. Of course, in warmer countries like Australia and California, the foliage may be left on the vine to protect the grapes from sunburn.

At this time, the vines are sprayed with copper sulphate — and there must be constant vigilance to control mildew and oidium. Next are the further treatments necessary to protect the vine, particularly against the *ver de la grappe*, a caterpillar which damages the grapes. Once the berries have been attacked by the caterpillar, rot follows inevitably. In Chablis, these treatments have been refined in recent years — where formerly a sort of blanket treatment took place, now gradually a more ecologically balanced program is evolving, with, for

example, moth traps among the vines. Since 1991, other trials in experimental parcels have been started.

Lots of enemies of the vine: exist. Already mentioned, oidium and mildew are the principal ailments of the vine; if it is not treated against these, the vine will eventually produce nothing. These are the main problems. Phylloxera, although endemic in most of Europe, has not been a major problem for many years, since nearly all vines are grafted on to resistant American rootstock. However, not all rootstocks are equally resistant and in California a recurrence of phylloxera has been permitted by the use of insufficiently resistant rootstock.

A fungal disease, eutypiose, that has recently spread to vines, has as yet no cure, but may not prove too serious a threat. Weather can be a greater danger, with the threat of frost damage. Successful flowering too is critical. It's much less spectacular and so less talked about: while a few hours of frost can wipe out the crop, days of rain and cold in June when the vines are in flower can mean that only 25 percent of them are fertilized successfully.

After 15 August the heavy work is complete, and' the *vigneron* can take two or three weeks off before preparing for the harvest. This usually begins in Chablis at the end of September and finishes towards 15 October. There is work in the *cuverie* making the wine until the end of October.

The cycle of the vine begins again at the start of November. Most of the wood is pruned then, though the secondary branches are not cut. This

work is left until the end of March or the beginning of April. If the branches are cut too soon, precocious growth is stimulated, and this will be more liable to frost damage. In warmer wine-growing countries, pruning obviously takes place earlier.

In terms of the division of labor, 1 hectare/2.47 acres of vines requires roughly 600 hours of manual work every year, excluding the work at vintage time. Of this total, 200 hours are devoted to the pruning of the vine between 1 November and 15 April. The remaining 400 hours are concentrated into the busy summer period from 15 May to 15 August.

ABOVE: The vines are sprayed to protect them from disease in Coonawarra, South Australia.

LEFT: There are many labor-intensive tasks in the vineyard apart from the work involved in the harvest. Pruning, an important step in the cycle of the vineyard, is one of these.

ABOVE: A mechanical harvester in action. There are some wine makers who doubt the efficacy of this machine, feeling it can be inimical to quality wine production.

Mechanical Harvesters

When the grapes are in perfect condition, a harvesting machine is not necessarily a bad idea, but its use requires care. With a machine as many as half the grapes may be broken, and will lose their juice, so that what is brought to the press will be both grapes and juice. This allows skin-contact maceration for a couple of hours — the average time taken for harvesting, transport and pressing. Some acidity is lost by using the machine because of this damage and delay. When winemakers are aiming for high quality, and especially when there has been rot and it is necessary to sort the grapes, then the machine is the wrong tool; it cannot make the necessary selection. The important thing in winemaking is not to produce volume, but quality, and that seems to meet consumer demand, too.

Vinification

Throughout the seventies and much of the eighties, the skills of the winemaker seemed all important both in Europe and the New World, and viticulture was given less attention. Happily, in recent years, there has been a growing realization that great wine is made in the vineyard.

Twenty-five years ago, clonal selection of wines was introduced to provide heavier yields and a better income for wine growers. This led to abuses and a corresponding drop in quality. Now the watchword is sensibly restricted yields with more rigorous selections of the right rootstocks. Micro-vinification in retorts of 1 liter/2.1 U.S. pints capacity allows one virtually to identify individual rootstocks, and even to pinpoint an individual vine that can produce a degree more alcohol than its neighbor within the same parcel. Wine growers in the classic regions of France have turned full circle and are going back to rootstocks chosen for quality.

Problems remain. Leading Chablis growers say, for instance, that during the last twenty-five years the generality of Chablis wines have lost 10 percent of their acidity. That is bad news, for acidity is vital to Chablis. The cause, in part, seems to be the excessive use of fertilizers in the vineyard. Too much potassium has been used, and potassium becomes concentrated largely in the skin of the grape. When liberated, it precipitates tartaric acid and thus causes the total acidity of the must to fall.

Ironically, the development of modern grape reception bays during the last twenty-five years has also contributed to a loss of aromas in wine. The grapes are brought in on trailers to the winery. Pumps, agitation of the grapes, high pressure in the piping; all these handling processes diminish the richness and complexity of the wine. Some cellars prefer to move grapes and must about by gravity only, and keep handling of the grapes to a minimum.

White Wine Vinification

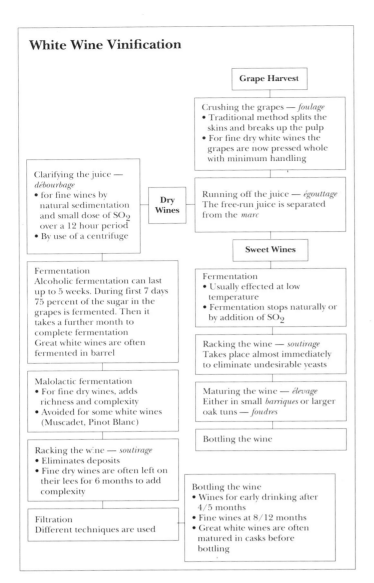

Grape Harvest

Crushing the grapes — *foulage*
- Traditional method splits the skins and breaks up the pulp
- For fine dry white wines the grapes are now pressed whole with minimum handling

Clarifying the juice — *débourbage*
- for fine wines by natural sedimentation and small dose of SO₂ over a 12 hour period
- By use of a centrifuge

Dry Wines

Running off the juice — *égouttage*
The free-run juice is separated from the *marc*

Sweet Wines

Fermentation
Alcoholic fermentation can last up to 5 weeks. During first 7 days 75 percent of the sugar in the grapes is fermented. Then it takes a further month to complete fermentation
Great white wines are often fermented in barrel

Fermentation
- Usually effected at low temperature
- Fermentation stops naturally or by addition of SO₂

Malolactic fermentation
- For fine dry wines, adds richness and complexity
- Avoided for some white wines (Muscadet, Pinot Blanc)

Racking the wine — *soutirage*
Takes place almost immediately to eliminate undesirable yeasts

Maturing the wine — *élevage*
Either in small *barriques* or larger oak tuns — *foudres*

Racking the wine — *soutirage*
- Eliminates deposits
- Fine dry wines are often left on their lees for 6 months to add complexity

Bottling the wine

Filtration
Different techniques are used

Bottling the wine
- Wines for early drinking after 4/5 months
- Fine wines at 8/12 months
- Great white wines are often matured in casks before bottling

For white wines, the vinification cycle begins with the pressing of the grapes that are, if possible, un-bruised and intact. It should be done with the minimum of handling. Traditionally, the grapes are de-stalked and then crushed; but pneumatic presses that gently squeeze the grapes rather than crush them are likely to become more common throughout the nineties. With the addition of a little sulfur dioxide (SO₂), perhaps 25-35 milligrams per liter/.79-1.1 grains per U.S. pint, the must is then allowed to clear itself naturally through precipitation over a twelve hour period. The residue is treated separately and filtered so that no large particles are retained; these heavier elements produce coarse, gross aromas and militate against finesse. It is essential to ferment clear juice without going to extremes: over-refined juice produces wines with less aroma.

The juice then undergoes its alcoholic fermentation in stainless steel or glass-lined vats or in wooden casks. In recent years, makers of white Burgundies and indeed the best Chardonnays of the New World have been experimenting with an intermediate technique. Fermentation begins in temperature-controlled vats at about 15°-19°C/59°-66°F for the first seven days, during which 75 percent of the sugar is fermented. Then the wine is put into casks of 225-500 liter/66-132 U.S. gallons capacity to finish the fermentation which takes another month. Many winemakers feel that when the wine is partially fermented in cask, the character of the wood is more harmonious and better integrated. The disadvantage of fermenting wholly in cask is that it is much more difficult to control the temperature, hence the preliminary use of modern vats for the

first week, although in small casks the temperature seldom rises high enough to be a problem. Léonard Humbrecht in Alsace has perfected a system of temperature-controlled fermentation in the traditional large oak *foudres*, a technique he created after a visit to Australia.

By the end of November (or May in the southern hemisphere) the alcoholic fermentation is over. In certain white wines the malolactic fermentation — which converts the hard malic acid into the softer lactic acid — is avoided. For wines like Muscadet or Alsace Pinot Blanc, whose freshness is their charm, the "malo" would make them flaccid and lifeless. But for more complex Chardonnays, be they from Meursault, Carneros or even Chablis, the malolactic

ABOVE: The pressing of Pinot Noir grapes at Moet et Chandon. There is a need for high-quality grapes in top condition and for care in pressing, in order to maintain the standards of excellence for which *grande marque* Champagnes are renowned.

BELOW: Chardonnay grapes passing through a modern grape crusher.

RIGHT: Grapes being loaded mechanically into a high-tech stemmer and crusher in northern California for the production of red wine.

is almost universally employed. "It gives complexity and interest to the wine," says Michel Laroche. "In Chablis we need to retain acidity by taking every precaution in the vineyard and winery rather than avoid the malo." The malolactic fermentation usually ends about Christmas. High quality wines then remain on their lees for about six months, since the fine lees add greater richness to the wine.

The vinification of sweet white wines implies grapes that have high levels of sugar. Part of this sugar is converted into alcohol, but the fermentation is sometimes arrested before its natural conclusion by the addition of sulfur dioxide (SO_2) and the elimination of yeasts by racking or the use of a centrifuge. The great dessert wines of Sauternes, Vouvray, Coteaux du Layon and Alsace are very rich in alcohol (15 to 16 percent by volume) and sugar (80 to 100 grammes per liter/6 to 7.4 ounces per U.S. pint). Their concentrated flavor is achieved by noble rot or *Botrytis cinerea* (see photo on page 65)which develops on the grapes in the warm, humid conditions of early autumn.

Rosé wines, sometimes known as *vins gris*, vary in color from very pale pink to a stronger hue that more resembles a light red. Generally speaking, rosé wines are classically vinified by a light pressing of

black grapes followed by the *saignée* method. *Saignée* literally means "bled": a vat is filled with black grapes, and maceration as for a classic red wine proceeds — but just for a few hours, sufficient to ensure the desired coloring of the juice. This is then run off and vinified separately.

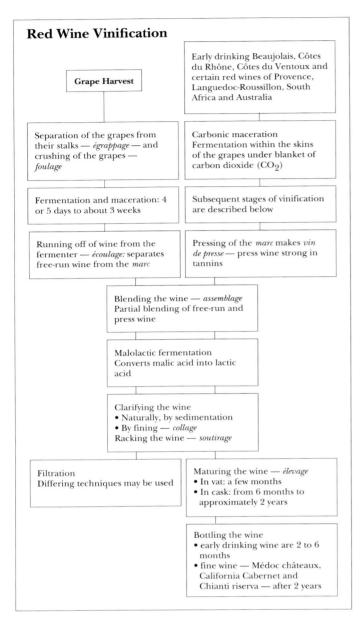

Red Wine Vinification

Grape Harvest	Early drinking Beaujolais, Côtes du Rhône, Côtes du Ventoux and certain red wines of Provence, Languedoc-Roussillon, South Africa and Australia
Separation of the grapes from their stalks — *égrappage* — and crushing of the grapes — *foulage*	Carbonic maceration Fermentation within the skins of the grapes under blanket of carbon dioxide (CO_2)
Fermentation and maceration: 4 or 5 days to about 3 weeks	Subsequent stages of vinification are described below
Running off of wine from the fermenter — *écoulage:* separates free-run wine from the *marc*	Pressing of the *marc* makes *vin de presse* — press wine strong in tannins
Blending the wine — *assemblage* Partial blending of free-run and press wine	
Malolactic fermentation Converts malic acid into lactic acid	
Clarifying the wine • Naturally, by sedimentation • By fining — *collage* Racking the wine — *soutirage*	
Filtration Differing techniques may be used	Maturing the wine — *élevage* • In vat: a few months • In cask: from 6 months to approximately 2 years
	Bottling the wine • early drinking wine are 2 to 6 months • fine wine — Médoc châteaux, California Cabernet and Chianti riserva — after 2 years

For red wines, in most cases, the grapes are first de-stalked, crushed, and everything — pulp, skins and pips — goes into the fermentation vat. By comparison with white wines, the room for maneuver in making red wines is immense. In places like Hermitage in the northern Rhône red wine can have a very long maceration of up to three weeks at temperatures as high as 30°C/86°F. The same time on the skins is allowed in a great Médoc château like Mouton-Rothschild, where by the time the alcoholic has ended, the malolactic has begun.

In Burgundy's Côte d'Or, the best domains still use fifteen-day vatting periods to extract tannin and color. The traditional Burgundian method for red wine involves fermenting in an open wooden vat, with *pigeage*, a procedure carried out by workers who submerge the "cap" of skins and pips with their feet; the technique is nowadays often achieved by compressed air. In other areas, winemakers will just use *remontage*, a pumping-over of the wine which ensures a thorough rinsing of the "cap". *Pigeage* and *remontage* will be carried out at the same rate, two or three times a day. At the same time, these processes also contribute an aeration of the must which aids fermentation at this early stage. These traditional methods produce well colored, powerful, tannic wines which age well.

There is also the Accad method, named after a contemporary Dijon enologist. This is cold maceration over a lengthy period before fermentation, which accentuates the varietal characteristics of Pinot Noir.

Of course, the inconvenience of traditional methods is that they produce high levels of tannin so that the wines cannot be drunk immediately. Carbonic maceration is used for making red wines like Beaujolais and Côtes-du-Rhône which are meant to be drunk within a few months of the vintage. Here the maceration is carried out with whole grapes, the berries are not crushed and the fermentation begins within the individual berry; this technique accentuates the fruity character of the eventual wine.

LEFT: The process of *pigeage* — the submerging of the "cap" of the skins and pips to extract all the juices and color — introduces air into the must in the open vat. This is achieved in Burgundy by workers using their feet.

ABOVE: The *remontage* or pump-over of Cabernet Sauvignon in this American vineyard is a process carried out to extract color and flavor and to moisten the skins of the grapes.

RIGHT: Barrel – fermented Pinot Noir, the great grape of Burgundy, is a rising star in parts of the New World.

There are other innovations, one of them rather risky. In the case of some *vins de primeur* there is a new technique to raise the temperature of the harvest in the vat to something like 60°C/140°F for a period of an hour or so, thus releasing all the coloring matter so that pressing can take place immediately and begin a fermentation like that of a white wine but with colored juice. This can be a dangerous exercise for if things go wrong there is a chance of losing the whole harvest.

Recently there has been a great deal of progress in determining the ideal time to mature and bottle a wine. Thirty years ago, many Burgundian growers were notorious for their ignorance of enology. They didn't know if the fermentation had ended and so tended to leave the wines a very long time in cask to be sure that there was nothing fermenting inside. Often this resulted in wines that were very oxidized and lacking in freshness and fruit; they had a character quite different from those of today. The white wines especially were often very yellow. Nowadays fermentations are allowed to run their full course, being controlled and analysed without juices being allowed to cool and without being racked to separate the wine from its lees before the fermentation has finished. This takes place around Christmas time in the northern hemisphere, after which the period of maturing the wine begins.

During the seventies and early eighties, there was a tendency to store dry white wines in sealed vats. As a result the wines were too little oxidized, and lacked air to aid their development. This was a serious fault. Through experience, quality-conscious winemakers have learned that the function of barrels is less to give a woody character than to allow some necessary oxidation. Barrel fermentation and maturation is now more widely used — but most wines are aged not entirely in new wood but in two or three year old casks, so that a white wine can remain for six to eight months and a red wine for eighteen months without acquiring too woody a taste. When the Chablis growers started using casks again in the eighties they became obsessed with the character of the wood: with hindsight, it is now clear that this attitude was a sort of caricature; wine after all must convey the character of the grapes and the

soil from which it comes. Using barrels in winemaking is like salt and pepper in cooking — without them a dish will be bland: with too much it will be a disaster.

After the fermentation process has ended, there follows a period in late winter when the sediment will settle and the wine will become clear, and time is needed for the assimilation of the primary aromas of the fermentation. A white wine when three months old can taste more like grapefruit juice than wine. A red wine, on the other hand, may resemble black currant cordial. One must wait at least until the spring to taste a wine with any claims to quality, if any clear idea is to be formed of the wine's potential. Many growers agree that the best time to bottle a white wine is about eight months after the harvest. For a red wine, eighteen months to two years after the harvest for bottling is the best timing.

ABOVE: Tasting the young wine from the barrel in a cellar in Germany. When the sediment settles the wine which now looks like grapefruit juice, will become clear.

The Appreciation of Wine

by Steven Spurrier

ABOVE: A tasting of Spanish wines in the open air among the vines. Not, perhaps, the perfect place for an analytical tasting, but just the right *al fresco* ambience to enjoy a glass.

All one needs to taste wine are the senses of sight, smell and taste, plus the faculty of memory. "Tasting" should not be thought of as an off-putting word, for the only difference between tasting and drinking is one of degree. Many professionals separate tasting wine into the categories of "analytical" tasting, assessing the wine for potential faults and qualities; and "hedonistic" tasting, drinking for pleasure. For most people, however, the difference between tasting and quaffing lies simply in paying attention.

This said, for the tasting rather than the drinking approach, there are certain guidelines to follow. These are the time of day, the place, the glass, the ambiance, your state of mind, even your state of health. Tasting, being the critical analysis of a wine or spirit, requires concentration and a mixture of involvement and detachment. Professional wine tasters prefer to taste in mid-morning, when their palates are fresh, and generally in their own tasting room or laboratory, in which they will be at ease and undisturbed.

Concentration, especially the absence of distractions, is most important. Some years ago, I was giving a tasting to a small group at L'Academie du Vin in Paris and, to prove the strength of outside influences, I had them taste a wine in the quiet of the classroom, and then the group repeated the exercise in the middle of the Place de la Concorde. The noise of the traffic, added to the fear of looking ridiculous and/or being knocked down, left the group incapable of retaining even the slightest impression.

All tasters have on and off days. The most common causes for off days when tasting wine are bad health, stress or other related troubles. Tasting is rather like skiing: once learnt, never forgotten, but more impressive and enjoyable when on form.

The tools of the trade are few: a clear, tulip-shaped glass (the International Standards Organization, or I.S.O., glass is designed just for this and is used internationally), good, clear lighting, a white background against which to check color, a notepad and a spittoon.

It is wiser to spit out when tasting, particularly if a large number of wines is under review, for the full impact of a wine can be gained without swallowing, and several swallows, however small, will result in blurred judgment. The palate, which in tasting terms includes the nose, tires very quickly, and even the most experienced tasters will pause every half a dozen wines for a sip of water, or a piece of bread.

Most tastings, professional or amateur, should be built around a theme. If I am tasting samples for purchase, I taste by region or style, seldom by color. Importers and shippers, who offer tastings to the trade, will present their wines regionally, white, rosé and red within the regions, and not by color. If they are showing only one region, the wines will be tasted by vintage. The looser the theme, wines from many different regions or grape varieties, for example, the smaller the range should be, for the taster has to assess each wine with a different set of values. Conversely, if only one style of wine is tasted, 1989 white Burgundies, for example, a much larger number can be examined without fatigue.

What is a large number? The average taster is supposed to tire after tasting ten or so wines, while Beaujolais *négociant* Georges Duboeuf will taste approximately two hundred and fifty wines a day when he is choosing his Beaujolais Nouveau. For the amateur, I would recommend tasting a maximum of twenty light, dry wines, but as few as six, if the wines are very sweet or very tannic. If a wine has a marked characteristic, such as acidity in young Rieslings, sweetness in Sauternes or tannin in Médocs, the palate will tire more easily than if the wines are less assertive.

Wines should be served in a logical order, generally young to old, light to heavy, dry to sweet, unless

they are purposefully served "blind". A blind tasting is one where the theme is disclosed, possibly down to the region or vintage, but the actual wines are not identified. A "double blind" tasting is one in which neither the identity of the wines, nor the region, nor style is disclosed.

Having set the scene, one can now pass to the action: discussing the various steps involved in actually tasting wine. Drinking wine for pleasure, to appreciate what the wine has to say, what it tastes like and perhaps why it tastes that way, is a little different from tasting in the analytical sense. Here, pleasure is not the aim: information is. The taster should enjoy the exercise, but it is an exercise nonetheless, involving three clear steps during which the wine is picked apart, and a fourth during which it is restored to a whole.

The first steps examine the color and general appearance of the wine, and its aroma or bouquet; the third step, the flavor and weight of wine in the mouth, and the fourth, and final step, the overall impression and degree of harmony. This step-by-step approach holds good as much for the absolute beginner as it does for the most experienced professional. The professional's advantage is that, as a result of experience, he can taste quicker and if necessary make a snap decision.

Given a correct wine glass, clear lighting and a white background against which to check color, the eye should pick up three things: the "disc", or surface of the wine, its color or "robe" and its viscosity, or "legs". The disc is just the top of the wine, which, when looked down on, should be clean and bright, free from all dust or solid matter.

Most wines today are cleanly, and sometimes over-cleanly bottled, so it is rare to find one that is "off" at first sight. However, if the disc is matt or murky, the wine will have a problem if one dares to taste it. The robe or color should be examined for its hue and its intensity.

These two factors change together as the wine ages and are clear indications as to its condition, quality and age. The visual impact of a wine, for pleasurable as well as analytical purposes, cannot be understated, and we have gone into this in depth on pages 35-8. As with the disc, if the wine is not clean, it is faulty: acceptable neither in a tasting room nor in a restaurant.

A wine's color should correspond to the origin and vintage of what is in the glass: pale yellow for a young Chablis, full gold for an old Sauternes; and the intensity is indicative, in principle, of quality. The lighter in color a wine is, the lighter — more delicate, even perhaps lacking in substance — will be the taste. However, color can be deceptive: a very bright wine may have been over-filtered and lack flavor; a very intense wine may result from too much *vin de presse* (juice obtained from pressing the skin and pulp left in the vat after the free-run juice has been drawn off) and be inelegant on the palate.

Color is the least exactly described of the steps in wine tasting. Remarks like "fine, intense, youthful", "light and rather washed out" are more common in tasting notes than chromographic descriptions. Yet color, being the first introduction to a wine's character, leaves the most marked impression.

The basic rule of tasting is that a wine with a good, appealing color has a better chance of tasting good than one that looks below par. As wines age, white wines and rosés take on color and become darker, a process known as "maderization"; red wines slowly lose color. This fading is evident from the rim of the disc, and the wine will finally become "oxidized".

To assess the "legs" or viscosity of a wine, the taster needs to pick up the glass, always by the stem, give it a twirl or shake and watch as the wine runs back down the sides of the glass. Once the wine is still, tears or legs will form that descend slowly. These are indicative of the richness of the wine in question, being formed by glycerols and residual sugar together with alcohol. Pronounced legs may just mean sweetness or high alcohol; their absence merely means that the wine is light. While not in

BELOW: The tasting room at Llano Estacado Winery, Lubbock, Texas. A relaxed atmosphere encourages tasting, which often leads to an eventual purchase.

RIGHT: Preparation for a tasting at Sterling Vineyards, Napa, California. The wines, arranged in "flights", await the tasters. The natural light adds an element of serenity to a studious tasting.

In simple terms, if a wine looks "off", it is off; if it smells "off" it is off. There is no point in tasting the wine at this stage, except to learn more about why it is off. Thus, in a restaurant, all the wine needs is a visual and nasal examination before accepting or rejecting it. An overbearing wine waiter will find it less easy to browbeat a client who refuses a wine on its aroma than on its flavor.

When tasting, or drinking wine for pleasure, there is almost continuous motion between admiring the color, "nosing" the wine and savoring the wine in the mouth. In an analytical tasting, there is so much information to be gained from the aroma (for a young wine) or bouquet (for a mature wine) that a taster may go back several times before he is at all satisfied.

To release the full aroma, the glass, always held by the stem, should be swirled vigorously, so that the wine rises up the sides of the glass, creating not only a vortex that pushes the aroma towards the nose, but also releasing the aroma by aeration.

The nose is then plunged into the glass and a few short sniffs should give an overall impression. The nose tires faster than the palate, so the taster should put the glass down, exhale deeply, and begin again. As color denotes the age of a wine, so will smell: young wines will retain their primary fruit aromas: blackcurrant, raspberry, strawberry, cherry for red wines, apricot, peach, sometimes banana for whites. These primary aromas refer to the fruity quality of the different grape varieties, and it is by these that varietals are most easily identified. Certain grape varieties are floral (Chardonnay, Sémillon), vegetal (Sauvignon Blanc, Cabernet Sauvignon), fruity (Cabernet Franc, Pinot Noir), spicy (Syrah), mineral (Riesling): all of these differences can be detected from those first few short sniffs of the wine.

Secondary aromas are concerned more with the transformation of wine during fermentation and aging. The presence of oak aging can be detected by vanilla aromas, even a certain toastiness, apart

themselves an indication of quality, since all fine wines have both body and substance, the presence of legs is a positive element.

The nose is the single most important organ used in assessing a wine. The sense of smell is so closely linked with the sense of taste, as anyone with a bad cold can testify, that the palate is really a confirmation of what is found on the nose, enhancing the flavors already perceived and adding the elements of weight and texture.

RIGHT: Sterling Vineyards, the tasting in action. Although the aim is comparative tasting for enlightenment rather than drinking for pleasure, the sense of expectancy and enjoyment are clearly present.

from the obvious smell of new wood, which most often is an indication that the wine is too young to drink.

A mature wine will have more complex aromas, a mixture of secondary and tertiary aromas that are referred to as "bouquet". These are less easy to recognize, less easy to describe from just the smell, and at this point the taster has more need of the palate to pinpoint the flavor, which is straightforward in a young, fruity wine, more complex in an older one.

To judge the taste of a wine requires the nose and palate to act in unison. The tongue distinguishes four basic types of flavor: sweet on the tip of the tongue, salty just behind the tip and on either side of the tongue, acid on the sides and bitter at the back. Those four flavors are modified by the sensations of temperature, weight and texture. The real flavors, the coloring of the picture and the underlining of the first impressions, will only come by rolling the wine around the tongue for a few moments, while at the same time breathing in through the mouth.

This process (which sounds acrobatic, but becomes second nature with practice) opens the retro-nasal passage and allows the nose and the palate to function as one. In order that the flavors can be fully registered and appreciated one should hold the wine in the mouth for several seconds. A distinction should be made between the first impression, or "attack", the general overall impression and the aftertaste.

The aftertaste is the summary of a wine. An inexpensive, young fruity wine will not linger very long on the palate: the pleasure is immediate, satisfying, but in tasting terms "short". A fine mature red Bordeaux should leave a clear impression that persists for several seconds before fading into memory. In tasting terms this type of lasting impression is referred to as "long".

Although length of flavor is an extremely important factor when assessing a wine, more important in fact, is the harmony and balance of a wine. A well-balanced wine, of any quality, is one that maintains a rhythm from the visual analysis, through the nose, onto the palate and in the aftertaste. Some tasters perhaps place too much importance on the aftertaste. The same tasters will probably spend longer "nosing" a wine, for although the nose gives little hint of the structure of a wine — that is the body and weight in the mouth — it fairly well describes balance.

Much has been made in recent years of the merits of different scoring systems for wines. The prestigious University of California at Davis works to a scale of twenty, which consists of specific points for specific elements in each wine. The British wine trade also tends to use a twenty-point scale, but this is less specific and not at all concerned with characteristics such as clarity or intensity of color, acidity, sugar levels, but with overall quality. A wine receiving a mark below ten is firmly below average, and the lower the mark, the more faulty the wine is. Eleven is an acceptable rating, twelve to thirteen quite good, fourteen to fifteen good, sixteen to eighteen very good and nineteen to twenty rates a wine exceptional.

Since the quality of winemaking in the world in general has improved so much technically, it is

ABOVE: Tasting in a cellar in Aloxe-Corton. The owner, Philippe Senard, tastes barrel samples with potential customers. Color, depth of fruit and structure in these young wines will determine their future.

more rare now to find wines with faults, although there are still too many wines that lack positive character. As a result, the British twenty-point scale much resembles the American one-hundred-point scale, which actually begins at fifty. The simple five-point scale is often used, or even a system of stars from one to four, with an extra star for something extraordinary.

Whatever the significance of a scoring system, it is more important to write down impressions, however brief or personal. Such tasting notes should describe in simple language what you see, smell and taste. For some years, wine tasting has been elevated to a sort of art, which is not at all what it should be. Plainly, tasters with more experience will find more in a wine and be able to describe that wine more fully than a novice: an art critic in front of a painting will have the same advantage. But that is not to say that the impression of a wine will be any stronger for the expert than for the novice. Very often the reverse is true.

The aroma and taste of wine derives most directly from the grape variety or varieties from which the wine is made. In young wines the flavor is still dominantly floral and fruity and the grape variety dominates the aroma. The grapy aroma of a Muscat, the strawberry or cherry fruit of the Pinot Noir, the blackcurranty spice of the Syrah are simple to identify and quite unmistakable.

As the wine matures, the influence of soil and climate — grouped together as *terroir* in France — emerges to a greater or lesser extent: an attractive *vin de pays* from the Merlot grape will seldom show many regional characteristics, while the soil at Château Pétrus in Pomerol overrides the grape from the very beginning.

Although the European system of controlled appellations is taking root in the New World (witness the A.V.A.s or Approved Viticultural Areas in California) more and more wines are being sold today by their grape variety, rather than their appellation (for example, Volnay) or brand (for example, Château Latour). The result is that consumers looking for specific fruit or floral aromas and flavors will find these things in varietal wines from all over the world. It is therefore important to look at the different styles of the major grape varieties.

Red Grapes

Cabernet Sauvignon ▶

The acknowledged head of the Cabernet family, this is a late-ripening grape variety, with small, very dark berries. The wines produced are deep in color, with a striking black currant aroma when young. Black currant blends with the aroma of bell peppers if the grapes come from climates warmer than their native Bordeaux. Cabernet Sauvignon has a firm, tannic-backed flavor with great depth and potential for aging. Being of a very pronounced style, Cabernet Sauvignon is planted with great success across the world. The finest examples are to be found tempered with a little Cabernet Franc and Merlot.

Cabernet Franc ▶

In principle, Cabernet Franc is a lighter variety than the Cabernet Sauvignon, but one with a ripe, aromatic fruit that is best personified in Château Cheval Blanc in Saint-Emilion. The planting of this grape represents two-thirds of the Château Cheval Blanc vineyard. The nose is more suggestive of violets or raspberries than of black currants, and except in very hot years in Touraine and Anjou, where it is planted almost to 100 percent, or in hot climates, the impression is one of a refreshing fragrance rather than one of intensity.

Merlot ▶

This variety is planted in more vineyards in Bordeaux than the two Cabernets together. Merlot has the advantage over the Cabernets of early ripening. However, this grape variety has the disadvantage of being more susceptible to rot. Merlot gives a dark-colored, rich, fleshy wine, supple and velvety, but mostly lacking the firm backbone of the Cabernets, to which it is a perfect foil. The ripe, plummy fruitiness of the Merlot *and* the absence of harsh tannins have made it one of the most popular red grape varieties.

Pinot Noir ▶

The traditional grape of Burgundy is a fragile variety compared to the Cabernet family. It grows best in a cool climate. In warm climates the typical strawberry, cherry fruit and lingering flavor is masked by concentration and alcohol. Acidity is generally higher than tannin, which allows the Pinot Noir to be drunk quite young, given the ripe fruit of a good year. This same wine will, however, age gracefully. The pure Pinot fruit has great clarity of expression, and is much sought after. If blended with other grapes, Gamay, for example, it loses this individuality.

Syrah ▶

Syrah is a dark-colored grape, which ripens late in a warm climate. Native to the northern Rhône valley, where it produces wines with an intensely deep color, a distinctive aroma of blackberries and black currants overlaid with spice and a rich, robust flavor, it has now spread to other, warmer regions in France, as well as to California, Australia and South Africa. The finest wines from this grape age as well, if not better than those from the Cabernet Sauvignon, losing their "chunky" fruit and gaining in elegance. The Hermitage La Chapelle 1961 has often been mistaken for a first growth 1961 from the Médoc.

Mourvèdre ▶

This is a grape variety of Spanish origin from which wines are produced of even greater depth of color and aging potential than from the Syrah. Mourvèdre is often blended with Syrah in Châteauneuf-du-Pape or Bandol. The grape has a black curranty robustness of fruit, but is too massively concentrated to be often used alone. It is more frequently used to add structure to the fleshy wines from the Grenache.

Grenache ▶

Another popular grape variety of Spanish origin is known as the Garnarcha in the Rioja. The Grenache is an early budding and early ripening grape. However it is prone to spring frost and to rot. The Grenache also has a tendency to overripeness, leading to high alcohol and low acidity, thus diminishing aroma and flavor. It is at its best in the southern Rhône valley, where it exudes a rich, ripe warmth of flavor, requiring the Syrah and the Mourvèdre to provide spiciness and structure to the wines of the region. The fleshy fruit of the Grenache, blended with the lean fruit from the Cinsaut, is also the base for some of the most successful rosés in the southern Rhône.

Gamay ▶

A grape which is so closely associated with the Beaujolais region that it is sometimes called Gamay-Beaujolais, the Gamay prefers coolish climates. It is one of the rare red grapes to retain its attractive fruit aromas even with yields of 60-70 hectoliters per hectare/3.5-4 tons per acre. This bouncy, rather obvious fruit, with a flavor sometimes reminiscent of pear-drops, is at its most marked when the wine is in its first year.

White Grapes

Chardonnay ▶

The Chardonnay produces many of the world's greatest dry white wines, of which those whites from Meursault, and the Montrachet family, are recognized as the benchmarks. This variety prefers growing conditions which offer a lightish soil and coolish climate, but adapts remarkably well to richer terrain and greater warmth. The wines will be noticeably richer when the soil is rich and weather warm. Color should always have a certain depth, often with green tints when the wine is young. The aroma is elusive, with apple-like, buttery or nutty overtones. The flavor has plenty of fruit and good acidity. It is this balance of alcohol and acidity that gives Chardonnay wines their capacity to improve with age.

Riesling ▶

The Riesling grape is to Germany what Chardonnay is to France. Both varieties have seen great success in the vineyards of the New World. The Riesling is a late-budding and hence late-ripening grape that is at its best in years when the fall is dry and sunny, resulting in extraordinary concentration of grape sugar to produce wines that combine great richness with high acidity. Indeed, the distinctive Riesling fruit, which shows a marked purity of style and lemony acidity (even at its sweetest), transcends differences in region and climate.

Gewürztraminer ▶

Although a native of Germany, the Gewürztraminer is at its best in Alsace and parts of California, Australia and South Africa. It has a musky, spicy, rose-scented aroma, often leaning towards exotic fruits like lychees and a ripe richness of fruit, with just enough acidity to give balance. It is an exuberant variety, with none of the steely reserve of the Riesling.

Chenin Blanc ▶

Chenin Blanc is a grape planted throughout the world, but it only produces great wine in the Loire valley. There it is also known as the Pineau de la Loire and can produce wines that are very dry, softly *demi-sec*, or lusciously sweet. Properly ripened, the Chenin Blanc shows an aroma of honeysuckle, honey and flowers, quince and apricot, always with a firm acidity which allows for lengthy aging in bottle.

Sauvignon Blanc ▶

Sauvignon Blanc is an extremely versatile variety, also known as the Fumé Blanc. It produces dry, sometimes aggressively fruity wines, and can even, if the conditions are right, be affected by noble rot to produce a rich, luscious dessert wine. The principal characteristics of the Sauvignon Blanc, with its redcurrant/gooseberry aroma that is sometimes a little vegetal or "catty", and with its crisp, slightly tart finish, are exemplified by the wines from Sancerre. In Bordeaux, it forms an elegant partner to the more fleshy Sémillon, for its redcurrant aromas are here less obvious. It is one of the most popular varieties and is planted throughout the world.

Sémillon ▶

The principal grape variety in the make-up of the great sweet wines of Bordeaux, the Sémillon is now regaining favor for dry white wines as it adds soft, ripe depth of fruit to the rather tart Sauvignon. When aged, especially if planted in Australia, Sémillon wines take on a mellow "waxiness" and the weight, but not the acidity, of a fine Chardonnay.

Muscat ▶

The finest Muscat grapes are white, from the Muscat à Petits Grains. In Alsace, this varietal is vinified dry, to produce a wine with the pronounced grapy Muscat fruit, best drunk as an aperitif. In the southern Rhône valley and in Languedoc-Roussillon, it produces heady, fortified *vins doux naturels*. In Italy it is used for the delicious, sparkling Moscato d'Asti and Asti Spumante.

Pinot Gris ▶

This variety, known as the Tokay-Pinot Gris in Alsace, is a derivative of the Pinot Noir, as is the Pinot Blanc. It makes wine with breadth of flavor, seemingly low in acidity, whose main characteristic is weight and flavor on the palate, rather than aroma.

Other, less noble grapes like the red Carignan, produce distinctive styles of wine, but are more influenced by where they are grown than by their own inherent aroma and flavor. Rare white varieties, such as the Viognier, retain their aromatic and flavor qualities wherever they are grown; but to date so little is planted that these varieties have not created a recognizable international style.

Learning from the Label

In many countries, including the member states of the European Economic Community, all bottled wines sold to the consumer must be labeled and the labels must carry particular information. Besides often being a legal requirement, labels are considered by the producer to be important in the selling of the wine. For the consumer, labels display information which can be revealing and help in deciding which bottle to buy.

FRENCH LABELS

The name of the château

Grand Cru Classé: this term can only be used in Bordeaux if the property is an officially classed growth

GRAND VIN
CHATEAU
LYNCH · BAGES
GRAND CRU CLASSÉ
PAUILLAC
APPELLATION PAUILLAC CONTROLEE
J. CAZES, Propriétaire à PAUILLAC (Gironde)
75cl
PRODUCE OF FRANCE

Pauillac is the commune in the Médoc from where the wine comes

Vintage — 1976

Appellation: all the famous communes in Bordeaux have a specific appellation

Name and address of the proprietor of the château, JeanMichel Cazes, an owner of a number of leading Bordeaux châteaux

Contents

Vintage
1988
APPELLATION HAUT-MÉDOC CONTROLÉE
CRU BOURGEOIS

From the Médoc appellation

Cru Bourgeois: this group of good quality wines are not part of the 1855 classification but represent good value for money

The name of the château

CHATEAU REYSSON
HAUT-MÉDOC

MIS EN BOUTEILLE AU CHATEAU
S. C. DU CHATEAU REYSSON, PROPRIÉTAIRE À VERTHEUIL (GIRONDE) FRANCE
PRODUIT DE FRANCE   PRODUIT DE FRANCE
NET CONT. 756 ML · ALC. 12% BY VOL.   CONTAINS SULFITES   RED BORDEAUX WINE
SHIPPED BY PIERRE CARTIER & FILS – BORDEAUX - FRANCE
IMPORTED BY
MONSIEUR HENRI WINES, LTD WHITE PLAINS, NY 10604

The owner

Bottled at the château

Contents   Alcoholic strength

The style is very dry

Name of wine (Champagne)

The date of the vintage. This is an example of vintage Champagne, made only in outstanding years. It is considered superior to non-vintage Champagne

CHAMPAGNE 1983
Veuve Clicquot Ponsardin
REIMS
FRANCE
1983   BRUT
PRODUCE OF FRANCE

Town where producer is located

The marque, the name of the house (or grower) who produced the wine. The house of Veuve Cliquot is one of the oldest and most distinguished in Champagne

The name of the wine: the term Grand Cru can only be used in Chablis if the wine comes from one of the seven officially recognized Grand Crus vineyards.

Chablis Grand Cru
"Les Preuses"
APPELLATION CHABLIS GRAND CRU CONTROLÉE
Mise à la Propriété
ALC. 13.5% VOL   René et Vincent DAUVISSAT, PROPRIETAIRES A CHABLIS (YONNE) FRANCE
Contents   750ml

Alcoholic strength

The specific Grand Cru

Appellation: the Grand Cru has a specific appellation

Name of the proprietors (growers)

Bottled at the domaine (by the grower)

The wine was bottled at the domaine

This wine comes from Gevrey-Chambertin in the Côte de Nuits, one of the best village appellations in Burgundy

VINS FINS DE BOURGOGNE
Mis en bouteille à la propriété
GEVREY-CHAMBERTIN
PREMIER CRU
CAZETIERS
APPELLATION CONTRÔLÉE
DOMAINE BRUNO CLAIR
Viticulteur à Marsannay-la-Côte, Côte-d'Or France
13% vol   75cl
Produit de France

This is a top class Premier Cru wine from the Cazetiers vineyard

The name of the producer

Alcoholic strength

Contents

Name of wine (Mâcon-Villages) with trademark (Jadot "La Fontaine")

FONDÉE   EN 1859
MACON-VILLAGES JADOT
"LA FONTAINE"
Appellation Mâcon-Villages Contrôlée
MIS EN BOUTEILLES PAR
LOUIS JADOT
LOUIS JADOT, NÉGOCIANT-ELEVEUR A BEAUNE - CÔTE-D'OR - FRANCE
PRODUCE OF FRANCE   KOBRAND   750 ml
ALC. BY VOL. 13%   Wines   Spirits   WHITE BURGUNDY TABLE WINE
IMPORTED BY KOBRAND CORPORATION, NEW YORK, N.Y., SOLE U.S. IMPORTERS

Appellation Controlée governing name of wine (Mâcon-Villages)

Bottled by Louis Jadot, the négociant (merchant)

Alcoholic strength

Contents

Name of importer

Appellation: one appellation (Alsace) covers all the wines of the region

Name of wine and grape variety: Alsace wines are invariably named according to the grape variety used. The exceptions are labels for Cremant d'Alsace, the local sparkling wine and those for bottles of blended grape varieties, sometimes called Edelzwicker

VIN D'ALSACE
APPELLATION ALSACE CONTROLÉE
PRODUCE   OF FRANCE
René Schmidt
ALSACE
13,5% VOL.   Gewurztraminer   750 mL
Mis en bouteille par: BAUMANN - SCHMIDT A RIQUEWIHR HT-RHIN (FRANCE)

The name of the producer

Wine region

Alcoholic strength   Contents

Bottled by the producer

Name of the domaine

PRODUCE OF FRANCE
Domaine de la Vieille Chaussée
ALCOHOL   NET CONTENTS
12% BY VOLUME   750 ML
MUSCADET de SÈVRE & MAINE
WHITE LOIRE WINE   SUR LIE
APPELLATION MUSCADET DE SÈVRE & MAINE CONTRÔLÉE
MIS EN BOUTEILLE AU DOMAINE
BOTTLED & SHIPPED BY: MOREAU FRÈRES, 44690 CHATEAU-THEBAUD, FRANCE

Country of origin specified for export market

Contents

Alcoholic strength

Name of wine

Name of grower (and bottler)

Bottled on its lees to maintain maximum weight and freshness

Bottled at the domaine

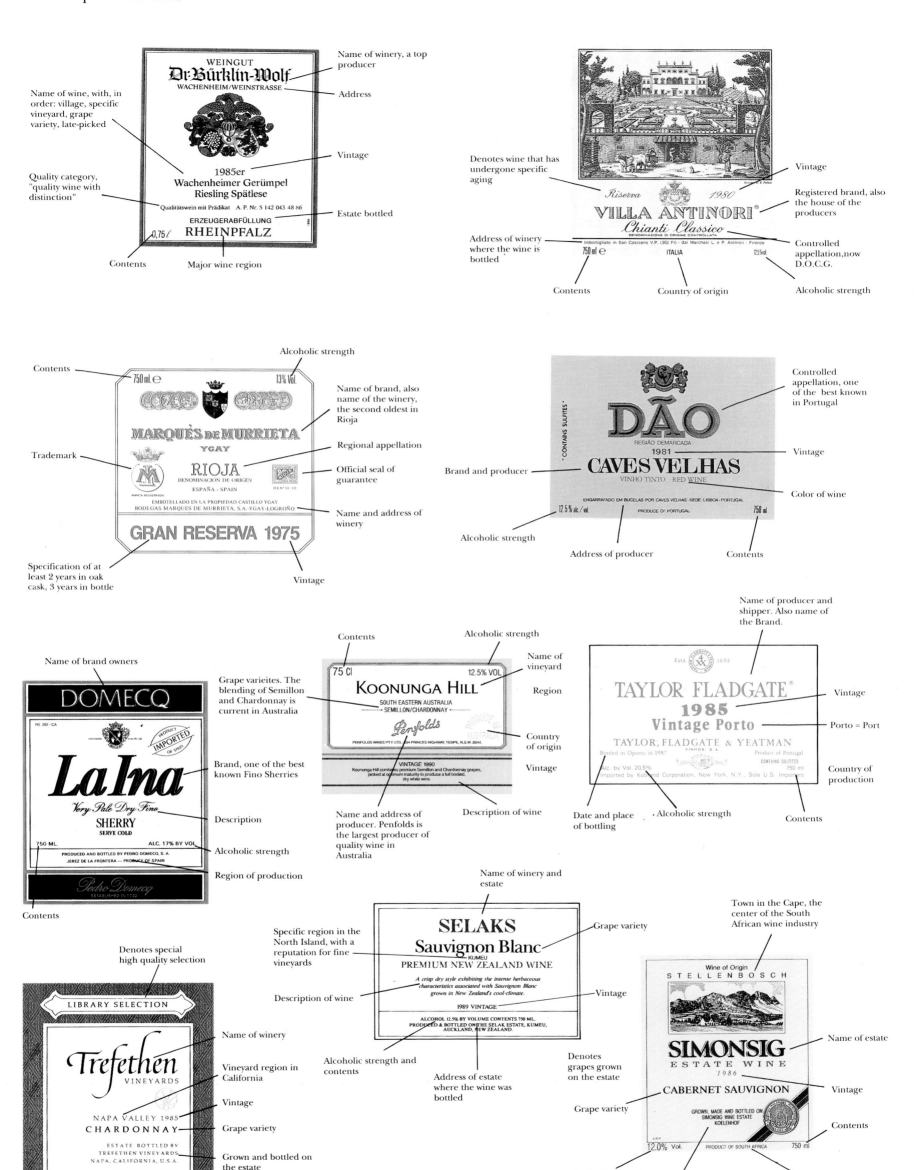

Name of winery, a top producer

Address

Name of wine, with, in order: village, specific vineyard, grape variety, late-picked

Vintage

Quality category, "quality wine with distinction"

Estate bottled

Contents

Major wine region

Denotes wine that has undergone specific aging

Vintage

Registered brand, also the house of the producers

Address of winery where the wine is bottled

Controlled appellation, now D.O.C.G.

Contents

Country of origin

Alcoholic strength

Contents

Alcoholic strength

Name of brand, also name of the winery, the second oldest in Rioja

Trademark

Regional appellation

Official seal of guarantee

Name and address of winery

Specification of at least 2 years in oak cask, 3 years in bottle

Vintage

Controlled appellation, one of the best known in Portugal

Brand and producer

Vintage

Color of wine

Alcoholic strength

Address of producer

Contents

Name of brand owners

Grape varieites. The blending of Semillon and Chardonnay is current in Australia

Contents

Alcoholic strength

Name of vineyard

Region

Name of producer and shipper. Also name of the Brand.

Brand, one of the best known Fino Sherries

Country of origin

Vintage

Description

Alcoholic strength

Region of production

Name and address of producer. Penfolds is the largest producer of quality wine in Australia

Description of wine

Vintage

Porto = Port

Date and place of bottling

Alcoholic strength

Country of production

Contents

Contents

Denotes special high quality selection

Name of winery and estate

Town in the Cape, the center of the South African wine industry

LIBRARY SELECTION

Specific region in the North Island, with a reputation for fine vineyards

Grape variety

Name of winery

Description of wine

Vintage

Vineyard region in California

Vintage

Grape variety

Grown and bottled on the estate

Alcoholic strength and contents

Address of estate where the wine was bottled

Denotes grapes grown on the estate

Grape variety

Name of estate

Vintage

Contents

Alcoholic strength

Address of estate

Country of origin

The Color of Wine

We have discussed the color of wines briefly on page 27, saying that color, being the first introduction to a wine, often leaves the most marked impression. Professional tasters vary in their approach to the value of color, but it is generally agreed that if the color is good, the wine, barring other faults, will be as well. The better the color, the better the wine. The wines in the following illustrations cover the main styles of wine, from dry to sweet and light to robust, and the major grape varieties. The wines have also been selected from a number of different wine-producing countries and regions of the world in order to provide a further source of comparison.

WHITE WINES

Muscadet sur lie 1990. Domaine de la Batardiere.
The palest of pale yellows gives the impression of lightness, a crisp dryness and youth. Refreshing and slightly tart, these wines should be drunk young.

Sancerre 1990. Cave du Clos la Perrière. Pale yellow with a hint of green, the Sauvignon grape gives this more weight and fruit than the Muscadet, while retaining a lively acidity.

Wehlener Sonnenuhr Riesling Spatlese (Mosel) 1990. J.J. Prum.
Very pale, almost colorless, the lack of color comes from the Riesling grape growing at the northern limit of the vine, and the lightness in alcohol. This wine will last for many years, gain color slightly with age, but not lose its freshness.

Puligny-Montrachet 1988. Gerard Chavy.
A full-bodied, pale, buttery yellow color shows the potential richness of flavor the Chardonnay grape has if it comes from a good vineyard in a good year, while keeping a natural acidity.

Chardonnay 1988. Joseph Phelps Vineyard, Napa Valley.
Pale to medium-yellow, with more ripeness and richness than the Puligny-Montrachet of the same year, due to the heavier soil and warmer climate of the Napa valley. Full-bodied but not heavy.

Chardonnay 1990. Wolf Blass, South Australia.
Medium-yellow, with a ripeness and richness that is almost exotic and although it is two years younger than the two wines at left, this South Australia Chardonnay will have riper, broader flavors, almost masking the acidity.

Gewürztraminer Sélection de Grains Nobles 1983. Trimbach.
Medium-yellow with green tints, very rich and unctuous, this wine shows no sign of age. Incredible sweetness will be balanced by a good acidity, which will keep the color from maderizing.

Champagne 1985 Perrier-Jouët.
Pale, firm yellow, with a profusion of tiny bubbles rising regularly to the surface, the epitome of a fine vintage Champagne that can be kept for several years.

ROSÉ WINES

Côtes de Provence rosé 1989.
Medium rose, with just a hint of orange, this wine clearly comes from a warm climate, yet still looks fresh and young.

Tavel rosé 1990 Domaine de Longval.
A year younger, but deeper-toned and more robust than the Côtes de Provence, the Grenache-based Tavel rosés are full and fleshy, and are drunk more with food than as an aperitif.

RED WINES

Brouilly 1990. Château de La Chaize.
A vibrant deep carmine, with a violet-colored rim, shows off the youth of this Beaujolais, which is packed with Gamay fruit. The immediate impact on the palate is as pleasurable as the color.

Chinon 1988. Charles Joguet.
A deep red, with a firmness of body and no real aging, the depth of color comes from old Cabernet Franc vines after careful vinification. This wine will age in the manner of a good Médoc.

Château La Grave à Pomerol 1988.
Pomerol.
Full, ripe, robust red, the color going right to the rim, this shows the plummy ripeness of the Merlot in an excellent year, as well as the firmness of a top Pomerol; a classic example.

Merlot 1988. Sterling Vineyards.
A full warm red, with only the faintest hint of maturity on the rim differentiating this Napa Valley Merlot from the Pomerol. Ripe fruit is evident from the color extraction.

Château Lynch-Bages 1986. Pauillac.
Very deep, intense red, with the color firm right to the rim. Only two years of extra age have left this Pauillac less opaquely intense than the previous wine. This very fine wine is still many years from maturity.

Cabernet Sauvignon 1986 Wolf Blass, South Australia.
A very deep, concentrated color, but slightly less intense than the Lynch-Bages of the same year. Maturity is beginning to show at the rim, but it will continue to improve.

Château Pichon Longueville-Baron 1988.
Pauillac.
Very intense, deep, almost opaque in the center, laden with deep fruit from the Cabernet Sauvignon, the intensity shows an extraction of color that could hardly be greater, and presages rich firm flavors and ripe tannins.

Châteauneuf-du-Pape 1989. Domaine la Roquette.
Very concentrated, intense and full-bodied, this Grenache-dominated wine shows the ripeness of the grapes from the sun-filled Châteauneuf-du-Pape vineyards. Such youthful intensity suggests a great vintage and a long life for the wine.

Barolo 1982. Cerreguio/Cantina di Marengo.
Full, deeply solid, mature red with mahogany-tawny rim, showing the intensity of color and fruit extraction. This is still young for a Barolo of this quality.

Zinfandel 1989. Ravenswood.
Vibrant, black-cherry red, of the same depth as the Chinon, this wine shows concentration and lively fruit extract without heaviness.

Zinfandel 1976. Ravenswood.
A very full, deep, warm, robust red, with mahogony tints and the rim beginning to fade, this is a remarkable color for a 1976 Zinfandel, due to old vines giving a low production of very ripe grapes.

Corton 1988. Domaine Bonneau de Martray.
Fine deep red; the Pinot Noir tends to show a watery edge early, can lose color with age, but does not lose fruit. From a good vintage, this is still many years away from maturity.

Corton 1987. Domaine Bonneau de Martray.
Almost as deep-colored as the proceeding wine, the brickiness of the red and the more faded rim denote a lesser vintage and one more year in the bottle. This color will hold for some years.

Corton 1986. Domaine Bonneau de Martray.
A fraction less youthful, but virtually identical to the 1987, with possibly a little more ripeness of fruit. The 1986 shows good depth of color from a good but not great vintage.

Corton 1981. Domaine Bonneau de Martray.
Full maturity can be seen by the tawny rim, but the color is still deep, solid and full of life. From an average year in Burgundy, this wine shows the firmness and extract of a Corton *Grand Cru*.

The Wine Regions
of the World

FRANCE

Introduction by Rosemary George, M.W.

The viticultural face of France is rich and varied, for it provides more of the world's truly great wines than any other country. It sets the standards to which all others aspire: remove its contribution from the world wine scene and the loss would be sorely felt. Where else can you find a sparkling wine with the subtlety and finesse of Champagne, dry white wines with the depth and complexity of white Burgundy and a spectrum of red wines from delicate red Burgundy through richly-flavored clarets to peppery Hermitage and Côte Rôtie? Among sweet wines Sauternes has few rivals, while the pungent flavors of Sauvignon Blanc from the Loire and the spicy fruit of Gewürztraminer set a challenge for the winemakers of the New World.

The wine map of France with its six classic areas, Bordeaux, Burgundy, Champagne, Alsace, the Rhône and the Loire, is largely defined by rivers. In the Middle Ages rivers provided an easy means of transport; early reputations were often made by such practical factors. The one exception is the Côte d'Or, which has no obvious outlet by water. Both the Loire, with its many tributaries, and the Rhône are lined with vineyards. The Dordogne and the Garonne flow into the Gironde, bringing wine to Bordeaux and, for centuries, trade to the port. Alsace has the Rhine, while the Seine and its tributaries, on which Chablis and Champagne depend, carried wine to Paris.

In very broad terms, the vineyards of France can be divided into three according to grape varieties and climate. The western half of the country has a maritime climate, benefiting from the moderating influence of the Atlantic Ocean. Winters and summers are rarely extreme. The grape varieties here are Cabernet Sauvignon, Cabernet Franc, Merlot and a few lesser vines for red wines, and Sauvignon, Sémillon and Chenin Blanc for white wines. The first two are known principally as the grape varieties of Bordeaux, but they spill into southwest France as well, and the last comes principally from the western half of the Loire valley.

Northeastern France, particularly Champagne and Burgundy, is dominated by Chardonnay, Pinot Noir and Gamay. Theirs is a more extreme continental climate, with harder winters and hotter summers. East meets west in the upper reaches of the Loire. In the appellation of Sancerre, Sauvignon Blanc is the variety for white wine, while Pinot Noir makes the red and rosé.

The third area comprises the vineyards of Languedoc-Roussillon, stretching from the Spanish border to the southern half of the Rhône Valley and then into Provence as far as Nice. The island of Corsica can be included here, for there are some similarities with the mainland. Vines flourish in the Mediterranean climate, with hot dry summers and mild winters. The most characteristic grape varieties are Grenache, Cinsaut and Carignan for everyday wines, and Syrah and Mourvèdre for more distinctive flavors.

The Midi meets the southwest in the Côtes de la Malepère and Cabardès, two little known *Vins Délimités de Qualité Supérieure* (V.D.Q.S.) to the south and north of the city of Carcassonne. In this area close to the watershed of the Mediterranean and the Atlantic, a variety of microclimates provide the condition for both Grenache and Cabernet Sauvignon to be grown.

The northern Rhône is dominated by Syrah for red wines and Viognier for whites, as well as some Marsanne and Roussanne. All of these now feature to some extent in the Midi, though in some instances they are being grown on an experimental basis.

History has somewhat isolated the vineyards of Alsace from the rest of France. They have more in common with those of Baden on the other side of the Rhine, with grape varieties that are not found elsewhere in France, notably Riesling and Gewürztraminer.

France has also given the example of its wine law to the rest of the world, with a system of *appellation contrôlée* (A.O.C.). This is based on the precise provenance of the grapes, that provenance itself being based on what is generally called *terroir.* *Terroir* means much more than just soil and includes aspect, altitude and even climate.

The first appellations were created in 1936, initially as a measure against fraud. They covered (and still do cover) grape varieties, yields, viticultural practices and methods of vinification.

The more recently formulated V.D.Q.S., *Vins Délimités de Qualité Supérieure,* is the category immediately below A.O.C, with equally exacting regulations, but covering lesser vineyards, such as Bugey or Côtes du Marmandais. Many of the appellations outside the classic regions—Corbières, Minervois, Coteaux d'Aix-en-Provence, for example—started life as V.D.Q.S.

Vin de table covers much of the anonymous wine of France while *vin de pays* raises some wine above the anonymity of *vin de table* and offers some regional identity.

Outside the classic wine regions, France abounds with pockets of vineyards. These produce wines as diverse as Gris de Toul, from the country's northernmost vineyards outside Metz; white Bellet, made from Rolle in the suburbs of Nice; the Mançois of the Aveyron in Marcillac; *vin de paille* from the Jura, and not least the remaining vineyards of Paris, of which the best known is the tiny Clos de Montmartre behind the Sacré Coeur. The variety is infinite.

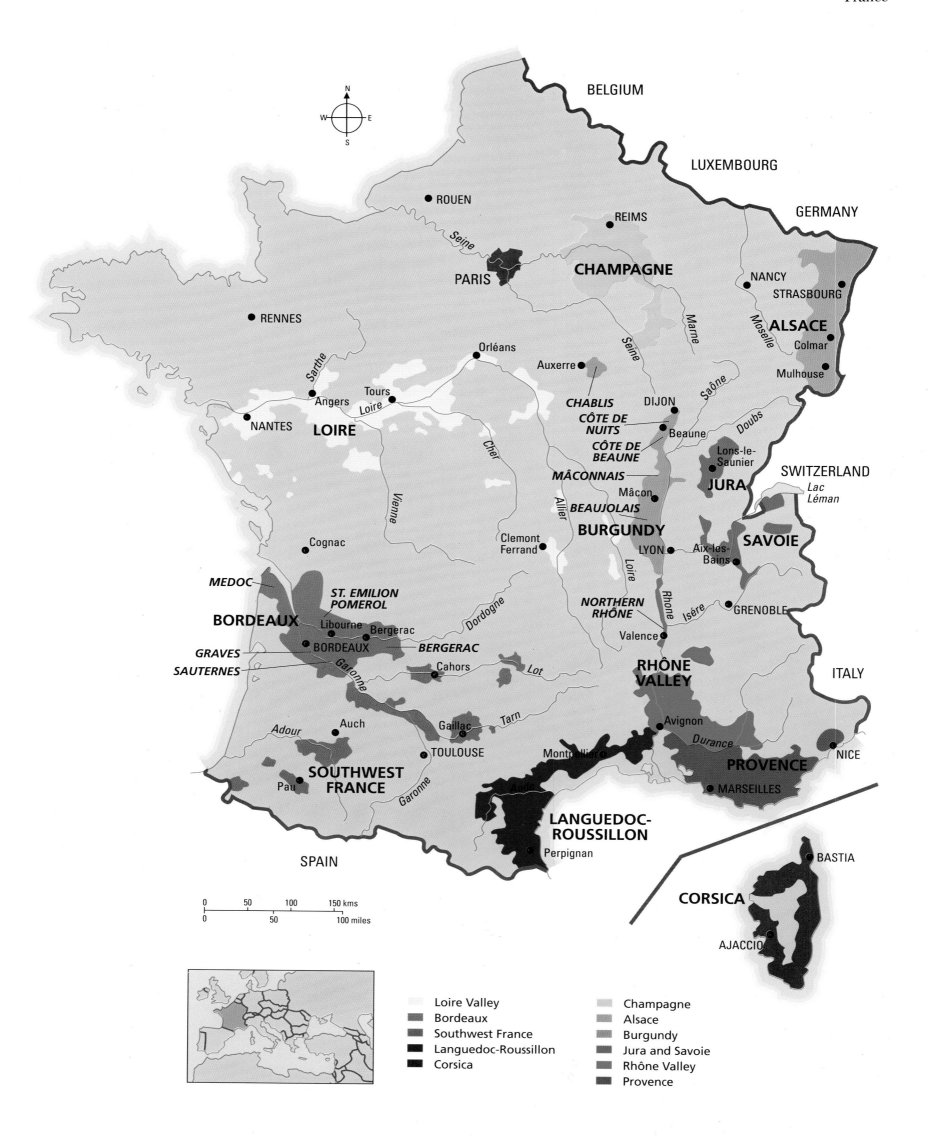

BELGIUM

LUXEMBOURG

GERMANY

• ROUEN

• REIMS

PARIS

CHAMPAGNE

NANCY •

STRASBOURG

ALSACE

Colmar

Mulhouse

Seine

Marne

Moselle

• RENNES

Orléans •

Auxerre •

CHABLIS

Saône

Sarthe

Tours •

Angers •

Loire

DIJON

CÔTE DE
NUITS

Beaune •

Doubs

NANTES

LOIRE

Cher

CÔTE DE
BEAUNE

MÂCONNAIS

Lons-le-
Saunier •

JURA

SWITZERLAND

Lac
Léman

Vienne

Allier

Mâcon •

BEAUJOLAIS

BURGUNDY

SAVOIE

Cognac •

Clemont
Ferrand •

LYON •

Aix-les-
Bains •

MEDOC

ST. EMILION
POMEROL

Loire

NORTHERN
RHÔNE

Isère

GRENOBLE •

BORDEAUX

Libourne •

Bergerac •

Dordogne

Valence •

Rhône

GRAVES

BORDEAUX •

BERGERAC

ITALY

SAUTERNES

Garonne

Cahors •

Lot

RHÔNE
VALLEY

Tarn

Avignon •

Adour

Auch •

Gaillac •

Durance

SOUTHWEST
FRANCE

TOULOUSE •

Montpellier •

PROVENCE

NICE •

Pau •

Garonne

Aude

MARSEILLES •

SPAIN

LANGUEDOC-
ROUSSILLON

Perpignan •

BASTIA •

CORSICA

AJACCIO •

0   50   100   150 kms

0   50   100 miles

	Loire Valley		Champagne
	Bordeaux		Alsace
	Southwest France		Burgundy
	Languedoc-Roussillon		Jura and Savoie
	Corsica		Rhône Valley
			Provence

41

BORDEAUX

by Anthony Rose

ABOVE: The contours of the Bordeaux region are defined by its two great rivers, the Garonne and the Dordogne. The two rivers converge into the Gironde estuary, separating the plains of the Médoc from the hillsides of Bourg and Blaye.

Setting the Scene

Bordeaux, the world's greatest fine wine region, is a living patchwork of trading towns and rural villages, of vineyards and châteaux. This historic region speaks of culture, architecture, of generations of aristocrats, merchants and peasants. But to the world beyond, it speaks of one export above all others: wine. Like the mechanism of a very fine watch, the whole is far greater than the sum of its parts. Its features interlock, all bent towards a common goal: the production of a unique wine of quality dedicated to the art of civilized living.

Bordeaux is a name that evokes both the grandeur of wine at its best and a centuries-old tradition of vinous cultivation and commerce. Bordeaux wine is produced in a range and variety of styles, yet it always speaks quality. Quietly evolving and constantly refining its techniques in pursuit of this goal, Bordeaux has set standards for others to follow. In the wine industries of the New World from California to Australia, the red wine of Bordeaux is the one most flattered by emulation, the role model other countries have tried hard to reproduce, with varying degrees of success.

Bordeaux can appear aloof and inhospitable. Its flat contours can suggest a region that has had to make up for lack of natural splendor by building châteaux. It is not a region that yields up its treasures lightly or takes its pleasures spontaneously. Few and far between are the properties advertising free tastings or cellar door sales. The Bordelais seem to prefer to run marathons rather than dance and sing. Tourists of less than serious intent are tol-

erated rather than welcomed. On the left bank of the Garonne River there is a certain formality, a discreet drawing-room ambiance in the air, an almost English kind of stiff-upper-lipness — at least on first acquaintance.

The right bank of the Dordogne is different. Around the bustling town of Libourne, where the monoculture of the vine seems to cover every nook and cranny of hillside and plain, the comfortable scale reflects a more rural tradition of sharecropping and mixed agriculture. Commerce and wine estates themselves operate on an altogether smaller, more human, scale in this part of Bordeaux. The whole region, in fact, owes its prosperity to several driving forces. These are a preoccupation with order and good name, a determination to be one step ahead of the game, a highly competitive spirit and a considerable talent for organization.

It is strange to think that by the time of the defeat of Talbot, Earl of Shrewsbury, in 1453, England had already been trading in the wines of Bordeaux for almost exactly three centuries. In 1152, Henry Plantagenet married Eleanor of Aquitaine, a union that secured the future of the Bordeaux wine trade.

The first château built for the purpose of producing wine was Haut-Brion at Pessac in 1525. The modern era really began, however, in the second half of the seventeenth century with the arrival of the Dutch. By draining the Médoc and regulating its streams, they laid the foundations, literally, for the establishment of its great estates. With the discovery in the same period of the dual benefits of corks and bottles, wines could be shipped and cellared for drinking many years after the harvest. This was the beginning of the concept of vintage-dated wines. Pioneers such as Arnaud de Pontac, owner of Château Haut-Brion, planted widely. Estates expanded into the Médoc and Graves. Other great families followed suit, and now-familiar names began to appear on the map: Château Margaux, for example, created by the Marquis d'Aulède de Lestonnac, and the vineyards of Châteaux Lafite and Latour, founded by the Ségur family.

At the end of the seventeenth century and the beginning of the eighteenth century, Protestant merchants came to Bordeaux from Holland, the British Isles, Denmark and Germany, setting up shop in the Chartreux suburb of Bordeaux. The merchants, or Chartrons, as they became known, were to benefit from the leveling process of the Revolution, and eventually established a stranglehold on the Bordeaux wine trade that lasted a century and a half.

The eighteenth century was the heyday of Bordeaux. During this period, the great estates established export markets and prospered. By 1855 the Bordeaux Chamber of Commerce was able to draw up a hierarchy of fifty-eight châteaux based on the prices each wine had fetched over almost a century: the 1855 classification was born.

The nineteenth century was a time of fine vintages and speculation. The disease oidium (powdery mildew) caused the shortages that fuelled the speculation, and huge amounts of wine were bought *sur souche*, or still on the vine. Fortunes were made and unmade. Châteaux proliferated, and the château concept spread to the whole of Bordeaux. In 1855 the commercial classification of Bordeaux secured the reputation of its wines throughout France and abroad. But like some latter-day version of the plagues visited on the Egyptians, two natural disasters, downy mildew and phylloxera, struck Bordeaux after oidium. Oidium, a fungus that attacks the green parts of the vine and reduces the yield, first appeared in the 1850s, and within six years was being treated with applications of sulphur. Downy mildew appeared in 1883. Like oidium, it attacked the leaves of the vine, but, unlike oidium, it actually ruined the wine by spoiling the flavor — a fact not necessarily discovered until long after bottling. The cure for downy mildew was found to be a treatment of copper sulphate, now known as Bordeaux mixture. But there was no cure for a bad bottle.

The phylloxera, which arrived from America, is an aphid that sucks the lifeblood from vines and kills them. It is such a tiny insect, with its destructive activity going on underground, that, not surprisingly, the solution — grafting the vines onto phylloxera-resistant American rootstocks — took years to discover. A major replanting of the vineyards took place over a period of decades. Ironically this adversity was the foundation of the modern Bordelais vineyard. It created the necessary opportunity for château proprietors to select the combination of grapes that best suited their soils. All told, it took three generations for the region to recover from a combination of plague and poor vintages. More significant still, economic depression fed by a vicious circle of a collapse in export markets and an absence of manpower meant that growers had nothing to plow back into the upkeep of their neglected vineyards.

It was during this period that the blueprint for the modern laws of *appellation contrôlée* gradually began to come into effect. The original incentive was the damage caused to the reputation of Bordeaux by systematic fraudulent adulteration with wines from North Africa and the south of France. In each area covered by the new laws, considerations such as the nature of the soil, exposure, drainage, grape varieties, pruning and limits on production were taken into account. At the same time, the idea of bottling wine at the château was dreamt up by a young château-owner, Philippe de Rothschild, in 1924. This idea was to have far-reaching consequences. Eventually it helped shift the balance back towards the châteaux in the saga of their long-running tussle with the merchants for control of the wine trade.

After World War II, the replanting of the Bordeaux vineyard brought both steady recovery and a gradual shift in emphasis from white to red wine. When in 1970 A.O.C. red wine topped the 2 million hectoliter/52,836,000 U.S. gallons mark for the first time, beating A.O.C. white into second place, the shift became irreversible. But there were still setbacks. The first came in the form of devastating February frosts that killed a huge number of vines in 1956. The second setback was man-made and an episode Bordeaux would no doubt rather forget.

Capitalizing on the relative success of the 1970 and 1971 vintages, the 1972 was offered and bought speculatively at unrealistically high prices. Merchants were left with wine in their cellars and egg on their faces. The crisis culminated in the Cruse scandal of 1973/4, when one of Bordeaux' most respected merchant houses was caught fiddling its books. If the fall of the house of Cruse was symbolic,

ABOVE: Ever since Château Lafite, run by Baron Eric de Rothschild, was ranked first in the 1855 classification of Bordeaux, it has become a byword for elegance.

the crisis hastened the end of the era of the domination of the great merchants. The result was a shift in the balance of power back to the château proprietors. They capitalized on new techniques in winemaking and new equipment to liberate themselves from the merchant yoke.

Newcomers with fresh capital arrived, lured by the chance to build on this newfound independence. The Mentzelopoulos, Moueix and Forner families and, latterly, foreign investors, banks and insurance companies have all played a part in transforming the face of Bordeaux. The fine vintage of 1975 signaled the beginning of the Second Golden Age, which reached its full glory in the eighties. Thanks to a series of fine vintages and success in marketing the product, the streets of Bordeaux have been paved with the gold of a hundred importing nations. Barring a second equally remarkable ten years, the 1980s will go down in history as the decade of the century.

Geography, Climate, Soil and Grapes

The vineyard of Bordeaux is vast and as varied as the wines it produces — dry and sweet, red and white, still and sparkling. Its great sweet wines rank among the finest in the world. Its fine white Graves have undergone a great revival in recent years. Above all, though, Bordeaux today is synonymous with fine red wine. In its range and quality red Bordeaux is unequaled anywhere. It was not always so. The story of Bordeaux wine since the end of World War II is the story of changing tastes and demands and the modification of the structure of Bordeaux from white wine to red to meet the challenge of the modern palate.

It is also the story of great strides in quality as table wine has been virtually eliminated in favor of *appellation contrôlée*. In the postwar period the total vineyard area has decreased from 140,000 hectares/345,800 acres in 1950 to just over 100,000

hectares/247,000 acres. Better control of pests and diseases, the use of fertilizers and work on productive vine clones and rootstocks have resulted in a doubling of yields in just two decades. In the five years between 1986 and 1990, Bordeaux delivered the three biggest harvests in its history — the equivalent of some 6.5 million hectoliters/1.7 billion U.S. gallons annually.

Within its huge framework, the variety of styles of Bordeaux reflects the changing make-up of geography and climate, the different grapes used, and the handling of those grapes by the winemaker or owner who may be — and often is — one and the same person.

Climate determines the general style of the wines. Weather on the other hand is the perennial joker in the pack; it tests the parameters of the known to keep everyone on his toes. It is the unpredictable element that gives each vintage, like different children in a family, its own distinct characteristics.

The weather may favor the Merlot in some years, such as 1985, or the Cabernet Sauvignon in others, such as 1986. Those who appreciate vintage variation can rest assured that despite the technological progress of recent years, it has been impossible to iron out the vicissitudes of the weather to the extent of producing a standardized vintage year in, year out. Weather destroyed the Merlot harvest in 1984, and wrought havoc again in 1991 when April frosts decimated the crop. Progress does not mean that Bordeaux will always have good vintages. Rather, it reduces the chances of a really bad one. Then again, localized weather conditions, even varying from one vineyard to the next, create different results that ensure, like games of chess, that no two vintages turn out the same.

In essence Bordeaux' climate is one of mild winters, plenty of rain, warm summers and long, dry falls. An analysis of the geography and microclimates of the region shows its heterogeneous nature: permutations of soil and grape varieties produce subtle nuances in style.

Bordeaux sits in the administrative department of Gironde. Bisecting the entire region, the Gironde River estuary diverges just north of the city of Bordeaux, which squats at the heart of the region like an exceedingly fat spider.

The Garonne and Dordogne rivers converge 14.5 kilometers/9 miles north of the city, creating three distinct geographical units, each of which sits astride one of the three river axes of the region. At its western border, the Atlantic Ocean lies behind a protective cladding of dense pine forest. Straddling the Gironde are the low-lying, gravelly peninsula of the Médoc and, on the other side, the Côtes, comprising the undulating districts of Bourg and Blaye, whose medieval citadel on the Gironde opposite Cussac, Fort Médoc, testifies to ancient trading ties with Britain.

To the east, Fronsac sits on a bluff dominating the town and port of Libourne, the hub of a busy commercial network. Here on the right bank of the Dordogne River sits the historic, ravishingly pretty fortified town of St. Emilion. The vineyards of St. Emilion and Pomerol form the nucleus around which a cluster of satellite towns are built on soils of clay and limestone. From the southern banks of the Dordogne towards the Garonne sprawls the vast tri-

angular sub-region of the Entre-Deux-Mers, a charming patchwork countryside of vineyard, cereals and pasture accounting for roughly one-third of all A.O.C. Bordeaux. As it approaches the Garonne, it turns into the Premières Côtes, a strip of vineyards towering over the Garonne and, on its left bank, the Graves.

It was the phylloxera scourge of the late nineteenth century that was the ultimate process of natural selection, helping Bordeaux to reduce its grape varieties — some sixty of them in the eighteenth century — to, for all practical purposes, just five for red wines and three for white. The starring role for red wines is usually reserved for the Cabernet Sauvignon. The Merlot is Best Supporting Actor, while the Cabernet Franc, Malbec and Petit Verdot are the essential spear carriers that in varying proportions constitute the rest of the Bordeaux blend. For white wines, the Sauvignon and Sémillon play more equal roles, sometimes one dominating, sometimes the other, while the Muscadelle gets a mention for its support.

The Cabernet Sauvignon is the classic variety of the Médoc and Graves. At around 18 percent of the Bordeaux vineyard, it is second in quantity terms to the Merlot, but its name is so well-known that it has virtually acquired the status of a brand. Even in its heartland, however, it is rare to find more than three-quarters of an estate planted with Cabernet Sauvignon. Flourishing on hot, gravelly soils, it is a thick-skinned variety that can have difficulty ripening in cooler years. At its best, it produces wines of a rich, deep ruby hue and the most wonderful fruitiness, often reminiscent of black currants in its austere youth, and maturing into silky textures with the fragrance of cedar and sandalwood and sometimes a hint of game. Combined with good natural acidity and backbone from the tannins in the skins, the Cabernet Sauvignon produces wines of great finesse with the structure and power for long aging.

The Merlot is Bordeaux' other great red variety. It is also the most widely planted, covering roughly 32 percent of the vineyard area. It tends to favor the cooler, more water-retentive soils of the right bank and the hillsides of the Côtes. Despite its usually inferior status alongside the Cabernet Sauvignon, it can produce wonderfully appealing wines. The highly-prized Château Pétrus, for instance, is almost entirely made from Merlot. But this is rare. Most of the great right bank châteaux, though they often favor Merlot, are rounded out with significant proportions of either Cabernet Franc or Cabernet Sauvignon, and usually both. Merlot is a higher-yielding, earlier-ripening variety than Cabernet Sauvignon, and has higher natural sugars and softer skins that are more susceptible to wet weather and hence to rot. The wine produced from the Merlot is unmistakably aromatic, soft-centered, succulently black curranty and seductively juicy. Though it can last, its relative lack of backbone makes it generally earlier-maturing than Cabernet Sauvignon.

Three other red varieties also play their parts. The Cabernet Franc, a country cousin of the Cabernet Sauvignon, is most widely planted in the St. Emilion district, producing wines that are finely perfumed. The Petit Verdot's late-ripening qualities make it a difficult grape to grow and hard to justify economically. Yet this high-quality grape can pack in flavor and punch. As an ingredient in the blend, it can produce fabulous wines of great structure and finesse. Although some growers will not touch it, others, such as Bernadette Villars of Château Chasse-Spleen, and May-Eliane de Lencquesaing of Château Pichon-Lalande swear by it. The earlier ripening Malbec is the blending grape par excellence, producing a soft, highly-colored wine of at best medium quality.

White wines are made up of two principal grapes, the Sauvignon Blanc and the Sémillon, with sometimes a proportion of Muscadelle for its attractive aromatic and fruity qualities. Winemakers and drinkers alike are divided on the question of whether it is the Sauvignon or the Sémillon that is Bordeaux' greater grape variety. But in the end it is an academic question. As often as not, it is the two grapes in tandem that best bring out the qualities of white Bordeaux. The Sauvignon loses the distinctly herbaceous qualities it develops in the cooler, northern climate of Sancerre to give a fuller-bodied, finer wine whose aromatic qualities and fresh acidity can nevertheless act as an excellent counterpoint to the Sémillon, which develops its character in bottle, imparting richness and a lovely honeyed roundness to the final wine.

Bordeaux — the Wine

The longevity of Bordeaux wines affords an occasional glimpse of the way in which the wines of today have evolved from those of yesteryear. According to Christian Moueix, the debonair proprietor of Château Pétrus, low yields and concentration of fruit are the reasons why the wines of half a century ago are hard, if not impossible, to emulate. If yields were once smaller, there were other differences too. Alcohol was generally lower and acidity higher. This is because the grapes used to be picked before they achieved optimum ripeness to minimize the risk of the fermentation stopping before all the sugars had fermented into alcohol.

This is not to suggest that things have changed for the worse. On the contrary. When it was good, Bordeaux was clearly very, very good. But when it was bad, it was disastrously thin, sour, acetic or tasting of rot — particularly in poorer vintages. The climate has not changed, nor has the soil. Apart from the natural selection of quality grape varieties since phylloxera, the vine varieties, though fine-tuned for the most productive, disease-resistant clones, are in essence the same.

BELOW: The international wine press is given its first glimpse of the new vintage in early April each year. Despite the bottles and labels, these wines are all, in fact, drawn from the cask for the specific purpose of the annual tasting.

So where do the changes for the better come from? The answer is from the hand and brain of man. A greater understanding of what goes on in the vineyard and the cellar is part of it; the rest is the wherewithal to invest in the most up-to-date material and equipment. The last twenty years have seen radical improvements.

The importance of the winemaker lies in the experience he or she can bring to bear, the skill in fashioning the raw material and the elevation of attention to detail to an art form. Decisions such as how to prune the vine, the date of harvest and when to bottle the wine are all crucial and will make lasting differences to the quality of a wine. Other seemingly trivial decisions, such as how to clean barrels or what sort of harvesting basket to use, may seem by comparison of little consequence. But for the potential of a fine wine to be realized, it is the sum of the hundreds of decisions made throughout the winemaking year that counts. Attention to detail can make the difference between a fine wine and a just a good one, between a good wine and an ordinary one. It is a kind of obsessiveness bred in the Bordelais bone, and it is what helps Bordeaux stay one step ahead of the competition.

In the words of Professor Emile Peynaud of the Bordeaux Institute of Enology, "Great wine is made in the vineyard". Certainly the efforts made in the vineyard, although often less apparent than those in the cellar, have made a vital contribution to progress in Bordeaux. The fact that yields have doubled since the war is a manifestation of the increased health and vigor of the vine as well as the effect of higher-density planting. Ronald Barton of Château Léoville-Barton used to complain that modern fertilizers and sprays had caused today's vineyards to overproduce. Ironically he died in 1986, a year that produced an all-time record yield.

Diseases and pests have indeed been controlled by modern chemicals, but the increase in yields has not sent quality plummeting. Fine years such as 1982, 1986 and 1989 have been years of superabundance. Perhaps more important than maximum yield per se is optimum yield, which varies according to grape variety and weather conditions. The Pinot Noir of Burgundy, for example, quickly loses its distinctive character when it crops too heavily. This is less obvious in Bordeaux. And legal controls on yields, which vary from one appellation to the next, help to keep overall quality within certain strictly defined parameters. Nevertheless where excessive yields have made it harder for the vine to ripen adequately, the wines have rightly attracted criticism. In 1990, château proprietors conscientiously carried out bunch-thinning in July, a practice developed in the vigorous, sun-drenched vineyards of the New World and brought to Bordeaux where it is known as *vendange verte* by pioneers such as Christian Moueix. But perhaps they did not get it quite right: 1990 was another bumper crop.

Truistic as Professor Peynaud's oft-quoted dictum about wine being made in the vineyard may sound, it at the same time underestimates the key role of enological research in the revival of Bordeaux' fortunes. Peynaud himself has been a major contributor to this. His discoveries, together with those of his colleague Jean Ribéreau-Gayon, have taken much of the random chance out of winemaking. By methodically sampling grapes for ripeness, Peynaud was able better to predict optimum harvesting dates. By subjecting bacteria to microscopic examination, the scientists were able to advise on how to avoid bacterial spoilage in wines. Peynaud was responsible for instance for the virtual elimination of old, hard-to-clean wooden fermentation vats in favor of cement or stainless steel. The discovery of the secrets of malolactic fermentation, the second natural fermentation that changes the sharp, malic acidity in a wine into the softer lactic acid, and makes the wine more stable, helped to prevent this fermentation occurring in bottle.

From the sixties onwards, enological research increasingly bridged the gap between laboratory and cellar. In particular, advocacy of the use of new oak barrels for maturing the wine gave Bordeaux more than just greater complexity of flavors. Through controlled aeration, the effect of maturation in wood is to smooth the hard edges of the wine and, like a child educated at a good school, prepare it for improvements ahead in bottle. Peynaud was instrumental too in spreading the gospel of selection.

When you read on an old label the words *Grand Vin,* this was not Bordeaux puffing itself up with false claims of greatness, whatever the words have come to mean now. They indicated that this was the final blend, and was considered worthy to bear the château label.

This selection of the best casks has resulted in the widespread practice of creating a second wine. Put out under a different label, these reject wines, usually a blend of the wines of young vines and vats considered unworthy of the top label, have allowed the great châteaux to fine tune the quality of their top wines. At the same time they have given the consumer a cheaper, earlier-maturing product to enjoy while waiting for the top wine to develop.

The multiplicity of equipment and gadgetry in the cellars of Bordeaux is enough to make one's eyes glaze over. It testifies to a restless search for perfection fueled by an innate competitiveness.

Optimum temperature control, length of vatting and manipulation of grapeskin tannins: all these are part and parcel of the winery scene. Majestic cellars of classical proportions house computer consoles straight out of *Star Trek.* Thanks to quality control, handling practices such as sorting the grapes on reception to remove unripe or rotten ones, the restless quest for improvement will continue for as long as Bordeaux itself thrives.

BELOW: In even the most traditional cellars, such as those of Cordier seen here, the use of stainless steel has enabled producers to bring to winemaking the benefits of improved cellar hygiene and temperature control.

The Médoc

by Anthony Rose

Lying between the Altlantic Ocean and the Gironde estuary, the Médoc peninsula takes its name from the Latin, *in medio aquae.* Starting at Blanquefort, north of the city of Bordeaux, and coming to a point at the Pointe-de-Grave even further north, the distinctive 80.5-kilometer/50-mile-long tongue of land has no corresponding distinction of landscape. It is testament to the entrepreneurial vision and engineering skills of the Dutch that they could have spent time and energy draining what was for the most part bleak marshland in the seventeenth century, regulating the streams, known as *jalles,* for drainage and dotting the whole surface with windmills. It is no coincidence that part of the northern Médoc was for long known as *La Petite Hollande.* The featureless and windy countryside must have made them feel at home.

Today, as you amble along the *Route des Châteaux,* the very flatness of the countryside serves to emphasize the splendor of the great estates. Erected in some cases before the Revolution and proliferating during the Second Empire in the latter half of the last century, the châteaux of the Médoc are the most tangible symbols of the wealth, power and prestige of the gentry and merchant classes.

Once the winemaking viability of the poor soils of the Médoc was established, the proximity of the city assured the ascendancy of the Médoc's wines over those of all other regions of Bordeaux. By 1855, when the now famous classification of Bordeaux was carried out, only one of the fifty-eight classified properties (later to become sixty-one after sub-divisions within estates), Haut-Brion in the Graves, came from outside the Médoc.

The vineyards of the Médoc hug the banks of the Gironde in a narrow strip some 80.5 kilometers/50 miles long but measuring only eleven kilometers/seven miles at its widest point. The soil consists principally of layers of gravel more than ten meters/eleven yards in depth carried down over the centuries from the Pyrénées and the Massif Central. The well-drained nature of this soil is one of the secrets of the Médoc. It is also soil that allows the roots of the vine to search perhaps 5 meters/5.5 yards down for sustenance and to take up water at the optimum rate for quality wine production. Deep-rooted vines are highly resistant to both drought and summer storms. Warm, stony soils are also the ideal home for the late-ripening Cabernet Sauvignon, which reaches its finest expression along

LEFT: This windmill standing in the windswept vineyards of Château La Tour-Haut-Caussan dates from 1734. Restored in 1981, it is a monument to the engineering skills of the Dutch, who drained the Médoc in the seventeenth century.

the banks of the Garonne in the four communes, from south to north, of Margaux, St. Julien, Pauillac and St.-Estèphe.

"The best vines are those which can see the water", say the Bordelais, especially those with estates on river banks. Certainly the climate provided by the conjunction of estuary, coniferous forest to the west and the humidity of the Gulf Stream creates ideal local conditions for the Cabernet Sauvignon to thrive. Yet even within this narrow strip, the myriad permutations of grape varieties, imperceptible gradients in the lie of the land, geological sub-structure and latitudes and the different approaches to winemaking from château to château ensure that the Médoc remains a sub-region producing wines of a thousand subtle nuances.

Covering an area of nearly 13,000 hectares/32,110 acres, just under half the 25,000 hectares/61,750 acres it accounted for in the days before the phylloxera struck, the Médoc comprises eight appellations and accounts for over one-tenth

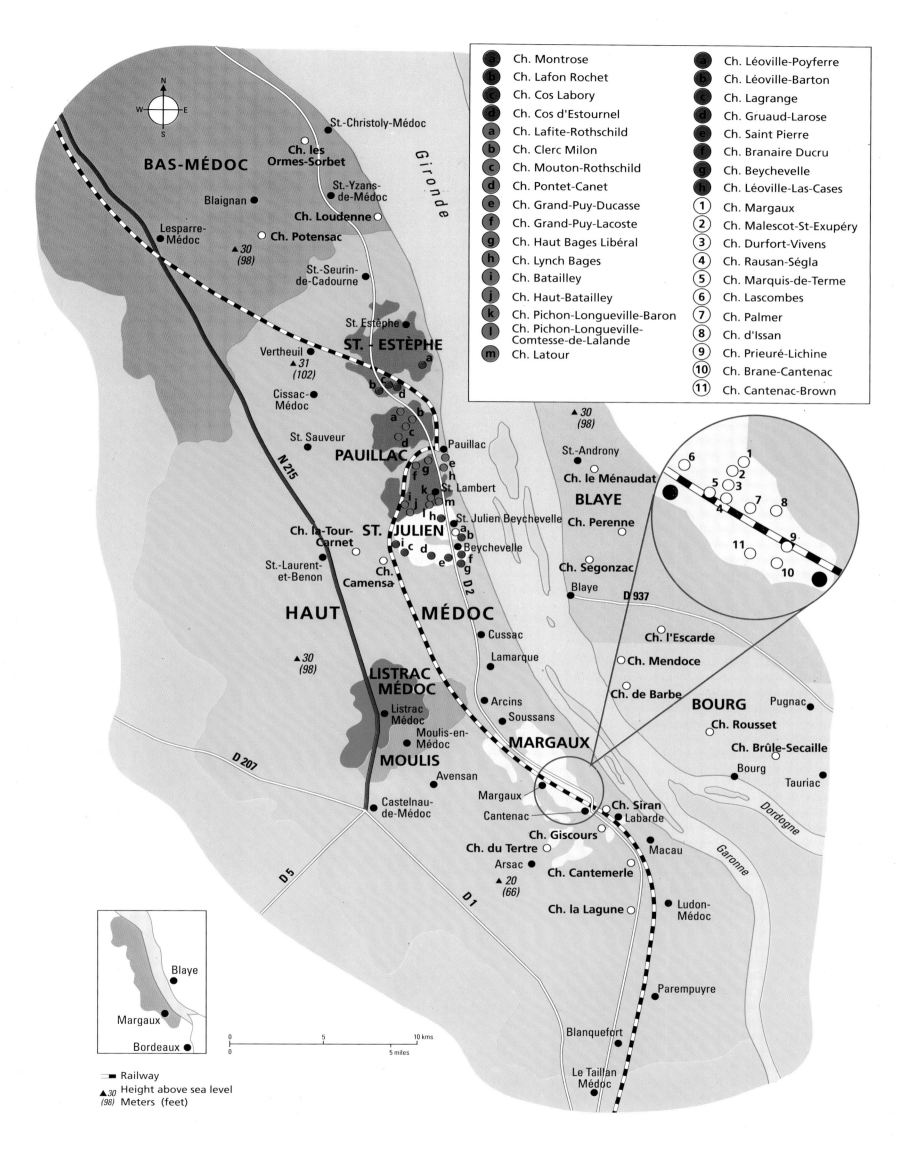

(a)	Ch. Montrose	(a)	Ch. Léoville-Poyferre
(b)	Ch. Lafon Rochet	(b)	Ch. Léoville-Barton
(c)	Ch. Cos Labory	(c)	Ch. Lagrange
(d)	Ch. Cos d'Estournel	(d)	Ch. Gruaud-Larose
(a)	Ch. Lafite-Rothschild	(e)	Ch. Saint Pierre
(b)	Ch. Clerc Milon	(f)	Ch. Branaire Ducru
(c)	Ch. Mouton-Rothschild	(g)	Ch. Beychevelle
(d)	Ch. Pontet-Canet	(h)	Ch. Léoville-Las-Cases
(e)	Ch. Grand-Puy-Ducasse	(1)	Ch. Margaux
(f)	Ch. Grand-Puy-Lacoste	(2)	Ch. Malescot-St-Exupéry
(g)	Ch. Haut Bages Libéral	(3)	Ch. Durfort-Vivens
(h)	Ch. Lynch Bages	(4)	Ch. Rausan-Ségla
(i)	Ch. Batailley	(5)	Ch. Marquis-de-Terme
(j)	Ch. Haut-Batailley	(6)	Ch. Lascombes
(k)	Ch. Pichon-Longueville-Baron	(7)	Ch. Palmer
(l)	Ch. Pichon-Longueville-Comtesse-de-Lalande	(8)	Ch. d'Issan
		(9)	Ch. Prieuré-Lichine
(m)	Ch. Latour	(10)	Ch. Brane-Cantenac
		(11)	Ch. Cantenac-Brown

Railway

▲30 Height above sea level
(98) Meters (feet)

48

of the surface area of Bordeaux. Its average annual production is around 77 million bottles. Furthest north lies the open, rather bleak backwater of the Bas-Médoc, a windswept, wide-open-spaced appellation on the road to nowhere comprising sixteen communes of mainly *crus bourgeois, petits châteaux* and cooperatives, producing sound, everyday, relatively early-maturing styles of wine labeled simply Médoc. The Bas-Médoc covers 3,770 hectares/9,312 acres, just under a third of the entire Médoc, and produces an average of 23 million bottles. Recommended wines here are La Tour-Haut-Caussan, Potensac, Loudenne and Les Ormes Sorbet.

The Haut-Médoc begins at Blanquefort and continues for some 50 kilometers/124 miles north to Saint-Seurin de Cadourne. At 3,500 hectares/8,645 acres, it is slightly smaller in vineyard area than the Bas-Médoc, comprising 15 communes, and containing only five classified châteaux: Camensac, Belgrave, la Tour Carnet, the superior La Lagune and refined Cantemerle. The backbone of the Haut-Médoc however are its 90 *crus bourgeois*, those literally middle-ranking estates, many of which, thanks to investment and improvements in vinification, offer amongst the best value in red Bordeaux.

The heart of the Haut-Médoc has been cut out to form the six juiciest slices of the region, the four great commune appellations mentioned, plus Moulis, the smallest, and Listrac, the "roof of the Médoc", which reaches all of 43 meters/140 feet above sea level. Among the best of the nonclassified Haut-Médoc wines are the following: Citran, Lanessan, Lamarque, Liversan, Beaumont, Cissac, Ramage-la-Batisse, Sénéjac, Tour-du-Haut-Moulin, Sociando-Mallet, Soudars.

Driving north from the city center, Margaux, lying almost in line with the confluence of the Dordogne and Garonne rivers, is the first appellation you reach. Of the six commune appellations, Margaux is the largest and at the same time the most diffuse, encompassing the five communes of Arsac, Cantenac, Labarde, Soussans and Margaux itself, a total area of some 1,250 hectares/3,088 acres. It produces around 54,000 hectoliters/1,426,572 U.S. gallons of wine. Margaux is the only commune taking its name from its most prestigious and only *Premier Cru*, Château Margaux itself. This is made easier by the fact that neither St. Julien nor St.-Estèphe contains a first growth, and Pauillac boasts three, which would make such a choice invidious. With no fewer than twenty-one classified properties one *Premier Cru*, five seconds, ten thirds, three fourths and two fifths, the concentration of fine wine is staggering, accounting as it does for the lion's share of the appellation both in vineyard area and production.

Margaux's soil is fine gravel flecked with small white pebbles that can resemble the aftermath of a hailstorm, but the character of its wines can be the hardest of all six communes to define. It is their very differences that make them so hard to pin down, but if it is possible to generalize without becoming trite, the wines tend to be more fragrant and silky-soft, more delicate and with greater finesse than those of other communes. This may be in part because, with only four exceptions including Château Margaux itself, none of the classified properties is planted with more than three-quarters of the Cabernet Sauvignon grape. Conversely,

GROWER'S VIEW

Great wines are above all the expression of the genius of a *terroir*, that is to say, that unique combination of natural factors, in particular the soil and the climate. The genius of man lies in harnessing the best of these natural factors and refining, little by little, the techniques of vine cultivation and the development and production of wine. It is really nature that creates and gives birth, while man educates, shapes and models.

The business of producing wine provides, first of all, a lesson in modesty before becoming — and sometimes justifiably — a source of pride. It is for this reason that I do not like the word "winemaker". If one is going to use a word, I should prefer "wineservant." The "maker," that is to say the creator, feels that he has ultimate power, to the extent of going too far in his experimenting; sometimes even verging on the ridiculous. A servant has first to feel respect for his "product/master." He acts in a measured fashion, looking more for harmony and balance than excess and strength.

For the greatest wines are first of all wines of perfect harmony where nothing is lacking and nothing upstages, where everything is included but nothing in particular is overpowering. These wines are powerful, certainly, but it is a controlled power, civilized, almost hidden; rich in tannin without being tannic; bursting with perfume and flavor but so well blended that no one element asserts itself.

Paul Pontallier

CHATEAU MARGAUX

BELOW: These four châteaux from the Haut-Médoc all rank as *crus bourgeois* apart from Château Cantemerle, a fifth growth, which is one of the few classified châteaux outside the four communes of St.-Estèphe, Pauillac, St. Julien and Margaux. If there were a new classification today, Château Chasse-Spleen in Moulis would undoubtedly be included.

ABOVE: Pauillac and Margaux between them contain all four first growth properties. The fortunes of Château Margaux have prospered under the Mentzelopoulos family, who acquired the estate in 1976.

RIGHT: Although Château Palmer was classified as a third growth in 1855, it is today generally acknowledged to be equal to the leading second growths. Château Palmer produces an elegant, rich wine of considerable finesse, thanks to the high proportion of Merlot in the blend.

many, notably Châteaux Palmer, Lascombes, Malescot-Saint-Exupéry, Prieuré-Lichine and Marquis de Terme, grow a good proportion of Merlot.

Top of the Margaux tree is without question Château Margaux itself, which under the direction of the Mentzelopoulos family, who bought it in 1976, and their gifted winemaker Paul Pontallier, has improved from a period in the doldrums to such an extent that it is now consistently one of the top wines of the vintage. Third-growth Palmer now vies for second place with Rausan-Ségla which since 1982 has improved beyond recognition. Below these two, a clutch of classified châteaux are making considerable efforts to catch the leaders, notably d'Issan, Cantenac-Brown, Giscours, du Tertre, Las-

combes, Prieuré-Lichine, Malescot-Saint-Exupéry, Brane-Cantenac and Durfort-Vivens. Margaux also boasts a number of excellent *crus bourgeois.* Both Monbrison and d'Angludet are up to classified-growth standard and would surely be promoted in the unlikely event of a new classification, while Siran, Labégorce-Zédé and La Gurgue are also potential candidates for promotion.

Curiously, meadow and woodland isolate Margaux from the three adjacent communes to the north, St. Julien, Pauillac and St.-Estèphe. St. Julien is the smallest with 850 hectares/2,100 acres and remarkable in that it contains eleven classified châteaux. Between them, they occupy three-quarters of the appellation and at the same time provide perhaps the highest concentration of consistent performers in the classification. Of the eleven, five are second growths, two third growths and four fourth growths. Although still predominantly gravel, there is a little more clay in St. Julien's soils, as a result of which its wines stand somewhere between Margaux in elegance and Pauillac on full throttle fruit. The vineyards producing wines with the greatest finesse are those situated on the slopes over the Gironde, in particular Ducru-Beaucaillou and Léoville-Las-Cases.

Ducru-Beaucaillou is the jewel in the crown of Jean-Eugène Borie, one of the few château owners to live on the premises. He also runs Lalande-Borie and, in Pauillac, Haut-Batailley and Grand-Puy-Lacoste. Léoville-Lascases, with one of the strictest selection policies of any château, has been honed to near first-growth standard by the single-minded efforts of the reclusive Michel Delon. Next in line, Beychevelle, Gruaud-Larose, Branaire-Ducru, Léoville Poyferré and Léoville Barton all produce excellent wine today, the last having considerably improved in the latter half of the eighties and become noteworthy too for its sensible pricing policies. Château Lagrange has made great strides since its renovation by the Japanese owned Suntory

LEFT: Château-Gruaud-Larose in St. Julien was bought by the Cordier family after World War I. A restoration monarchy favorite, the label still boasts the motto "Le Roy des Vins, le Vin des Rois".

group, and St. Pierre, now run by the son-in-law of the late mayor, Henri Martin, is a property to watch. The same goes for Château Gloria, the *cru bourgeois* which is also under the same new management.

Sitting on the Gironde like some tatterdemalion port in a seedy, low-budget B-movie, the town of Pauillac hardly does justice to the magnificent properties whose reputations have spread its prestige far and wide. The magical names of Latour, Lafite and Mouton Rothschild make Pauillac, if not the geographic center, then certainly the spiritual heart of Bordeaux. Archetypal claret, deep-hued, long-lived, richly fruity, fine and black currant, is made here. If Margaux lays claim to the highest number of classified vineyards, Pauillac takes the title for the commune with the largest classified vineyard area, some 750 out of 1,100 hectares/1,850 out of 2,717 acres of A.O.C. Pauillac, although it has eighteen to Margaux's twenty classified châteaux, with no fewer than twelve relatively lowly fifth growths. Pauillac's

soil is poor and varied with much iron-rich gravel producing varying styles that are for the most part full-bodied, concentrated, long-lived and with supreme finesse.

Of the three first growths, Château Lafite is the wine with the lowest Cabernet Sauvignon and highest Merlot content. Perhaps for this reason, it possesses the most ethereal, divine bouquet and elegance. Latour is made of sterner stuff, often good in off-vintages, but powerfully fruity and incredibly long-lasting in great ones. After a mildly disappointing performance in the early eighties, Latour appears to be right back on song. Its second wine, Les Forts de Latour, is easily the best of the seconds and worthy of classified status in its own right. Mouton-Rothschild, with one of the highest proportions of Cabernet Sauvignon planted (85 percent), is a monument to the efforts of Baron Philippe, whose 55-year reign saw Mouton elevated to first-growth status in 1973. It is the only change ever

BELOW: While the labels of two of the great first growths of Pauillac, Lafite and Latour, appear timeless, those of Mouton-Rothschild change every year, as part of a policy pursued by Baron Philippe de Rothschild from 1946 onwards, to commission a different artist to design the label for each new vintage.

ABOVE: The exotic oriental architecture of Château Cos d'Estournel in St.-Estèphe, with its Chinese pagodas, conceals the fact that there is no château, only a cellar.

RIGHT: In the cool, dark underground cellars of Château Lafite, old bottles of wine lie undisturbed apart from a periodical recorking to prevent the corks from becoming saturated and the wine leaking.

BELOW: Labels from estates in St.-Estèphe, the most northerly of the Haut-Médoc's famous four communes, including the two best-known properties in the commune, Montrose and Cos d'Estournel.

made to the 1855 classification. Mouton is gloriously, exotically perfumed with aromas of cedar and black currants, the epitome of great Pauillac and on splendid form since 1982.

Pauillac's two second growths, both great wines, are also great rivals: Pichon-Longueville, and its neighbor across the road, Pichon-Lalande. While May-Eliane de Lencquesaing has worked wonders to produce in Pichon-Lalande one of Bordeaux' most seductive wines, Jean-Michel Cazes has, as manager of the estates of the insurance group, Axa-Millésimes, revitalized Pichon-Longueville. It too has been making richly concentrated, superb wine since 1986.

A string of fifth growths is headed by Cazes' own excellent Lynch-Bages and Jean-Eugène Borie's Grand-Puy-Lacoste, consistently good value. In the wines-to-watch category, Clerc-Milon, Haut-Bages-Libéral, Pontet-Canet and Grand-Puy-Ducasse are all making strides, as are the solid soldiers of Batailley and Lynch-Moussas. There are relatively few *crus bourgeois* in Pauillac, but the best are probably Fon-

badet and the little Château Pibran, now also part of the Axa empire.

With around 1,200 hectares/2,964 acres St.-Estèphe vies for size with Margaux, but with only five châteaux classified and forty-eight *crus bourgeois* and *petits châteaux,* a number exceeded only in Margaux, the impression here is more of reliable solidity. Gravel, chalk and sand and, further to the north, clay, are found in St.-Estèphe's varied soils, once again making it difficult to pinpoint a communal style by reference to soil alone.

Here the leading estate was until recently without question Château Cos d'Estournel. Run with passion and intellectual rigor by Bruno Prats, Cos is as stylish as the exotic oriental architecture of its *chai* is distinctive. Since 1986, Montrose has proved the equal of Cos. Facing the nuclear-power station at Blaye, Montrose is a long-distance runner, a powerful, deep-colored wine that since the late eighties has been getting increasingly exciting.

Of the remaining classified châteaux, both Lafon-Rochet and Cos Labory have made strides in the eighties and usually represent good value.

As befits the leading *cru bourgeois* commune, there are a number of wines here worthy of classified status. Château de Pez, under the quiet care of

Robert Dousson, is consistently classy. Phélan-Ségur has once again returned to form having been bought by ex-Champagne Pommery and Lanson magnate Xavier Gardinier. Haut-Marbuzet with its high proportion of Merlot and new oak, has great sensuous appeal. Les Ormes de Pez is another reliable performer.

The two remaining appellations of the Médoc, Moulis and Listrac, respectively 500 and just over 600 hectares/1,255 and just over 1,482 acres, tend to be considered rather as afterthoughts, mainly because they contain no classified estates. Being inland, they are also a little more remote. Yet both, Moulis in particular, produce wines of fine fruit flavors and good keeping qualities, usually offering good value for the money. In particular is Chasse-Spleen, a big, rich wine with uncompromisingly powerful style that keeps and keeps. Poujeaux, little known until recently because of its commercial ties with Belgium, is another excellent, supple, classy wine. Maucaillou, Dutruch-Grand-Poujeaux and Gressier-Grand-Poujeaux can be excellent value. Listrac tends to produce a slightly harder style of wine, but the leading properties, Fourcas-Hosten, Fourcas-Dupré and Clarke, manage to extract plenty of fruit and flavor.

The Graves and Pessac-Léognan, Entre-Deux-Mers

by Anthony Rose

Though in the shadow today of its more illustrious northern neighbor, the Graves is the ancient vinous heart of Bordeaux, its wines preeminent centuries before the emergence of the Médoc in the early eighteenth century. Taking its name from the underlying gravelly soil, the Graves was the name for the whole of the left bank of the Garonne and Gironde before the Médoc established its superiority. Mention of Château Haut-Brion in Samuel Pepys' diary of 1663 as "a sort of French wine called Ho Bryan that hath a good and most particular taste that I ever met with" provides the first recorded mention in English literature of an individual Bordeaux estate. Over the centuries, the gradual suburban sprawl of the city of Bordeaux has resulted in a corresponding contraction of the vineyards of the Graves. Of the 10,000 hectares/24,700 acres of vines 100 years ago, only one-third remain today. In 1850, for instance, Mérignac had twenty-two wine-producing estates. Today it has one, and an international airport.

Bounded to the west by the sandy soils of the pine forests of the Landes and to the east by the Garonne River, the Graves begins where the Médoc ends, at the Jalle de Blanquefort north of the city of Bordeaux. It encompasses the city itself before traveling some fifty-six kilometers/thirty-five miles and ending south of Langon. More wooded than the Médoc, the Graves' attractively rural landscape is the setting for some of Bordeaux's most notable medieval monuments, notably Château La Brède, the thirteenth-century moated castle where Montesquieu was born and wrote, and Château de Roquetaillade, a massive fourteenth century fortress.

Although similar in composition to the Médoc, the soil of the Graves is more ancient, with Pyrenean gravel terraces, rich in ironstone, forming the left bank of the Garonne. The gravel combines in places with sandy and clay soils.

Until the 1970s, Graves were predominantly white wines and for the most part on the sweet side. Today only around 500 hectares/1,235 acres of vineyard are reserved for the production of Graves Supérieures, the semi-sweet style, while almost twice that amount goes to the production of dry white

BELOW: Bordeaux' famous wine quays lie on the Garonne River, which flows out through the Gironde estuary to the Atlantic. Centuries of control of the wine trade have brought prosperity to the citizens of Bordeaux.

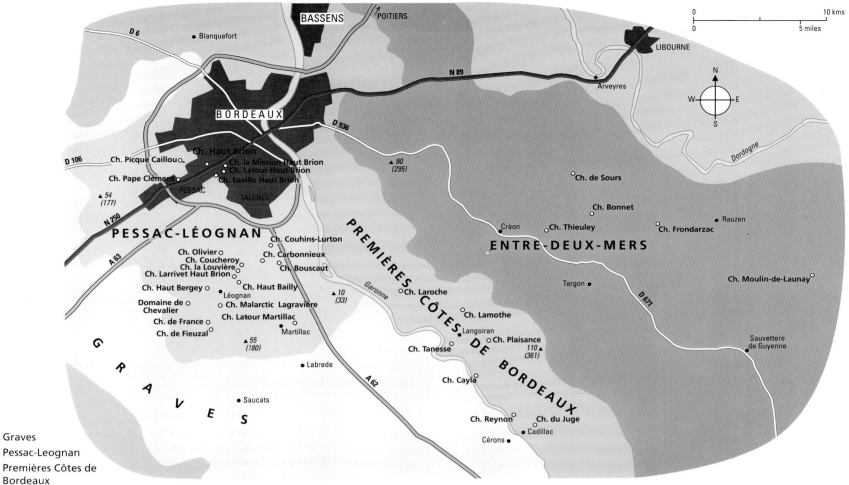

Graves

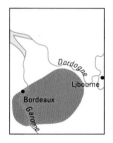

Pessac-Leognan

Premières Côtes de Bordeaux

Entre-Deux-Mers

○ Vineyard

━━ Autoroute

▲54 Height above sea level
(173) Meters (feet)

BELOW: Labels from some of the up-and-coming properties in the southern districts of Bordeaux. Both Château Bonnet and Château Thieuley have made something of a name for themselves with their modern-style, crisp but fruity, dry white wines.

wines. The Graves now produces slightly more red than white. The Graves was redefined in the eighties into two separate appellations: Pessac-Léognan in the northern half, which from 1987 includes all the *crus classés*, and the Graves, an area roughly twice the size incorporating the less well-regarded vineyards of the southern half. The vineyards of the Graves were officially classified in 1953 and 1959, listing, alphabetically, thirteen red wines and eight white.

It is hard to pinpoint the character of the Graves. The dry whites have improved out of all recognition from the stale, tired wines of yesteryear. Thanks to the pioneering work of Pierre Coste, André Lurton and Denis Dubourdieu, there has been a revolt into style. Temperature control, clean stainless steel equipment and barrel fermentation have introduced aromatic qualities, fresh fruitiness and a degree of complexity once lacking in all but the very few top wines. Graves reds generally contain a slightly lower proportion of Cabernet Sauvignon and higher proportions of Merlot than their Médoc counterparts. While resembling them in their blend of spice and vanilla aromas and black currant

fruitiness, they tend to be softer, lighter in body and earlier-maturing, sometimes with a giveaway earthy, floral or tobaccoey character.

Haut-Brion, subtle, delicate, approachable but slow to show its true colors, is the best wine of the Graves. Indeed many believe that in 1989 it produced the wine of the vintage. Across the road, La Mission Haut Brion, its old sibling rival, has been under the same ownership since 1983, and is capable of producing superb wines in less than great vintages, as in 1981 and 1987. Domaine de Chevalier and, since its return to form in 1985, Pape-Clément, are neck-and-neck, the former richly oaky, spicy and fine, the latter now a wine of considerable concentrated fruit and finesse. Beneath these four, I would place Haut-Bailly, de Fieuzal, Malartic-Lagravière and Smith-Haut-Lafitte, with the non-classified reds of Larrivet-Haut-Brion and La Louvière both worthy of classification. Among the less well known, good value properties: de France, Haut-Bergey, Cruzeau, Picque-Caillou and Cabannieux.

Three estates, Malartic-Lagravière, Couhins-Lurton and Smith-Haut-Lafitte use only Sauvignon Blanc. Most like to blend the Sauvignon Blanc

LEFT: Château Haut-Brion was the only Graves to be included in the 1855 classification of Bordeaux. Although not always consistent, today its place in the pantheon of fame is fully justified.

and Sémillon together, occasionally with a touch of Muscadelle. The feeling seems to be that while the Sauvignon gives a wine aroma and freshness, the Sémillon, especially when barrel fermented, adds weight and complexity which develops into a lovely honeyed richness. For a long while, Haut-Brion, expensive but outstandingly good, Laville-Haut-Brion and Domaine de Chevalier have been islands of quality in a dull Graves sea. Since the mid-eighties, however, there has been nothing short of a revolution in the Graves. With its biggest property, Carbonnieux, improving under the influence of Professor Denis Dubourdieu of the Bordeaux Institute of Enology, others have followed suit, notably de Fieuzal, La Louvière, La Tour Martillac, Couhins-Lurton and Smith-Haut-Lafitte. Look out too for Clos Floridène, Piron, Montalivet, Coucheroy and Cruzeau.

On the right bank of the Garonne, the Premières Côtes de Bordeaux extends in a narrow, fifty-six kilometer/thirty-five-mile strip of wooded hills of clay and limestone overlooking the Graves. It stretches from Ormont, northeast of the city, all the way to St. Macaire in the south. Over 2,000 hectares/4,940 acres of the appellation are devoted to red wine. The dry white is labeled simply as A.O.C. Bordeaux Blanc. For the most part the reds are medium bodied and attractively fruity, many having improved enormously thanks to considerable investment by the bourgeoisie of Bordeaux. Wines of note include Châteaux Lamothe, Laroche, du Juge, Reynon, Cayla, Tanesse and Plaisance.

Next to this strip, the triangular wedge of land that stretches to the Dordogne in the north is known as the Entre-Deux-Mers. It includes the enclaves of St. Macaire, Haut-Benauge, Ste. Foy in its northeast corner, and, opposite Libourne, Graves de Vayres. At some 3,000 hectares/7,410 acres the largest of all Bordeaux's sub-regions, the Entre-Deux-Mers is also one of the prettiest, its undulating countryside punctuated by churches, rivers and sleepy little towns. The appellation is reserved for dry white wines, although owners sometimes prefer to use the simple A.O.C. Bordeaux Blanc appellation. With improvements in technology, the wines can be delightfully fragrant and fruity and represent very good value. Names to look out for in Entre-Deux-Mers include Châteaux Bonnet, de Sours, Thieuley, Fondarzac and Moulin-de-Launay.

BELOW: Cadillac was a new appellation created in 1973 to provide a sharper focus for the better sweet-white-wine producing communes of the southern Premières Côtes de Bordeaux, but by 1986 only 16,000 cases of appellation Cadillac were made.

St. Emilion, Pomerol and Satellites

by Anthony Rose

If a great wine region has to have its tourist attractions, then the picturesque, fortified town of St. Emilion provides plenty of meat for the camera and drink for the palate. Originating in Roman times, the town takes its name from the hermit Aemilianus, who settled here in the eighth century long after all trace of the Roman Empire had vanished. The Benedictines laid the early foundations in the seventh century, to be developed later by new religious orders, notably Franciscans and Dominicans. Here, above Aemilianus' cavern in the eleventh and twelfth centuries, the Eglise Monolithe, Europe's largest underground church, was carved out of the surrounding limestone by Benedictine monks. Equally famous is the Eglise Collégiale, whose chapter governed the town until the French Revolution together with the secular Jurade, instituted by John, king of England, in 1199.

Next to St. Emilion, and on the Dordogne, the town and port of Libourne is the trading center of the region, established in 1270. Its history is intimately connected with that of St. Emilion and the surrounding appellations. With its hybrid religious and secular organization, its smaller estates and comparative remoteness from the city of Bordeaux, St. Emilion's trading priorities were for long very different from those of Bordeaux.

If not exactly shunned, St. Emilion was ignored by the *négociants* and pooh-poohed by the *noblesse de robe* of the Médoc until comparatively recently. None of the properties of St. Emilion was considered worthy of classification in 1855. It was only in the second half of the last century, with shortages caused by natural disasters, that the merchants of Bordeaux began to cast their net in the general direction of St. Emilion.

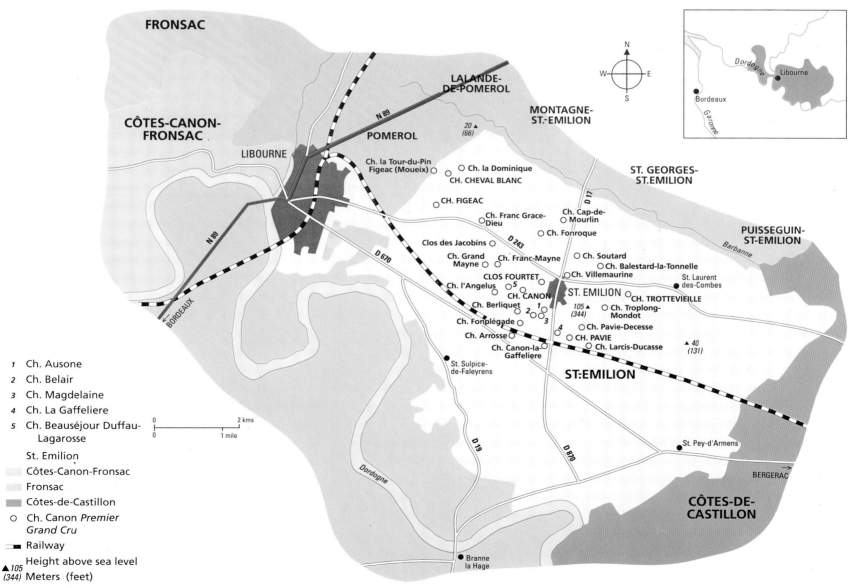

1 Ch. Ausone
2 Ch. Belair
3 Ch. Magdelaine
4 Ch. La Gaffeliere
5 Ch. Beauséjour Duffau-Lagarosse

St. Emilion
Côtes-Canon-Fronsac
Fronsac
Côtes-de-Castillon
○ Ch. Canon *Premier Grand Cru*
▬ Railway
▲105
(344) Height above sea level
Meters (feet)

St. Emilion differs in a number of respects from the Médoc and Graves. Estates are smaller and more compact, averaging from 10 to 20 hectares/24.7 to 49.5 acres in size compared to three times that and more on the left bank. Vines here seem to occupy every available space, and although at 5,200-odd hectares/12,800-odd acres, St. Emilion covers less than half the vineyard area of the Médoc, production is correspondingly higher. In 1986, it reached 40 million bottles. The main differences in the wines however arise from distinctions in terrain, grapes and climate.

The soils of St. Emilion are so varied that Henri Enjalbert, a geologist, made the study of them his life's work. Even so, according to Bernard Ginestet, author of *The Ginestet Guide to St. Emilion* (1990), Enjalbert "got lost in the geological maze". For our purposes, it is sufficient to sub-divide the appellation into three main parts. Most of the best vineyards lie on the limestone plateau and hill that slopes south towards the Dordogne River. To the west in the direction of Pomerol, the smaller gravel-

ly area houses two of St. Emilion's finest châteaux, Cheval Blanc and Figeac. It is no coincidence that Figeac contains the highest proportion of Cabernet Sauvignon of all St. Emilion's classified properties. Between the two is an area of ancient sandy soils on a bed of limestone.

Because of the different composition of the soils, grape varieties vary too. The Merlot is the dominant grape and characteristically planted in inverse proportion to its plantations in the Médoc and Graves. Only Cheval Blanc, with 66 percent Cabernet Franc, and Figeac, with equal parts Cabernet Sauvignon and Franc, are planted with less than half Merlot. Ausone is half Merlot, half Cabernet Franc. The early-ripening, delicate Merlot favors the cooler, richer clay and limestone soils of the region. It produces higher yields than the Cabernet Sauvignon, and wines whose extra alcoholic strength and more evident sweetness have obvious charm and immediate appeal. Producing wines with a tendency to be aromatic, plump in texture and fruity in flavor but with balanced tannins, the wines of St. Emilion are

ABOVE: Built on a hillside, the charming medieval town of St. Emilion with its narrow, winding streets, its monuments and views of the vineyards beyond, is the epitome of the French wine town.

57

Named after the fourth-century Roman poet Ausonius, whose villa is said to have stood on this site, Château Ausone sits on a unique soil of clay and sand on limestone.

generally more appealing and approachable young than those of the Médoc. They are quick developers and not quite so long-lasting, although the best of them have considerable staying power.

The two great wines of St. Emilion are Cheval Blanc and Ausone, the former powerful, subtle and complex, the latter, under the stewardship of master craftsman Pascal Delbeck, delicate and tantalizing in its bouquet, the most ethereal of all Bordeaux wines. Of the remaining *grands crus classés,* Canon, Magdelaine, Figeac and Pavie stand apart as wines of tremendous style. Next in rank Belair and Clos Fourtet are making rapid strides.

Perhaps the most difficult task for the consumer, given the bewildering number of classified wines, is to sort out the current, most consistent performers. Not in any particular order, these are some of the high fliers: Angélus, Cap de Mourlin, Larmande, L'Arrosée, Couvent des Jacobins, la Gaffelière, Canon la Gaffelière, Fonroque, Franc-Mayne, Franc-Grâce-Dieu, Grand-Mayne, La Tour du Pin Figeac, Soutard, Larcis Ducasse, Troplong-Mondot, Pavie-Decesse, La Dominique, Balestard la Tonnelle, Berliquet, Villemaurine and Fonplégade.

There are even more *grands crus,* some two hundred in all. Names to look out for here include Bellefont Belcier, Ferrand, Fombrauge and particularly Le Tertre Rôteboeuf.

Surrounding St. Emilion mainly to the north and north east are the so-called satellites of Montagne, Lussac, Puisseguin and Saint-Georges, covering a large area of some 3,300 hectares/18,150 acres. There is a tendency to more Merlot in the blend, hence softer, earlier-drinking wine. Among the best of the satellites are Château Bel-Air (Puisseguin), Belair-Montaiguillon, Calon, Lyonnat, Roudier, de Roques, St. André-Corbin and St. Georges.

If size were the only criterion, you might say that Pomerol has made a disproportionate noise on the world stage. But although Château Pétrus, or simply Pétrus as it likes to be known, the most expensive of all red Bordeaux, has helped to put tiny Pomerol on the map, it is largely the driving force of the family

behind the château, the Moueix family, that has really been responsible for the dramatic upturn in Pomerol's fortunes. Pétrus actually won a gold medal at the Paris exhibition in 1878. Yet Pomerol has been recognized as a distinct entity only since 1923. Even then, to the irritation of the orderly-minded, it has never had its own classification.

With just 730 hectares/1,803 acres of vineyard, and no village or much else to its name apart from wine estates, Pomerol is so inconspicuous you need a map as much to find your way in as to find your way around. And once you are there, you must admit, the place is pretty undistinguished — except for the wine, of course. On a plateau which to all intents and purposes is as flat as a pancake, Pomerol is really an extension of Libourne, the town from which it quietly plied its wines for decades until it was "discovered" by Jean-Pierre Moueix, an urbane businessman from the Corrèze with a nose for the finest things in life. He managed to convince the château's redoubtable owner Madame Loubat that he understood Pétrus. Then it was seized upon by the Americans, who adored the heady, spicy, sheer voluptuousness of Pétrus. When, following the 1982 vintage, itself one of the most exotic in years, the influential American critic Robert Parker latched on to Pétrus, its fortune, and that of Pomerol along with it, was secured. Since then, it has become the fashion to call a wine the Pétrus of this, the Pétrus of that. Who knows, perhaps the word *pétrus* will yet find its way into the dictionary.

What is the special character of Pomerol? At its heart, the Pomerol plateau is gravelly with Pétrus sitting in an island of sandy clay. Surrounding the top of the plateau is a gravelly terrace mixed with clay and sandy soils which slopes imperceptibly to the sandier, alluvial soils of the Dordogne. In places there is a hard, iron-rich *crasse de fer* which many owners claim gives Pomerol its special qualities, but how much belongs to folklore and how much to scientific fact is impossible to determine. Suffice it to say that Enjalbert's one paragraph on the subject (out of 150 pages on the soils of the Libournais) is inconclusive on the point. The wines of

ABOVE: Château Pétrus, known simply as Pétrus to connoisseurs, is the jewel in the crown of Pomerol, with a price to match its starring role.

OPPOSITE PAGE, BOTTOM: Labels of four of St. Emilion's top properties, indicating, in contrast to the system in the Médoc and Graves, that the comparatively recent classification of St. Emilion is actually incorporated into the appellation.

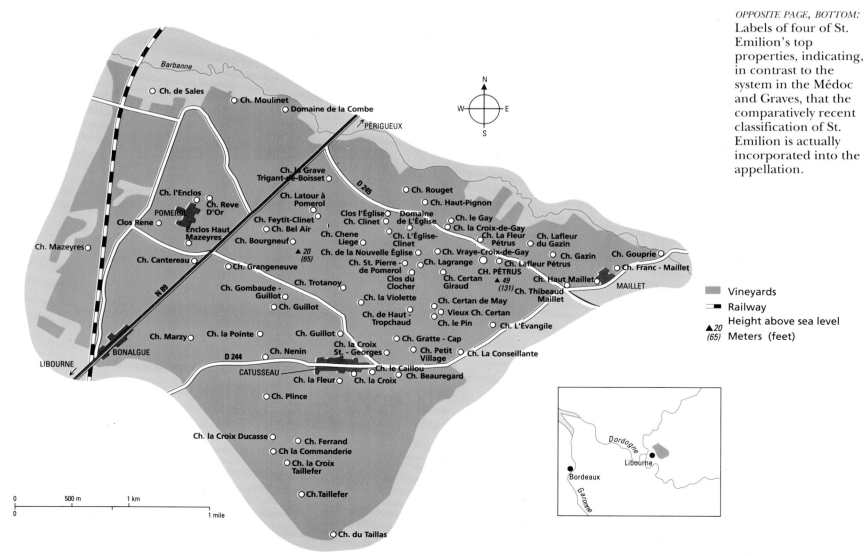

L'Enclos, Le Bon Pasteur, Nenin, La Pointe, de Sales. Across the Barbanne River, Lalande de Pomerol, larger than Pomerol itself, produces some excellent-value drinking from such châteaux as Siaurac, Moulin-à-Vent, La Croix St. André, Bertineau St. Vincent, Grand Ormeau and Hauts Conseillants (also known as Hautes-Tuileries).

─── GROWER'S VIEW ───

There is no one way of making wine, but several. From the same starting point, a different approach can produce different results and varying degrees of quality. It would be pretentious to think that you can know everything or that you have invented everything. You only have to look at the variety of wines from Europe and outside to see that that is an impossibility. With a product as subjective as wine, taste can never conform to just one stereotype. From an exceptional vineyard and microclimate at L'Angélus and quality grape varieties, what I have always sought in terms of technique is to combine the most simple with the most scientific and at the same time the most practical. Although one has to be receptive to passing fashions in taste, my aim is to produce a wine that will stand the test of time: a product in harmony with its environment, the typical character of its soil, the soul of its creator and the pleasure of the consumer.

Without passion and faith in your vineyard, you cannot make a wine that reflects those strong emotions. Color, aroma, bouquet, texture and richness are just some of the quality elements. But nothing is definitive in wine. The greatest wines have evolved over a period of time. What counts is elegance, breed, finesse and modesty and the conviction that you are on the right track.

Hubert de Bouard
CHATEAU L'ANGÉLUS

ABOVE: Thanks to their voluptuously fruity character, demand for the wines of Pomerol is in inverse proportion to supply.

Pomerol tend to be well-structured and firm, spicy and rich, with a greater finesse and delicacy than those of St. Emilion.

There are fifty-one châteaux in Pomerol. After Pétrus, there are a number of properties producing magnificent wine, but the speculation fever that hit Pétrus has rubbed off on others. Prices can be ferocious. In the first rank after Pétrus come Certan de May, Clinet, La Conseillante, L'Eglise-Clinet, La Fleur de Gay, Lafleur, L'Evangile, Lafleur, Latour-à-Pomerol, Petit-Village, Le Pin and Vieux Château Certan. Other properties demonstrate that despite the demand for Pomerol, it is still possible to find good value, in particular La Croix de Gay, Le Gay, Gazin, Beauregard, Feytit-Clinet, Clos René,

RIGHT: Vieux Château Certan has usually been regarded as one of the leading Pomerol properties, jostling for first place with Pétrus. From the mid-1980s a policy of reduced yields and other improvements has led in recent years to the production of wines of exceptional depth and finish.

Fronsac and the Côtes: Bourg, Blaye, Castillon and Francs

by Anthony Rose

Fronsac

A stone's throw northwest of the town of Libourne, the picturesque wooded hills and valleys of Fronsac stand in marked contrast to the altogether flatter vineyards of Pomerol on the opposite bank of the little river Isle. With close to 1,100 hectares/2,717 acres of vineyard, Fronsac is larger than Pomerol, although it is two centuries since its reputation was superior to that of its now more illustrious south-eastern neighbor. Fronsac is divided into two separate appellations, Canon-Fronsac and Fronsac, of which the former, accounting for roughly one-third of the total area under vine, produces generally superior wines. Improvements in vinification practice and care in the vineyards owe much to increasing investment in the area by the highly successful Moueix family and other Libournais merchants.

Standards have improved to the point where Canon-Fronsac and, to a lesser extent, Fronsac too, stand on the verge of recognition as quality districts in their own right and compare favorably for value

with similarly priced reds throughout the rest of Bordeaux. The limestone soils of Fronsac and a tendency to blend slightly more Cabernet Franc and Malbec with the Merlot than in St. Emilion and Pomerol give the fruity wines of Fronsac an added dimension of acidity and tannin. This provides the structure to allow them to age well in bottle for five to ten years. Among the leading estates of the area are, in Canon-Fronsac, Châteaux Canon, Canon-de-Brem, Canon-Moueix, Mazeris Bellevue, Vray-Canon-Boyer, Moulin-Pey-Labrie; and, in Fronsac, La Dauphine, de la Rivière and Villars.

Côtes de Bourg

The ancient port of Bourg-sur-Gironde sits on the Dordogne opposite the Bec d'Ambès, the northern strip of the Entre-Deux-Mers district that juts into the Gironde estuary at the confluence of the Dordogne and Garonne rivers. Bourg's reputation as a producer of full-bodied red Bordeaux was established long before the Médoc was even a twinkle in

ABOVE: Château de la Rivière in Fronsac, one of the most picturesque districts of Bordeaux. After a period in the doldrums, Fronsac is beginning to reproduce the quality for which its wines were once renowned.

ABOVE: Thanks to modern viticulture and winemaking, as well as a better perception of the market, the producers of the Côtes are providing wines of good value for everyday drinking.

the eye of the Dutch engineers. Until the early 1970s, the wines of Bourg were used to a great extent by Bordeaux's merchants as vins *médecins*, sturdy wines ideal for blending. Since the crash of 1973/1974, however, the small-scale growers of Bourg have had to fend for themselves, as has been the case in so many of Bordeaux' minor regions. Roughly half of Bourg's 1,100 growers sell their grapes to cooperatives. Improvements, such as careful selection, temperature control, stainless-steel fermentation vats and oak barrels for aging, have raised quality standards considerably.

The fertile, undulating countryside of Bourg, with its compact vineyards on clay-limestone and clay-gravel soils, contrasts favorably in aesthetic terms with the monotony of the Médoc on the opposite bank. Bourg contains just two appellations for red and white wines, but its 3,300 hectares/8,151 acres are devoted almost exclusively to the production of red Bordeaux. Like those of Blaye, the wines of Bourg's little-known *petits châteaux*, supple-textured blends mostly of Merlot, with an added mix of Cabernet Sauvignon, Franc and Malbec, can provide excellent value for the money and should be drunk ideally at between three and five years of age, although the best of these wines will mature for up to ten years. Leading estates include de Barbe, Brûlesé-caille, Cana, Rousset, Mendoce, Guerry and the Tauriac cooperative.

Côtes de Blaye

The citadel of Blaye, completed as a military bulwark against the British in 1689 by Vauban, is linked by ferry with Lamarque on the left (Médoc) bank of the Gironde. The town of Blaye has a tiny population of 5,000, but the region, extending about fifty kilometers/eighty miles to the north of Bordeaux, is almost as extensive as the Entre-Deux-Mers region. With some 4,000 hectares/9,880 acres under vine, it makes a significant contribution to Bordeaux' total production of wine.

There are two red appellations for Blaye. The better wines come from the Premières Côtes de Blaye, which is restricted to the two Cabernets, Merlot and Malbec, and cannot be produced from vines on the alluvial soils in the river valley. A typical blend might be one-half Merlot and a quarter Cabernet Sauvignon with the balance made up of Cabernet Franc and Malbec. Then there is plain Blaye, which allows the addition of local grape varieties and can come from the richer alluvial soils.

There are three appellations for the white wines of Blaye. Premières Côtes de Blaye is limited to the three varieties Sémillon, Sauvignon and Muscadelle, with a more restrictive yield than the Côtes de Blaye which also allows Folle Blanche, Ugni Blanc and Colombard, the grape varieties that spill over from Cognac country, the Charente.

The least distinguished appellation is plain Blaye. Partly because of its remoteness, Blaye has developed a significant direct sales trade within France, and over 200 growers bottle and market their own wine, while 50 to 60 percent of production is sold by Bordeaux' wine merchants. The reds of Blaye, with its diverse soils of chalk, clay and gravel, tend to be softer and fruitier than those of neighboring Bourg, and easier to drink young, although they should keep improving in bottle for up to five years. Basic whites can be pretty undistinguished, although at Premières Côtes level it is possible to find an increasing number of fresh, crisp, fruity wines, sometimes with a light touch of oak for greater complexity. Among the best of Blaye are Châteaux Les Moines, Haut-Bertinerie, Crusquet-Sabourin, L'Escadre, Haut-Sociando, Pérenne, Segonzac, Peybonhomme-les-Tours, Marinier (white) and Le Menaudat.

Côtes de Castillon and Francs

Adjacent to the satellites of St. Emilion in the east are the two appellations of Côtes de Castillon and Côtes de Francs. At the frontier of the neighboring Dordogne region, where the Bergerac appellation begins, the gently rolling hills of Castillon, with some 2,600 hectares/6,422 acres of vineyard in the appellation, overlook Castillon-la-Bataille on the right bank of the Dordogne. John Talbot, Earl of Shrewsbury, died here in the battle that brought the curtain down on three centuries of English rule when the French defeated the English forces on July 17, 1453. The soils consist mainly of gravel, sand and clay closer to the river, becoming more chalky as the vineyards rise to the north. The wines, with their high Merlot and Cabernet Franc content, can be deliciously fruity and robust, with the best maturing well for a good five years upwards. About 25 percent of Castillon's production is sold through the cooperative.

At around 300 hectares/741 acres, the Côtes de Francs to the north, created in 1967, is one of the four smallest red appellations in Bordeaux (the others in ascending order of size being St. Georges St. Emilion, Graves de Vayres Rouge and Canon-Fronsac). There is a small cooperative and around twenty *petits châteaux* within the appellation, the soils of which are mainly clay-chalk. Leading Castillon estates include Châteaux de Pitray, de Belcier and La Terrasse. Among the best estates of the Côtes de Francs are Châteaux de Francs, Puygueraud, La Claverie and Puyfromage.

Sauternes

by David Peppercorn, M.W.

LEFT: The fortified medieval Château of Lafaurie-Peyraguey, with the trees of its park clearly visible, predates the fame of the vines which now surround it.

Sauternes is a unique gift of nature. Human skills have combined, with a special relationship of soil and climate, to produce a wine unlike any other sweet wine in the world.

The appellation Sauternes-Barsac is in effect an enclave in the southern Graves region, just west of Langon. It covers the five communes of Sauternes, Barsac, Fargues de Langon, Bommes and Preignac. While the Sauternes appellation covers all five, Barsac has its own separate appellation and can label its wines as Barsac or Sauternes, or indeed Sauternes-Barsac. This is because Barsac has always enjoyed its own persona with wines tending to be less liquorous than the other Sauternes as well as less botrytis affected.

The special element in the production of Sauternes is a form of rot called *Botrytis cinerea* or, more commonly, noble rot. The ideal chain of events is as follows: first, the grapes must fully ripen, when they become golden in appearance. Then they progress to being *grains pourris pleins,* that is affected by botrytis spores, but with smooth, brownish skins, and still full of juice. In the final stage they are known as *grains rôtis,* when the botrytis gradually dehydrates the grapes so that they become completely dessicated.

Sweet wines are made in other parts of the world with the assistance of noble rot — notably the great German Trockenbeerenauslesen, and more recently in some of the New World vineyards — though, in some cases, the botrytis in California and Australia is inoculated, and not spontaneous. But nowhere else do the particular climatic conditions produce ripe grapes by early October, followed by the mild, damp weather which is necessary to induce the botrytis to spread, on such a consistent basis.

Now for a more detailed look at what goes into the making of these great wines. The best grapes — in terms of their susceptibility to botrytis — are Sémillon. Some properties, such as Château Climens, use virtually 100 percent Sémillon, but most, including Château d'Yquem, opt for 80 percent Sémillon and 20 percent Sauvignon.

This produces less liquorous wines of elegance and helps to give balance to the final blend. Small quantities of Muscadelle are also found in many vineyards. This gives very aromatic, fruity wine which complements the other two varieties.

The next distinctive feature of Sauternes is the picking itself. Unlike red grapes, or those used for the production of dry white wines, the grapes are not picked in a single continuous operation, but in a succession of passages through the vineyard known as *tries.* This allows the pickers — and this is an operation where only experienced pickers from the region are used — to select only those grapes

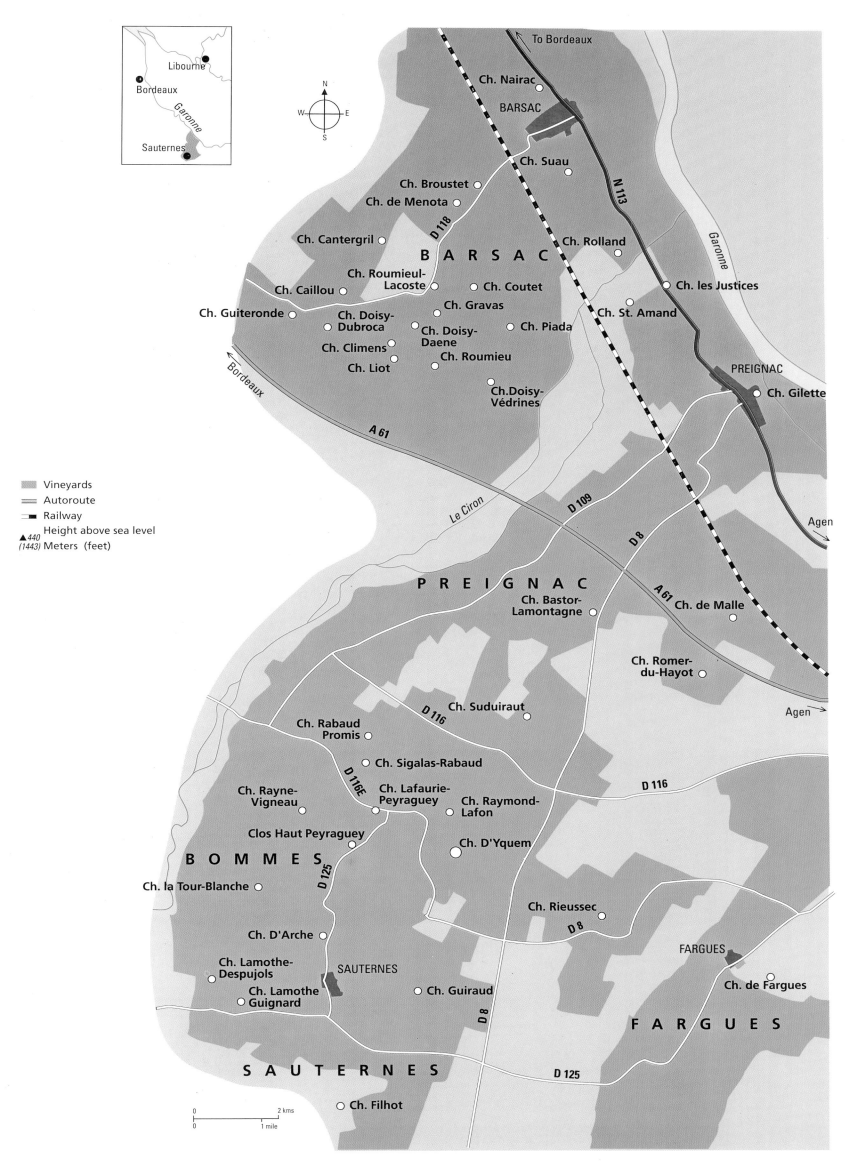

Libourne

Bordeaux

Garonne

Sauternes

N
W E
S

To Bordeaux

Ch. Nairac

BARSAC

N 113

Ch. Suau

Ch. Broustet

Ch. de Menota

D 118

Ch. Cantergril

B A R S A C

Ch. Rolland

Garonne

Ch. Roumieul-
Lacoste

Ch. Caillou

Ch. Coutet

Ch. les Justices

Ch. Guiteronde

Ch. Gravas

Ch. Doisy-
Dubroca

Ch. St. Amand

Ch. Doisy-
Daene

Ch. Piada

Ch. Climens

Ch. Roumieu

PREIGNAC

Bordeaux

Ch. Liot

Ch.Doisy-
Védrines

Ch. Gilette

A 61

Le Ciron

D 109

Vineyards
Autoroute
Railway
▲440 Height above sea level
(1443) Meters (feet)

P R E I G N A C

D 8

A 61

Ch. de Malle

Ch. Bastor-
Lamontagne

Ch. Romer-
du-Hayot

Agen

D 116

Ch. Suduiraut

Ch. Rabaud
Promis

Ch. Sigalas-Rabaud

D 116E

Ch. Lafaurie-
Peyraguey

D 116

Ch. Rayne-
Vigneau

Ch. Raymond-
Lafon

Clos Haut Peyraguey

Ch. D'Yquem

B O M M E S

D 125

Ch. la Tour-Blanche

Ch. Rieussec

D 8

Ch. D'Arche

FARGUES

Ch. Lamothe-
Despujols

Ch. de Fargues

Ch. Lamothe
Guignard

SAUTERNES

Ch. Guiraud

F A R G U E S

S A U T E R N E S

D 8

D 125

0   2 kms
0   1 mile

Ch. Filhot

which are absolutely ready and usually botrytized. Typically, a vintage may require four to eight *tries* over a period of four to eight weeks, and may vary from picking individual berries to cutting parts of bunches, or even whole bunches. All this will depend on the degree of concentration of sugar in the grapes which, in turn, depends on the extent of the botrytis. In practice, a completely botrytized crop would result in musts which would be too rich to ferment, or would produce a wine too sweet and alcoholic, lacking the style looked for in Sauternes. So the secret is to achieve a balance between the various elements in the vineyard, in order to produce a wine with between 13.5 percent and 14.5 percent alcohol by volume, and between about 70 and 120 grams of residual sugar. If the alcohol gets much higher than this, the wine acquires an alcohol "burn" on the palate and will lack finesse; if it is sweeter, the wine again loses its essential balance and fruitiness.

Fermentation traditionally takes place in cask but today some top châteaux use stainless steel for easier temperature control, and then transfer the new wines to cask. Because the action of botrytis on the grapes punctures the skins and allows the water content of the grapes to evaporate, thus concentrating the sugar and acidity, the yields in Sauternes are far lower than elsewhere in Bordeaux. The A.C. allows for a maximum of 25 hectoliters per hectare/1.5 tons per acre compared with 50-60 hectoliters per hectare/2.9-3.5 tons per acre in other parts of Bordeaux. In practice, in a good typical year, the best châteaux seldom make more than 15 hectoliters per hectare/.9 tons per acre while at Yquem the yield is only 7 hectoliters per hectare/.4 tons per acre. Sauternes needs to be expensive if it is to survive.

The assembling of the finished wine in Sauternes is a far more complex matter than in red wine châteaux. With a number of pickings often made in different weather conditions, over a period of time, with the resulting wines matured in cask, there will be a huge number of different elements involved. The blending is usually done shortly before bottling, after eighteen to twenty-four months in cask (forty-two months at Yquem).

The leading wines of the region were classified in 1855, along with those of the Médoc. Here, were there a new classification, there would be far fewer changes. Yquem still stands alone as the supreme expression of Sauternes, and is one of the great wines of the world. After a period of inconsistency, it has been in top form since 1967.

The 1980s have been both a period of outstanding vintages, and a time when the commercial fortunes of the region at last improved. With this improvement came a raising of winemaking standards. Among the stars has been Climens — often second only to Yquem in excellence, but with a lighter style of great elegance, as befits a Barsac. From 1983 to 1990, it was always among the best two or three wines of any vintage. Lafaurie-Peyraguey came back strongly after a disappointing period from 1967 to 1978, and is now consistently among the best. Rieussec, historically one of the great wines of Sauternes, received a well-deserved fillip when acquired by Domaines Rothschild (which also owns Lafite) in 1984. Since 1986, it has produced some of the outstanding wines of the region.

Guiraud, with one of the largest vineyards, is another *cru* which has been given a new lease of life under new management. With more Sauvignon in its makeup than other *crus classés,* very good wines and high prices have been the order of the day since 1983. Finally, in this group, comes Suduiraut, one of the finest properties in Sauternes. It made great wines in the fifties and sixties, but faltered badly in the seventies. In the eighties, it made a comeback, though without quite reaching the same heights. Not quite among the top growths, but commendably consistent with small quantities of attractively luscious wines, is Sigalas-Rabaud.

Then comes a group of wines which had been performing poorly, sometimes for only a short period as at Coutet, or had never really hit the headlines at all, as with Clos Haut-Peyraguey.

Coutet was also regarded as the close rival of its Barsac neighbor, Climens. In recent years, it has been lighter, drier and less consistent. There are

ABOVE: A good illustration of how grapes in different stages of development can be found on the same bunch. The fungus called "noble rot" is clearly visible, while other grapes are still green.

BELOW: Evolving fashions in labels, from the classic simplicity of Yquem, unchanged for 150 years, to the modern typography of Lafaurie-Peyraguey.

Sauternes Vintages

Clearly, given the exacting requirements for producing Sauternes, there are fewer successful vintages than elsewhere in Bordeaux, and these do not always coincide with the best red wine vintages.

Exceptional vintages — 1990, 1989, 1947
Great vintages — 1988, 1986, 1983, 1976, 1967, 1962, 1961
Very good vintages — 1985, 1981, 1975, 1971, 1970
Good vintages — 1980, 1979, 1966
Irregular years, but with a few good wines — 1987, 1984, 1982, 1978

---

now signs of an improvement. At Clos Haut-Peyraguey, the wines were simply unremarkable, with no hint of the fine position of the vineyard. Since 1986 there has been a marked improvement. Rabaud-Promis, a fine property once united with Sigalas as Château Rabaud, made thoroughly dull, commercial wines, but the eighties have seen a great improvement. Rayne-Vigneau, another victim of the years of depression, with dull, anemic wines, has seen an upturn since 1983. Finally, La Tour-Blanche, a famous old property now run by the French Ministry of Agriculture, was for many years the victim of bureaucratic experimentation, but there have been clear improvements and a new dedication in the management of late.

The second growths have suffered even more than the first growths from the chill winds of depression. But a few *crus* always kept up their standards and reputations. Outstanding among these is Doisy-Daëne, where Pierre Dubourdieu has been the greatest innovator of his generation. The emphasis is on freshness and elegance, and the wines are consistently fine and attractive, the quintessence of Barsac. At Doisy-Védrines, another Barsac, the wines are richer and fatter, sometimes at the expense of finesse, but some beauties have been made in the eighties. The final Doisy, Dubroca, is run in conjunction with Climens — so the wines are beautifully made and traditional. Filhot has the advantage of being both famous and beautiful, but the wines recently have proved variable, often clumsy, and seemingly over-botrytized. De Malle has owed its reputation as much to its glorious buildings and garden as to its wines, but in the mid-eighties these improved and are now deliciously fruity and elegant.

Of the remaining *crus*, d'Arche is a well-placed vineyard which, under new management, has restored its reputation since 1981 with fine rich wines. Broustet also emerged from the shadows in this decade, to produce wines which are rich, but not very liquorous. Caillou is sold mostly direct in France, so is not often seen on export markets. Some fine wines are made which age well.

The vineyard of Lamothe is divided in two: one part, now known as Lamothe-Guignard, has made an excellent reputation for itself since a change in ownership in 1981; the wines are very stylish and fruity. The other Lamothe produced very unimpressive wines until a fine 1986. Nairac was rescued from near oblivion in the seventies, and now makes consistently stylish Barsac, rich but not very liquorous. Romer-du-Hayot produces fresh, fruity wines sold at very reasonable prices, while the least known *cru*, Suau, has a very small production, so is hard to find. At its best, it is delicate and fine.

Among the unclassified wines, two stand out: de Fargues and Raymond-Lafon. Both sell at *cru classé* prices — indeed de Fargues, under the same management and with the same exacting standards as Yquem, is actually more expensive than any of the *crus classés* except Yquem. These are wonderful wines, but less luscious than Yquem. Raymond-Lafon's vineyard adjoins Yquem at one point and belongs to the family of the former manager of Yquem. The wines are distinguished, of *cru classé* quality, with prices to match.

Other consistently attractive wines sold at value-for-money prices are Bastor-Lamontagne, Guiteronde — under the same ownership as Romer-du-Hayot — Les Justices, de Rolland and St. Amand, also sold as La Chartreuse.

Other botrytis-affected sweet wines are also made across the river on the hillside vineyards of Ste.-Croix-du-Mont and Loupiac, and in certain communes of the Premières Côtes adjoining Loupiac, but they are lighter and less luscious. In Cérons, adjoining Barsac, most growers now opt to make Graves rather than the sweet Cérons.

GROWER'S VIEW

In 1939, at the age of sixteen, Pierre Dubourdieu found himself making his first vintage. Over fifty years later, people say he is still the *enfant terrible* of Sauternes-Barsac, and still searching restlessly for ways of making better wines.

So, what has changed in this lifetime of winemaking in Sauternes-Barsac? Nothing and everything! The principles remain the same — and, indeed, are reaffirmed and confirmed by modern research and experience. The patient picking in *trie* [going through the vineyard many times to select only ripe and botrytized grapes] and fermentation in cask turns out to need no temperature control — unlike in vat — to achieve the best results.

Pierre Dubourdieu believes that the greatest single advance will prove to be cryo-extraction — the removal of surplus water from grapes by freezing before pressing — because this will supplant chaptalization and enable growers to improve quality in vintages such as 1987 and 1991. It preserves the character of botrytized grapes, which is essential for the distinctive character of Sauternes-Barsac. He believes in supplanting the old dependence on sulfur. Hygiene, a greater understanding of the action of yeasts, and cold treatment, to arrest fermentation, are all parts of the answer. He has also banished volatile acidity from his wines.

He looks for an ideal balance of 18.5 Baumé/32.7 Brix in the must at Doisy-Daëne, which will convert into about 14 percent alcohol and 4 grams residual sugar. The result is great elegance and an emphasis on fruit and freshness.

Pierre Dubourdieu
CHATEAU DOISY-DAËNE

COGNAC

by Michael Edwards

Cognac may be the world's most famous brandy, but it is one that is still poorly understood.

The word "Cognac" applies exclusively to spirits made from grapes (mainly Ugni Blanc) grown, vinified and distilled in the delimited Cognac region. This consists of some 101,175 hectares/250,000 acres within Charente and Charente Maritime, both departments of western France. There are six sub-regions or *crus:* Grande Champagne, Petite Champagne, Borderies, Fins Bois, Bons Bois and Bois Ordinaires.

Cognac's potential as an exceptional brandy rests firmly on the geology and physical characteristics of its chalky soil. The best type of chalk is found in Grande Champagne, and the very finest Cognacs tend to come from this area. Yet parts of Petite Champagne, particularly around Archiac, produce Cognacs as good as those of Grande Champagne. The Borderies can be lovely examples of the spirit, with a nutty, round flavor which is much favored by Martell as a key ingredient in its blends. And the best pockets of the seriously underrated Fins Bois near Jarnac account for delicious early-maturing Cognacs of marked fruitiness.

Most Cognac is a blended product, and the above four regions are prime sources for the best blends. Bons Bois, with a few exceptions, and Bois Ordinaires are far less good, the latter in particular pro-ducing coarse, acid spirits, which are avoided by quality-conscious Cognac houses.

Cognac is made from white wine distilled twice in pot stills to a maximum strength of 72 percent. Then, before sale the Cognac is reduced in strength to about 40 percent. The reduction process must be carried out with care, for the quality of the Cognac depends greatly on the quality of the reduction.

Most firms use distilled water to reduce their Cognacs. But as water and Cognac produce an adverse chemical reaction, this technique needs to be implemented gently over many months.

The other crucial factor which shapes the quality of a great Cognac is its maturation in oak casks. The particular type of oak used for the cask will significantly influence the style of the resultant brandy. Some firms like Limousin oak because the wood is porous and tannic, the tannins giving the Cognac both structure and a chestnut-toned color. Consistency of color in nearly all commercial brands is obtained by adding caramel. This does not affect the flavor. Other houses prefer the tighter-grained Tronçais oak which helps to produce paler, less obviously "woody" Cognac.

A classic chronology of cask aging might be as follows: a maximum of nine months in new oak casks, then five to fifteen years prior to reduction in used Cognac casks.

LEFT: A traditional Cognac producer, Pierre Ferrand is blending in his tasting room.

ABOVE AND RIGHT: The styles of Cognac labels are varied. Vintage Cognac is not usually permitted under the governing regulations; an exception is "early-landed" Cognac, which is shipped in barrels and matured outside France, sometimes for as long as thirty years before bottling.

TOP LEFT: Demi-johns of old Grande Champagne Cognac dating from the nineteenth century in a producer's cellar.

BLENDER'S VIEW

Once distilled, *eau-de-vie* is kept in cask in a warehouse to await its eventual bottling.

A good warehouse for aging Cognac should be damp to allow the spirit to lose alcoholic strength, for it is the water molecules in suspension in the atmosphere of the warehouse which attract the molecules of alcohol of the *eau-de-vie*. Over a period of many years a slow evaporation takes place by capillary action through the wood of the cask.

During its years of aging, an *eau-de-vie* loses on average 0.4 percent of alcohol each year. We talk about an average because the warehouse, above ground and rarely air-conditioned, is susceptible to fluctuations of temperature and humidity. In a wet year the loss of alcohol is appreciable: in a dry one it may be negligible.

In principle, then, it is necessary to wait fifty years for an *eau-de-vie* to lose 20 percent alcohol and become a Cognac with a natural strength of 49 percent. Assuming that the *eau-de-vie* is of top quality and that its maturation has been faultlessly supervised, the probable result will be a remarkable Cognac — a rarity that would be worth a fortune.

But the practical reality is that when we speak of old Cognacs, generally we mean brandies with ten to twenty years of cask age.

Even after twenty years, the spirit will still show 61 percent alcohol and generally is reduced in strength shortly before bottling. Very few people wish to taste an *eau-de-vie* with a very high degree of alcohol, which in itself prevents the spirit from developing the aromas so sought after by lovers of fine Cognacs.

We must remember that one of the properties of alcohol is a slowing down of oxidation. While the level of alcohol in an *eau-de-vie* remains high, little aging can take place. Not until the alcoholic degree has dropped to around 58 percent can the spirit begin to mature and develop.

Given the difficulty of naturally reducing the strength of a Cognac, reduction is achieved by adding distilled water to the spirit.

A good *eau-de-vie* must age naturally in cask for a period of four to seven years. Only then can reduction be undertaken and the spirit begin its slow transformation into Cognac.

The two phases of aging, before and after reduction, are equally important. If the first period is long, fifteen to twenty-five years, and the second short — maybe just twelve months — the Cognac will be undistinguished. To achieve a great Cognac, the period of aging after reduction must be lengthy, from ten to twenty years.

The consideration of reduction or non-reduction can give no clear indication of a Cognac's eventual quality. Reduction properly carried out allows the harmonious development of the *eau-de-vie*, enabling it to reach its full potential.

Pierre Voisin

COGNAC LÉOPOLD GOURMEL

BURGUNDY

by Frank Prial

Burgundy is one of the two or three great wine regions of the world. But even more than this, it is a state of mind. It is the cellar at the Hospices de Beaune on a crisp November morning. It is market day in Meursault. It is perfectly trimmed vines in the tiny enclosure that is Le Montrachet. It is five hundred guests laughing and singing and drinking great wine in the vast hall at the Clos de Vougeot.

Burgundy is the solid peasant, a scruffy cap jammed on his round head, who each year makes a few barrels of wine that the whole world wants to buy. Burgundy is the ramparts of Beaune on a soft summer night, it is back-country villages, just off the main roads but happily lost in time. It is the tranquil Canal de Bourgogne and the humming *autoroute*. It is an unending stream of tourist buses bringing stolid Teutons, excited Latins and diffident Anglo-Saxons to an unforgettable rendezvous with the good life.

Burgundy is Chablis, a scant 161 kilometers/100 miles from Paris and closer, in fact, to Champagne than to the fabled Côte d'Or. The Mâcon region, with its oceans of solid white wines, is Burgundy; so is Beaujolais where the juice of the Gamay is drunk

as wine two months after the grapes are picked. Burgundy is the land of Cluny and Pontigny and Cîteaux and monks who made good wine not long after the time of Christ.

It is a country of fat cows and plump chickens; of good sausage and better cheese; of real butter and real cream, and of cooks who know how to use all these things. And of course, it is a land of glorious wines. To true Burgundy lovers, they are the only wines in the world.

By rights, Burgundy is too far north to make good wine. And, in fact, in many vintages, the wine is poor. Memories are short and, in the wake of a fortuitous string of fine vintages in the late 1980s and early 1990s, there is a tendency to forget the bad times. Between 1960 and 1985, for example, there were really only three outstanding vintages in Burgundy: 1969, 1976 and 1985.

Burgundy has always been popular, and there has never been enough of it. But the current demand for it is without precedent and the temptation to stretch, to overcrop and to vinify too quickly is fierce. In the 1930s Burgundy went through a period of dire poverty and neglect. Today it is experiencing a period of almost incalculable success. There are those who say Burgundy will have a more difficult time surviving the good times than it did enduring the bad.

LEFT: Typical Burgundian winemaker doles out a few precious drops for a customer. A Burgundy man is never happier than when he's showing his wines.

BELOW: Each November, wine lovers of the world descend on Beaune for a three-day wine festival. The main event of the weekend is the Sunday auction to benefit the Hospices de Beaune shown here.

Chablis

by Frank Prial

RIGHT: The real Chablis. The name of Chablis has been appropriated by winemakers from Australia to California by way of Spain, for wines that have only the barest of resemblances to their namesake.

There is an old saying that a bad year for the Côte d'Or will certainly be worse in Chablis, and that a good year in the Côte d'Or may still be bad in Chablis.

If ever there was an example of man's indomitable urge to tame nature, it is in the vineyards of Chablis. Pounded by violent hailstorms in the summer and subject to bitterly cold winters, Chablis is a textbook example of a place not to make wine.

But wine has been made here since ancient times. Vines ran up to the walls of Auxerre in the seventh century and the monks at Pontigny, 20 kilometers/12.4 miles away, were working at least 174 hectares/430 acres of vines early in the twelfth century.

Chablis, and the other villages of the Auxerre region, were the vineyard of Paris for centuries. It is difficult to comprehend now but in the eighteenth century, there were 32,400 hectares/80,000 acres of vines planted in the area. A hundred years later there were 40,500 hectares/100,000 acres, three-quarters of which were turned into red wine.

Auxerre and Chablis were in their time the most important part of Burgundy. Today there are less than 2,830 hectares/7,000 acres, not 7 percent of

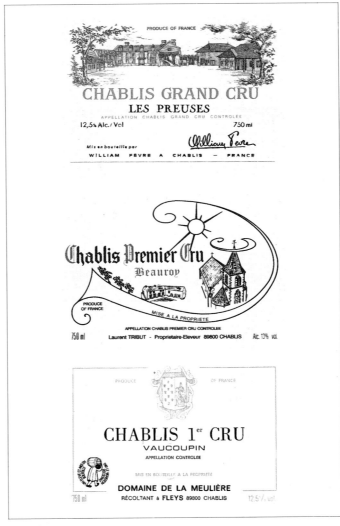

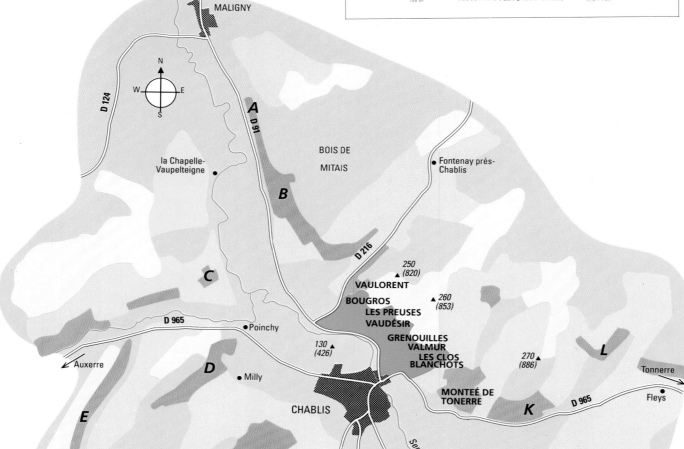

LEFT: Chablis' classification system follows that of the rest of Burgundy, and whereas in Bordeaux a *Premier Cru* is the best, in Burgundy a *Grand Cru* tops everything.

A L'homme Mort
B Fourchaume
C Beauroy
D Côte de Lechet
E Vaux de Vey
F Vaillions
G Montmains
H Vaugiraut
I Vasgros
J Vaucopin
K Mont de Milieu
L Les Fourneaux

A.O.C. Chablis *Grand Cru*
A.O.C. Chablis *Premier Cru*
A.O.C. Chablis
Petit Chablis
▲270 Height above sea level
(886) Meters (feet)

what it was a century ago. And they are virtually all planted with white grapes.

The late nineteenth century saw the Chablis vineyards destroyed, as were practically all of France's vineyards, first by mildew and then by phylloxera. But the growers of Chablis, and Milly and Fontenay and the seventeen other towns and villages that make up the region had a more insidious enemy: history.

In time, thanks to American rootstock, the vineyards of France came back. But the time of phylloxera was also the time of the railroad. By 1890, the lush vineyards of the Midi had become closer to Paris than Chablis had been fifty years before.

And the Midi was fruitful as Chablis had never been. Much earlier, most of the growers in Chablis had abandoned the elegant Pinot Noir and its cousin the Chardonnay, for the cheaper but more prolific Gamay and the inferior white wine grape called Sacy. The wines were often thin and acidic compared to the lush, fat, high-alcohol wines from the Mediterranean littoral.

What's more there was the weather. There were years when there simply was no Chablis — or very little. And there are no years when the Midi doesn't gush forth a river of wine.

Chablis has yet another problem: its name. It is, in fact, a wonderful name, pronounceable in virtually any language. Which, of course, is why it has been coopted by winemakers and wine merchants around the world.

There have been at one time or another, Chilean "Chablis," South African "Chablis", Australian and Spanish "Chablis". California has had so many different kinds of spurious "Chablis" (including "Pink Chablis") that the word has for many people become synonymous with white wine.

Some wine-producing countries have passed laws restricting the use of generic names such as Chablis. Also, the trend to varietal wines, wines named after the grape from which they are made, has stemmed somewhat from the promiscuous use of "Chablis" to describe any cheap white wine, but the damage has been done.

It will take a long time, another generation perhaps, for genuine Chablis to recover the reputation it deserves. After all, Chablis at its best is a superb white Burgundy. It can stand alongside Meursault and Puligny-Montrachet, and can best all but a few of the wines of Pouilly-Fuissé.

The fashion for Chablis has returned. Virtually forgotten in the years just after World War II Chablis made a dramatic comeback in the late 1960s and 1970s. Once ridiculously cheap, the better Chablis are now as expensive as any wine of comparable quality from the Côte d'Or.

What's more is that even though Chablis' area in vines is pitifully small compared with the area of the nineteenth century, it is three times what it was thirty-five years ago. Just between 1967 and 1978, the vineyard area in Chablis increased dramatically by 50 percent.

Then, average production of Chablis was not much more than 100,000 cases. Today, thanks to better vinification methods and better frost control, average production is around 700,000 cases a year. In fact, the average is misleading in terms of what Chablis can do. In the best years, production easily surpasses a million cases.

In fact, growth is probably Chablis' biggest current problem. Some growers want to enlarge the area of production; others, generally those who own the best land, want to restrict it. Most objective observers believe that there are, even now, wines bearing the Chablis appellation that are not truly up to what a genuine Chablis should be.

There are four Chablis appellations as defined in 1938 by the Institut National des Appellations d'Origine Contrôlée. They are Chablis, Chablis Grand Cru, Chablis Premier Cru and Petit Chablis. The only grape from which any of them can be made is the Chardonnay.

There are only seven *Grand Cru* vineyards and they all adjoin each other on the same hillside just north of the town of Chablis itself. They are called Vaudésir, Les Clos, Grenouilles, Valmur, Blanchots, Les Preuses and Bougros. Together they comprise 100 hectares/247 acres and their total production even in a good year, does not quite reach 75,000 total cases.

There are over forty vineyards, totaling about 650 hectares/1,605 acres, entitled to be called *Premiers Crus*. To keep the names from becoming completely confusing, the growers and shippers have regrouped their *Premiers Cru* vineyards so that only about a dozen of their names ever appear on labels. Among the most favored are Vaulorent and Montée de Tonnerre, both of them hard by the *Grand Cru* vineyards on the right bank of the little Serein River.

Total area in the ordinary Chablis appellation is about 2,120 hectares/5,236 acres, while Petit Chablis accounts for about 260 hectares/640 acres of vines. Much of this wine is blended and bottled, not by the vineyard owners but by shippers who buy from various growers. It is important to look for the best shippers' names when buying these wines. Among the larger shipping concerns the leading names include Laroche and Moreau and the La Chablisienne cooperative; among growers, names to look for include Raveneau, René Dauvissat, William Fèvre, Louis Michel, Droin, Jean Collet, Durup, Pico-Race, Claude Laroche (Domaine de la

BELOW: Three *Premiers Crus* Chablis, two from top individual producers and one from the famous La Chablisienne cooperative. J. Moreau is one of the best-known Chablis makers.

Meulière), Jean Defaix, Etienne Defaix and Alain Geoffroy.

The four appellations are spread over about twenty towns and villages and only a portion of the land entitled to the appellations is actually cultivated in vines. The *Grand Cru* area probably cannot be expanded geographically but the other appellations can. In fact, a new *Premier Cru* was created in the late 1970s called Vaudevey. Its first crop was in 1984. It is estimated that the size of the Chablis vineyard area legally in production could be much increased with ease.

The best Chablis has what the locals call a *goût de pierre à fusil,* or gunflint taste: a smoky, flinty flavor that could equally well be a metaphor for the rock-like austerity of the wine that combines perfectly with its underlying Chardonnay fruit.

Each of the seven *Grand Crus* has its individual style and, inevitably, its staunch advocates. Alexis Lichine, who bought his first Chablis in the 1930s and returned regularly over the next fifty years, preferred Les Clos and Les Preuses as being the longest-lasting wines and having the greatest depth of taste.

These days the growers argue over the value of aging their wines in oak. Some of the *Grand Cru* wines spend some time in oak while most of the *Premier Cru* wines spend all their time in stainless steel so as not to mask the fruit. Most Americans, familiar with over-oaked California Chardonnays, find the unoaked Chablis too austere.

Chardonnay may dominate the vineyards in this part of France, but it is not the only grape grown. St. Bris le Vineux grows Sauvignon Blanc, the only village in Burgundy to do so; the wine, currently a V.D.Q.S., is called Sauvignon de St. Bris. Aligoté is grown here as well, and Crémant de Bourgogne is produced at Bailly-sur-Yonne. Irancy produces a red from a blend of Pinot Noir and César, and Auxerre, in the form of the Clos de la Chainette, produces some *vin gris* and some white.

GROWER'S VIEW

The flinty-dry taste of true Chablis is determined by our Kimmeridgian soil, which is a unique mix of chalk and clay. Our best vineyards are those on south-facing hillsides protected from bitter winds. In the Yonne, we are at the northern extremity for the cultivation of the vine, so the Chardonnay has to struggle to survive the mortal danger every year of a late spring frost.

Chardonnay, like most noble grape varieties, only really becomes interesting from vines between twenty-five to thirty years of age, and in Chablis it is important to restrict yields to 40 hectoliters per hectare/2.4 tons per acre if we are to make exceptional wine. In the vineyard, we use very little fertilizer and we do not like to see too much foliage on the vine. After a successful flowering in June, we practice a *vendange verte* where necessary, which in simple terms means picking off as much as 50 percent of the green infant grapes so that those which remain will be more concentrated and make better wine. We usually harvest our grapes quite late when they are fully ripe, and hand picking is an important element in the wine's eventual quality.

Our best *Premier* and *Grand Cru* wines are fermented in oak barrels, which ideally are not less than three years old. The wines then spend a maximum of six months in cask, after which they are stored in stainless-steel vats to await bottling. This takes place nine to twelve months after the harvest. It is quite fashionable nowadays to stir the lees of the wine in the cask with a wooden *baton.* There is no conclusive evidence that this ritual adds much to the wine.

Michel Laroche

DOMAINE LAROCHE

ABOVE: The Domaine Laroche. Michel Laroche is one of a new breed of Chablis makers who combine all the latest techniques with traditional winemaking skills.

LEFT: The vineyards at Chablis. These manicured vineyards produce some of the finest white wine in the world, when the rugged winter weather permits.

Côte de Nuits

by Frank Prial

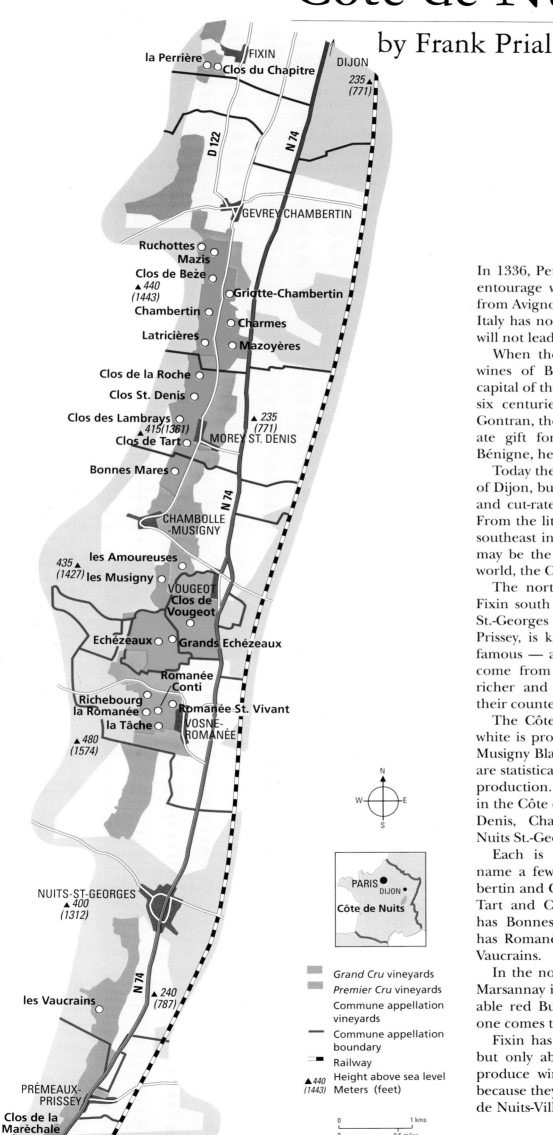

In 1336, Petrarch discovered why the pope and his entourage were so reluctant to return the papacy from Avignon to Rome. "The truth is", he said, "that Italy has no Beaune wine, and they think that they will not lead so happy a life without this liquid".

When the Italian poet penned those lines, the wines of Burgundy — Beaune is the unofficial capital of the region — had already been famous for six centuries. Perhaps longer; in A.D 581. when Gontran, the King of Burgundy, sought an appropriate gift for the monks of the Abbey of Saint-Bénigne, he gave them the vineyards of Dijon.

Today there are no more vines in the bustling city of Dijon, but just south of it, where the used-car lots and cut-rate furniture stores end, the vines begin. From the little village of Fixin the vineyards stretch southeast in a 48 kilometer/30 mile carpet of what may be the most valuable agricultural land in the world, the Côte d'Or, Burgundy's Golden Slope.

The northern portion of the Côte d'Or, from Fixin south through Gevrey-Chambertin and Nuits St.-Georges to the little hamlets of Prémeaux and Prissey, is known as the Côte de Nuits. The most famous — and expensive — of all red Burgundies come from the Côte de Nuits. They are bigger, richer and longer-lived, generally speaking, than their counterparts from the Côte de Beaune.

The Côte de Nuits is red-wine country. A little white is produced and an exceptional wine it is — Musigny Blanc. But its several hundred cases a year are statistically insignificant compared with red-wine production. There are five important communities in the Côte de Nuits: Gevrey-Chambertin, Morey-St.-Denis, Chambolle-Musigny, Vosne-Romanée and Nuits St.-Georges.

Each is surrounded by famous vineyards. To name a few, Gevrey-Chambertin has its Le Chambertin and Clos de Bèze, Morey-St.-Denis its Clos de Tart and Clos des Lambrays, Chambolle-Musigny has Bonnes Mares and Musigny, Vosne-Romanée has Romanée-Conti, and Nuit-St.-Georges has Les Vaucrains.

In the north of the Côte de Nuits, the village of Marsannay is an increasingly good source of affordable red Burgundy. But the first major commune one comes to is Fixin.

Fixin has about 243 hectares/600 acres of vines but only about one-sixth of them are allowed to produce wine bearing the name Fixin. The rest, because they produce a lesser wine, must call it Côte de Nuits-Villages. There are six important vineyards

in Fixin, the two largest being La Perrière and Clos du Chapitre.

Gevrey-Chambertin is the first of the important wine communities. It is also the beginning of the twisting little road known as the *Route des Grands Crus* that wanders for 16 kilometers/10 miles or so through the perfectly preserved little wine villages. Besides Chambertin and Clos de Bèze, there are about a dozen truly famous vineyards, including Latricières, Mazis, Charmes, Ruchottes and Griotte.

As is the case throughout Burgundy, a number of owners share each of these renowned vineyards. Domaine Trapet, Louis Latour and Joseph Drouhin are among the principal owners of Chambertin and Clos de Bèze.

Morey-St.-Denis is the home of the Clos de Tart, Clos de la Roche and Clos St.-Denis vineyards, along with a small portion of Bonnes Mares, most of which is in the adjoining town of Chambolle Musigny. It is interesting to note that the wines from the Morey-St.-Denis side of the vineyard are consistently different from the Bonnes Mares made from grapes in Chambolle. They are harder when young and longer lasting, just like other Morey-St.-Denis wines.

The two most prestigious vineyards in Chambolle-Musigny are Musigny and Bonnes Mares and Musigny is considered the best of those two. The wines — both of them — are rich in flavor yet delicate. They have an unforgettable bouquet and they are exceptionally long-lasting on the palate. Musigny constitutes 11 hectares/27 acres; Bonnes Mares 16 hectares/40 acres in Chambolle and 1.9 hectares/4.6 acres in Morey-St.-Denis.

One of the leaders among the second rank of vineyards in Chambolle-Musigny, after the two *Grands Crus,* is Les Amoureuses. It is just below the vines of Musigny on the line that separates Chambolle-Musigny from Vougeot, and is considered first among the *Premiers Crus* vineyards of the commune. In good years, it displays elegance and a feminine delicacy that make it a delicious but ligther echo of Musigny.

Just north of Vosne-Romanée is the separate enclave of the Clos de Vougeot, whose magnificent château has come to be the most familiar landmark in all of Burgundy. The vineyard — *clos* means a walled vineyard — was first planted in the eleventh century by the monks of the abbey of Cîteaux about seven miles away. The great château was built five centuries later by Dom Jean Loysier, the forty-eighth abbot of Cîteaux.

The building is now owned by the Confrérie des Chevaliers du Tastevin, a fraternal and promotional organization whose members don vaguely medieval garb and indulge in good food and, naturally, Burgundy wine. The Chevaliers hold splendid dinners in the château at regular intervals when as many as six hundred guests dine regally, sing songs and pledge their devotion to Burgundy and its wines.

The Clos is one of the biggest single vineyards in Burgundy, totalling some 50 hectares/124 acres. But it is shared by many owners: some seventy-five individuals and shippers, in fact, and there are more than one hundred plots of vines.

The complexities of the Clos de Vougeot vineyard illustrate the problems confronting any consumer trying to understand Burgundy. Each of the seventy-five proprietors sells his wine individually and, while

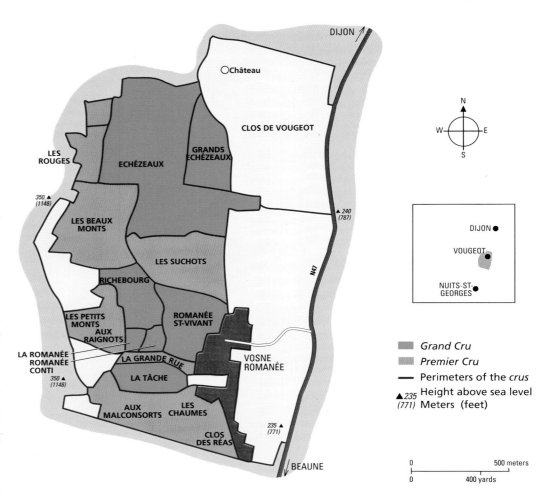

the vineyard is classified as *Grand Cru,* the highest classification in Burgundy, the wines can vary widely in quality. It becomes, then, not so much a question of a bottle of Clos de Vougeot, but whose Clos de Vougeot.

There are a few vineyards in Vougeot outside the weather-beaten walls of the Clos, good ones, too, but in reputation, they are completely overshadowed by their illustrious neighbor.

Up the slope behind the Clos de Vougeot are the vineyards of Flagey-Echezeaux. Only the vineyards, because the town of Flagey-Echezeaux is down on the plain, across the highway and the railroad tracks in an area where no quality grapes are grown at all. The two principal vineyards are Echezeaux and Grands-Echezeaux and they produce some of the finest of all Burgundies. In style they are somewhere between the best Vougeot and the lighter wines of Vosne-Romanée. The Domaine de la Romanée-Conti owns over a third of Grands Echezeaux and about a seventh of Echezeaux.

Vosne-Romanée might be described as the Beverly Hills of Burgundy. There is a greater concentration of superstars here than in any other wine village: La Tâche, Richebourg, Romanée and Romanée-Conti. Plus, technically, the two Echezeaux, which are actually in the commune of Flagey-Echezeaux.

Romanée-Conti has long been considered the best of the best in Burgundy, something like Lafite in the Médoc and Pétrus in Pomerol. The vineyard is entirely owned by the Domaine de la Romanée-Conti. So is La Tâche. The Domaine also owns about half of Richebourg and about one quarter of Romanée-St.-Vivant.

The wines of Vosne-Romanée, at their best, are certainly the equal of any wine in Burgundy, and occasionally better than them all. They have the best attributes of Burgundy, depth, richness, softness, lingering aftertaste and magnificent perfume, and all beautifully balanced. Certainly they are among

75

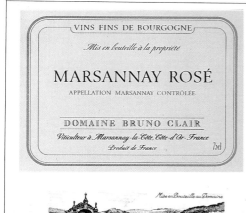

ABOVE: The two top labels, for a Marsannay rosé and a Fixin blanc, represent two of Burgundy's lesser-known gems. They are from two of the northernmost appellations on the Côte d'Or, just south of Dijon.

BELOW: Four famous vineyards and four equally prominent growers. Louis Jadot, also an important *négociant,* is owned by Americans. The Domaine de la Romanée-Conti is Burgundy's one great superstar.

the most expensive wines not only in Burgundy but in the world.

But they have their detractors. There are two schools of thought about Burgundy-making. One prefers its wine big and robust, what they refer to as "old-time" Burgundy. Others like their wine lighter, more delicate. It is the latter school that criticizes the Domaine, saying they are too intense, too alcoholic. The public, which will pay an average man's weekly wage for a bottle, evidently disagrees.

The last important wine commune in the Côte de Nuits is Nuits-St.-Georges itself. More of a small city than a town, its side streets are lined with the warehouses of shippers, and on crisp fall days, the smell of young, fresh wine is everywhere. The vines begin north of the town and end abruptly at the town line. They pick up again where the town ends to the south. The commune of Prémeaux, just south of Nuits-St.-Georges, uses the Nuits-St.-Georges appellation and is home to what is probably the best-known of all the Nuits-St.-Georges vineyards, the 9.7 hectare/24 acre Clos de la Maréchale, all of which is owned by the Faiveley shipping firm. As might be

expected, the Nuits wines are a bit softer in texture than their neighbors to the north. Even so, they are deceptively hardy and can be quite rough when they are very young.

GROWER'S VIEW

There is a great diversity of soils in the vineyards of the Côte d'Or. Limestone is a common constituent of the Burgundian earth but you will also find sandstone and marl. Moreover, the depth of the soil is very different from one parcel to another.

Most vineyards in the Côte de Nuits and Côte de Beaune face southeast but there are some important exceptions: Corton-Charlemagne faces southwest and the Les Jarrons vineyard at Savigny-les-Beaune northeast. The *Grands Crus* and *Premiers Crus* vineyards are usually on the hillsides, but the steepness of the slope is no indicator of the vineyard's potential. Le Chambertin, for example, is situated on a gentle slope.

Because our climate is semi-continental, the favorable southeasterly aspect of the best Burgundian vineyards is important. In these sites, the vine gets more sunshine and the morning mists dissipate very early. The climatic features of the Côte are, of course, the microclimates. Because of the varying contours, exposure to sunshine is determined by the slopes.

The Pinot Noir is the most suitable varietal for our soil and climate. Pinot Noir in Burgundy is like a hand in a glove, since it is the soil which fashions its character. Like all noble grape varieties, Pinot Noir needs to be of a certain age to give good quality. Harvesting by hand is absolutely essential since only a gentle treatment of the vine allows it to live a long life. The vine stock itself must be healthy and virus-free, for how can a vine with a cold perform properly?

We employ classical vinification methods with partial destalking of the grapes, and maceration of the wine on its skins for 9 to 14 days. We think it essential to taste the fermenting must every day to determine the optimum time to stop fermentation. Extraction of the maximum aromatic potential of the Pinot Noir fruit through *pigeage* and *remontage* is vital. The goal of vinification for us in Gevrey is to give full expression to our remarkable *terroir.*

Only wooden casks guarantee the development of a *grand vin.* New oak brings to the wine fine tannins and a touch of vanilla. The proportion of a new wood should be subtle. Basically, Pinot Noir is a very aromatic grape and cannot support too much oak. That's why at the domain we use only 20 percent new wood for our village *appellation* wines: 33 percent for our *Premiers Crus.* For our *Grands Crus,* such as Le Chambertin, that proportion may be as much as 50 percent.

Nicolas Rossignol

DOMAINE ROSSIGNOL-TRAPET

Côte de Beaune

by Frank Prial

The Côte de Beaune is, quite simply, the southern half of the Côte d'Or. It stretches from the town line separating Ladoix-Serrigny and Aloxe-Corton in the north to the hilly country due west of the commercial town of Chagny in the south; about twenty-four kilometers/fifteen miles.

But what a great fifteen miles it is! Le Corton, Corton-Charlemagne, Beaune Clos des Mouches, Beaune Cent-Vignes, Volnay Champans, Meursault Charmes, Bâtard-Montrachet, Le Montrachet. Great reds, greater whites; nowhere on earth has nature's bounty been more fully realized.

Someone once said that if Paris be France's head, and Champagne her soul, then Burgundy is her stomach. Somehow, the axiom seems to be more relevant here in the southern end of the Golden Slope where the land is more spacious and open, more remote from the workaday world. If anything, the towns are even more unspoiled than those on the Côte de Nuits. Except of course for Beaune.

But Volnay, Monthélie — which no one seems to be able to find — Meursault and Puligny-Montrachet are truly rural and untouched. Even the three towns north of Beaune, the northern outposts of the Côte de Beaune, are a bit slower, a bit more *folklorique,* than some of the renowned villages of the Côte de Nuits. Santenay and Pernand-Vergelesses, both hidden away from the main road, are as untouched as they were forty years ago.

The Côte de Beaune is about the same length as the Côte de Nuits to the north, but because the slope is less precipitous, it is much wider. Production is more than double that of the Côte de Nuits and, if there are more indifferent wines than in the Côte de Nuits, there are enough great ones to give any area proper competition.

The border town of the Côte de Beaune is not Beaune itself but Aloxe-Corton, about 6.5 kilometers/4 miles beyond the northern reaches of the town of Beaune. One can see Beaune from the edges of Aloxe, and the stream of traffic on the *autoroute* to the south. But this little village somehow remains untouched by time. This the home of Corton-Charlemagne, of Le Corton, of Les Bressandes, Le Clos du Roi and Les Renardes. The Romans were here once; the ruins prove it. Charlemagne owned land here and, in the eighth century, donated some of his best vines to the Abbey of Saulieu.

BELOW: Legend has it that Aloxe-Corton, one of the loveliest of the Côte d'Or villages, was once the site of the vineyards of the Emperor Charlemagne.

RIGHT: Prices paid at the annual November wine auction for the Hospices de Beaune tend to set the pattern for all the prices of Burgundy wine in the year ahead.

There is a story, almost certainly false, about how Corton-Charlemagne came into being. It seems — so the story goes — that the emperor's wife was irritated by his sloppy drinking habits, the way he soaked his beard with red wine. Drink white wine, she told him, and have a beard fit for an emperor. So he ordered that some of his best land be turned over to white-wine grapes. Chardonnay? In the eighth century? For the sake of the story, why not?

Whatever the origin of the Corton-Charlemagne vineyard, it is one of the two or three greatest white wines of Burgundy. The reds which have their detractors, are slow to age. A ten-year-old Corton Les Bressandes from Daniel Senard, or a Corton from the Domaine Rapet will stand up to — and face down, if need be — almost any red wine in Burgundy. But these wines do need time.

Back behind the Montagne de Corton is the delightful village of Pernand-Vergelesses, best known for its reasonably-priced, accessible reds and a few whites, including even a few excellent Corton-Charlemagnes from the area where that famous vineyard slips over the town line. The best vineyard: the Ile des Vergelesses. The best bargain: Louis Jadot's Pernand-Vergelesses-Clos de la Croix Pierre.

The second of these two villages hidden up behind Aloxe, and the more attractive, is Savigny-lès-Beaune. The frenetic atmosphere of Beaune during the tourist season and at harvest time is missing here. There is a tranquility that, given the slightest encouragement, one could say is reflected in the wines.

The wines are light, fresh and unpretentious and yet, at their best, classically Burgundian, with the unmistakeable *goût de terroir* that fine Burgundy possesses. Simon Bize is an exceptional producer to look for.

Chorey-lès-Beaune is just outside Beaune, on the right as one comes down from the *autoroute* overpass on the N.74 road to Dijon. There are no great but some good wines at good prices. Bargains? Well, yes, as bargains go in Burgundy these days. Leroy, Daniel Senard and Tollot-Beaut all make some decent Chorey.

And then we are in Beaune. It is safe to say there is no more inviting wine city anywhere. With its medieval ramparts, its carefully preserved buildings, including the magnificent Hôtel-Dieu, Beaune's world-famous hospital, its attractive shops, good hotels and even better restaurants, Beaune is a must for any wine enthusiast who has a chance to visit.

Nor is everything that is good and beautiful only on the surface in Beaune. The old town is honeycombed with wine cellars that have been in use for hundreds of years. Some are open to the public and in season are filled with shuffling, bored tourists. If you have a favorite shipper — Latour or Jadot or Drouhin — make an appointment in advance. It will be well worth the effort.

But Beaune is more than a repository for history and aging wine. Its vineyards, which circle around the town to the north and the west, are among the most famous along the Côte d'Or. There are no *Grands Crus* in the Beaune appellation, but there are twenty-eight *Premiers Crus*. The best include Les Marconnets, Les Fèves, Les Bressandes, Les Cent Vignes, Les Grèves, Les Epenottes, Clos du Roi and Clos des Mouches.

Each year, on the third weekend of November, Beaune is host to a three-day wine festival called *Les Trois Glorieuses*. Wine professionals, wine writers and wine hangers-on from all over the world make their way to Beaune to feast, to drink, to mingle and to buy. The celebration begins with one of the dinners mentioned earlier at the Clos de Vougeot, six hours of rich food, off-key singing and great wine.

On Sunday, the wine auction to benefit the Hospices de Beaune indicates what the prices for Bur-

gundy might be in the coming year. Since the profits go to the hospital, prices tend to be inflated, but experts can interpolate and gauge quite accurately how the market will go for the new wines. On Monday, there is yet another feast, the famed Paulée de Meursault, a lunch attended by as many as four hundred people, most of them winemakers and all of them carrying a dozen or so bottles of their best wine to share with everyone else.

Ten minutes southeast of Beaune lie the vineyards of Pommard. Unfortunately there is a tendency in the United States, even among waiters, to confuse it with Pomerol, in the Bordeaux region on the other side of France. Pommard found its way to the United States in the 1950s and 1960s and Burgundy lovers in that country tend to be suspicious of it. But Pommards from reputable growers such as André Mussy can be good muscular wines. There are individual vineyards to look for, Les Epenots and Les Rugiens among them.

Just south of Pommard lies Volnay, one of the oldest and most quality-conscious wine communes in Burgundy. The most famous vineyards are the Clos des Ducs, Bousse d'Or, Les Caillerets, Clos des Chênes and Taille-Pieds. Producers to seek out are the Domaine de la Pousse d'Or and Michel Lafarge.

Volnay borders on Meursault, which is the largest producer of white wine on the Golden Slope and the first of the great white-wine communes that distinguish the last few miles of the Côte d'Or. Interestingly enough, along the line where Volnay and Meursault meet, some winemakers conveniently — and quite legally — change colors. Les Santenots, a Meursault vineyard, produces only red wine. So it's called Volnay. Similarly, whatever white wine is made in Volnay is called Meursault.

At its best, Meursault is a superb white wine; it never reaches the intensity of the Montrachets, perhaps, or the richness of Corton-Charlemagne, but, when it comes from the Les Perrières, Les Charmes and Genevrières vineyards, it can have a special elegance all its own.

The problem in Meursault is the large quantity of lesser wine made from grapes grown on the flat plain west of the N.74 road. These wines, usually sold to shippers who sell it as simple Meursault, do more harm than good for the appellation. They are not cheap but they are no better than some inexpensive wines of the Mâconnais; St. Véran, for example, produced many miles to the south.

The Château de Meursault, now owned by the Patriarche firm in Beaune, has been the site in recent years of the Paulée luncheon on the Monday after the Hospices de Beaune auction. The château also produces some excellent Meursaults, but the best come from the smaller growers such as Jean-François Coche Dury, François Jobard, the Comtes Lafon, Pierre Morey, Olivier Leflaive and Guy Roulot. Louis Jadot, the Beaune négociant firm, also produces superb Meursaults.

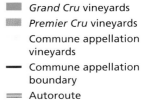
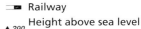
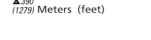

Grand Cru vineyards
Premier Cru vineyards
Commune appellation vineyards
Commune appellation boundary
Autoroute
Railway
▲390 (1279) Height above sea level Meters (feet)

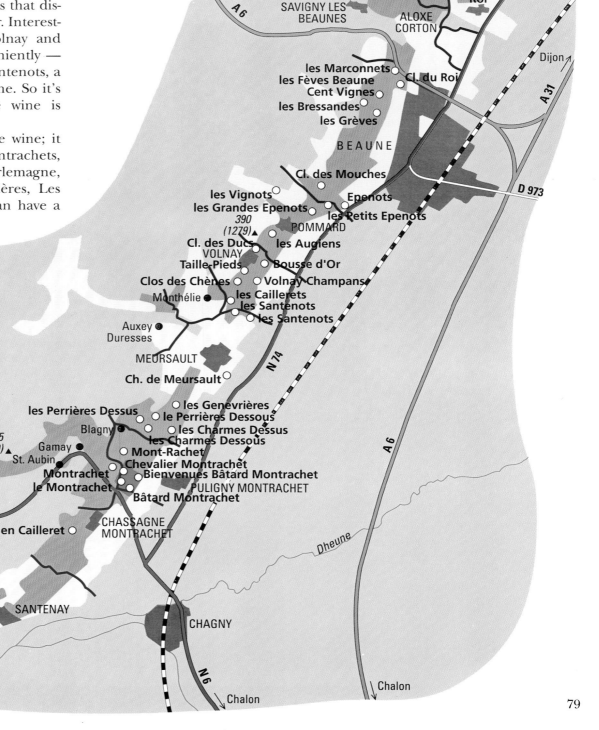

ABOVE: Volnay, an old wine village south of Beaune, is the home of the Marquis d'Angerville, courageous fighter against fraud and shortcutting in Burgundy.

Up in the hills west of the town of Meursault are the small communes of Monthélie and Auxey-Duresses. The white-wine vineyards of Auxey are really extensions of some of the best vines in Puligny and Meursault and the wine they produce can be truly delicious. They mature fast and fade fast, however, so must be consumed when they are young. Monthélie, which has been called the forgotten little sister of Volnay, only became known when the price of better-known Burgundies became prohibitive. The reds are a bit coarser than Volnay but

GROWER'S VIEW

The most important consideration in making good wine is the soil. The soil gives the wine its individuality, and its flavor and finesse. Ninety percent of the taste of the wine, in my view, comes from the soil. The next most important factor is the way in which the winemaker produces the wine. We are very traditional. We ferment in wood and use barrels that we know will go well with the wine. For white wine we use barrels mainly from the Allier in Central France and for reds it is principally barrels from the Jura, but always a mix of new and old oak. The proportion depends on the year or on the appellation. For *Grand Cru* about 30 to 35 percent of the barrels we use are very new oak, while for Puligny-Montrachet Village we put about 15 percent of the wine in new oak. With straightforward Bourgogne Rouge or Bourgogne Blanc about 5 to 10 percent goes into new barrels. Leflaive wines spend twelve months in barrels and four months in stainless-steel vats, compared to the usual practice of most Burgundian producers, who keep their wines for twelve months in the barrel and only a few weeks in the vats.

For me, the quality of wine also comes from the balance. This means three things: alcohol, acidity and the structure of the wine. These three things, taken together, affect the quality of the wine. With barrels it is the same thing. If you put all your wine into new oak barrels, the balance would be unsatisfactory because the wine would just taste of wood. When you have light years, you should put less wine into new oak barrels and proportionately more should go into new barrels if it is a vintage where the wine is particularly powerful. As I say, balance is the key if you want the wine to have finesse.

People like to say that such and such a year was the best of the decade and another year was the best year of the century. I do not think that way. Each year has its own character. It also depends whether you are talking about white or red wine. Taking white wine first as I am principally a maker of white wine, 1988, for example, was a very light year with very fruity wine that lacked structure, but it had good acidity whereas the following year the wine was more concentrated. It depends on what you ask or expect from wine. With red wines you get a big year like 1988 when the wine was well structured, powerful and full of tannin. However, there are people who do not like tannin and who would prefer a rounder wine that they can drink earlier, so a 1988, for example, would not be a good choice for them.

In summary, I would say that finesse and elegance are more important than fruit in the production of wine. Our methods are very traditional in Burgundy. We let nature do the work — usually nature knows best.

Olivier Leflaive

DOMAINE LEFLAIVE

LEFT: Some of the greatest expressions of the Chardonnay grape are to be found in the white wines of Montrachet and Meursault.

they are delicious at three or four years of age and still reasonably priced.

To the south of Meursault is Puligny, a modest little town that to many wine lovers is the greatest white-wine community in the world. Puligny, it may be said, represents the apotheosis of the Chardonnay grape. First of all, it is home to the small — 7.7 hectare/19 acre — Le Montrachet vineyard with its annual production of about 2,500 cases and a waiting list that guarantees prices unmatched by almost any other dry white wine. Le Montrachet is generally acknowledged to be the best white wine in the world. Which is not to say that indifferent wine has never been made here.

But Puligny's other wines are, some of them, only slightly less famous: Bâtard-Montrachet, Bienvenues Bâtard-Montrachet, Chevalier-Montrachet and Puligny-Montrachet. These are long-lived wines; Le Montrachet can thrive for thirty years and a fine Bâtard-Montrachet for twenty. Most Burgundy lovers put Chevalier Montrachet at the top of the list after Le Montrachet, but there are years when Bâtard, with its haunting smoky taste and bouquet, reigns supreme. Top growers in Puligny include the Domaine de la Romanée-Conti and Ramonet for Le Montrachet, Etienne Sauzet for Bâtard and the Domaine Leflaive for Chevalier.

The last of the three famous white-wine villages of the Côte de Beaune is Chassagne-Montrachet, which shares Le Montrachet and Bâtard-Montrachet with Puligny and has its own Montrachet, the 1.4 hectare/3.5 acre Criots Bâtard Montrachet. The Les Grandes Ruchottes, En Cailleret and La Boudriotte vineyards produce wine to equal almost anything in Puligny and usually at slightly lower prices. Chassagne actually makes more red wine than white

but its reputation is solidly based in what it does with the Chardonnay grape.

The newest appellation in Burgundy is Les Maranges. Created in 1989, it includes three villages at the very southern tip of the Côte de Beaune: Cheilly-les-Maranges, Dézize-lès-Maranges and Sampigny-les-Maranges. The wines, mostly red, are pleasant but unexceptional. They relate more to the wines of the Chalonnais to the south than to Côte de Beaune to the north.

LEFT: A winemaker gets only one chance a year to show what he can do. Anyone who knows the wines of the Domaine Leflaive, knows that Frank Grux accepts the challenge every year, and invariably wins.

OPPOSITE PAGE, BOTTOM: Some of the great wines of the Côte de Beaune are sold by the famous merchant houses such as Drouhin while others come to the market directly from the domain like the outstanding Corton and Volnay wines whose labels are shown here.

The Chalonnais

by Frank Prial

BELOW: The Château de Rully is in the Côte Chalonnais, a region just south of the Côte d'Or, which still manages to produce excellent Burgundy at reasonable prices.

The vineyards of the Chalonnais region are merely an extension of those of the Côte de Beaune but, while they produce similar wines, they rarely achieve the quality of their neighbors directly to the north. The name comes from bustling Chalon-sur-Saône, a rail center and manufacturing city about sixteen kilometers/ten miles east of the vineyards.

The principal communes of the Chalonnais are Givry, Mercurey, Montagny, Rully and Buzeron. For many years, much of the region's production went into sparkling Burgundy, an inexpensive Champagne substitute that was produced in both white and red versions.

As Burgundy prices began to climb twenty years ago, the growers in the Chalonnais realized that they could do better with still wines than with sparkling, and they have concentrated on them ever since. The best come from Mercurey, the home of the famous Clos de Myglands vineyard of J. Faiveley. The Faiveleys cultivate some 61 hectares/150 acres

MAP

BOUZERON
• Bouzeron

RULLY
RULLY

Chagny

N 981

▲366
(1200)
MERCUREY
■ Clos de Myglands

D 978

MERCUREY

St. Martin-
sous-Montaigu

▲317
(1040)

■ GIVRY

GIVRY
• Poncey

N 80

MONTAGNY
LES BUXY

BUXY

D 977

MONTAGNY

CLUNY

• Chagny

Chalon-sur-
Saône

Givry •

Saône

0   3 kms
0   2 miles

■ Vineyards
▲317 Height above sea level
(1040) Meters (feet)

GROWER'S VIEW

With 600 hectares/1,482 acres under vines, those vines being 95 percent Pinot Noir and 5 percent Chardonnay, our commune of Mercurey is the largest red wine producing commune of Burgundy. The vineyards are between 260 and 320 meters/850 and 1,050 feet above sea level, and the soil is a mixture of clay and limestone, with the latter predominating on the slopes.

Mercurey offers a wide range of differing exposures too; the hillsides form a ring with an opening towards the east. The *Premiers Crus* are found on the southern slopes (Clos des Barraults), with variations to the southeast (Clos l'Eveque) and southwest (Les Champs Martins and Clos Tonnerre). The climate is continental, and gives us 700 to 800 millimeters/28 to 31 inches of rainfall per year and some 1,900 hours of sunshine.

The age of the vines varies greatly from holding to holding, yet qualitatively speaking a vine is at its best between the ages of fourteen and fifty-five years, a period which corresponds with the working life of the grower. We pick our grapes by hand, and in 1991 sixty pickers worked for eleven days.

We bring the bunches of grapes in whole, destalk them. Then we vinify in open vats in 50 hectoliter/1,320 U.S. gallon units. The grapes are macerated at 16°C/60°F over five days in order to obtain color. The alcoholic fermentation lasts from four to seven days at a temperature no higher than 32°C/89°F after which we allow the maceration to continue for a further two to three days. Throughout this period of *cuvaison* and fermentation we alternate *pigeage* and *remontage* to a maximum of twice a day. The wine is then ready to be drawn off, both the free-run wine or *jus de goutte* and the press wine, or *jus de presse* obtained from its residue, the latter being left to settle for 48 hours in order to eliminate the heavier deposits.

Blending may then take place and the wine goes out into casks which may be new or up to six years old. For us maturing in cask is synonymous with quality. The malolactic fermentation takes place in cask, and once this been completed, the first racking of the wine is carried out. The process of maturing in cask lasts from fourteen to eighteen months.

Michel Juillot

DOMAINE MICHEL JUILLOT

BELOW: Of the four appellations of the Côte Chalonnais, Mercurey produces the greatest volume of wine. Joseph Faiveley is largely responsible for Mercurey's fame with the Clos du Roy and Clos des Myglanges vineyards.

---

in Mercurey, mostly Pinot Noir, and make wines that rival many lesser offerings from the Côte de Beaune.

Rully's best wines are whites. Givry produces both but the red is the best. It is said to have been the favorite of Henri IV, but then so are many other French wines. Montagny produces white wines exclusively. Bouzeron makes both red and white but only its white wine, made from the Aligoté grape, qualifies for village A.O.C. status, and is on the wine maps mostly because of Aubert de Villaine, who makes both when he isn't working at the Domaine de la Romanée-Conti, of which he is half-owner.

The Mâconnais

by Michael Edwards

The Mâconnais is the home of affordable white Burgundy, providing great quantities of attractive wine from the Chardonnay grape. The locals claim, indeed, that the world's best-known variety takes its name from the little village of Chardonnay, a few miles west of Tournus.

This is southern Burgundy, a transitional, bucolic land which lies between the Côte d'Or and Beaujolais. On a summer's day the sun feels much hotter than in Beaune, a mere sixty-four kilometers/forty miles to the north, but in fact the Mâcon climate is changeable and treacherous. February can be bitterly cold, spring frosts are a regular danger and hailstorms a constant fear in May, June and August.

The Mâconnais is essentially a chain of small hills running north-south for about forty-eight kilometers/thirty miles. The vineyards are bordered to the north by the Côte Chalonnaise, to the south by the Beaujolais border at St. Amour, to the east by the river Saône, and to the west by the foothills of the Charollais.

The total area of wine production is approximately 6,000 hectares/14,820 acres. The main grape is the Chardonnay which accounts for two thirds of the planted vines. The Gamay grape, accounting for a quarter of production, yields an astringent, earthy red wine on the Mâcon soils. A small amount of Pinot Noir is also made. It is always much less distinguished than the great red wines of the Côte d'Or or the increasingly impressive ones of the Côte Chalonnaise, though a few Mâconnais growers like

BELOW: The limestone and marl-based soil beneath the cliffs of Vergisson in the southern Mâconnais produces some of the best Chardonnay of the area.

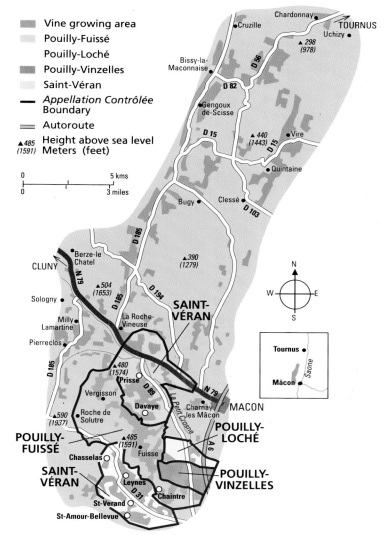

the Belgian-born Guffens Heynen now make a Pinot Noir which is a pleasure to drink.

Winemaking in the Mâconnais is dominated by the cooperatives, which represent 85 percent of the region's production. The quality of cooperative wines varies widely, overcropping of the Chardonnay in particular being an endemic problem. The best cooperatives, however, are admirable providers of wines that offer exceptional value for money. The Groupement de Producteurs de Prissé, for example, has one of the best winemakers in the region.

Most cooperatives specialize in Mâcon Villages wines made from Chardonnay; these account for as much as 70 percent of each cooperative's production. Of the forty-two villages entitled to the Mâcon Villages appellation, names to look out for include Mâcon-Charnay, Mâcon-Prissé, Mâcon-Clessé,

Mâcon-Viré and Mâcon-Lugny. These last three come from the northern Mâconnais, and produce wines which are more flowery in style than the steelier ones from further south.

Yet a good Mâcon Villages should always be fresh and fruity, a wine to be drunk between one and three years of the vintage. Temperature-controlled fermentation at 18° to 20°C/64° to 68°F is now the general rule; in this way the aromas of Chardonnay are fully retained.

The commune of Clessé-Quintaine deserves particular mention because of its microclimate. This village is close to the Saône, and autumn fogs from the river shroud the vineyards at vintage time. In warm, humid Octobers like those of 1983 and 1989, noble rot (*Botrytis cinerea*) develops on the Chardonnay grapes, creating a wonderfully rich *demi-sec* wine that matches fruit-based desserts perfectly. One of the finest exponents of botrytized Chardonnay is Jean Thévenet of Quintaine, a brilliant winemaker who looks like a monk from the Abbey of Cluny. His 1989 Domaine la Bon Gran Cuvée Tradition is surprisingly complex and should still be drinking well in the year 2000.

Clessé-Quintaine is something of an exception among the Mâcon Villages, for the best white wines of the Mâconnais generally come from the southern vineyards of the region. Beneath the magnificent rock cliffs of Solutré and Vergisson, the soil is based on a deep bedrock of marl and limestone, which gives the wines of this area greater depth of flavor and longer life.

This is the home of Pouilly Fuissé, Pouilly Vinzelles, Pouilly Loché and St. Véran. Prices of these wines vary wildly, though their quality and style are much alike. Pouilly Fuissé is the most famous name and commands the highest price. From excellent growers like Jean-Jacques Vincent, Guy Burrier, Claude Manciat and Madame Ferret, Pouilly Fuissé can be a splendid wine which develops a honeyed richness akin to a good Meursault; examples from great years will continue to improve for a decade. But there is also a lot of inferior Pouilly Fuissé produced in the high-yielding vineyards of Chaintré; this wine is generally much less interesting than a good St. Véran, and costs considerably more.

St. Véran is often a bargain. The appellation dates from 1971 and the wine is still little known,

but the standards of winemaking are probably the highest in the Mâconnais. St. Vérans from growers like Roger Luquet and Bernard Léger-Plumet, a local doctor, combine a ripe richness with a steely length of flavor. They age well for three or four years.

ABOVE: A vineyard in Pouilly Fuissé, whose wines are the most famous in the Mâconnais.

ABOVE: The labels represent four of the principal white wines of the Mâconnais and the red and rosé wines of Mâcon-Pierreclos.

GROWER'S VIEW

We firmly believe in using the most natural methods possible, both in the vineyard and in the cellar.

Although the weeding of our vines is done mechanically, the greater part of any fertilizer we may use is of plant or animal origin. So far as possible, any treatments of the vines are limited to the use of sulfur and Bordeaux mixture — we aim to avoid using chemical pesticides.

Harvesting takes place when the grapes are fully ripe — often as late as the middle of October — with most of them showing *pourriture noble* (noble rot). This phenomenon is a special gift of nature in our commune.

Chaptalization is used only in years when

there is a lack of sun, as for example in 1980, and then only within the limits laid down by law.

It is vital to restrict the yields of Chardonnay if we are to make a complex, fine wine. Annually our yields average 40 hectoliters per hectare/2.3 tons per acre against a maximum permitted yield of 72 hectoliters per hectare/4.2 tons per acre.

Fermentation takes place in its own time, which may be as long as six to eight months. No commercial bacteria or yeasts are added.

Jean Thévenet

QUINTAINE PRES CLESSE

Beaujolais

by Michael Edwards

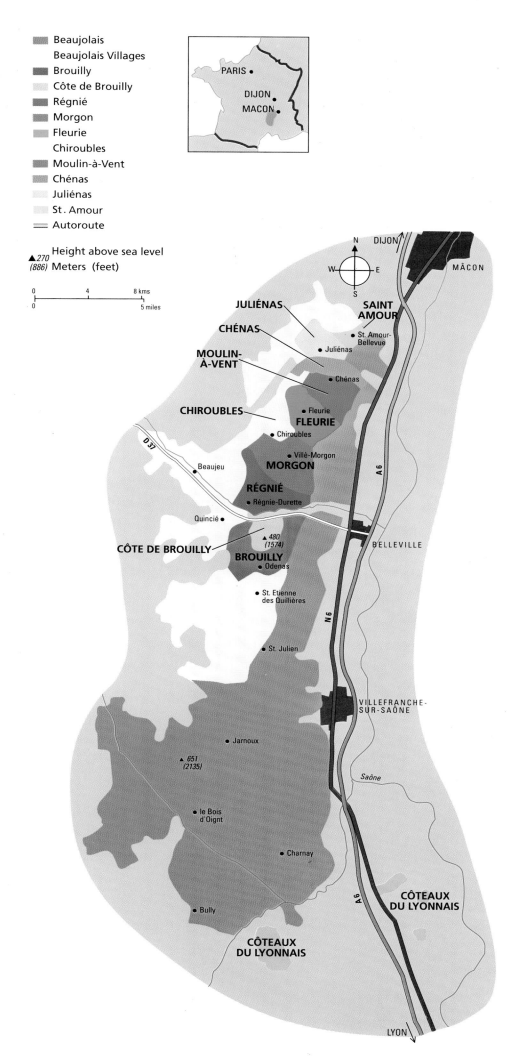

Beaujolais
Beaujolais Villages
Brouilly
Côte de Brouilly
Régnié
Morgon
Fleurie
Chiroubles
Moulin-à-Vent
Chénas
Juliénas
St. Amour
Autoroute

▲270
(886) Height above sea level
Meters (feet)

0   4   8 kms
0   5 miles

PARIS •
DIJON •
MACON •

Beaujolais is one of the best-loved French wines for the good reason that it is delicious to drink when very young, yet certain wines from the best growers in the *cru* villages can be at their best after two or three years. The phenomenal success of Beaujolais Nouveau internationally owes a lot to adroit marketing, but quite a bit too to the style of the wine, which combines freshness, fruitiness and extrovert fragrance. But it has to be said that the image of Beaujolais as a simple country wine is outmoded. The better wines are of higher quality than that, and the lesser wines are expensive; Parisians who first led the fashion for drinking very young Beaujolais are now turning to alternative and affordable *vins nouveaux* from the Gamay growers of Touraine. This competition is no bad thing, for the Beaujolais region has a great deal more to offer than the new purple wine released on the third Thursday of November every year.

The Beaujolais is thought of as part of Burgundy, but it is a quite separate wine region of considerable size and importance: in 1990 1,200,000 hectoliters/ 31,701,600 U.S. gallons of wine were produced from the 22,000 hectares/54,340 acres of cultivated vineyards. This represents about 40 percent of the total wine production of Burgundy and in terms of volume is equivalent to that produced in the whole of Alsace. What sets Beaujolais apart is the Gamay grape, which grows on the northern granite hills of the region and yields a wonderfully vivacious light red wine — at its best the finest example of Gamay in the world.

The Beaujolais region is bordered to the north by the Mâconnais, to the south by the Lyonnais, to the east by the broad valley of the Saône and to the west by the picturesque hills known as Les Monts du Beaujolais. The vineyards, never more than sixteen kilometers/ten miles wide, extend southwards for about fifty-six kilometers/thirty-five miles from the Mâconnais commune of La Chapelle de Guinchay down to La Turdine, close to the city of Lyon. The vast majority of wine made is red, though a small amount of racy dry white wine called Beaujolais Blanc is produced in vineyards which intermingle with those in the Mâconnais zone of St. Véran. Beaujolais Blanc represents about two percent of the entire region's production. A benchmark example is made by Bernard Dalicieux of Leynes. A tiny amount of Beaujolais rosé is also produced by several growers.

Beaujolais stands on the exact latitude which divides northern France from the Mediterranean South. The climate is semi-continental with quite big differences of temperature: in August it can exceed 40°C/104°F, in winter the thermometer can register -7° to -10°C/19.4° to 14°F. Conditions are very favorable for the cultivation of the vine, with long, hot summer days and cool nights.

Beaujolais is the only red wine region in France where automatic picking machines are banned at vintage time in order to keep the Gamay grapes unbruised and intact. This is a crucial prerequisite for the special winemaking technique now used at all quality levels of Beaujolais — both for Nouveau and for the more serious Villages and *cru* wines released in the following spring and summer. The technique is an adapted form of carbonic maceration. Whole uncrushed grapes are put into a large, loosely-covered vat; the weight of the upper grapes causes the lower ones to split, setting off a normal fermentation and an attendant release of carbon dioxide, thus protecting the upper grapes from contact with air. It is important that the vat should not be over-filled with grapes so that the carbon dioxide can form a blanket between thè vat cover and the fermenting must. Fermentation for Beaujolais Nouveau lasts for a maximum of three to four days, that for Villages and *cru* wines for six to seven days, sometimes longer, at relatively cool controlled temperatures of 20° to 25°C/68° to 77°F. In this way, the aromatic constituents of the grapes are preserved, and the wines show good color and fruit, but less tannin. "Un bon Beaujolais est glissant" say the locals; a good Beaujolais slips down.

Viticulturally, Beaujolais is divided into two parts, reflecting a sharp difference of soils. The Haut Beaujolais, the northern part of the region, has an essentially granite soil and produces all the best wines; the Bas Beaujolais is based on clay and limestone, giving the wines an earthier flavor. The hierarchy of wine quality in Beaujolais consists of four levels. In ascending order of price they are: Beaujolais, Beaujolais Supérieur, Beaujolais Villages and the ten Beaujolais *crus*.

Beaujolais is the simplest wine of the region, mainly produced in the Bas Beaujolais, which is also a major source of Beaujolais Nouveau. Beaujolais Supérieur, which must have a minimum alcoholic content of 10.5 percent compared to Beaujolais' 9.5 percent, is normally released in December following the harvest. In practice, Beaujolais Supérieur is often superior to straight Beaujolais in name alone.

There is, however, a jump in quality to Beaujolais Villages. This appellation covers thirty-nine villages in the Haut Beaujolais. The granite soil, the higher altitude, the longer spell in vat all account for wines of greater depth of flavor. Before the Nouveau fad of the 1970s, this generalization was true without exception. But nowadays most leading producers make a Beaujolais Villages Nouveau, which they say lasts longer than a simple Beaujolais Nouveau. This seems a waste of better vineyard land. Those Villages wines that do spend a full winter in vat before bottling, by contrast, offer the consumer the best quality: price ratio in the Beaujolais region, with an interesting range of styles. The commune of St. Etienne-des-Ouillières is known for supple wines with a primary smell of the grape; Quincié is

ABOVE: A Haut Beaujolais vineyard in winter. This vineyard with its high altitude often needs a sunny year to produce its best vintages.

RIGHT: The Clos des Garands vineyard in Fleurie produces wine with a silkiness and fruitiness characteristic of this *cru*, but with added body and structure deriving from the higher mineral content of its soil.

BELOW: At the highest echelon of the Beaujolais hierarchy are the ten *crus*, each of which is represented below.

tougher, more tannic, capable of long life. The most reliable source of good blended Beaujolais Villages is the small band of local négociants, whose leader is Georges Duboeuf. Duboeuf's success has been based on innovative winemaking and imaginative marketing. Other excellent merchants include Pierre Ferraud and Sylvain Fessy. There is also some Beaujolais Villages which can match the Beaujolais *crus* in quality. These wines are unblended and come from particular estates. Jean-Charles Pivot in Quincié, for example, makes a powerful, tannic wine which can match a fine Morgon.

The ten *crus* are the aristocrats of Beaujolais, entitled to bear their village names on their labels. The best *crus* show individual personality and an extra dimension of flavor; but as a result of strong consumer demand too many wines have become depersonalized through an excessive use of chaptalization, the addition of sugar to the fermenting wine in order to increase the alcoholic content.

Brouilly is the largest of the *crus,* and is also the most forward, delicate and fruity. The best part of Brouilly is a steep blue granite hill called the Côte de Brouilly which has its own A.O.C. and which usually produces a richer wine needing a year in bottle to reveal itself. André Large, a member of the Eventail du Beaujolais group of growers, makes excellent, delicately poised wines in both appellations. Chiroubles is a *cru* to be drunk in the spring and summer following the vintage, but because of its high altitude and racy acidity, it needs a sunny year like 1989 to show its stylish paces. An exception to the rule of easy, early drinking is the superb long-lived wine of Georges Boulon.

Practically all the Beaujolais *crus* are distinguished by the fresh grapy flavor of the Gamay. This characteristic is less marked in Morgon, where the wine tends to show a richer taste redolent of cherries, plums, even apricots. But this is a large commune, producing 5,900 hectoliters/155,886 U.S. gallons of wine in a plentiful year, and quality is variable. It is as well to remember an old Morgon saying: "il faut taper dans le rognon," which means one must persevere to find the best wines. As a general rule, these tend to come from the decomposed slaty soil of Morgon's Côte de Py and the neighboring Les Charmes vineyard.

Morgon wines have a reputation for aging well. A minority of growers, such as Jacky Janodet, Gérard Brisson and Michel Gutty, do make splendid wines built to last, though those of the outstanding vigneron, Jean Descombes, often taste perfect after just twelve months in bottle.

Fleurie is perhaps the most currently fashionable *cru,* with floral scents, generous fruit, firm body and a lovely velvety texture. The vineyards of Les Moriers and Les Garands, close to the Moulin-à-Vent boundary, have a more minerally soil which gives the wines extra substance and structure.

Recent Beaujolais Vintages
1990 — Elegant breed, very frank and typical
1989 — Fleshy, open and profound
1988 — Well-balanced and agreeable
1987 — Fine and subtle, underrated
1986 — Pleasant, easy to drink
1985 — Outstanding; harmonious, appealing, structured

Juliénas is one of the most northerly *crus* with a reputation for powerful wines. Sadly this reputation is based on tradition rather than current reality. Certainly there are some excellent, deep-flavored wines from growers like André Pelletier and Gérard Descombes, but many other wines from this commune are much too light.

By contrast, the wines of Chénas are a model of round, frank fruit and admirable consistency. Chénas is perhaps the least known of the *crus*, but it frequently shows the Burgundian power of neighboring Moulin-à-Vent at a more reasonable price. Outstanding producers include Fernand Charvet, Daniel Robin, Château de Chénas and Pierre Ferraud, the largest buyer of Chénas wines.

Moulin-à-Vent is the most famous Beaujolais *cru*. The element of manganese in the sub-soil gives the wines great color and a fleshy weight which deserves a couple of years in bottle to show to best advantage. Some critics maintain that Moulin-à-Vent is capable of very long life, though others point out that the wine tends to lose the grapy succulence essential to Beaujolais if it remains in bottle after five years. Those commentators who claim that mature Moulin-à-Vent tastes like a Burgundian Pinot Noir may be indulging in a bit of wishful thinking. Nonetheless, sources of first-rate wines are Jean-Pierre Bloud, Jacky Janodet, GFA Les Marquisads and Bernard Diochon.

St. Amour is the forgotten Beaujolais *cru*, the boundaries of the commune being entirely in the Mâconnais. Here the soil is clay and limestone, which shapes the style of the wine. St. Amour is discreet and subtle with less of the exuberant fruit of the other *crus*, but though little known it rarely disappoints. The leading producers are Domaine du Paradis, Janin, Jean-François Echallier and Georges Trichard.

Régnié was elevated to *cru* status in 1988. It is too early to say whether the wines of the commune as a whole deserve this promotion. There is certainly a wide disparity of qualities and styles. Champions of Régnié say that the wine should show the easy fruit of Brouilly with the firm character of Morgon. This is not always apparent in the glass, but vibrant Régnié wines come from Paul Cinquin and Jean-Charles Braillon.

GROWER'S VIEW

The Charter of Quality, launched in Beaujolais in 1991, is a happy initiative which allows for the protection of the grape and the wine against new factors, brought into play by technical progress, which could depersonalize them. This initiative also has the advantage of compelling those engaged in the profession to think about what they are doing.

Technical progress, carelessly applied, always carries the risk of impairing the traditional character of our product. For example, I think it is a pity that very little Beaujolais nowadays spends any time in wood before bottling. I still use large 50 hectoliter/1,320 U.S. gallon *foudres* made of Czechoslavakian oak to age my Beaujolais *crus* for a few months. This type of old wood is low in tannin, and both supports and softens the wines so they may release fully the individual aromas and flavors of their respective appellations.

Pierre Ferraud

PIERRE FERRAUD ET FILS S. A.

Coteaux du Lyonnais

Coteaux du Lyonnais is an appellation dating only from 1984. The zone of production covers some 350 hectares/865 acres spread across forty-nine communes. The vineyards are bordered to the east by the Massif Central, to the west by the Rhône and Saône rivers, to the north by the vineyards of Beaujolais, and to the south by those of the Rhône Valley or Côte Rôtie. The predominant grape is the Gamay, which is vinified by the Beaujolais method of carbonic maceration. The red wines produced are fresh and lively, though they lack the fruitiness of good Beaujolais. They do however provide consistent drinking, full of character, and at more affordable prices.

BELOW: Old vines of Moulin-à-Vent on a granite and manganese soil. This soil contributes to the fullness and relative aging qualities for which this *cru* is renowned.

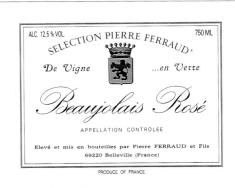

LEFT: White and rosé Beaujolais represent under one percent of the appellation but can often be fine wines, while the famous Nouveau or Primeur accounts for over half the Beaujolais produced.

THE LOIRE

by Michael Edwards

The Loire is France's longest river. It rises in the Massif Central, flows north as far as Orléans, swings left past the magnificent Renaissance châteaux of Touraine and Anjou, and reaches the sea at Nantes. Along its course of nearly 1,070 kilometers/665 miles, 80,000 hectares/197,600 acres of vines produce as much as 3.5 million hecto-liters/92,500,000 U.S. gallons of wine in a good year. Loire wines show a unified style of delicacy and freshness, shaped by the gentleness of the climate and the constant presence of water; in all other ways, however, they vary greatly.

For reasons of completeness, the scattered vine-yards of the upper Loire bordering the Massif Central should be mentioned, but essentially there are four main regions producing A.O.C. wines: the Sancerre and Pouilly-sur-Loire area of central France; Touraine; Anjou and the Pays Nantais. These are among the most northerly vineyards in France, and the best sites generally are those on sheltered south-facing hillsides. Annual rainfall is less than 600 millimeters/23.6 inches, but the winds coming off the Atlantic can be fierce.

The soils and geology of the Loire change, of course, all along its length. The gravel of St. Pourçain, the *perruches* flint of Vouvray, the chalky *tuf* of Chinon, the granite and schist of Saven-nières, all strongly influence the flavor of their re-spective wines. Grape varieties, too, change according to the region. At the western end of the Loire, where it empties into the Atlantic, the Mus-cadet grape, which makes the pale, crisp wine of the same name, rules the vineyards. At Savennières, one of the great white grapes of the Loire, the Chenin Blanc, enters the picture, and is even better known when it comes from Saumur. There are reds and rosés from the latter, too, both made from Caber-net, and some Champagne-method sparkling wine. Anjou produces all styles and grows a whole range of grapes: varieties like Groslot or Pineau d'Aunis as well as the more familiar Chenin Blanc, Gamay and Cabernet. These last two, plus Pinot Noir, are the main red grapes of the Loire; Cabernet Franc makes the reds of Chinon and Bourgueil; Pinot Noir the equally fashionable reds of Sancerre. Vouvray specializes in Chenin Blanc for still and sparkling, dry and sweet wines, and in Touraine, and further east in Sancerre and its neighboring regions, the third major white grape of the Loire comes into its own. Sauvignon Blanc makes the aro-matic, racy wines from here which for many people are the epitome of Loire whites and which have become the benchmark by which Sauvignon Blancs worldwide are judged.

The wines from the far reaches of the upper Loire do not compare in quality with those of the central region, but they offer interesting drinking at

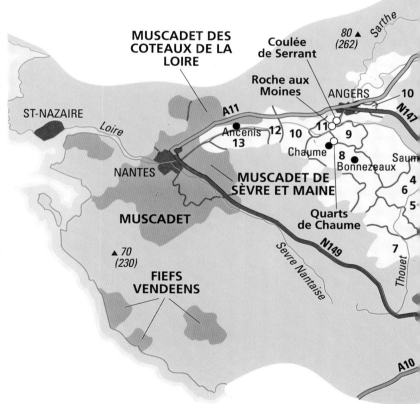

affordable prices. Both the Côtes d'Auvergne and the Côtes du Forez on the eastern edge of the Massif Central provide bright, positive red wines from the Gamay grape; in the former, look out for the names of the sub-districts of Boudes, Chanturgues, Châteaugay, Corent and Madargues. The Côtes du Forez boasts of one of France's better cooperatives, and even better Gamays come from the Côte Roannaise, an hour's drive west of the Beaujolais, whose fresh, fruity charm they share. St. Pourçain is the home of crisp, racy white wines, their character deriving from the Chardonnay, Sauvignon Blanc, Tressallier grapes; there are also reds from Pinot Noir and Gamay. And the small, 80-hectare/198 acre appellation of Châteaumeillant is famous for its *vin gris*, a delicious rosé Gamay of fine texture and delicate fruit.

The Sauvignon is the dominant white grape of the central part of the Loire, and shows to particular advantage at Sancerre, 48 kilometers/30 miles east of Bourges. The vineyards of Sancerre are among the steepest in France, extending to 1,900 hectares/4,693 acres spread across 14 communes.

ABOVE: The Loire River looking east at Tours. The surrounding Touraine appellation includes the red wines of Bourgueil and Chinon and the famous sweet wines of Vouvray.

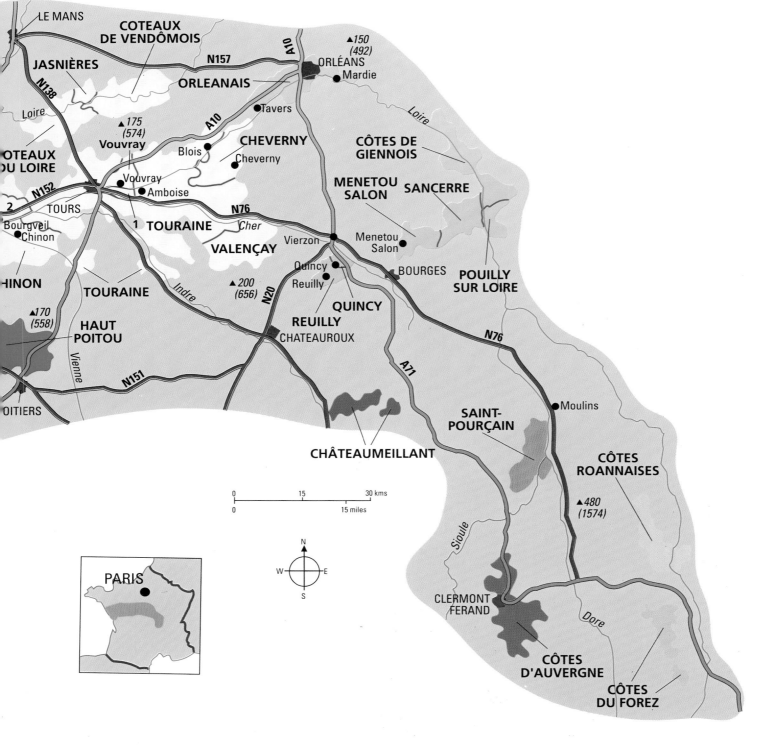

1   Montlouis
2   Bourgueil
3   Saint Nicholas de Bourgueil
4   Saumur-Champigny
5   Côteaux de Saumur
6   Saumur
7   Thouarsais
8   Côteaux du Layon
9   Côteaux de l'Aubance
10 Anjou-Côteaux de la Loire
11 Savennières
12 Côteaux d'Ancenis
13 Anjou
▨   Pays Nantais
    Anjou-Saumur
    Touraine
▨   Central Loire
▨   Haut Poitou
▨   Châteaumeillant
▨   Saint-Pourçain
▨   Côtes d'Auvergne
    Côtes Roannaises
    Côtes du Forez
━   Autoroute
▲480 Height above sea level
(1574) Meters (feet)

ABOVE: The medieval town of Sancerre sits astride a steep hilltop with the south and east facing vineyards situated on similarly sharp inclines.

TOP: The Sauvignon Blanc grape produces virtually all of the white wine of the Sancerre region but with some differences in style between the intensity of Sancerre, the opulence of Pouilly Fumé and the floral character of Menetou-Salon.

vine — the Sancerrois is on the same latitude as Dijon — and the variety ripens late. Traditionally red Sancerre is light and fruity, often vinified for only a short period to accentuate the same crisp freshness that is found in white Sancerre. But there has been a trend in recent years to macerate Pinot Noir for a longer time to produce a red wine of deeper color and richer flavor. New oak barrel aging is as much the mode in Sancerre as it is in California, but too often the aggressive wood flavors completely mask the fragile fruit of Pinot Noir grown in a cold climate. Sancerre rosé, on the other hand, can be a wine of real delicacy, its subtle pale pink tint and its discreet lingering fruit placing it among the better rosés of France.

Opposite Sancerre are the vineyards of Pouilly Fumé and Pouilly-sur-Loire. Chasselas is the main grape for the white wines labeled Pouilly-sur-Loire, but it is being replaced by Sauvignon, the only permitted grape for Pouilly Fumé. The soil is less chalky, the land flatter, the wine fuller, more *vineux*

--- GROWER'S VIEW ---

Above all, a grower's wine must please him when he tastes it. A grower who does not love wine cannot be a good grower.

His heart must go out to his vines, so that they produce fine grapes in adequate but not excessive quantity in order that his essential raw material may be healthy, ripe and of irreproachable quality. As regards vinification, it is vital that the *chai*, the *cuves*, everything associated with winemaking should be immaculately clean. The fermentation itself requires minute and constant attention and control. In the case of white wines, I think a fermentation which takes place at 20°C/68°F is ideal, producing wines with maximum fruit and richness. Racking must be carried out with extreme care to exclude air and a consequent loss of the aromas of the wine.

Joseph Balland

DOMAINE BALLAND-CHAPUIS

The main factor that determines the nuances of style in Sancerre is the soil, which is a Jurassic stratum of limestone similar to that found at Chablis, 97 kilometers/60 miles to the northeast. In fact there are two main types of soil in the Sancerrois. The chalky *caillottes*, found in the central part of Bué, yields wines of pronounced aroma and elegant fruit for relatively early drinking. By contrast, the white *terres blanches*, with a higher proportion of marl and clay, produces firmer, more structured wines, which are austere when young but which show length and complexity of flavor after a year or two in bottle. The village of Verdigny is particularly known for *terres blanches* yet the Domaine Daulny, one of Verdigny's best estates, makes an exceptional wine, its exquisite balance given by grapes grown on both types of soil.

Pinot Noir is the grape used for the red and rosé wines of Sancerre, accounting for about 500 hectares/1,235 acres of planted vineyards. But growing Pinot Noir here is hazardous: this is near the northern extremity for the cultivation of the

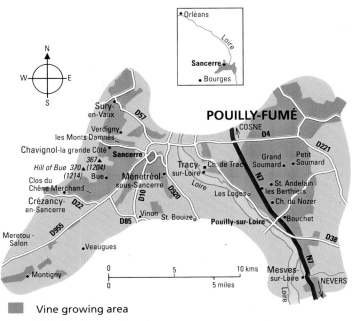

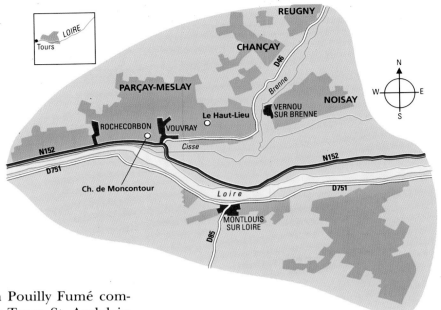

Vineyards

than in Sancerre. Of the seven Pouilly Fumé communes, the most important are Tracy, St. Andelain and Les Loges. The steep vineyard of Les Berthiers is one of the few which suffers less from the danger of frost. Complexity is achieved in the wines of Domaine Chatelain, Roger Pabiot (particularly his Coteau des Girarmes) and Didier Dagueneau.

To the west of Sancerre lie the communes of Menetou-Salon, Quincy and Reuilly. The same Sauvignon grape and similar climate and soils produce realistically-priced alternatives to Sancerre, though they often lack the elegance and definition of flavor of the latter. Henry Pellé and Etienne Daulny in Menetou-Salon, Domaine Mardon in Quincy and Claude Lafon in Reuilly make excellent wines in their respective appellations.

Downstream from Sancerre and Pouilly, the Loire skirts the Côteaux du Giennois, a good red and white wine source. Sauvignon from Balland Chapuis, who also has vines in Sancerre, is good. Further north, the vineyards of the Orléanais cover both banks of the Loire from Mardié to Tavers. Red wines made from Pinot Noir (known here as Auvergnat Rouge) and white ones from Chardonnay (Auvergnat Blanc) can show good varietal character, but need a sunny year to offset their high acidity.

Touraine is still *la vieille France*, a land of subtle beauty and rich culture, where superb châteaux are as numerous as vineyards. The Atlantic climate cedes to more continental influences here and the French notion of *terroir* — that combination of soil, exposition and microclimate — is perfectly illustrated at Vouvray. Here on the slopes and valleys above the northern banks of the Loire east of Tours, the south-facing vineyards catch the full strength of the sun, ripening the Chenin Blanc which derives a depth of flavor strongly influenced by the famous *perruches* and limestone *aubuis* soils. Yet as Noël Pinguet, winemaker at Domaine Huet in Vouvray says, "The sugar content from the juice of the Chenin Blanc grape is highly variable, according to the weather. Nature dictates the style of the wine." Vouvray can thus be bone dry (*brut*) medium (*demi-sec*) or intensely sweet (*doux*) — the latter wine being made from strict selections of botrytis-affected grapes. Sweet Vouvrays can be magnificent dessert wines which in great vintages like 1989 can easily live for fifty years. Montlouis, on the opposite

bank of the Loire, is often called Vouvray's poor relation, but it has several fine growers who are making rich, elegant wines from Chenin Blanc. Names to look for are Yves Chidaine and Domaine Delétang.

West of Tours is the home of the red wines of the Loire. At the confluence of the Vienne and the Loire lies Chinon, dominated by the ruins of its medieval castle. On the hillsides of limestone, known as *tuf*, the Cabernet Franc can yield Chinons capable of aging for ten to fifteen years when from exceptional vintages, but it is also a versatile grape that gives a delicious fragrant wine full of youthful fruit if grown on the lower sandy gravel soil within the Chinon appellation. Charles Joguet, a leading grower who is also a sculptor, produces a lovely aromatic wine called Varennes du Grand Clos as well as a wine from old vines, Clos de la Dioterie, that shows ripe tannins and power sufficient to justify keeping the wine for at least six years before drawing the cork.

Tannic power is an even more pronounced characteristic of Bourgueil, Chinon's rival appellation, eleven miles to the north. The Bourgueil village of Benais has a clay soil, where densely-structured and extremely complex red wines, as great as any on the

BELOW: These labels show some of the great range of red and white wines to be found in the center of the Loire valley.

ABOVE: Some growers believe that only Muscadet kept in wooden barrels as in this cellar, can justify the term *sur lie*, as keeping wine in contact with its lees in stainless steel vats is unlikely to enhance its quality.

river, are made by Pierre-Jacques Druet in his Grand Mont and Vaumoreau *crus*. St. Nicolas de Bourgueil is a neighboring appellation. The wines are lighter, more charming. Joel Taluau makes a fine example which is a vivid expression of pure Cabernet Franc.

The generic Touraine appellation covers vineyards partly situated in the *département* of the Cher and partly in that of Indre et Loire. This is an expanding, dynamic appellation, providing 150,000 hectoliters/ 3,962,700 U.S. gallons a year of all colors and most styles. The principal red grape is the Gamay, though on more calcareous soils the Cabernet and the Côt contribute wines of greater body and staying power. Sauvignon de Touraine is a brisk, herbaceous, all-purpose dry white. A Sauvignon that rises above the honest rustic character of the appellation to show delicacy and class is produced at Domaine Gibault in Noyers.

Touraine also produces sparkling wines, and a good deal of rosé is also vinified. Of the smaller Touraine appellations, mention must be made of Jasnières and Azay-le-Rideau, where fine, dry, age-worthy white wines are made from Chenin Blanc. Around Blois the Cheverny vineyards give clean-flavored Gamays, Cabernets and Pinot Noirs, and light whites in which Sauvignon, Chenin and Chardonnay are taking over from the indigenous white Romorantin grape.

BELOW: These Anjou labels represent four of the most underestimated white wines in France.

Anjou produces more wine than anywhere else along this long river. Across two hundred communes and twenty-five appellations, 60,000 hectoliters/1,585,080 U.S. gallons of white wines and 90,000 hectoliters/2,377,620 U.S. gallons of red and rosé are made. Rosé production dwarfs all else. At its best it is generally called Cabernet d'Anjou, and is normally sweet in flavor; straightforward Rosé d'Anjou, also rather sweet, is made from Cabernet, Côt, Pineau d'Aunis, Gamay and Groslot.

The best kept secrets of Anjou are the great white wines of Savennières, Quarts de Chaume, Coteaux du Layon and Bonnezeaux. All are made from Chenin Blanc. Savennières, with its blue-violet schist soil, encloses the two *crus* of Coulée de Serrant (look out for the wines of Nicolas Joly — dry, with great persistence of flavor, and needing seven or eight years to reach full maturity) and Roche aux Moines. Very fine, less expensive Savennières wines are made by Jean Baumard, a local négociant, by the Soulez brothers at Château de Chamboureau and by Madame Bizard de Raynal at Château d'Epiré.

The trio of vintages of 1988, 1989 and 1990 produced exceptional sweet wines in Quarts de Chaume and Coteaux du Layon, where the star growers are Jacques Lalanne and Vincent Ogereau respectively. Both appellations yield luscious but delicate wines shaped by a fine acidity. Bonnezeaux wines are similar in style though they often show an earthy note which is an acquired taste. Château de Fesles is a leading Bonnezeaux estate. In a good vintage, all these wines will live ten to fifteen years.

The red wines of Anjou have improved in recent years, coinciding with the appearance of a new Anjou Villages appellation. Made from Cabernet Franc and Cabernet Sauvignon, they can, however be very tannic, needing a sunny year to reveal their fruit. The Domaine Richou makes a weighty red to rival a good Bourgueil. More immediately attractive wines come from the appellation of Saumur Champigny, where immaculate vinification emphasizing the Cabernet Franc fruit is achieved at Château de Targé and Domaine Filliatreau.

Saumur is also the home of an important sparkling wine industry, the wines made into full *méthode champenoise mousseux* or the slightly less sparkling Crémant de Loire. Significantly one of the best producers, Bouvet-Ladubay, is owned by a Rheims Champagne house.

The Nantes region produces one of the best known dry white wines of the Loire. Muscadet is the name of the wine and the grape from which it is made. This variety is Burgundian in origin, traditionally known as Melon de Bourgogne. The area of production of the Nantais is some 13,000 hectares/ 32,110 acres situated in the *département* of Loire-Atlantique. The vineyards, mainly planted on sunny hillsides, are strongly influenced by the Atlantic Ocean. There are three appellations: Muscadet, Muscadet des Coteaux d'Ancenis and Muscadet de Sèvre-et-Maine. Sèvre-et-Maine is the most highly thought of district, and most of the finest wines come from Vallet. In an exceptional year, Muscadet de Sèvre-et-Maine can develop a vinous flavor akin to a minor white Burgundy, if allowed to mature in bottle for two to three years. Yet Muscadet is essentially a wine to be drunk young in the twelve months following the harvest. Look for the words *sur lie* on the label. Wines aged on their lees

in this way do not undergo the *malolactic* fermentation. Instead, the lees increase the richness of the wine by maintaining its freshness.

Of local négociants, Louis Métaireau and Sauvion et Fils produce excellent wines. Among the best estates are Château La Noé, owned by the bookish Comte de Malestroit, and Léon Boullault's Domaine des Dorices. Boullault practices organic viticulture, his Cuvée de Grande Garde having a capacity to age for up to ten years.

Within the Nantes region, the V.D.Q.S. zone of Gros Plant du Pays Nantais produces rasping, bone dry white wines from the Folle Blanche. The locals drink Gros Plant with oysters, but the wine has never sold well outside the region.

ABOVE: High-quality sparkling wine such as this Gratien Brut, this domain-bottled Muscadet and a red Saumur emphasize the range and quality of Loire wines.

GROWER'S VIEW

Great red wine needs mature vines. The balance comes from replacing failing vines with new young ones. Old vines, by which I mean those which are fifty to eighty years old, tend to give wine with a shut-in nose but also great persistence on the palate. Young vines contribute aroma.

You cannot make great red wine without the right soil. In the Bourgueil appellation, vines on gravelly, sandy *terroir*, do not produce wines for aging, there is a lack of the right acids, so these plots are better for *vins de primeur*. It is on the chalky *tuf coteaux* that the Cabernet Franc makes wines that age well. Our own commune of Benais has a particularly heavy clay soil which gives wines of extraordinary tannic power and complexity — a fact that is little known, even by wine experts.

I use the simple *guyot* method to prune my vines. The shoot is tied down to restrict the sap flow: too much vigor gives grapes that are too big for quality. I use manure and minerals where necessary and I try to take advantage of modern techniques without abusing the soil, the plant or the product.

Choosing the exact date at which to harvest the grapes is a game of poker in our northern climate. The grapes are normally ripe one hundred days after the flowering of the vine, but there is always a leeway of a week or two when you can hold back or start picking. It is a nail-biting decision.

Pierre-Jacques Druet
LE GRAND MONT

Calvados

Calvados is the world's best known apple or cider brandy, whose name derives from the department of Calvados in Normandy, northwest France. The first apple brandy was distilled there in 1553. It is a lush, green land of apple orchard and pasture, where apples and the other local specialty, cream, feature strongly in the cooking.

The apple or cider brandies of Calvados are defined by their own *Appellations d'Origine Contrôlées*. The original Calvados A.O.C., and the one still reckoned to produce the finest, most complex eaux-de-vie, is the central production area of the Pays d'Auge. The second division Calvados, which come from districts surrounding the Pays d'Auge, are: Avranchin, Pays de Bray, Calvados, Cotentin, Pays de Merlerault, Perche, Pays de la Risle, Vallée de l'Orne and Domfrontais.

In the Pays d'Auge, cider is distilled twice in a Charentais pot-still which gives more substance and power to the resulting brandy. In the other appellations, a continuous still is used to convert the cider into apple brandy. These "B" team Calvados lack the complexity of a great Pays d'Auge from outstanding producers like Roger Groult or Morice. However they can be delightfully light and fruity. Distilleries in Domfrontais, in particular, use pears as well as apples for their base ciders which result in "apple" brandies of marked aroma.

Exports of Calvados have increased significantly in recent years. Sales to Britain have doubled since 1989, and the United States is a growing market.

Most Calvados is drunk very young in France, at three to four years of age, but those for export on average are at least six or seven years old. Hors d'age Calvados, the top of the range, are usually about ten years old, but they can be magnificent at twenty.

LEFT: The apple harvest is the first step in the production of Calvados, which, from the making of cider from apples crushed in the traditional manner to distillation, follows the time-honored and strict procedure of its own appellation.

CHAMPAGNE

by Steven Spurrier

Champagne has a glamour that makes it the supreme wine of celebration. Christenings, marriages, birthdays and election night victories all call for the world's most famous sparkling wine. There is always a sense of excitement as the cork pops out of the bottle and the pale gold bead of tiny bubbles rises in the tall flute glasses.

Champagne is a unique wine, a constant reviver of the spirit which may be drunk at any time of the day or night. Its secret lies in the chalky soil of the vineyards and the meticulous way in which the wine is blended and aged. Sparkling wine may be made

anywhere in the world, and even the method by which Champagne is made is not unique. Finding that particular balance of richness and leanness of wine that ages beautifully yet maintains its freshness is a very different matter.

The vineyards of Champagne are the most northerly in France, spreading across five *départements*. Of a possible 34,000 hectares/83,980 acres approved as suitable land for the production of Champagne grapes, just under 25,000 hectares/61,750 acres are actually planted. The department of the Marne has 80 percent of the area under vines and the Aube 15 percent, with the remainder scattered in much smaller pockets across the Aisne, the Haute-Marne and Seine-et-Marne.

The central area of production is around Rheims and Epernay, comprising the Montagne de Reims, the Côte des Blancs and the Vallée de la Marne. The vineyards of the Aube are isolated 75 kilometers/47 miles to the southeast, while the vineyards at the extremities of the Champagne region are currently being replanted. Although the last two regions do not, on their own, produce the best bottles of Champagne, their wines are certainly used in some of the finest blends.

Three grape varieties only may be planted in Champagne. The Pinot Noir accounts for 28 percent of the vineyard. It is mainly planted on the Montagne de Reims, ripening well on the chalky-sandy slopes, and gives wines of balanced richness and finesse. The sturdier Pinot Meunier is more resistant to bad weather and is well adapted to the richer soil of the Vallée de la Marne and the Aube. Representing 48 percent of the vineyard area, Pinot Meunier is a dependable and prolific grape, so it is an important source of wines for non vintage Champagne blends, to which it contributes a supple, soft flavor. The Chardonnay shows itself to best advantage on the pronounced chalky soil of the Côte des Blancs, where it is the sole authorized grape. Less vulnerable to spring frosts than the early-flowering Pinot Noir, Chardonnay has a higher yield. It is above all appreciated for its delicacy and refinement, which balance the richness and fullness of the Pinot Noir. A Champagne *blanc de blancs* is one made from pure Chardonnay.

Champagne is unique among the *appellation contrôlée* wines of France in that it omits any mention of A.O.C. on its labels. Nevertheless, the wine is subject to rigorous controls. The maximum permitted yield

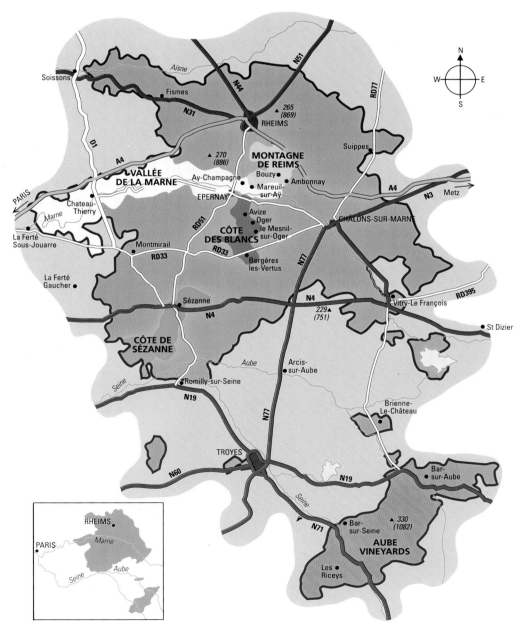

Vineyards	
	Vallée de la Marne
	Montagne de Reims
	Côte des Blancs
	Côte de Sézanne
	Aube Vineyards
—	A.O.C. Region of Champagne
═	Autoroute
▲330 (1082)	Height above sea level Meters (feet)

is 85 hectoliters per hectare/5 tons per acre, and in an average year the total production of Champagne will be about 250 million bottles.

The process by which still wines are made sparkling in Champagne is known throughout the world as the Champagne method. There are other, quicker ways of achieving sparkle in a wine, to be sure, and they are usually cheaper. But Champagne is fermented twice, once to turn it from grape juice into wine, and again in bottle, with a little sugar added to the new wine and some more yeast also added to ferment the sugar. The bottles are kept sealed as the wine ferments for the second time; with nowhere to escape, the carbon dioxide that is the by-product of fermentation stays in solution in the wine, to emerge in the form of fine bubbles when the wine is eventually opened and poured.

Champagne is, however, not the only wine made in the region. The appellation of Coteaux Champenois dates only from 1974, and it defines the still wines which were formerly known as Vins Natures de la Champagne. Coteaux Champenois wines, red, white or rosé, are made from the same grape varieties and in the same cultivated area as those carrying the appellation Champagne. Often wines from the *cru* villages are marketed unblended, identified on the label by the name of the village, Avize say, or Bouzy.

The best and most consistently successful of the white wines are those made from Chardonnay

grapes in the *Grands* and *Premiers Crus* of the Côte des Blancs, like Moët & Chandon's Château de Saran and Laurent Perrier's Blanc de Blancs de Chardonnay. Better known are the red wines of the Montagne de Reims, from the communes of Ay, Mareuil and Ambonnay. Best known of all is Bouzy Rouge, which is made from *Grand Cru* Pinot Noir in a village famous for Bollinger's holdings of ungrafted vines. The rosés are a rarity, and are seldom seen outside France.

Rosé de Riceys is the third appellation of the Champagne region. It defines a still, pale rosé wine made from Pinot Noir in the commune of Les Riceys on the far southern edge of the Aube, beyond the Seine. This rare wine is produced by a short maceration of the skins in the juice: its level of natural alcohol must be no lower than 10 percent by volume. After two to four days maceration, the wine must be taken off the skins at a precisely timed moment if it is to have the special but elusive *goût de Riceys*. If the wine has too little or too much color, if the taste is not characteristic, the wine is declassified. Production is tiny, averaging around 7,500 bottles, as only the grapes of the south-facing slopes ripen sufficiently. The remainder goes into Champagne.

But Champagne, like all wines, begins in the vineyard. The grapes are picked in small quantities, and sorted to discard poor or damaged berries. They are handled very gently to avoid breaking the skins

ABOVE: The easy slopes of the Montagne de Reims, with its chalky soil and excellent drainage, are perfect for Pinot Noir.

LEFT: Based in the *Grand Cru* village of Ay, Deutz produces one of Champagne's finest *blanc de blancs* from another *Grand Cru* village, Avize. Bruno Paillard is the most recently formed house in Champagne, and specializes in hand-crafted wines. Taittinger's Comtes de Champagne is amongst the leaders in the luxury *cuvée* market with this superb *blanc de blancs*.

ABOVE: Henri (left) and Remi Krug creating the blend that will end up as Krug Grande Cuvée.

BELOW: A *remueur* at work. The more traditional houses still prefer the human hand to the automatic *gyropalette* for this vital task.

before they are pressed, which could cause discoloration of the must. For the same reason the grapes are pressed as quickly as possible in large, low presses, 4,000 kilograms/8,818 pounds at a time. From each such unit a total of 2,666 liters/704 U.S. gallons may be obtained by three separate pressings. The first, the *cuvée*, produces 2,050 liters/541 U.S. gallons, the second 410 liters/108 U.S. gallons and the third 206 liters/54 U.S. gallons. As the pressing repeats itself, the must becomes progressively darker and more tannic, and so less desirable for the making of Champagne. Many houses only use the *cuvée*, selling the second and third pressings, the *taille* and *deuxième taille*, to other firms whose standards are lower than their own.

Impurities in the must are allowed to eliminate themselves by precipitation, and the alcoholic fermentation nowadays takes place in stainless steel vats rather than traditional oak casks, although Krug, for example, still uses oak casks. Malolactic fermentation follows in most cases, to reduce the acidity on the palate. At this stage the wine is very like any other dry white wine, but the blending, and the second fermentation, transform it.

It is the skill of the blender, and of course the influence of the soils and microclimates, that set Champagne apart from lesser sparkling wines. Each year the blender aims to create a wine that corresponds to the established style of his house. To do this he may use a greater or lesser number of wines from the current year, together with a smaller volume of the reserve wines available to him from previous years. Vintage wines, though following the house style, will also reflect the individual characteristics of their year.

Once the blend has been completed, sugar dissolved in old wine, plus yeasts, are added in carefully controlled quantities, and the wine is bottled and cellared to await its second fermentation in bottle. This fermentation is called the *prise de mousse* and must be undertaken very slowly, over many months, in order to achieve a constant, regular stream of very small bubbles once the wine is in the glass. The pressure created inside the bottle is normally five or six times that of the atmosphere, or three to four times that in the case of a *crémant* Champagne.

As this second fermentation takes place, with the bottle lying on its side, deposits are formed, mostly of dead yeasts. These are then removed by the

---

Champagne Bottle Sizes

Champagne is bottled in many sizes, but only the half-bottle, bottle and magnum are sold without exception in the bottle in which they underwent the second fermentation. Generally speaking, the jeroboam and larger sizes are decanted under pressure from ordinary 75-centiliter/25.4 U.S. ounce bottles. The same practice applies to quarter bottles. The different sizes with their total liquid volumes are as follows:

Quarter bottle 18.7 centiliters/6.3 U.S. ounces
Half bottle   37.5 centiliters/12.7 U.S. ounces
Bottle   75 centiliters/25.4 U.S. ounces
Magnum (two bottles)
Jeroboam (four bottles)
Rehoboam (six bottles)
Methuselah (eight bottles)
Salamanazar (twelve bottles)
Balthazar (sixteen bottles)
Nebuchadnezzar (twenty bottles)

---

process called *remuage*. For this the bottles are placed almost horizontally in racks called *pupitres* and are turned and tilted daily, eventually arriving at an almost vertical position, neck downwards, which causes the deposit to settle on the cap or cork. This labor-intensive work is now usually carried out by automatic machines called *gyropalettes*, which do the job more quickly and cheaply than *remueurs*, as the skilful men who used to do the job everywhere were called.

At this point the bottles are taken from the *pupitres* or *gyropalettes* and stored vertically, upside-down, to mature gently in preparation for the technique known as *dégorgement*. The bottles are kept in their vertical position and then passed through a conveyor machine that freezes the liquid in the neck of the bottle, in this way imprisoning the sediment in a tiny pellet of frozen wine. The bottle is then up-ended by a *dégorgeur*, who removes the cap or cork, allowing the pressure of the gas to expel the

LEFT: The Bollinger RD, for *Récemment Dégorgé*, spends up to ten years in the cellars before *dégorgement*. The most prestigious of the smaller houses, Billecart-Salmon produces firm, long-lasting wines. Cristal is one of Champagne's most sought after *cuvées*, bottled in a clear glass bottle based on one supplied to the Russian court.

little block of ice from the wine, leaving that which remains, clear and bright.

To compensate for the loss of wine, an equivalent amount of *liqueur de dosage*, a solution of cane sugar and still Champagne, is added to the bottle; both the amount and the sugar content of the *liqueur* will determine the wine's style and relative sweetness. The addition of 1 percent of *liqueur* will produce wines classed as *brut,* 1 percent to 3 percent *extra-sec,* 3 percent to 5 percent *sec,* 5 percent to 8 percent *demi-sec,* and 8 percent to 15 percent *doux,* the old-fashioned dessert Champagnes. The finest *cuvées* are always earmarked for the *brut.* In relatively few instances, no *liqueur* is added, the topping-up being done with the equivalent quantity of the same wine. This produces extremely dry Champagne, classified as *extra brut,* but also known as *brut intégral, brut zéro, brut 100 pour-cent* or *brut non-dosé.*

After *dégorgement* and *dosage,* the Champagne will be returned to the cellar to mature further, or it will be packaged for sale. Although the minimum permitted period between bottling and sale is one year, many quality-conscious houses allow three years, and five or more for their vintage wines.

While Champagne is essentially a blended wine that corresponds to the established style of each house, a wide range of individual styles is available in vintage Champagnes. Vintage Champagnes are only made in outstanding years, which in the eighties were 1982, 1983, 1985 and 1986. Eighty percent of the year's harvest may be used, the remainder going into the production of non-vintage wines.

Non-vintage wines are a blend of wines from several years, with the youngest wine predominating. Wines from the reserves of previous years are added to the new wine at the time of blending, in proportions chosen by each blender. Roughly 75 percent of all Champagne produced is non-vintage, and these are the flagship wines of the producers.

Just as *blanc de blancs* is white Champagne made only from white grapes, so *blanc de noirs* is wine made only from the black grapes Pinot Noir and Pinot Meunier. What little is made comes from the *Grand Cru* villages of the Montagne de Reims, and shows a deeper color and more substance than a *blanc de blancs* or a blended wine.

Crémant is Champagne with a pressure of 3.6 atmospheres, as against the more usual five or six atmospheres. Its gentler mousse foams or creams, hence the name. *Crémant* is always made with a high proportion of Chardonnay grapes.

Rosé Champagne became fashionable again in the 1980s. It is the only rosé in the European Community which may be made by the blending of red and white wine, the amount of red varying according to the color and weight of wine the blender wishes to create. Champagne rosé may also be made from red grapes left in the juice to color the must. Whichever method is chosen, the color of pink Champagne can vary from pale red to *oeil de perdrix,* the palest of them all.

Cuvées de Prestige, as their name implies, are showpiece wines, elegantly presented, from the leading houses. Some are rightly famous, Dom Pérignon and Roederer Cristal being probably the best known. They are always expensive and usually of excellent quality, though the jump in quality is not

LEFT: The deep *crayères,* quarried for chalk in Roman times, provide the perfect cellars for maturing Champagne.

LEFT: Gratien is one of the most traditional small houses, whose Champagnes are always well-matured. Blason de France is a prestige *cuvée* of rosé from Perrier-Jouët. Billecart-Salmon is always supremely elegant.

RIGHT: The Krug brothers do not approve of their Grande Cuvée being described as "non vintage" but prefer "multi-vintage." Bollinger, one of the few houses still remaining in family hands, represents Champagne tradition at its best. Perrier-Jouët, a prestigious house based in Epernay, underlines its fame during the "Belle Epoque" through its label design.

BELOW: The Abbaye of Hautvillers, home of Dom Pérignon and his order, now houses a museum devoted to the history of Champagne.

always as high as the jump in price; standard vintage Champagnes may be better value.

Champagne labels, particularly on the export market, are dominated by the strong brand images of the *grandes marques*. Contrary to the carefully cultivated façade of an exclusive club of top quality producers, *grande marque* Champagne houses account for more than twenty firms some of whose wines are grand in name alone and do not justify their high prices. Those that do provide consistently excellent Champagne can be swiftly listed.

Top of the tree is Krug which represents Champagne in its most traditional and uncompromising expression. The splendidly structured Grande Cuvée non vintage is released at six years of age as opposed to the normal three. Laurent Perrier is known for its exceptionally fine Grand Siècle *cuvée* and one of the best Coteaux Champenois *blanc de blancs*.

Bollinger is a very distinguished house, its own vineyards accounting for 70 percent of its needs. Pinot Noir is the dominant variety in the non-

vintage. Deutz is one of the most discreet *grandes marques* providing Champagnes of exceptional flavor and balance from the firm's holdings on the Montagne de Reims, and in exceptional years its vintage *blanc de blancs* is excellent. Perrier-Jouët makes a good meaty non vintage, while Pol Roger is an outstanding house with a classically elegant non-vintage wine and the very finest vintage Champagnes. Veuve Clicquot provides model examples of well structured, consistent, non vintage *cuvées*. The small family house of Billecart Salmon makes a delicately fruity non vintage, a subtle rosé and a superb *blanc de blancs*. The 100 percent Chardonnay vintage Dom Ruinart, the product of the oldest recorded house in Champagne, has the edge over Billecart Salmon.

Apéritifs and Digestifs of the Champagne Region

Ratafia de Champagne is an apéritif made in Champagne of two thirds grape juice to one-third marc.

Fine de la Marne is the local grape brandy of the Champagne district which is made by the distillation of the still white wines of Champagne. Fine de la Marne should not be confused with Fine Champagne which is a greatly superior brandy coming from the Grande Champagne or Petite Champagne zones of the Cognac district.

Marc de Champagne is a strong brandy distilled from the residue of crushed skins which remain after the Champagne grapes have been pressed and the juice has run off to be converted to wine. It is normally distilled to a high strength — between 40 percent and 50 percent alcohol by volume. Though powerfully flavored, Marc de Champagne has a less pungent style than Marc de Bourgogne. The Champenois *marc* is usually more digestible, particularly when it is made from the residue of white Chardonnay grapes.

There has been a big increase in the availability of high quality Champagnes beyond the magic circle of the *grandes marques*. The smaller *récoltants-manipulants* (growers) and the cooperatives now account for 87 percent of vineyards in Champagne and 36 percent of production. Champagne Jacquart is a typical success story. This cooperative recently became a private company and is now the sixth largest producer in the region. Continuity of supply is excellent, through the vineyard holdings of its 800 member growers. The cooperative at Avize is another first class producer of keenly priced Champagnes. Of the smaller *récoltants*, among the best are Michel Arnoux, who also grows for Bollinger, Vilmart Père et Fils, and R. & L. Legras.

The *cru* system in Champagne differs from those in Burgundy or Bordeaux. While it has a definite geographical base, it is essentially an index of price, based on quality, of grapes from individual vineyards. The scale of quality was first applied in 1919, as part of the restructuring of the Champagne industry after the First World War. At that time the finest grapes of the *grands crus* were assessed at 100

percent, with the percentage dropping with declining quality to 50 percent.

Today the scale rates the poorest grapes at 77 percent; those of *deuxième cru* status are rated at 80 percent to 90 percent, the *premiers crus* at 90 percent to 99 percent, with the seventeen *grands crus* remaining at 100 percent.

From 1960, this qualitative scale governed the price of grapes under the terms of the *contrat interprofessionnel*, which was an agreement negotiated annually between the growers and the *négociants*. A per kilogram (1 kilogram equals 2.2 pounds) price was fixed each year before the harvest, and the proportion of this price available to the grower was dictated by the percentage rating of his grapes. Thus grapes from a *grand cru* would sell for 100 percent of the declared price, and others according to their relative status on the index. The quality of Champagne is very closely linked to the quality of the grapes used to make it, and few serious houses will use grapes averaging below 90 percent.

In April 1990, the growers and *négociants* failed to renew the contract. A provisional agreement, valid for three years, has replaced it. This allows grape prices to fluctuate from a *prix indicatif*, a reference price, which has to be agreed each year, and it places limits on the buying of individual houses. This price ceiling is designed to prevent the richest firms from overflexing their purchasing power by taking too large a share of the grapes available. What replaces this provisional agreement will depend on future negotiations.

GROWER'S VIEW

As small *récoltants-manipulants* we believe in making Champagne in the most traditional and natural way possible. We are lucky enough to own 11 hectares/27 acres of vines in the *Premier Cru* village of Rilly La Montagne, made up of 50 percent Chardonnay, 30 percent Pinot Noir and 20 percent Pinot Meunier.

There are no stainless steel fermenters in our cellar; we use big oak casks or *foudres* for the fermenting and maturing of the young wines. We believe that the wood adds a complexity, depth and extra dimension to the finished Champagne.

We are vehemently opposed to the use of herbicides and pesticides, and we use only organic fertilizers. We also hoe the soil by hand. All this makes the working of the vineyards highly labor intensive and therefore quite expensive.

In making rosé Champagne, it is essential to use the traditional method of allowing the skins of the Pinot Noir grape just enough contact with the fermenting juice to give the wine a bright natural salmon pink color, neither too dark nor too pale.

The style of Champagne we aim to produce emphasizes purity of fruit rather than the taste of dead yeasts that so often characterizes more commercial blends.

Laurent Champs

CHAMPAGNE VILMART

ALSACE

by Michael Edwards

Alsace lies at the heart of Western Europe, an outpost of France on the German border. It is extremely beautiful and has kept its special character and traditions, even its own language, through many centuries of oppression and hardship.

Germany has frequently been an occupying power in the province, but the people of Alsace have remained both fiercely French and intensely proud of their own culture. To the *Alsacien,* life is precious and should be lived to the full. So good eating and good drinking are very important, and this hedonistic approach is reflected in the sensuous, distinctive flavors of Alsace wines.

The vineyards are mostly on the foothills of the Vosges mountains. They rise out of the broad plain of the Rhine to form a natural barrier between Alsace and the rest of France; they also give Alsace its exceptional climate by restricting much of the wind and rain coming from the West. Thus Colmar, the center of the Alsace wine region, enjoys one of the driest and sunniest summer climates in France,

with an average annual rainfall of just 500 millimeters/19.7 inches. The sun has an almost Mediterranean warmth here, yet this is well to the north of frost-prone Chablis. It is the differing microclimates, created by the various aspects and elevations of the Vosges foothills, which play a key role in the disposition and quality of the vineyards.

Another striking feature of Alsace is the extraordinary complexity of its soils. In the very early period of the earth's formation, the mountains that are now the Vosges and Black Forest ranges rose as a single entity above the surrounding waters. During the Tertiary period, about 60 million years ago, the middle part of this massif began to sink, forming a fault which much later became a plain. As a result, nearly all the deposits of earth which accumulated during the course of subsequent geological periods were exposed on this fault.

It is possible to find almost every type of soil in the region. There is chalk and limestone, sandstone and schist, clay, loess and various volcanic sedi-

ments. Most Alsace wine communes have four or five distinct soil formations. The individual grape varieties flourish on different soils: Riesling grown on the granitic uplands produces wines of great aroma and delicacy, while Gewürztraminer gives good results on richer, alluvial land near the bottom of the valley.

The Alsace vineyards total some 13,000 hectares/32,110 acres, producing roughly 1,200,000 hectoliters/26,418,000 U.S. gallons of wine each year. Grape yields are among the highest in France: the Beaujolais region by comparison produces approximately the same amount of wine from a total vineyard area of 23,000 hectares/56,810 acres.

The average size of an Alsace vineyard holding is very small, approximately 0.1 hectare/0.25 acres, and there are over 8,150 growers. The zone of production extends southwards for about 113 kilometers/70 miles through the departments of Bas Rhin and Haut Rhin.

The Bas Rhin, from Wasselone in the north down to Sélestat, is much the smaller of the two, and its wines are less highly regarded. This is unfair, for the best Bas Rhin wines are refreshing and quietly elegant: they also offer an excellent quality: price ratio. The drier, more austere grape varieties like Riesling are often successful, particularly if grown on the schistous outcrop around the picturesque little town of Andlau. Further north, André Pfister's *Grand Cru* Engelberg vineyard at Dahlenheim is based on chalk, which extends to a depth of 20 meters/22 yards below the topsoil. His Engelberg Rieslings are steely, vigorous and very long-lived.

The Haut Rhin stretches from Sélestat to Thann. This is the heartland of Alsace with a heavy concentration of the finest vineyard sites, some of which were famous in the Middle Ages. Alsace's most southerly vineyard, the Rangen at Thann, was well known at the court of the Capetian Kings of France in the thirteenth century. Warm autumn days in the Haut Rhin are especially favorable for the development of extra ripe grapes needed to make successful *Vendange Tardive* wines.

Alsace wines, with their Teutonic names, present a blurred image to the consumer. They are often confused with the wines of Germany, to which they bear little resemblance. Alsace wines are mainly dry and fruity, their essential appeal lying in the maximum development of the aromatic constituents of the grapes. This perhaps explains why in Alsace the wines are named after the grape variety from which they are made, rather than the vineyard or *cru* in which the grapes were grown, as is the case in Burgundy to the southwest.

It is sensible to divide Alsace grape varieties into two groups: one includes the staple varietals for everyday drinking, the second the noble grapes which produce the outstanding wines of the region.

Chasselas, also known as Gutedel, was until the 1950s the workhorse grape of Alsace. Since then its area has sharply declined and now represents 2.5 percent of the total area under vine. Chasselas is an early-ripening grape and makes a neutral-flavored wine destined for the Edelzwicker blends that are the staple *vins de carafe* of brasseries in Strasbourg and Colmar. A good Edelzwicker needs the bolstering flavor of Pinot Blanc and a touch of the aromatic Muscat to offset the bland neutrality of Chasselas.

Sylvaner used to be one of the most widely

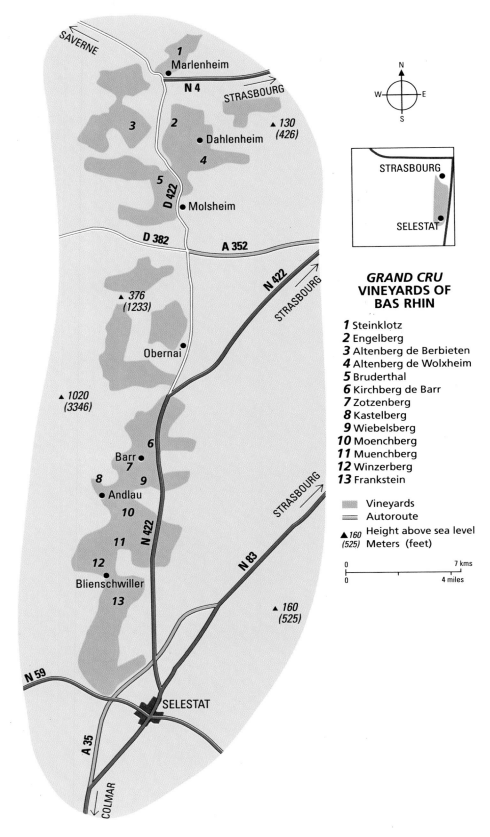

GRAND CRU VINEYARDS OF BAS RHIN

1 Steinklotz
2 Engelberg
3 Altenberg de Berbieten
4 Altenberg de Wolxheim
5 Bruderthal
6 Kirchberg de Barr
7 Zotzenberg
8 Kastelberg
9 Wiebelsberg
10 Moenchberg
11 Muenchberg
12 Winzerberg
13 Frankstein

▨ Vineyards
═ Autoroute
▲*160* Height above sea level
(525) Meters (feet)

0   7 kms
0   4 miles

planted grapes in Alsace, but it too is dropping in popularity. When produced on low-lying land, the wine can be sharp, thin and dull — yields of 100 hectoliters per hectare/5.9 tons per acre are quite common for Sylvaner, hence the dilute flavor. But if cultivated in sensibly limited quantities on sandstone or limestone slopes, this grape can produce lively, fragrant and altogether more interesting white wine. Jean-Pierre Dirler, a perfectionist grower, makes a superb Sylvaner from old vines on the best sandstone slopes above the village of Bergholtz. This practice of growing a modest grape on an exceptional site finds a parallel in Burgundy, where the simple Aligoté has traditionally given excellent results in the Bonneau du Martray domain of Corton-Charlemagne fame.

Pinot Blanc is the current success story of Alsace grape varieties. It now accounts for nearly 20

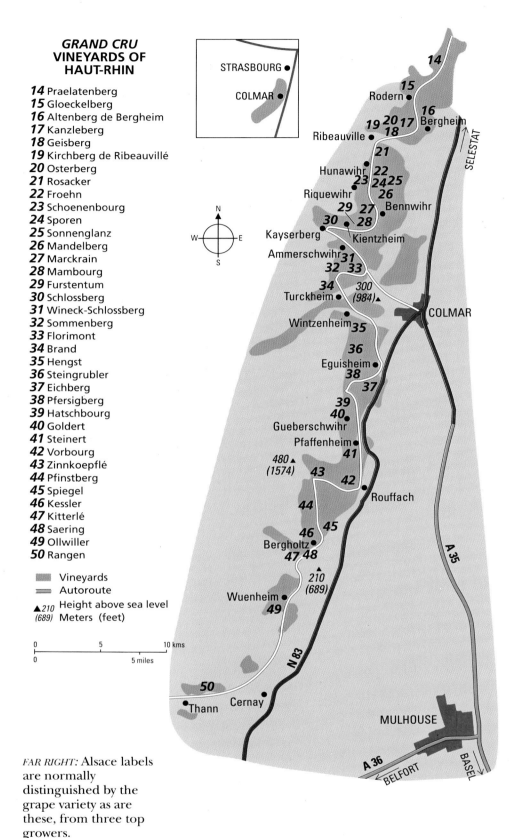

GRAND CRU VINEYARDS OF HAUT-RHIN

14 Praelatenberg
15 Gloeckelberg
16 Altenberg de Bergheim
17 Kanzleberg
18 Geisberg
19 Kirchberg de Ribeauvillé
20 Osterberg
21 Rosacker
22 Froehn
23 Schoenenbourg
24 Sporen
25 Sonnenglanz
26 Mandelberg
27 Marckrain
28 Mambourg
29 Furstentum
30 Schlossberg
31 Wineck-Schlossberg
32 Sommenberg
33 Florimont
34 Brand
35 Hengst
36 Steingrubler
37 Eichberg
38 Pfersigberg
39 Hatschbourg
40 Goldert
41 Steinert
42 Vorbourg
43 Zinnkoepflé
44 Pfinstberg
45 Spiegel
46 Kessler
47 Kitterlé
48 Saering
49 Ollwiller
50 Rangen

■ Vineyards
━ Autoroute
▲210 Height above sea level
(689) Meters (feet)

0   5   10 kms
0   5 miles

FAR RIGHT: Alsace labels are normally distinguished by the grape variety as are these, from three top growers.

percent of all varieties grown in the region, production having doubled since 1979. Combining freshness, body and suppleness, Pinot Blanc is a credible substitute for basic Chablis and it is more acceptably priced. Confusingly, Pinot Blanc is often blended with the Auxerrois grape and then labeled as "Pinot" or "Klevner", a traditional Alsace name which covers both varieties. Some growers sell a pure Auxerrois. High in acid and natural alcohol, the best wines can live for a surprisingly long time. A 1983 Auxerrois from Rolly Gassmann had lost none of its fruit when tasted in 1989.

Of the most interest to the serious wine drinker are the four "noble" varieties: Riesling, Tokay-Pinot Gris, Muscat and Gewürztraminer.

Riesling is thought of as Alsace's finest wine, though many growers see as much potential in Pinot Gris. Good Alsace Riesling has an elegant bouquet and shows delicate fruit allied to that pronounced

RIGHT: Labels from both the traditional, and the up and coming in Alsace. Colette Faller of Domaine Weinbach has long been regarded as one of the greatest exponents of Gewürztraminer while the young Christian Koehly is producing wines of great elegance and balance.

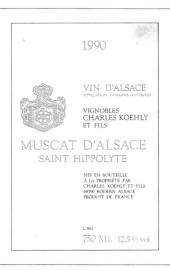
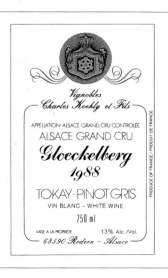

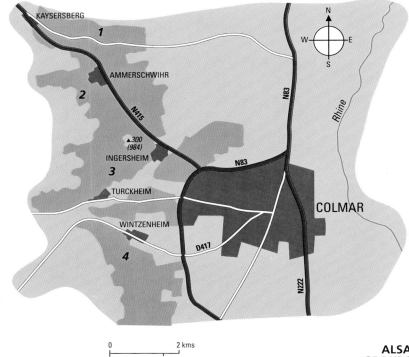

Vendange Tardive is a term used in Alsace for wines which have been late harvested, usually towards the end of October. *Sélection de Grains Nobles* (S.G.N.) signifies very late harvested wines made from individually selected grapes which have been affected by *Botrytis cinerea* or noble rot. Grapes destined for S.G.N. wines are picked as late as November or December following the vintage.

In March 1984, a new decree defining Alsace *Vendange Tardive* and *Sélection de Grains Noble* wines came into force. Only wines made from one of the four noble grape varieties are entitled to these designations. The minimum quality requirements are among the most stringent in France. For example, a grower must declare in advance his intention to harvest these special wines; an official quality inspection must take place before harvesting begins; and prior to selling the wines in bottle, a tasting panel of local experts must approve the wines at a date not earlier than eighteen months after the date of the harvest.

Vendange Tardive wines come in a variety of styles, depending on the amount of residual sugar left unfermented in the wine. Those styles where most of the sugar is fermented out taste rich and spicy but with a dry finish. The sweeter styles are close to traditional dessert wines. *Vendange Tardive* wines will age for at least eight years.

Sélection de Grains Nobles wines are unquestionably sweet and concentrated, though they are less luscious than a great Sauternes. In exceptional years like 1963, 1976 and 1989 they can easily live for 20 years and more.

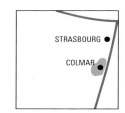

ALSACE GRANDS CRUS

1 Schlossberg
2 Sommersberg
3 Brand
4 Hengst

Vineyards
Height above sea level
▲300 (984) Meters (feet)

acidity which gives it the potential to improve with aging. The style, however, is to a large extent determined by the soil. The *Grand Cru* Brand at Turckheim is based on granite giving early-maturing wines of pronounced aromas, while the *Grand Cru* Altenberg of Bergheim has a soil of marl and limestone producing Rieslings of steelier structure. Certain Rieslings develop a characteristic *goût de pétrole* with age, their viscous, rich textures acting as an ideal foil to smoked fish, which is one of the most difficult foods to match with wine.

Tokay-Pinot Gris used to be known here just as Tokay, but it has no similarity in flavor to the great white Burgundy. Pinot Gris is found in the Côte d'Or where it is called Pinot Beurot: the Germans name the same grape Rülander; in Italy it is Pinot Grigio. Pinot Gris is a low-yielding varietal which is difficult to grow, but it has the potential to produce complex wine of great distinction in the Alsace *terroir*. Its flavor is richer than many Burgundian Chardonnays, releasing aromas of coffee or toast; and it is an exceptionally adaptable wine with a wide range of dishes such as foie gras, salmon, guinea fowl, offal, strong cheeses and desserts.

By contrast, Muscat makes Alsace's best apéritif wine. Usually classified as a single grape variety, there are in fact two types of Muscat used in Alsace wine-making. Muscat d'Alsace, also known as Muscat Blanc à Petits Grains, has a delicious grapy flavor, while the earlier maturing Muscat Ottonel imparts a fine, flowery quality. Indeed the smell of Alsace Muscat is close to that of spring flowers, though uniquely among the Muscats of France, the wine tastes completely dry with a crisp acidity.

Gewürztraminer is the Alsace grape variety par excellence, producing the best-known wine of the region and its most distinctive. The currently planted variety is a particularly spicy form of the Traminer family of grapes, *gewürz* meaning spice in German. Gewürztraminer is also grown in Austria, Italy, Australia, New Zealand and California. In these countries the wine, though rich, tends to be

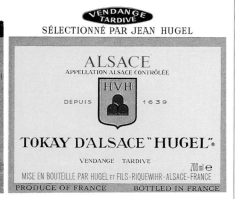

LEFT: Apart from the individual growers, the other producers in Alsace are the cooperatives, such as this one from Beblenheim and the great négociant houses like Trimbach and Hugel who continue to dominate the export market.

sweet, even cloying. On the palate Alsace Gewürztraminer is naturally unctuous, but if made from low-yielding grapes in favored sites, it also has an impressive refinement unmatched by Gewürztraminers elsewhere in the world. In warm falls, suitable for the development of *Vendange Tardive* and *Sélection de Grains Nobles* wines, Alsace Gewürztraminer can reach a potential alcoholic strength of 20 percent by volume.

Pinot Noir is an increasingly important grape variety in Alsace. By 1990 it accounted for nearly 1,000 hectares/2,470 acres under vines. Once known as a pleasant rosé for local consumption, the grape which makes red Burgundy is now being as seriously vinified in Alsace as it is in California and Oregon. Experiments with aging the wine in new oak barrels are quite fashionable. However, there are some outstanding winemakers like Colette Faller and Christian Koehly who believe that it is a mistake for Alsace Pinot Noir to ape red Burgundy, since the variety in the Haut and Bas Rhin has a much frailer constitution.

The Alsace wine trade is in a state of flux. Until recently, *négociants* and cooperatives accounted for 40 percent and 35 percent respectively of Alsace wine production. In the 1990s the picture is changing with the *négociants'* share of business declining at the expense of that of individual grower-winemakers. The cooperatives appear to be holding their own.

Of every ten bottles of Alsace, three are exported. *Négociants* still dominate the export market and certainly the whole region is lucky to have been represented abroad by such *grandes maisons* as Hugel, Trimbach and Dopff au Moulin, whose probity and standards of winemaking were, and are, high.

Quality Alsace wines are usually named after the grape variety from which they are made. The *négociants,* in order to protect their market share, have generally preferred to market their better wines under their own merchant names and under *cuvée* names particular to themselves, for example "Trimbach Riesling Cuvée Frédéric Emile" or "Hugel

Gewürztraminer Réserve Personnelle". Rarely have the *négociants* mentioned the exact vineyard of origin on the labels of their wines. These *cuvées* in effect amount to brand names, and the only way the consumer can tell where each ranks on the quality ladder is by drinking them.

In preferring the *cuvée* as opposed to the vineyard designation, the Alsace merchants have followed the practice in Champagne rather than that in Burgundy. Yet Alsace has a diversity of vineyard sites every bit as complex as Burgundy's Côte d'Or. The notion of classifying the *crus* of Alsace, though, is a new one.

In 1975 the I.N.A.O. introduced a new "Alsace Grand Cru" appellation. The *Grand Cru* designation was restricted to wines made from one of the four noble varieties — Riesling, Muscat, Pinot Gris and Gewürztraminer. The minimum alcoholic strength was fixed at 10 percent for Riesling and Muscat, and 11 percent for Pinot Gris and Gewürztraminer. Yields were reduced to 70 hectoliters per hectare/4.1 tons per acre.

In 1983, twenty-five *Grands Crus* were recognized by the authorities. By 1992 a further twenty-five were awaiting final classification, and whether the total will increase beyond fifty *Grands Crus* remains to be seen.

The choice of *Grands Crus* was controversial from the start. Certain vineyards which did not merit *cru* status were included, others that did were omitted. Moreover, the exact boundaries of the *Grands Crus* have still to be definitively delineated. In 1991, a team of viticulturists from the Institut National de la Recherche Agronomique was involved in a major cartographic project to map out the *Grands Crus* boundaries.

Classifications of vineyards *per se* do not make great wines. One has only to taste a selection of *Grand Cru* wines from, say, Gevrey-Chambertin — ranging from the sublime to the mediocre — to illustrate the point. In Alsace, as in Burgundy, a better guide to quality is the name of the winemaker.

BELOW: The Clos St. Urbain of the Rangen *Grand Cru*, Alsace's most southerly vineyard, is based on volcanic soil.

Chardonnay is a ubiquitous white wine grape around the world and winemakers seem preoccupied with making it in small oak barrels. So we *Alsaciens* have a chance to re-emphasize our own inimitable expression of other great grape varieties — Riesling, Pinot Gris, Gewürztraminer — and our very different approach to white winemaking.

Maximum extraction of aromas, purity of fruit and clear, *vif* acidity — these are what set us apart. That means generally avoiding a malolactic fermentation during vinification, for the reduction in acidity can make our wines flaccid and lifeless. I also try to minimize oxidation and the use of sulfur dioxide, which are the errors besetting winemaking in our region. Oak barrels are not as indispensable an aid to quality as some Alsace estates would have you believe.

But it is really the diversity of soils in Alsace which holds the promise of the future for the *vigneron*. Take my own village of Rodern. The Gloeckelberg vineyard is essentially granitic. The soil heats up quickly. This makes the wine elegant and aromatic. Altenberg de Bergheim, by contrast, is based on marl and limestone with a stratum of sandstone. This soil yields wines of depth and structure with a touch of femininity given by the sandstone. Our soils are truly astounding and give us the opportunity to reclaim that cultural heritage that has been diminished by branded varietal wines.

Christian Koehly

CHARLES KOEHLY ET FILS

ABOVE: *Grand Cru* vineyards planted on terraces that follow the natural contours of the hillside.

Superb wines continue to be made by Alsace merchants under a simple *Cuvée Personnelle* label. And there are a few exceptional estates in Alsace — Domaines Weinbach and Schlumberger are good examples — which still prefer the *cuvée* designation rather than the name of the vineyard for their best wines.

But these are exceptions to the general trend. More and more Alsace growers are bottling wines from particular parcels of land separately to show the characteristics of each *terroir*. In a sense, Alsace has turned full circle, returning to an old practice, which dates from the Middle Ages, when wines were named after the commune or vineyard of origin. Mixed plantings of Riesling, Pinot Gris and Pinot Blanc were commonplace in the nineteenth century, when it was generally agreed that a blend of these grapes made the best wines. A champion of Alsace *vins de terroir* is Léonard Humbrecht of Domaine Zind-Humbrecht. He has planted Chardonnay at his Clos Windsbuhl at Hunawihr. Chardonnay is not, of course, a recognized noble grape variety in Alsace, but Humbrecht's intention is to blend the grapes of this variety with the Pinot Gris also grown in the Clos. The resulting wine is likely to be simply labeled Clos Windsbuhl without mention of the grapes used. It will not, of course, be entitled to A.O.C. status, but it could well rival a great white Burgundy.

Alsace Digestifs

Alsace is distinguished from other wine regions in France by the production of a full range of brandies made by fermenting and distilling the great quantities of soft fruits and berries grown locally. These, when unsweetened and colorless, are known collectively as *alcools blancs*. They are stored in glass vessels rather than in wooden casks to preserve their water-whiteness. Some, however, are sweetened and have the natural color of the fruit: they are then called, for example, Crème de Framboise.

Among the principal *eaux-de-vie* of Alsace are Framboise (raspberry); Fraise (strawberry); Kirsch (cherry); Myrtille (bilberry); Prunelle Sauvage (sloe); Poire William (William pear); Mirabelle (yellow plum); Quetsch (red plum).

All make first-rate *digestifs*, particularly after large Alsace meals, and are best served in chilled glasses, the cold helping to accentuate the powerful bouquet. *Eaux-de-vie* are made by many producers, among the most notable being Marcel Windholtz and Jos Meyer.

Most wine regions in France produce their own *marc*, a spirit distilled either from the lees or from the pips, skins and stalks left after pressing. Marc d'Alsace is colorless and is often distilled from Gewürztraminer and Muscat grapes. Jean-Pierre Dirler of Bergholtz provides a particularly good example of the latter.

THE RHÔNE

by Giles MacDonogh

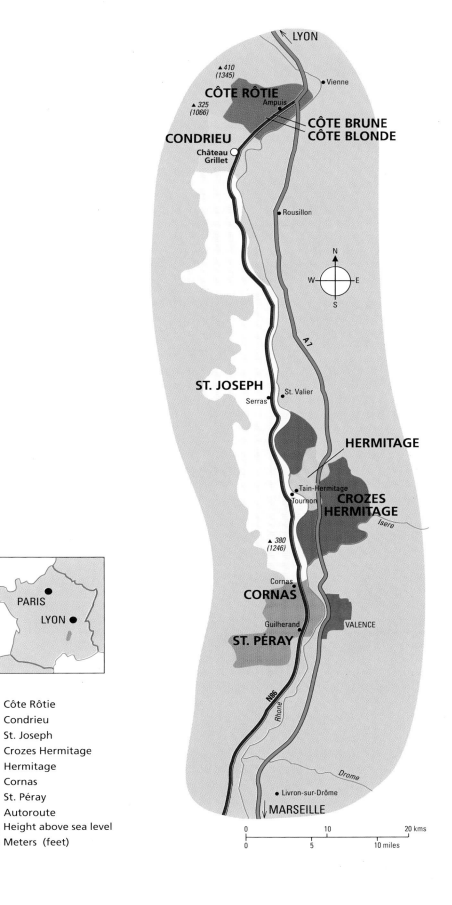

Côte Rôtie
Condrieu
St. Joseph
Crozes Hermitage
Hermitage
Cornas
St. Péray
Autoroute
▲380 Height above sea level
(1246) Meters (feet)

0   10   20 kms
0   5   10 miles

The charm of the Rhône Valley is its backwardness. Things are designed on a small scale here, and machines simply do not accord with the geological conditions. This is one of the last regions in the world where the wines are hand-made: and what more can you expect from a grower with two hectares/five acres, in eight different sites, making 2,000 bottles of wine a year? In Bordeaux the wines may be made by machines and designed by computers; not here.

It is for this reason that the great *crus* of the Rhône Valley have almost never been successfully copied. Stand at the base of the Côte Rôtie and it will become obvious: no one in his right mind would plant a slope like that. This is the clue to the wines of the region: anyone who chooses to plant on the best sites of the northern Rhône has to give up his life to them.

In the south conditions are different. Most of the wines are already more Provençal in style: aromatic and generous. Only one *cru* stands out, and that is Châteauneuf-du-Pape. Its quality came about almost by accident but now it is firmly established as the one wine from the unfashionable Grenache grape which commands world respect.

But it is logical, when looking at the Rhône, to start in the north. The swollen village of Ampuis lies only a few miles south of the Roman city of Vienne. Vienne itself is not so far from Lyon. For more than two millennia, proximity to these two conurbations has provided little Ampuis with a dual role: growing vegetables on the flat, alluvial lands beside the Rhône and producing the very best of the region's red wines on the "roasted slope" of Côte Rôtie.

In Ampuis the distinction between the "flatlanders" and the "hillsiders" has always been blurred: some families contain both while others plump for one or the other. Intermarriage complicates the issue still further. One thing, however, is certain: those growers who have elected not to soil their hands with potatoes and leeks have little time for their cousins on the riverbanks below.

For generations the divide between flatlanders and hillsiders produced no rancor and little jealousy; that is until competition from the South cut the price of vegetables, and the rediscovery of the Côte Rôtie in Paris, London and New York sent the prices of the wines up through the roof. Now the flatlanders are finding every excuse to come up the hill, while the hillsiders' scorn has taken on a bitter, resentful air.

But whatever the people do, the Syrah vine, with its small bunches of inky blue-black berries is in its element on this precipitous, granite slope. At least one grower likes to challenge the accepted wisdom that the Syrah was brought to the Rhône Valley from Persia or the Lebanon by the Phoenicians or the Greeks; Marcel Guigal (who incidentally owns rather more of the slope that anyone else) maintains that the Syrah is a chance mutation of a wild grape wholly indigenous to Côte Rôtie itself.

Of all the top *crus* of the northern Rhône, Côte Rôtie has always stood out for its elegance alongside the robust wines of Hermitage or Cornas. The best has the intense scent of violets, carnations and peonies associated with granite-grown Syrah, allied to an opulent redolence of peaches or apricots that is imparted by a judicious addition of Viognier grapes. The growers of Côte Rôtie have the right to add as much as twenty percent of the perfumed Viognier to their vats, though these days few of them exceed ten percent. Traditionally, the Viognier played a greater role in the tougher, longer-lasting wines of the iron-rich topsoils of the Côte Brune; the sandier Côte Blonde is thought not to need it. The Côte Rôtie is comprised of these two Côtes together, and Brunes are masculine, they say, Blondes are feminine; it may help as a rule of thumb, but there are exceptions: Pierre Barge, for example, makes a deliciously feminine Brune, using large wooden casks and a smidgen of Viognier; his son Gilles makes a dense, masculine, long-lasting Blonde, and adds no Viognier at all.

Most Côte Rôtie, however, is a blend of grapes from both soils, allowing these wines to express all that feminine delicacy in youth while giving the wine the backbone to age for twenty years and more. The whole question, though, of how wines from the northern Rhône age is a puzzle. It is obvious that they do age, but since some of the communes here only started to bottle their wines separately relatively recently (Cornas in 1969, for example), in many cases the old bottles from which one could judge aging capacity simply do not exist. So overall judgement must simply be reserved for a few more decades.

The "greats" to look out for in Côte Rôtie are Gilles Barge, Pierre Barge, Burgaud, Champet, Gentaz, Guigal, Jamet, Jasmin and Rostaing.

Just five kilometers/three miles to the south of Ampuis are the vines of Condrieu. Once again there is granite, while the subsoil is not unlike that of the Côte Brune, but with traces of mica. The easy distance between the two means that some of the growers' names are interchangeable: Barge, Vernet and Delas all own vines, while Marcel Guigal buys in grapes to make a very fine Condrieu.

Here in Condrieu, all the wine is white; and, with

ABOVE: Viognier vines in Condrieu. Until recently Viognier was unknown outside this small site in the northern Rhône.

the exception of a few clumps of Chasselas, all the grapes are the aromatic Viognier. And it is here that Viognier reaches its apogee. Many a grower in the Midi regards Viognier as the great white hope of southern whites, but all too often, Viognier grown away from Condrieu lacks the aromas and the texture that it shows here. It may be a question of soil; it could also have something to do with the age of the vines here: until the recent fashion for Viognier started, most were over fifty years old.

The superb peach and apricot bouquet of Condrieu develops at around eighteen months, and there is little sense in hanging on to bottles over four years old. In the past some semi-sweet Condrieu was made. Most people who knew these semi-sweet Viogniers heave a sigh of relief to hear that they are no longer to be found on the market.

LEFT: Guigal's basic wine is the Brune et Blonde. Delas makes a reliable and modestly priced Côte Rôtie Seigneur de Maugiron. Guigal's La Landonne is one of the region's top wines, a Côte Brune with great power to age gracefully.

RIGHT: Alain Paret makes a dense, long-lasting Saint Joseph with old fashioned "breed". Alain Graillot is the best grower in Crozes Hermitages and his La Guerande is a sensational new release. Georges Vernay is the uncrowned king of Condrieu.

Within the 100 hectare/247 acre area of Condrieu (only a little over 30 hectares/74 acres is in fact planted with vines) is one of France's smallest A.O.C.s, Château-Grillet. The 2.5 hectare/6 acre property is planted entirely with Viognier and gives its wines slightly more barrel aging which makes them slower to mature. Château-Grillet could be thought of as a superior Condrieu. However, recent examples have been exceptional but mostly for their high price.

The best growers of Condrieu include Cuilleron, Dézormeaux, Dumazet, Multier (Château de Rozay), Niero et Pinchon, Perret, Vernay and Delas.

The history of the Saint Joseph A.O.C. has been a sorry tale of compromise and pusillanimity. The wines of the communes of Tournon and Mauves on the western side of the Rhône opposite the hill of Hermitage had for centuries enjoyed a well-merited reputation for quality. In 1956 it was decided to create an A.O.C. which would encompass six communes around the town of Tournon, thereby recognizing the quality of the wines made there. But it was already too late: standards had fallen, in most cases the vines had already quit the steep hillsides for the alluvial roadside plains and very little good wine was being made at all.

Then came the decision in 1979 to extend the A.O.C. to twenty-three communes to the north, taking in more poor land and some growers who did not deserve the higher appellation (as well as a few who did). The result was that Saint Joseph became a band 70 kilometers/44 miles long producing red wines from Syrah and some white wines (chiefly Marsanne with a little Roussanne) of immensely variable quality, for the simple reason that most of the grapes were grown in the wrong places.

Not all stories of this sort have happy endings, but this one does. A small group of dedicated growers led by the cousins Gripa or Grippat (the family spells its name in different ways) has worked to ensure that a large part of the vines are returning to the slopes. So far the focus has been on the *lieu-dit* of Saint Joseph itself, which lies on the borders of Tournon and Mauves; most recently Jean-Louis Grippat has done astonishing work in clearing the hillsides above the town of Tournon, presenting Hermitage across the river with a vine-façade of equal majesty. Work finished on Jean-Louis' new vineyard only in 1991, so keep an eye out for the wines in the future.

To the south of Mauves in the commune of Châteaubourg, the Courbis family is doing similar good work on its slopes.

The best growers of Saint Joseph include Chapoutier, Chave, Courbis, Coursodon, Gripa, Grippat and Florentin (Clos de L'Arbalestrier).

The mistakes committed in Saint Joseph were no more than a larger-scale repeat of the errors made in extending the A.O.C. in Crozes-Hermitage. The Crozes-Hermitage A.O.C. was created in 1937 to cover the vines to the north of the great hill of Hermitage. Here, with modest yields, the Syrah grape for the reds and Marsanne and Roussane for the whites could produce wines of breed and concentration. Then came the compromise: in 1952 the A.O.C. was extended to cover not only the better hill villages to the north and east like Gervans and Erôme, but also the flat land to the south of Tain. Now the plains account for the majority of Crozes and with the exception of those growers listed below the watchword is *caveat emptor*.

Growers to look for are Chapoutier, Bernard Chave, Desmeure, Fayolle, Ferraton, Graillot, Jaboulet (particularly his Domaine de Thalabert), Pochon (particularly his Château de Curson) and Tardy et Ange.

Still moving south, Cornas has a curious atmosphere, more like Burgundy than the Rhône Valley; it reminds many visitors of Gabriel Chevallier's novel *Clochemerle*. Nobody appears to like anybody else; curtains twitch at the approach of a stranger; visitors are interrogated for hours in order to find out where the next-door-neighbor is selling his wine. Everything in Cornas is done on a small scale. Cellars are minute and cramped and the barrels are often old and crumbly, but for all that there is a handful of instances where the wines are simply out of this world.

Cornas is very fashionable now. Since the dark days following the last war the vineyard has grown dramatically, and vines are everywhere: in the back gardens of the village houses; smack next door to the cemetery; or on the flat land where no good wine will come of them. Quality is to be found above all on the steep slopes where careful growers restrict the yields of their ancient vines and have the

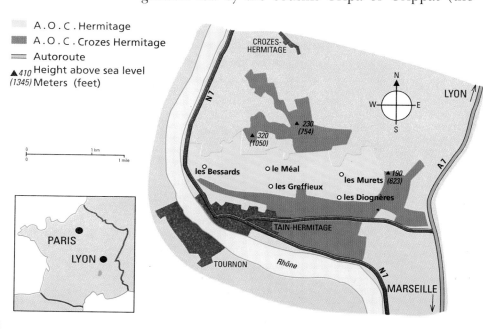

A.O.C. Hermitage
A.O.C. Crozes Hermitage
Autoroute
▲410 Height above sea level
(1345) Meters (feet)

courage to keep the wine from the lower vineyards out of the main blend.

Cornas has recently been shaken up by the arrival of a Bordeaux-trained enologist called Jean-Luc Colombo and now the village speaks of little else. Colombo has not stuck to advice and analysis; he has acquired some vines and begun to demonstrate his theories by making his own wine. He calls for regular replacement of barrels and the use of new or secondhand Burgundian *barriques;* he advocates extracting the maximum from the grapes by means of *pigeage* (or the breaking up of the cap to keep the skins in contact with the juice); he also believes in the old Bordeaux system of hiking up the prices of his wine until it is so high that everyone believes it must be great simply because they can no longer afford to drink it. So far only Jean Lionnet has become an unreserved "Colombien", but others teeter on the brink.

With the exception of a few more supple styles (notably that of Guy de Barjac), Cornas is the biggest and most unreservedly masculine wine of

the northern Rhône. Made from one hundred percent Syrah untempered by any white grapes, the wines are dark and brooding. After they shed their early charm they can take eight to ten years to reveal not only that distinctive violet, Syrah character, but also something more earthy, gamy and animal; as such they provide an excellent counterpoint to well-hung game and the most powerful and pungent of cheeses.

Among the best growers in Cornas are Clape, de Barjac, Juge, Lemenicier, Jean Lionnet, Michel, Noël Verset, Voge and Courbis.

The reputation of the great red wines of Hermitage dates back to the time of Louis XIV, if not further. Their fame was no doubt aided by the fact that the commune lies directly on the route to Rome taken by so many grand tourists from the seventeenth century onwards. Everyone who was anyone had to have a view as to the wine's quality and aging potential. The Scottish writer Tobias Smollett, on his way to Italy, for example, thought it overrated; on his return he changed his mind.

ABOVE: The chapel above Hermitage which gives its name to the top Jaboulet wine, la Chapelle. In the distance are the newly replanted vineyards of Tournon across the Rhône.

ABOVE: The soil at Hermitage varies enormously; Jaboulet, Delas and Chave can all boast vineyard holdings in different parts of the appellation that balance tannin against fruit, denseness against aroma. Robert Michel is one of the stars of Cornas, where quality can be variable.

In the nineteenth century, however, decline set in. Hermitage began to play a rather shameful role in Bordeaux as a *vin médecin* to beef up claret in off-vintages. After phylloxera the growers were slow to replant; even in the 1930s the hill was still largely bare of vines. If Hermitage has returned to form in our own day it is probably due to the trouble taken by the older generation of the Jaboulet family to ensure that the wine once again graced the tables of wine connoisseurs the world over.

From far away the great hill seems all of a piece; but geologically speaking this is anything but true. The rock itself is granite; but the topsoils vary considerably, making blending indispensable for anyone wanting to make great wine.

Basically the hill divides into three mounds represented by the main vineyards of Les Bessards (to the east), where the soil is composed of fractured granite; Greffieux and Méal, in the center, with Méal at the top, where the soil varies between sand and clay; and finally Murets and Dionnières where the soil is chalky. The clay soils of Les Greffieux are largely used for the white wine made from Marsanne and Roussanne grapes, which represents about a quarter of the Hermitage crop.

The ideal solution has always been to own a chunk of each soil type; only then may the balance be achieved between the dense, bitter and tannic wines obtained from some and the fragrant, aromatic wines derived from others.

It is for this reason that the leading merchants and the local cooperative enter the battle with one hand tied behind their backs. The *négociant* houses of Chapoutier, Delas and Jaboulet can all rely on their extensive holdings on the hillside to produce archetypical Hermitage. Of the growers themselves only Gérard Chave has that advantage.

That does not mean that the merchant houses are above reproach. Both Chapoutier and Delas have been through bad patches; in Chapoutier's case the problems seem to have been largely cleared up since Michel Chapoutier took over the wine making. Delas went through a very bad patch in the 1970s

RIGHT: Vines on the terraced slopes of Hermitage produce some of the world's most long-lasting wines and have been famous to travelers since the seventeenth century.

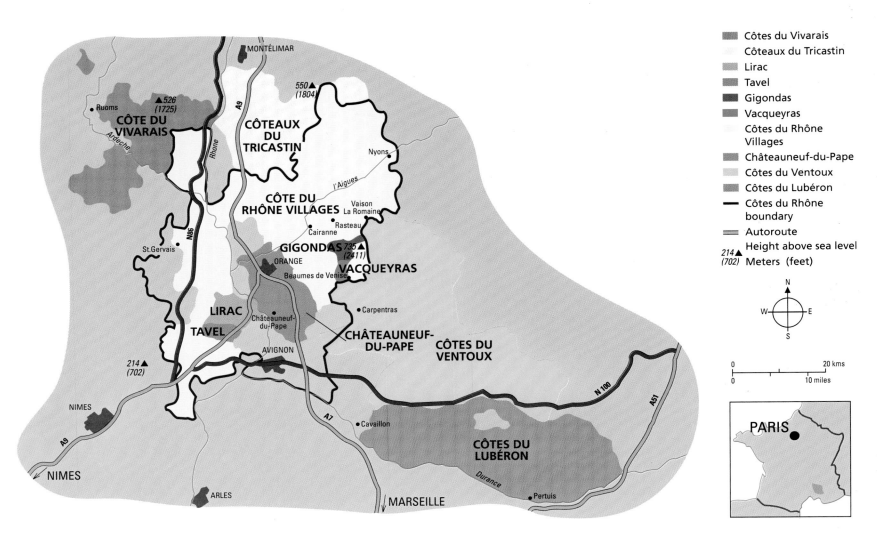

Côtes du Vivarais
Côteaux du Tricastin
Lirac
Tavel
Gigondas
Vacqueyras
Côtes du Rhône Villages
Châteauneuf-du-Pape
Côtes du Ventoux
Côtes du Lubéron
Côtes du Rhône boundary
Autoroute
214▲ Height above sea level
(702) Meters (feet)

but now makes highly attractive Hermitages; more recently Jaboulet's La Chapelle has come under attack for its inconsistent bottling.

Of the minor league, Desmeure makes a wine reminiscent of Delas, up-front and appealing and perhaps rather more typical of the grape than of the commune; both Faurie and Fayolle make old-fashioned wines in small quantities, Faurie being the more reliable; Jean-Louis Grippat makes minute amounts of very stylish wine; Sorrel makes huge, tough, tannic wines which are clearly built to last for decades and Thierry Allemande should also be sought out.

Saint Péray used to be a town of *négociants* second only to Tain, but no longer. The name of Saint Péray is now better known for white wines made primarily from the Marsanne grape (the more sickly Roussanne is seen less and less). Some of this is rendered sparkling by the Champagne method. At its best Saint Péray can be a nice, white fruit-and-almond-scented wine with sufficient body to deal with quite highly-spiced river fish dishes. The sparkling wine is consumed locally as an aperitif.

Twenty kilometers/twelve miles south of Valence on the eastern side of the Rhône is the last outpost of 100 percent Syrah wines in the valley. The wines from the Colline de Brézème on the Drôme are not perhaps among the Rhône's finest, but they have curiosity value.

Among the best producers of Saint Péray are Bernard Gripa, Jean Lionnet and Voge. The best in Brézème is Jean-Marie Lombard.

Châteauneuf-du-Pape is greatly misunderstood; few if any wines generate so much confusion. To a very great extent this has been caused by the continuing presence on the market of Châteauneuf wines, bottled by *négociants* outside the commune, which bear no stylistic resemblance whatsoever to Châteauneuf-du-Pape. Further problems have been

caused by a certain amount of fecklessness within the appellation itself where growers embarrassed by the nature of the wine have tried to alter its character by resorting to carbonic maceration in the hope of achieving a lighter, less alcoholic style. They were encouraged in their efforts by French women's magazines which constantly urge their readers not to drink wines over 11 percent alcohol by volume, when the Châteauneuf A.O.C. actually stipulates a minimum of 12.5 percent.

More confusion is created by the famous thirteen grape varieties which formed part of the original A.O.C. decree. These thirteen were, even then, a museum collection; many varieties had to be obtained from elsewhere in the Midi. The original idea of using those varieties came from a Commandant Ducos who soon after phylloxera decided to recreate the vineyard at the Château La Nerthe. His idea for blending Châteauneuf was eccentric, to say

BELOW: Châteauneuf-du-Pape. The quality of the wine here is often attributed to the smooth pebbles or *galets* which absorb heat by day, feeding it back to the vines at night.

113

ABOVE: Beaucastel makes atypical wines with a strong pungency which develops with age. Fortia is the former home of the Baron Le Roy, where his son now makes one of the most traditional wines in the region. The estate of Vieux Télégraphe has made wines of consistently high quality for a decade and more. The large Mont-Redon estate controls the lion's share of the great, sunscorched plateau of Mont-Redon which lends its character to the wine.

the least. Had the Bordelais shown the same enthusiasm for creating a living museum of their ancient vines after phylloxera, Château Latour would perhaps still be made from the dozen or so largely obscure grapes from which it was blended in the 1840s.

Châteauneuf is essentially Grenache; Grenache with enough Syrah and/or Mourvèdre to allay a few of its shortcomings. A typical blend would be Brunier's Vieux Télégraphe, with 70 percent Grenache Noir, and 15 percent of both Syrah and Mourvèdre; or Paul Avril's Clos des Papes with the same quantity of Grenache but with 20 percent Mourvèdre and only 10 percent Syrah. As for the other varieties, when they are used at all it is only in minuscule amounts. The most popular is the Cinsaut, which gives a pleasant raspberry-fruitiness to the wine, but not much else. Recently the Counoise grape has enjoyed a renewed popularity on the basis of its peppery character.

Growers are rather less certain just what, if anything, is to be gained by the admixture of Muscardin, Terret Noir, Picpoul Noir or Vaccarèse. The

remaining five cultivars are white and as such were generally reserved for the rare white wines of Châteauneuf: Roussanne, Clairette, Picpoul Blanc, Bourboulenc and Picardan. Most people also seem to get away with using Grenache Blanc, too.

Another myth surrounding Châteauneuf is its stony soil. The stones are vital to the style of Châteauneuf, say the textbooks; they absorb the heat during the day and reflect it back on to the grapes at night. In fact, quite a lot of the appellation is made up of clay soils which result in lighter wines. It is the high plateau of Mont-Redon that boasts those shining, heat-retaining stones. The high plateau was not in fact cleared of its cherry trees and olives until earlier this century, and the use of the land for grapes added another dimension to the wines of Châteauneuf: as they will tell you locally, the herby, tobacco-scented character of the wines is a result of this sun-baked sector to the north.

Like a great many other regions of France (notably Cornas to the north) Châteauneuf is currently being shaken up by an enologist bent on re-shaping the wines of the district. In Châteauneuf this is Noël Rabot, who is keen to introduce small oak barrels (preferably new ones), vats with automatic *pigeage* and uniform bottlings. This last is an essential reform in Châteauneuf where too many estates bottle only when the orders come in, meaning that the wine from the same vintage may have been taken from cask any time over a period of eighteen months. Rabot works with the following estates: Monredon, La Nerthe, La Gardine, Les Fines Roches, Vieux Lazaret and Beaurenard.

By no means everyone in Châteauneuf feels that they have need of this sort of reforming hand; many estates have elaborated highly individual styles of winemaking over the years which have a wide following. One which uses an uncharacteristically modest amount of Grenache is Château de Beaucastel, where the father of the present owners devised a process of flash-heating the skins of the grapes before pressing, making wines of immense weight and flavor. Châteauneuf also has a high proportion of eccentrics, ranging from Baron Le Roy, who likes to present tasters with broken glasses, to the highly-acclaimed Henri Bonnot, who makes the wine from his six hectares/fifteen acres in his kitchen sink. The most eccentric of them all is Jacques Reynaud of Château Rayas. Reynaud uses as much as 100 percent Grenache and somehow manages to produce great wine in conditions that would make hygiene-minded New World producers throw up their hands in horror.

The best wines of Châteauneuf can be among the most warming and invigorating of them all; great Châteauneuf should combine a bouquet of licorice, dried herbs, cigarettes, spices and leather with a palate of raspberries, figs, cherries, plums and dark chocolate. The whites used to suffer from being rather flabby and oxidized but are now made with rather more care; generally from Clairette and Grenache Blanc with a little Bourboulenc. They can have a good deal of charm with plenty of apricot fruit. One exceptional white Châteauneuf is the Perrins' Vieilles Vignes from Château de Beaucastel, made from 100 percent old Roussanne vines.

The best of Châteauneuf-du-Pape includes Château de Beaucastel, Henri Bonnot, Bosquet des Papes, Clos des Papes, Fabrice, Font de Michelle,

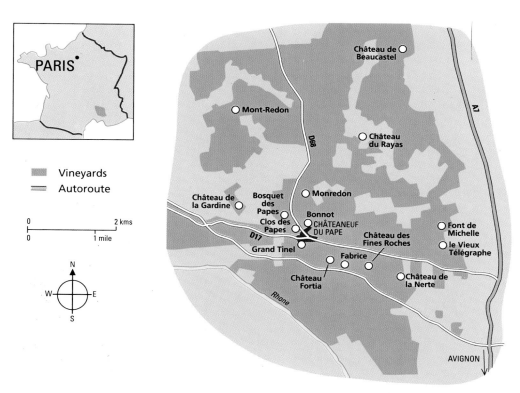

Château Fortia, Grand Tinel, Mont-Redon, Château Rayas and Vieux Télégraphe.

The warm-hearted Grenache Noir also lends its character to most of the wines of the southern Rhône, from the handful of individual A.O.C.s to the Côtes du Rhônes Villages (of which there are now sixteen) and the simple wines of the Côtes du Rhône.

The best wines come from regions ike Gigondas ("le Châteauneuf des pauvres"), Vacqueyras and Lirac, as well as from certain of the villages which have achieved a reputation over the years and will probably follow Gigondas and Vacqueyras up to A.O.C. status before too long.

Many of the villages have some charm or specialty to offer. Rasteau has its Grenache-based *vin doux naturel;* Beaumes de Venise has its popular Muscat. Côtes du Ventoux used to be a favorite *bistrot* wine in Paris where its seeming lightness masked its ever-present alcoholic strength. Over the past decade the neighboring Coteaux du Tricastin has made considerable progress in making deep-colored wines with the help of a large addition of Syrah. White wines can be found in the village of Laudun, particularly from Domaine Pelaquié. France's most famous rosés come from Tavel and Lirac, and are made from Grenache and Cinsaut but with more and more Mourvèdre. A good Tavel, indeed, is just what you need to complement a summer lunch in the southern Rhône.

The best growers of Gigondas include Raspail-Ay, Les Pallières, Saint-Gayan. In Vacqueyras look for Combe (Fourmone), Pascal, Richard (Couroulou); in Tricastin, Bour (Grangeneuve); in Ventoux, Swan (Ange); in Lirac, Assémat (Garrigues), Sabon; in Tavel, Château d'Aquéria; in Rasteau, La Soumade; in Séguret, Château La Courançonne; in Cairanne, Rabasse-Charavin; in Côtes de Rhône, Châteaux de Fonsalette, du Grand Moulas, de Saint Estève and Coudoulet de Beaucastel.

ABOVE: Vidal Fleury is a Gigondas that is bottled by a top Ampuis *négociant.* Lirac is famous for its rosés and reds made with a high proportion of tannic Mourvèdre. The wines of the Côtes du Ventoux have improved in the last decade and are no longer the stuff of cheap Parisian bars.

GROWER'S VIEW

The first thing you have to consider is geology. In the Rhône Valley you will find the most varied of all terrains: primary rock (granite and schist); Alpine rocks (limestones and chalk) and clay. Côte Rôtie was the limit of the glaciers. Here we sit on "multiple geology". Personally, I'm very attached to the notion of *terroir.* When your yields are low it is geology which expresses itself through the wine; when they are high the variety speaks. Herein lies the attraction of varietal wines: in California they'll tell you that *terroir* counts for naught and that the only thing that matters is climate: that is because they have yields of eighty-five hectoliters per hectare/five tons per acre, so it is quite normal that they think *terroir* is unimportant. The Rhône (and this includes even generic Côtes du Rhône) has the lowest yields in France. I also hate this idea of "second wines", it drives me crazy with rage.

They really are careful about yields in the southern Rhône, and now that they have mastered cooler temperature fermentation these are good wines. Just look at the differences between Gigondas, Rasteau or Châteauneuf; they are all made from the same grapes! It is not like that in Burgundy. There it is the producers who create the taste of the wine; here the grower comes second to the soil. Châteauneuf is the subtlest wine in the Rhône Valley simply because its yields cannot rise above 35 to 40 hectoliters per hectare/2 to 2.3 tons per acre. Cabernet and Chardonnay do not suffer at these levels but Grenache does. Over 25 hectoliters per hectare/1.5 tons per acre it needs a pair of crutches in the form of Syrah and Mourvèdre. Jacques Reynaud knows this, that is why he can make pure Grenache Châteauneuf: his yields are only 15 hectoliters per hectare/.9 tons per acre.

There are two sorts of Rhône whites: the easy-drinking wines from the south and the long lasting whites from the north. I take umbrage at the marketing concept of skin contact. It is artificial. The wines simply fall apart within a year. With malolactic fermentation our whites keep for forty years. We are not frightened of their suppleness. Professor Ribéreau-Gayon castigates low acidity because he comes from Bordeaux and knows grapes like the Sauvignon Blanc. We need the *malo* here, if we do not do it the wines need too much sulfur dioxide. People complain of headaches.

The Roussanne? That has virtually disappeared because it was too sickly. As for Viognier, that needs to be drunk young. If you will excuse the expression, Viognier is a bit of a whore as far as aromas are concerned; to master it you need to keep yields right down. It also needs granite or schists; those estates in the south simply do not have the soil. They should be planting Muscat.

Michel Chapoutier
CHAPOUTIER

SOUTHWEST FRANCE

by Rosemary George, M.W.

Côtes de Duras
Bergerac
Cahors
Entraygues et du Fel
Estaing
Marcillac
Côtes du Marmandais
Côtes de Buzet
Côtes du Bruhlois
Lavilledieu
Madiran
Jurançon
Côtes du Frontonnais
Gaillac
Limoux
Tursan
Côtes de St. Mont
Côtes de Béarn
Irouléguy
Armagnac
① Bas Armagnac
② Tenarèze
③ Haut Armagnac
Autoroute
▲655 Height above sea level
(2181) Meters (feet)

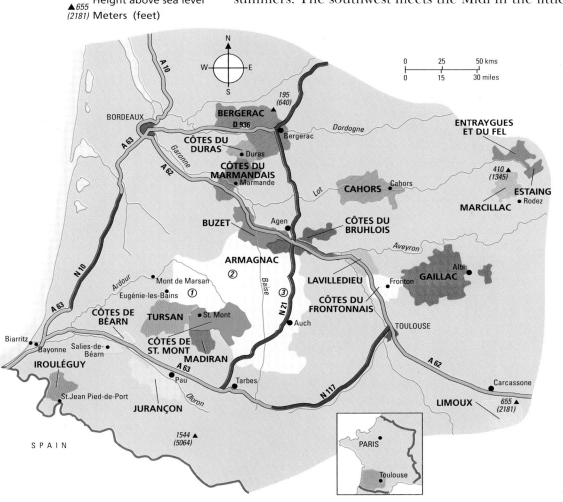

Bordeaux is the inevitable starting point for the wines of southwest France. Claret provides the model for the reds, with Cabernet Sauvignon, Cabernet Franc and Merlot the base for many of them. As recently as the beginning of this century, many of these wines were blended with those of the Gironde to be sold as claret, and in the Middle Ages they shared a history of commercial strife and rivalry. There is a similar parallel in the white wines, with Sauvignon and Sémillon accounting for many of the appellations of the southwest. However in both instances, the further you travel from Bordeaux, the more different the grape varieties become, with more deviations from the Bordeaux recipe.

All of southwest France enjoys a maritime climate, benefiting from the tempering influence of the Atlantic Ocean. Further inland and towards the Mediterranean the effect lessens and temperatures become more extreme, with hotter and drier summers. The southwest meets the Midi in the little known areas of Côtes de la Malepère and Cabardès, situated to the south and north of the walled city of Carcassonne, where a variety of microclimates make it possible to grow both Cabernet Sauvignon and Grenache.

The appellations closest to Bordeaux, namely Bergerac and Côtes de Duras, are only separated from it by the departmental boundary. The attractive country town of Bergerac gives its name to a wine that borders the vineyards of St. Emilion, with which Bergerac Rouge has some affinity in taste. Whites are usually dry, sometimes pure Sauvignon, while Côtes de Montravel and Saussignac are slightly sweet. Pécharmant provides an enclave of more solid, long-lasting red wine, while Monbazillac can in the best vintages produce lusciously sweet wines from nobly rotten grapes. Good producers include Château la Jaubertie, Château Court-les-Mûts, Château Belingard and Château Tiregand in Pécharmant. The leading producer of Monbazillac is M. Vidal at Château Treuil de Nailhac.

There is little to distinguish Côtes de Duras, from vineyards around the town of Duras, with its imposing château, from simple red and white Bordeaux. Like Bergerac, Côtes de Duras is gradually establishing its own identity, as is Buzet, further down the Garonne. Here too the grape varieties and methods are the same as Bordeaux, while the V.D.Q.S. of the Côtes du Marmandais, which lies between them, around the town of Marmande, allows for a local and otherwise unknown grape called Abouriou which can give the red wines a distinctive regional flavor. Production in the Côtes du Marmandais and Buzet is dominated by cooperatives, and while the Côtes de Duras has two large cooperatives, there are individual producers too, such as Domaine Durand, Domaine Ferrant, Château de Conti and Domaine la Grave-Béchade.

To the east along the Lot valley is the appellation of Cahors, for red wine alone. The emphasis changes here, for Auxerrois, otherwise known as Malbec in Bordeaux or Cot in the Loire Valley, is the principal grape variety. There is Merlot too, and Tannat, but unusually no Cabernet Sauvignon. Cahors was once famed for its "black wine", from which a legend has developed of a wine that is sturdy, tannic and long-lasting. Today, although Cahors has become softer and more accessible, it remains one of the finer wines of the southwest. There has been considerable investment and reno-

ABOVE: The imposing sixteenth century Château de Monbazillac dominates the vineyards of the appellation of Monbazillac.

vation in both cellar and vineyard, the results of which can be tasted in the glass. There are numerous good estates, such as Château Haute-Serre, Château St. Didier, Prieuré de Cenac, Clos Gamot, Château de Cayrou, Château de Chambert, Domaine Eugénie, Domaine des Savarines, Clos Triguedina and Domaine de Gaudou as well as a successful cooperative called Les Caves d'Olt, which markets the wines of several members' châteaux.

Further east still, in Gaillac, in vineyards close to the Toulouse-Lautrec town of Albi, there is a wealth of different grape varieties. Red wine may include the Bordelais varieties of Cabernet Sauvignon, Cabernet Franc and Merlot as well as a local grape, Duras, others from the southwest such as Négrette and Fer Servadou, and even Syrah from the Rhône Valley. Gamay is grown too, but only for a *vin nouveau.* As for white Gaillac, there is Sémillon and Sauvignon as well as the local grapes Loin de l'Oeil and Mauzac. Consequently the appellation of Gaillac covers a wide spectrum of taste; the white can be dry, sweet, *moelleux,* sparkling or *perlé,* which describes a wine in which a little carbon dioxide from the malolactic fermentation has been retained, with bubbles looking like tiny pearls. Red Gaillac is usually based on Duras, to which is added either the Bordeaux grapes, or Fer Servadou and Syrah. Even so there is an enormous variation in flavor amongst red Gaillacs. Leading estates in Gaillac include Domaine Jean Cros, Château Larroze, Domaine des Trois Cantous, Domaine de Labarthe, Mas Pignon and Château de Lastours.

Nearby Fronton or Côtes du Frontonnais, situated on a plateau northwest of the city of Toulouse,

depends upon Négrette for its individuality. Several other varieties are allowed in the appellation, of which Cabernet Franc and Sauvignon and Fer Servadou are the most usual. Négrette must account for a minimum of half the blend, thus maintaining the typicity of flavor. Château Bellevue-la-Forêt is the best known estate. The nearby V.D.Q.S. of Lavilledieu and Côtes du Brulhois borrow grapes from both Bordeaux and the Pyrenees and for the moment are rarely seen outside their own locality.

Further east still in the upper reaches of the Lot Valley are the red appellation of Marcillac and the two tiny V.D.Q.S. of Estaing and Entraygues et du Fel, where an extraordinary mixture of grape varieties has been retained. Some of these are local, some are from Bordeaux and some are from eastern France. However it is Fer Servadou, locally known as Mansois, that gives the red wines, Marcillac above all, their character.

Further south towards the Pyrenees, the grape varieties change again. In Madiran, which is one of the rising red stars of southwest France, Tannat is the main variety. As the name implies, it is a sturdy, tough-skinned grape, making a solid mouthful of wine, which needs to be toned down with other varieties, namely Cabernet Franc, Cabernet Sauvignon and a drop of Fer Servadou, and aged in wood for several months. Look for Château Arricau-Bordes, Château d'Aydie, Château Montus, Château Bouscassé and Domaine Teston, amongst others. The adjoining white wine is a mouthful of a name, Pacherenc du Vic-Bilh, coming entirely from obscure Pyrenean varieties, namely Gros Manseng, Petit Manseng, Courbu, as well as Arrufiat, a local

variety which accounts for some of the character of Pacherenc.

However, the most noteworthy white wine of the Pyrénées is undoubtedly Jurançon, from vineyards in the foothills of the mountains, south of the town of Pau. Jurançon can be both dry and sweet. The sweet wine is made from grapes that are picked in late autumn, after being left on the vines to dehydrate in the wind in a process called *passerillage*. The grape varieties of Jurançon are Gros Manseng, Petit Manseng and Courbu, but it is Petit Manseng above all that provides the quality of these delightfully honeyed wines, as in the wines of Domaine Cauhapé. Also try Clos Uroulat and Château Jolys. Dry Jurançon has an attractive pithy, fruity flavor and is occasionally aged in oak.

Further north on the edge of the pine forests of the Landes is the little known V.D.Q.S. of Tursan, where Baroque makes the white wine. It is somewhat deficient in aroma, but improvements in vinification methods are helping to make the wine fresher and fruitier. Red Tursan is a rather rustic blend of Tannat and Cabernets, both Franc and Sauvignon. The local cooperative is responsible for most of the production.

The tiny, recently promoted V.D.Q.S. of the Côtes de Saint Mont benefits from the energetic experimental work of one of France's leading cooperatives, the Union de Plaimont, which incorporates the smaller village cooperative of St. Mont. Improvements in vinification methods and work on the local grape varieties are helping to put all three colors of Côtes de St. Mont firmly on the wine map of the Pyrénées.

Irouléguy is one of those unexpected islands of vineyards with which France abounds. The village nestles in the heart of the Pyrénées, close to the Spanish border, and produces red and pink wine from Tannat, Cabernet Sauvignon and Cabernet Franc. The nearby appellation of Béarn is rather broader, acting as a second wine for both Jurançon and Madiran, with more vineyards around the town of Salies-de-Béarn. A little white is made from the usual Pyrénéan grape varieties, namely Manseng, Courbu and Raffiat de Moncade, while red from Cabernet and Tannat is most successful. Rosé de Béarn has declined in popularity.

BELOW: Labels from two leading producers, both pacesetters in their appellations. *Vendanges tardives* refers to the practice of leaving the grapes to dry on the vines, in order to make Jurançon *moelleux*.

GROWER'S VIEW

Of all the wine appellations from the southwest of France, it is Monbazillac that particularly attracts me at the moment, because it is undergoing a wine revolution.

The appellation covers 1,400 hectares/3,458 acres, and five communes: Monbazillac, Pomport, Rouffignac-Colombier and St. Laurent. Until the late 1950s, the region's leading estate, the Château de Monbazillac, was considered to be on a par with Château d'Yquem and Château Rayne-Vigneau in Sauternes, and other châteaux had the right to be called "Grand Cru".

Their downfall came in the 1960s and 1970s. Substantial yield increases, less selective fruit picking and the introduction of mechanical harvesters all led to a wine not even worthy of being called the poor man's Sauternes.

Now, despite all the modern technology available, the best way to success for the producers seems to be to follow their grandfathers' traditional methods. The Syndicat Interprofessionnel de Monbazillac, the region's governing body for wine, has made some brave decisions. Each property now is limited to only the best areas for making Monbazillac, and pruning has been modified to reduce yields. Selective hand picking is now obligatory, and must be proved. The minimum sugar level of the grapes at the time of the harvest has been increased, and oak barrels have started to reappear in the wineries.

Sadly, the immediate reaction from the majority of the locals was negative. But it is only these restrictive measures that can save the honor of Monbazillac — and I believe the future looks bright.

Hugh Ryman

H.D.R. Wines

RIGHT: The label of Clos la Coutale depicts the medieval, fortified bridge of Valentré which crosses the river Lot at Cahors. Château de Haute-Serre was bought by Georges Vigouroux, a leading Cahors *négociant* in 1970. The vineyards have been replanted and the cellars renovated. Sigoulès is one of the better village cooperatives of Bergerac.

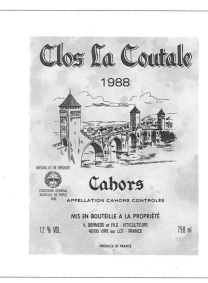

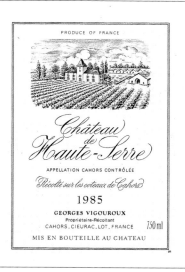

ARMAGNAC

by Michael Edwards

Armagnac claims to be France's oldest brandy. As early as the twelfth century, the peasants of this region came into contact with the Moors of Spain and Portugal, who probably taught them the art of distillation. A document in the archives of the Haute Garonne records that in 1411 Antoine of Toulouse distilled wine into *aygue ardente* or *eau-de-vie.*

Armagnac, a rustic backwater 160 kilometers/100 miles southeast of Bordeaux, differs from its main rival Cognac. The soils are more varied. The Ténarèze, a mix of clay and chalk produces fine floral brandies; in the Bas-Armagnac, generally reckoned to be the best district, the soil is sandier, yielding sweeter, fuller Armagnacs with a concentrated fruit. The smaller Haut Armagnac production district near Auch produces coarser, less fine Armagnac.

Folle Blanche, also known as Picpoul, with its unmistakable violet aroma, used to be the great grape of Armagnac. Sadly this variety is fast disappearing from the vineyards as it is particularly susceptible to gray rot.

The quality and character of great Armagnac is determined partly by the use of the traditional continuous still — *a jet continu* — which is banned in Cognac. Ironically, it is its very inefficiency as a distillation tool, only extracting 50 to 52 percent alcohol, that allows the continuous still to shape the distinctive character of Armagnac. Because the spirit is less refined, more of the grape's character survives the distillation process resulting in greater richness and more congeners, (residual chemical components that add flavor), in the finished brandy. The Cognaçais pot still is becoming more widely used.

Great Armagnac may taste both richer and closer to nature than Cognac, but no other spirit needs such careful handling or longer maturation. Armagnac is traditionally aged in barrels made from the local black oak from the Monlezun Forest, which gives a rounded aroma and flavor to the brandy. In recent years, Limousin and Tronçais oaks have been used for cask maturation. Better Armagnacs spend nine months in new wood, then as much as twenty years in older casks so that they may gently mature.

As in Cognac, distilled water is generally used to reduce the alcoholic strength of Armagnac to a salable strength of 40 percent to 43 percent by volume. Most of the label designations follow the same rules as those for Cognac — V.S.O.P., Napoléon, Extra and so on — but broadly speaking the average age of the *eaux-de-vie* used in Armagnac blends is much older than in Cognac.

Armagnacs may carry a vintage label, but vintage Armagnacs must be at least ten years old when they are released.

GROWER'S VIEW

Armagnac is a highly individual brandy, and that individual character is determined by the different soil of each district. Take the Bas-Armagnac. Here the yellowish sandy soil is relatively poor and acid, and so it's particularly suitable for the cultivation of wine grapes for *eaux-de-vie* which are fruity, light and delicate.

The characteristics of the soil and of our climate, which is much influenced by the Atlantic Ocean, combine to produce white wine of high acidity and low alcohol, ideal for the making of quality *eaux-de-vie*. Armagnac is distilled from white wines, are vinified traditionally, with a minimum of treatment, and kept on their lees, isolated from the atmosphere. It is vital that distillation takes place as soon as possible after fermentation to avoid any deterioration of the wine, and to maximise the release of aromatic substances during the heating process.

As it leaves the still, the spirit is put immediately into 400 liter/105.6 U.S. gallon oak casks. This wood aging is essential to the development and enrichment of the *eaux-de-vie* which come about as a result of the complex chemical reactions through which the tannin and the aromatic elements of the oak are dissolved in the alcohol.

Philippe Layus-Coustet

ARMAGNAC LAFONTAN

LEFT: Armagnac, unlike most Cognac, may be vintage-dated. It can be slower to mature than Cognac, and the brandies used in blends are usually older.

THE MIDI, PROVENCE AND CORSICA

by Rosemary George, M.W.

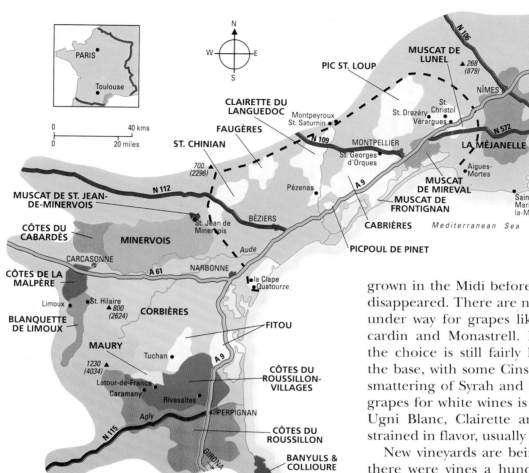

Legend:
- Costières de Nîmes
- Clairette du Bellegarde
- Coteaux du Languedoc
- Minervois
- Muscat de St. Jean-de-Minervois
- Corbières
- Fitou
- Blanquette de Limoux
- Côtes de la Malpère
- Côtes du Roussillon-Villages
- Maury
- Côtes du Roussillon
- Banyuls and Collioure
- Boundary of Coteaux du Languedoc
- Autoroute
- ▲800 (2624) Height above sea level Meters (feet)

The vast vineyard of Languedoc-Roussillon, covering the four departments of Pyrénées-Orientales, Aude, Hérault and Gard, is full of contrasts and contradictions. The production of *vin ordinaire* is still the principal activity of many a conservative wine grower, but these growers are a dying breed and over the last ten years the winds of change have swept through the region at near gale force. The wine lake is drying up and innovation is the order of the day, with an urgent quest for quality and technology that makes the region one of the most exciting in France today.

Quality begins in the vineyard, for you cannot make good wine from bad grapes. Over the last ten years the move away from Carignan, as well as hybrids such as Alicante Bouschet, has gathered momentum. Grenache, Syrah and Mourvèdre are all essential ingredients in the appellations of the Midi and some growers would like to include Cabernet and Merlot too. They are resentful of the iron grip that the Bordelais have on the Institut National des Appellation d'Origine (I.N.A.O.), enabling them to retain a monopoly of these grape varieties. It has been widely recognized for several years that the ubiquitous Carignan badly needed an injection of interest, but many of the different grape varieties

grown in the Midi before the phylloxera crisis have disappeared. There are now experimental plantings under way for grapes like Calitor, Counoise, Muscardin and Monastrell. However for the moment the choice is still fairly limited. Carignan remains the base, with some Cinsaut, some Grenache and a smattering of Syrah and Mourvèdre. The choice of grapes for white wines is also pretty restricted, with Ugni Blanc, Clairette and Macabeo, all fairly restrained in flavor, usually providing the base.

New vineyards are being planted on land where there were vines a hundred years ago, but which were abandoned with the shift from the infertile foothills of the Massif Central, where yields were low and cultivation difficult, to the fertile coastal plains, where yields of 200 hectoliters per hectare/12 tons per acre were common. Subsidies provide a small incentive for pulling up some of these coastal vineyards, but many will disappear anyway with the passage of time, as the older generation gives up the vines that are of no interest to its children.

Vinification methods have improved too, not just with an increased understanding and an appreciation of the importance of hygiene and temperature control, but with the development of a fermentation technique called *macération carbonique*. Used traditionally in Beaujolais, this has made a dramatic improvement to the taste of the ubiquitous Carignan, bringing out its fruit while masking some of its defects. Investment and interest from outside the area, notably by Hardys, a large Australian wine company, has had a further impact on quality.

The vineyards of Roussillon are dominated by the appellation of Côtes du Roussillon together with the more restricted Côtes du Roussillon Villages, which includes two named villages, Latour-de-France and Caramany. The wines are warm and rugged, like the countryside. Village cooperatives dominate production, but two exceptions are Château de Corneilla and Château de Jau. This is also a region of *vins doux naturels*, with wines like Banyuls, (Domaine du Mas Blanc) Maury (Mas Amiel) and Rivesaltes (Domaine

du Sarda-Malet). Fitou, notably in Château de Nouvelles, and Collioure, especially from Domaine du Mas Blanc, are two other sturdy red wines.

Corbières and Minervois form twin appellations on either side of the valley of the Aude. Corbières lies in the foothills of the Pyrénées while Minervois depends upon those of the Massif Central. For both, red is the dominant color, with a significant improvement in flavor partially motivated by their promotion to appellation status in 1985. There are really exciting flavors to be found, with herbs and spice and depth. In Corbières try Château de Lastours, Château St. Auriol, Domaine de Fontsainte, Domaine de Villemajou, Domaine la Voulte-Gasparets and Château la Baronne. There is little doubt that quite the best producer of Minervois is Daniel Domergue (see Grower's View, page 122) but also try Château de Gourgazaud, Domaine Ste. Eulalie, Château Fabas, Château de Paraza, and Domaine Maris.

The tiny village of St. Jean-de-Minervois, within the appellation of Minervois, is also known for its Muscat wines. Nearby is an enclave of sparkling wine, Blanquette de Limoux and, new and even better, Crémant de Limoux, made from the Mauzac grape with some improving Chenin Blanc and Chardonnay. Local tradition attributes the monks of the abbey of St. Hilaire with the development of sparkling wine, a century or two before Dom Pérignon. The local cooperative dominates production, with brand names like Sieur d'Arques.

The Coteaux du Languedoc covers a wide expanse of vineyards from just south of Narbonne, along the Mediterranean past Béziers to the east of Montpellier, as far as the Costières de Nîmes. The Coteaux du Languedoc include fourteen *crus*. Traveling roughly west to east, they are Quatourze, La Clape, St. Chinian, Faugères, Picpoul de Pinet, Cabrières, St. Saturnin, Montpeyroux, St. Georges d'Orques, Pic St. Loup, Méjanelle, St. Drézery, St. Christol and Coteaux de Vérargues. It is not unlike the appellation of Bordeaux, with a basic appellation for the whole area and specific villages of particular quality singled out for special mention. Apart from Picpoul de Pinet, which is made from the white Picpoul grape, all are predominantly red. Faugères and St. Chinian, which were initially appellations in their own right, have the widest following outside their region. Cooperatives dominate the production of the Coteaux du Languedoc, but there are some good individual producers, especially in Faugères (Château de Haut-Fabrègues, Gilbert Alquier) and St. Chinian (the cooperative at Berlou, Château Coujan), and also the Prieuré de St. Jean de Bébian near Pézenas. There is also a little known white appellation, Clairette du Languedoc, as well as some Muscat based *vin doux naturel* from Frontignan, Mireval and Lunel.

The vineyards of the Languedoc end with the Costières de Nîmes, formerly called Costières du Gard. This is where the Languedoc meets the Rhône. The wines are mainly red, while there is a small white appellation called Clairette de Bellegarde. As in the Coteaux du Languedoc, Carignan is the principal grape variety, with some Grenache and Cinsaut and some improving Mourvèdre and Syrah. Again, the small amount of white comes from Ugni Blanc, Grenache Blanc and Macabeo. As elsewhere in the Midi, experimentation with

more unorthodox grape varieties is officially limited to *vins de pays*. Château du Rozier, Château du Campuget, Domaine de l'Amarine and Domaine de St. Louis-la-Perdrix are working well for their appellation.

To the east of Languedoc-Roussillon are the vineyards of Provence, and if you have ever vacationed on the Côte d'Azur, sat at a café in St. Tropez, eaten bouillabaisse in Marseille and sipped the local wine, the chances are that you drank a pink Côtes de Provence from an amphora-shaped bottle. But the wines of Provence are so much more than pretty pink wines for holidays and picnics. There are serious reds and whites in this region offering a myriad of tastes.

The largest and best known appellation of the area is Côtes de Provence, and it can be red and white as well as pink. Domaines Ott at Clos Mireille and Château de Selle are considered the best and also most expensive producers. Also try Domaine de la Bernarde, Château Minuty and Commanderie de Peyrassol. Around the town of Aix-en-Provence are the vineyards of Coteaux d'Aix-en-Provence, with a sub-region, Coteaux des Baux-de-Provence, with vineyards on the foothills of the Alpilles. Domaine de Trévallon is the outstanding estate here, with several others working well, such as Domaine des Terres Blanches, Château de Calissanne, Château Fonscolombe and Mas de la Dame.

Between these two appellations lies the Coteaux Varois, a recent promotion from *vin de pays* to V.D.Q.S. for red and pink wine. Then there are four smaller, more prestigious appellations. Cassis, with

ABOVE: The village of Minerve, which takes its name from the Roman goddess of wisdom, perches on steep cliffs above the Cesse River.

BELOW: Domaine du Révérend is an up and coming estate in Corbières, now run by Peter Sichel of Château d'Angludet in the Médoc. The spicy red wine comes from sixty year old Carignan vines, as well as Grenache and Syrah. La Clape, named after a rocky mountain just east of Narbonne, is one of the fourteen *crus* of the Coteaux du Languedoc and produces some of the most individual white wine of the Midi.

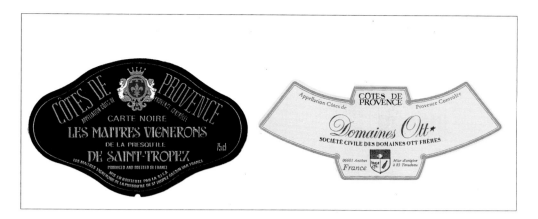

ABOVE: Two leading producers of Côtes de Provence. These neck labels suit the typical elongated bottle of the appellation much better than the classic wine label.

Domaine de Paternel and Clos Saint-Magdeleine, has a reputation for its white wine, while Bandol is known above all for substantial red wines, based on the distinctive Mourvèdre grape, which flourishes in the terraced vineyards behind the fishing port. Domaine Tempier is the best, but good wines are also made at Domaine du Pibarnon, Mas de la Rouvière, Domaine de Terrebrune, Moulin des Costes and Château de Vannières, amongst others.

Outside Aix-en-Provence is the tiny appellation of Palette, where the Rougier family at Château Simone, the only estate of significance, maintains the traditional methods of Provence, with great success. Hidden in the suburbs of the city of Nice itself are the vineyards of Bellet, with some stylish white wines from the unusual Rolle grape.

Provence meets the Rhône in the new appellation of the Côtes du Lubéron, with vineyards around the town of Apt on the foothills of the Montagne du Lubéron. Château Val-Joanis and Château la Canorgue make the best wines. The adjoining and much less well-known V.D.Q.S, Coteaux de Pierrevert, is a sleepy backwater of Provençal viticulture.

The vineyards of Corsica are covered by three appellations, Patrimonio, Ajaccio and Vin de Corse, with the *crus* of Calvi, Sartène, Figari, Porto-Vecchio and Cap Corse, as well as the appropriately named Vin de Pays de l'Ile de Beauté. The most exciting flavors come from indigenous grape varieties not found on mainland France, namely Sciacarello and Nielluccio for reds and Vermentino for whites. Other island varieties like Carcagiolu, Barbirossu, Pagadebit and Bianco Gentile are less important.

The enormous influx of *pieds noirs,* the French ex-colonists who returned to France from North Africa in the 1960s, had a dramatic effect on Corsican viticulture. The immigrants planted the varieties they had grown in North Africa — Grenache, Cinsaut, Carignan and Alicante-Bouschet — expecting to produce wine in the same prolific quantity. Many of their vineyards have now been pulled up, although Grenache, Carignan and Cinsaut remain.

The third strand to Corsican viticulture comes from the recent introduction of grape varieties such as Cabernet Sauvignon, Merlot, Chardonnay and Chenin Blanc. For the moment these can only be included in *vin de pays,* and the traditionalists of Sartène and Ajaccio are anxious that these varieties do not infiltrate the island appellations.

Names to watch include Domaine de Peraldi in Ajaccio, Dominique Gentile, Yves Leccia and Antoine Arena in Patrimonio, Clos Nicrosi in Cap Corse and Domaine de Torraccia at Porto-Vecchio.

GROWER'S VIEW

At the beginning of the seventies the Languedoc, in terms of wine, was viewed as the French California. Everything seemed set fair for a dramatic improvement in quality. The noblest grapes were being planted, or had been in the past. There were excellent and often unsuspected *terroirs*. Progress seemed assured, and yet, twenty years on, it is clear that the Languedoc is a land of missed opportunity.

It is universally recognized that the quality of our wine has improved spectacularly, but this progress has been in the wrong direction. We are trapped within the framework of adequately made, simple, good value wines.

The root problem is that about a century ago our region chose to adopt a banal grape brought from Spain. A hundred years later we are still stuck with the drab and deadly Carignan, yet grapes like the Pinots, the Côt and the Fer Servadou, as well as the admirable Cinsaut can be regarded as native to the Languedoc.

Just as the grape varieties that are supposed native are not always so, so it is sometimes the man most faithful to local traditions who is the least recognized.

Daniel Domergue

CLOS CENTEILLES

Provence appelations
- A Coteaux d'Aix-en-Provence
- B Coteaux-des-Baux-en-Provence
- C Palette
- D Côte de Provence
- E Coteaux Varois
- F Bandol
- G Cassis
- H Bellet
- Autoroute
- ▲810 (2657) Height above sea level Meters (feet)

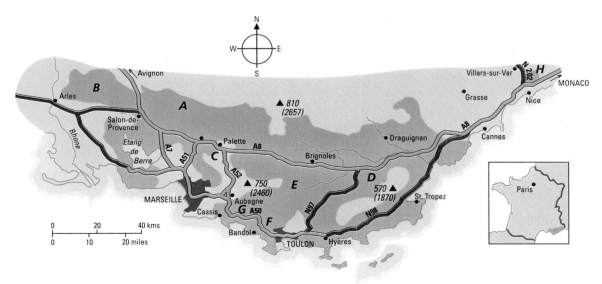

JURA AND SAVOIE

by Rosemary George, M.W.

Mountains seem to enhance individuality in wines, cutting a region off from other influences. This may explain why the Jura, situated as it is, in a remote corner of eastern France on the borders of Switzerland, is the home of some of the country's most original wines. There are grape varieties and flavors that are not found anywhere else; not only red, white and pink wines, still and sparkling, but also the distinctive *vin jaune,* which is the nearest France comes to producing anything resembling Sherry, as well as the luscious *vin de paille,* a remnant of old-fashioned winemaking that has survived in this isolated region.

The overall appellation is Côtes du Jura, covering all the vineyards not included in the other small appellations of Château-Chalon, L'Etoile and Arbois. In addition to the local grape varieties, white Savagnin and red Trousseau and Poulsard, the historical links with Burgundy are maintained with Pinot Noir and Chardonnay. White wines may be pure Chardonnay or Savagnin or a blend of both, or even include some Poulsard; likewise reds and pinks may come from a single variety or be a blend of two or three varieties.

Château-Chalon is the appellation of Vin Jaune, an unusual white wine, made from Savagnin alone, that is left to mature for six years in small barrels, without any topping up, thereby upsetting the accepted rules of enological practice. The dividing line between oxidation and otherwise is very fine. Jean Macle is the best producer of Château-Chalon, while Christian Bourdy makes stylish *vin jaune.* L'Etoile is a white appellation, at its best in the hands of Jean Gros at Domaine de Montbourgeau. Arbois is better known for its red wines. It is also the home of the Jura's largest producer, Henri Maire, who more than anyone has put the Jura on the wine map of France. Other good Arbois producers include Rolet Frères and Lucien Aviet, while names to look out for in the Côtes du Jura include Château d'Arlay, Luc Boilley, Château de Gréa and Jacques Richard.

The vineyards of Savoie are scattered over a large area of the departments of Savoie and Haute Savoie, with pockets of vines mingling with fields of cereal and pasture land. The city of Chambéry is the natural center of the region, with vineyards stretching from the valley of the Isère south of Chambéry, through the Combe de Savoie and along the shores of the Lac du Bourget, as far as Lake Geneva on the Swiss border. The principal appellation of Savoie is quite simply Vin de Savoie, which currently includes fifteen possible *crus,* some of which are better known than others. Abymes and Apremont produce slaty white wine from the Jacquère grape (le Vigneron Savoyard, Pierre Boniface at Domaine des Rocailles), while the village of Chignin also has its own separate appellation of Chignin-Bergeron for wine made from the Roussanne of the northern Rhône (Raymond Quénard). No one knows quite

ABOVE: Densely planted Savagnin vines in the Jura for making the distinctive Vin Jaune.

FAR RIGHT: The Bourdy family is one of the leading producers of the tiny appellation of Château-Chalon, the most original appellation of the Jura.

Côtes du Jura
Arbois
Château-Chalon
L'Etoile
Height above sea level
▲520 (1706) Meters (feet)

RIGHT: View of the rolling Savoyard countryside. Vineyards are interspersed with pasture and fields of grain.

BELOW: Abymes is one of the better known *crus* of Vin de Savoie, taking its name, not from a village, but from the debris left by a colossal landslide back in the thirteenth century. Unlike those of Savoie, labels from the Bugey tend to feature the grape variety. Chardonnay is the most successful white.

how there came to be a pocket of Roussanne in this one village. Further down the valley Arbin has a local reputation for red wine from the Mondeuse (Louis Magnin), while the village of Ayze is an island of severely dry sparkling wine made from the local Gringet grape.

Roussette, sometimes called Altesse, is a Savoyard grape variety with its own appellation, Roussette de Savoie, which confusingly may include some Chardonnay. However the four *crus* of Roussette de Savoie, namely Frangy, Marestel, Monthoux and Monterminod, must be pure Roussette. Closer to the border, the influence of Swiss viticulture is felt, as the dominant grape variety changes to Chasselas in wines like Ripaille (Château de Ripaille) and Marin (Claude Delalex) as well as in the small appellation of Crépy (Fichard, Mercier, Métral).

The town of Seyssel sits astride the Rhône and the appellation, which bridges Savoie and the Bugey, has a reputation for sparkling wine made from Roussette and Molette. As for the rest of the Bugey, this is a lost region, contained in a large loop of the Rhône, with the town of Belley at its center. Like Vin de Savoie, the V.D.Q.S. Vin du Bugey has several *crus,* produced from a hodge podge of grape varieties including Jacquère, Aligoté, Molette, Roussette, Chardonnay, Pinot Noir, Gamay and Mondeuse, making dry whites and fruity reds, wines which rarely travel far. The Caveau Bugiste and Eugène Monin are the best exponents of the Bugey, while Seyssel is exemplified in the wines of Varichon & Clerc and Mollex.

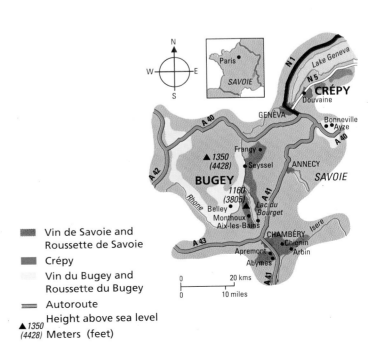

Vin de Savoie and Roussette de Savoie
Crépy
Vin du Bugey and Roussette du Bugey
Autoroute
Height above sea level
▲1350 (4428) Meters (feet)

VINS DE PAYS

by Rosemary George, M.W.

There are *vins de pays* all over viticultural France, from the Yonne to the Pyrénées, but it is in the Midi, in the four departments of Pyrénées-Orientales, Aude, Hérault and Gard, where there is the greatest concentration. The *vins de pays* were born of an urgent need to give the vast quantities of anonymous wine produced in the Midi some identity and to encourage a move towards an image of quality. The first tentative steps towards their creation were taken in 1973 and six years later they were defined by an official government decree. By 1976 there were seventy-five *vins de pays,* and the total at the last count now reaches 141, from fifty-four departments.

There are three categories of *vins de pays.* The broadest is *vins de pays régionaux,* of which there are four, Vin de Pays du Jardin de la France, which covers the whole of the Loire Valley; Vin de Pays d'Oc which encompasses the whole of the Midi; Vin de Pays des Comtés Rhodaniens for the Rhône Valley and Vin de Pays du Comté Tolosan, for a large part of the Southwest. Next come the *vins de pays départementaux,* which are limited by departmental boundaries, such as Vin de Pays de l'Aude. Then within these are the *vins de pays de zone,* such as the evocative sounding Vin de Pays de la Vallée du Paradis or Vin de Pays des Collines de la Moure.

Unlike appellations, *vins de pays* are demarcated by political and administrative geography rather than by geology. The sole exception is the Vin de Pays des Sables du Golfe du Lion, where the sand dunes are the deciding factor. Essentially *vins de pays* are seen as superior *vins de table,* but with some regional character. The criteria of production are much stricter than for *vins de table* and more flexible than for an appellation or a V.D.Q.S. Yields are restricted to 90 hectoliters per hectare/5.3 tons per acre, and the minimum alcohol level is 10 percent by volume, as opposed to 8.5 percent for *vin de table.* The wines have to pass analytical and organoleptical tests, so that levels of sulfur and volatile acidity are also controlled.

The *vins de pays* regulations also allow for an imaginative flexibility as to which grape varieties may or may not be planted. There are two lists for each department, of grapes that are recommended and those that are authorized. Authorized varieties are not as good as recommended ones, but not bad enough to be banned completely. If a grape variety is mentioned on the label, the wine is made from that variety alone. This flexibility has allowed more adventurous growers to plant unusual varieties under the guise of experimentation, with some exciting results.

The proliferation of *vins de pays* in the last few years means that many of them are hardly known outside their own locality. Some have been created in order to satisfy growers who have known how to pull strings in high places. Some will become better known because they have dynamic producers who will create a reputation for themselves and their wines. Les Salins du Midi and their Vin de Pays des Sables du Golfe du Lion is just such an example. Others will never progress beyond the official decree that created them and will remain shrouded in obscurity until they ultimately disappear.

There are few vineyard areas without a *vin de pays.* In the classic regions of Burgundy or Bordeaux they can be used for the wine from vines too young for the appellation, such as Vin de Pays de l'Yonne. In the Midi they are an exciting source of experimentation, for growers who do not want to be hampered by appellation regulations. Depending on the producer, a *vin de pays* can be very much better, or very much worse than the parallel appellation. The most exciting *vins de pays* tend to be made in areas where there are no competing appellations or V.D.Q.S. and no constraints to follow the "usages locaux, loyaux et constants", thereby allowing for unorthodox grape varieties and providing an outlet for the increasing number of Midi growers who want to experiment not only with Cabernet and Chardonnay, but also Viognier, Chenin Blanc, Pinot Noir and other noble varieties.

The most famous example of a *vin de pays* that has acquired a reputation and a price to compete not just with its neighbors, but with appellations from the classic regions of France is Mas de Daumas Gassac, which according to the label is a humble Vin de Pays de l'Hérault. The wine, however, is far from simple. It has been described as the Lafite of the Languedoc and it represents an exciting example of just what can be achieved with ability and talent, as well as money. In little more than ten years — the first vintage was 1978 — it has become a pacesetter for other producers in the Midi, setting an inspiring example and helping in the reassessment of the wines of the south of France.

A few of the more recently created V.D.Q.S. such as Côtes de Saint Mont and Côtes du Brulhois began life as *vins de pays.* Another *vin de pays* whose

RIGHT: The vines of Clos du Montmartre, in the very heart of Paris, are the last vestiges of an important medieval vineyard.

growers may wistfully hope for promotion is the Vin de Pays des Côtes de Gascogne, a rising star of the southwest, and a wine born of the decline in Armagnac sales. Wine produced for distillation requires minimal attention to hygiene or vinification details, so some changes were required, but turning from white wine production to red would have been still more drastic, and Vin de Pays des Côtes de Gascogne has become a dry pithy white wine with fruit and flavor. Sometimes it is aged in oak barrels, or the grapes may even be picked late to make some delicately sweet wine. A parallel, but less successful transformation has happened with Cognac and Vin de Pays Charentais, but this wine has the disadvantage of a cooler climate which sometimes makes for rather acidic wines.

Other *vins de pays* with a high profile include Vin de Pays des Coteaux de l'Ardèche. Again, there is no parallel appellation, and dynamic producers have activated the region. Négociant Louis Latour chose the Ardèche as a supplementary source of Chardonnay, which provided the local growers with an incentive for improvement. The nearby Coteaux des Baronnies are also establishing a reputation for varietal wines from Syrah, Cabernet Sauvignon and Chardonnay.

Many of the good *vins de pays* are in the hands of a dynamic local cooperative, while others depend upon a talented producer. As with most wines it is the person who makes the wine who determines its final quality.

The production of many *vins de pays* is dominated by village cooperatives. However, there are some good private estates. Among those in Languedoc-Roussillon are Mas de Daumas Gassac; Domaine de l'Arjolle; Domaine St. Martin de la Garrigue; Domaine Limbardie; Domaine de la Baume; Les Salins du Midi, with Domaine de Jarras, Domaine du Villeroy and Domaine du Bosquet; Skalli with their Fortant de France label; Domaine du Bosc; Domaine de la Grange Rouge; Domaine de la Fadèze; Domaine de la Gardie; Domaine St. Victor; Domaine des Pourthié; Mas Chichée. In the Coteaux des Baronnies look out for Domaine de la Rosière, and in the Côtes de Gascogne, Domaine de San Guilhem, Domaine de Tariquet, Domaine Mestre Duran and Domaine de Rieux all producing wines which can be recommended.

RIGHT: A selection of *vins de pays* labels, each for a grape variety that is not traditional to the region, such as Chardonnay and Merlot in the Midi and Gamay in the Rhône.

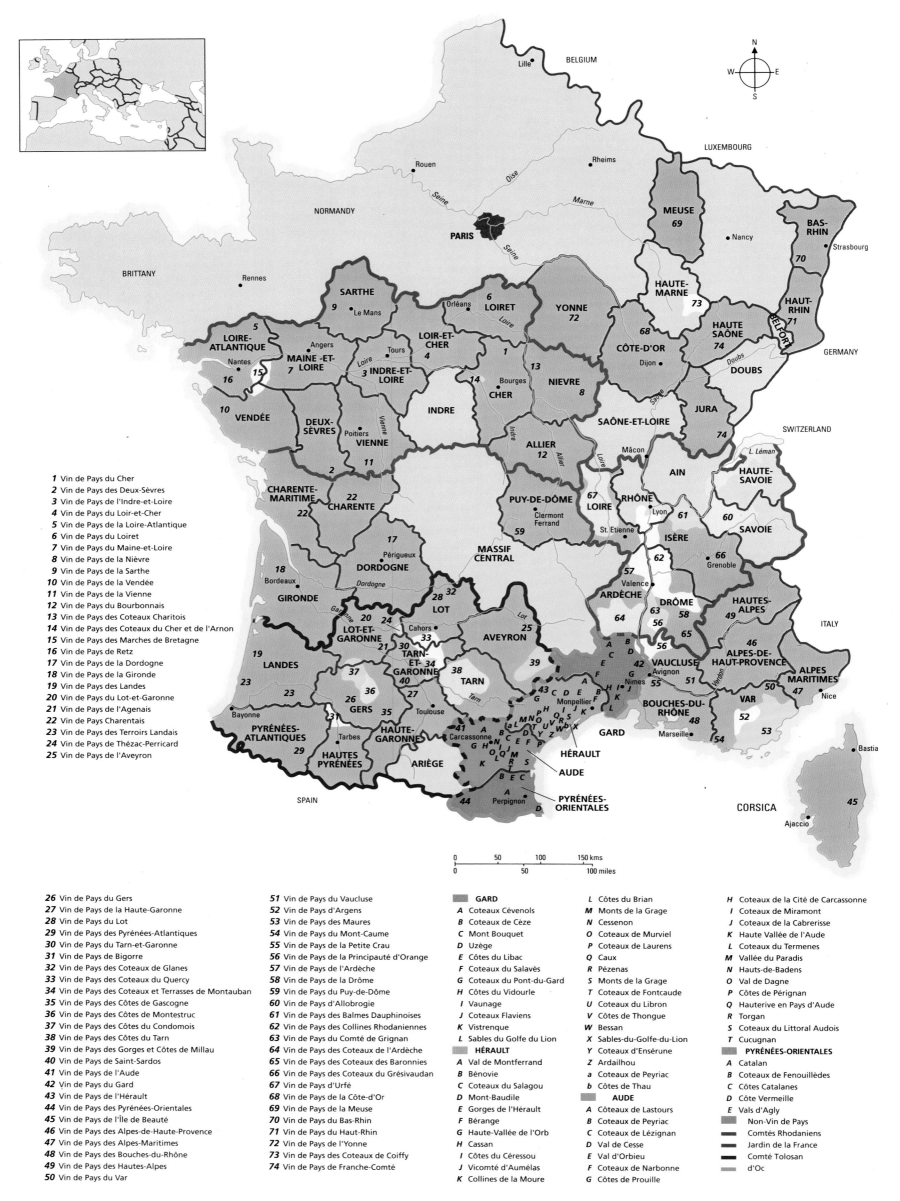

1 Vin de Pays du Cher
2 Vin de Pays des Deux-Sèvres
3 Vin de Pays de l'Indre-et-Loire
4 Vin de Pays du Loir-et-Cher
5 Vin de Pays de la Loire-Atlantique
6 Vin de Pays du Loiret
7 Vin de Pays du Maine-et-Loire
8 Vin de Pays de la Nièvre
9 Vin de Pays de la Sarthe
10 Vin de Pays de la Vendée
11 Vin de Pays de la Vienne
12 Vin de Pays du Bourbonnais
13 Vin de Pays des Coteaux Charitois
14 Vin de Pays des Coteaux du Cher et de l'Arnon
15 Vin de Pays des Marches de Bretagne
16 Vin de Pays de Retz
17 Vin de Pays de la Dordogne
18 Vin de Pays de la Gironde
19 Vin de Pays des Landes
20 Vin de Pays du Lot-et-Garonne
21 Vin de Pays de l'Agenais
22 Vin de Pays Charentais
23 Vin de Pays des Terroirs Landais
24 Vin de Pays de Thézac-Perricard
25 Vin de Pays de l'Aveyron

26 Vin de Pays du Gers
27 Vin de Pays de la Haute-Garonne
28 Vin de Pays du Lot
29 Vin de Pays des Pyrénées-Atlantiques
30 Vin de Pays du Tarn-et-Garonne
31 Vin de Pays de Bigorre
32 Vin de Pays des Coteaux de Glanes
33 Vin de Pays des Coteaux du Quercy
34 Vin de Pays des Coteaux et Terrasses de Montauban
35 Vin de Pays des Côtes de Gascogne
36 Vin de Pays des Côtes de Montestruc
37 Vin de Pays des Côtes du Condomois
38 Vin de Pays des Côtes du Tarn
39 Vin de Pays des Gorges et Côtes de Millau
40 Vin de Pays de Saint-Sardos
41 Vin de Pays de l'Aude
42 Vin de Pays du Gard
43 Vin de Pays de l'Hérault
44 Vin de Pays des Pyrénées-Orientales
45 Vin de Pays de l'Île de Beauté
46 Vin de Pays des Alpes-de-Haute-Provence
47 Vin de Pays des Alpes-Maritimes
48 Vin de Pays des Bouches-du-Rhône
49 Vin de Pays des Hautes-Alpes
50 Vin de Pays du Var

51 Vin de Pays du Vaucluse
52 Vin de Pays d'Argens
53 Vin de Pays des Maures
54 Vin de Pays du Mont-Caume
55 Vin de Pays de la Petite Crau
56 Vin de Pays de la Principauté d'Orange
57 Vin de Pays de l'Ardèche
58 Vin de Pays de la Drôme
59 Vin de Pays du Puy-de-Dôme
60 Vin de Pays d'Allobrogie
61 Vin de Pays des Balmes Dauphinoises
62 Vin de Pays des Collines Rhodaniennes
63 Vin de Pays du Comté de Grignan
64 Vin de Pays des Coteaux de l'Ardèche
65 Vin de Pays des Coteaux des Baronnies
66 Vin de Pays des Coteaux du Grésivaudan
67 Vin de Pays d'Urfé
68 Vin de Pays de la Côte-d'Or
69 Vin de Pays de la Meuse
70 Vin de Pays du Bas-Rhin
71 Vin de Pays du Haut-Rhin
72 Vin de Pays de l'Yonne
73 Vin de Pays des Coteaux de Coiffy
74 Vin de Pays de Franche-Comté

GARD
A Coteaux Cévenols
B Coteaux de Cèze
C Mont Bouquet
D Uzège
E Côtes du Libac
F Coteaux du Salavès
G Coteaux du Pont-du-Gard
H Côtes du Vidourle
I Vaunage
J Coteaux Flaviens
K Vistrenque
L Sables du Golfe du Lion

HÉRAULT
A Val de Montferrand
B Bénovie
C Coteaux du Salagou
D Mont-Baudile
E Gorges de l'Hérault
F Bérange
G Haute-Vallée de l'Orb
H Cassan
I Côtes du Céressou
J Vicomté d'Aumélas
K Collines de la Moure

L Côtes du Brian
M Monts de la Grage
N Cessenon
O Coteaux de Murviel
P Coteaux de Laurens
Q Caux
R Pézenas
S Monts de la Grage
T Coteaux de Fontcaude
U Coteaux du Libron
V Côtes de Thongue
W Bessan
X Sables-du-Golfe-du-Lion
Y Coteaux d'Ensérune
Z Ardailhou
a Coteaux de Peyriac
b Côtes de Thau

AUDE
A Côteaux de Lastours
B Coteaux de Peyriac
C Coteaux de Lézignan
D Val de Cesse
E Val d'Orbieu
F Coteaux de Narbonne
G Côtes de Prouille

H Coteaux de la Cité de Carcassonne
I Coteaux de Miramont
J Coteaux de la Cabrerisse
K Haute Vallée de l'Aude
L Coteaux des Termenes
M Vallée du Paradis
N Hauts-de-Badens
O Val de Dagne
P Côtes de Pérignan
Q Hauterive en Pays d'Aude
R Torgan
S Côtes du Littoral Audois
T Cucugnan

PYRÉNÉES-ORIENTALES
A Catalan
B Coteaux de Fenouillèdes
C Côtes Catalanes
D Côte Vermeille
E Vals d'Agly

Non-Vin de Pays
Comtés Rhodaniens
Jardin de la France
Comté Tolosan
d'Oc

127

ITALY

Introduction by Maureen Ashley, M.W.

RIGHT: However up to date Italy's wine cellars may be historical landmarks are never far from the vineyards as here at Badia a Passignana in Tuscany.

Italy is both the most and least traditional winemaking country; the most homogeneous but most diverse; the most fascinating and most frustrating.

Winemaking in Italy goes back at least to Etruscan times, although it was with the Greeks that it became widespread. Yet many of the wines poured today may have little connection with those drunk throughout history; modern know-how and Italians' reawakened sense of self-worth have intertwined to ensure massive improvements.

The vine is grown in every one of the country's ninety-five provinces, making Italy vie with France for the role of the world's largest producer of wine. The importance of wine is taken for granted everywhere, since wine is an accompaniment to every meal and a part of Italian culture. Trends and fashions in wine production and consumption spread rapidly throughout the country. The types and styles of wines produced are so numerous and so varied that they could easily represent the output of the world, not just one small country within it.

There are wines of sheer genius, of utter delight, grand structure and serious demeanor, as well as wines of light, simple drinkability. There are also squabbles and disputes, labels that reveal little, laws made only to be broken, producers of little worth and wines that lighten the palate somewhat less than the pocket. In Italy, the drinker may find disappointing wines as easily as wines about which to be enthusiastic. It is generally the better wines that are exported. Italy and its wines are anything but dull.

It is not surprising that there are so many different wines. Italy stretches over 1,500 kilometers/932 miles from its boundary with Austria where there is a cool, Alpine, continental climate, to the warmth and dryness of Sicily. Within that span there is an infinite number of growing conditions. Much of Italy is mountainous. The Apennine chain in particular forms a solid backbone to the country, in places stretching almost to the coast. Thus at every degree of latitude there are innumerable altitudes, aspects and exposures, not to mention soil types, microcli-

mates and other elements affecting vine growth.

There is also an abundance of grape varieties. The existing number is estimated as thousands; at least a hundred distinct varieties are of some importance. Most of these are indigenous and grown in some small area of the country only, apart from in experimental plots, which are springing up everywhere. The abundance of grape varieties gives a huge range of flavors to Italian wines.

There is no unified way of pruning these vines. The steepest slopes of the north may use a *pergola*; the traditional planting of the south is a low, bush-like *alberello* but other forms are widespread too. One of the more common is *spalliera*, a wire-trained system similar to *guyot*, but varying from place to place in height, number of shoots, number of buds, curvature of shoots and so on. Recent times have also seen the proliferation of *tendone*, the *bête noire* of most quality-minded wine producers. This high-trained system has an X-shaped horizontal canopy and encourages vines to be as prolific as they can be. Yields can be four times higher than with *spalliera*, but the wines are correspondingly dilute.

Even in the new Italy, developments in the vineyards follow those in the cellar. New plantings with many more vines per hectare or acre are the most visible sign of this, but the establishment of new, improved clones of grape varieties and research into the most suitable rootstocks for them continues, with the refinement of husbandry techniques.

In the cellar white winemaking first underwent a complete overhaul. Italian whites, yellow-colored, dull and fruitless, are now only a bad memory. Temperature-controlled fermentation made them fresher and crisper. At first this new process was used over-enthusiastically, resulting in acidulous wines that tasted of little else. Producers quickly learned the best temperatures for their grapes to allow varietal flavors to shine through.

Red wines were also subjected to temperature control at considerably higher temperatures than the whites. It was the aging of the reds that most engaged (and still engages) producers. Italian red wines have traditionally been aged in large barrels of (usually) Slavonian oak known as *botti*, bought only occasionally and kept for generations. Depending on how these are treated, they may cede little or no oak character to a wine, even after several years. Gradually the idea spread of using *barriques*, small barrels of French oak, bought regularly and replaced after about three years' use. These impart a richer, more voluptuous, vanilla-like oakiness. Wines from some grape varieties are improved by this treatment, but many are not.

By choosing between *barriques* of different ages and *botti*, or some combination, and by controlling the time in each medium, winemakers now have the potential to find the best aging techniques for their wines. It is often not until a number of years after bottling that a red wine becomes mature, so it takes some time to see the results of any aging system.

Another remarkable difference between today's Italian wines and those of just a few years back is their distinctive livery. The shape of the bottles, the colors of the glass and capsule and, most importantly, the design of the label have become of great importance, resulting in wines that share with many other Italian goods the pre-eminence of design.

Italy's wine nomenclature deserves an explana-

LEFT: Sturdy, bushy vines, staked for support, are still much in evidence, although more often replaced by easier cultivated wire-trained systems.

tion, because it inspires heated opinions. Nominally, at least, Italy follows other European Community countries, with a system of controlled origin wine, supposedly "quality" wine, and less-controlled "table" wine. Controlled origin wine is labeled *Denominazione di Origine Controllata* (D.O.C.) or, for a few wines, *Denominazione di Origine Controllata e Garantita* (D.O.C.G.). D.O.C.G. wines are theoretically superior to D.O.C.s but in reality the distinction is anything but clear-cut.

The criteria for D.O.C.(G.) are quite rigid. Most D.O.C.s, in addition, were created before the revolution in winemaking practices started to spread. The result is that there has been no official category that catered satisfactorily to forward-thinking winemakers who wanted to make high-quality wines using methods or grapes not prescribed in the D.O.C. or D.O.C.G. rules. They are reduced to labeling such wines as "table wine", ostensibly the category for the cheap and cheerful. They then avoided confusion with the lowlier sort of table wines by bottling their high-quality versions in expensive bottles, and charging prices that were among the highest in Italy.

Each producer gave his own version a made-up name displayed prominently on the label. This meant that there were hundreds of wine names in circulation but the important thing was that each was a representative of quality-conscious thinking or experimentation. Wines labeled D.O.C.(G.) may have benefited from modern developments in vine growing and winemaking, but their style was essentially traditional.

However, a complete revision of the wine law has been passed, which begins to remove some of these anomalies. Given the complexities of the old system the revision in the wine law will need time to take effect.

NORTHWEST ITALY

by Maureen Ashley, M.W.

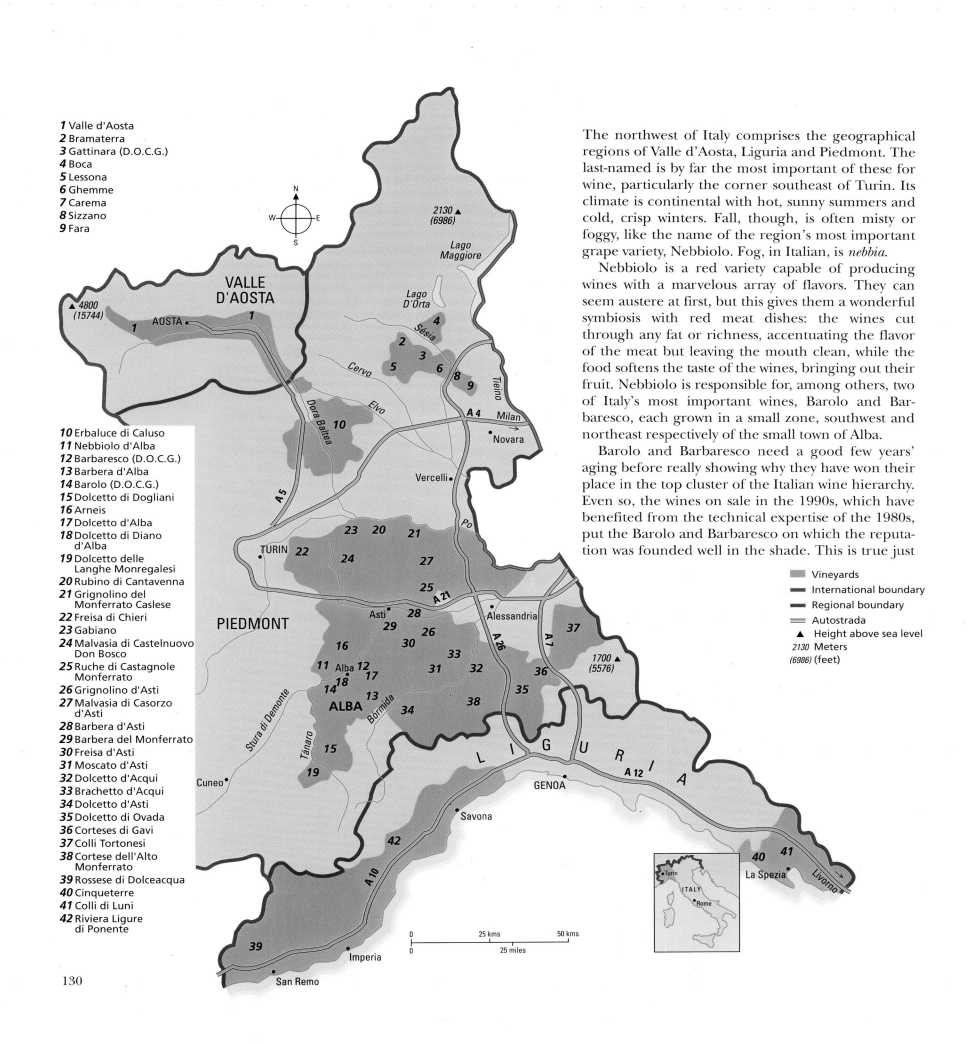

1 Valle d'Aosta
2 Bramaterra
3 Gattinara (D.O.C.G.)
4 Boca
5 Lessona
6 Ghemme
7 Carema
8 Sizzano
9 Fara

10 Erbaluce di Caluso
11 Nebbiolo d'Alba
12 Barbaresco (D.O.C.G.)
13 Barbera d'Alba
14 Barolo (D.O.C.G.)
15 Dolcetto di Dogliani
16 Arneis
17 Dolcetto d'Alba
18 Dolcetto di Diano d'Alba
19 Dolcetto delle Langhe Monregalesi
20 Rubino di Cantavenna
21 Grignolino del Monferrato Caslese
22 Freisa di Chieri
23 Gabiano
24 Malvasia di Castelnuovo Don Bosco
25 Ruche di Castagnole Monferrato
26 Grignolino d'Asti
27 Malvasia di Casorzo d'Asti
28 Barbera d'Asti
29 Barbera del Monferrato
30 Freisa d'Asti
31 Moscato d'Asti
32 Dolcetto d'Acqui
33 Brachetto d'Acqui
34 Dolcetto d'Asti
35 Dolcetto di Ovada
36 Cortese di Gavi
37 Colli Tortonesi
38 Cortese dell'Alto Monferrato
39 Rossese di Dolceacqua
40 Cinqueterre
41 Colli di Luni
42 Riviera Ligure di Ponente

The northwest of Italy comprises the geographical regions of Valle d'Aosta, Liguria and Piedmont. The last-named is by far the most important of these for wine, particularly the corner southeast of Turin. Its climate is continental with hot, sunny summers and cold, crisp winters. Fall, though, is often misty or foggy, like the name of the region's most important grape variety, Nebbiolo. Fog, in Italian, is *nebbia*.

Nebbiolo is a red variety capable of producing wines with a marvelous array of flavors. They can seem austere at first, but this gives them a wonderful symbiosis with red meat dishes: the wines cut through any fat or richness, accentuating the flavor of the meat but leaving the mouth clean, while the food softens the taste of the wines, bringing out their fruit. Nebbiolo is responsible for, among others, two of Italy's most important wines, Barolo and Barbaresco, each grown in a small zone, southwest and northeast respectively of the small town of Alba.

Barolo and Barbaresco need a good few years' aging before really showing why they have won their place in the top cluster of the Italian wine hierarchy. Even so, the wines on sale in the 1990s, which have benefited from the technical expertise of the 1980s, put the Barolo and Barbaresco on which the reputation was founded well in the shade. This is true just

Vineyards
International boundary
Regional boundary
Autostrada
▲ Height above sea level
2130 Meters
(6986) (feet)

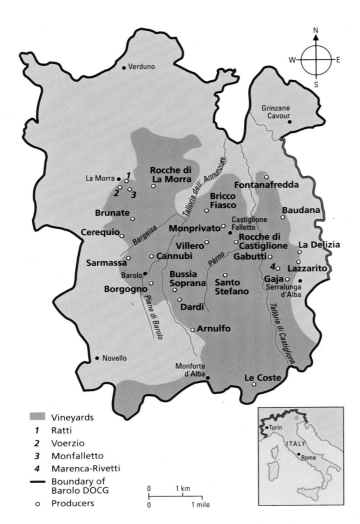

Vineyards
1 Ratti
2 Voerzio
3 Monfalletto
4 Marenca-Rivetti
— Boundary of Barolo DOCG
o Producers

as much of the so-called traditionalists aiming for powerful, intense wines of great structure and longevity, such as Aldo Conterno, Giacomo Conterno, Bruno Giacosa, Bartolo Mascarello, Giuseppe Mascarello, Prunotto, Scarpa, Vietti and others, as of the much vaunted modernists who put fruit much more strongly into the equation, for example, Altare, Clerico, Marchesi di Gresy, Sebaste and Roberto Voerzio.

The Aging of Piedmontese Reds

Red Piedmontese wines made from the Nebbiolo variety, most notably Barolo and Barbaresco, are wines that require several years' aging to be at their best. This does not mean that there is any hard and fast rule on how long they need to age; that depends both on the characteristics of each vintage (which vary considerably) and one's own tastes (which will vary every bit as much). Nor does it mean that there is just one year when a wine will be at its peak; the development of fine wines is like a long curve which rises gently, has a long, nearly flat top, then slowly descends. Italian wine law insists that the first three years of the aging of Barolo (two of which must be in wood) and the first two years of Barbaresco (one of which must be in wood) take place before the wines are released for sale. For certain vintages this aging will suit the palates of some people. Others like to see even the simplest wines being given five years or so, while leaving the more important vintages, for example, 1990, 1989, 1985 and 1982, to improve for ten years or more. If in doubt, though, it is always better to drink a wine a little too young than too old.

ABOVE: Barolo labels range from the staunchly traditional such as those of Borgogno and Renato Ratti to ultra-modern Roberto Voerzio.

LEFT: The village of Barolo, home of Italy's most revered wines, seen from the densely planted vineyards of producer Ceretto.

BELOW: Barbaresco may have fewer producers than Barolo but the labels are no less distinctive, as this selection shows.

BELOW: Carema is a small area in the alpine northwest producing Nebbiolo wine. Pio Cesare and Franco Fiorina produce fine wines.

BOTTOM: White wines of Piedmont: sparkling Asti Spumante; still wines made from the same Moscato grapes; firm, dry Arneis and steely Gavi.

Piedmont is in essence a red wine region with several other major red varieties planted alongside Nebbiolo. Most important of these are Dolcetto, which makes gulpingly fresh but nevertheless quite robust wines, and Barbera, which gives an invigorating zing and a fruit-packed punch to its wines, which can be quite remarkable. Both varieties are grown widely in the region's southeast and in a variety of styles. Dolcetto is probably at its best when young and freshly vibrant, like the example produced by the Viticoltori dell'Acquese, whereas Barbera is more flexible and shines just as well as a robust wine with a few years' aging potential, as made by Cascina Castlèt, for example, or even with *barrique* aging, notably by Giacomo Bologna or Coppo. Many Nebbiolo producers also make Dolcetto and Barbera wines, often to very good effect.

Other red Piedmontese varieties include Grignolino (as typified by Bricco Mondalino), Freisa (Vajra and others), Ruché (Rabezzana, Scarpa) and the light, strawberry-like Brachetto, exemplified by Giacomo Bologna or Scarpa.

There are some whites as well, however. There's Gavi, from the Cortese grape, produced in the extreme south of the region, not far from Genoa. Its steely-firm, subtle style is one that has enabled it to stay in fashion in Italy far longer than most. La Scolca is widely regarded as being the best Gavi but La Giustiniana, Castello di Tassarolo, La Battistina and others are also excellent.

Also fashionable is Arneis, produced mainly north of Alba. This grape was virtually extinct until, in the early 1980s, growers started to take an interest in varieties that had earlier fallen from grace. Results from Arneis, ranging from elegantly perfumed, as made by Deletto, Malabaila, Malvirà or others, to nuttily full, for example Castello di Neive, were such a pleasant surprise that they rapidly took off. Experimenters have also recently planted the international variety, Chardonnay, with promising results.

Most important, though, is the Moscato grape. It produces light, delicate, slightly sweet wines; the complete antithesis of the region's muscular reds. Often they have a bit of a bubble, too. Moscato's ambassador has long been the fully sparkling Asti Spumante but Moscato d'Asti is the wine that really shows the grape to perfection. Rivetti is often considered the king of Moscato but there are a good dozen pretenders to the crown.

── GROWER'S VIEW ──

Monforte d'Alba is a small village in the heart of the Langhe where three important D.O.C. wines are produced: Barolo from Nebbiolo, Dolcetto d'Alba and Barbera d'Alba.

While maintaining the Piedmontese traditions for vine cultivation, we are aiming at wines of great quality and so prune very short to get a maximum yield of 60 quintals of grapes per hectare (equivalent to 40 hectoliters per hectare/2.4 tons per acre), a quantity much lower than the wine laws permit.

However, for us the most important factor in producing great wine is the weather conditions in any year.

Around fourteen years ago, I made a study of the land in collaboration with various experts in the field. As a result I tried planting Chardonnay and Pinot Noir vines and made two wines, L'Angelica Chardonnay and Pinonero, which have turned out extremely well. Once other producers of the zone saw the great success I was achieving they began to follow my example.

Valentino Migliorini

PODERE ROCCHE DEI MANZONI

CENTRAL NORTH ITALY

by Maureen Ashley, M.W.

Central northern Italy (the regions of Lombardy and Emilia-Romagna) is atypical of Italy in that much of it is flat. Great swathes of land form the fertile plain of the Po River — much more suited to grains and fruit farming than viticulture — and a large area is covered by the city of Milan and its sprawling, industrial hinterland. Despite this, there is no shortage of wine; the vine flourishes wherever a few hills appear and, in one case, on the plains too.

The one case is Lambrusco, the name of both the wine and the grape that makes it. Unusually, Lambrusco vines grow well in the flat Po valley countryside around the town of Modena, near Bologna. The wine often used to stop fermenting before all the sugar had been turned to alcohol. There was also often a tendency for the fermentation to restart after bottling. All that was necessary was to control and refine these processes to turn out a wine that has captivated large chunks of the wine-drinking world. Lambrusco is mostly red, with a cherry-like flavor, slightly sparkling and usually sweetish; it is neither serious nor complicated, just fun, and it is in its element with rich foods like salami.

Although Lambrusco is a red grape, pink and white versions of the wine have been introduced in the last few years and have been wildly successful.

Further southeast, on the Apennine foothills towards the Adriatic, three other grapes dominate: red Sangiovese and white Trebbiano and Albana. The first two of these grow in many other areas of Italy too, Trebbiano being particularly widespread. Grower's pride, therefore, is principally invested in Albana. Fattoria Paradiso is the leading producer and Trerè and Cesari are both in the vanguard. Nevertheless, the wines of all three grapes will need to see continued improvement to keep up with standards already achieved elsewhere.

At the western end of the central North is another cluster of vine-covered hills, straddling the boundary between the regions of Lombardy and Emilia-Romagna. The part in Lombardy is called Oltrepo'Pavese, the other, Colli Piacentini. Aptly, the area's top estate, Castello di Luzzano, sits on the border of the two regions, with land in each. A dozen varieties are grown, not all by each estate, giving wines that may be red or white, sweet or dry, still, lightly or fully sparkling. A touch of sparkle is most popular locally but the area's flagship is Gutturnio, a cherry-and-chocolate-flavored red made from a mix of Barbera and Bonarda grapes.

LEFT: The broad, sluggish river Po has a strong influence on the climate of the plainlands of central north Italy, bringing winter mists and fogs and raising summer humidity.

The next area of upland eastwards, Franciacorta, is even more inclined towards the bubble, even if it produces some fine still reds and whites too. Franciacorta sparkling wines, made from Pinot Blanc and Chardonnay grapes, rank among Italy's finest and hold their own on the world stage, too, especially since the area's top producers, Bellavista and Ca' del Bosco, kept their eyes firmly on Champagne while developing their wines.

Lombardy's north is sub-alpine, with conditions suitable for vine-growing on only a thin slither of land, the Valtellina. The wines are made from Nebbiolo and are not totally dissimilar from those from Piedmont. The estates of Negri and Rainoldi dominate this small area. Lombardy's east, on the other hand, borders Lake Garda and has, among others, Trebbiano planted, producing a soft, light, dry white called Lugana which is steadily gaining attention, most notably those of Ca' dei Frati and Zenato.

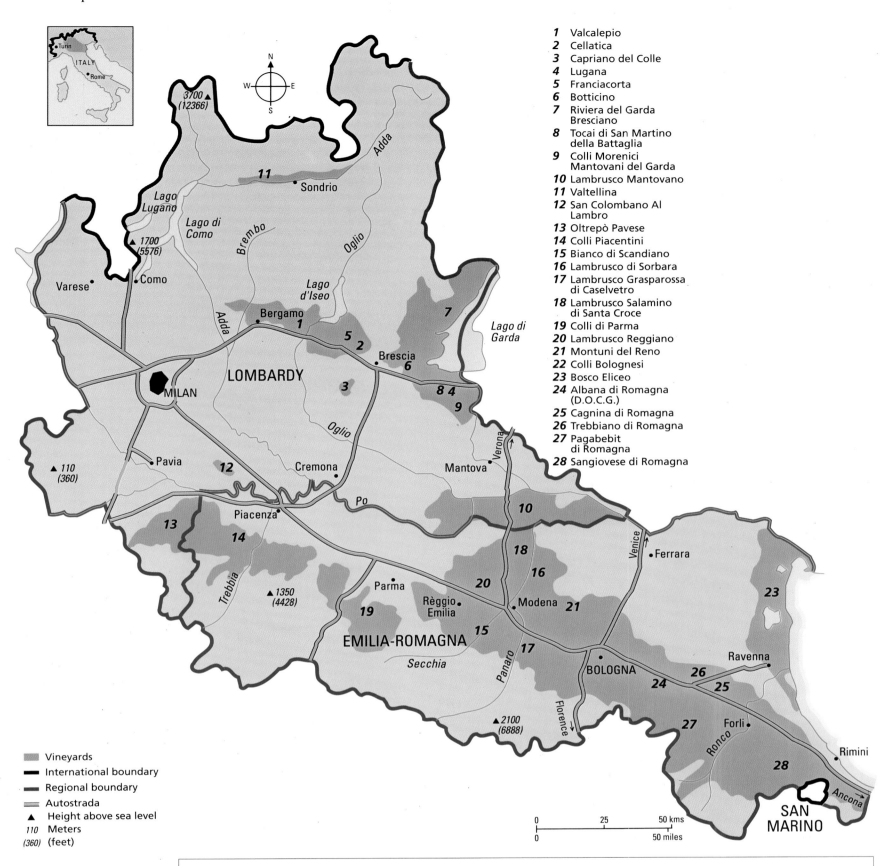

1 Valcalepio
2 Cellatica
3 Capriano del Colle
4 Lugana
5 Franciacorta
6 Botticino
7 Riviera del Garda Bresciano
8 Tocai di San Martino della Battaglia
9 Colli Morenici Mantovani del Garda
10 Lambrusco Mantovano
11 Valtellina
12 San Colombano Al Lambro
13 Oltrepò Pavese
14 Colli Piacentini
15 Bianco di Scandiano
16 Lambrusco di Sorbara
17 Lambrusco Grasparossa di Caselvetro
18 Lambrusco Salamino di Santa Croce
19 Colli di Parma
20 Lambrusco Reggiano
21 Montuni del Reno
22 Colli Bolognesi
23 Bosco Eliceo
24 Albana di Romagna (D.O.C.G.)
25 Cagnina di Romagna
26 Trebbiano di Romagna
27 Pagabebit di Romagna
28 Sangiovese di Romagna

Vineyards
International boundary
Regional boundary
Autostrada
▲ Height above sea level
110 Meters
(360) (feet)

RIGHT: An Oltrepo' Pavese Pinot from Guarnazzola, a Lambrusco Reggiano from Riunite and a Lugana from Zenato are all from north-central Italy and each shows *Denominazione di Origine Controllata* under the wine's denomination. For a *vino da tavola*, named for the esteemed Maurizio Zanella, the wine's producer, no classification is specified.

NORTHEAST ITALY

by Maureen Ashley, M.W.

Northeastern Italy starts east of Lake Garda with the Veneto region and spreads to the region bordering Austria (Trentino-Alto Adige) and that adjoining Yugoslavia (Friuli-Venezia Giulia).

In the Veneto, there is no shortage of viticultural areas but those of any importance are in the west of the region, starting at Lake Garda, and well within striking distance of Verona. The wines, Soave, Valpolicella and (to a lesser extent) Bardolino are household names and sell in vast quantities but, even here, there's more to them than their simple image conveys. Soave and Valpolicella were first produced just on hill sites. As they became more popular, cultivation spread to the surrounding plains, to the detriment of quality. Wines now coming from the hilly heartland are labeled *classico*. Their quality is several notches up from basic, so it is a distinction well worth noting. In addition, the *classico* wines of top Soave producers such as Anselmi or Pieropan, or Valpolicella estates such as Allegrini, Le Ragose, Quintarelli and others are so fine that they redefine the terms for examining these household names.

Bitter-cherry-like Bardolino resembles a lightweight Valpolicella but Valpolicella itself, regardless of producer, can reach heights of distinction and concentration that would surprise many. This super-Valpolicella is called *amarone* and is made from Corvina, Rondinella and Molinara grapes that have been left to shrivel and dry out for three months or more between the harvest and pressing. The water evaporates, the juice is concentrated and after a slow fermentation a big, powerful, alcoholic, intense wine emerges. Occasionally the fermentation is stopped before all the sugar has been converted to alcohol and the resultant sweetish wine is called *recioto*. Producers sometimes beef up their ordinary Valpolicella by letting the recently made wine ferment again on the lees of *amarone*. Unfortunately, labels never indicate whether this highly beneficial process has occurred.

The Garganega grape gives Soave its almondy character and bitter almonds aftertaste. Bianco di Custoza is not dissimilar but has a little more fruit and zip, the result of being made from other grapes together with Garganega, and a large number of producers, for example, Cavalchina, Fraterna Portalupi, Gorgo, Le Vigne di San Pietro and Zenato, are exploiting the blend to obvious good effect.

Near Vicenza are the vineyards of Breganze, turning out a smart range of wines, mainly from

ABOVE: All top Soave producer Anselmi's vineyards are in the hilly *classico* zone where better exposure, better drainage and lower yields ensure superior wine.

GROWER'S VIEW

Among the elements that give a wine its personality none dominates. The final result is a synergy of micro-elements, of small thoughts rather than single actions. The real catalyst is man. A grower knows what he wants from his vineyard: quantity or a top class product. This dichotomy has been one of the principal causes of the loss of image of Veronese winemaking. Man treasures everything natural conditions give him and everything that technology and human endeavor suggest to him in order to obtain the product he envisaged on planning his vineyard.

We, at Allegrini, have tried to fulfill the legacy of our father who wanted to achieve precisely the wine he had imagined on acquiring the La Grola vineyard. To that end he molded all the elements of the site and devised a planting system, a grape mix then so innovative for the Valpolicella zone that he is now regarded as well ahead of his time.

Franco Allegrini
AZIENDA AGRICOLA ALLEGRINI

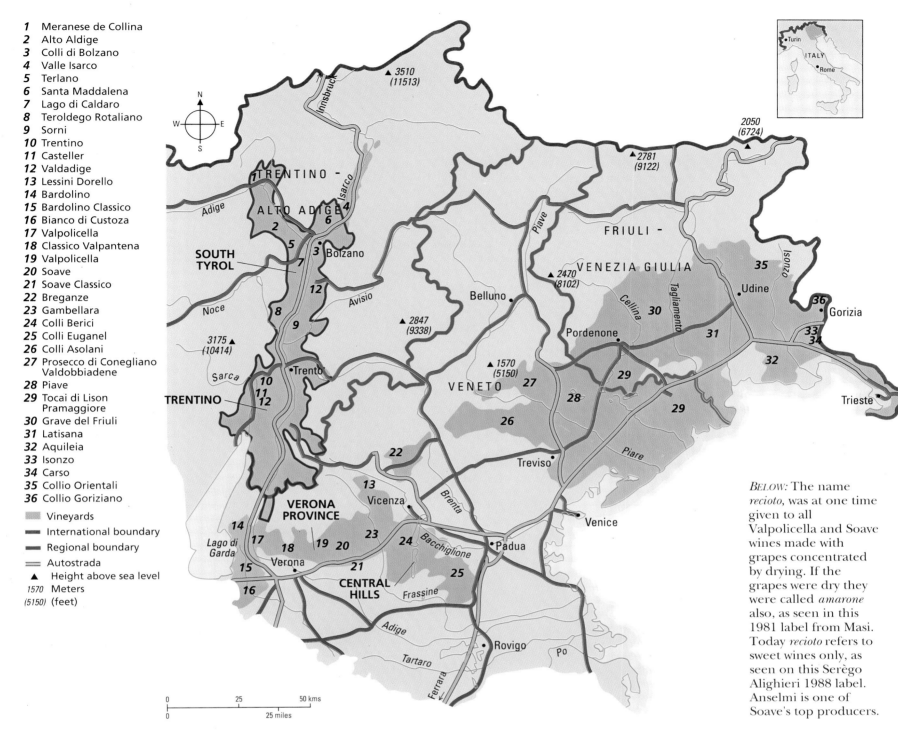

1 Meranese de Collina
2 Alto Aldige
3 Colli di Bolzano
4 Valle Isarco
5 Terlano
6 Santa Maddalena
7 Lago di Caldaro
8 Teroldego Rotaliano
9 Sorni
10 Trentino
11 Casteller
12 Valdadige
13 Lessini Dorello
14 Bardolino
15 Bardolino Classico
16 Bianco di Custoza
17 Valpolicella
18 Classico Valpantena
19 Valpolicella
20 Soave
21 Soave Classico
22 Breganze
23 Gambellara
24 Colli Berici
25 Colli Euganel
26 Colli Asolani
27 Prosecco di Conegliano Valdobbiadene
28 Piave
29 Tocai di Lison Pramaggiore
30 Grave del Friuli
31 Latisana
32 Aquileia
33 Isonzo
34 Carso
35 Collio Orientali
36 Collio Goriziano

▒ Vineyards
▬ International boundary
▬ Regional boundary
═ Autostrada
▲ Height above sea level
1570 Meters
(5150) (feet)

BELOW: The name *recioto*, was at one time given to all Valpolicella and Soave wines made with grapes concentrated by drying. If the grapes were dry they were called *amarone* also, as seen in this 1981 label from Masi. Today *recioto* refers to sweet wines only, as seen on this Serègo Alighieri 1988 label. Anselmi is one of Soave's top producers.

grape varieties originating in France and dominated by the producer Maculan. Further east is the domain of a classically Veneto grape: Prosecco. Prosecco wines are light and white with a milky softness, an apple-like crispness and a spicy tang. A large number of estates are producing wines that fully reflect the grape's charms: Bisol, Canevel, Carpenè Malvolti, Le Case Bianche, Le Groppe, Zardetto and others. Prosecco wines may be dry or medium dry and are more often sparkling than still.

The vineyards of Trentino-Alto Adige carpet the hills on either side of the fast-flowing Adige River. In Alto Adige, the northern part of the region, the valley is steep and narrow, in Trentino it is a little wider and gentler. The zone has sharp diurnal temperature swings, which tend to boost the grapes' aromatic elements, and the wines are among Italy's most perfumed. Nearly all are made from single grape varieties, and large numbers of varieties, of French, German and Italian origin, are grown, the spread of altitudes providing rapidly changing conditions suitable for a wide range of grape types. The wines usually have very pure toned varietal characteristics together with slightly restrained flavors.

It is the white wines of Alto Adige that best represent the area, although the reds are produced in much greater quantities. Labels of Alto Adige wines may well be in German as well as, or instead of, Italian since the province belonged to Austria until 1918. Germanic culture still runs strong. Lageder and Tiefenbrunner lead a long list of quality-conscious producers. In Trentino, firmly Italian, reds share the stage with whites, notably because of the red varieties, again indigenous: Teroldego (most notably by Foradori) and Marzemino (De Tarczal, I Vini del Concilio, Simoncelli). The former is a grassy, plummy, peppery, spicy wine and the latter is lighter and fresher with more redcurrant-like fruit.

Much of the land of Friuli-Venezia Giulia is no more than gently undulating; it is only at its eastern boundary that a major hill ridge appears. Like Trentino-Alto Adige, the wines are made from a significant number of single varieties. The wines of the region are, however, broader, gentler, with more pervasive flavors. Until recently, the white wines were far superior to the reds but efforts have been made to improve the red wines, with good results. Wines from the hill ridge are named precisely for where they come: Collio Goriziano, Colli Orientali del Friuli and Grave del Friuli and Carso. Apart from the more internationally known varieties, grapes that typify the region are the red Refosco and the white Ribolla, Verduzzo and, for sweet wine, Picolit. Fine estates are numerous but the wines of Jermann, Puiatti and Schiopetto each have a particular style that puts them just ahead of the others.

ABOVE: Alto Adige's vineyards, usually pergola-trained and often grown at unimaginably high altitudes vie for attention with craggy, snow-capped mountains.

LEFT: Whether from top producer Lageder in Alto Adige or Pojer & Sandri further south in Trentino, label designs reflect the proximity of Trentino-Alto Adige to Austria.

GROWER'S VIEW

Culturally, linguistically and historically South Tyrol's affinities are with the Germanic nations of the north and are noticeable in vine growing and winemaking. Yet South Tyrol stands on its own, as a producer of wines recognizably South Tyrolean.

In the vineyards we have great respect for natural balances. We operate as organically as possible and intervene with the minimum of treatments. We make a very careful selection of the grapes to obtain wines of unique character and personality.

We have directed our energies for twenty years towards white wines, continuously experimenting for more successful results. Recently we have been concentrating on the vinification of full-bodied reds, visiting and exchanging information with producers in the famous red wine areas of the world. We are highly encouraged by our results.

As far as maturation is concerned we have been returning to aging in oak barrels, both for reds and whites, as well as experimenting with *barrique* aging. Our recent acquisition of the Hirschprunn estate, with 31 hectares/76.5 acres of vineyards marks the beginning of a new and very challenging phase in our development. Our aim is maximum quality — always.

Alois Lageder

AZ. VITIVIN ALOIS LAGEDER

CENTRAL EASTERN ITALY

by Maureen Ashley, M.W.

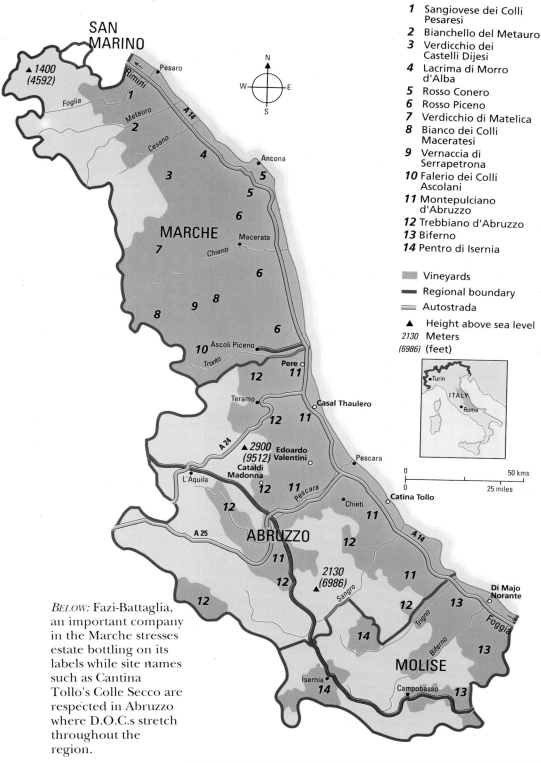

1 Sangiovese dei Colli Pesaresi
2 Bianchello del Metauro
3 Verdicchio dei Castelli Dijesi
4 Lacrima di Morro d'Alba
5 Rosso Conero
6 Rosso Piceno
7 Verdicchio di Matelica
8 Bianco dei Colli Maceratesi
9 Vernaccia di Serrapetrona
10 Falerio dei Colli Ascolani
11 Montepulciano d'Abruzzo
12 Trebbiano d'Abruzzo
13 Biferno
14 Pentro di Isernia

Vineyards
Regional boundary
Autostrada
▲ Height above sea level
2130 Meters
(6986) (feet)

BELOW: Fazi-Battaglia, an important company in the Marche stresses estate bottling on its labels while site names such as Cantina Tollo's Colle Secco are respected in Abruzzo where D.O.C.s stretch throughout the region.

The central east's regions of Marche, Abruzzo and Molise follow the Adriatic coast from just past Rimini to the spur that marks the beginning of Italy's 'heel'. Although the climate throughout is Mediterranean, conditions get steadily more torrid towards the South. It would be too hot for wine production there were it not for the hills, with their cool temperatures and occasional rain.

Although the Marche produces a number of good red wines, most notably Rosso Conero and Rosso Piceno, both from different blends of Sangiovese and Montepulciano grapes, the region's flagship is one white wine, Verdicchio dei Castelli di Jesi. The wine is made from the Verdicchio grape, which gives plenty of crisp, lemony acidity and a minerally tang. Its fame might have remained little more than local, had not the company Fazi-Battaglia come up with the marketing masterstroke of putting the wine in a distinctive, curvaceous, amphora-shaped bottle, which was rapidly dubbed "la Lollobrigida". At one time it seemed that the bottle was all the wine had to offer, but then Verdicchio started bouncing back, thanks to estates such as Fratelli Bucci and Zaccagnini in particular, Garofoli, Monte Schiavo and Umani Ronchi. Verdicchio, picked fully ripe, often from special vineyards or *crus*, can be a wine of an almost buttery richness.

Abruzzo is dominated by the red Montepulciano grape (unconnected with the Tuscan town of the same name). Montepulciano d'Abruzzo is a blackberry-like, fruit-packed, gutsy wine. The top selections of cooperatives such as Tollo's Colle Secco and Casal Thaulero's Orsetto Oro, or estates such as Barone Cornacchia, Illuminati, Camillo Montori and the remarkable Edoardo Valentini show this wine to full advantage. Surprisingly, there is also another version, Montepulciano d'Abruzzo Cerasuolo, that appears as a fresh, bouncy rosé. Cataldi Madonna has high repute in the area for Cerasuolo (which means cherry-colored), although most good Montepulciano producers make a good Cerasuolo too. White wine in the region comes from the Trebbiano grape but with few exceptions (notably Valentini, Montori) it is uninspiring.

Molise has less to offer; the region would be best ignored were it not for one estate, Di Majo Norante, making a striking range of wines, sold under the zonal name, Biferno, the estate's brand name, Ramitello, or as part of the series of *Nuovi Vini d'Antichi Vitigni* (New Wines from Ancient Varieties).

TUSCANY

by Rosemary George, M.W.

The winescape of Tuscany is dominated by Chianti. This is the wine that everyone knows. It is cheerful and unassuming, but on better acquaintance you begin to realize that it has unsuspected facets to its character.

Chianti is produced over a large part of Tuscany, with seven different sub-zones recognized in the D.O.C.G. regulations. Chianti Classico comes from the heart of the area, from the enchanting hills between Florence and Siena, dotted with medieval castles and Renaissance villas. This is where most of the best Chiantis are made, wines with length and complexity. There are several talented producers, amongst whom are Isole e Olena, Felsina Berardenga, Fontodi, Vignamaggio, Antinori, Castello di Ama, Castello di Volpaia, Badia a Coltibuono, Riecine and Montagliari.

The small area of Rufina also produces some long-lived wines, notably from Selvapiana, Frescobaldi and Villa di Vetrice, but most Chianti from the other areas, namely the Colli Fiorentini, Colli

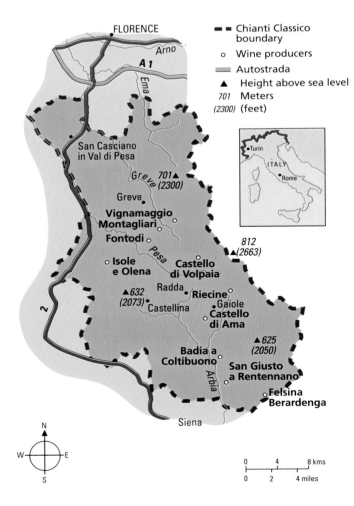

LEFT: View of the vineyards of Peppoli, formerly Villa Terciona, and one of Antinori's recent acquisitions in Chianti Classico.

Aretini, Colli Senesi, Colline Pisane and Montalbano, tends to be lighter, for earlier drinking.

Chianti has undergone an enormous transition in the last twenty, or even ten years. Its reputation had been sadly tarnished. The Sangiovese grape is the mainstay of Chianti and indeed of all the red wines of Tuscany. The D.O.C. regulations of 1967 allowed for as much as 30 percent of white grapes, in the making of the red wines of Chianti. The 1960s also saw the dismantling of the *mezzadria* or sharecropping system of landholding and agriculture, which had been a part of Tuscan life since the Middle Ages. This brought radical changes in land ownership and the abandon of the *cultura promiscua*, the growing of mixed crops which had provided the traditional framework of the countryside. Instead specialized vineyards were planted, often without thought and with the wrong grape varieties. The market became awash with bad Chianti, resulting in a crisis of confidence. Chianti lost many friends.

The thinking grower realized that something had

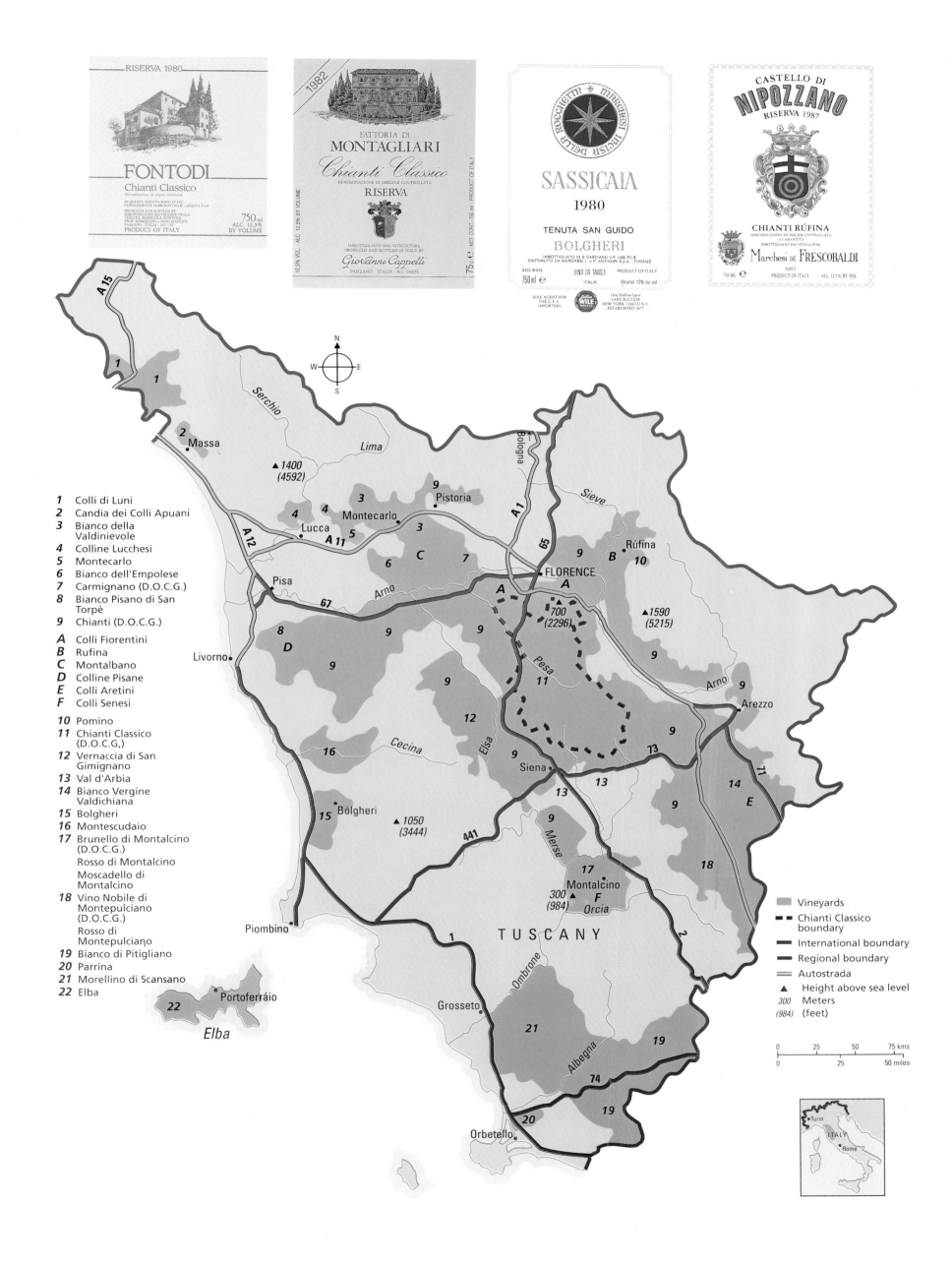

RISERVA 1980

FONTODI

Chianti Classico
Denominazione di origine controllata

DI QUESTA ANNATA SONO STATE
CONFEZIONATE 33.460 BOTTIGLIE - QUESTA È LA

PRODUCED AND BOTTLED BY
IMBOTTIGLIATO ALL'ORIGINE NELLA
TENUTA AGRICOLA FONTODI
PROP. DOMIZIANO E DINO MANETTI
PANZANO - ITALIA -1981 FI
PRODUCT OF ITALY

750 ml
ALC. 12,5%
BY VOLUME

FATTORIA DI
MONTAGLIARI
Chianti Classico
DENOMINAZIONE DI ORIGINE CONTROLLATA
RISERVA

IMBOTTIGLIATO DAL VITICOLTORE
PRODUCED AND BOTTLED IN ITALY BY
Giovanni Cappelli
PANZANO · ITALIA · R.I. 740/FI

1982

12,5% VOL. - ALC. 12,5% BY VOLUME

75 cl e · NET CONT. 750 ml · PRODUCT OF ITALY

SASSICAIA
1980
TENUTA SAN GUIDO
BOLGHERI

IMBOTTIGLIATO IN S. CASCIANO V.P. (302 FI) E
DISTRIBUITO DA MARCHESI L. e P. ANTINORI S.p.A. · FIRENZE
RED WINE   VINO DA TAVOLA   PRODUCT OF ITALY
750 ml   ITALIA   Alcohol 12% by vol.

SOLE AGENT FOR
THE U.S.A.
IMPORTERS

WILE

One Hollow Lane
LAKE SUCCESS
NEW YORK 11042 U.S.A
ESTABLISHED 1877

CASTELLO DI
NIPOZZANO
RISERVA 1987

CHIANTI RÚFINA
DENOMINAZIONE DI ORIGINE CONTROLLATA
E GARANTITA
IMBOTTIGLIATO DAI VITICOLTORI
Marchesi de' FRESCOBALDI
SIECI
750 ML e   PRODUCT OF ITALY   ALC. 12,5% BY VOL.

1 Colli di Luni
2 Candia dei Colli Apuani
3 Bianco della
  Valdinievole
4 Colline Lucchesi
5 Montecarlo
6 Bianco dell'Empolese
7 Carmignano (D.O.C.G.)
8 Bianco Pisano di San
  Torpè
9 Chianti (D.O.C.G.)

A Colli Fiorentini
B Rufina
C Montalbano
D Colline Pisane
E Colli Aretini
F Colli Senesi

10 Pomino
11 Chianti Classico
   (D.O.C.G,)
12 Vernaccia di San
   Gimignano
13 Val d'Arbia
14 Bianco Vergine
   Valdichiana
15 Bolgheri
16 Montescudaio
17 Brunello di Montalcino
   (D.O.C.G.)
   Rosso di Montalcino
   Moscadello di
   Montalcino
18 Vino Nobile di
   Montepulciano
   (D.O.C.G.)
   Rosso di
   Montepulciano
19 Bianco di Pitigliano
20 Parrina
21 Morellino di Scansano
22 Elba

Vineyards

Chianti Classico
boundary

International boundary

Regional boundary

Autostrada

▲ Height above sea level

300 Meters

(984) (feet)

to be done. The introduction of the D.O.C.G. regulations (stricter than the previous D.O.C. rules) in 1984 reduced the permitted percentage of white grapes, and certainly helped to eliminate some bad wines. It also gave producers a much needed boost of confidence. More exciting, however, is the wave of revolutionary winemaking outside the regulations that has swept through Tuscany in the last few years. The pace was initially set by Sassicaia from the Tenuta San Guido near Bolgheri, which was quickly followed by Antinori's Tignanello, a wine with a Tuscan flavor but designed for the international market, combining the Sangiovese with Cabernet Sauvignon. Its success surprised even Antinori, but many others have followed its example.

Over the last ten years Tuscany has seen the creation of an astonishing number of new wines. Most attention has been paid to Sangiovese, which is now recognized as a fine grape variety in its own right; varieties from outside Tuscany have also been planted. These changes in the vineyards have been accompanied by an enormous improvement in winemaking techniques, not least in the aging of the wine, with the increasing use of French *barriques* in preference to the traditional large *botti*. Few are the serious estates, particularly in Chianti Classico, that have neither Cabernet Sauvignon nor French *barriques*. These *vini da tavola* (they cannot be D.O.C. or D.O.C.G. as they conform to no regulations) sometimes called Supertuscans, are by no means all super. Some are over-oaked and over-priced to match, but the best show just what superb wines Tuscany can produce. Look for Brunesco di San Lorenzo, Cepparello, Coltasala, Fontalloro, Grosso Sanese, Il Sodaccio or Vinattieri Rosso, which are pure Sangiovese, and Balifico, Bruno di Rocca and Sammarco, which include some Cabernet Sauvignon. Even better, the quality of Chianti has improved in their wake.

As well as Chianti, Tuscany has three other D.O.C.Gs, Brunello di Montalcino, Vino Nobile di Montepulciano and Carmignano. Brunello di Montalcino comes from vineyards around the delightful hilltop town of Montalcino and is made only from the Sangiovese grape, locally called Brunello, which must be aged for a minimum of three years in wood. It is a wine of great stature and depth and capable of considerable longevity. Rosso di Montalcino is the parallel D.O.C.G., a lighter and younger version from the same grapes and vineyards. Biondi Santi was the leading producer, but has been superseded by others, such as Il Poggione, Altesino, Case Basse, Il Paradiso and Caparzo.

Vino Nobile di Montepulciano, a D.O.C.G. from vineyards around Montepulciano, and the Rosso di Montepulciano wines, are made from the same grape varieties as Chianti, and sometimes there is little to distinguish between the two. Avignonesi, Poliziano and Boscarelli are the best producers here. Carmignano is unique in that the regulations allow for the inclusion of a percentage of Cabernet Sauvignon, which was introduced to that part of Tuscany, not recently, but in the early eighteenth century. Tenuta di Capezzana is the leading estate and Fattoria di Ambra also makes excellent wines.

The tiny D.O.C. of Pomino, which is dominated by Frescobaldi, also allows for Cabernet Sauvignon, as well as Cabernet Franc, Merlot and Pinot Nero. Again these are no recent introductions, but date

from the last century. The white wine is equally full of character, with Pinot Bianco, Pinot Grigio and Chardonnay, as well as the ubiquitous Trebbiano. This is the mainstay of most of the white wines of Tuscany, such as Bianco di Pitigliano, Bianco Val d'Arbia, Bianco della Valdinievole, Bianco Pisano di San Torpè and Bianco Vergine della Valdichiana. Malvasia is the other common white grape, and has a little more flavor, but rarely a great deal, and therein lies the problem with most of the white wine of Tuscany. Galestro, which was born of the surplus of white wine in Chianti, allows for an injection of a little extra flavor, but still tends towards a rather neutral taste.

Vernaccia di San Gimignano, from vineyards around the town of San Gimignano, depends upon the unique Tuscan grape variety of Vernaccia rather than Trebbiano or Malvasia. This Vernaccia bears no relation to the Vernaccia grape grown elsewhere in Italy. It has a firm nutty taste and is occasionally aged in *barriques*. Teruzzi e Puthod, Falchini, Pietraserena, Fattoria di Cusona and Le Colonne

ABOVE: Vineyards of Caparzo which makes traditional Brunello as well as *barrique*-aged Chardonnay.

OPPOSITE PAGE: The wines of Fontodi benefit from the expertise of Franco Bernabei. Montagliari makes long-lasting Chianti Classico. Sassicaia is the pacesetter in the new wave of Tuscan winemaking. Castello de Nipozzano is the largest estate of Chianti Rufina.

BELOW: Labels from leading producers in Montalcino and Montepulciano.

The two principal wines are Morellino di Scansano and Bianco di Pitigliano, from hilltop towns dating back to the Etruscans. Morellino, yet another synonym for Sangiovese, is at its best in the hands of Erik Banti. Mantelassi and Le Pupille are good too. La Stellata is the best in Pitigliano. La Parrina near Orbitello is one of the smallest D.O.C.s of Tuscany, while Val di Cornia is the newest, and uses a mix of grape varieties grown in the hills behind Piombino. Even the island of Elba has its own styles. La Chiusa, makes palatable reds and whites from Sangiovese and Trebbiano, and Lupi Rocchi has a reputation for Moscato and Aleatico.

Variations of Vin Santo are to be found in other parts of Italy, but there is something quintessentially Tuscan about this wine. Made with dried grapes, it may be either sweet or dry. It is the wine that every peasant farmer makes for home consumption and to offer to family and friends. Outstanding Vin Santo is made by Isole e Olena, San Giusto a Rentannano, Montagliari, Avignonesi and Fattoria di Sassola, among others.

ABOVE: A Vernaccia di San Gimignano is one of a long list of Tuscan wines from Cecchi. Frescobaldi is virtually the sole producer of the tiny D.O.C. of Pomino. Vin Santo labels from two of the larger producers of this most individual wine. As yet no D.O.C. regulations control its production in Chianti so that it is a *vino da tavola.*

RIGHT: Cecchi, large Tuscan merchants, have recently acquired vineyards in San Gimignano. Their label is pictured above.

are good producers. Montecarlo, from the hills east of Lucca, includes Roussanne, Sémillon, Sauvignon, Pinot Grigio and Pinot Bianco, which were brought to the area in the middle of the last century. The red is less exciting, while the nearby Colline Lucchesi makes more successful red than white.

Candia dei Colli Apuani is a little-known wine in a remote corner of Tuscany. The town of Montescudaio, near the Colline Pisane, gives its name to both a red and a white wine. The Maremma covers the coastal lowlands and the wild hills behind Grosseto.

GROWER'S VIEW

Work in the vineyard is the key to quality in Tuscany. In the last ten years many new grape varieties, such as Cabernet Sauvignon and Chardonnay, have been planted. These need to be reconsidered. We should not diversify so much, but concentrate on Sangiovese, which is the traditional grape variety that gives us our individuality.

Sangiovese is a good variety, but it is tempermental like Pinot Noir. However, we must take into account not just the grape variety, but also the different soils in the vineyards of Chianti. Local conditions, what the French call *terroir*, must be considered, for Sangiovese is sensitive to different growing conditions. We should plant vines that are selected locally, in the right soil, and provide the right growing conditions, so that we obtain the right yields. We need to improve our vineyards so that our best wine represents a much higher proportion of our total production. At the moment it is often only as little as 10 percent. Working in this way, I have started to recognize a particular Isole e Olena style in my wines.

If we get the vineyards right, what happens in the winery takes second place. We must work properly, respecting our raw material. Too many people still use too many old *botti* which remove the fruit from the wine. Much better are 500 liter/132 U.S. gallon barrels, and also some *barriques*. My Chianti *normale* spends less than a year in wood, while Cepparello, a pure Sangiovese, which is my *riserva*, (except that the law does not allow me to call it that) is aged for at least twelve months in oak or longer, for richer vintages. I use more *barriques* if the wine is heavier.

Paolo de Marche

ISOLE E OLENA

CENTRAL ITALY

by Maureen Ashley, M.W.

Politically, the center of Italy is Rome. The surrounding region, Latium, is geographically central as well, lying halfway down the Mediterranean coastline. Although a good number of wines are produced in this area, only one wine really matters: Frascati.

Frascati comes from the Castelli Romani, a large, semi-circular ridge of hills overlooking the city to its southeast, and made from Trebbiano and Malvasia grapes in any proportions. With more Trebbiano it is crisper, steelier and nuttier, as exemplified by Fontana Candida; with more Malvasia, as made by Colli di Catone, it is softer and fatter with flavors of buttermilk and apricots. Casale Marchese, Conte Zandotti, Mastrofini and Villa Simone are among other good estates.

Other wines from the Castelli Romani, Marino, for example, are made from the same grapes as Frascati, are produced in the same way and quite predictably taste very similar. Any differences in taste would only be discernible to a winemaker of the region.

Even more central than Latium is the region of Umbria. The region is landlocked between the Mediterranean and the Adriatic and situated midway between the Alps and the instep of Italy. Orvieto was the wine that first put Umbria on the viticultural map. Orvieto, a white wine, is made from a blend that depends on Trebbiano for bulk and Grechetto for character.

Once usually made with some sweetness (sweeter examples of Orvieto are labeled *amabile*), the wine is now more commonly dry (*secco*) and, at its best, can be an intriguing creamy mix of walnut, greengage and pear flavors. Although a number of estates (Barberani, Decugnano dei Barbi, Palazzone and others) are producing fine examples of the wine, Bigi's *cru* Torricella is the archetype.

Umbria also houses the small area of Torgiano, near Perugia, a zone dominated by the family-owned company Lungarotti, which single-handedly turned it into one of Italy's earliest pace-setting areas. Red Rubesco (Lungarotti's trademark) Riserva *cru* Monticchio and San Giorgio (a "table wine" from a Sangiovese-Cabernet mix) top a large range of wines.

For anyone attracted by the unusual, Umbria's red Sagrantino di Montefalco (made from the Sagrantino grape) is a big, powerful wine, but production is limited.

1 Colli di Luni
2 Candia dei Colli Apuani
3 Bianco della Valdinievole
4 Colline Lucchesi
5 Montecarlo
6 Bianco dell'Empolese
7 Carmignano (D.O.C.G.)
8 Bianco Pisano di San Torpe

9 Chianti (D.O.C.G.)
10 Pomino
11 Chianti Classico
12 Vernaccia di San Gimignano
13 Val d'Arbia
14 Bianco Vergine Valdichiana
15 Bolgheri
16 Montescudaio
17 Brunello di Montalcino (D.O.C.G.)
   Rosso di Montalcino
   Moscadello di Montalcino
18 Vino Nobile di Montepulciano (D.O.C.G.)
   Rosso di Montepulciano
19 Bianco di Pitigliano
20 Parrina
21 Morellino di Scansano
22 Colli Altotiberini
23 Colli del Trasimeno
24 Colli Perugini
25 Torgiano (D.O.C.G.)
26 Montefalco
27 Colli Martani

28 Orvieto
29 Est! Est! Est! di Montefiascone
30 Aleatico di Gradoli
31 Cerveteri
32 Bianco Capena
33 Frascati
34 Colli Albani
35 Velletri
36 Zagarolo
37 Marino
38 Montecompatri-Colonna
39 Colli Lanuvini
40 Aprilia
41 Cori
42 Cesanese di Olevano Romano
43 Cesanese del Piglio
44 Cesanese di Affile
45 Elba

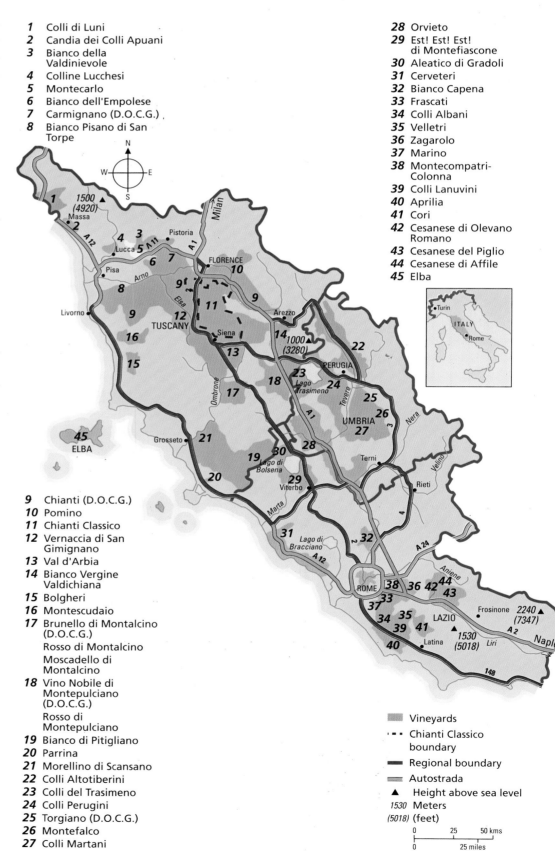

Vineyards

- - - Chianti Classico boundary

Regional boundary

Autostrada

▲ Height above sea level

1530 Meters

(5018) (feet)

0   25   50 kms

0   25 miles

143

RIGHT: Dr. Lungarotti proudly displays one of his fine reserve wines in his Rubesco cellars in Umbria.

BELOW: Terms referring to aging (*riserva*), vineyard heartlands (*classico*), additional alcohol (*superiore*) or sweetness (*amabile, secco*) often adorn central Italian labels such as these from Lungarotti, Fontana Candida, Colli de Catone and Antinori.

GROWER'S VIEW

Frascati has been well known since the time of the Roman Empire, when Marcus Porcius Cato, a fanatical grower of vines, advised everyone to plant vines. Since then some things have changed appreciably, although not the nature of the land, which is well suited to vine cultivation, being mainly hilly and of volcanic origin, rich in potassium and with a good quantity of phosphorus, calcium, magnesium and iron. In addition, winter rains and an almost complete absence of water for the rest of the year give an excellent climatic base for wine production.

Several grape varieties, such as Malvasia del Lazio and Greco, which until a few years ago had almost disappeared from Frascati vineyards, because of their unfashionably low yield despite their unsurpassable quality, are today gradually returning to vogue. It was, however, just the use of Malvasia del Lazio on which I first based my philosophy of high quality many years ago, and which remains the central tenet of winemaking at Colli di Catone.

The fundamental and most important thing for me has always been not to lose touch with tradition completely. This made me turn aside from new technologies whose only merit seemed to be in depersonalizing wines, rendering them all more or less identical. So, from this starting point I continue to work towards the right balance between technology and tradition and try to produce ever better wines, some of them new like Colle Gaio and Casal Pilozzi, which are having an enormous success.

Antonio Pulcini
COLLI DI CATONE

SOUTHERN ITALY AND THE ISLANDS

by Maureen Ashley, M.W.

The north has made great strides forward in wine-making techniques; the south is some way behind, although it is catching up fast. Italian wines of real distinction are less numerous in the south than in the north and, generally, are the results of the efforts of individual winemakers rather than of topography. Even so, topography is vital in the south. It is the cooler upland and mountain terrain that makes serious winemaking possible in this sun-baked part of the Mediterranean.

The South

On the western side is Campania, centered around Naples. In the north is the home of Falernum, an ancient wine of great renown. It has recently been brought back to life as Falerno by the Villa Matilde estate, employing equal respect for historical authenticity and modern winemaking know-how. The white is from the Falanghina variety, the red from Aglianico and Piedirosso, three southern grapes of indisputable pedigree, which are used in Campania to great effect. Piedirosso shows its class even more clearly in the same estate's reincarnation of Caecubum (Cecubo), another wine that once kept the ancient world enthralled.

Other producers taking an interest in realizing the potential of local varieties include Mustilli and Vinicola Ocone. Otherwise Campania is dominated by the company Mastroberardino, based inland near Avellino, in the center of the region. It practically had a monopoly on production of the wines of the area: smoky, minerally, white Greco di Tufo (from Greco); intriguing, floral, vegetal, white Fiano di Avellino (from Fiano); and slow-maturing, coffee and damson-like, red Taurasi (from Aglianico), but now a number of small growers, notably of Fiano di Avellino, are trying their luck at producing wine themselves, with increasing success.

Calabria forms the toe of Italy. Although vineyards are scattered widely throughout, there is only one wine, Cirò, that is seen much outside the region. This is primarily due to the vitality of one company, Librandi. Cirò comes in red, white and rosé versions. All three are big, powerful wines.

Basilicata, the instep, also tends to be a one-wine region: Aglianico del Vulture, from the Aglianico grape grown high on the cool, east-facing slopes of the volcanic Mount Vulture. It is a full red that is

tough when young but steadily softens to an impressively spicy, earthy, smoky and chunky wine, expressed most fully by Fratelli d'Angelo and Paternoster.

In Puglia, the heel of Italy, there is a wealth of wine names. The wines may be divided essentially into four groups. There are reds from the north (for example, San Severo), made with Montepulciano and Uva di Troia; reds from the center (such as Castel del Monte), made mainly from Uva di Troia; reds from the south, made with Puglia's most promising grape, Negroamaro (Salice Salentino, Copertino, Brindisi) or from Primitivo (Primitivo di Manduria); and whites, notably the light, fresh Locorotondo, from Verdeca. It is rare to find more than one producer per wine zone exploiting its potential to the full.

Sicily

Sicily is the largest island in the Mediterranean and it is probably the most misunderstood, for Sicily is so much more than Mafia and Marsala. Nevertheless, both do exist, both originate from the west of the island and some would say both are equally damaging to Sicily's reputation. For years Marsala meant little more than some thick, sweet, strangely-flavored, alcoholic wine whose place was in the kitchen. It was left to one man, Marco De Bartoli, to fight a hard, lonely battle to keep supplies of true,

ABOVE: In the south, as here at Copertino in Puglia, vines are as much a part of the countryside as other Mediterranean plants such as prickly pears or olives. Plots are still sometimes shared in mixed cultivation, echoing earlier ages.

145

RIGHT: As the urge to experiment overtakes the south, increasing numbers of new style wines are appearing using international grape varieties such as Chardonnay, mastered by Torrebianco. New vinification and aging techniques are used by Mirafiore to make their blush wine and Mastroberardino to produce the stylish Radici. As a result old favorites like Lacryma Christi risk being overlooked.

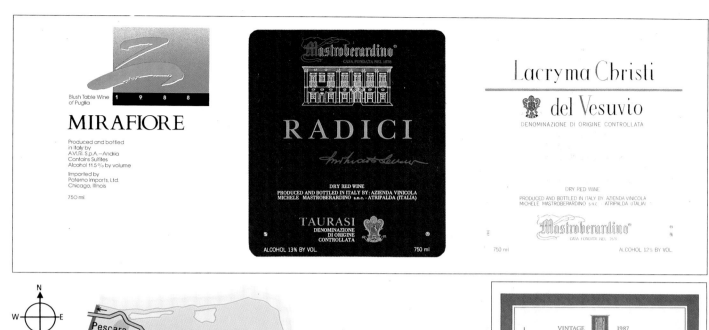

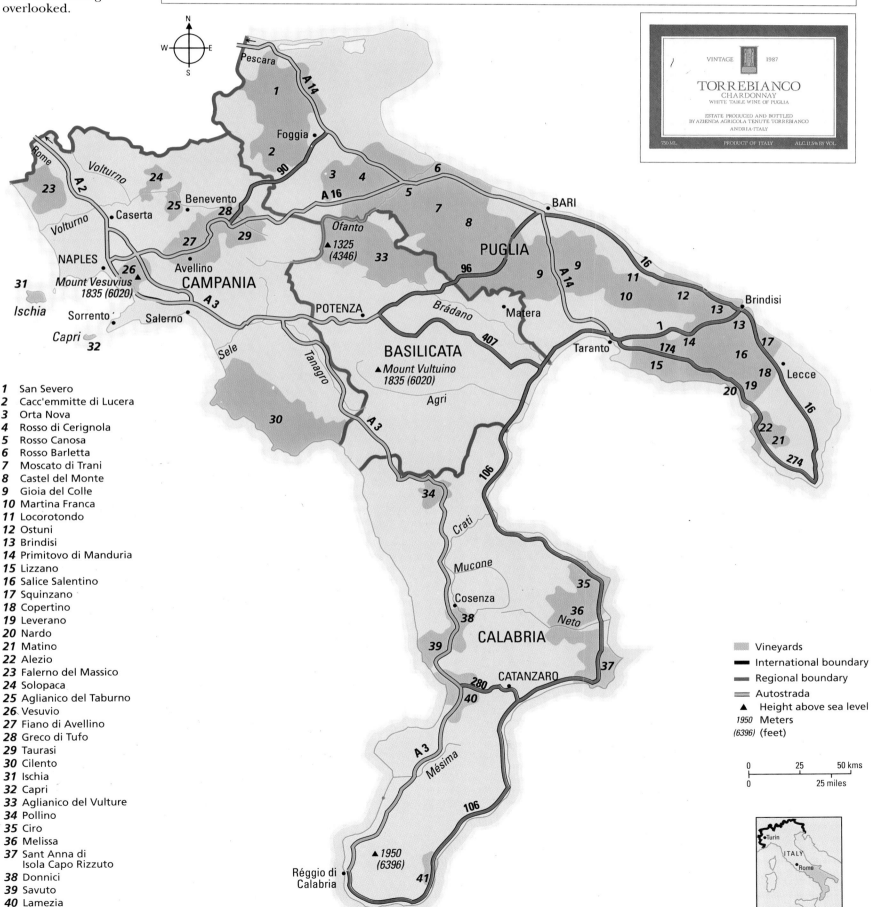

1   San Severo
2   Cacc'emmitte di Lucera
3   Orta Nova
4   Rosso di Cerignola
5   Rosso Canosa
6   Rosso Barletta
7   Moscato di Trani
8   Castel del Monte
9   Gioia del Colle
10 Martina Franca
11 Locorotondo
12 Ostuni
13 Brindisi
14 Primitovo di Manduria
15 Lizzano
16 Salice Salentino
17 Squinzano
18 Copertino
19 Leverano
20 Nardo
21 Matino
22 Alezio
23 Falerno del Massico
24 Solopaca
25 Aglianico del Taburno
26 Vesuvio
27 Fiano di Avellino
28 Greco di Tufo
29 Taurasi
30 Cilento
31 Ischia
32 Capri
33 Aglianico del Vulture
34 Pollino
35 Ciro
36 Melissa
37 Sant Anna di
     Isola Capo Rizzuto
38 Donnici
39 Savuto
40 Lamezia
41 Greco di Bianco

Vineyards
International boundary
Regional boundary
Autostrada
▲ Height above sea level
1950 Meters
(6396) (feet)

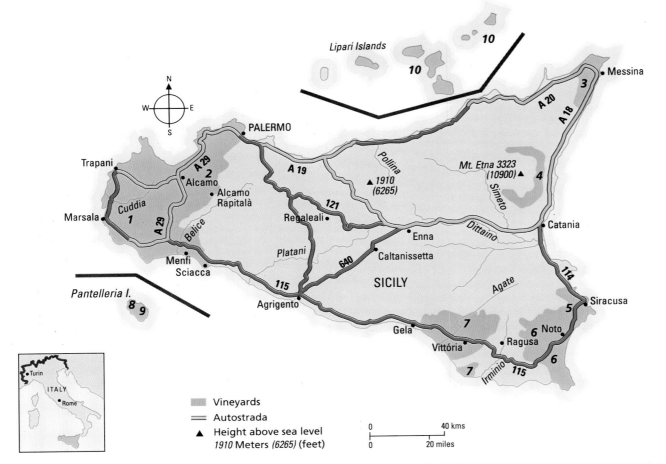

1 Marsala
2 Alcamo
3 Faro
4 Etna
5 Moscato di Siracusa
6 Moscato di Noto
7 Cerasuolo di Vittoria
8 Moscato di Pantelleria
9 Passito di Pantelleria
10 Malvasia delle Lipari

Vineyards
Autostrada
▲ Height above sea level
1910 Meters (6265) (feet)

0   40 kms
0   20 miles

BELOW: Labels representing a geographical cross-section of Sicilian wines: the sweet orange-amber Malvasia from the islands of Lipari; the distinguished red wine of Regaleali, a leading innovative estate of central Sicily; Colomba Platino, the premium white of Corvo from near Palermo; and Cerasuolo di Vittoria, the unusual cherry-red wine of the southeast.

high-quality Marsala available. His greatest weapon was Vecchio Samperi, a dry, naturally strong, long-aged, fine, nutty wine produced from the best grapes in the area, made to show what Marsala was like before fortification by the addition of grape brandy became compulsory and sweetening commonplace.

Marsala comes in a number of styles and there is a plethora of explanatory terms on the label. *Oro* (gold), *Ambra* (amber) and *Rubino* (ruby) indicate color. *Fine* (one year), *Superiore* (two years) and *Vergine* (five years) are some of those indicating aging. Dryness or sweetness (*secco, semi-secco, dolce*) may also be shown, apart from Marsala Vergine which is always dry. In essence, though, it is made by adding a small amount of grape brandy and a variable amount of *cotto* (grape must reduced by heating to a thick, sweet syrup) or other approved sweetening agent (not sugar) to a normally-made wine and then aging in large barrels until the various elements are well amalgamated. Real Marsala can be a very high quality fortified wine, in the same league as the finest Sherry or Madeira. There is not all that much made, but signs are that the more dynamic companies such as Curatolo and Florio are putting a little more weight behind these top wines. Marsala flavored with egg or anything more exotic no longer bears the name and is called Cremovo.

Sicily's satellite islands, Pantelleria and the Aeolian archipelago, produce mainly traditional *passito* wines, sweet wines made from grapes laid out in the sun after picking to dry out and concentrate their flavors. Those from Pantelleria (most notably from De Bartoli) are made from the Moscato grape, those from the Aeolian (or Lipari) islands from Malvasia (led by Hauner).

Otherwise Sicily is alive with development and in-

BELOW: Over two centuries ago the British created Marsala as we know it today. Old bottles on display in Florio's showroom recall leading names.

GROWER'S VIEW

To make a wine that pleases eye, nose and mouth, and at the same time evokes a plethora of sensations, the grape itself must have a particular typical aromatic note to its taste supported by a certain sapidity. That we achieve this is due without doubt to our calcareous, gravelly soils of marl or clay and to microclimates characterized by sharp temperature shifts from day to night and summer to winter, as well as lands facing mainly north for white grapes and south for reds.

Critical factors for our wines include our very special situation; clones; planting density; age of vineyard; cultivation methods; and harvesting after careful monitoring of the grapes' taste and several chemical parameters. Just as important are vinification and aging. I believe that in the cellar you can achieve a "lesser" product from a "greater" but never a "greater" from a "lesser". Therefore our cellar techniques are aimed at obtaining the best of what a grape has overall while emphasizing a few of its characteristics.

All this can be achieved by thoughtful use of stainless steel and various woods, of indigenous yeasts chosen to maintain typicality, of techniques such as skin contact to enhance some aspects in the wine, and a critical consideration of ancient vinification practices linked to rediscovering extinct indigenous vines. In conclusion you can love the cellar only after loving the land.

Maurizio Micciche'

TERRE DI GINESTRA

---

novation, resulting in some quite delightful wines. Whites are in the forefront, based usually on the native Catarratto or more aromatic Inzolia grapes. Wine names tend to be producers' brand names: Terre di Ginestra, Corvo, Regaleali, Rapitalà, Libecchio, Cellaro, Settesoli, Donnafugata and so on. Reds, from Nero d'Avola, Nerello Mascalese, Frappato and Perricone, are catching up fast and the same brand names apply, with the exception of the rich, vibrant Cerasuolo di Vittoria, from an area around Vittoria in Sicily's southeast and best handled by the estate C.O.S. Sicily also produces a number of refreshingly fruity rosés, the Nerello Mascalese variety being ideally suited to this task.

Sardinia

Sardinia is farther from mainland Italy than Sicily and has retained its individuality of attitude and culture. Reminders of its Spanish-owned past abound. Wines fall broadly into two types: the traditional (less often seen these days) hefty, alcoholic and often sweetish; and modern, light, uncomplicated, wines for easy drinking. The lightest of reds are made from Monica, the fuller and somewhat more serious ones from Cannonau (the local name for Grenache, and the island's most esteemed red variety). Everyday white comes from Nuragus; floral, minerally, vegetal white from Torbato, produced only by the large company Sella & Mosca, and richer, more buttery white from Vermentino, which is at its best in the Gallura area of the Northeast and can be most impressive (Tenute Capichera, for example). Most of the production is handled by cooperatives; Dolianova is far and away the most progressive.

BELOW: The Nuragus di Caliari is the principal everyday drinking wine of Sardinia. Its mass-produced nature perhaps is attested by the fact that it has the highest consented yield of any Italian D.O.C.

Vineyards

Four D.O.C's.
Cannonau di Sardegna
Moscato di Sardegna
Monica di Sardegna
Vermentino di Sardegna
cover the whole island

▲ Height above sea level
1235 Meters *(4051)* (feet)

D.O.C. Vermentino di Gallura
D.O.C. Moscato di Sorso-Sennori
D.O.C. Malvasia di Bosa
D.O.C. Vernaccia di Oristano
D.O.C. Campidano di Terralba
D.O.C. Mandrolisai
D.O.C. Arborea
D.O.C. Naragus di Cagliari
D.O.C. Carignano del Sulcis
D.O.C. Girò di Cagliari
D.O.C. Malvasia di Cagliari
D.O.C. Monica di Cagliari
D.O.C. Moscato di Cagliari
D.O.C. Nasco di Cagliari

Spirits

To many Italians the only spirit worthy of mention is malt whisky. Fine brandies are produced in Italy and so are spirit-based *amari* (bitters). The archetypal *amaro*, flavored with herbs and spices, is Averna, from Sicily, but there is also Cynar (artichoke), the medicinal Fernet Branca, Unicum, Braulio (Alpine herbs) and China Martini (quinine bark).

The most important spirit is *grappa*, made by distilling the residues from winemaking or lees. Production of high-quality, *grappa* is a serious business. The sooner the residues reach the distillery the better the quality purity and flavor of the *grappa*. If lees start to referment, unwanted by-products are produced. Finer *grappa* is also made from lees which are gently pressed leaving maximum flavor in the mix. Some *grappas* are aged in oak, others remain "white". There is great interest in single-varietal *grappa*, particularly among the more aromatic varieties (notably Moscato).

Grappa production is concentrated in the north. Nonino is the more revered producer. A number of Tuscan estates produce small quantities of *grappa*, but the northern conditions are better for its production. However, Giovanni La Fauci from Sicily makes *grappa* of a quality to rival the best of the north.

SPAIN

by Richard Mayson

Spain strikes you with its size. Separated from the bulk of Europe by the Pyrenees, it behaves more like a self-contained continent than a country. A number of different peoples, from the Celts to the Moors, chose to settle in this western European *cul-de-sac*. Great *cordilleras* or mountain ranges split the Iberian land mass into distinct natural regions. Cool, green Galicia and the Basque country in the north, each with its own language and culture, seem to have little in common with arid Castile or Mediterranean Andalusia in the south.

These regional differences are embodied in the wines. Galicia has delicate, dry whites; Catalonia produces sparkling wines; the reds from Rioja and the Duero are rich and oak-aged. Finally, there are aperitif and dessert wines from Andalusia.

Spain lays claim to more land under vine than any other country in the world. At the center of the Iberian peninsula there is a vast expanse of parched earth covered by nearly 1 million hectares/2.5 million acres of vineyard — a fifth of the total area of the country. But production figures belie these dimensions. With an average annual harvest of between 30 and 35 million hectoliters/792.5 and 924.6 million U.S. gallons, Spain ranks fourth in the world wine production league behind Italy, France and the old Soviet Union, or third in the absence of the U.S.S.R.

On the whole, vineyard yields are depressingly low. With an average altitude of 650 meters/2,130 feet, Spain is the second highest country in Europe. Vines have to be widely spaced to survive the climatic extremes. The soil is frequently shallow and infertile and vineyards are split among peasant smallholders with little or no technical expertise. Compared to France, where yields average 60 hectoliters per hectare/3.5 tons per acre, and Germany, where many growers top 100 hectoliters per hectare/5.8 tons per acre, Spain produces a paltry average of 23 hectoliters per hectare/1.4 tons per acre from her mesh of scrubby vines.

The Spanish claim to have 600 different grape varieties, though just twenty take up 80 percent of the country's massive vineyard. Understandably, farmers looking to maximize the return on their land favor the grapes that are best adapted to the climate. The white Airén is the most popular. This hardy vine is the world's most planted variety, all because of that blanket of vineyard covering central Spain. Garnacha Tinta, a grape that flourishes in

ABOVE: Parched vineyards, like these in Alto Turia northwest of Valencia, yield only very small amounts of wine.

arid, windy conditions, comes in second. Neither variety is highly regarded for quality but, like the mules that still trudge through the fields, they are old faithfuls, trusted by idle growers.

But Spain is waking up. In certain parts of the country there is now an encouraging move to replace poor quality vines with grapes that produce better wines. The native Tempranillo is the most fashionable and it crops up throughout Spain masquerading under various local names. But with a lack of indigenous quality, varieties like Cabernet Sauvignon and Chardonnay are straying across the border from France.

With improvements in the vineyard there is a revolution occurring in the winery. Modern winemaking methods have been slow to reach Spain where "tradition" has been used as an excuse for poor standards. Until recently, few producers had either the finance or the incentive to change. But since the death of General Franco in 1975 and the restoration of the monarchy, the growth of a consuming middle class has created a seemingly insatiable new market for quality wine. An investment program begun in the early 1980s has been helped

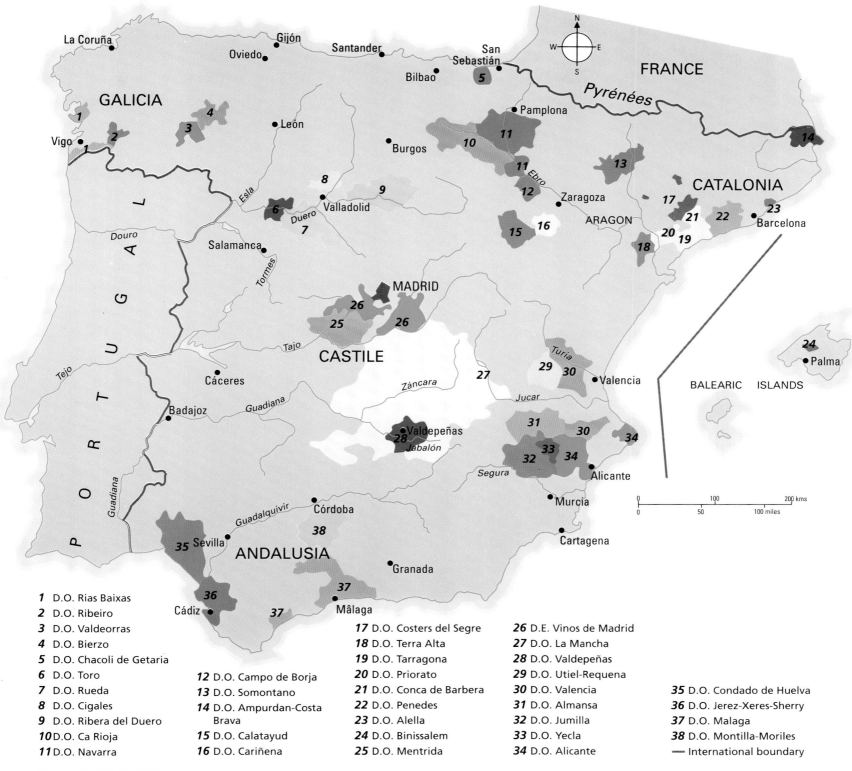

1 D.O. Rias Baixas
2 D.O. Ribeiro
3 D.O. Valdeorras
4 D.O. Bierzo
5 D.O. Chacoli de Getaria
6 D.O. Toro
7 D.O. Rueda
8 D.O. Cigales
9 D.O. Ribera del Duero
10 D.O. Ca Rioja
11 D.O. Navarra

12 D.O. Campo de Borja
13 D.O. Somontano
14 D.O. Ampurdan-Costa Brava
15 D.O. Calatayud
16 D.O. Cariñena

17 D.O. Costers del Segre
18 D.O. Terra Alta
19 D.O. Tarragona
20 D.O. Priorato
21 D.O. Conca de Barbera
22 D.O. Penedes
23 D.O. Alella
24 D.O. Binissalem
25 D.O. Mentrida

26 D.E. Vinos de Madrid
27 D.O. La Mancha
28 D.O. Valdepeñas
29 D.O. Utiel-Requena
30 D.O. Valencia
31 D.O. Almansa
32 D.O. Jumilla
33 D.O. Yecla
34 D.O. Alicante

35 D.O. Condado de Huelva
36 D.O. Jerez-Xeres-Sherry
37 D.O. Malaga
38 D.O. Montilla-Moriles
—— International boundary

further by Spain's entry into the European Community in 1986.

It is no coincidence that Spanish wine laws correspond closely to those worked out by the French. There are four tiers to the pyramid. *Vino de mesa* (table wine) covers all wine made from unclassified vineyards, most of which is drunk by thirsty locals or sent for compulsory distillation in an effort to prevent Europe's wine lake overflowing. Just above the basic (but only just), *Vino de la tierra* covers wine from a specific but usually large region provided that the growers obey certain local laws. This category purports to be the equivalent of the French *vin de pays* but few wines are of an exportable standard. The mainstay of Spanish quality control is the *Denominación de Origen* (D.O.). This is supposedly equal to the French *Appellation Contrôlée* though, as they proliferate, the significance of the D.O. is debased. (There are currently thirty-nine D.O.s in Spain.) As if to rectify this, the Spanish authorities have recently introduced a new category: *Denominación de Origen Calificada* (D.O.Ca). So far, only Rioja has made the grade.

Galicia

Spain's northern fringe defies the country's traditional travel poster image. Galicia has lush green fields, dairy cattle and sturdy granite farmhouses. Cool winds blowing off the Atlantic and the Bay of Biscay make this a very wet part of Europe. The rocky, deeply indented coastline around Cape Finisterre looks more like southwest Ireland instead of Spain.

Galicia is geographically and culturally closer to Portugal than Madrid. The locals speak *Gallego*, a variety of Portuguese. The wines show strong similarities to those of Portugal. Vines are widely planted, many of them trained over pergolas as in Vinho Verde country. Albariño and Loureiro are the grapes that have recently shot to stardom in one of the newest D.O. regions, Rias Baixas. Both make fragrant, delicate, dry white wines. The D.O.s of Valdeorras and Ribeiro tend to produce stronger, coarser wines, though progress is being made with grapes like Treixadura for white wines and Mencia for reds.

LEFT: Galicia's Albariño grape (for left and center) has a cult following in fashionable restaurants all over Spain. Ribeiro produces delicate white wines from a blend of Treixadura, Loureiro and Torrontes grapes.

Navarra and Aragón

Navarra, sloping gently up from the Ebro River to the foothills of the Pyrenees, lives in the shadow of its neighbor, Rioja. It has been trying to match Rioja with soft, vanilla-flavored reds but most wines suffer from a high proportion of rather brutish Garnacha. Other grapes, like Tempranillo and Cabernet Sauvignon, are now creeping into the region's vineyards and *bodegas* like Ochoa and Chivite are busy carving a new identity for D.O. Navarra's red wines. Most of Navarra's effort goes into fresh, fruity rosé for which Garnacha is well suited.

Aragón, a little closer to the furnace at the center of Spain, tends to make coarse reds, mainly from overripe Garnacha grapes. But there does seem to be room for improvement. Of the four D.O.s in the province, Somontano in the cooler hills southwest of Huesca is currently showing the most promise. Foreign grape varieties are creeping in and *bodegas* like Covisa and Lalanne are making the most of Chardonnay, Gewürztraminer and Cabernet.

Rioja

The Cantabrian Cordillera, a westerly spur of the Pyrenees, acts as a climatic shield for inland Spain. The effect of the mountains is most evident if you take the motorway from Bilbao to Haro, the wine capital of Rioja. Clouds piling up over the *sierras* give way to bright sunshine as you descend into the Ebro valley on the southern side.

This is ideal winemaking country. Gentle south- and west-facing slopes and long, warm summers help the grapes to ripen slowly and evenly. The French recognized this in the late nineteenth century. When Bordeaux was suffering from shortages caused by the phylloxera epidemic, winemakers journeyed across the border to Rioja. They refined production techniques and introduced the 225 liter/59.4 U.S. gallon oak cask or *barrique* (*barrica* in Spain) for aging wines.

Rioja held the upper hand over all other Spanish wine regions for nearly a century. Little went for

BELOW: The castle at Olite, formerly the seat of the kings of Navarra, is pictured on Ochoa's labels. Vinicola Navarra, founded in the nineteenth century, is now one of the largest producers in the region.

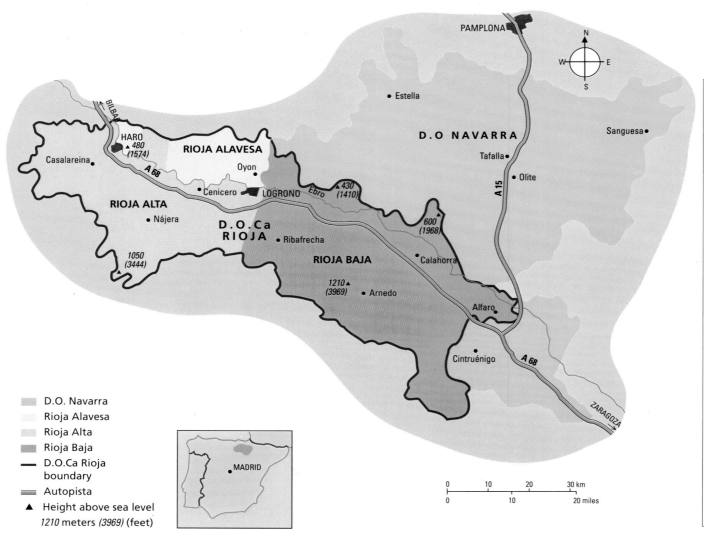

D.O. Navarra
Rioja Alavesa
Rioja Alta
Rioja Baja
D.O.Ca Rioja boundary
Autopista
▲ Height above sea level
1210 meters *(3969)* (feet)

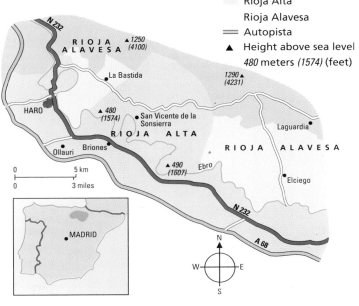

ABOVE: Rioja's finest oak-aged red wines become smooth and silky with age. Lopez de Heredia, La Rioja Alta and Marqués de Murrieta make classic *gran reservas.* C.V.N.E. produces one of Rioja's best oak-aged whites.

export but, to Spaniards dining out in good restaurants, Rioja had the reputation of Bordeaux and Burgundy rolled into one. The region was discovered by the outside world in the mid-1970s, and since then Rioja has become a household name.

Rioja divides into three sub-regions. Rioja Alta and Alavesa in the cooler upper reaches of the Ebro valley are planted predominantly with Tempranillo. Further south and east, in the hotter Mediterranean country downstream from the city of Logroño, Rioja Baja grows Garnacha. Most Riojas are blended from all three districts, Garnacha adding flesh to the more delicate and sometimes stern Tempranillo. But the key to a really fine Rioja is its ability to develop with age. All except the plainest and most inexpensive wines spend time in *barricas* made from American oak. Riojas labeled *crianza* spend a minimum of six months in *barrica, reservas* spend a year and *gran reservas,* wines from the best vintages, are left in cask for at least two years before bottling. The wine softens as it ages, taking on the round vanilla character that is the hallmark of high-quality Rioja.

Outside Galicia (see page 150), Rioja has one of the most complex systems of land holding in Spain. Some 17,000 growers farming 90,000 vineyard plots sell their grapes to some fifty wineries or *bodegas.* Not all of them make wine to the same standard but most have been forced to raise prices in recent years as growers demand more for their grapes. *Bodegas* La Rioja Alta, Riojanas, C.V.N.E., Marqués de Murrieta and Lopez de Heredia are among the best and most traditional, making wines that develop well. Marqués de Cáceres, Berberana and Campo Viejo are larger modern producers making some good, ripe-flavored reds, though their wines tend to be lighter and mature earlier. Martinez Bujanda, a small family-owned concern at Oyon, also make fragrant, deliciously oaky red wines in the lighter modern idiom. Because of the fragmented pattern of vineyard plots, there are few single-estate wines but Remelluri and Contino are worth seeking out for individuality and quality.

Most *bodegas* make smaller amounts of wine from the Viura grape. On its own this popular but productive grape tends to be rather bland. However, blended with a proportion of Malvasia, white Rioja can taste round and peachy. A touch of oak adds more character. C.V.N.E. and Murrieta are now almost alone with their rich, buttery cask – aged whites.

GROWER'S VIEW

At Remélluri we are convinced that the quality of our wines depends exclusively on the quality of the fruit that we obtain from our vines. Our main objective is to control yields and so improve the wine.

Our vineyards at La Bastida are some of the highest in the region. We therefore harvest late so that the tannins are fully ripe and levels of acidity are balanced by the natural sugars that ferment to alcohol. The wine then becomes smooth and silky with age; essential, in my opinion, for a *Reserva* Rioja.

The *bodega* is close to the vineyard. Regular deliveries of grapes reduce the time between picking and the start of fermentation, so keeping oxidation to a minimum. Once the grapes have been crushed and the juice is in the vat we take

the greatest care to preserve the primary character of Tempranillo, the grape that is the backbone of our wine.

While the wine is in the *bodega* we keep treatments to a minimum. We reject the idea of adjusting our wine with additives as we think that it is fundamental to keep the balance produced in the vineyard by the fruit itself. The only treatments that take place are regular rackings and a final clarification with egg white. In this way we manage to produce a wine reflecting the vineyard site: a single-vineyard Rioja.

Telmo Rodriguez Hernandorena
RÉMELLURI

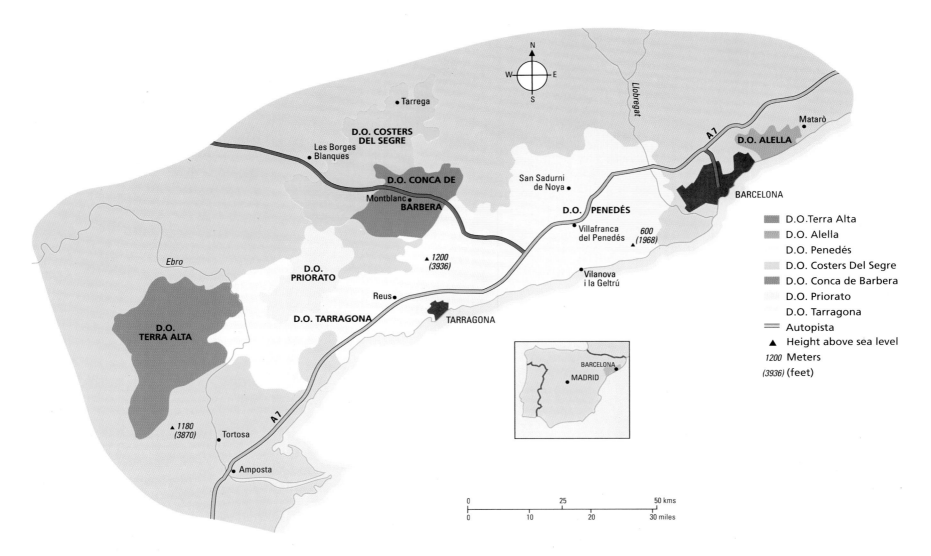

Map labels:
- N / W E / S (compass)
- Tarrega
- Llobregat
- D.O. COSTERS DEL SEGRE
- Les Borges Blanques
- Mataró
- A7
- D.O. ALELLA
- D.O. CONCA DE
- BARBERA
- Montblanc
- BARCELONA
- San Sadurni de Noya
- D.O. PENEDÉS
- Villafranca del Penedés
- 600 (1968)
- ▲ 1200 (3936)
- Ebro
- D.O. PRIORATO
- Vilanova i la Geltrú
- Reus
- D.O. TARRAGONA
- TARRAGONA
- D.O. TERRA ALTA
- ▲ 1180 (3870)
- Tortosa
- A7
- Amposta
- BARCELONA
- MADRID

Legend:
- D.O. Terra Alta
- D.O. Alella
- D.O. Penedés
- D.O. Costers Del Segre
- D.O. Conca de Barbera
- D.O. Priorato
- D.O. Tarragona
- Autopista
- ▲ Height above sea level
- 1200 Meters
- (3936) (feet)

0   25   50 kms
0   10   20   30 miles

Catalonia

The triangle of land bordered by France, Aragón and the Mediterranean is almost a country in its own right. Certainly, many fervent Catalans like to think so. They have their own language, a provincial flag and in Barcelona, a flamboyant and cosmopolitan capital that feels closer to Paris than Madrid.

The densely populated countryside around the city is a hive of enterprise and industry. It is therefore no coincidence that Catalonia has been at the vanguard of Spain's twentieth-century revolution in winemaking. The region began to stir over a hundred years ago when Don José Raventos brought Champagne-method sparkling wine to the small town of San Sadurní de Noya. His foresight generated Cava, one of the world's best-selling sparkling wines.

Besides Cava, which has its own national denomination, Catalonia has eight D.O.s: Alella, Ampurdán-Costa Brava, Conca de Barberá, Costers Del Segre, Penedés, Priorato, Tarragona and Terra Alta. Penedés, rising like a series of steps from the Mediterranean southwest of Barcelona, is by far the most important for both quantity and quality. This is where the big-name winemakers are concentrated.

The best known is that of Miguel Torres, whose family *bodega* in Villafranca has been the center of progress in Penedés over recent years. Alongside traditional grapes like Garnacha, Monastrell and Ull de Llebre (Catalonia's name for Tempranillo), Torres has introduced classic varieties from abroad. Cabernet, Merlot and Pinot Noir seem to be well-suited to the warm growing conditions of Medio Penedés, the second landing on the three-flight staircase that is Penedés. Further up in Penedés Superior, Chardonnay, Riesling, Gewürztraminer and

the Spanish Parellada ripen slowly enabling Torres to make crisp, fragrant, dry whites. A number of smaller firms, in particular Jean León, Masia Bach and Ramon Ballada, also add to the eclectic range of Penedés wines.

Most Medio Penedés vineyards, however, are tied to the Cava industry. Three grapes, Xarel-lo, Parellada and Macabeo, produce a pleasantly fresh but neutral dry base for turning into soft, inexpensive

BELOW: This vertical press belonging to Freixenet, one of the Cava giants, is a relic from the past. The winery alongside is equipped with the very latest technology.

In the Mediterranean region it is important that the soil is of the right texture and able to retain water. During the long, dry summers, the soil has to act like a sponge, holding water and releasing it slowly. This is totally alien to the Bordeaux philosophy where drainage is the all-important factor.

In Penedés, unlike most growers, I believe in planting 4,500 to 5,000 vines per hectare/ 11,115 to 12,350 per acre. In this way the foliage shades the ground and the roots can reach all the moisture there is. The vine has to struggle more, and its vigor is reduced. The yield remains about the same but the quality of the wine is greatly improved. Less vigorous vines are also less prone to disease.

Since 1975, I have been practicing "ecological viticulture" avoiding the use of insecticides to combat pests, and generally trying to preserve the local fauna. Pests are eliminated by the introduction of natural predators. This preventative policy has been so successful that we only have to spray once a year, usually with a natural product such as copper sulfate to prevent mildew.

In the winery, I pioneered the use of cold fermentation for white wines, but I believe that a wine should reflect its local environment: the soil, the climate and the vine. In some cases we are returning to traditional methods, fermenting in small oak casks and leaving the wine on its lees until May following the harvest. My philosophy of mixing old and new also applies to grape varieties. I am committed to local Penedés varieties but believe that they are often planted in the wrong place. By planting them higher in the mountains we have achieved some astonishing results with white grapes like Parellada.

Miguel Torres

VINEDOS TORRES

ABOVE: Everyone to their own taste: excellent Catalan fizz (Cava) from Miro, Freixenet, Juve y Camps and Pedro Domecq.

sparkling wine. A few of the more progressive growers are planting Chardonnay to lend more character to Cava but, so far, there is insufficient Chardonnay to go round. Codorníu (belonging to the Raventos family) and Freixenet are the big names.

Elsewhere in Catalonia, Costers del Segre is the name of the denomination drawn around the huge Raventos-owned Raimat estate set in near-desert conditions close to Lerida. Without the irrigation channel that cascades down from the Pyrénées there would be no ripe Raimat reds.

There is more to Catalonia than high-technology and big business. Priorato, in remote, mountainous country behind Tarragona, makes some of Spain's most inspiring reds using methods that have barely changed since the Carthusian priors first planted vines there in the Middle Ages. Two unfashionable grapes, Garnacha and Cariñena, yield tiny quantities of dark, sweet juice which ferments up to an incredible 18 percent alcohol by volume. Masía Barril and Scala Dei are the leaders of Priorato with their big, black, pungent wines.

BELOW: Two of Spain's most innovative growers, Miguel Torres and Jean León, make rich "minty" wines from well-ripened Cabernet Sauvignon grapes.

Old Castile and the Duero

The Duero is fast becoming one of Europe's great wine valleys, comparable in stature to the Loire or Rhône. The river starts life in the mountains near Sorria and cuts a gash through Old Castile, changing its name to the Douro when it reaches Portugal. From the source to the sea, vineyards are never very far away.

Old Castile, centered on the medieval university city of Valladolid, is a relative newcomer to quality wine, and Ribera del Duero, awarded D.O. status in 1982, is already challenging Rioja. Admittedly, the region's reputation was helped by Bodegas Vega-Sicilia, Spain's self-styled "first growth", planted in the 1860s. But for over a century the vineyards languished on their own among beetroot farms on the banks of the Duero.

Other winemakers are now trying to make up for

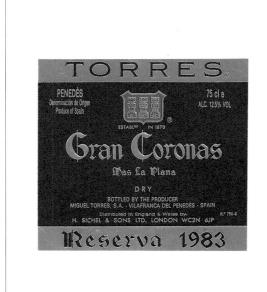

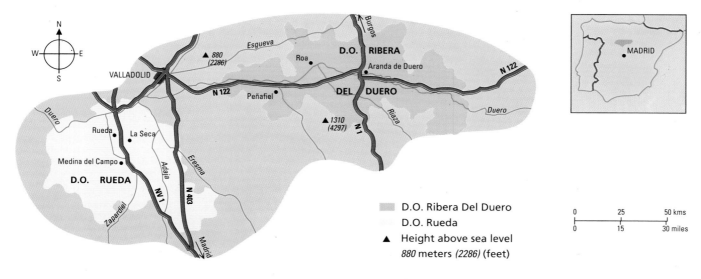

D.O. Ribera Del Duero

D.O. Rueda

▲ Height above sea level
880 meters *(2286)* (feet)

ABOVE: Vega-Sicilia is a legend in itself but growers like Alejandro Fernandez (Pesquera), Bodegas Fariña (Colegiata) and Angel Lorenzo Cachazo (Martivilli) are making some fine red and white wines in the Duero valley.

TOP: The castle at Peñafiel towers over the vineyards of the Duero in the heart of Old Castile.

ABOVE: Vega-Sicilia was one of the first properties in Spain to plant Cabernet Sauvignon.

BELOW: Bodegas y Bebidas (Casa de la Viña and Tres Puentes), Bodegas los Llanos and Bodegas Foix make some of the most distinctive wines in central Spain.

lost time. Mauro, Bodegas Alejandro Fernandez (whose brand is Pesquera) and Perez Pascuas all make dark, dense, oak-aged reds from Tinto Fino or Tinto del País, both local names for Tempranillo. Recent fame has brought fortune to Ribera del Duero along with questionably high prices for some wines.

There is better value to be had downstream, from the vineyards of D.O. Toro. Despite the harsh climate, the Tinto de Toro grape (another alias of Tempranillo) makes big, stony reds that respond well to aging in oak. The best examples come from Bodegas Fariña.

Sandwiched between Toro and Ribera del Duero, the gravelly plateau around the village of Rueda makes white wines. At one time, these were fortified *palidos* and *dorados*; coarse *fino* and *oloroso*-style wines made from the Palomino grape, the variety used to produce Sherry. All but the most traditional *bodegas* have now been converted, and Rueda has earned a D.O. for its refreshing, apple-like dry white made

mainly from Verdejo. The cooperative at La Seca, Marqués de Riscal and the Sanz family with Bodegas Castilla La Vieja and Vinos Sanz, make the best quality Rueda. Look out for white wines under the Marqués de Griñon label.

New Castile and La Mancha

Mountains divide Old Castile from the great, flat tableland or *meseta* at the hub of Spain. But apart from Madrid, strategically placed by Philip II in the center of the country, New Castile is an enormous void. Straight roads glisten in the bright sunlight for as far as the eye can see. On either side, rows of stubby vines puncture the hard, brown earth until they merge with the horizon.

This is Spain at her most extreme. Winters are long and raw with temperatures dipping well below zero for days on end. The summer bites back with fierce heat and little, if any, rain falls between May and September. Castilians who have to live with this talk about "nine months of winter and three months of hell".

La Mancha, *Don Quixote* country south of Madrid, is Europe's largest demarcated vineyard region. Behind dazzling white walls, the *bodegas* are awash with wine. Most of it is rather alcoholic, lackluster white, made in large, old-fashioned cooperatives from Airén grapes. Modern stainless-steel technology is helping to improve quality, but as the bulk of Manchegan white is made for distillation, few winemakers have any incentive to do better.

Red wines have a brighter future. Tempranillo is the principal grape, posing under the local name of Cencibel. Where it is used unblended, it produces simple, sappy reds like Vinicola de Castilla's Castillo de Alhambra, but all too often the wines are diluted with a generous dollop of white Airén. Valdepeñas, a separate enclave with its own D.O. on the southern edge of the great central plateau, is home to some of the best red wine in central Spain. Bodegas Los Llanos have introduced oak *barricas* to imitate a soft, vanilla-flavored Rioja at a fraction of the price, and Casa de la Viña is a single estate producing elegant red wines with flavors unaffected by the heat.

Outside the D.O. Carlos Falco (the Marqués de Griñon himself) teamed up with Bordeaux guru Emile Peynaud to overcome the odds. In a remote vineyard near Toledo, Cabernet Sauvignon and Merlot combine with new French oak to make an exciting Franco-Spanish red.

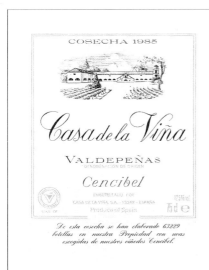

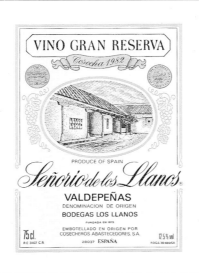

The Levante

Valencia, Spain's third city and largest port, is the capital of the Levante, which consists of four provinces facing the Mediterranean. Behind the ribbon of highrise tourism that mars this once beautiful coast, there are lush *huertas* growing oranges and paddy fields for *paella* rice. Vineyards play an important part in the rural economy. Near the coast, vines grow sweet table grapes for export whereas inland, large stretches of hillside produce more wine than anywhere outside La Mancha.

The Levante divides into five D.O. regions: Alicante, Jumilla, Utiel-Requena, Valencia and Yecla. Red wines predominate. Black, overripe Bobal and Monastrell grapes are sometimes picked with 16 or 18 percent head-splitting potential alcohol. One of two *bodegas* in Jumilla and Yecla are now turning out jammy reds fit for drinking but Valencia has become the world's bargain basement for bulk wine.

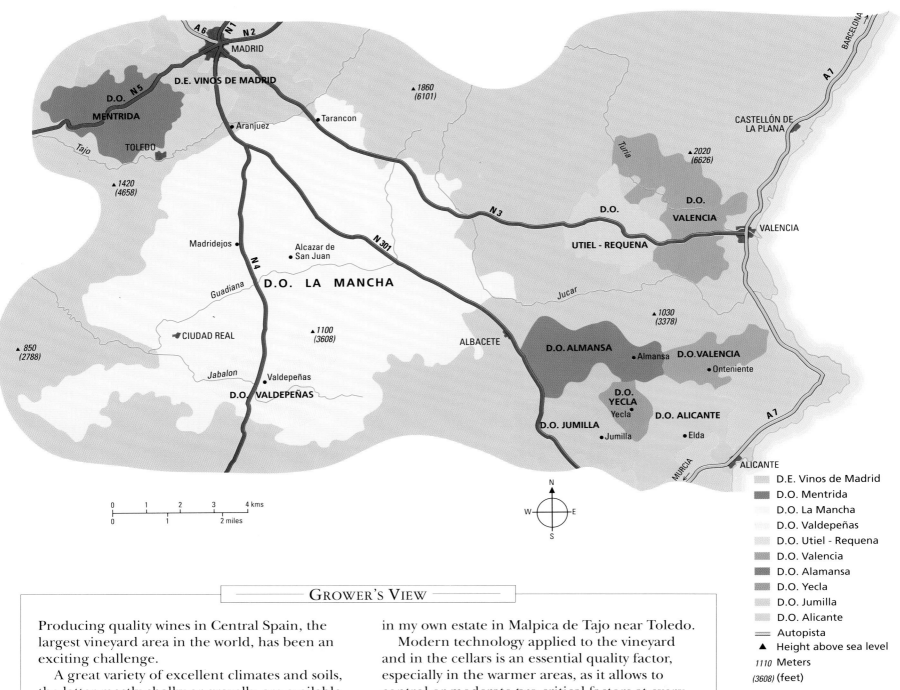

Legend:
- D.E. Vinos de Madrid
- D.O. Mentrida
- D.O. La Mancha
- D.O. Valdepeñas
- D.O. Utiel - Requena
- D.O. Valencia
- D.O. Alamansa
- D.O. Yecla
- D.O. Jumilla
- D.O. Alicante
- Autopista
- ▲ Height above sea level
- *1110* Meters
- *(3608)* (feet)

GROWER'S VIEW

Producing quality wines in Central Spain, the largest vineyard area in the world, has been an exciting challenge.

A great variety of excellent climates and soils, the latter mostly chalky or gravelly, are available. The coolest (Winkler 1 and 2) are located along the Duero River Valley in Old Castile. The highest part of the Tagus River is warmer (Winkler 3). (For an explanation of the Winkler scale see page 357 of the Appendices).

Among a range of grape varieties, I have picked three Spanish — Tempranillo, Garnacha Tinta and Verdejo — and four imported — Cabernet Sauvignon, Merlot, Syrah and Sauvignon Blanc — all of which have great potential in the right soil and climate.

Since the Spanish varieties and the Sauvignon Blanc are already available, the latter in Rueda, I have decided to grow the imported red varieties in my own estate in Malpica de Tajo near Toledo.

Modern technology applied to the vineyard and in the cellars is an essential quality factor, especially in the warmer areas, as it allows to control or moderate two critical factors at every stage: humidity and temperature. The most important tools being used are vineyard training, drip irrigation, grape cooling, controlled fermentation and air-conditioned cellars.

Of course, there is no substitute for picking ripe, good-quality grapes. We therefore try to select for our Spanish grapes vineyards that are old (at least twenty years) and northeast orientated; we harvest only when the berries are fully ripe.

Carlos Falco

MARQUÉS DE GRIÑON

157

ABOVE: Clay pots or *tinajas,* like these fifteenth-century examples in Requena, are still used by wine makers in central and southern Spain.

RIGHT: One of a dying breed, Scholtz is one of the few remaining firms to produce deliciously sweet Málaga dessert wine.

Andalusia

Brilliant whitewash, lively flamenco and moody gypsies bring a certain mysticism to Andalusia, the southernmost part of Spain. This is primarily Sherry country (see page 159-60), but there are two other wines firmly rooted in Andalusia's *tapas*-eating, hand-clapping, singing and dancing tradition.

Montilla-Moriles comes from the two towns of those names situated in one of the hottest parts of Spain a short way south of the Moorish city of Cordoba. The Pedro Ximénez grape (or P.X. for short) parallels the Palomino in Jerez, making wines that range from dry and austere to rich and sweet. Large earthenware pots called *tinajas* are used to ferment grape juice into wine with up to sixteen percent alcohol. The best Montillas drunk locally in *tapas* bars are fortified, and wines like Bodegas Alvear's nutty, dry *fino*, aged under the influence of *flor*, and bitter-sweet *oloroso*, taste every bit as good as their Sherry counterparts. Sadly, due to tax regimes in other countries, the dry, medium and cream Montilla shipped abroad is unfortified. These price-sensitive wines are a poor substitute for the real fortified thing.

Málaga, on the coast, is better known today as an airport on the way to the Costa del Sol than it is for wine. But long before the days of mass tourism, Málaga, or "Mountain" as it was sometimes called, was widely appreciated as an opulent dessert wine. Phylloxera dealt a cruel blow to the steeply terraced vineyards overlooking the city and the arrival of tourism eliminated any prospect of revival. A handful of *bodegas* cling to tradition, making unctuous fortified wines from super-ripe P.X. grapes. The arrival of Lairén (alias the Airén of La Mancha) has contributed to a general decline in quality, but Scholtz and López Hermanos continue to bottle some wonderfully concentrated, sticky old wines.

Sherry

by Julian Jeffs

Sherry is one of the great wines of the world. It is also one of the most underrated and least understood. For those reasons it is also one of the most underpriced. No other wine at the moment offers such value.

Sherry is a geographical name derived from the ancient Moorish name for Jerez de la Frontera in Andalusia. All real Sherry comes from Spain and is grown on rolling downlands of limestone soil that shine brilliantly snow-white under the clear southern sun; hence its name of *albariza*. The best vineyards are roughly in a triangle between the inland town of Jerez de la Frontera and the seaside towns of Puerto de Santa Maria, at the mouth of the Gaudalete River, and Sanlúcar de Barrameda on the estuary of the Guadalquivir River — ports whence the Conquistadors set out to discover and conquer the new continents of America.

Nearly all the wine is produced from grapes grown on Palomino Fino vines, a variety that is not exclusive to the Sherry area but which produces quite different wines (and not very interesting ones) when grown elsewhere. The only other variety of any significance is the Pedro Ximénez, which is not widely grown.

The picturesque days when the grapes were trodden by foot have almost completely disappeared. They are crushed now with the most modern presses and are always fermented right out, so that all the natural grape sugar is turned into alcohol. Often the fermentation takes place in stainless-steel vats that are temperature controlled, but some of the most traditional growers still ferment in oak casks. There is a great demand for these casks from whisky distillers all over the world, who find that they impart a special quality to their spirits.

Sweet wines for blending, to provide medium, cream and sweet sherries, are produced by shrivelling grapes in the sun, so they are almost like raisins, with a great concentration of sugar. A little alcohol is added during fermentation so that the yeasts which bring about the fermentation stop working while the wine is still sweet.

When the must is fermented naturally, it can develop in several ways. Some casks develop a film of natural yeasts on the surface of the wine, known as *flor* (flower) — these are yeasts of much the same kind that bring about the fermentation in the first place. When this happens the wine is said to be a *fino*. It is very pale in color and has a special, very

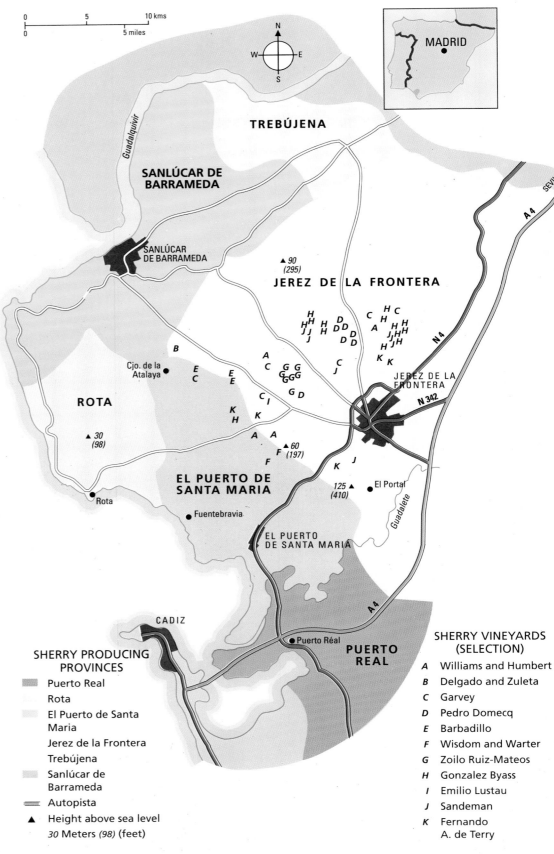

SHERRY PRODUCING PROVINCES

- Puerto Real
- Rota
- El Puerto de Santa Maria
- Jerez de la Frontera
- Trebújena
- Sanlúcar de Barrameda
- Autopista
- ▲ Height above sea level
- *30* Meters *(98)* (feet)

SHERRY VINEYARDS (SELECTION)

- A Williams and Humbert
- B Delgado and Zuleta
- C Garvey
- D Pedro Domecq
- E Barbadillo
- F Wisdom and Warter
- G Zoilo Ruiz-Mateos
- H Gonzalez Byass
- I Emilio Lustau
- J Sandeman
- K Fernando A. de Terry

159

ABOVE: Sandeman's great vineyard El Corregidor. The white *albariza* soil can be seen clearly between the rows of vines.

characteristic and delightful aroma. When a *fino* ages it darkens in color, deepens in aroma and acquires a special flavor that has been described fairly as nutty. At this stage it is an *amontillado.* All *amontillados* in their natural state are bone dry, and as they are the products of aging they cannot be cheap. Unfortunately the term has been much misused and on the export markets it has simply come to mean a medium sherry. The real thing is well worth seeking out, and its higher price is fully justified.

Manzanilla is a special form of *fino* matured in the cool seaside atmosphere of Sanlúcar de Barrameda, where the *flor* grows with great abundance to give wines that are notably fresh, crisp and fragrant, with a slight salty tang.

Those casks on which the *flor* does not grow provide *oloroso* sherries. *Oloroso* is Spanish for fragrant. Their fragrance is shallower and less penetrating than that of *finos.* But it has a charm of its own, and the wines are much darker in color, golden brown when young and deeper brown with age.

Just a little of the wine turns into *palo cortado,* which is a kind of *oloroso* but having more of the nose of an *amontillado*: a very special kind of wine much favored by connoisseurs.

BELOW: Two labels exemplify what is best in Sherry: a fine dry *oloroso* from Sanlúcar de Barrameda and a light *flor* fino from Jerez de la Frontera.

Sherry is not matured as vintage wine but rather on the *solera* system. This is a method of fractional blending that is achieved by taking a cask of mature wine of the required kind and drawing off perhaps a third for use. Then the void is filled with a similar but slightly younger wine. After six months the process begins again. The blending process can involve a hundred or more casks at a time. These in turn are refreshed with wine from a hundred more, which are in turn refreshed with a slightly younger

wine still. Each age of wine is known as a scale, and there may be six or seven of them, or even more. The final, mature scale is the *solera,* the younger ones being numbered in sequence and known as *criadera,* or nurseries.

All *solera* wines are bone dry. To make the popular, sweeter kinds of Sherries — the medium sherries, creams, and dessert *olorosos* — *solera* wines are blended with the specially prepared sweetening wines already mentioned. Finally there is a slight fortification with grape alcohol.

Sherry is often thought of as an aperitif, but it is much more than that. *Finos* are best drunk slightly chilled and should never be served in the horrible thimbles hotels favor. Worst of all are the Elgin glasses which curve inwards in the middle. Dock glasses are the best, or their smaller version, *copitas,* broad at bottom, tapering inwards towards the top. A glass should be filled not more than one third so the nose can develop and be enjoyed. To get the very best from sherry, try it with a little food. The Spaniards serve a great variety of snacks, or *tapas.* *Finos,* too, are excellent to drink with meals, particularly fish and poultry, and are robust enough to stand up to an *hors d'oeuvres.*

Other kinds of Sherry should be served at room temperature, though some people prefer them chilled. The sweet ones are good with sweet food and are particularly good with nuts. As with all things, you get what you pay for. A glass of a fine sherry can give more pleasure than two of a cheap one.

GROWER'S VIEW

To my mind the real future of the Sherry trade lies in its fine wines. I have never gone in for cheap bulk wines. They do not interest me at all. The only cheap wine I produce is a limited amount for the catering trade.

We have been involved in producing and shipping Sherry for centuries. My family was here as wine growers in the fifteenth century though we do not have complete records and I doubt whether there are any that go back beyond the seventeenth century. Frankly I have never looked. It does mean, though, that we have large stocks of old wine and it is those that I am concentrating on. Although I have been fermenting a small part of my vineyards' products in stainless steel for the last three years, 85 percent of my wines are still fermented in the wood which gives them a special individuality. It is more expensive but I think it is better. Each cask can develop in its own way and that gives me the wide range of wines that I want. I like to produce well matured wines of every possible style.

I also like to produce single-vineyard wines. My Fino Inocente, for instance, is a single-vineyard wine that is cask fermented.

I am sure that the pendulum is swinging and that first-class Sherry will soon come back into favor. Our future lies in producing top-quality wines, not in cheap bulk wines.

Miguel Valdespino

A.R. VALDESPINO S.A.

PORTUGAL

by Richard Mayson

Portugal is a paradox. This seafaring nation perched on the bow of Europe helped to discover much of the New World. Today, relieved of the burden of an overseas empire, Portugal is a small, sedate country clinging firmly to the Old World. Cross her borders and you take a step back in time.

Portugal's wine industry reflects this. Her winemakers belong to the old school of rustic charm. Anyone searching for disinfected, high-tech flavors should look elsewhere; the Portuguese old guard have so far resisted the Cabernet/Chardonnay bandwagon that seems to be rolling uncontrollably through the world's main wine-producing regions, and have stuck loyally to their indigenous grape varieties. With a big improvement in the standard of winemaking helped by entry into the European Community, the treasures that Portugal once kept for herself are now being slowly released for the outside world to see, smell and taste.

Portugal is, however, the home of one of the greatest international wine success stories in recent years. Slightly fizzy, not too sweet, or dry rosé caught the imagination of a new band of wine drinkers after World War II and brands like Mateus and Lancers took off. Such wines are not much drunk in Portugal, but sales of rosé continue to be about half of all Portugal's table wine exports.

This small rectangle of land, 560 kilometers/348 miles long and no more than 200 kilometers/125 miles wide, is full of contrasts. Imagine a rich, fiery glass of Port and a crisp, fresh Vinho Verde. No two wines could be more different. Yet they are produced in adjoining regions. Climate plays a part. The wines produced on Portugal's flat, fertile littoral are much influenced by the moderating effect of the Atlantic. The climate becomes more extreme, with baking summers and biting winters, the closer one comes to the Spanish border.

Vines cover Portugal from the Minho River in the north to the Algarve coast in the south. There are nearly 400,000 hectares/1 million acres of vineyards, making Portugal the world's seventh largest wine producing country. It is divided up into forty-one officially recognized winemaking regions with a top tier of thirteen regions. Until Portugal settles on one or the other term, these may describe themselves as *Região Demarcada* (R.D.) or *Denominação de Origen Controlada* (D.O.C.). The two terms are roughly equal to the French *Appellation Contrôlée*. There is a second, new string of twenty-eight areas,

A family affair: pocket-sized plots of wines in Vinho Verde country. Vines are trained to grow high on *pergolas* in order to make the best use of available space. The leaves of the vines, using this system, protect the fruit from the hot sun.

each with the title of *Indicacão de Proveniencia Regulamentada* (I.P.R.). These are candidates for promotion to R.D. status, but it seems doubtful whether many of them will make the grade.

Vinho Verde, Portugal's largest demarcated wine region, covers the entire northwestern corner of the country. The landscape is a riot of vegetation, like a kitchen garden run wild. Vines clamber everywhere; up houses, trees and over specially constructed pergolas. This is the part of Portugal that makes crackling "green wine". Vinho Verde can be either red or white. Both are equally acidic and often have a slight effervescence. Red Vinho Verde, which still amounts to about half the region's total output, is ink black with the rasping astringency of sandpaper. White Vinho Verde is aromatic, naturally bone dry and austere. It is usually sweetened to make it more attractive in export markets. Good commercial brands include Gazela and Casal Garcia, but the single-estate (*quinta*) wines made from either Alvarinho or Loureiro grapes have more character.

The Douro River bisects the hard, northern mountains and lends its name to the demarcated region famous for Port and increasingly well known for table wine. Our ancestors used to call these deep, dark, tannic reds "blackstrap", but new methods are helping to make something softer and more approachable from Port grapes. Ferreira's Barca Velha is one of Portugal's best reds but is expensive and difficult to find. Quinta do Côtto Grande Escolha is excellent and more affordable.

Dão, enveloped by the high granite mountains

161

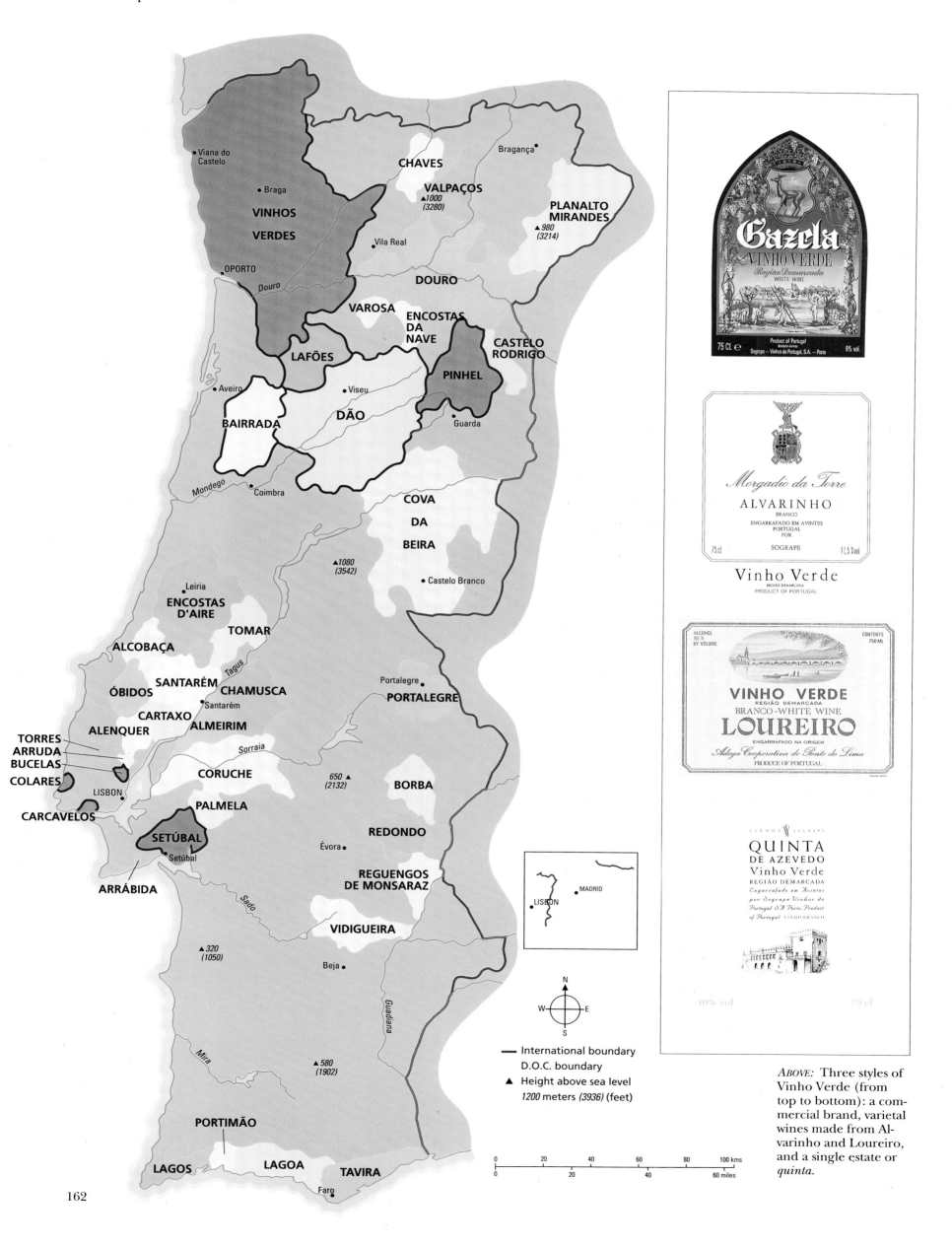

• Viana do Castelo

• Braga

VINHOS

VERDES

OPORTO

Douro

• Bragança

CHAVES

VALPAÇOS
▲1000
(3280)

• Vila Real

**PLANALTO
MIRANDES**

▲ 980
(3214)

DOURO

VAROSA

**ENCOSTAS
DA
NAVE**

LAFÕES

• Aveiro

BAIRRADA

• Viseu

DÃO

**CASTELO
RODRIGO**

PINHEL

• Guarda

Mondego

• Coimbra

COVA

DA

BEIRA

▲1080
(3542)

• Castelo Branco

• Leiria

**ENCOSTAS
D'AIRE**

TOMAR

ALCOBAÇA

SANTARÉM

Tagus

CHAMUSCA

Portalegre •

PORTALEGRE

ÓBIDOS

CARTAXO

ALENQUER

• Santarém

ALMEIRIM

TORRES

ARRUDA

BUCELAS

Sorraia

COLARES

LISBON

CORUCHE

650 ▲
(2132)

BORBA

CARCAVELOS

PALMELA

SETÚBAL

• Setúbal

REDONDO

• Évora

ARRÁBIDA

**REGUENGOS
DE MONSARAZ**

Sado

VIDIGUEIRA

▲ 320
(1050)

• Beja

Guadiana

Mira

▲ 580
(1902)

PORTIMÃO

LAGOS

LAGOA

TAVIRA

• Faro

162

N
W–E
S

——— International boundary
        D.O.C. boundary
▲ Height above sea level
1200 meters (3936) (feet)

0   20   40   60   80   100 kms
0   20   40   60 miles

LISBON   • MADRID

LISBON

Gazela
VINHO VERDE
Região Demarcada
WHITE WINE

75 CL ℮
Product of Portugal
Bottled in Avintes
Sogrape - Vinhos de Portugal, S.A. - Porto
9% vol.

Morgadio da Torre
ALVARINHO
BRANCO
ENGARRAFADO EM AVINTES
PORTUGAL
POR
SOGRAPE   11,5 %vol
75 cl

Vinho Verde
REGIÃO DEMARCADA
PRODUCT OF PORTUGAL

ALCOHOL
9.5 %
BY VOLUME

CONTENTS
750 ML

VINHO VERDE
REGIÃO DEMARCADA
BRANCO-WHITE WINE
LOUREIRO
ENGARRAFADO NA ORIGEM
Adega Cooperativa de Ponte do Lima
PRODUCE OF PORTUGAL

VINHOS SOGRAPE

QUINTA
DE AZEVEDO
Vinho Verde
REGIÃO DEMARCADA
*Engarrafado em Avintes
por Sogrape Vinhos de
Portugal SA Porto. Product
of Portugal.* VINHO BRANCO

10% vol.   75 cl

ABOVE: Three styles of Vinho Verde (from top to bottom): a commercial brand, varietal wines made from Alvarinho and Loureiro, and a single estate or *quinta*.

south of the Douro, is the home of Portugal's best-known red table wine. Standards have slipped owing to shoddy winemaking over recent years and many wines taste hard and lean. The Vinicola do Vale do Dão bottles good, spicy wine under the Grão Vasco label, and Caves São João makes a deep, concentrated red, called Porta dos Cavaleiros, that ages well.

Grown on the heavy clay coastal soils south of Oporto, Bairrada tends to be more reliable. Reds are made predominantly from the Baga grape, which produces big, tannic wines packed with blackberry fruit. The best, from winemakers like Luis Pato and Caves São João, need time to soften, although lighter wines from Caves Aliança may be drunk young. Sogrape, the firm that popularized Mateus Rosé, also makes a fresh, aromatic dry white Bairrada.

South of Bairrada and the university city of Coimbra, the Oeste and the Ribatejo regions produce great quantities of jug wine as well as some of Portugal's best *garrafeiras*, the mature red wines selected from the cream of the crop. Caves Velhas and Carvalho, Ribeiro and Ferreira uphold the tradition.

Lisbon has all but absorbed three small wine regions near the Tagus estuary. Carcavelos has one vineyard and Colares, famous for its *phylloxera*-free Ramisco vines which grow in sand, has nearly disappeared. There is still a flicker of life in Bucelas, a small village making dry white wine from the acidic Arinto and Esgana Cão (or Dog Strangler) grapes.

The south of Portugal starts at the Tagus, where mountains yield to a broad expanse of plain. The Setúbal Peninsula immediately south of Lisbon is one of the country's most innovative wine regions largely because of two firms: José Maria da Fonseca and João Pires. Both have benefited from New World-inspired winemaking, although Portuguese grape varieties like Periquita retain the upper hand. Setúbal itself is a demarcated region for a sweet fortified wine made predominantly from Moscatel grapes.

The Alentejo, south and east of Lisbon, is relatively new to commercial winemaking. Five wine-producing enclaves have recently been designated as I.P.R.s. Borba, Redondo and Reguengos de Monsaraz are the names to look out for on the labels of these vibrant, warming red wines. Last and almost certainly least comes the Algarve; a distinctly Old World player making flabby whites and hot climate reds.

GROWER'S VIEW

I am a great believer in the potential of Portuguese grapes. The world is tired of Cabernet Sauvignon and Chardonnay, and Portugal has around sixty different indigenous alternatives. Of these, I think that there are twelve which are outstanding.

At José Maria da Fonseca, we produce 80 percent of our wine from indigenous varieties. Since we installed stainless-steel fermentation tanks, we have been adapting our winemaking to our grapes. We are learning how and where to plant different vines, taking factors like soil and exposure into account. Although the national legislation obliges us to plant certain varieties in certain areas, I feel that we should be experimenting with as many different combinations as possible in order to find the best results. That is the way forward.

In recent years we have been conducting micro-vinifications based on a dozen or so plants. Having identified what we believe to be the grapes with the most potential we are now conducting experiments with three thousand vines, fermenting each variety separately and in a number of different ways. In this way we find out about the quality of our own grapes.

Although we use small amounts of Cabernet, Chardonnay and Gewürztraminer to round off some of our blends, varieties with unfamiliar names like Castelão Frances, Trincadeira, Touriga Nacional, Antão Vaz and Arinto have a great future ahead. In adapting our vinification methods, my aim is to make Portuguese wines that are easy to drink, without losing their Portuguese character.

Domingos Soares Franco

JOSÉ MARIA DA FONSECA SUCCRS.

BELOW, FAR LEFT: A white from a good producer in Bairrada, a Portuguese region with a recently acquired reputation for remarkable wines, and the label of fine Dão, a *garrafeira*, the highest mark of quality for Portuguese red wine, based on a minimum of aging in barrel and bottle.

BELOW: For such a small country, Portugal produces a broad range of wines: a sweet fortified Moscatel, a full-flavored dry white, Catarina, from the Setubal region, and two solid reds from Bairrada and the Douro.

Port

by Andrew Jefford

ABOVE: Sandeman is one of the many shippers to moor a *barco rabelo* along the Gaia waterfront. Once these craft were the sole means of transporting wine downriver and empty casks back up. On June 24 each year the boats are raced in from the river's mouth at Foz do Douro to Gaia.

Port is an absolute, an extreme. No wine is stronger, darker or more powerfully flavored than this fortified wine from the wild and rocky Douro Valley in northern Portugal. It is served as the climax to grand meals, its rich, sweet fruit exploding in the mouth.

The Douro Valley was one of the first wine regions in the world to be demarcated — in 1756, at the instigation of the Portuguese reformer the Marquis of Pombal. The Port-producing zone stretches to both sides of the Douro River from the Spanish border (in Spain, the Douro is known as the Duero) westwards to the mountain range centered on the Serra de Marão. It forms an island of schist in a sea of granite. Combined with the water-retentive properties of schist the high mineral content helps the Douro's vines survive and be fruitful over the length of the long, very dry and very hot Douro summer.

The vineyards are among the most spectacular in the world. Flanks of rock rise steeply up from the river (now a series of long, thin lakes, dammed for hydroelectricity), and most cultivation is on terraces. The terraces give this wild and rugged region an almost manicured look. Douro's vineyards are classified into one of six categories, based on potential quality, and this classification governs how much of the crop a vineyard's owner is allowed to make into Port. The rest becomes table wine. Most of the best vineyards, classified either A or B, are in the Cima Corgo area — the central part of the

Douro, around Pinhão. The Douro Superior, the most remote and eastern region, also produces high-quality Port, but is sparsely planted; the lower lying Baixo Corgo, centered on Peso da Régua, produces a large quantity of lower quality, bulk Ports, and is intensively planted.

Port has traditionally been made from a large number of grape varieties, but in recent years attention has focused on five: Touriga Nacional, Touriga Francesa, Tinta Barroca, Tinta Roriz and Tinto Cão. Many of the new vineyard plantings in the Douro are based on these five varieties alone, as are all of those created under the World Bank scheme to bring greater economic development to the area.

How is Port made? The principles are simple: it is made in exactly the same way as any red wine, except that the juice is run off the skins midway through fermentation, and fortified with high-strength brandy to produce a finished wine of around 20 percent alcohol. The brandy stops any further fermentation from occurring, since the yeasts cannot survive in solutions of above 16 percent alcohol. The result is that natural grape sugars remain in the wine, providing Port with its sweetness. The main difficulty in Port vinification is the extraction of sufficient color, extract and tannin from the grape skins during the short period (two to three days) between the beginning of fermentation and fortification. The ideal implement for this extraction is the human foot.

After the harvest, Port rests *in situ* up at the *quinta* (farm) where it was made, before being taken down to Vila Nova de Gaia, across the Douro from Oporto, for blending. It is in Vila Nova de Gaia that the Port shippers have their lodges, and the Port ages quietly in these dark, cobwebby warehouses, in seasoned 534 liter/141 U.S. gallon wooden casks called *pipes,* until bottling. Port is, in nearly every case, a blended wine, and the blender's art is as important as the winemaker's. From the vast palette of materials stored in the lodge the shipper prepares his range of Ports.

Among the best shippers and producers are the following (asterisks indicate producers of outstanding vintage port); Burmester, Cálem, Churchill, Dow*, Ferreira, Fonseca*, Gould Campbell*, Graham*, Kopke, Martinez, Niepoort*, Offley Forrester*, Poças Junior, Quinta do Côtto, Quinta do Noval*, Ramos-Pinto, Sandeman*, Smith Woodhouse*, Taylor*, Warre*.

Port Types

Ruby Port: basic, fruity young Port

Tawny Port: also a basic young Port, but one blended from both red and white Port to give a mellower, less overtly fruity style.

White Port: Port made in the usual way, but from white grapes. Varies from very sweet (*lacrima*) to almost dry (misleadingly labeled "Very Dry"). "Light" versions are also produced, containing 17.5 percent alcohol, rather than the usual 20 percent.

Vintage Character Port: Premium ruby Port: young, but richly fruity. (Its name may be altered in the future.)

Late Bottled Vintage Port: Port of a single year, bottled between the fourth and sixth years after the harvest. May in some cases require decanting—the back label should make this clear. L.B.V. should be a deep, fruity Port of character and style, ready for drinking when sold. (Its name may be altered in the future.)

Port with an indication of age: Sold as "10 years old", "20 years old", "30 years old" or "over 40 years old", these are true tawny Ports — in other words, Ports that have aged in pipes rather than in bottles for long periods. Only the last two, however, achieve a true tawny color. The "indications of age" are neither a minimum age nor even an average age, but correspond to styles approved by the Instituto do Vinho do Porto, one of the governing bodies of the Port trade, as authentic for such wines. They do not improve in bottle.

Colheita Port: this is single-vintage tawny Port. *Colheita* Port may be sold the seventh year after the harvest. Generally it is kept much longer, stored in *pipes* until an order comes through, when it is bottled. It is often a more characterful tawny than the "Port with an indication of age". It does not improve once bottled, so should be drunk soon after purchase.

Crusting Port: this in some ways more nearly resembles vintage Port than so-called "Vintage Character". It is a vigorously fruity wine requiring some years' storage (during which it throws a deposit or "crust") before being decanted and drunk. Crusting ports, however, are blended from several vintages.

Single Quinta Port: these are wines sold under *quinta* (farm) names. As yet, legislation does not oblige them to be the produce of that *quinta* alone, nor does a *quinta* name imply a certain style of Port. A number of large shippers use *quinta* names to sell vintage Ports of non vintage years — in which case the label will also say "Vintage Port".

Vintage Port: powerfully fruity Ports from the very finest years (vintage years), bottled between the second and third years after the harvest. Vintage Ports need long aging (a minimum of ten to fifteen years) and decanting before being drunk. Most shippers regard their vintage Ports as their finest products — though some would place their best *colheitas* on a par with their best vintage Ports.

ABOVE: Since damming, the once-muddy Douro River has become an attractive, placid mirror, reflecting light back up towards the terraced vineyards and thereby, some feel, improving fruit quality. The small town of Pinhão lies at the heart of the finest Port-producing area, with vineyards of uniform excellence romping up the surrounding hills.

GROWER'S VIEW

Port always improves with blending, and all Port should be blended, in my opinion. The only exception I would make to this rule is for fine vintage Ports from single *quintas* (farms) — and from one vat only.

At Cálem, where I work as consultant, almost all the Ports we buy are made under our supervision. Occasionally we purchase a very old tawny for blending into our "Ports with an indication of age", and then it is age I look for above all, though general quality — nose and taste — are important, too. In a young Port intended for ruby or L.B.V., I look for depth of color in addition to a good general quality standard.

An average day involves a couple of hours' tasting, usually in the morning. The rest of the day is taken up with checking results, planning future blends, planning the vintage, checking on lodge installations, and overseeing stocks.

Few people realize how important stocks are to the success of a Port house. Take our "over 40 years old" tawny, for example. Annual sales are small, since this is a fine wine — about 100 cases. In order to meet regulations and ensure continuity,

we need to have 39 times that amount, plus additional quantities to compensate for the 2.25 percent evaporation rate we experience on all stocks. So our stock of "over 40 years old" is some 50,895 liters/192,788 U.S. gallons — and we have to source it from a circuit of progressively younger tawnies (30, 20 and 10 years old), each of which has to be maintained as a viable stock in its own right, with all blends kept consistent from year to year. It is a complicated business.

The big moment of the year for me, as for all blenders, comes in early February, when we have to taste and classify all the new vintage wines. This is our marathon.

I think the three Ports I'm probably proudest of are Mackenzie 1955, which I blended alongside my father in 1957; Taylor 1977, a wine which does justice to that superb year; and Cálem 1985, almost my first job on joining the company, and a Port that brought Cálem the serious attention it had not been accorded previously.

Jeremy Bull

CALEM

RIGHT: Guimaraens, a second label of Fonseca, is used for vintage releases from second-quality (but still vintage-worthy) years like 1978. Dow's 1963 is fine vintage Port, approaching its peak in 1992, while Graham's 40-year-old tawny is at its peak when sold.

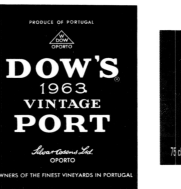

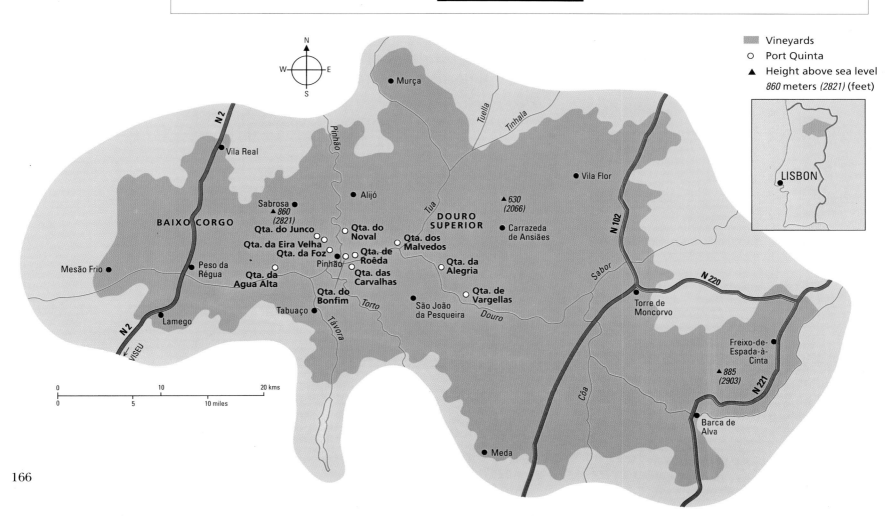

Madeira

by Richard Mayson

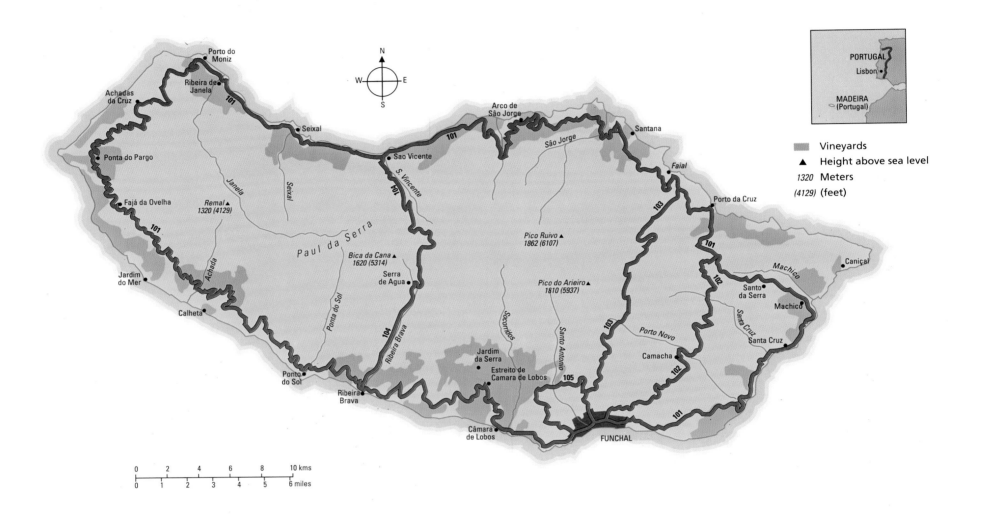

Madeira rises out of the Atlantic 700 kilometers/450 miles off the coast of Morocco. Behind the exotic, subtropical shoreline, a mass of tiny shelf-like terraces pile up the hillside until they disappear from view in the almost perpetual clouds that cover the mountain peaks. The isolation, the breakneck terrain and the warm, damp climate make this an unlikely place to find one of the world's most distinctive wines.

Madeira was discovered by the globe-trotting Portuguese in 1420 and, after the mountains had been cleared of the thick woods that gave the island its name, vines were planted for the benefit of the early settlers. As overseas trade developed, Madeira quickly established itself as an ocean-going service station for ships *en route* to Africa and the East. They replenished their empty holds with wine. Alcohol, probably distilled from locally grown cane sugar, was added to Madeira wine in order to help it survive the long sea voyages.

With the colonization of America in the seven-teenth century, Madeira gained an important export market on the eastern seaboard of that continent. It was found that the wine tasted better after pitching and rolling through the Tropics and a fashion developed for *vinho da roda*; wines that had done the round trip across the Equator and back.

When the taste for Madeira reached Britain, merchants started to look for ways to simulate the long, costly Tropical sea voyages that were so beneficial. They built *estufas*; rooms full of huge vats with fires underneath to heat and advance the development of the wine.

Today, the bulk of Madeira is still produced this way. The cheaper wines, predominantly made from the all-purpose Tinta Negra Mole grape, are heated to between 40 and 50°C/104 and 122°F for a minimum period of 90 days. Most enter the system unfortified, as valuable alcohol is lost through evaporation in the *estufa*. Brandy is therefore added afterwards and the wines are sweetened according to style. The greater the heat, the more rapidly the

FAR RIGHT: Vines with a view: the spectacular vineyards on the north side of Madeira.

wine develops, but short *estufagem* at high temperatures tends to make wine that smells and tastes stewed. Much of this inexpensive Madeira is shipped in bulk to France where it is used by cooks to make *sauce madère.*

The finest Madeiras are produced without any artificial heating. These wines, made only from the so-called noble Sercial, Verdelho, Bual and Malvasia grapes, are fortified early on and then left to age slowly in 600 liter/158 U.S. gallon casks or pipes stowed in attics warmed naturally by the subtropical sun. Some spend fifty or a hundred years maturing, topped up at regular intervals to replace wine lost through evaporation. This robust treatment would turn most wines into vinegar but it gives Madeira an unequalled nervy intensity of flavor and a resilience that seems to defy the test of time.

Traditionally, different styles of Madeira were distinguished by the grapes from which the wines were originally made. Sercial produces the driest wine with a distinct acidic tang; Verdelho is softer and medium-dry; Bual is richer and medium-sweet and Malvasia or Malmsey is the most unctuous with raisin-like intensity and sweetness.

But with most Madeira now made from the versatile but inferior Tinta Negra Mole grape, producers are being obliged to alter their labels to comply with European Community law. From the beginning of 1993, all Madeiras labeled Sercial, Verdelho, Bual and Malmsey must be produced from at least 85 percent of the stated grape variety. Other wines will be limited to using the terms *seco* (dry), *meio seco* (medium-dry), *meio doce* (medium-sweet) and *doce* (sweet) to indicate style.

The age and quality of Madeira is indicated on the label by the following generally accepted hierarchy of terms:

Finest: basic three-year-old wines made predominantly from Tinta Negra Mole and bottled after *estufagem* and aging in bulk. Many suffer from having a coarse, baked, cheesy character.

Reserve: a blend of five-year-old wines most of which are made from Tinta Negra Mole and will have undergone *estufagem* in bulk. Again, many reserve wines have cooked aromas and flavors.

Special Reserve: this is where Madeira begins to be worthwhile. These are ten-year-old wines aged in wood, usually without recourse to the *estufa.* The base wine should contain a high proportion of one of the noble grapes. The firms of Blandy and Henriques & Henriques make fine examples.

Extra Reserve: a category no longer recognized officially but, where used, it denotes a high-quality fifteen-year-old wine. Look out for bottles of an exceptional Sercial from Lomelino.

Solera: the *solera* system, used in Spain to age and blend Sherry, is also used for Madeira, although sadly this category is slowly being discontinued. Some firms, particularly Henriques & Henriques, pride themslevs on *soleras* established in the last century.

Vintage: wines of the very highest quality from a single year, bottled after spending at least twenty years aging in cask. Once in bottle, vintage Madeiras develop little but may be kept indefinitely (provided the cork remains in good condition), such is their resistance to oxidation. Pereira d'Oliveira, Barbeito, Blandy and Cossart Gordon maintain good stocks of wonderful vintage wine.

FAR RIGHT: One of the world's most resilient wines, vintage Madeira keeps for seventy years or more.

GROWER'S VIEW

A tricky question in relation to Madeira is when to pick the grapes. Being a small island in the Atlantic, on the same latitude as Casablanca, it is fairly warm but quite humid. As the grapes ripen they are prone to fungal diseases, and growers are not always diligent about spraying their vines. Fortunately the wetter north side of the island is also subjected to strong winds, which tend to dry the grapes and topsoil and thus reduce the risk of rot.

Madeira is unique among wines in undergoing a heating or *estufagem* process. This blunts the vigor of the young wines, but imparts to them exceptional characteristics which set Madeira apart.

There is no doubt that it is age that brings out the best in Madeira. A well-made ten-year-old Malmsey will have a marvellous richness on the palate and yet the characteristic acidity of Madeira will avoid any hint of cloying. Equally, a ten-year-old Sercial will be mellow and without harshness yet will have the clean acidity which makes it such an effective aperitif.

In making up the blends for these wines the blender must choose most carefully the wines which will show the characteristics of mellowness, acidity and length on the palate in the most flattering proportions.

James Symington

THE MADEIRA WINE COMPANY

GERMANY

by Ian Jamieson

It used to be said that German wines were unique, and the lightest in the world. The claim remains true in those parts where the climate sets the pattern for wines with an intense, fruity aroma, long flavor and refreshing but not sharp acidity. Rieslings from the Mosel producer Dr. Loosen, or from von Hövel and the Rautenstrauch Karthäuserhof estate in the Saar and Ruwer valleys are classic examples of the breed. They are unique because their delicacy and style, common to good wines from the northern German regions, cannot be reproduced elsewhere. Their quality depends on the local climate and the skill of the winemakers in guiding the transformation of sometimes relatively sour grapes into wines of distinction.

Moving south to the Rheingau, Rheinhessen and Rheinpfalz the summers become progressively warmer and the wines gain in alcohol. In the Rheinpfalz, the Burgunder (or Pinot family) grapes on estates such as Lingenfelder and Knipser can develop as much as 13.5 percent alcohol or more. Tannic, dark red wines for which no chaptalization was necessary are much less rare than they were in the mid-1980s, but the German wine most popular abroad remains white, light and medium-sweet. For millions Liebfraumilch is the archetypal German wine.

As far as the outside world was concerned, German wines used to be either Hock or Moselle. These days, however, there is more emphasis on the regions of origin. The regional name gives a broad indication of the likely style of wine but says nothing about its true quality. The law judges matters in a way of its own and as a result some 95 percent of German wine is classified in accordance with European Community regulations as "quality wine".

ABOVE: The Calmont, one of Germany's steepest vineyards, is shared between the villages of Bremm and Eller. The vineyards climb sharply for 186 meters/610 feet directly from the banks of the Mosel. The south-facing slopes of gray weathered slate can only be worked by hand and with great difficulty. The Riesling wines are known locally for their concentrated, steely flavor and character.

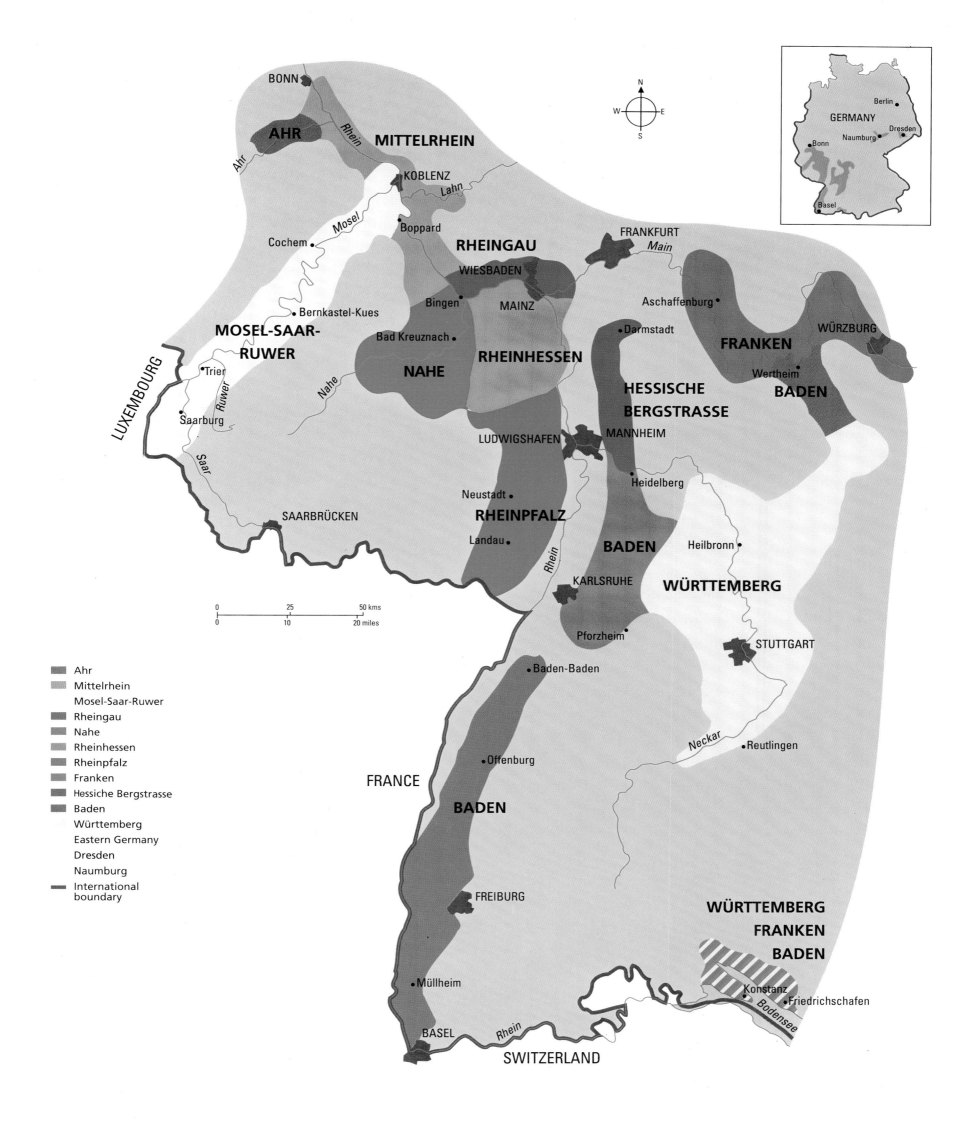

GERMANY

Berlin

Naumburg Dresden

Bonn

Basel

BONN

AHR

MITTELRHEIN

Ahr Rhein

KOBLENZ

Lahn

Mosel Boppard

Cochem RHEINGAU

FRANKFURT Main

WIESBADEN

Bernkastel-Kues Bingen MAINZ

MOSEL-SAAR-RUWER

Bad Kreuznach RHEINHESSEN

Aschaffenburg

Darmstadt

FRANKEN

WÜRZBURG

Wertheim

NAHE

BADEN

HESSISCHE

LUXEMBOURG Trier Ruwer

Nahe BERGSTRASSE

Saarburg

LUDWIGSHAFEN MANNHEIM

Saar

Heidelberg

Neustadt

SAARBRÜCKEN RHEINPFALZ

Landau Rhein BADEN

Heilbronn

KARLSRUHE

WÜRTTEMBERG

Pforzheim

STUTTGART

Baden-Baden

FRANCE

Offenburg

BADEN Neckar Reutlingen

FREIBURG

WÜRTTEMBERG

FRANKEN

BADEN

Müllheim

Konstanz

Friedrichschafen

BASEL Rhein Bodensee

SWITZERLAND

Ahr
Mittelrhein
Mosel-Saar-Ruwer
Rheingau
Nahe
Rheinhessen
Rheinpfalz
Franken
Hessiche Bergstrasse
Baden
Württemberg
Eastern Germany
Dresden
Naumburg
International boundary

0   25   50 kms
0   10   20 miles

The first quality assessment is made at the harvest. It is based on the sugar content of the grape juice, or must weight, measured on a scale devised by Ferdinand Oechsle, a particularly inventive early nineteenth-century scientist and notable amateur musician from Württemberg. The minimum legal levels of must weight can vary according to the grape variety and the region, with Baden in the southwest requiring higher levels than other regions. This does not necessarily imply that Baden wine is the best, but in its middle-priced versions it does sometimes have more substance than those from further north.

The grapes in a German vineyard rarely ripen in unison and so in the last century it became the practice to gather the harvest over several weeks. Grapes picked at different times are vinified and bottled separately. The result is a range of officially recognized categories of wine based on factors such as the date of the harvest, the sugar content of the grapes, or the way in which they were gathered. Usually over half the German vintage is classified as simple Qualitätswein bestimmter Anbaugebiete (Q.b.A.), meaning "quality wine from a specified region", with almost all the rest being Qualitätswein mit Prädikat or Q.m.P., meaning "quality wine with distinction". The first of these "distinctions" is Kabinett and here the description of "the lightest white wine in the world" is often legitimate — particularly in the Mosel-Saar-Ruwer region. A medium sweet Kabinett wine from the Mosel may have less than eight percent of actual alcohol, but if it is well made it will not taste thin or too insubstantial. The alcohol content of a Q.m.P. cannot be increased by adding sugar to the fermenting must, which shows how German thinking on cellar procedure varies from that of Burgundy or Bordeaux, where such "enrichment" is a regular practice at all levels of quality. The producers of the cheapest German wines consider the minimum legal must weights as sufficient, but good estates with different aims set their own, much higher, analytical standards. It is therefore possible (though unusual) to find a producer such as Klostergut St. Lamprecht in the Rheinpfalz offering Kabinett wine with over twelve percent alcohol. Perhaps it would assist the consumer if the Germans set maximum as well as minimum levels of must weight for each quality category, as happens in certain instances in Austria.

The higher categories of Q.m.P. should not be cheap and if a late picked or Spätlese wine is offered at a low price it is unlikely to be a bargain. Many of the best modern, drier German wines are gathered late in the season which gives them sufficient alcohol to balance their relatively high acidity and lack of residual sugar. If the Germans preferred their wines in the 1960s to taste sweet, a noticeable acidity seems to be a common attraction in the 1990s. What constitutes harmony in wine is open to debate and a matter of personal opinion, but excessively high or low levels of acid are not welcomed by the international wine trade.

The fruity-tasting tartaric acid that comes from a slow ripening of the grapes is the backbone of all good German wine. Its flavor and feel are quite different from that of the sharp and short-tasting malic acid of any early gathered grape in a hot climate. Even so, it can be too strong if it is not matched by a little sweetness, and that is why the amount of bone

dry wine produced in the Mosel-Saar-Ruwer is proportionately less than that from further south in Germany.

If the name of a region suggests wine of a particular style and flavor, the grape variety, the presence or otherwise of the words *trocken* or *halbtrocken* (dry or medium-dry), and finally the official quality category, lead to a specific type of wine. Searching for top quality is an exercise in which the name of the producer is one's best guide. A lesser wine from a good estate is much more interesting than a wine of legally superior quality from an indifferent bottler. In truth, the official control system to which all Q.b.A. and Q.m.P. wines are subject in Germany is concerned more with the elimination of faulty or uncharacteristic wines rather than with what is generally understood by the word quality. This may be a weakness but it is nevertheless the only nationwide attempt in the European Community to maintain a standard of quality wine by tasting every bottling.

Riesling produces its most distinguished and complex wines in the northern German regions, where it can be successful at all quality levels. To produce wine in the Auslese category in the Rhine, it almost always needs the concentrating effect of noble rot, thus limiting the amount that can be produced and the frequency with which it can be harvested. The yield from Riesling Beerenauslese and Trockenbeerenauslese grapes is tiny, and the rain-free but humid conditions in the fall necessary for their production seldom occur more than twice in a decade. By pressing frozen, ripe grapes that have been harvested at -8°C/17°F or thereabouts (artificial refrigeration or cryoextraction, currently being tested in France, is not allowed in Germany), the sugar content of the must can be increased by 40 percent or more. The result, Eiswein, can be marvelous, as the State Cellars at Eltville in the Rheingau and the Mosel estate of Max Ferd. Richter frequently demonstrate. Like Beerenauslese, Eiswein is immensely sweet, and its concentrated acidity will keep it fresh for years, but it lacks the complexity and honeyed flavor of a top-quality Beerenauslese. The preference for drier wines that developed in Germany in the mid-1970s has meant that on some estates even the sweeter, richer wines are now more alcoholic and drier than they were. To this extent, Beerenauslese from the Rheinpfalz and Sauternes have drawn closer together in style.

Many of the innovative producers who are still in their thirties or forties received a more extensive formal education in winemaking than their fathers. They are scattered throughout Germany, often and excitingly in areas not well known for interesting wines. In the southern part of the Rheinpfalz, for example, growers such as Siegrist, Rebholz, Dr. Wehrheim and others have built a reputation for concentrated, serious wines from low yields. Where appropriate, they use the popular techniques of fermenting and aging in new 225 liter/59.4 U.S. gallon casks (*barriques*), particularly for wines from the Burgunder vine varieties. In internationally famous wine regions it may be less easy to attract attention, as the competition is already so strong. In spite of this, the new-style Rheingau wines of Becker of Walluf, and Kesseler of Assmannshausen, rightly bring them much publicity.

The range of German wines is starting to be more comprehensible, but there are so many names

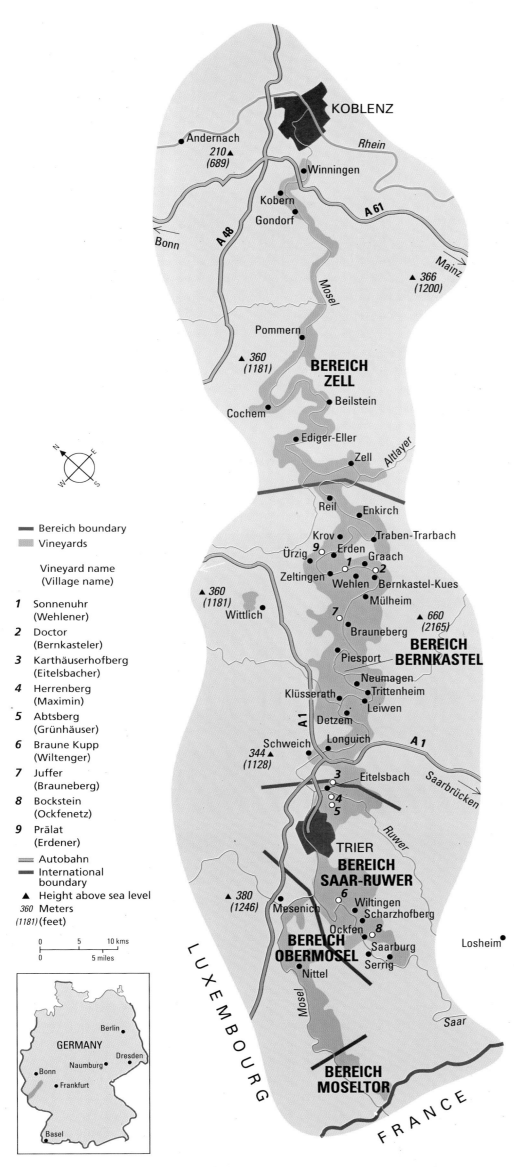

Map labels

Andernach
210 ▲
(689)

● Winningen

Kobern

Gondorf

A 61

A 48

Bonn

Mosel

Mainz

▲ 366
(1200)

● Pommern

BEREICH
ZELL

▲ 360
(1181)

● Beilstein

Cochem

● Ediger-Eller

Zell

Altlayer

Reil

Enkirch

Krov

Traben-Trarbach

Ürzig 9 Erden
1

Graach
2

Zeltingen

Wehlen

Bernkastel-Kues

▲ 360
(1181)

Wittlich

7

● Mülheim

Brauneberg

BEREICH
BERNKASTEL

▲ 660
(2165)

Piesport

Neumagen

Klüsserath

Trittenheim

Leiwen

Detzem

A 1

Schweich

Longuich

A 1

344 ▲
(1128)

3

Eitelsbach

Saarbrücken

4
5

Ruwer

TRIER

BEREICH
SAAR-RUWER

▲ 380
(1246)

Mesenich

6

Wiltingen
Scharzhofberg

Losheim ●

Ockfen
8

Saarburg

BEREICH
OBERMOSEL

Serrig

Nittel

Mosel

Saar

BEREICH
MOSELTOR

Legend

— Bereich boundary
▨ Vineyards

Vineyard name
(Village name)

1 Sonnenuhr
(Wehlener)

2 Doctor
(Bernkasteler)

3 Karthäuserhofberg
(Eitelsbacher)

4 Herrenberg
(Maximin)

5 Abtsberg
(Grünhäuser)

6 Braune Kupp
(Wiltenger)

7 Juffer
(Brauneberg)

8 Bockstein
(Ockfenetz)

9 Prälat
(Erdener)

═ Autobahn
— International
boundary

▲ Height above sea level
360 Meters
(1181) (feet)

0   5   10 kms
0   5 miles

GERMANY

Berlin

Bonn
Naumburg
Dresden

Frankfurt

Basel

LUXEMBOURG

FRANCE

under which it can be sold that few become familiar. As always, there are complaints about the effects of the wine laws, but price lists can be simplified without a change in legislation, as the various Wegeler-Deinhard estates, and Gunderloch in the Rheinhessen have shown. The pricing of some of the newer, interesting red wines ignores the competition on the international market, but they have an enthusiastic following in Germany and, if anything, demand exceeds supply.

Some cooperative cellars, particularly in Baden and in the Rheinpfalz, appear to be settling down to producing the sound, fairly priced white wines that attract export customers. The marketing pretensions of others lead them to Italian-designed bottles and innovative artist's labels; neither of these devices suggests much pride in the geographical origin of the wine. The value of these new creations may well decline if their present rate of appearance continues, and once again price-cutting will doubtless be seen as a way out of a difficulty. Those large merchants who follow a policy of "anything you can do, I can do cheaper" do nothing for the reputation and health of the German wine industry. The successful new selling initiatives in the future will be those that take an improved quality of wine as their starting point. In the meantime, skilled and committed estate owners or administrators are becoming better known and understand that a carefully thought out marketing plan is essential to their future business. There have been no bad vintages in recent years, with the trio of 1988, 1989 and 1990 showing an almost unparalleled run of high quality. In spite of difficulties, good German wine looks in better shape than it has for many years — even if much of it is still relatively unknown abroad.

The area under vine in Germany of roughly 100,000 hectares/250,000 acres is about a tenth of that in France or Italy. As throughout Europe, the average vineyard holding per grower is small, and viticulture is mainly a part-time occupation. In the 1980s yields averaged 104 hectoliters of must per hectare/6.1 tons per acre. They were at their highest in the Mosel-Saar-Ruwer region (120 hectoliters per hectare/7 tons per acre) and at their lowest in the Rheingau and the Ahr valley (81 hectoliters per hectare/4.8 tons per acre). On top estates the yield would be about 30 percent less than that of the regional figure. The average price of quality wine was at its highest in the Ahr valley, the Rheingau, and Franken, and at its cheapest in the Rheinpfalz. Over a quarter of German wine is exported, of which nearly 60 percent is sold in the United Kingdom.

Mosel-Saar-Ruwer

Germany's most widely known wine region follows the Mosel from the French border to its confluence with the Rhine at Koblenz. At its upper end the vineyards of the Saar and Ruwer valleys can produce superb Riesling wines. Even more than those of the *Bereich* or district of Bernkastel in the central section of the river, Saar wines have strong acidity, an easy-to-recognize flavor from the soil and a powerful aroma. Their attraction is obvious and much appreciated by the Dutch and other visitors who drive to the district to buy wine directly from the producer.

The large estates based on Trier — the Bischöfliche Weingüter, von Kesselstatt, the Vereinigte Hospitien and the Friedrich Wilhelm Gymnasium — own vineyards on the Saar as well as in the better-known villages of the Bereich Bernkastel. The best-known producer, resident in the Saar, is Egon Müller with a holding in the finest part of the Scharzhofberg vineyard, but it is invidious to highlight one estate when others, such as Forstmeister Geltz of Saarburg or Fischer of Ockfen, can also claim attention.

All the best wines of the Mosel-Saar-Ruwer are Rieslings from steep, slate-covered vineyards, which may all look very much alike but yet produce wines with many variations of structure and flavor within a common style. Quality in this northern region can vary greatly from year to year with the local climate having a strong influence. A good winemaker aims to retain the individuality of each wine, while the cheaper products of large bottling establishments have a more generalized and less subtle style. The Müller-Thurgau vine and some more recent crossings of *Vitis vinifera* are the main source of ordinary Mosel but above Trier in the Obermosel, agreeably rustic wine has for centuries been made from Elbling.

Full, classy and long in flavor describes the best wines of Piesport. The Braunebergers of Fritz Haag are exquisitely delicate, a good Bernkasteler Riesling is firm and solid, and Wehlen is internationally known for the wines of J.J. Prüm from the better part of the Sonnenuhr vineyard. The good wines from each village have a constant style which can easily be lost by heavy handling. A blemish in light Mosel without excessive sweetness is obvious, as the wine does not have the robustness that comes from a high alcohol content.

Downstream Mosel, more correctly known as the Bereich Zell, is at last starting to achieve some of the recognition it deserves, thanks to the high standards of a few estates and an association of growers calling themselves the Erzeugergemeinschaft Deutsches Eck. Their Riesling wines from low-yielding vines are steely in flavor and have the body of a Rhine wine rather than the delicacy of a Mosel. As yet few are exported.

LEFT: Bernkasteler Doctor. The 3.26 hectare/8 acre Doctor vineyard, the glory of Bernkastel, was once known for its red wine but since the eighteenth century has been famous for its Rieslings. Many of the ancient vines are ungrafted and help to enhance the flavor from the Devon slate soil. The gradient of 60 to 70 percent, the southern aspect and the reflection of warmth from the roofs of Bernkastel below, all help to produce a wine that can rise to heights of unrivaled distinction.

FAR LEFT: The Saar, which joins the Mosel near Trier, has a more severe climate. The village of Ockfen and the Scharzhofberg vineyard are among the best producers of Riesling wines of stunning quality in good years, characterized by a strong, fruity bouquet, with a long and deep flavor.

ABOVE: The Braunebergers of Fritz Haag are exquisitely delicate, and a good Bernkasteler Riesling is firm and solid.

GROWER'S VIEW

In the Mosel-Saar-Ruwer region the Riesling forms a perfect union with the slaty soil. The result is vibrant and beautifully poised wine that is full of flavor.

I see it as our task to bring out the individuality and subtle differences of our Riesling wines, which come from the unique climate and the soil of our steep vineyards. We must guard the originality and the richness of a tradition of 2,000 years of vine growing.

To be successful we have to respect nature and look after the soil and the vine. The grapes are hand-picked at their moment of optimum ripeness and care is taken to see that the young

wine in 1,000 liter/264 U.S. gallon oak casks, or *Fuder*, is protected from oxidation. The speed of fermentation is controlled by temperature so that the bouquet of the wines is delicate and complex, and the acidity and sweetness are well balanced.

Riesling wines need time to show all their charm and wealth of flavor. I like our wines to give a clear reflection of the philosophy of our estate. The Riesling vine makes this possible.

Dr. Dirk Richter

WEINGUT MAX FERD. RICHTER

RIGHT: Rheingau after *Flurbereinigung.* Nearly 60 percent of Germany's vineyards have been rebuilt under a state-supported scheme, *Flurbereinigung.*

BELOW: The bottles of many well-known Rheingau estates bear labels that recall their noble and ancient origins.

OPPOSITE PAGE, LEFT: Rheinhessen labels today vary from the traditional, complex and highly informative, to the simple and easily understood.

OPPOSITE PAGE, RIGHT: The original Liebfraumilch vineyards at Worms now produce a flavory wine, estate-bottled by Valckenberg.

Rheingau

"There are no bad vintages in the Rheingau — only wines that take longer to mature". The administrator of the Schloss Schönborn estate, Robert Englert, could have been speaking for all good wine producers in Germany. Successful wines in off-vintages can be a delight after aging has overcome the handicaps of their year of birth, and Rheingau Rieslings do need time to develop in bottle. The home market is more attracted by the latest vintage, but as good wine takes time to move through the channels of trade on the export market, mature bottlings are often obtainable abroad.

Anyone whose experience of Riesling is limited to wines from hot climates may wonder if the praise of Rheingau Riesling is exaggerated, but it is not. At its best, the balance can make it one of the very few great white wines of the world.

The Rheingau has a higher proportion of top-quality estates in relation to its size (a modest 2,904 hectares/7,260 acres) than any other region in Germany. They begin with Weingut Graf von Kanitz at Lorch and follow the Rhine to Walluf, to appear once more at Hochheim on the Main. Traveling upstream, the vineyards leave the Rhine gorge near Rüdesheim and gently climb to the edge of the Rheingauer Wald. The climate is dry, the soil varied, with the difference in the height of a vineyard and its distance from the Rhine often determining the type of wine produced.

Rheingau vineyards have been reconstructed and modernized in recent years, and the process still continues. If soil and microclimate permit, Riesling is planted, usually with a variety of clones from the vine-breeding institute at Geisenheim.

Although Riesling is famous for its sweeter wines, many Rheingaus today taste dry — although, analytically and officially, they may be medium-dry. Wines of this sort are most easily found from estates such as Schloss Vollrads which are members of the *Charta* association. Their bottles and capsules are embossed with a Romanesque double arch.

The red vine varieties reached the Rheinland before the white, and since the eighteenth century Assmannshausen in the Rheingau has been known for its Spätburgunder (or Pinot Noir). It is now enjoying the Germans' recent interest in their own red wine as an accompaniment to food, which has led to Spätburgunder being planted on many Rheingau estates as a supplement to Riesling.

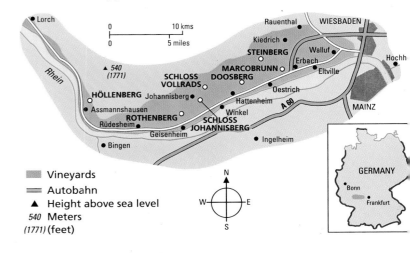

Rheinhessen

The Rheinhessen is best known abroad as a source of cheap, medium-sweet white wine, sold under the names Niersteiner Gutes Domtal, Oppenheimer Krötenbrunnen and Liebfraumilch. Much is bottled by merchants outside the region and is sold particularly successfully in the United Kingdom. But there is another side to Germany's largest wine region, represented by the vineyards that climb away from the west bank of the Rhine between Bodenheim and Mettenheim. This area, known as the Rheinterrasse, amounts to about 14 percent of the whole of the region.

High-quality wine has also been made for centuries by a handful of producers further north at Ingelheim and Bingen. Often, as the vineyards of the Rheinterrasse are improved or rebuilt, Riesling is replacing other vine varieties. A dry Rheinhessen Riesling is firm, fresh and sometimes has an attractive taste of the soil. Late-picked versions from good estates in Nierstein, Oppenheim or Nackenheim sell well in Germany. In the search for characterful, good-quality Rheinhessen wine, the name of the bottler is particularly important.

Silvaner has long been associated with the region of Rheinhessen but today's dry wine from low-yielding vineyards is quite unlike some of the soft, oxidized wines of twenty years ago. Good examples of Rheinhessen Silvaner from a number of producers can be found under the admirably simple name of R.S.

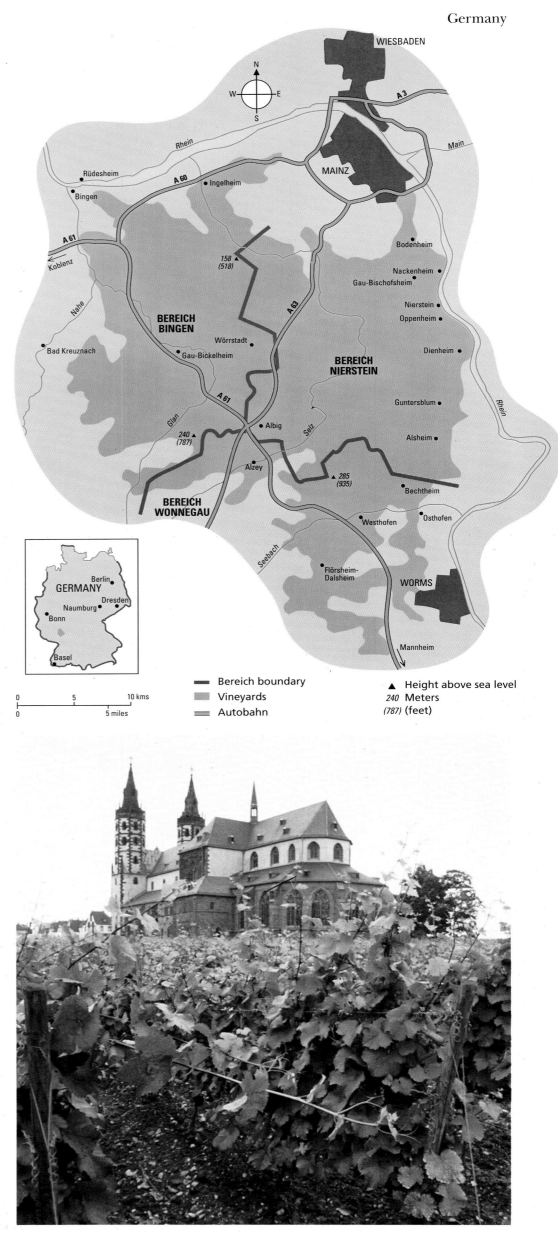

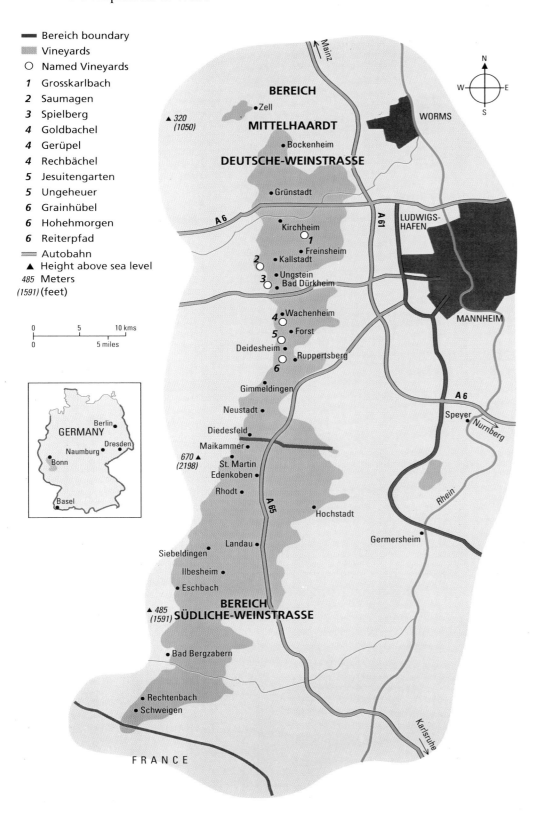

Legend:
- ━━ Bereich boundary
- ▨ Vineyards
- ○ Named Vineyards
- 1 Grosskarlbach
- 2 Saumagen
- 3 Spielberg
- 4 Goldbachel
- 4 Gerüpel
- 4 Rechbächel
- 5 Jesuitengarten
- 5 Ungeheuer
- 6 Grainhübel
- 6 Hohehmorgen
- 6 Reiterpfad
- ▤ Autobahn
- ▲ Height above sea level
- 485 Meters
- (1591) (feet)

Rheinpfalz

The Pfalz, to use the shortened name, offers a wider range of top-quality wine than any other region in Germany — as well as much that is ordinary and rightly cheap. In the Mosel-Saar-Ruwer and the Rheingau, all the best white wines are from Riesling, and the Pfalz also has its stunning examples. They are fresher and have more acidity than was the case

BELOW: The Rheinpfalz, "the sleeping giant of German fine wine production", is a rich source of both white and red wines.

fifteen years ago and to this extent some resemble wines from the northern regions. Besides the Rieslings, Ruländer, or Grauburgunder as its modern, crisp form is often called, is very successful. It reaches more than 13 percent alcohol without being overburdened with flavor. The Gewürztraminers are also impressive, but those of Alsace over the border and to the south are usually more concentrated. For a vine that is uniquely German and is not grown much elsewhere, Pfälzer Scheurebe from estates such as Pfeffingen of Bad Dürkheim or Lingenfelder of Grosskarlbach produces wines with the expected blackcurrant flavor and some of the elegance of Riesling.

During the 1990s, the quality of the region's red wines will continue to improve as the vines become older. The decade may start to show how good Pfälzer Spätburgunder can be, and if growers such as Müller-Catoir can add complexity to its other virtues, middle-priced Burgundy could be faced with a rival nearer to it in style than any other wine. Dornfelder from Thomas Siegrist in the Süd Pfalz and from similarly innovative private estates is a deep-colored, intensely flavored red wine which can improve by aging in new oak casks. Weaker, cheaper and more commercial bottlings of Dornfelder can be bought from cooperative cellars, but it seems a pity when pale colored Blauer Portugieser is widely available as a thirst quencher.

Until the start of the 1980s, Kallstadt, Bad Dürkheim, Wachenheim, Forst, Deidesheim and Ruppertsberg were almost the only Pfälzer villages known outside Germany for their wine. For hundreds of years, their vineyards below the Pfälzer Wald have been the largest suppliers of the best wine in the region. Others, on rolling slopes further north, are now seen to have tremendous potential

---

GROWER'S VIEW

The quality of our wines is determined in the vineyards. In the cellar we try to let the grape express its potential at the time of picking to the fullest extent. Good wine cannot be produced from poor fruit.

In fact, we do not see ourselves as the makers of wine. Chardonnay wine is often *made* but wines from Riesling, Pinot Noir and Scheurebe should be allowed to create themselves. We merely prepare the right environment in which the wine can come into existence and thrive. Obviously you need to know what to do in the cellar if a year's work in the vineyard is not to be wasted, but the birth of a wine is a process which we leave to nature. We are only the midwife.

Therefore, our aim is to let the original character of the wine speak for itself. It might derive from depth or complexity of flavor, elegance and lightness, or maybe a combination of several factors. It matters not which, but it is important that nothing should diminish a wine's natural characteristics. That is our aim.

Rainer Lingenfelder

WEINGUT K. u. H. LINGENFELDER

— when they are in the right hands — and the same is true of vineyards in the Süd Pfalz. Here the quality of inexpensive varietal wine from the largest cooperative cellar in the region — the Gebiets-Winzergenossenschaft Rietburg — has been recognized abroad. Even allowing for its success so far, the Rheinpfalz could be the sleeping giant of German fine wine production.

Baden

In a region that is over 400 kilometers/249 miles in length there is bound to be a great variety of wine, and so it is with Baden. The natural tendency is for Baden wines to be more alcoholic and less acidic, although this is by no means always true. Their virtues are therefore different, and their style is often of a generalized, European sort which is perhaps both an advantage and a disadvantage.

As the cooperative cellars control over 80 percent of the production, they have access to the best as well as the more ordinary vineyards. A third of the Baden harvest is handled by the Badischer Winzerkeller in the Kaiserstuhl district, where it is bottled by robots at a rate of 36,000 bottles per hour. Judged by the quality of the Winzerkeller wines the robots work well and consistently. Throughout the region there are small village cooperatives, some of which operate very much like privately owned estates. That is to say there is a close working relationship between the grape growers and the winemakers.

The region has two districts with reputations that stretch well beyond their borders. The Ortenau on the slopes of the Black Forest has some fine estates in spectacular and steep vineyards around Durbach, and Kaiserstuhl near Alsace produces characterful wines from Burgunder family grapes. Nearly a quarter of the region's area under vine is planted in Spätburgunder. Where the yield is high the wine lacks grip and is of little interest outside Germany, but serious red wine is also being made by cooperative and private estates alike, showing what might be achieved in the future.

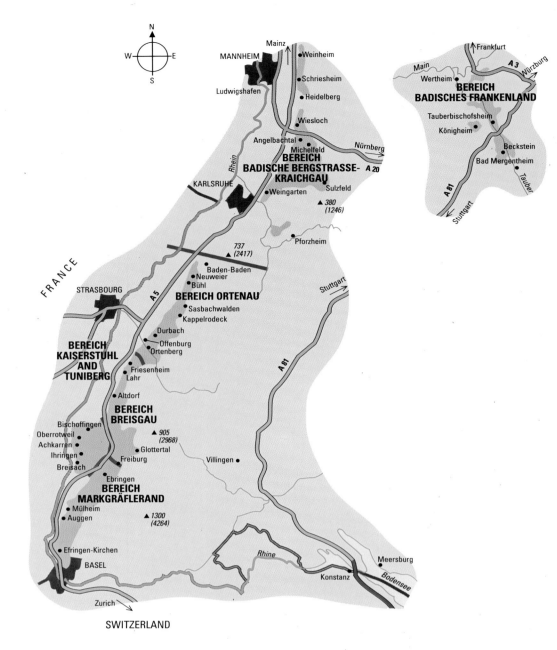

Bereich boundary
Vineyards
Autobahn
International boundary
▲ Height above sea level
1300 Meters
(4264) (feet)

LEFT: Baden is known for its many good cooperative cellars and for a few private estates. The Pinots and Rieslings can be most impressive.

Nahe

The Nahe has far fewer well-known estates than the Rheingau but for connoisseurs its Rieslings can be among the best in Germany. Indeed, the leading estate, the Staatliche Weinbaudomäne at Niederhausen-Schlossböckelheim, is one of the great wine producers of the world. Freshness and high acidity are characteristic of good Nahe, and the Rieslings in particular respond sensitively to variations in site and soil.

Most of the good vineyards of the Bereich Schlossböckelheim, upstream from Bad Kreuznach, lie close to the Nahe River. In some places the flavor of their wine is influenced strongly by the neighboring porphyritic rocks, which also increase the average temperature in the vineyard to good effect. At Kreuznach, the Anheuser family has now been making wine for thirteen generations, and the true worth of the local wine was recognized in Germany

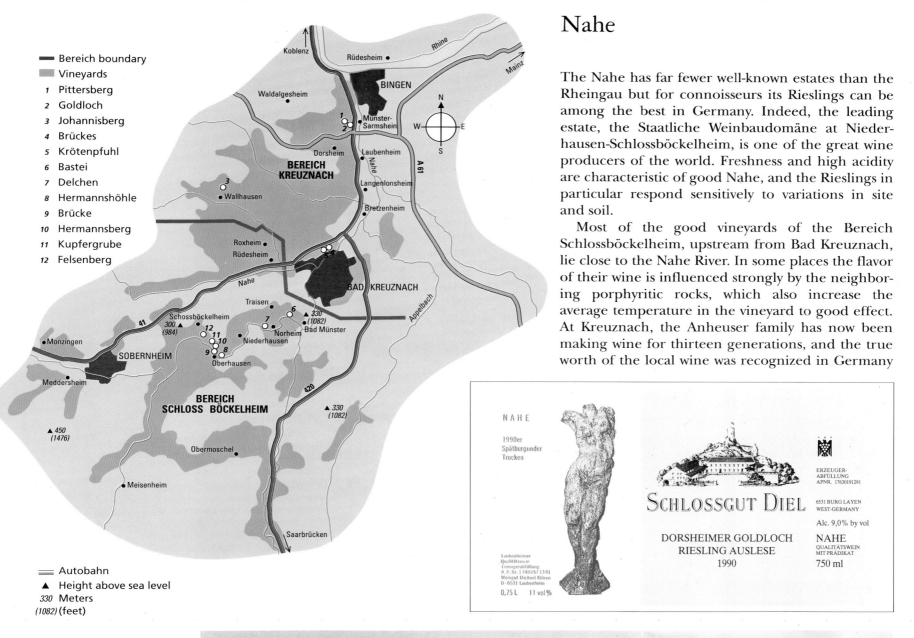

Bereich boundary
Vineyards
1 Pittersberg
2 Goldloch
3 Johannisberg
4 Brückes
5 Krötenpfuhl
6 Bastei
7 Delchen
8 Hermannshöhle
9 Brücke
10 Hermannsberg
11 Kupfergrube
12 Felsenberg

Autobahn
▲ Height above sea level
330 Meters
(1082) (feet)

NAHE

1990er
Spätburgunder
Trocken

SCHLOSSGUT DIEL

DORSHEIMER GOLDLOCH
RIESLING AUSLESE
1990

ERZEUGER-
ABFÜLLUNG
APNR: 17630191291

6531 BURG LAYEN
WEST-GERMANY
Alc. 9,0% by vol

NAHE
QUALITÄTSWEIN
MIT PRÄDIKAT

750 ml

ABOVE, RIGHT: The labels of many estates in the Nahe are simple and admirably clear. Some of the Rieslings are amongst Germany's best.

RIGHT: Village of Ebernburg, near Bad Münster am Stein. The vineyards at the foot of the steep Rotenfels cliff-face near Bad Kreuznach produce strongly – flavored Rieslings with a noticeable *goût de terroir.*

long before the town became a spa. Like the Rheinpfalz, the Nahe also has some outstanding young winemakers in villages so far unknown to the export market. The cheapest wines of the region, based on Müller-Thurgau, resemble those of neighboring Rheinhessen in quality and style.

Franken

At their best the wines of Franken are truly impressive. They have class, a long, strong flavor influenced by the soil, and a powerful aroma. The large and historic estates based on Würzburg and the Castell estate on the edge of the Steigerwald to the east are responsible for much of the most distinguished wine. There are, of course, other good producers scattered throughout the region making wines that are characterful and well worth tasting, in particular those of Hans Wirsching of Iphöfen.

The vineyards often suffer from frost so that recent yields have ranged from 13 hectoliters per hectare/0.8 tons per acre in 1985 to 155 hectoliters per hectare/9.1 tons per acre in 1989. Franken Q.b.A. wine, of which about a half is dry, is often sold in liter/2.1 U.S. pint bottles, but the better wines are offered in the traditional flagon known as a *Bocksbeutel*. So far little is exported. Over 40 percent of the harvest is processed by cooperative cellars, which achieve average prices nearly three times higher than those on the Mosel. To an outsider, cheap Franken wine seems expensive, while prices for top-quality wine are high but fair.

GROWER'S VIEW

Our wines from 64 hectares/160 acres of steep or sloping vineyards are born with their own particular character from the dry continental climate and the deep soil of the Steigerwald. It is my aim to avoid anything that might reduce their individuality and so each wine is vinified separately according to the vine variety and the vineyard from which it comes. Castell wines are naturally fruity, earthy and almost spicy, with a good backbone of acidity; these are the qualities we appreciate most.

If our wines have 10 percent potential alcohol we are happy not to add any sugar but to let them develop as fresh, light and digestible simple Q.b.A. wines. Over 90 percent are *fränkisch trocken* or Franconian dry, with less than 4 grams per liter/0.5 Brix of unfermented sugar.

Although our region is mainly concerned with white wines we have been encouraged by the results we have been getting from Spätburgunder and Domina. After their alcoholic and malolactic fermentations the red wines mature in oak casks or in small *barriques*.

I think you could say the winemaking in our three-hundred-year-old cellars is traditional except where modern methods are best.

Graf Wolfgang Castell

FÜRSTLICH CASTELL'SCHES DOMÄNENAMT

BELOW: Fifty percent of Franken wine is sold in a flagon-shaped *Bocksbeutel*. Müller-Thurgau and Silvaner predominate.

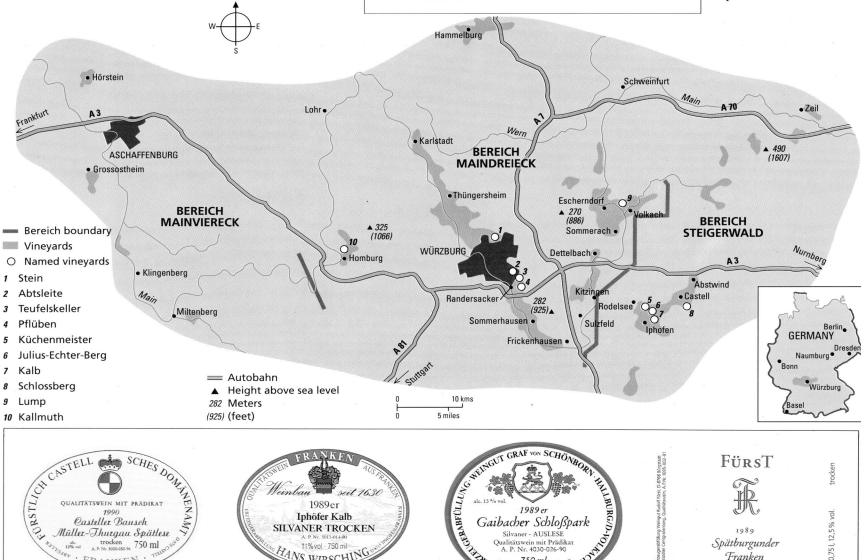

Key:
- Bereich boundary
- Vineyards
- ○ Named vineyards
1 Stein
2 Abtsleite
3 Teufelskeller
4 Pflüben
5 Küchenmeister
6 Julius-Echter-Berg
7 Kalb
8 Schlossberg
9 Lump
10 Kallmuth

Autobahn
▲ Height above sea level
282 Meters
(925) (feet)

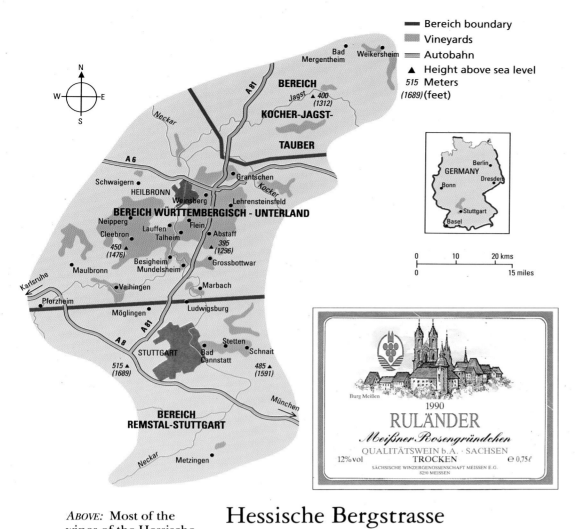

ABOVE: Most of the wines of the Hessische Bergstrasse are drunk in the region. Standards are high and the best Rieslings are remarkable.

Hessische Bergstrasse

This is a small region of less than 400 hectares/1,000 acres, with sloping vineyards looking towards the Rhine from the edge of the Odenwald. At Bensheim there are distinguished Rieslings from the Staatsweingut which taste like a variation on the Rheingau theme with a shade less acidity, and there is also a good regional cooperative cellar. Worth a detour, if not a journey.

Ahr

BELOW, RIGHT: Spätburgunder is the leading vine in the steep and sometimes terraced vineyards of the Ahr. It is a picturesque wooded region, loved by coach parties from the Ruhr.

The typical wine of the Ahr Valley not far from Bonn is a Spätburgunder that is low in tannin, high in acidity, and slightly sweet. Some more internationally acceptable red wine is also starting to be produced but it is bought by visitors to the Ahr almost as soon as it is bottled — at surprisingly high prices.

Württemberg

To anybody outside the region the wines of Württemberg are among the least impressive in Germany. They are pleasant enough, but quality suffers through overproduction. Although over half of the vineyard area is planted in red vine varieties, the average yield per hectare/acre for the whole of the region is among the highest in Germany. Many of the vineyards are steep, sometimes terraced, and therefore very expensive to operate, so that costs could only be covered by producing top-quality wine or, as is the case, by a large crop. The result is that Württemberg wines often lack grip and body, but they are much enjoyed by a well-trained local community willing to pay prices twice as high as those on the Mosel or in the Rheinpfalz. In fact the region drinks more wine than any other in Germany, and it is really only in Württemberg that wine becomes an everyday drink of the people — a *Volksgetränk*.

There are a few producers whose wines have the concentration normally associated with serious winemaking, but nearly 95 percent of the harvest is delivered to cooperative cellars, whose big task is to keep the supply of café wines rolling.

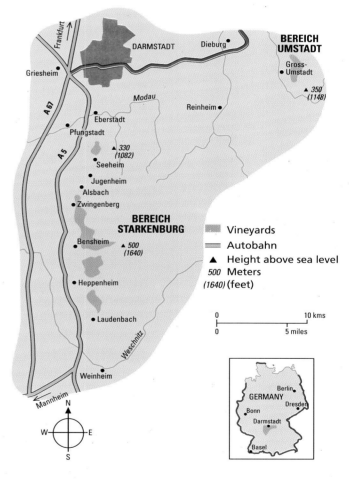

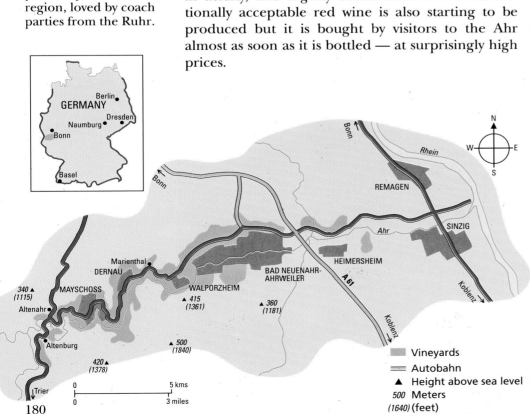

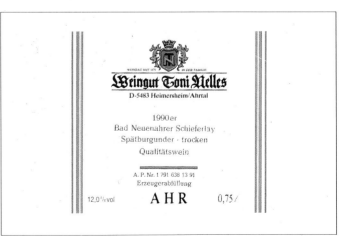

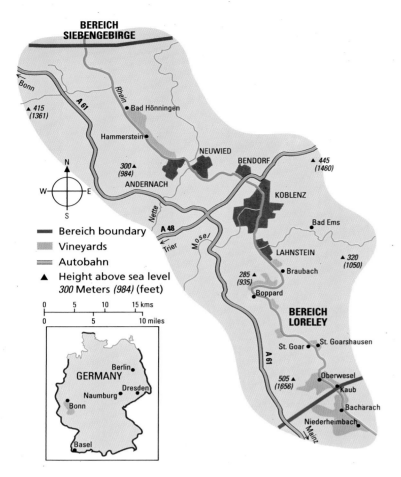

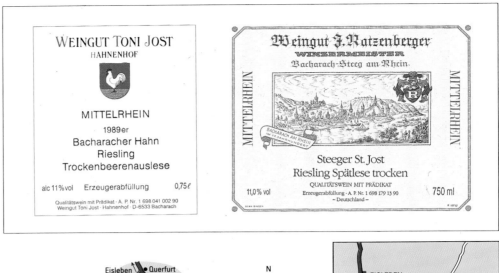

Mittelrhein

The Mittelrhein is a small but beautiful region whose steep Riesling vineyards rise above the romantic Rhine downstream from Lorchhausen. Much of the wine is sold through local wine bars and restaurants but a few private estates are now becoming known abroad. Some of the best are members of the association of top German estates — the V.D.P. — whose wines are identified by an eagle emblem on the capsule.

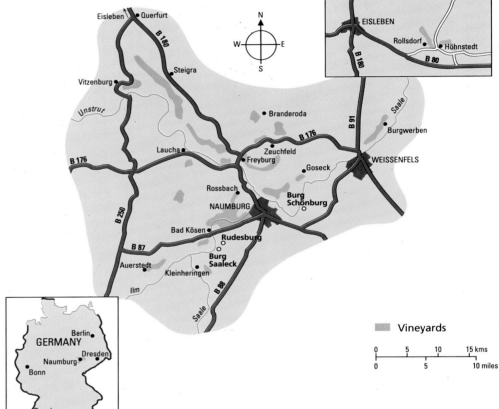

ABOVE: In the romantic vineyards of the Mittelrhein, Riesling grows in all its variations from base wine for Sekt to fine estate-bottled wine.

LEFT: The pleasantly rural eastern German vineyards produce dry wines of a quality similar to those of Luxembourg. Standards should now improve.

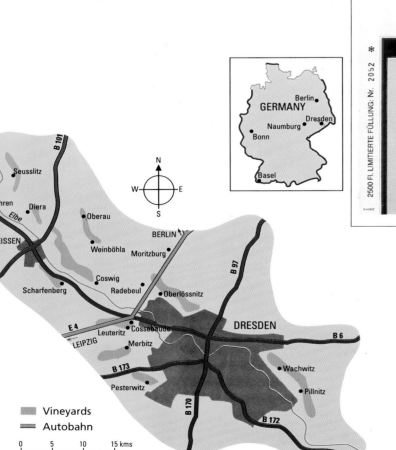

Eastern Germany

The two wine-producing regions of eastern Germany cover 735 hectares/1,838 acres and follow the rivers Saale and Unstrut, and the Elbe valley. In a continental climate even more variable than that of Franken, 45 percent of the vineyard area is planted in Müller-Thurgau, 15 percent in Weissburgunder and 10 percent each in Silvaner and Traminer. Everything needed for the production of wine has been in short supply or unavailable for years, so that matters can only improve in the 1990s.

AUSTRIA

by Ian Jamieson

ABOVE: Falkenstein, a famous Weinviertel village, where the growers work closely together, producing dry, crisp wines.

OPPOSITE PAGE, LEFT: Vines in the center of Vienna. Vienna and wine are almost inseparable, and the capital of Austria is itself a wine region.

OPPOSITE PAGE, RIGHT: Austria's wine labels are as varied as its wine. Both have improved in the last five years.

Austria's vineyards lie in the eastern half of the country where the summers are warmest, the winters not too cold and the rainfall is adequate. Fifty-eight percent is in the varied landscape of Niederösterreich or Lower Austria; 36 percent is in the Burgenland; 5 percent is on the steep slopes of the Steiermark, or Styria, and a tiny 1 percent is in the suburbs of Vienna, supplying the city's famous wine bars, the *Heurigen.* In the 1990s Austria is producing stylish dry white wines, particularly but not exclusively in the Wachau in Lower Austria. To the south of Vienna, the sunny area around the Neusiedlersee in Burgenland has luscious dessert whites which a kind climate provides in relative profusion. The best of these are now outstandingly good and some might say they were the result of hard times, for in 1985 Austria lost her good name. It was discovered that Diethylene glycol was being used to falsify sweet wine, but the international scandal that followed,

and the creation of a new and strictly implemented law, led to a marked improvement in quality. After the trauma of the past the mood is distinctly upbeat.

Most of Austrian wine is uncomplicated, light, dry, white and fruity. If much is offered in the 1 liter/2.1 U.S. pint or 2 liter/4.2 U.S. pint bottles required by the restaurant trade, serious wines in 750 or 700 milliliters/23.7 or 25.4 U.S. ounce bottles are selling well, reflecting an increasing interest in individual, characterful wines with a concentrated flavor. Some of the dry white wines from Riesling, Weissburgunder, Grauburgunder and Grüner Veltliner are outstandingly successful. For many producers, acid levels are as important as sugar content when deciding the moment to start the grape harvest, and white wines with high acidity are sought after.

Austrian red wine has tended to be somewhat wishy-washy in the past but where the yield is low and traditional French methods of vinification are

followed, results are very different. Blauburgunder (Pinot Noir) and a little Cabernet Sauvignon are grown but there is a belief that preference should be given to indigenous vines such as St. Laurent or Zweigelt Blau. The producers work hard marketing their wines, sometimes jointly owning and staffing a simple wine bar for passing tourists and regular visitors. At their *Vinotheken,* or wine shops, it is possible to experience the revival of quality winemaking.

GROWER'S VIEW

My family has been involved with wine since the eighteenth century, and our links with the past and experience of the international wine market encourage us to work closely with others of similar outlook in our region. We bought the old monastery of Kloster Und in 1987 and built it into a center for wine culture. Over one hundred different wines from leading local producers can be tasted daily.

In cooperation with our neighbors, we installed an irrigation system in our steep vineyards to cope with the dry summers. The aim is for the grapes to be ripe enough to make de-acidification or added sugar unnecessary. Most of our wines are fully fermented and of *Kabinett* quality. We believe the characteristics of the individual vineyards should be clearly noticeable.

Although we were the first to grow Müller-Thurgau in Austria (and, incidentally, amongst the first to sell wine in bottle), we concentrate today on Grüner Veltliner, and Riesling with a low yield of about 45 hectoliters per hectare/2.6 tons per acre. In the loess terraces of our Wachtberg vineyard we also have the last plantation in Austria of yellow Traminer—a rarity which many of our customers appreciate.

Erich Salomon

WEINGUT UNDHOF

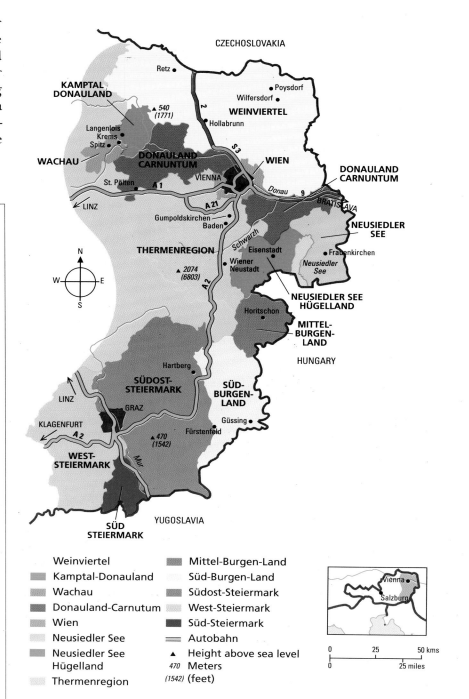

Weinviertel
Kamptal-Donauland
Wachau
Donauland-Carnutum
Wien
Neusiedler See
Neusiedler See Hügelland
Thermenregion
Mittel-Burgen-Land
Süd-Burgen-Land
Südost-Steiermark
West-Steiermark
Süd-Steiermark
Autobahn
▲ Height above sea level
470 Meters
(1542) (feet)

SWITZERLAND

by Ian Jamieson

RIGHT: Vineyards of St. Saphorin with southern exposure on the shores of Lake Geneva. At the eastern end of the Lavaux above Lake Geneva, the vineyards are planted mainly in Chasselas.

Switzerland is not a country one usually expects to rush headlong into change. These days, however, her vinous conservatism is threatened by the increasing strength of the European Community. Self-imposed practices aimed at improving quality are being introduced at community and cantonal level, with the intention of making Swiss wine more competitive in a possibly enlarged, possibly unified European wine market. Experiments in winemaking techniques, such as the partial evaporation of the juice of the unpressed grape in hermetically sealed wind tunnels, suggest a new approach to cellar procedure; the Swiss are also susceptible as anyone else to the current fashion for aging wine in new *barriques*.

There are vineyards in almost every canton, with nearly two-thirds being in the Valais on either side of the Rhône and in Vaud, overlooking the Lake of Geneva. Most of the white wine vineyards are planted in Chasselas — a fairly neutral grape which allows flavor from the soil to show through. As a general rule the Swiss like wines with less acidity than other European nations, but some growers in the hot climate of the Valais are producing a crisper style by harvesting Chasselas when it is not yet fully ripe. A lighter, slightly sparkling and cheaper Chasselas is produced between Lausanne and Geneva. The most elegant versions are likely to come from the very steep and expensive-to-work vineyards of the Lavaux or from Chablais Vaudois, between the Lake of Geneva and the start of the Valais.

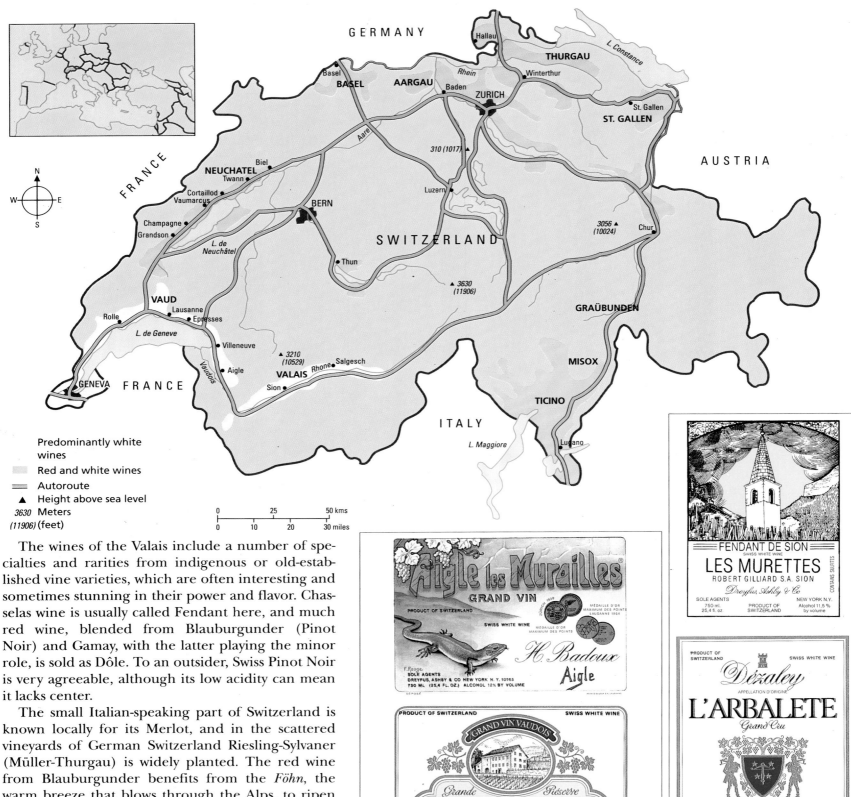

The wines of the Valais include a number of specialties and rarities from indigenous or old-established vine varieties, which are often interesting and sometimes stunning in their power and flavor. Chasselas wine is usually called Fendant here, and much red wine, blended from Blauburgunder (Pinot Noir) and Gamay, with the latter playing the minor role, is sold as Dôle. To an outsider, Swiss Pinot Noir is very agreeable, although its low acidity can mean it lacks center.

The small Italian-speaking part of Switzerland is known locally for its Merlot, and in the scattered vineyards of German Switzerland Riesling-Sylvaner (Müller-Thurgau) is widely planted. The red wine from Blauburgunder benefits from the *Föhn*, the warm breeze that blows through the Alps, to ripen the grapes and reduce the likelihood of rot.

Practically all Swiss wine is dry, and much good wine is produced in large merchants' cellars and by cooperative cellars. The best remains in Switzerland.

ABOVE: Swiss wine labels are among the most colorful of any wine region in Europe. This selection represents top producers from Chablais Vandois, the Valais and the lakeside appellation of Dézaley.

GROWER'S VIEW

Swiss wine enjoys a high popularity at home which may have made us a little complacent. We should now see our wines from an international point of view. It is more a matter of being familiar with them, than of their intrinsic quality. Take Chasselas as a case in point. In Switzerland we love its delicate, almost neutral character, but abroad its low acidity and tangy taste of the soil are often considered odd.

In fact we have a wide range of styles of wine, including a number of vine varieties that are unique to Switzerland. The production of these specialties is limited but they are much enjoyed by the adventurous foreign wine lover. I believe our Chasselas too could become suited to foreign palates, but it needs to be produced differently and with more acidity. For the export market we should concentrate at first on Chardonnay and Pinot Noir.

We must diversify to become less dependent on our home market and to establish our image as one of Europe's classic wine-producing countries. This is particularly important in the light of developments in the European Community. Switzerland is no longer an island.

Charles Rolaz

ROLAZ AND COMPANY

ENGLAND

by Jim Ainsworth

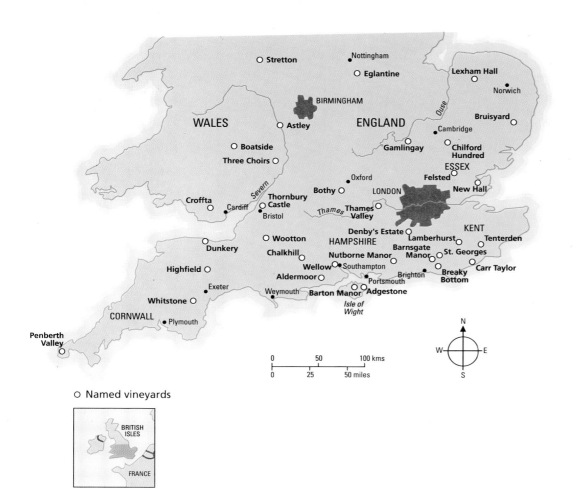

○ Named vineyards

BELOW: The label from one of the wineries which has pioneered the cultivation of Seyval Blanc in England, a grape generally regarded as having enhanced the quality of English white wines.

Breaky Bottom

Dry White Table Wine

Estate grown and bottled by Peter Hall
Breaky Bottom Vineyard, Rodmell, Sussex, UK
Produce of United Kingdom
75cl   11% vol

As marginal climates go, England's is nearly off the scale. Only a moderating maritime effect makes wine-growing in England possible. Estimates of the total number of vineyards vary, because many are tiny and still at the hobby stage, but 440 are registered with the English Vineyards Association, which represents about 70 percent: relatively few of these, however rate as a significant commercial proposition.

About one third of English vineyards are planted with the white Müller-Thurgau, a variety noted in Germany more for volume than character. In England it turns out attractive, crisp, flowery wines which owe some of their distinction to that fact that yields are generally about a quarter of those achieved in Germany.

One grape variety, Seyval Blanc, has caused a particular problem because it is a hybrid. Although it produces some of the country's most stylish wines, it is outlawed by the European Community for the production of "quality wine". A little red is made, sometimes from Pinot Noir, sometimes from Germanic red varieties.

A system for the control of quality wines suddenly sprang into existence in 1991, without benefit of a pilot scheme to iron out any difficulties. Seyval Blanc is not allowed in quality wine, although it is anticipated that the regulations will be reviewed in due course.

---- GROWER'S VIEW ----

I do not have any background as a winemaker, but I do have strong family associations through my French mother, which have influenced my approach to winemaking.

In 1974 I planted the vineyard at Breaky Bottom, mostly with Seyval Blanc. This variety ripens well in England, thrives in my chalk soil, crops well and shows good disease resistance.

The vineyard is only 5 kilometers/3 miles from the sea, an isolated dry chalk valley hidden in a fold in the South Downs. The soil is similar to Champagne with a high pH.

Grape quality is crucial and the vineyard must be netted against birds to get full ripeness. I pick in November. I stop spraying at least eight weeks before picking to ensure a clean crop.

Yields can be pretty erratic. In 1989, with a Burgundian summer, I produced 27,000 bottles, but production can fall to 1,000 in a poor year. I don't restrict the crop in prolific years. Experience shows me that Seyval makes full and flavorsome wines. What is more, they age well. My 1982 Seyvals are still wonderfully alive with the depth of a good Sancerre or Chablis.

Harvesting is by hand, pressing with a modern horizontal 1.5 tonne/1.5 ton Vaslin press. I like to press hard, looking for extra tannin and zip from the skins, pips and stalks. I don't like the fruit to dominate, and this method gives the wine a more vinous character — a good fruit/alcohol balance. The must is chaptalized and fermented fast on a Champagne-type yeast, in glass fiber vats, and bottled around April.

Peter Hall
BREAKY BOTTOM VINEYARD

EASTERN EUROPE

by Jim Ainsworth

Bulgaria

Why has Bulgarian wine done so much better in the West than that of other east European countries? One reason is that it got off to an early start, thanks to specialization within Comecon countries, the East European Communist counterpart to the European Economic Community, under Krushchev during the 1950s. During the 1970s Bulgaria successfully exploited the western predilection for Cabernet Sauvignon (which now accounts for one in four vines), and since then it has never looked back.

Production has fluctuated during the 1980s. As exports to the Soviet Union dropped during this period, vines were pulled up, reducing output by a quarter. Years of drought in the late 1980s reduced it further, from 4.5 million hectoliters/118,881,000 U.S. gallons in 1985 to a mere 1.8 million hectoliters/47,552,400 U.S. gallons in 1990. But the 1990 vintage was "the best in forty-five years" according to the Bulgarian Vintners Company (B.V.C.). Rain during 1991 relieved the worst effects of the drought, and production approached normal levels.

Short harvests in the early 1990s moved Bulgaria from fifteenth to about twentieth in the volume league table of wine production. It was the second largest exporter of bottled wine in the world up to 1990.

Political changes have affected the structure of the industry. Following elections in the summer of 1990 Vinprom (the state organization responsible for wine production under communism) was disbanded. Vinimpex, its export arm, survived because it was the hard currency earner and took over some of Vinprom's functions, as well as the job of trying to introduce the industry to market-based ideas. B.V.C., which used to market all Bulgaria's wines in the West, now faces competition, since individual wineries will be able to make their own direct agency deals. It has also faced the end of cheap government loans and price controls, which helped to make Bulgarian wines so competitive on export markets.

The new government helped, or possibly hindered, progress by introducing the Land Reform Act in February 1991. This piece of legislation enabled people to claim back land that had been theirs (or their family's) prior to 1945. In the long

LEFT: A low-tech hand-bottling line in Bulgaria. How long will such labor-intensive practices last?

run, and in theory, private ownership of land should encourage personal enterprise and initiative, and perhaps a free market in grapes, similar to that which successfully underpins good quality wines elsewhere in the world. In the short-term, though, it is more likely to produce chaos. Another change has been that wineries, which previously had to pass on 70 percent of foreign earnings to the government, can now keep all their profits, providing investment capital and extra cash for the rapidly increasing price of grapes.

One of the jobs Vinimpex is tackling is that of renewing the quality control system. Regional designations currently use adminstrative rather than viticultural criteria. A new regional map, taking due account of grape varieties, soils and climatic differences, is in preparation. For the present, the old system remains in place.

Quality levels begin with standard Table Wine, which does not indicate an area of origin. Country

ABOVE: These labels illustrate the range of grape varieties grown in Bulgaria, from the indigenous Mavrud or Assenovgrad producing arguably Bulgaria's most distinguished red wines, to more familiar varietals such as Merlot and Sauvignon Blanc, which successfully compete in the international market.

Wine does, and is made from specified grape varieties. Wines of Declared Geographical Origin (D.G.O.) carry a specific district designation. *Controliran* Wines (equivalent to A.O.C. in France, for example) have to be made from specified grape varieties grown in designated vineyard sites in one of the twenty-six D.G.O.s. Both D.G.O. and *Controliran* wines can claim Reserve status if they have been matured in oak (two to three years for whites, three to four years for reds) and have some potential for aging.

Of the regional designations Shumen, Varna and Targovishte in the Eastern Region have the best track record for white wines, including Chardonnay. Oaky Khan Krum is best known outside the country, but Novi Pazar and Preslav also produce moderately good Chardonnays.

Suhindol, Pavlikeni and Pleven in the Northern Region are best known for Cabernet Sauvignon, Merlot, and the native Gamza which produces full-bodied, chunky wines that can age well. Svischtov and Lozitza Cabernet Sauvignons are particularly rich.

Assenovgrad in the Southern Region is home to the native Mavrud variety, producing hearty, plummy wines that age well over five years and more. Plovdiv, Sakar Mountain, and Oriachovitza Cabernet Sauvignons and Cabernet-Merlot blends

are particularly good. Finest of all are the Reserve Merlots from Stambolova.

The pride of the Southwest Region is Melnik, a grape and a place, as well as a wine. Melnik is a thick-skinned variety, grown in Damianitza and Harsovo, that produces weighty, tannic wines for long keeping.

Controliran Wines	
Suhindol Gamza	Assenovgrad Mavrud
Sakar Merlot	Novi Pazar Chardonnay
Svischtov Cabernet	Oriachovitza
Sauvignon	Cabernet-Merlot
Lozitza Cabernet	Varna Chardonnay
Stambolovo Merlot	Yantra Valley Cabernet
Preslav Chardonnay	Sauvignon
South Coast Rosé	Pavlikeni Gamza
Rozovata Dolina Misket	Sungurlare Misket
"Treasure of Kralevo"	Novo Selo Gamza
Khan Krum Traminer	Harsovo Melnik
Russe Riverside White	Liaskovetz Aligoté

Czechoslovakia

Like Germany, Czechoslovakia is equally at home with grapes and grain. Beer dominates the Bohemian north, and wine the Slovakian south (along the borders with Austria and Hungary) as well as parts of Moravia.

Little of the 2 million hectoliters/52,836,000 U.S. gallons of wine escapes the country. Three quarters of it is white, and much of it — made from Welschriesling, Grüner Veltliner and Müller-Thurgau — bears a family resemblance to the Austro-Hungarian styles to the south. Limberger or Frankovka (Blaufränkisch in Austria, Kékfrankos in Hungary) makes attractively soft and easy red wine.

Although less well known than Hungary's version, Czechoslovakia produces a Tokay from Furmint and Hárslevelü, with a little help from Muscat.

Hungary

Anybody taking a historical perspective, and many Hungarians do, will recall the extent and wealth of the Austro-Hungarian Empire. Hungary's association with fine wine goes back farther than any other country in the Eastern Bloc, including Bulgaria.

Under communism the wine industry was monolithic. State farms and state cooperatives produced state wine. Now Western buyers are asking for later-picked grapes, for more body and character, more complexity, and early bottling for freshness. Although international varieties do well, native grape varieties could be the strongest card Hungary has to play in a world bursting with Chardonnay and Cabernet. Whether world markets will take to the style that Hungarians enjoy is an open question. They look for medium body, without too strong or intrusive a varietal character, and a certain honeyed warmth. That is, when they can afford it. The future success or otherwise of winemaking here, as throughout eastern Europe, is tied inextricably to the country's economic well-being.

Of the whites, Olasz Rizling grows abundantly in

Tokay

Tokay is the finest wine of Hungary, even though it accounts for only a small proportion of Hungary's total annual output of 3.8 million hectoliters/100,388,400 U.S. gallons. It is made from Furmint and Hárslevelü grapes near the Czech border. Tokay Szamorodni (literally "as it comes") may be dry (*szaraz*) or sweet (*edes*); it is Tokay Aszú and Tokay Aszú Essencia that most resemble the Tokay of legend, the wine that was reputed to last for centuries.

Tokay, like all great sweet wines, relies on *Botrytis cinerea* for its character. The botrytized, shrivelled grapes, called *Aszú,* are put into *puttonyos,* or wooden tubs, and left while a small amount of free-run juice collects at the bottom. This juice is *essencia* and is used for adding to other musts. The contents of the *puttonyos,* minus the *essencia,* is crushed to a paste and added to dry base wine made from non-botrytized grapes. The sweetness of the final wine depends on how many *puttonyos* are added, and the label of a bottle of Tokay Aszú will state the number. Tokay Aszú Essencia contains around eight *puttonyos.*

Today's Tokay, though not the same as that of previous centuries, will still keep well. It has a Sherry-like nose (oxidation being a deliberate part of the winemaking process), and becomes richer in flavor over perhaps fifteen years. Old Tokays, of thirty years plus, can still taste very fresh.

the Great Plain south of Budapest; most is undistinguished, but the best comes from around Mount Badacsonyi, a south-facing volcanic outcrop overlooking Lake Balaton. Furmint, an ingredient of Tokay, also makes worthy dry wine of its own accord. Leanyka ("little girl"), and Ezerjo ("thousand blessings"), which makes its best wines around Mór, are both underrated, perhaps because they produce rather delicate wines. Kéknyelü ("blue stalk") and Hárslevelü ("lime-leaf") are both native too, the latter making good medium-sweet wines in Mátraalya. Szürkebarát, which also does well in the Mount Badacsonyi region, is a variant of Pinot Gris or Ruländer.

Among red grape varieties, Kadarka produces big gutsy wines, particularly at Szekszárd in the Great Plain. Kékfrankos (the Austrian Blaufränkisch) turns out light quaffing wines. Zweigelt, another Austrian import, makes attractively soft and succulent reds. Bull's Blood or Egri Bikavér, blended from Kadarka, Kékfrankos and Merlot, is made around the city of Eger and briefly captured the West's imagination during the 1970s.

— International boundary
▲ Height above sea level
1328 Meters
(4537) (feet)

LEFT: The famous Bull's Blood red wine from Hungary is a blend of principally local grape varieties. Furmint is also made from varietals and the result is a dry wine of quality.

BELOW: The three styles of Tokay: the basic Szamorodni, the Aszu and Essencia, made entirely from *Botrytis*-affected grapes. The latter two types most closely resemble this Hungarian wine of legend.

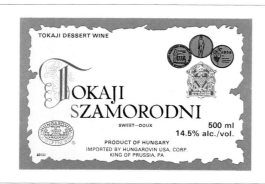

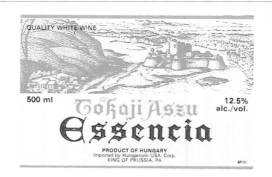

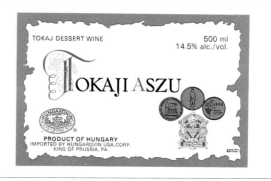

ABOVE: A small Hungarian vineyard, located in Eger.

BELOW: The Vranac grape, exclusive to Yugoslavia, produces wine of remarkable robustness and aging potential. The Tarnave region of Romania is notable for crisp, white wines of quality such as this Premiat Sauvignon Blanc.

Yugoslavia

Yugoslavia makes good Merlots, Cabernet Sauvignons, Pinot Noirs and beefy reds from local grapes: lively Vranac, robust, full-bodied Postup and Prokupac, alcoholic Dingac, lighter Plavina and Plovdina, and a sweet, nutty, tawny, dessert wine, Prosek.

Yugoslavia's potential for quality has always been greater than its achievement. Drinkable, uninspiring, whites made from Laski Rizling have been the export norm. Slovenia's vineyards at Ljutomer and Ormoz provide much of the ordinary white wines that reach the West. But delicate flavors are possible in the Julian Alps where Riesling and Traminer are leading a drive for better quality.

Vojvodina, Kosmet, the Fruska Gora hills, and Kosovo are jewels in Serbia's crown. Croatia has one third of the country's vineyard area and includes Dalmatia, where whites tend to be rich and earthy; Posip, Bogdanusa and Vugava are among the names to look for. An oxidized Sherry-like wine called Grk is made on the island of Korcula. The structure of the industry, state-controlled until now, will doubtless undergo considerable revision in the near future.

VRANAC® 1989
KONTROLISANA OZNAKA PORIJEKLA
APPELLATION D'ORIGIN CONTROLEE
MONTENEGRO
PRODUCE OF YUGOSLAVIA
11,5% VOL   75 cl
A   N° 3024145
ESTATE BOTTLED BY AGROKOMBINAT "13 JUL"
TITOGRAD AND IMPORTED BY
VITKOVITCH BROTHERS, LONDON SE1 7 EF

PREMIAT®
SAUVIGNON BLANC
WHITE WINE FROM THE TARNAVE REGION
1987
PRODUCT OF ROMANIA
IMPORTED BY MONSIEUR HENRI WINES, LTD., WHITE PLAINS, N.Y. 10604
ALCOHOL 12% VOL   CONTENTS 750 ML

GROWER'S VIEW

Each of our growers, all eagerly awaiting an economic miracle from the West, contributed a plot of land from 0.5 hectares to 3 hectares/1.2 acres to 7.4 acres. Most are around the village of Mad, traditionally among the best communes in Tokay. Browsing through a bookshop in old Buda, I came across Anthony Szirmay's *Topografica Politica Zempleniensis*, printed in Buda in 1803, which contained the complete 1789 classification for Tokay — divided into first, second and third growths —but also the names of winemaking families living in each village at the time.

Some of those original names, like the Molnars, Szepsys, Bodnars, Orosz and Kiss families, are among our present group of growers. Of their 100 hectares/247 acres, 51 hectares/126 acres are second growth, and the remaining 2 hectares/4.9 acres are third growth. Under the state monopoly these wines were simply blended into anonymity with all the rest.

The grape varieties nowadays are mainly Furmint, a high-yielder with good acidity, which rots easily, giving strongly sappy, velvety and high-flavored wine; Hárslevelü, a dry climate late-ripener; and a tiny amount of Muscat. Other varieties such as Weissling-Feher Szölö and Augster-Gher are no longer used, but it would be interesting to know what qualities, if any, they brought to the old Tokays.

The project is a long-term one. The vines are young, mostly under ten years old. But the resurrection of the old classification is already seeing the gradual return of a winegrowing community's pride and self-respect.

Peter Vinding-Diers

THE ROYAL TOKAY WINE COMPANY

The Former Soviet Union

When the republics of the Soviet Union were united their output, at 40 million hectoliters/1,056,772,000 U.S. gallons, was the third largest for a country in the world. It is unlikely ever to be considered in these terms again.

Very little wine in the past was exported to the West, and until quality improves, the wine is unlikely to succeed in foreign markets. But improvement is unlikely unless there is foreign input in the form of know-how, equipment and money.

The most potential is to be seen in four republics: Georgia, which, together with Armenia and Azerbaijan, constitute the oldest producing region, dating back to Noah's time at least; Moldavia; Russia itself; and the Ukraine, including the Crimea and the site of Massandra, from where wine made for the tsars, and drunk by Stalin, was eventually shipped to the West for sale by Sotheby's in London.

Grapes are bewildering in their variety, from the

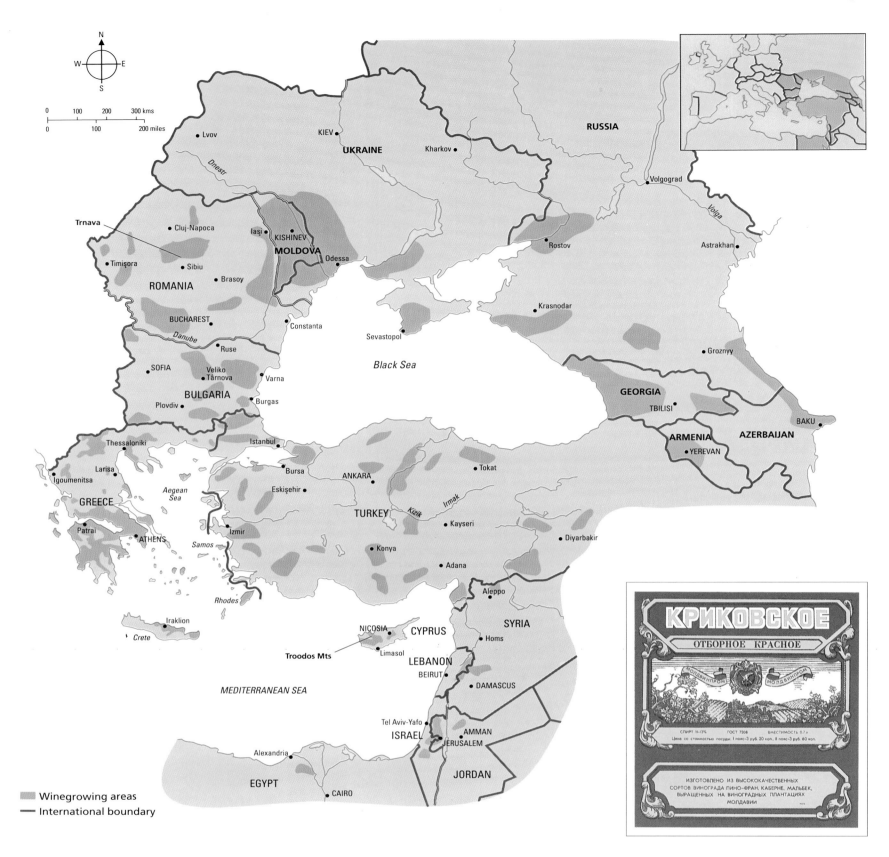

ubiquitous white Rkatziteli and red Saperavi, to the likes of Grasnostok Zolotovskij or Tsimljanskoje, which, however good they taste, are unlikely to end up as popular varietals in the West. Styles run the whole gamut, but the sweeter and more sparkling they are, the more domestic consumers seem to like them. The native sparkling wine, called Champanski, is made sweet for the domestic market, but dry for tourists.

Romania

Like other east European countries Romania has the sort of climate, and a sufficiently mixed bag of native and international grape varieties, to make good wines. But there has been little opportunity for its annual production of 7.5 million hecto-liters/198,135,000 U.S. gallons to create an impression abroad in recent years. Its present wine

industry is soundly based on a mixture of tradition and sensible, if limited, use of technology.

Cotnari, from Moldavia, is the most famous white wine, made sweet in a vaguely Sauterne style. Tami-ioasa is an attractive medium-sweet wine made from a member of the Muscat family, while Feteasca Alba (Hungary's Leanyka) is the country's staple white grape. The Babeasca grape makes savory, spicy reds, while Feteasca Negra makes soft and full-bodied ones. There are also widespread plantings of Muscat, Gewürztraminer, Chardonnay, Riesling and Ruländer, as well as Cabernet Sauvignon, Merlot and Pinot Noir.

Romania's crispest, freshest whites come from Tirnave in the northern mountains. The Banat Plain in the west has rarely produced wines of more than drinkable standard. Dealul Mare in the south-east is home to international varieties including Pinot Noir. Murfatlar near the Black Sea makes dessert wines based on Muscat.

ABOVE: This label of a Moldavian wine, produced from Merlot and Cabernet Sauvignon, represents one of the former Soviet Union's finest red wines. Much prized by former Communist Party bosses and consequently once restricted in supply, today these wines are increasingly available in the West.

191

GREECE AND THE LEVANT

by Maggie McNie, M. W.

ABOVE: A view towards the Aegean from the beautiful vineyards of Domaine Carras.

BELOW: Attica is the best area for Retsina. Naoussa is a red wine made from the ancient Xynomavro grape.

Greece

The Greeks were the finest winemakers of the Classical era, admired throughout the known world, but many centuries of Turkish occupation meant that winemaking was reduced to a village activity with no thought of quality. The renaissance began some thirty years ago, but owing to the prevalence of retsina and local barrel wine in most tourist resorts, rather than the finer wines, few consumers, both Greek and foreign, are aware of the quality Greek wines now being produced.

Greece has many indigenous grape varieties which give new and often very interesting flavors to wine, such as the Agiorgitiko (St. George) which makes the soft and fruity Nemea, or the Xynomavro of Naoussa and Goumenissa, the Robola of Cephalonia, or the blend of Assyrtiko, Athiri and Aedani which make the powerful wine of Santorini. In addition, there is now a system of appellations for the better wines, including the famous Muscats of Samos and of Patras, as well as the great Mavrodaphne wines, remotely reminiscent of tawny Port.

Production in the past has been centered on the great firms that owned some vineyards but also bought in grapes, such as Achaia Clauss, Boutari, Cambas, Kourtakis and Tsantalis. But in the late 1960s a wealthy ship owner, John Carras, started the vineyards of Domaine Carras (today with the appellation Côtes de Meliton) making estate wines. Assisted by Professor Peynaud of Bordeaux, in addition to Greek grape varieties, the estate planted some French varieties, including Cabernet Sauvignon, Cabernet Franc, Merlot and Cinsaut. The success of these wines undoubtedly encouraged the development of other small estates, such as the wines of Château Semeli and Stroliloa, thus changing the face of Greek wine, which today, if it can only shake off the image of retsina and barrel wine, can certainly make a contribution to the quality wine of the world.

Retsina

The practice of adding pine resin to white wine is an old one, dating back to the ancient Greeks, who sealed the amphorae in which wine was stored with pine resin. The resin tainted the wine and was believed to preserve it; it was but a short step, then, to add the resin during fermentation, as happens nowadays.

The majority of Greek wine sold abroad comes under the heading of retsina, although strictly speaking retsina is an aromatized wine, like vermouth. It goes well with Greek food, but it is an image that the more adventurous Greek producers are keen to leave behind.

The qualitative potential of Greek white wine stems from the many excellent indigenous varieties — indeed, I would hesitate to declare one of them to be the best for fear of doing injustice to the others.

Each variety displays certain unique characteristics, assuming it is grown under the right climatic and soil conditions. Among the best I would mention Malagousia, Robola, Assyrtiko, Athiri and Moshcofilero, although I would also mention the white variety that produces the *vin doux naturel*, the Muscat of Samos.

Malagousia is a grape whose name is familiar in Greece, but has never been grown and vinified on its own; indeed, until recently it was believed that it had vanished. In the experimental vineyard of Porto Carras, where the late Professor Logothetis had concentrated almost all the Greek white varieties, five Malagousia vines were found. Ten years ago I commenced experimental

vinifications which proved that this variety produces a very aromatic and pleasant wine.

Future work on red wines must be in two directions. The first is the improvement of vinification of the indigenous Greek varieties — Agiorgitiko, Limnio, Xynomavro, Negoska and Kotsifali — which produce the appellation wines of Nemea, Côtes de Meliton, Naoussa, Amyntaion, Goumenissa and Peza. The second is the production of foreign varieties. After twenty-three years of growing French vines at the Porto Carras vineyard, we have proved that grapes such as Cabernet Sauvignon, Cabernet Franc, Petite Sirah and Grenache can be acclimatized and produce high-quality wine.

E. Gerovassiliou

DOMAINE CARRAS AND GEROVASSILIOU ESTATE

Israel

The Jewish tradition of wine production goes back to Moses, and is mentioned throughout the Old Testament. Modern winemaking started during the 1880s with the encouragement of Baron Edmond de Rothschild. Vineyards were planted with mainly French varieties and two wineries were established, followed by a cooperative venture in 1906. The Wine Institute was founded in the late 1950s, but the most significant date was 1960, when a visiting professor from the University of California at Davis suggested that the Golan Heights, with its lower temperature (rarely more than 25°C/77°F particularly at night), might be suitable for fine wine production.

Planting commenced in 1977, with such classic varieties as Pinot Noir, Merlot and Cabernet Sauvignon for the reds, and Sauvignon Blanc, Chenin Blanc, Sémillon, Chardonnay and Riesling for whites. Sweeter styles have been available for many years. The market has recently seen good quality, fruity wines such as Gamla Cabernet Sauvignon and Yarden Sauvignon Blanc. Kosher wines were for years the most widely-sold wines in the United States.

Lebanon

In spite of its ancient vine-producing traditions, wine in the Lebanon really owes its existence to Christian communities which kept some vineyards in production during the centuries of Islamic domination. Modern statistics show a large amount of land under vine, but it is important to remember that most of the crop is sold as table grapes or as dried fruit.

The main wine-growing district is the Bekaa Valley, divided from Beirut and the coast by mountains. The valley floor is some 1,000 meters/3,300 feet above sea level, giving the cooler conditions needed to produce fine wine. The best vineyards are on the slopes, situated on gravel over limestone subsoil.

The leading winemaker is Serge Hochar of Chateau Musar, which was founded in 1930 by his father, Gaston. Despite the constant fighting, and

ABOVE: Gamla and Yarden show the modern face of Israeli wine using single variétals. Ben Ami is a traditional red wine.

LEFT: The claret-like wine produced at Chateau Musar is capable of long aging.

danger from tanks and jet fighters, the estate has produced vintages in all years except 1984, when fighting prevented the grape trucks reaching the winery in time — on arrival the grapes were fermenting and oxidized, in a condition that no wine-maker could use. Bordeaux-trained Serge Hochar produces a claret-style of wine, matured in wood and usually capable of aging well, from Cabernet Sauvignon, Syrah and Cinsaut, and has also made an interesting, as yet experimental, Chardonnay wine.

Other than Musar, little Lebanese wine is available, and those tasted have often shown crude, old-fashioned winemaking, although the grapes are often excellent. Given time and peace, the Lebanon has great potential.

Turkey

If Sumerian records are to be trusted, wine has been made here for over 4,000 years, and it appears to have been enjoyed in western Europe at the end of last century while *phylloxera* was devastating the French vineyards. However, although government policy, which follows that of Kemal Ataturk, is to develop the wine industry, Islamic tradition is still very powerful, and less than 3 percent of the grapes grown are actually turned into wine. Nonetheless, wine zones are being developed as the first step towards a full and enforceable wine regime.

The textbooks always mention Buzbag, a red wine from local grape varieties, and Trakya, a dry white from Thrace. However, from central Turkey come wines of the Diren, a small family concern run by the six children of the founder. Diren wines are grown traditionally, without artificial fertilizers and pesticides, near Tokat, and use the indigenous Narince for their white wines and Bogazkere and Okuzgozu grapes for their red and rosé wines, all made by modern controlled-temperature fermentation methods. Tekel, the state monopoly, makes about 60 percent of the country's wines, while another small, independent firm, Cavaklidere, also uses indigenous grapes. In Thrace and along the western coast, however, some interesting wines are being made from French varieties. Tastings suggest enormous but currently untapped potential in Turkey.

FAR RIGHT: Commandaria is the great specialty of Cyprus, while labels for Palomino and Riesling wines show how the Cypriot wine industry is developing.

BELOW: Local Turkish grapes are still cultivated according to traditional methods and are producing wines of rising interest to the international market.

Cyprus

Cypriot wines undoubtedly made their mark through the Sherry styles which in previous decades were highly successful on the United Kingdom market. The fall in demand for this style of wine, plus the European Economic Community's refusal to recognize them following Spain's accession in the mid-1980s, might have led to a collapse of the wine industry. However, in spite of recent local difficulties, it has survived, putting much effort towards the making of light, dry table wines, both red and white.

Free from *phylloxera,* the island grows mainly three varieties, the black Mavron, the Xynisteri, white but prone to oxidation (and therefore suitable for Sherry styles) and the Muscat d'Alexandrie, and much of the production is controlled by large firms in or near the port of Limassol, such as Keo and Sodap. In addition some Palomino is now being grown for Sherry-style wine.

The vines, however, are mostly grown on the Troodos Mountains, a considerable distance from the wineries, and one of the current problems arises from the time taken for the grapes to reach the wineries. However, an encouraging sign is the development of regional wineries much nearer the vineyards, resulting in much fruitier styles of wine.

The great speciality of Cyprus is Commandaria, a dessert wine of some antiquity, named by the Knights Templar and made from a blend of red and white grapes (Mavron and Xynisteri) sun-dried to concentrate the sugar and fermented slowly. The very best are well aged; the odd bottle has been known to last a hundred years.

NORTH AMERICA

by Frank Prial

LEFT: Highway 101 through Sonoma and Mendocino Counties is the arterial spine of California's world-renowned North Coast wine region.

Historians tend to date the beginning of the American wine adventure from the arrival of the Franciscan Junipero Serra in California in 1769 to found Mission San Diego, the first of a chain of twenty-one Catholic missions that would reach Sonoma in northern California over the ensuing fifty years.

While Padre Serra probably brought with him cuttings of the Criolla, or Mission grape, a European variety that was to produce California's first wine, it was not until at least a decade later that there were records of wine being made by the Franciscans, and it was made at Mission San Gabriel, east of the frontier settlement of Los Angeles.

But wine had been made in this country long before Padre Serra arrived. In his masterly *The Wines of America,* Leon D. Adams dates the first successful winemaking to 1562 when French Huguenots used the wild Muscadine — sometimes called Scuppernong — grapes they found growing near what is now Jacksonville, Florida. Both the Jamestown colonists in Virginia, in 1609, and the Pilgrims at Plymouth, Mass., twelve years later, fermented native grapes into wine.

But winemaking in North America goes back even further. As governor of New Spain — Mexico — Hernando Cortez oversaw the planting of extensive vineyards — probably the Criolla grape — as

early as 1524, and the first commerical Mexican winery was in operation at Coahuila, 800 kilometers/500 miles north of Mexico City, by 1593. It was from Mexico that winemaking spread south to Argentina and Chile and north to what was to become the United States.

The first successful vineyards in what was later to become the United States were planted near what is now El Paso, Texas, when it was part of Nuevo Mexico. In the far north, Jacques Cartier found wild vines on an island in the St. Lawrence in the 1530s, and some ninety years later, Jesuit missionaries in the same area began to make wine with which to celebrate the Mass. The grapes were probably not too different from those Lief Ericsson was supposed to have found when and if he landed at Newfoundland some six hundred years earlier.

The eastern seaboard of the United States, beginning with the Huguenots and going up to Thomas Jefferson, had a long and much more varied experience with viticulture well before it began in California, but with middling success.

In their 1941 book *American Wines*, Frank Schoonmaker and Tom Marvel wrote of the early settlers. "They strove to make the land conform to their ideas, or the ideas of overseas experts, instead of taking their cue from nature and adapting them-

195

RIGHT: Bottle from the Forbes Collection alleged to be 1787 Château Lafite from Thomas Jefferson's cellar. Its provenance has never been authenticated.

The native varieties proliferated. The Isabella was introduced in 1816; the pink Catawba in 1823, the Concord in 1854 and the Elvira in 1870. A report prepared by the British Legation in Washington in 1859 indicated that Ohio had 1200 hectares/3,000 acres of vineyards; Kentucky, Missouri and Illinois 200 hectares/500 each; Indiana, 400 hectares/1,000 acres, and the Carolinas, 200 hectares/500 acres. "At least 75,706 hectoliters/2 million gallons of wine are now raised in the United States," the report said, "the average value of which may be taken at a dollar and a half a gallon."

By 1880, according to the U.S. Department of Agriculture, Ohio had 4,000 hectares/10,000 acres, Missouri 3,000 hectares/7,400 acres and New York, which had not even been mentioned twenty-one years earlier, reported 31,134 hectares/12,600 acres of vineyards.

In the meantime, California had come into what could be called its first golden age of wine.

Even before the Gold Rush of 1849, Easterners and mid-Westerners had begun to see California as a paradise on earth waiting with open arms for

RIGHT: The legendary "Count" Agoston Haraszthy, Buena Vista's founder.

BELOW: Napa Valley pickers pause for a photographer during the 1882 harvest. By then, the center of the California wine business had moved north from Los Angeles and the wines were winning prizes around the world.

selves to conditions as they found them".

In other words, they tried to grow European vinifera grapes in hostile climates and soils. Jefferson, whose cellars were filled with fine French wines, is said even to have imported French soil in an attempt to get his European vines to grow. His decision, in 1823, to abandon the effort to grow vinifera and to concentrate on native varieties is a landmark in the gradual ascendency of native grape varieties in colonial America.

Jefferson's interest centered on the Alexander grape, which is said to have been discovered near Philadelphia by James Alexander, the gardener to Thomas Penn, William Penn's son. "I think it will be well to push the culture of this grape without losing time and efforts in the search for foreign vines, which it will take centuries to adapt to our soil and climate", Jefferson wrote.

Jefferson was off by about 140 years. European vinifera vines have grown successfully and produced good wines in Jefferson's own part of Virginia since the 1960s.

anyone with the energy to make the trip west. By 1830 there were already some 100,000 vines in Los Angeles, according to Leon Adams. By 1848, a year before the gold discovery, there were vineyards as far north as Napa and Sacramento counties. By 1856, California wines were being shipped in bulk to Great Britain, Germany, Russia, Japan and South America. That same year, the remarkable Agoston Haraszthy arrived in Northern California. A promoter and deal-maker in the best tradition of the American frontier, he had emigrated from Hungary as a self-styled political exile. He founded what is now Sauk City in Wisconsin, then turned up in San Diego in 1848.

Obsessed with grapes and wine, he planted vineyards unsuccessfully at several locations before happening on Sonoma in 1856. There he created what is now the original Buena Vista Vineyard. In 1861, he went to Europe representing the state of Califor-

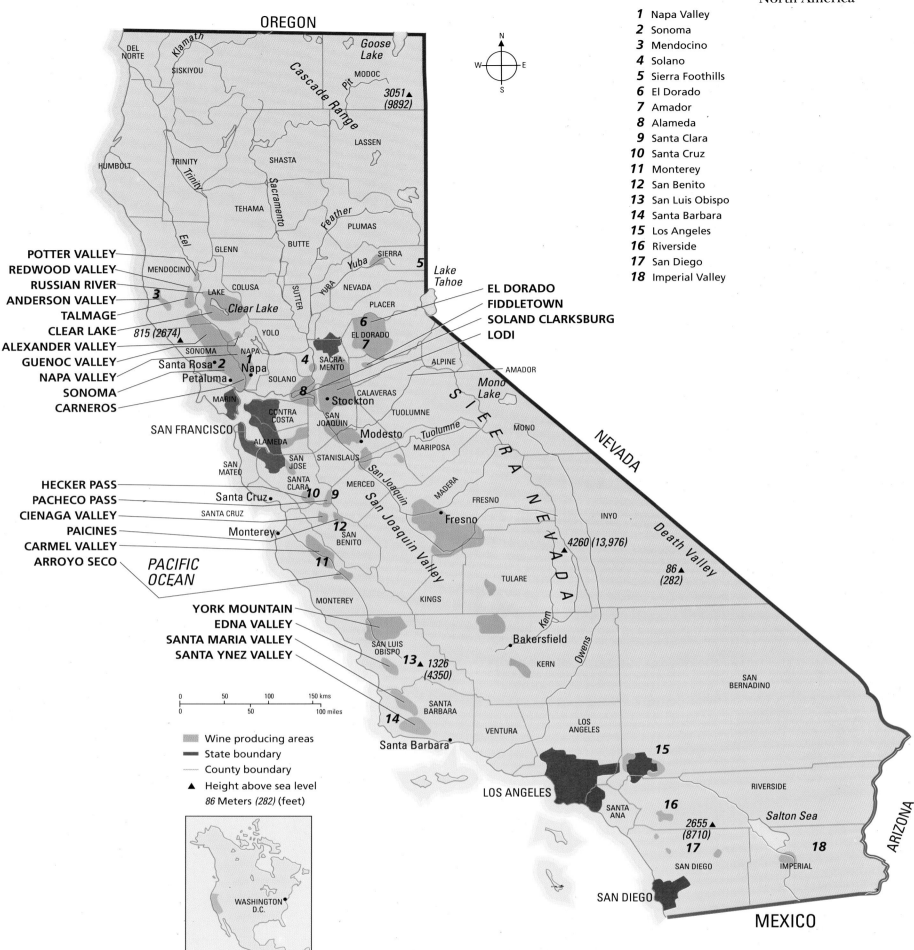

1 Napa Valley
2 Sonoma
3 Mendocino
4 Solano
5 Sierra Foothills
6 El Dorado
7 Amador
8 Alameda
9 Santa Clara
10 Santa Cruz
11 Monterey
12 San Benito
13 San Luis Obispo
14 Santa Barbara
15 Los Angeles
16 Riverside
17 San Diego
18 Imperial Valley

POTTER VALLEY
REDWOOD VALLEY
RUSSIAN RIVER
ANDERSON VALLEY
TALMAGE
CLEAR LAKE
ALEXANDER VALLEY
GUENOC VALLEY
NAPA VALLEY
SONOMA
CARNEROS

EL DORADO
FIDDLETOWN
SOLAND CLARKSBURG
LODI

HECKER PASS
PACHECO PASS
CIENAGA VALLEY
PAICINES
CARMEL VALLEY
ARROYO SECO

YORK MOUNTAIN
EDNA VALLEY
SANTA MARIA VALLEY
SANTA YNEZ VALLEY

Wine producing areas
State boundary
County boundary
▲ Height above sea level
86 Meters *(282)* (feet)

nia. He brought back 100,000 vines of more than three hundred grape varieties, converting California growers once and for all to the best European grapes. He became involved in the financial dealings surrounding Buena Vista and eventually fled to Nicaragua to make rum. He is supposed to have fallen into a stream and been eaten by crocodiles.

Haraszthy has been called "The father of the California wine industry", but he was considerably less than that. He did not, as has been claimed, introduce the Zinfandel grape to California, and he was not the first to bring superior grape varieties into the state. He did bring public attention to California wines through his writings but was, at best, a controversial and in fact highly dubious figure in the saga of California wine.

The California vineyards expanded rapidly in the years following the 1849 Gold Rush. Entrepreneurs and adventurers who flocked to the Pacific Coast to make their fortune did just that, in grapes and wine, not in gold. But in the mid-nineteenth century, the glory days of California wine were still in the future. It was not California that fascinated the world's wine drinkers then; it was Ohio. By 1860, Ohio was the most important wine-producing state in the nation, making a third of all the wine in the country and twice as much as California. The principal grape was the Catawba and the Ohio River was, for a brief

197

golden time, known as the Rhine of America.

Nicholas Longworth, a self-made millionaire, first planted grapes around Cincinnati in 1823. A quarter of a century later he had 4,047 hectares/10,000 acres of vines growing along the Ohio and his wines were featured in the great restaurants of New York and London. Then disaster struck. Black rot and powdery mildew, diseases for which there were then no cures, devastated the vines. By 1865 they were all dead.

Not all the Ohio growers were concentrated in the south. Those along the shore of Lake Erie, 322 kilometers/200 miles to the north, were spared the diseases that affected the vines around Cincinnati and prospered well into the twentieth century. Then they were stricken by another calamity; the vintners of Toledo and Sandusky survived black rot, but not Prohibition.

The end of the nineteenth century and the be-

ginning of the twentieth were roller-coaster years for the California wine industry. Boom-and-bust cycles ruined speculators and workmen alike at least four times in the years before Prohibition. Each time, prices climbed and more grapes were planted until, inevitably, the market broke and prices plunged.

But, more ominously, in those same years the temperance movement was gaining strength. Originally, it was aimed at spirits and beer but wine eventually was linked with them. By 1914, thirty-three states were "dry". Five years later, with the adoption of the eighteenth amendment to the Constitution, and the passage the following year of the Volstead Act, Prohibition was the law of the land.

In short order, many of the country's finest wineries had shut their doors and abandoned their vineyards. But then wine lovers discovered a loophole in the law. Anyone, it turned out, could make 758 liters/200 gallons of fruit juice in the privacy of his home. Overnight the demand for grapes and grape concentrate boomed. And if the juice fermented into something else, who was to know?

According to a University of California survey taken at the height of the Prohibition period, Americans made about 151,412 hectoliters/4 million gallons of illegal wine in 1910. In 1925, in the depths of Prohibition, they made 3,406,768 hectoliters/90 million gallons.

The home winemakers wanted big, fat juicy grapes, like the Alicante, and not tiny, intensely-flavored grapes used to make fine wine. Some speculators had moved into the abandoned vineyards, ripped out good grapes and replanted with cheap varieties destined to please a new, undemanding generation of winemakers.

When Repeal came in December 1933, it was wine made from these grapes, mostly raisin and table grapes, that flooded the market. Good wine grapes were scarce, especially those from the best

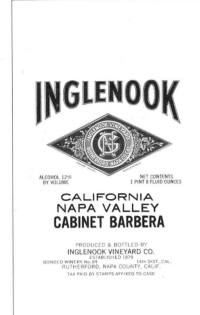

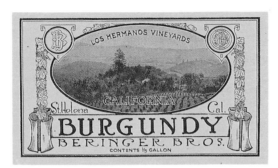

LEFT: Old California wine labels. Inglenook, Beringer and Foppiano still thrive. So does California Burgundy. But California Sauterne, Golden Chasselas and Cabinet Barbera disappeared long ago.

mountain vineyards, which had been abandoned more than a decade earlier. By the mid 1960s, according to Leon Adams, California's grape harvest was averaging more than 3,048,300 tonnes/3 million tons, but less than a fifth of it consisted of wine grapes.

And the demand for these grapes was growing. Americans, some of them at least, had once again discovered the pleasures of fine wine. Wineries that had subsisted on fortified wines, so-called Port and so-called Sherry and Muscatel, discovered that their customers were asking for dry table wines. Not many at first; mostly veterans who had served abroad during World War II, and the expanding middle class whose members were traveling for the first time and who had the discretionary income to buy, when they returned home, the wines they had come to enjoy on their trips abroad.

In 1968, for the first time, the consumption of table wines surpassed that of so-called dessert wines, the "Ports" and "Sherries" that most Americans had come to think represented what American wine was all about. What came to be known as the "wine revolution" was under way.

A major factor in the popularization of California's fine wines was the use of varietal names. For almost a century, American wines had usurped the names of the best French and Italian wines, presumably to make them more easily identifiable to the millions of first generation immigrants who were expected to buy them. "Claret", "Chianti", "Chablis" and "Burgundy" were used to describe any melange of grape types the winemakers happened to have on hand.

It was the writer and wine merchant Frank Schoonmaker who first convinced the Californians to identify their best wines by the grapes from which they were made. After some initial resistance, most premium wine producers adopted the practice and consumers learned to discuss the differences among various Cabernet Sauvignons or Zinfandels or Chardonnays.

But the laws required that only 55 percent of a varietal wine had to be from the named grape. Thus a wine billed as a Cabernet Sauvignon could actually contain 45 percent Carignane or some cheaper grape. Eventually the law was stiffened; the minimum is now 75 percent. Anything less and the varietal name cannot be used; the wine can be called only red — or white — table wine.

Ironically, just as the law was tightened up, many of California's best winemakers concluded that there were times when they needed more flexibility in blending. They decided that they would ignore the rule and blend as they saw fit. Most adopted proprietary names that they hope bespeak quality even when the wine is identified only as red or white table wine. Mondavi's Opus One, the John Daniel Society's Dominus and Francis Ford Coppola's Rubicon are examples of such *nouvelle vague* wines.

The "wine revolution", also known as the "wine boom", lasted until the early 1980s. Through the late 1960s and the 1970s, wine experts and wine publications routinely predicted that American wine consumption would double every three or four years well into the twenty-first century.

A quarter of a century earlier, in *American Wines*, Frank Schoonmaker and Tom Marvel wrote: "Nature seems to have planned the United States to be a nation of wine drinkers".

They were wrong. Both the figures and Schoonmaker and Marvel.

The United States produces some of the world's best wines and probably has some of the world's most knowledgeable wine consumers. But it is not a nation of wine drinkers. It never was and never will be. Accepting that fact is essential to understanding wine's status now and its future in North America.

Writing on the eve of World War II, Schoonmaker and Marvel were well aware of wine's notorious boom-and-bust past, but they had no way of knowing that wine's days were numbered, that in a few years wine would be in retreat on many fronts everywhere. Not because of moral strictures but because of economic realities. Wine had been important for thousands of years because it was more than a drink, it was a diet staple, an inexpensive source of nourishment in poor lands where most foods spoiled quickly and what little water there was often was contaminated.

The end of World War II saw astonishing economic strides taken in the traditional wine-drinking

ABOVE: The way it used to be. Hand-operated presses and open fermenters seen in this old-time harvest photo, are now just part of the California wine industry's heritage.

nations. Electricity, which meant refrigeration and water pumps, became available almost everywhere. Roads were cut through to remote vineyard regions bringing beer and soft drinks. Young people casting off the ways of their elders rejected wine. So rapid was the decline in wine consumption that by 1988, more than half of all French men and women were telling pollsters they never drank wine.

For a time, in the late 1960s and early 1970s, it seemed as if Schoonmaker and Marvel's dream for the United States might come true. Wine consumption doubled, then doubled again. Wineries, first in California, later in Oregon and Washington and eventually in some forty-three other states were opening at an astonishing rate. "People are bonding their garages and tool sheds", said an overworked government official in 1972, referring to the demand for official permissions to open wineries. There were times during the 1970s when five or six wineries would open in California in a single month. In 1970, there were 240 wineries in the state; by 1990 there were over 900.

The industry — and its investors — were ecstatic, until it was pointed out that, while production and sales were increasing dramatically, the number of wine drinkers was not. Marketers discovered, to their dismay, that the optimistic *per capita* figures were dangerously misleading; they discovered that the same group of people — dedicated wine drinkers all — was consuming more and more wine and that the vast majority of Americans were still not interested in wine. In the early 1980s, the inevitable happened. The market became saturated; sales flattened out, then began to slide.

Also, the substantial ethnic market, the immigrants and sons and daughters of immigrants who had loyally consumed millions of gallons of jug wines over the years, was dying out. The wine drinkers who had made E. & J. Gallo the largest wine company in the world and still managed to support a dozen Gallo competitors no longer existed. What's more, the newest wave of immigrants, people from Asia and Latin America, came with no tradition of wine drinking.

The wine industry in the 1990s became a victim of one of those cyclical changes in American thinking that marks a retreat from what is conceived as material excess. Health concerns became paramount; and the evils of driving under the influence of alcohol gained new urgency. Vainly, the wine industry tried to promote wine as the drink of moderation, as a food to be consumed with other foods. The new generation of prohibitionists, the so-called neo-prohibitionists, depicted wine as merely another form of alcoholic beverage and included it in their anti-alcohol campaigns.

The prolonged economic recession of the early 1990s also took its toll. For the first time in recent history, the faltering economy had its largest impact on middle-management, the sector of the job market that had grown most rapidly in the boom years. Many of the country's newest and most ardent wine enthusiasts came from this group. Since so few Americans had made wine a part of their lives, it was a discretionary pleasure to be set aside while times are hard.

At the same time, analysts detected an interesting and encouraging trend within a trend. Even though overall wine sales were down, sales of the very best wines, those selling for U.S. $20 and more, actually continued to improve. In the midst of a serious downturn, not a few wineries were doing so well that their wines were on allocation. Only old customers could buy them and then only in limited quantities. Industry observers saw a new wine market developing, a true luxury market. America might never become a wine-drinking nation, but it appeared that there was a growing group of Ameri-

cans who would pay a great deal for American wines if the quality was there.

The quality factor has led to remarkable innovations in American winemaking and in American wine styles. In the 1960s and 1970s, Cabernet Sauvignon and Chardonnay — originally called Pinot Chardonnay — took their places at head of the list of America's best wines. The great châteaux of Bordeaux were the inspiration of the Cabernet makers; the famous white wines of Burgundy inspired the creators of the best American Chardonnays. Merlot, long the most important grape of Bordeaux's Right Bank — St. Emilion and Pomerol — became an important variety in the 1970s and early 1980s.

Pinot Noir, the temperamental grape that makes the superb wines of Burgundy's Côte d'Or, had always eluded the skills of American winemakers. A few California wineries had made Burgundy-style Pinot Noir as early as the 1960s but it fell to Oregon's wine community first to tame the grape in the early 1970s. A handful of additional California winemakers had some success in the 1980s, and from the beginning of the 1990s good and occasionally excellent Pinot Noir emanated from American vineyards.

Meanwhile even more challenging projects were occupying some young and daring winemakers. An entirely new wine region was created in the 1970s and 1980s on Long Island, in New York. Where once potatoes were the principal crop, hundreds of acres of premium wine grapes now grow, and the wines made from them are remarkably good. With a climate similar to Bordeaux's, Long Island wines tend to resemble Bordeaux wines even more than California's.

In California, some winemakers have accepted the fact that their local climate is much more akin to that of Avignon than St. Emilion and have begun to produce wines in the style of the Rhône Valley. Grapes that were dismissed as coarse by California winemakers only a decade or so ago — Grenache, Syrah and Mourvèdre, for example — are the wine country's new stars.

Nor has the experimentation stopped there. Other innovators are working with Italian varieties such as Nebbiolo, Trebbiano and Sangiovese. The plantings were relatively new in the early 1990s and the first wines tentative, but noone close to the wine industry doubts that in a few years, these wines will be significant additions to the American wine scene.

Even more important, perhaps, has been what many feel is a long overdue change in the American philosophy of winemaking. Through the 1960s and 1970s, the emphasis was on technical wizardry and the skills of the winemakers, who talked of "sculpting" their wines in the cellars and laboratories. The wine press followed the comings and goings of winemakers the way sports writers followed quarterbacks and the food press lionized chefs.

As far back as the 1930s, University of California scientists had divided that state into regions based on climate. Each region had many microclimates and it was on this data that vineyards were planted and wineries built. The European emphasis on the importance of soil was downplayed or dismissed.

This approach always had its critics and, slowly, through the 1980s, the importance of soil began to take precedence. More and more, one would hear the phrase: "Wine begins in the vineyard". The trend to viticultural regions played an important role in this change in American viticulture. The first viticultural regions, similar to France's *appellation contrôlée*, began to appear, under the aegis of the Federal Government, in the 1970s. The regions are determined after consultation with the growers and winemakers in the regions concerned. As more and more winemakers began to demand their own official regions, they were forced to think about the correct boundaries. This, of course, meant they had to think about soil. Gradually many came to realize that, even within a specific microclimate, different parcels of vineyard produced different kinds of wine.

Closer contact with European counterparts also has helped to bring about this new — for America — approach. Twenty years ago, French and Italian

BELOW: Tank cars of bulk wine from Sebastiani Vineyards in Sonoma roll through the vineyards in the 1950s on their way east. Now a premium wine producer, 40 years ago Sebastiani was mostly a supplier of bulk wine to East Coast bottlers.

ABOVE: Monastery-like Sterling Vineyards seems about to be engulfed dramatically by a cool fog rolling up the Napa Valley from San Pablo Bay. One of the most striking wineries in California, Sterling is owned by Seagram's.

winegrowers tended to dismiss the brash Americans as upstarts. The Americans, on their part, pretended to dismiss the European experience as irrelevant. Over the years they have grown much closer. They meet regularly to exchange tips and research; they send their sons and daughters to work in each other's vineyards and cellars, and they drink each other's wines.

At the same time, more and more Europeans are taking an active part in the American winemaking. An earlier generation — among them Czechs, Serbs, French, Swiss, Germans, Italians, Hungarians and Russians — founded America's fine wine industry. Now another generation is buying American vineyards and wineries. Some, including, of course, the Japanese, come as investors, others to settle in the wine country and make a new life, just as their forebears did. America, they are saying by their actions, is still a land of promise and challenge.

The American wine experience has come full circle. It has come of age.

California

To most of the world, California wine and American wine are synonymous. California is the locomotive of the American wine industry, with one wine company, E. & J. Gallo, producing more wine annually than almost any state in the union and, in fact, more wine than most of the states put together.

But California wine is also part of the California dream — that there really is a paradise on earth where every prospect pleases. The capital of that California is the Napa Valley with its handsome

wineries and even handsomer people, all of them dedicated to making life more pleasant for the people who can afford their wines.

With the exception, perhaps, of Death Valley and the fog-shrouded forests of the northern coasts, there is wine everywhere in California. But the Napa Valley, unquestionably, is America's Pauillac. There are more great wines made in one relatively small area here than in any other part of the state, or the country, for that matter. At last count, there were some two hundred and forty wineries in the county. According to Leon Adams, twenty-one pre-Prohibition wineries were refurbished and opened in the valley at the beginning of the wine boom, and eighty-seven new ones were built just between 1979 and 1989. Another dozen opened in the early 1990s, and despite a downturn in wine sales more were on the drawing boards.

Some 16,188 hectares/40,000 acres of Napa Valley land had been exploited for vineyards and wineries by the end of the 1980s and little prime land was left for conversion to vines. Perhaps it was just as well; the cost of purchasing and developing a single acre of valley land for wine grapes had reached the formidable figure of U.S. $50,000.

The Napa names are a litany of the California wine nobility: Mondavi, Beaulieu, Inglenook, Heitz, Diamond Creek, Martini, Stag's Leap, Schramsberg, Krug, Grgich Hills, Joseph Phelps, Caymus, Silver Oak, Clos du Val, Stony Hill, Togni, Freemark Abbey, Coppola.

Their fame and the beauty of the valley itself, as it rolls north from San Pablo Bay in the lee of the

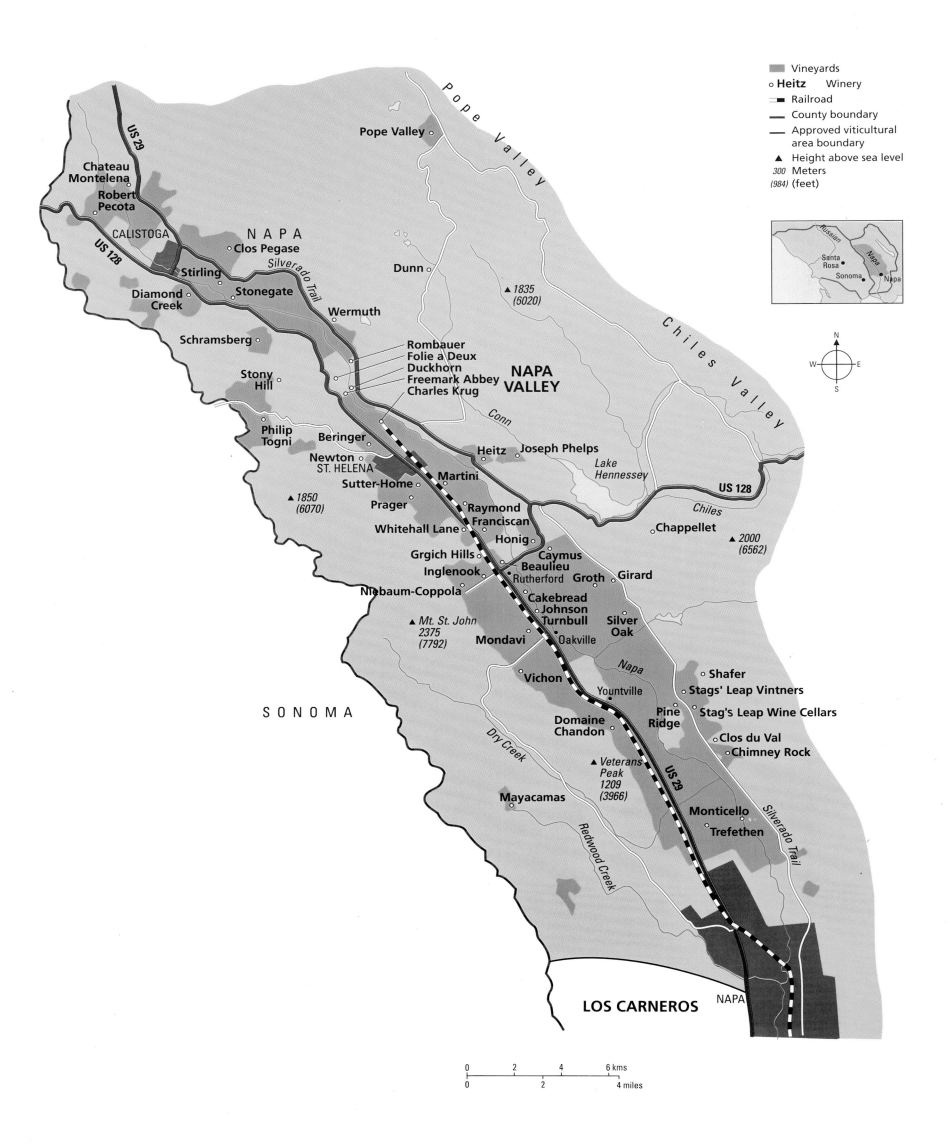

Vineyards
Heitz Winery
Railroad
County boundary
Approved viticultural
area boundary
▲ Height above sea level
300 Meters
(984) (feet)

US 29

**Chateau
Montelena**
**Robert
Pecota**
CALISTOGA
N A P A
Clos Pegase
US 128
Stirling
Stonegate
**Diamond
Creek**
Wermuth
Schramsberg

Silverado Trail

Dunn

Pope Valley
Pope Valley

▲ *1835
(6020)*

Chiles Valley

**NAPA
VALLEY**

Conn

**Stony
Hill**
Rombauer
Folie a Deux
Duckhorn
Freemark Abbey
Charles Krug

**Philip
Togni**
Beringer
Newton
Heitz
Joseph Phelps
*Lake
Hennessey*
ST. HELENA
Martini
▲ *1850
(6070)*
Sutter-Home
Prager
US 128
Chiles
Raymond
Franciscan
Whitehall Lane
Chappellet
Honig
▲ *2000
(6562)*
Grgich Hills
Caymus
Beaulieu
Inglenook
Rutherford
Groth
Girard
Niebaum-Coppola
Cakebread
Johnson
Turnbull
▲ *Mt. St. John
2375
(7792)*
Mondavi
Oakville
**Silver
Oak**

Napa
Vichon
Shafer
Stags' Leap Vintners
Yountville
**Pine
Ridge**
Stag's Leap Wine Cellars
S O N O M A
**Domaine
Chandon**
Clos du Val
Chimney Rock
Dry Creek
▲ *Veterans
Peak
1209
(3966)*
US 29
Mayacamas
Redwood Creek
Monticello
Silverado Trail
Trefethen

LOS CARNEROS
NAPA

0   2   4   6 kms
0   2   4 miles

Russian
Napa
Santa
Rosa
Sonoma
Napa

N
W   E
S

Mayacamas Mountains, have lured tourists from every where. And if the wineries reflect the fantasies of their wealthy owners, the chic restaurants, trendy inns, exclusive shops and traffic jams speak volumes about America's fascination with wine, not as food or drink but as a cultural phenomenon.

The winegrowers, many of whom came to the semi-rural Napa Valley to escape the pressure of city life, are unhappy about the hordes of visitors who have discovered their bucolic hideaway. Several years ago, a wealthy entrepreneur restored an old train to carry even more tourists up and down the valley. Winery owners along the "Wine Train's" route, while uneasy about the tourists (they do spend money, after all) decided the train was too much.

Everything that had gone wrong in the valley — the crowds, the commercialism, the sense of lost innocence — coalesced in the train, and the wine-growers set out to crush it. They lost. The train runs twice a day, introducing thousands of people a year to the valley and, in its dining and bar cars, the valley's wines. But not the wines of the people who tried to kill the train.

The *crème de la crème* of the Napa wineries and vineyards are found in two places, an area known as the Rutherford-Oakville Bench, along the southwest side of the valley, where the Robert Mondavi Winery and Beaulieu Vineyards are to be found, and in Stag's Leap, on the eastern edge of the valley along the Silverado Trail. Stag's Leap Wine Cellars, Chimney Rock, Shafer and Pine Ridge are some of the better known Stag's Leap wineries. Fine wines are made outside these two areas, but without the cachet these two names impart.

BELOW: This portion of the Stags' Leap Winery in the Napa Valley was once part of a hotel called Stags' Leap Manor. The building was restored in the 1960s by Carl Doumani. Both Stags' Leap Winery and its neighbor Stag's Leap Wine Cellars are located in the Stags' Leap viticultural region.

Stag's Leap Viticultural Area

The nearest American equivalent to the French controlled appellation is the A.V.A., or Approved Viticultural Area. The most famous A.V.A. is California's Napa Valley and it has been divided into sub-areas, one of the most important of which is Stag's Leap. This district lies in the southeastern part of the valley, along the Silverado Trail, north of the town of Napa.

Stag's Leap gained wide acclaim when its wines bested some top French wines at a competition in Paris in 1976. When the same competition was held ten years later, another wine from the area, Clos du Val, was the winner.

In 1985 some of the growers in the area proposed a 890 hectare/2,200 acre A.V.A. Several wineries to the north of the line objected and the issue dragged on for two years. In 1989, the Bureau of Alcohol, Tobacco and Firearms, which controls such things, announced an A.V.A. of 1,093 hectares/2,700 acres which included the original wineries, Chimney Rock Winery, Shafer Vineyards, Stag's Leap Wine Cellars, Stags' Leap Vintners, Pine Ridge, Silverado Vineyards and Stelzner Vineyards. The two wineries in the expanded section were Robert Sinskey Vineyards and S. Anderson Vineyard. Robert Mondavi Winery and the Joseph Phelps Vineyards also own vineyard land in the district.

All the Stag's Leap district growers have agreed to use the name only in conjunction with the Napa Valley appellation.

diamond creek

Volcanic Hill

Napa **1986** Valley

Cabernet Sauvignon

grown, produced and bottled on diamond mountain by
DIAMOND CREEK VINEYARDS   CALISTOGA, CA.

ALCOHOL 12½% BY VOLUME   CONTAINS SULFITES

STERLING VINEYARDS®

ESTATE GROWN & BOTTLED

1987
Sterling Reserve

NAPA VALLEY

62% CABERNET SAUVIGNON
29% MERLOT, 9% CABERNET FRANC, AND 9% PETIT VERDOT

GROWN, PRODUCED AND BOTTLED BY STERLING VINEYARDS
CALISTOGA, NAPA VALLEY, CA • ALC. 13.1% BY VOL. • BW CA 4553

CLOS DU VAL

1987
ESTATE BOTTLED
MERLOT
STAGS LEAP DISTRICT
Napa Valley

Produced and Bottled by
CLOS DU VAL WINE CO LTD
Napa California

Alcohol 13% by Volume

VINTAGE 1987	BOTTLED JUNE 1991
Bottle	of a total of 56,880 Bottles
Magnum	of a total of 2,400 Magnums

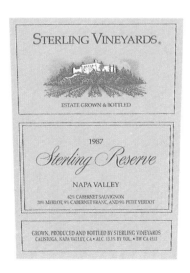

Beaulieu Vineyard

BV

GEORGES DE LATOUR
PRIVATE RESERVE

NAPA VALLEY
CABERNET SAUVIGNON
1986

PRODUCED & BOTTLED BY BEAULIEU VINEYARD
RUTHERFORD NAPA VALLEY CALIFORNIA
ALCOHOL 13% BY VOLUME

ESTATE BOTTLED

Carneros
PINOT NOIR
1988

SAINTSBURY

PRODUCED AND BOTTLED BY SAINTSBURY, NAPA, CALIFORNIA
ALCOHOL 13.2% BY VOLUME   CONTAINS SULFITES

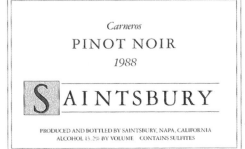

Heitz Cellar

NAPA VALLEY
CABERNET SAUVIGNON
ALCOHOL 13½% BY VOLUME
PRODUCED AND BOTTLED IN OUR CELLAR BY
HEITZ WINE CELLARS
ST. HELENA, CALIFORNIA, U.S.A.

ABOVE: Diamond Creek Vineyards produces one of California's most sought-after Cabernet Sauvignons. Owner Al Braunstein makes separate wines from each vineyard. Pictured here are Red Rock terrace in the foreground and Volcanic Hill on the right.

LEFT: Napa elite: six of the most famous wineries in the valley that are all known for their Cabernet Sauvignons, except Saintsbury, which specializes in Burgundy-style Pinot Noir. Heitz's Martha's Vineyard is the rarest of all.

RIGHT: Modern double-trellised vines in the De Loach Vineyard in the Russian River Valley region of Sonoma County. After years of technical innovation in their cellars, Californians now devote far more attention to their vineyards.

Some of the other regions within the Napa Valley viticultural area are Howell Mountain, Chiles Valley, Pope Valley and Carneros.

Sonoma County, California's second wine county in reputation, is big enough to have a variety of widely separated wine regions: the Sonoma Valley and parts of Carneros in the south; Green Valley in the west, Dry Creek in the northwest, the Russian River region in north central Sonoma, the Alexander Valley, which wanders the length of the Russian River before it turns west toward the ocean, Knights Valley, just north of the Napa Valley, and in the far south, its own share of the Carneros viticultural area. In all the county has about 165 wineries. Sonoma has its own honor roll of famous wineries, starting with Buena Vista, which was founded by Agoston Haraszthy in the 1860s.

GROWER'S VIEW

Fruit in the Napa Valley consistently reaches full maturity with excellent sugar and acid levels achieved naturally in the vineyard — a gift of our exceptional climate and the employment of proper handling techniques. Our climate, then, is what gave Napa Valley wines the richness and fullness of flavors we were seeking, in spite of the low-density, high-vigor vineyards we used to have.

All great wines are made first and foremost in the vineyard. One of the first steps to realizing Napa Valley's full potential is the adoption of the low-vigor concept, embracing techniques such as appropriate moisture management of the soil, which means more dry farming and less irrigation; along with canopy management and leaf removal to allow sunlight onto the fruit to give the wine a deeper color, fuller body, better acid balance and far better flavor.

When we implemented these techniques at the winery, we saw our yields drop while the flavors skyrocketed. In most cases now we impose low vigor on existing vines that were originally intended to be much more vigorous. In many vineyards, though, we are replanting to ensure low vigor through tighter spacing, pruning and trellising techniques.

The result of these changes in the vineyards, coupled with gentle handling in the cellar, is wines that express the soil and the vintage more completely. California wines today, and specifically those grown in the Napa Valley, possess more elegance, finesse and personality than ever before.

The Robert Mondavi Winery was founded in 1966, nearly thirty years after my father entered the Napa Valley wine business. Our goal has been constant since the first harvest: to produce world-class wines, to educate the American public about wine and its proper role as a mealtime beverage to be drunk in moderation and to promote the gracious way of life, integrating wine with all fine arts.

Tim Mondavi

ROBERT MONDAVI WINERY

BELOW: Four Napa Valley white wines: a late harvest Riesling, two rich Chardonnays and an exceptional mountain-grown Sauvignon Blanc from Philip Togni. Phelps' late harvest can rival the best German *beerenauslese* wines.

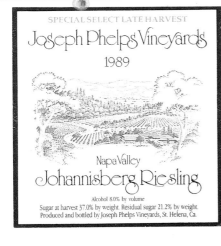

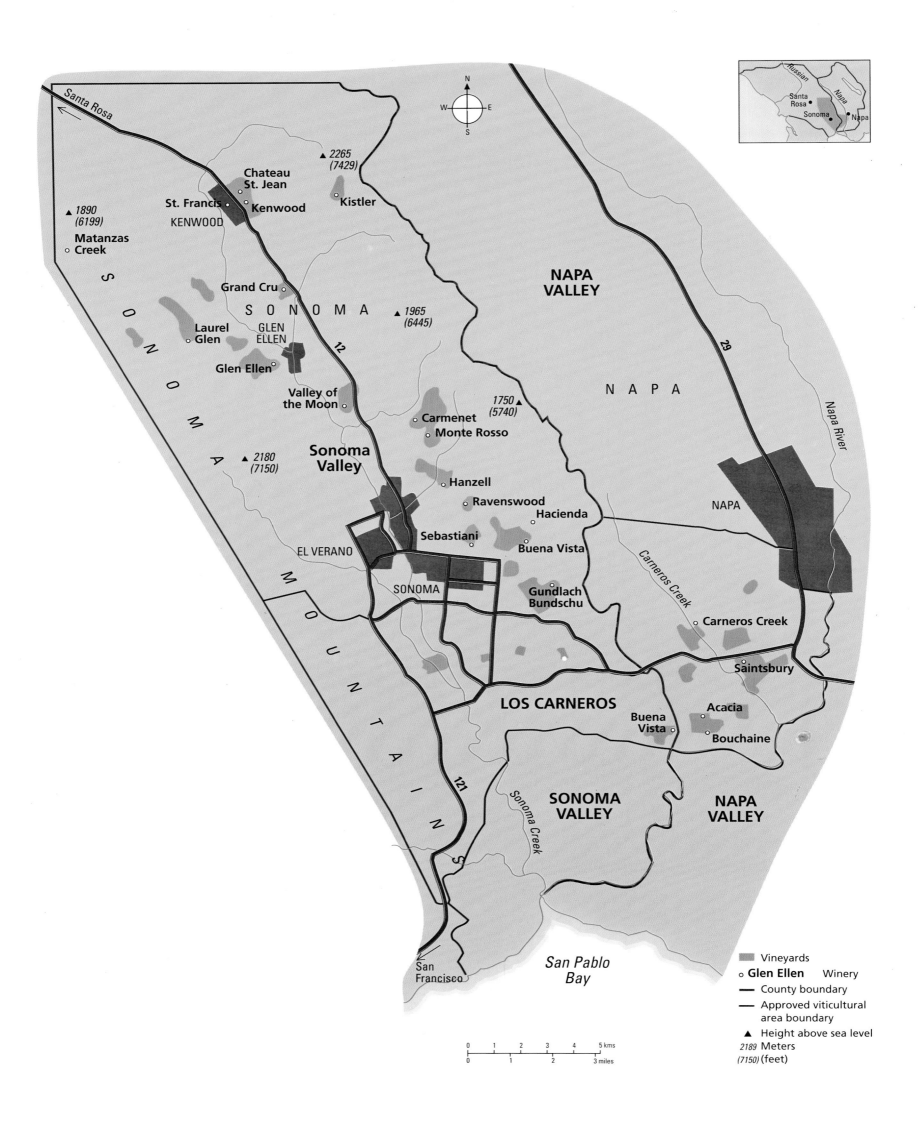

St. Francis
Chateau
St. Jean
Kenwood
KENWOOD
Kistler
▲ 2265
(7429)

▲ 1890
(6199)
Matanzas
Creek

Grand Cru

S O N O M A

Laurel
Glen
GLEN
ELLEN

▲ 1965
(6445)

NAPA
VALLEY

Glen Ellen

Valley of
the Moon

N A P A

Carmenet
Monte Rosso

▲ 1750
(5740)

▲ 2180
(7150)

Sonoma
Valley

Hanzell

Ravenswood
Hacienda

NAPA

Sebastiani

EL VERANO

Buena Vista

SONOMA

Gundlach
Bundschu

M O U N T A I N S

Carneros Creek

Carneros Creek

Saintsbury

Acacia

LOS CARNEROS

Buena
Vista

Bouchaine

121

SONOMA
VALLEY

NAPA
VALLEY

San Francisco

Sonoma Creek

San Pablo
Bay

Napa River

29

12

Santa Rosa

■ Vineyards
○ **Glen Ellen** Winery
— County boundary
— Approved viticultural
   area boundary
▲ Height above sea level
2189 Meters
(7150) (feet)

0 1 2 3 4 5 kms
0   1   2   3 miles

Russian
Santa
Rosa
Sonoma
Napa
Napa

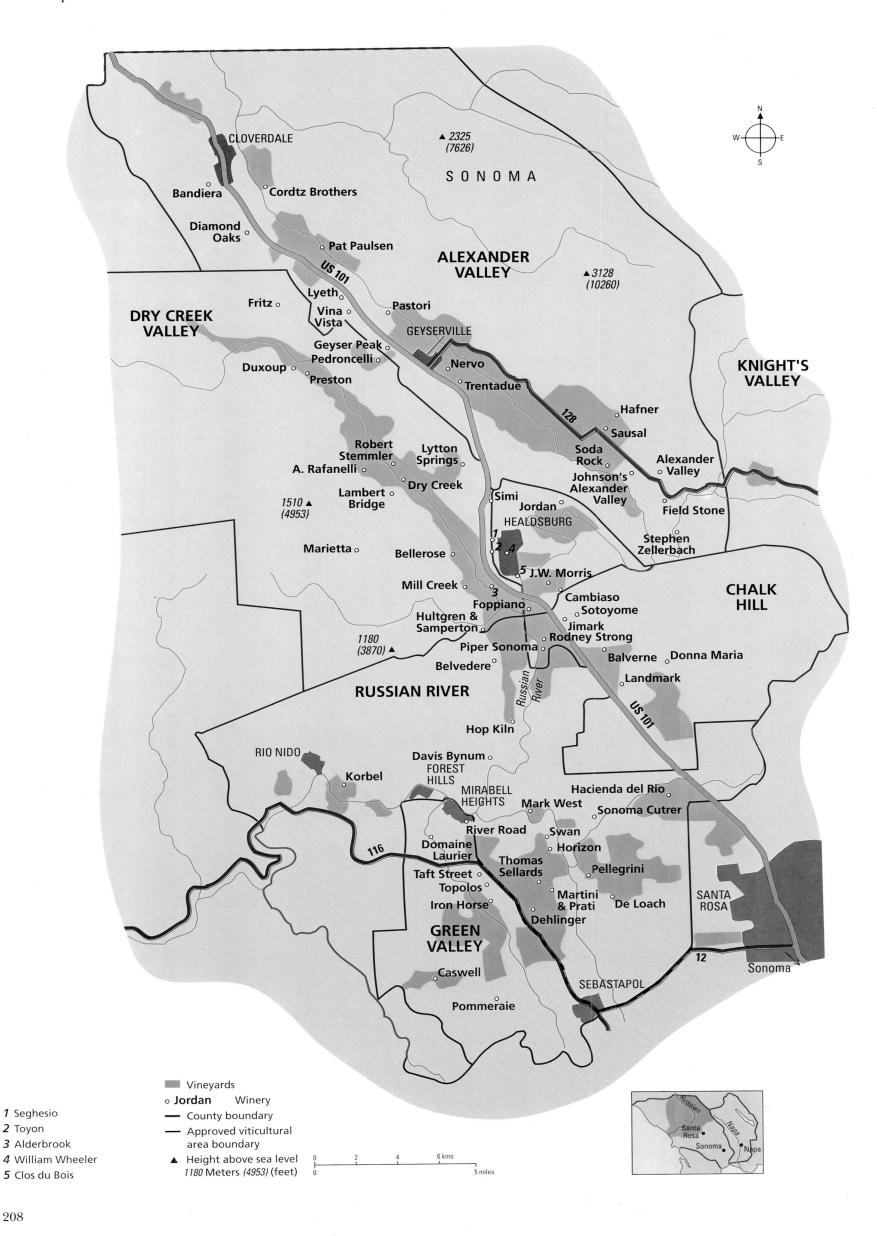

CLOVERDALE

Bandiera

Cordtz Brothers

Diamond
Oaks

SONOMA

▲ 2325
(7626)

Pat Paulsen

ALEXANDER
VALLEY

US 101

▲ 3128
(10260)

DRY CREEK
VALLEY

Fritz

Lyeth

Pastori

Vina
Vista

GEYSERVILLE

KNIGHT'S
VALLEY

Geyser Peak
Pedroncelli

Duxoup

Nervo

Trentadue

Preston

128

Hafner

Sausal

Robert
Stemmler

Lytton
Springs

Soda
Rock

Alexander
Valley

A. Rafanelli

Dry Creek

Johnson's
Alexander
Valley

Field Stone

Lambert
Bridge

1510 ▲
(4953)

Simi

Jordan

HEALDSBURG

1

Stephen
Zellerbach

Marietta

Bellerose

2 4

5 J.W. Morris

CHALK
HILL

Mill Creek

3

Cambiaso

Foppiano

Sotoyome

Hultgren &
Samperton

Jimark

Rodney Strong

1180
(3870) ▲

Piper Sonoma

Balverne

Donna Maria

Belvedere

RUSSIAN RIVER

Russian
River

Landmark

US 101

Hop Kiln

RIO NIDO

Davis Bynum

FOREST
HILLS

Korbel

MIRABELL
HEIGHTS

Hacienda del Rio

Mark West

Sonoma Cutrer

River Road

Swan

Domaine
Laurier

Horizon

Thomas
Sellards

Pellegrini

Taft Street

Topolos

Martini
& Prati

De Loach

SANTA
ROSA

Iron Horse

Dehlinger

GREEN
VALLEY

12

Sonoma

Caswell

SEBASTAPOL

Pommeraie

Vineyards

○ **Jordan**   Winery

— County boundary

— Approved viticultural
area boundary

▲ Height above sea level
1180 Meters *(4953)* (feet)

1 Seghesio
2 Toyon
3 Alderbrook
4 William Wheeler
5 Clos du Bois

0   2   4   6 kms

0   5 miles

Russian

Napa

Santa
Rosa

Sonoma

Napa

Buena Vista, Sebastiani Vineyards, Kenwood and Chateau St. Jean are all in the Sonoma Valley. Iron Horse, is the best-known property in Green Valley. In Windsor, the cruciform Rodney Strong Vineyards winery is one of the best-known wineries in California. In Healdsburg is the Simi Winery, which is owned by France's Moët-Hennessy and presided over by Zelma Long.

Sonoma winegrowers like to think of themselves as more unassuming than their Napa colleagues, but some of Sonoma's wineries are just as dramatic as Napa's. The spectacular Jordan winery in the Alexander Valley rivals anything the Napans, or the French, have to offer. Souverain, Pedroncelli, Geyser Peak, Foppiano, Clos du Bois and Glen Ellen are a few of the better-known Sonoma County wineries.

Although there are a few brave souls who grow grapes and make wine in the far northern reaches of the state, Mendocino County, just north of Sonoma, really marks the northern boundary of the California wine country. With several dozen wineries scattered about the beautiful Anderson Valley, a few more, northeast in Potter Valley, and the big Fetzer Vineyards facilities near Hopland and in the Redwood Valley, Mendocino is only beginning to become a major factor on the wine scene.

American Sparkling Wines

Someone described America as being afloat on a sea of bubbles. Where sparkling wine is concerned a bit of hyperbole is not out of order but, in fact, the Americans do down prodigious quantities of Champagne and other sparkling wines.

Sparkling wine is produced in at least twenty states but most of it comes from two — California and New York. The range is enormous, from the simple but clean bulk process of André of E. & J. Gallo Winery to the most refined *méthode champenoise* cuvées of Schramsberg.

Nowhere has the invasion of America by foreign winemakers been more evident than in the sparkling wine category. At the last count, European companies included Moët & Chandon, at Domaine Chandon; Lanson, at Scharffenberger; Roederer, at Roederer Estate; Piper-Heidsieck, at Piper Sonoma; Deutz, at Maison Deutz; Mumm at Domaine Mumm; Taittinger, at Domaine Carneros; Freixenet at Gloria Ferrer and Codorníu at Codorníu Napa. Laurent Perrier is involved in a cooperative venture with Iron Horse, and A. Charbaut & Fils has options on land in New York State.

Winemakers are just beginning to discover that New York's harsh northerly climate is much closer to that of the Champagne region in France than California's and may well be more hospitable to the Champagne grape varieties. Vinifera vines have not fared well in New York in the past but superior clones and modern vinifera methods are changing that. Superior vinifera sparkling wines have been produced by Great Western in the Finger Lakes and by Millbrook Vineyards in the Hudson Valley.

Not that hybrids cannot do well, too. Clinton Vineyards, another Hudson Valley winery, makes a splendid sparkling wine entirely from Seyval Blanc grapes.

In California, hardly a major winery has been able to resist the temptation to make a sparkling wine. Most recently, the Jordan winery unveiled its "J" to considerable acclaim. Robert Mondavi has been experimenting with sparkling wine for years but has only recently released one. Among the more popular labels, aside from André, are Korbel, Hanns Kornell and Paul Masson. The very top producers would include Iron Horse, Château St. Jean and Domaine Chandon, particularly the last named winery's Etoile.

LEFT: Jordan's soft Cabernet Sauvignon is appreciated for its early drinkability. Clos du Bois is a leader in Sonoma Merlot production. Ravenswood produces rich, muscular Zinfandels, while De Loach has become a star producer of fine Chardonnay.

BELOW: The best sparkling wines, including these four, are made in California by the *methode champenoise*— fermented in the bottle in which they are sold. Neither Iron Horse or Domaine Chandon call their wine "Champagne" insisting that true Champagne is made only in Champagne.

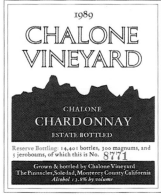

ABOVE: Six familiar California labels. Le Cigare Volant, from Bonny Doon, means flying cigar and the bottle's back label, not pictured here, explains what it means. Ridge Monte Bello is one of California's treasured Cabernet Sauvignons. Fetzer is a leader in organic grape growing.

Important wineries in the county include Parducci, Navarro and Scharffenberger and Roederer, the last two producers of sparkling wines. Lake County, east of Mendocino, was an important grape growing area before Prohibition. It is slowly coming back as a wine producing county, as well. Kendall-Jackson and Guenoc are two of the best-known Lake County names.

Alemeda County, across the Bay from San Francisco, boasts one of the oldest wine producing regions in the state, around Livermore. Two of the best-known wineries are Concannon and Wente Brothers.

South of San Francisco Bay, urbanization has driven many wineries and vineyards out of Santa Clara County. A few, such as Mirassou Vineyards, survive on the edges of San José, but most are in the Santa Cruz Mountains on the western border of the county. Best-known among them is Ridge Vineyards, near Cupertino. Ridge's Montebello Cabernet Sauvignon is one of the finest of all California Cabernets. Bonny Doon Vineyard in Santa Cruz County is a leader in the new effort to produce California versions of the wines of France's Rhône Valley. Randall Grahm, Bonny Doon's owner, is the unofficial leader of a group of young winemakers known as the "Rhône Rangers".

The remote mountains east of Soledad in Monterey County are home to Chalone Vineyards, where some of California's most successful Burgundy-style wines are made. Chalone is part of a publicly-owned company that owns three other wineries and has exchanged shares with the Rothschilds who own Château Lafite-Rothschild in Bordeaux.

San Luis Obispo and Santa Barbara counties in central California comprise the state's fastest growing wine region. Only a few of the wineries, such as Firestone Vineyards, Edna Valley Vineyards and Sandford and Benedict, are well-known but many north coast wineries grow and buy grapes here. Amador and El Dorado counties, near the state's eastern border with Nevada, an area called

the Sierra Foothills, are known for their strong Zinfandels. Montevina in Amador, now owned by the Sutter Home Winery in the Napa Valley, is one of the best-known names in this area.

California's wine industry started around Los Angeles and a few wineries still exist there, but the best wines in the southern part of the state come from around Temecula in Riverside County. Callaway Vineyard is the best-known Temecula winery.

Then, of course, there is the vast San Joaquin Valley, stretching from Lodi to Bakersfield, where America's jug wine is produced. This is Gallo country — the main E. & J. Gallo Winery is in

GROWER'S VIEW

Like Columbus, who sought a trade route to Asia, I set out in search of the great American Pinot Noir. I foundered in the shoals of astringency and lack of finesse and ended up running aground in the utterly unexpected New World of Rhône and Italian (under the Ca'del Solo label) varieties. I like to call this category "meridional wines" — wines of the sun, of the South (below the 45th parallel). Our New World efforts with these varieties are then quite literally on a common wavelength with those of our Old World *confrères*.

If there is a tragic flaw at Bonny Doon, it is, no doubt, excessive eclecticism. We are experimenting with scores of meridional (and some continental) varieties in the hopes of discovering which grape will marry well with the growing conditions (soil and climate) that obtain in our Santa Cruz Mountain and Monterey County vineyards.

The salient and recurring winemaking themes of Bonny Doon Vineyard/Ca'del Solo are:

• Having as much fun with the wine as the relevent governmental agencies will allow.

• Producing wines and wine labels that will scintillate the sensibilities of the most jaded imbiber.

• Retaining as much of the natural qualities of grapes (especially fragrance) through careful handling and minimal cellar treatment. Limpiditiy for its own sake is eschewed.

• Paying particularly close attention to the old axiom about wine being produced in the vineyard. After determining that a particular grape belongs in a certain spot, we seek the appropriate cultural practice (pruning style, yields and so on) that will lead to the fullest expression of the character of the variety.

I consider myself a champion of the strange and heterodox, the ugly duckling grape varieties too easily passed over, whose very existence is threatened by the dominant Cabo- and Chardocentric paradigm.

Randall Grahm
BONNY DOON VINEYARD

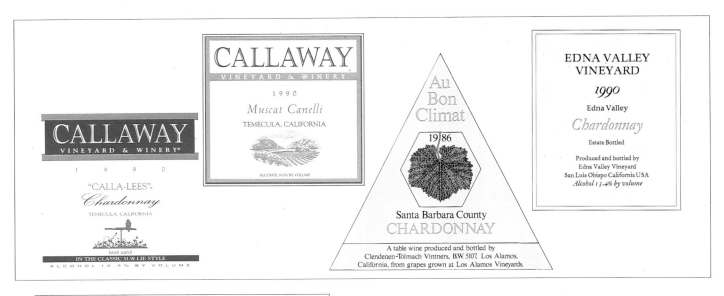

LEFT: Callaway, in Temecula, the state's southernmost winemaking region, makes only white wine. Edna Valley, managed and partly owned by Chalone Vineyards produces some of the best, moderately priced Chardonnays.

GROWER'S VIEW

As a winegrower, I see fine winemaking as secondary to selection of site, variety and viticultural techniques. Without an exceptional match of those elements in a single piece of ground, the winemaker, no matter how skilled, cannot make great wines.

I believe that what sets a great wine apart is its individual, identifiable character. The difference between a great wine and a very good wine lies in the quality and consistency of that character. Winemakers can draw wines from different vineyards in a number of microclimates to provide a spice rack of sorts from which to blend a wine of character.

On the other hand, when we allow a single great vineyard to determine the character of a wine, there is a consistency and depth to that character that we cannot match. Typically, in one vineyard there are going to be several soils and, on a slope, variations in exposure. With great Cabernet or Zinfandel, there are generaly several varieties on the same piece of ground.

The winemaker makes each variety and batch separately, then selects and assembles to bring out the character of the vineyard. He does not create a distinctive character; it is there in the vineyard. The great wines of the world have usually come from single vineyards. It is this connection to the earth and the cycle of life which attract winemakers so strongly.

Paul Draper
RIDGE VINEYARDS

Modesto, in Stanislaus County — and everything here is done on a large scale: big grapes, big wineries, and vast amounts of wine. Gallo is said to produce some 250,000 cases of wine a day.

Oregon

To wine enthusiasts, the name McMinnville does not connote anything particular, like, for example, Beaune, Margaux or Bernkastel. And yet McMinnville is the unofficial capital of one of America's most interesting wine regions, Oregon's Willamette Valley. Oregon's wine industry is minuscule compared to California's, and much of the winemaking is, as the

French say, *artisanal.* That is, it is done by hand.

Wine has been made in Oregon since the days of the Oregon Trail but the modern wine business dates from the 1960s, with Richard Sommer's Hillcrest Vineyard near Roseburg and David Lett's Eyrie Vineyard at Dundee in the Willamette Valley. In 1972, Dick Erath opened what was to become the Knudsen-Erath Winery a few miles from Eyrie.

Oregon winegrowers produce most popular vinifera varieties but it is their Pinot Noir that sets them apart. When California winemakers — with a few notable exceptions — were still struggling to master the stubborn grape of Burgundy, Oregon growers were already turning out wines to rival some of the best products of the Côte d'Or.

There was a period in the late 1980s when the spirit seemed to go out of the growers and their wines and that the promise of the 1970s and early 1980s had not been kept. It seemed that California would gradually outclass Oregon when it came to the Pinot Noir. Happily, by the early 1990s, Oregon vintners were back on track and the wines were good.

If one man can be said to have encouraged the Oregonian growers, just by his presence, it was the Frenchman Robert Drouhin, the head of Maison Drouhin, in Beaune, one of Burgundy's most famous growers and shippers. Drouhin had been impressed with Oregon's Pinot Noirs in the 1970s and had quietly watched them improve over the years. He bought 36.4 hectares/90 acres near Dundee in the early 1980s and set about building a U.S.$4.3-million winery. His first wines under the Domaine Drouhin label were introduced in 1991 to rave reviews. Oregon had shown what it could do.

Other labels from the state of Oregon worth seeking out include Ponzi, Sokol-Blosser, Tualatin, Adelsheim and Amity.

BELOW: Oregon is Pinot Noir country, as these labels indicate. Except for a shaky period in the late 1980s, Oregon wines have improved with each new vintage. Pinot Noir has an exciting future in the Willamette Valley.

Arbor Crest
WASHINGTON
COLUMBIA VALLEY
SAUVIGNON BLANC
1987
WAHLUKE SLOPE
CELLARED AND BOTTLED BY ARBOR CREST
SPOKANE, WASHINGTON, 99207, U.S.A.
ALCOHOL 12.5% BY VOLUME   (509) 927-9463

Ste. CHAPELLE

VINEYARD SELECT
1 9 9 0
Johannisberg Riesling
IDAHO
DRY
PRODUCED AND BOTTLED BY STE. CHAPELLE, INC.
CALDWELL, IDAHO. ALCOHOL 12.4% BY VOL. CONTAINS SULFITES.

Woodward Canyon Winery
1988
COLUMBIA VALLEY
CHARDONNAY

Produced and bottled by Woodward Canyon Winery
Route 1, Box 387 • Lowden, Washington
Alcohol by Volume—12.3%   Contains Sulfites

ABOVE: Beginning in the 1960s, Washington has become a major wine producing state. Arbor Crest in Spokane specializes in white wines. Woodward Canyon, a Chalone associate, makes superb Cabernet Sauvignon. Idaho's Ste. Chapelle specializes in Riesling.

RIGHT: The Ste. Chapelle Winery, near Caldwell, is dramatic proof that potatoes are not Idaho's only crop. In addition to its Rieslings, the winery makes a full line of wines from both Washington and Idaho grapes.

Washington and Idaho

When Frank Schoonmaker and Tom Marvel wrote *American Wines* in 1941, they devoted two quick pages to Washington State. "The best of the wines are undistinguished today", they said, "but they are improving, and they are sound". They added: "The entire industry ... is still in a sort of embryonic state and the most significant thing that one can say about it is that Washington, sooner or later, will produce fine wines and will rank among the best viticultural regions of the United States".

Fifty years later, that prediction has come true. Washington has indeed become a major producer of fine wines. Unlike Oregon, where the vineyards are clustered in the western part of the state, not far from the Pacific, Washington's grapes, and most of its wineries, are in the hot, dry Yakima Valley in the south central part of the state and further east near Walla Walla.

The state's most important winery, Ste. Michelle, keeps its vineyard here, east of the Cascade Mountains, but the winery is in Woodinville, twenty-four kilometers/fifteen miles from Seattle in the temperate Puget Sound area. Ste. Michelle, which is owned by the American Tobacco Company, makes the Columbia Crest Wines and has interests in wineries in California. André Tchelistcheff, the famous Napa Valley enologist, was the consultant in Ste. Michelle's formative years.

The Columbia Winery — no relation to Columbia Crest — was started by a group of university professors in the 1960s. Eventually, they formed a corporation, bought vineyards in the Yakima Valley and hired David Lake, a British-born Master of Wine, as winemaker. The winery is also in Woodinville, almost 322 kilometers/200 miles from its vineyards. Preston, Hogue Cellars, Covey Run and Woodward Canyon, now associated with the Chalone group in California, are among the Washington wineries to remember.

According to the history books, Idaho made wine almost before it got interested in potatoes. In any event the potatoes survived Prohibition but the vineyards did not. Now there are eight or nine wineries in the state, most of them in the southwest, near the Oregon border and not far from Boise. The best known is Ste. Chapelle, near Caldwell, which is named for the church on the Ile de la Cîté in Paris.

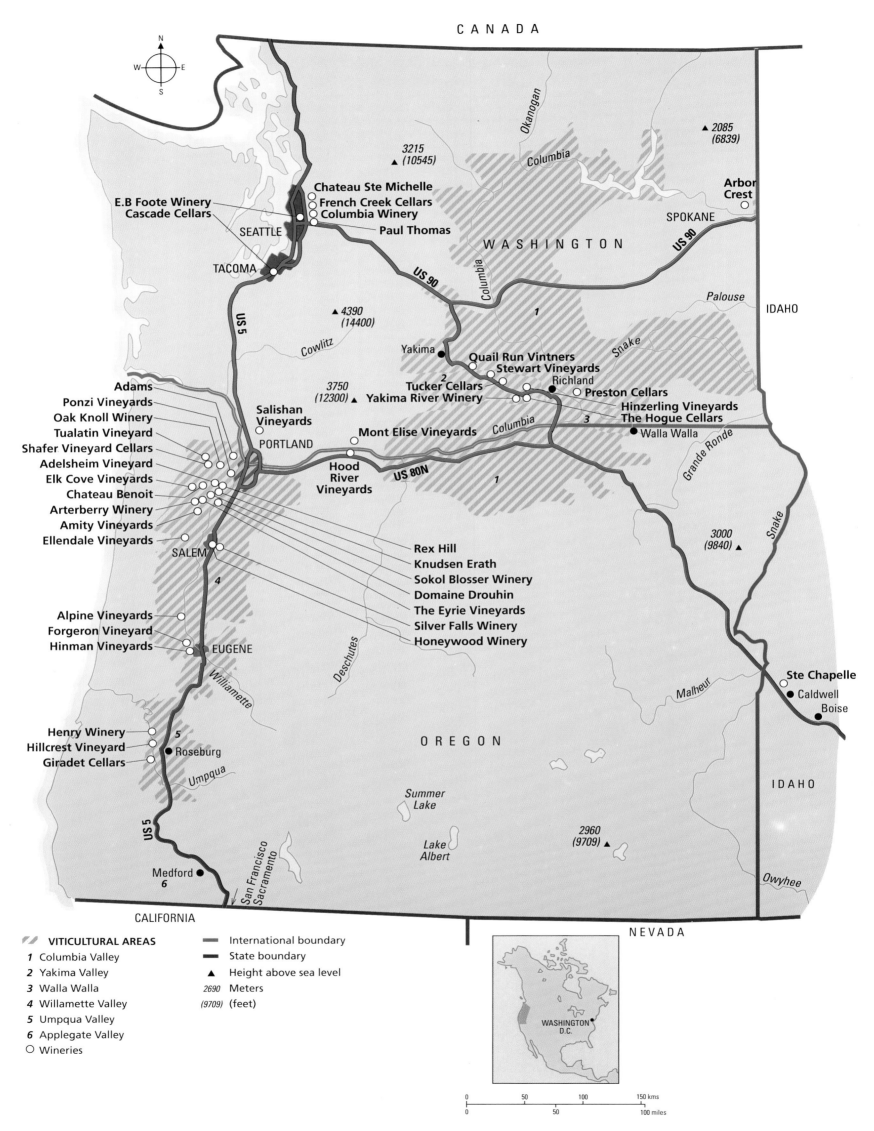

CANADA

N
W · E
S

▲ 2085
(6839)

Okanogan

Columbia

3215
(10545) ▲

**Arbor
Crest** ○

WASHINGTON

SPOKANE

US 90

Chateau Ste Michelle ○
French Creek Cellars ○
E.B Foote Winery ○
Cascade Cellars ○ **Columbia Winery**
SEATTLE **Paul Thomas**

Columbia

TACOMA

US 5

▲ 4390
(14400)

Cowlitz

Palouse

Snake

IDAHO

Yakima ●

Quail Run Vintners ○
Stewart Vineyards ○
Richland ●

2

3750
(12300) ▲

Tucker Cellars
Yakima River Winery ○ ○
○ **Preston Cellars**
Hinzerling Vineyards
The Hogue Cellars

Adams
Ponzi Vineyards
Oak Knoll Winery
Tualatin Vineyard
Shafer Vineyard Cellars
Adelsheim Vineyard
Elk Cove Vineyards
Chateau Benoit
Arterberry Winery
Amity Vineyards
Ellendale Vineyards

**Salishan
Vineyards**

PORTLAND

Mont Elise Vineyards

Columbia

3

Walla Walla ●

Grande Ronde

3000
(9840) ▲

Snake

**Hood
River
Vineyards**

US 80N

1

SALEM

4

Rex Hill
Knudsen Erath
Sokol Blosser Winery
Domaine Drouhin
The Eyrie Vineyards
Silver Falls Winery
Honeywood Winery

Alpine Vineyards
Forgeron Vineyard
Hinman Vineyards

EUGENE

Deschutes

Williamette

OREGON

Ste Chapelle ○
● Caldwell
Boise ●

Henry Winery
Hillcrest Vineyard
Giradet Cellars

5

● Roseburg

Umpqua

Summer
Lake

Lake
Albert

2960
(9709) ▲

IDAHO

Medford ●
6

San Francisco
Sacramento

US 5

Owyhee

CALIFORNIA

NEVADA

▨ **VITICULTURAL AREAS**
1 Columbia Valley
2 Yakima Valley
3 Walla Walla
4 Willamette Valley
5 Umpqua Valley
6 Applegate Valley
○ Wineries

— International boundary
▬ State boundary
▲ Height above sea level
2690 Meters
(9709) (feet)

WASHINGTON
D.C.

0   50   100   150 kms
0   50   100 miles

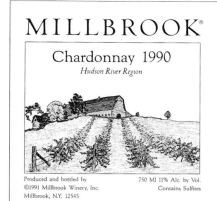
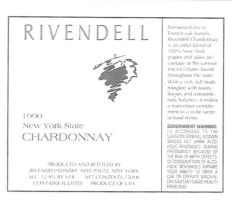
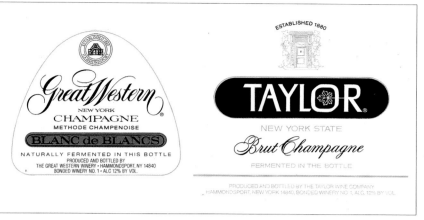

New York State

ABOVE: Millbrook Winery and Rivendell, both in the Hudson Valley, are two of New York State's newest wineries; jointly-owned Great Western and Taylor in Hammondsport, in the Finger Lakes, are two of its oldest. Great Western Blancs de Blancs Champagne rivals some of California's best sparklers.

New York State claims five separate wine districts. From west to east, they include an area near Westfield, on the shores of Lake Erie, known as the Chatauqua-Erie Grape Belt; another at Niagara Falls, just south of Lake Ontario; the Finger Lakes in the center of the state; the Hudson Valley, about halfway between New York City and Albany; and the newest region, on the eastern end of Long Island.

Wine has been made in New York since colonial times but, until very recently, it was the Finger Lakes region that dominated the industry in the state. Well into the American wine boom of the 1960s and after, the Finger Lakes wineries remained committed to native American grape varieties and particularly the unattractive Concord. Reluctantly, they switched over to hybrids and more recently, in spite of the bitter winters, have enjoyed considerable success with vinifera varieties, particularly Chardonnay and Riesling.

The Taylor Wine Company, in Hammondsport, is, with its subsidiary, the Pleasant Valley Wine Company, one of the largest producers of sparkling wine in the world. Its Great Western label is probably the best-known of all New York State wines. In nearby Canandaigua, Canandaigua Industries makes some 567,795 hectoliters/15 million U.S. gallons of wine a year, though not all of it comes from this plant. There are subsidiaries in Virginia, the Carolinas and California. One of Canandaigua's best-known wines is called Richard's Wild Irish Rose, a fortified wine that, while it is one of the largest-selling wines in the United States, has little in common with the wines that normally appeal to connoisseurs.

Bully Hill Winery, overlooking Keuka Lake, just north of Hammondsport is the lair of Walter S. Taylor, whose family founded the Taylor Wine Company. Walter was dismissed from Taylor for criticizing the way wine was made by the big New York State producers — using concentrated grape juice, for example. He started his own winery, concentrating on French-American hybrids and a few local varietals. When the courts enjoined him from using the Taylor name, he garnered immense publicity by hiring friends to ink out his name on his bottles.

Mr. Taylor's first winemaker, Hermann J. Wiemer, has his own vineyard and winery on nearby Seneca Lake where he has had considerable success with vinifera, notably Chardonnay and Riesling.

Hammondsport was also the home of the late Dr. Konstantin Frank, a Russian-born viticulturist who first proved that vinifera could be grown in the harsh Finger Lakes climate. Other prominent wineries in the area include Heron Hill, Wagner Vineyards and Glenora Cellars.

The Grape Belt produces half of New York's grapes, mostly for use in wineries elsewhere in the

RIGHT: Winters can be long and bitter on the shores of Keuka Lake in New York's Finger Lakes. Some growers have resorted to burying tender vinifera vines during the coldest months to protect them from sub-zero temperatures.

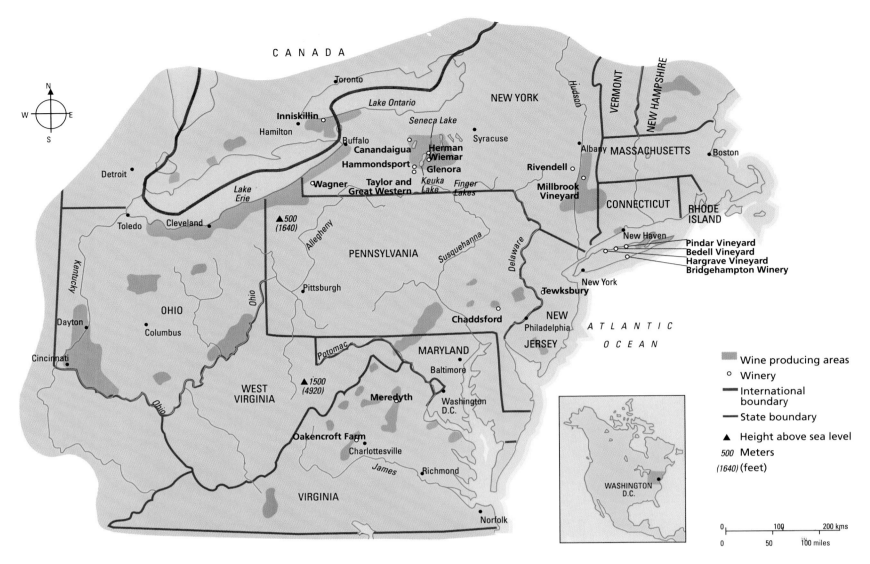

state. Once almost exclusively a Concord grape region, the Grape Belt now concentrates on hybrids and a few native varieties. A few wineries such as Woodbury Vineyards also produce excellent wines from vinifera varieties such as Chardonnay and Riesling. Nearby Niagara County produces significant quantities of wine grapes but has no wineries.

The Brotherhood Winery, at Washingtonville, New York, was for many years a popular tourist facility close to New York City, but the wines, made from purchased grapes, were mediocre. New owners, on the scene in 1990, promised vast improvements. The best-known winery in the region is Mark Miller's Benmarl, in Marlboro. A former magazine illustrator who lived in Burgundy for a time, Miller took over the Caywood vineyard in 1956 and planted vinifera and hybrids. Most of his wine is sold to members of his Societé des Vignerons, customers who buy vine rights that entitle them to buy at least

a case of wine a year.

At nearby Milton, the tasting room at the Royal Kedem kosher winery is a major tourist attraction. West Park Vineyards is a small winery, specializing in vinifera-based wines.

On the east side of the Hudson River, at Millbrook, John S. Dyson, once New York State Commissioner of Agriculture, established a winery and all-vinifera vineyard in 1981. He has had considerable success with some innovative systems for trellising his vines. Other notable wineries in the Hudson Valley include Clinton Vineyards, at Clinton Corners; Eaton Vineyards, in Pine Plains; Brimstone Hill and Baldwin Vineyard near Pine Bush in the Shawangunk Mountains; and, at New Paltz, the Rivendell Winery.

If there is a hero in the Long Island wine story, it has to be Alexander Hargrave, who first planted grapes at Cutchogue, on the island's North Fork in

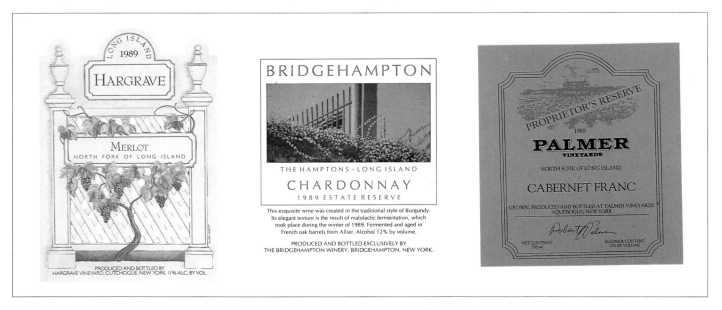

LEFT: New York State's newest wine region is the North Fork of Long Island where Cabernet Franc and Merlot show great promise. Hargrave, starting in 1972, was the pioneer. Bridgehampton, in the South Shore resort area, no longer grows its own grapes.

215

Other Regions

Rather than list the states where wine is made, one might simply note that there are only a few where it is not made: the Dakotas, Louisiana, Nebraska and Maine are, temporarily at least, out of the wine picture. Even Colorado, Hawaii, Montana and Nevada produce wine these days. In the southwest, Texas, Arizona and New Mexico are all wine-producing states now as they were two centuries ago under Spanish and later Mexican rule. Texas has twenty-five wineries, one of the largest being Domaine Cordier, near Bakersfield in West Texas. The operation is run by Cordier, a French firm that owns several famous châteaux in and ships wine from Bordeaux.

Texas is so huge that winegrowers encounter almost as many soil and climatic variations as can be found in France. Near Lubbock, in the high plains area, Llano Estacado and Pheasant Ridge are two of the best-known wineries. Near Austin, Fall Creek Vineyard and Cypress Valley are two of the prominent wineries along with Château Montgolfier, which is named after the eighteenth century French balloonist brothers. The owner has been known to inflate his own balloon and treat visitors to a serene ride over the vineyards.

In New Mexico, Anderson Valley Vineyards, near Albuquerque, one of about fifteen wineries in that state, makes a Zinfandel that matches all but a few to be found in California. In Arizona, the Sonoita Vineyard Winery near Elgin and the Webb Winery at Vail are two of the better-known wine producers.

The Southeast

Where Thomas Jefferson failed — one of his very few failures, actually — a current generation of Virginians has succeeded. Jefferson spent a good part of his life trying to grow vinifera vines in his native state, with no success. Modern viticultural and wine-making techniques have accomplished what Jefferson's enthusiasm could not — there are now some

ABOVE: Robert Palmer founded Palmer Vineyards in 1982 when he bought the 1792 Wells farmhouse in Aquebogue on Long Island's North Fork and planted 60 acres of vines. Palmer has produced outstanding Merlot and Cabernet Franc.

1973. More cautious enthusiasts waited until Hargrave's first wines proved to be excellent, then began turning potato fields into vineyards at a furious pace. Now more than a dozen wineries are making excellent wines on the island. Originally, it was thought that white wines would do best; more recently, it has been the reds, particularly Merlot and Cabernet Franc, that have succeeded in New York.

Long Island wineries worth noting include Palmer, Pindar, Bidwell, Bedell, Lenz, and, on the chic South Shore, the Bridgehampton Winery.

GROWER'S VIEW

To me, agriculture is analogy. I planted grapes on Long Island because the lay of the land struck me as being like Bordeaux, probably in much the same way as the Finger Lakes region, in upstate New York, was planted by Germans who saw similarity to the hillsides of their beloved Rhine.

The North Fork of Long Island is a narrow peninsula of land surrounded and moderated by large shallow bodies of water on three sides. All climatic and growing effects flow from this. There were a hundred technical reasons to plant vinifera vines on the Island, including a two hundred day, frost-free growing season, relative freedom from fog, moderate winter temperatures and a sandy well-drained soil — the best topsoil of New England thoughtfully bulldozed right to my farm by the last glacier.

The promise of Long Island is to make wines with nearly ideal balance; graceful and aromatic. But of all the factors, the feel of the warm, soft air

from off Great Peconic Bay was the most persuasive.

I do not make wine by numbers. I feel the old Roman way of delaying the harvest until the seed becomes dusky is a surer test of maturation than any sacchrometer or pH meter can provide. I feel the winemaker is only an arbiter of elements to which he can add none, only subtract. Since wine mirrors everything that happens to it, we are non-interventionists. We do the least possible at the last possible minute. We would rather deal with a headstrong child than a precocious one.

The only pedigree in wine comes from ripeness of fruit and patience in the cellar. That makes winemaking a vintage-to-vintage steeplechase the world over.

Alex Hargrave

HARGRAVE VINEYARDS

LEFT: Fall Creek Vineyards near Austin, Texas. Rancher and lawyer Ed Auler discovered winemaking studying cattle breeding in France. The result was Fall Creek. Quality whites—Chardonnay, Chenin Blanc, Riesling —are the main thrust of his production but good reds are made, too.

3,218 hectares/2,000 acres of wine grapes and, since around 1970, forty wineries. Ironically, the best wine country in the state is where Jefferson lived and labored fruitlessly in his own vineyard.

Among the best-known Virginia wineries are Meredyth Vineyard, near Middleburg, Piedmont Vineyard, which sold the first vinifera — Chardonnay — outside Virginia in 1977, and Felicia Warburg Rogan's Oakencroft Farm at Charlottesville. Mrs. Rogan is a tireless promoter of Virginia wines and hosts an annual Harvest Wine Festival at the Boar's Head Inn in Charlottesville, which was founded by her late husband.

Maryland has a thriving wine industry, with more than twenty-five wineries catering to a mostly local but enthusiastic clientele. But Maryland's claim to

ABOVE: Wine is made in unusual places: Chardonnay in Virginia, Cabernet Sauvignon in Mexico and Texas, and Riesling in Canada. The wines are good, if not yet world class, but they all have fervid local fans. Domecq in Baja, California is a name to watch.

wine fame rests on the reputation of one man, a retired editorial writer for the *Baltimore Evening Sun*, Philip M. Wagner. An amateur winemaker, he was among the first in Maryland to experiment with hybrid vines growing in France. Hybrids, crosses between native American and French varieties, proved highly resistant to East Coast winters and to the diseases that killed off vinifera vines east of California.

From Wagner's small operation, which he called Boordy Vineyards, the fame of his vines spread rapidly. New, hardier strains of vinifera have checked their popularity somewhat, but hybrids are still planted and turned into good wine throughout the United States and in Canada. Some of the better-known hybrids are Baco Noir, Chambourcin, Chelois, De Chaunac, Maréchal Foch and Seyval Blanc.

Canada

Like the United States, Canada has wine growing regions in both the East and the West. The newest, and easternmost, is on the southern, protected side of Nova Scotia. There are only a couple of wineries but, according to Leon Adams, the temperature is similar to that in the Mosel Valley. Perhaps one day there will be a Nova Scotian Bernkasteler Doctor.

The principal Canadian wine region stretches along the north shore of Lake Erie, with most of the grapes grown in the slim neck of land that separates

Lake Ontario from Lake Erie. Harsh winters dictate special care for vinifera vines and a heavy reliance on hybrids. The Bright's Winery, just outside the Canadian city of Niagara Falls, is the country's largest winery, producing a variety of wines, most of them from hybrids. The De Chaunac hybrid grape is named after Adhémar de Chaunac, who was Bright's winemaker for many years.

The Okanagan Valley, in British Columbia, is Canada's second most important wine region, running north from the United States border for about 161 kilometers/100 miles along both shores of Okanagan Lake. For most of their history, which began in the 1930s, the handful of wineries in the valley, plus several on Vancouver Island to the west, made most of their wine from imported California grapes. Previously, most of the wines had been made from berries, apples and foxy-tasting locally grown Labrusca grapes. Currently, half a dozen or more British Columbia wineries are making at least some of their wine from vinifera varieties.

Mexico

Vines and winemaking came to Mexico with the Conquistadors and followed them north into what is now the United States and south as far as present-day Argentina and Chile. At least one winery established near Mexico City in the sixteenth century is producing wines again today.

But the story of contemporary winemaking in Mexico begins with an Irishman. James Concannon, the founder of Concannon Vineyards in Livermore, California, came to Mexico in 1889 and convinced President Porfirio Diaz that he, Concannon, should create a wine industry in Mexico. He stayed until 1904 after planting wine grapes all over Mexico. He was followed in 1910 by Anton Perelli-Minetti, another California winemaker, who planted almost 405 hectares/1,000 acres of vines near Torreon. Some of modern-day Mexico's best vineyards and wineries were started by Perelli-Minetti. He left Mexico in 1916, tired of the ravages of the Revolution that had started six years earlier.

Wine is big business in Mexico, with almost 80,940 hectares/200,000 acres of grapes under cultivation in nine separate wine districts. The biggest two names that are central to the success of winemaking in Mexico today are Tchelistcheff and Domecq. Dmitri Tchelistcheff, the son of André Tchelistcheff and himself a famed oenologist, worked for Bodegas de Santo Tomas, the largest winery in Baja California, from 1962 to 1977. He planted better grapes, installed modern equipment and generally upgraded the quality of Mexican wines.

The Domecq family, of Spanish Sherry and Rioja fame, make both wine and brandy in Mexico in a dozen separate wineries and distilleries. They own the million-gallon Vides de Guadalupe winery in Baja California to make table wine and the Vinicola de Ensenada, which makes wine for Domecq brandy. Some of their Mexican table wines have been imported into the United States.

While the oldest winery in the country, founded in 1593 at Paila, in Coahuila, is only a ruin, the second oldest, the Madero family's Bodegas San Lorenzo, in the same region, is still in operation. It is a 378,530 hectares/10-million U.S. gallon winery.

SOUTH AMERICA

by Rosemary George, M.W.

Jesuit missionaries introduced viticulture to South America in the middle of the sixteenth century, first to Chile and then to Argentina. Wine has been made here longer than anywhere else in the New World, but production has concentrated on the domestic market that demands reds and whites made from the grape called Criólla in Argentina and Pais in Chile. The wines are kept too long in large oak barrels losing their freshness and fruit. Recently the Chilean wine industry has undergone a dramatic transformation, initiated partially by investment and interest from France, America and Spain. This is being imitated to a lesser extent in Argentina, and there is progress, too, in Brazil, with new plantings of *Vitis vinifera* replacing hybrids, and new vineyards across the River Plate in Uruguay. A handful of wineries in the Moquegua Valley and Ica region continue the four-hundred-year-old winemaking traditions of Peru in the foothills of the Andes.

Don Luis Cousiño brought the first French vine cuttings to Chile from Bordeaux in the middle of the last century, happily before *phylloxera* had crossed the Atlantic from North America. Today the flavors of Chile are dominated by France, with Cabernet Sauvignon and some Merlot and Malbec for reds and Sauvignon Blanc and Chardonnay for whites. Chilean winemakers are learning to control their fermentation temperatures and to master the techniques of barrel fermentation and the judicious use of oak for aging their wines. Some of the flavors can lack subtlety and for the moment reds tend to be more successful than the whites.

However Chile, apart from being one of the few parts of the world that is free of *phylloxera*, has a magnificent climate for growing healthy grapes. Around Santiago, where many of the vineyards are concentrated, the rainfall is very low and the melted snows of the Andes provide the much-needed irrigation water. Temperatures are moderated by the mountains and by the cool waters of the Pacific Ocean and rarely rise above 35°C/95°F even in the height of summer. The vineyards are in the Central Valley, which is in fact a plateau, flanked by two mountain ranges and crossed by the rivers Maipo, Maule and Aconcagua, among others. New vineyards are being planted further south, in the search for cooler conditions. Chile does have the elements of a system of *Denominación de Origen*, but so far there is no legal requirement to use a *denominación* on the label. Terms like *gran vino* and *reserva* are pretty

ABOVE: The snow-capped mountain range of the Andes forms a dramatic backdrop to the vineyards of Cousiño Macul, one of Chile's leading wineries.

meaningless too, serving merely as an indication of the producer's own perception of his wine. Leading producers in Chile include Santa Rita, Miguel Torres, Errázuriz, Cousiño Macul, Concha y Toro, Montes and Los Vascos.

Argentina is the world's fifth largest wine producer, making huge quantities of Criolla-based wine, aged for months, if not years, in fruit-sapping oak casks. There has, however, been a shift to European varieties: Malbec, Cabernet Sauvignon, small plantings of Riesling, Chardonnay and Chenin Blanc, and Torrontes from Argentina.

The principal wine regions in Argentina also depend upon the melted snows of the Andes for irrigation water. Mendoza, where Trapiche is not only the largest but also one of the most innovative producers, is the most important. The Rio Negro in northern Patagonia has one good producer Umberto Canale. Vineyards at an altitude of 1,700 meters/5,580 feet in the northern province of Salta benefit from the cool mountain air. Miguel Torino and Bodegas Etchart are two producers to note from Salta.

The other regions in Argentina are San Juan, known mainly for white wines, and grape concentrate; La Rioja, whose hot climate produces wines high in alcohol; and the smallest area, Catamarca, where the bulk of production is used for distillation into brandy.

Wine growing areas

Chile
- A Northern Zone
- B Central Zone
- C Southern Zone

Argentina
- D Norte
- E Occidente
- F San Juan
- G Córdoba
- H Littoral
- I Entre Rios
- J Mendoza
- K Rio Negro
- L Santa Fe
- M Buenos Aires

Wine growing countries

▲ Height above sea level
6206 Meters
(20362) (feet)

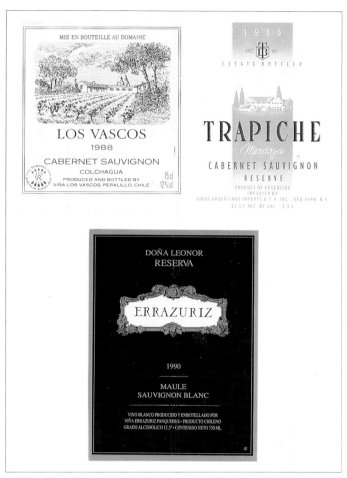

Peru's wine industry, with an annual production of less than a quarter of a million cases, is one of the smallest in South America. Some is exported, but by far the largest proportion is distilled into Pisco brandy. Most wines suffer from old-fashioned wine-making. A little is exported. Ecuador also produces a small amount of wine, from Labrusca vines. Most of the wine in Bolivia, produced in the La Paz region, is distilled into local brandy. There is limited production of table wine. In Paraguay the region of Villa Rica is the main source of the country's modest wine production. The Isabella grape is the most widely planted variety in Colombia. Principal producers include Bodegas Andaluzas, David and Eduardo Puyana and Bodegas Arejas.

ABOVE, RIGHT: Los Vascos, an estate in Colchagua, benefits from investment by the Rothschilds of Château Lafite. Trapiche is the largest Argentinian wine producer, now making some respectable Cabernet Sauvignon and other European varietals. Chilean Sauvignon Blanc improves with every vintage, as vinification techniques develop. Errázuriz is one of the most successful producers.

As yet there is no appellation system in Argentina, although labels are reliable as to grape variety and region. In both Argentina and Chile the producer's reputation is a key factor in choice. Some control over yields is necessary, for the notion that quantity equals quality still prevails in many quarters.

The vineyards of Brazil are concentrated in the province of Rio Grande do Sul, in the southern part of the country, and are mostly controlled by foreign companies, such as Moët & Chandon, Remy Martin and Heublein. In sharp contrast to Chile and Argentina, excessive rainfall and humidity are a problem, which hybrid varieties better withstand. It is only since the mid-1970s that *Vitis vinifera* varieties, such as Cabernet Sauvignon and Chardonnay, have been planted. Even so Isabella and Concord are still important on the domestic market.

Uruguay has some 55,000 hectares/135,850 acres under vine and produces generally old-fashioned wines from a large variety of grapes, among them Cabernet Sauvignon and Franc, Pinot Noir, Merlot, Nebbiolo, Grenache, Barbera, Pedro Ximénez, Riesling, Isabella, Sémillon, Sauvignon Blanc and Pinot Blanc. About half the vineyards are in the south; the rest in the northwest at Maldonado on the Plate River.

GROWER'S VIEW

We have many top-quality grapes in Chile. In the future it is important to try innovative blends. We have developed a blend that we call Montes Folly: it is 50 percent Chardonnay, 25 percent Riesling and 25 percent Gewürztraminer. We get an intense aroma of Riesling and Gewürztraminer combined with the elegance and character of Chardonnay.

We have been experimenting with growing Merlot and Pinot Noir in the cold climate of the south. The first results look good.

The central part of Chile is warmer and we have planted a small amount of Petite Sirah here; we feel this grape could do very well in the Central Valley. Areas near the coast and to the south have great potential for white grapes; warm valleys in the same areas, will also give excellent reds.

Aurilio Montes
DISCOVER WINE LTDA.

AUSTRALIA

by James Halliday

It may be because of some cartographer's trick of varying scales in world atlases, but it is quite remarkable how few wine-oriented visitors to Australia have any conception of the distances involved in travelling from one wine region to the next. For example, when Mitchelton, a medium-sized winery in Central Victoria, decided it would buy some Rhine Riesling from the Mount Barker region of Western Australia, it trucked the grapes (in a refrigerated semitrailer) the whole way. The journey took thirty-two hours of nonstop driving; the distance is the same as that from Madrid to Oslo.

It is hardly surprising, then, that Australia is able to produce every wine style. There are *flor* Sherry-styles; delicate Rieslings; luscious Chardonnays; Pinot Noirs; spicy Shiraz; Cabernet Sauvignons; sparkling wines; searingly intense botrytis Rieslings; mouthfilling botrytis Sémillons; tawny and vintage Port-styles and ultimately Australia's speciality, the fortified Tokays and Muscats of northeastern Victoria. Tokay in Australia, incidentally, is a synonym for the Muscadelle grape of Bordeaux. It should not be confused with the dessert wine from Tokay in Hungary.

But even here the pattern is more complex than might appear at first sight. By 1845 wine was being made in every Australian state except Queensland and the Northern Territory, and by the latter part of the century the viticultural map was just as complex and as far-flung as it is today. Grapes were grown and wine made in virtually every imaginable combination of climate and *terroir*: at the Great Intercolonial Exhibition of 1881, the Yarra Valley in Victoria (with a climate distinctly cooler than Bordeaux) did battle to the end for top position with the Hunter Valley (with a climate warmer than Provence). In the first half of the twentieth century that map shrank progressively, centering itself on the high-yielding, irrigated and hot Riverlands area of New South Wales, Victoria and South Australia, together with the Hunter Valley (N.S.W.), the Barossa Valley and Southern Vales (S.A.), the Swan Valley (W.A.) and a few anomalous outposts scattered without obvious rhyme or reason across the country.

It was a vinous dark age, not as severe as Prohibition, but one which saw fortified wine (much of it decidedly ordinary) come to dominate both production and consumption. The production of fine table

LEFT: Aerial view of the Barossa Valley. This is arguably Australia's most famous region but of declining importance, though it remains the production center for many of Australia's largest wine producers and a Mecca for wine tourists. Each year substantially more grapes from other regions are brought to the Barossa Valley for processing than are grown in it, and plantings on the valley floor decreased significantly during the 1980s.

221

Range with vineyards stretching from Inverell and Quirindi in the north to Tumbarumba in the Snowy Mountains to the extreme south. One small statistical illustration will suffice: in 1965 there were around twenty licensed wineries in Victoria; today there are almost two hundred.

Enough historical background: what of the overall style of Australian wine? Is there a style? Where are the wine styles headed? What are the strengths and the weaknesses? Where does the wine come from? How much wine is there, and where does it go?

ABOVE: Nothing much has changed at Morris's Winery in Rutherglen since the last century. These basket presses are much favored by winemaker Mick Morris for production of the superb fortified dessert wines made from Muscadelle (Tokay in Australia) and Brown Muscat.

wine continued thanks to the genius of now-revered makers such as Colin Preece at Seppelt Great Western (Vic.), Maurice O'Shea at McWilliams Mount Pleasant in the Hunter Valley (N.S.W.) and Roger Warren at Thomas Hardy in the Southern Vales (S.A.). But the volume of this wine was minuscule, its significance today being greater than it was at the time — with only a handful of bottles remaining in private cellars.

The renaissance had a distinctly improbable genesis: the ending of beer rationing in 1953 in the aftermath of World War II. The precise reasons and mechanisms are beyond the scope of this book, but it is no coincidence that in 1953 Max Schubert produced the first commercial vintage of Penfolds Grange Hermitage and that in 1953 Orlando beat a competitive field vying for hard-to-obtain import licences and imported the first stainless–steel pressure fermenter from Germany which was to revolutionize white wine making in Australia.

For the next fifteen years, from 1955 to 1970, technological advances in the winery and laboratory took the limelight. The decade thereafter (1970-80) saw a radical reshaping of vineyard plantings. First there was the shift from red wine production (dominant in the 1960s) to white wine, which outsold red by six to one by the end of the decade, then there was the emergence of the classic grape varieties led by Cabernet Sauvignon and followed by Chardonnay, supplementing the staples of Riesling (called Rhine Riesling in Australia), Shiraz (often called Hermitage) and Sémillon.

The last decade has seen the re-emergence of cool climate viticulture, spearheaded by Coonawarra — which, it is true, had been there all along — and Padthaway, which had been first planted in the 1960s, but which did not come into its own until the end of the 1970s. In Western Australia, the Margaret River blossomed and the Lower Great Southern sprawled improbably across an area not much smaller than Wales; in South Australia viticulture moved up from the floor of the Barossa Valley to the encircling East Barossa and Mount Lofty Ranges; Victoria blazed with activity just as it had during the gold rush days of the late nineteenth century (when Australia enjoyed the highest per capita income in the world) and before phylloxera took hold; while New South Wales began a still-tentative expansion along the western slopes of the Great Dividing

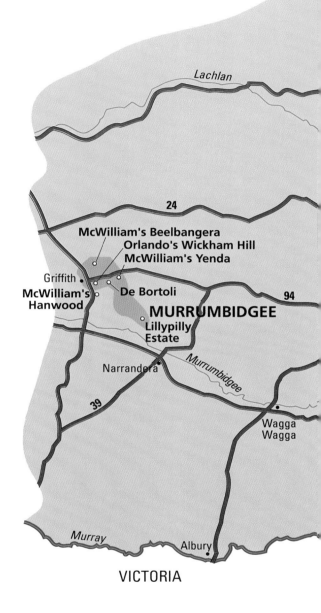

VICTORIA

The first and the last questions have a partially common answer. The wines, white and red, dry and sweet, table and fortified, have a common thread. They are soft, clean, fruity and easily understood: they are user-friendly. They reflect the sunshine, the clean air and the informal way of life. They say a surprising amount about the Australian lifestyle and attitude. They appeal as much to the heart (or perhaps the stomach) as to the mind, and they do not rely upon tradition to inflate their value.

These qualities have won increasing acceptance by overseas markets at the very time it is most needed. The neo-prohibitionist lobby is alive and well in Australia, as are ill-defined and ill-conceived concerns about health, accentuated by a largely-undeserved reputation as a nation of heavy drinkers. This reputation is undeserved because the annual per capita consumption of 8.31 liters/2.2 U.S.

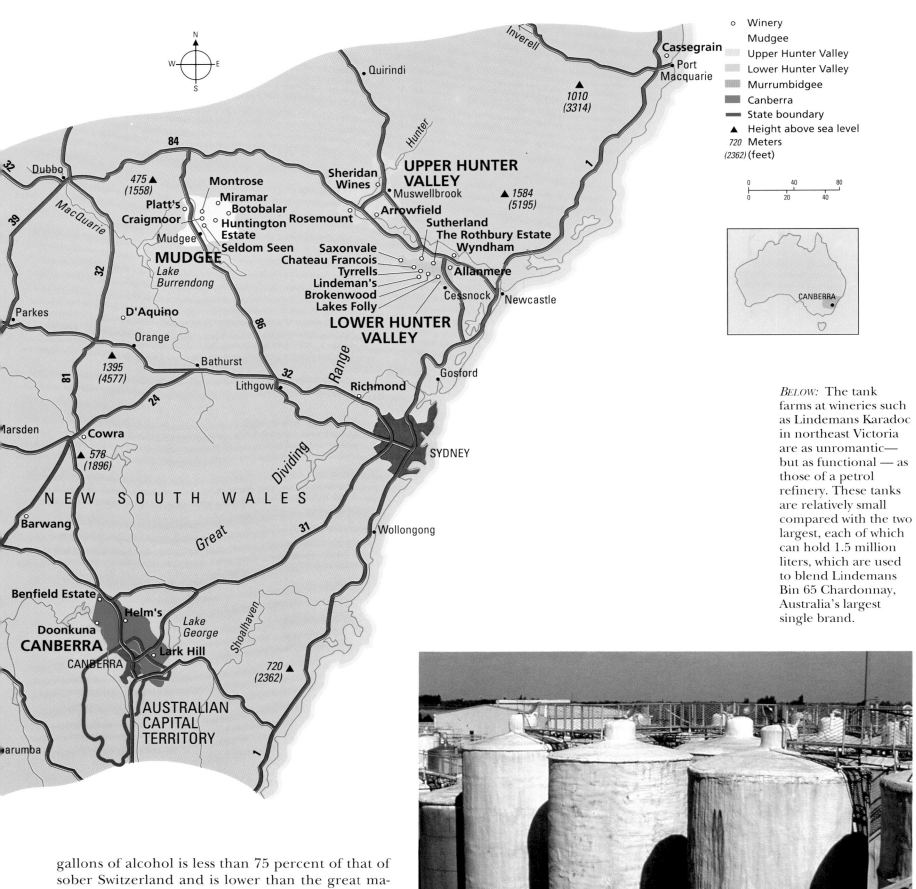

Legend:
- ○ Winery
- Mudgee
- Upper Hunter Valley
- Lower Hunter Valley
- Murrumbidgee
- Canberra
- State boundary
- ▲ Height above sea level
- *720* Meters
- *(2362)* (feet)

BELOW: The tank farms at wineries such as Lindemans Karadoc in northeast Victoria are as unromantic— but as functional — as those of a petrol refinery. These tanks are relatively small compared with the two largest, each of which can hold 1.5 million liters, which are used to blend Lindemans Bin 65 Chardonnay, Australia's largest single brand.

gallons of alcohol is less than 75 percent of that of sober Switzerland and is lower than the great majority of European Community countries.

However, such concerns have seen domestic wine consumption decline from its 1986 peak of 343,112 hectoliters/9,064,333 U.S. gallons to 1990 consumption of 311,000 hectoliters/8,215,998 U.S. gallons. The offset has been an increase in exports from 8,600 hectoliters/227,195 U.S. gallons in 1985 to 57,000 hectoliters/1,505,826 U.S. gallons in 1990-91, with the United Kingdom the largest market in terms of both volume and value, followed by Scandinavia and the United States.

South Australia remains by far the most important state, even if its peak of 80 percent of total production in 1946 has now diminished to 55 percent. In South Australia, Victoria and New South Wales

ABOVE: One of the Rosemount Estate wineries in the Upper Hunter Valley.

and southern Victoria; the Clare and Barossa Valleys, the Southern Vales, Coonawarra and Padthaway in South Australia, and the Swan Valley, Margaret River and Lower Great Southern in Western Australia. Other districts include the Granite Belt of Queensland, the Canberra district adjacent to the Australian Capital Territory, and Tasmania — each producing tiny quantities of wine, although there is endless fascination with Tasmania.

Rather than attempt to describe each of these regions and the wines they produce, it is better to focus on the major wine styles, thereby bringing the regions into play as they reflect and contribute to each style.

Chardonnay may have made a belated start, but it has made every post a winner since Murray Tyrrell of Tyrrell's Hunter Valley winery produced 1971 Vat 47, the first wine this century in Australia to be labeled Chardonnay. It is grown in every wine region and is as complaisant a variety in Australia as it is elsewhere in the world. It bends gracefully to every conceivable combination of *terroir*, climate and viticultural practice and is no less flexible and accommodating when it arrives in the winery.

So one finds a tremendous variety of style within an overall framework of clean wines in which varietal fruit flavor is usually given pride of place, usually framed within a substantial border of new oak.

At the most voluptuous extreme are the peachy, buttery, alcoholic Chardonnays of the Hunter Valley, the Southern Vales and the best of the Riverlands. Typically, these are made using techniques which make them extremely attractive at eighteen to thirty months after the vintage, and only the best examples mature with any grace thereafter, the lesser wines becoming rather blowsy and coarse as excessive phenols take over.

Tyrrells, in the Lower Hunter Valley with Vat 47, and Rosemount Estate in the Upper Hunter Valley, with Roxburgh and Show Chardonnay, would generally be regarded as leading exponents of this style, but there are numerous others who do very well— too numerous to mention, although Renmano Chairman's Selection Chardonnay Bin 104 from the Riverlands has an uncanny knack of rising way above its station.

At the other extreme are the far more elegant and subdued wines of the coolest parts of Victoria, South Australia (the Adelaide Hills), Western Australia and Tasmania, often made by small producers such as Petaluma, Mountadam and Pipers Brook, who are aiming towards a less overtly fruity and more complex style which can take four or five years (or more) to approach its peak.

Somewhere in the middle come the large-producer wines from areas such as Padthaway (notably Thomas Hardy and Lindemans) which have zesty, melon-grapefruit flavors set amid spicy oak and which mature with grace over a number of years.

As the 1990s opened, the endemic excess of demand over supply of Chardonnay eased — not surprising given the doubling of production between 1987 (18,600 tonnes/18,307 tons) and 1990 (34,700 tonnes/34,153 tons) and the forecast redoubling by 1994 to 67,200 tonnes/66,142 tons. This saw steep falls both in the price of grapes and the wines on the shelves (at the cheaper end) and foolish and naïve predictions that Chardonnay had had its day. The reality is that it will steadily grow in

alike the Riverlands (congregated along the vast Murray River in the first two states, the Murrumbidgee and the Murray in the last) dominate production in quantity, though not in quality terms.

It is these regions which produce the sea of wine which goes into the wine casks — the bags-in-boxes — which account for a staggering 65 percent of all wine sales in Australia. The technology which drives this production can only be described as exemplary, and it is small wonder that many wine-drinking Australians are content to have a cask in the fridge door as their sole source of wine. The quality is on a par with wines such as Lindemans Bin 65 Chardonnay, of which 4 million bottles were made in 1990 (and produced as a single blend); this single wine provided 20 percent of Australia's total exports to the United States. For the Riverlands are essentially white wine country, reflecting to the full the continuing four-to-one ratio of white to red production and consumption.

The wine for the middle and upper sectors of the market comes from the regions which one most frequently reads or hears about: the Hunter Valley and Mudgee in New South Wales; north eastern, central

Australia (legend)

- ○ Winery
- Murray River
- Great Western
- Pyrenees
- Central Victoria
- Goulburn Valley
- North East
- Bendigo
- Yarra Valley
- Geelong
- Mornington Peninsula
- Gippsland
- Tasmania

SOUTH AUSTRALIA

Murray
Mildura
Lindemans
12
McWilliams
MURRAY RIVER
Bullers
Murrumbidgee
20
75
NEW SOUTH WALES
39
31
Snowy Mountains
N
W E
S

V I C T O R I A
Loddon
Murray
Mount Prior
St Leonards
Albury
79
Monichino
CENTRAL VICTORIA
GOULBURN VALLEY
Bullers
Morris
Campbells
Wangaratta
NORTH EAST
Baileys
8
Balgownie Estate
Shepparton
Brown Brothers
▲ 2230 (7315)
Passing Clouds
Bendigo
1985 (6512)
PYRENEES
Chateau Leamon
Longleat
Chateau Tahbilk
Mitchelton
Paul Osicka
GREAT WESTERN
Taltarni
Heathcote
Harcourt Valley
Garden Gully
Glenelg
Boroka
Ararat
Virgin Hills
890 (2920) ▲
Great Dividing Range
Best's
Seppelts
Gisborne
YARRA VALLEY
De Bortoli
St. Huberts
Mount Langi Ghiran
Yellowglen
Healesville
Yarra Yering
BENDIGO
Ballarat
8
Graiglee
Coldstream Hills
Wantirna
Nicholson River
Tarcoola
MELBOURNE
Bannockburn
Briagolong
Idyll
1
Geelong
Elgee Park
Sale
Prince Albert
Dromana Estate
Bass Phillip
McAlister
GEELONG
Merricks
GIPPSLAND
MORNINGTON PENINSULA

— State boundary
▲ Height above sea level
1750 Meters
(5151) (feet)

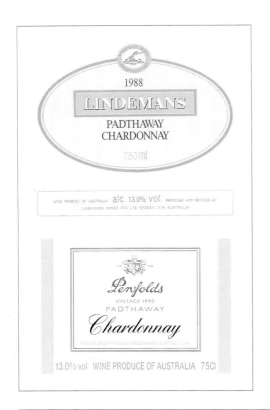

1988
LINDEMANS
PADTHAWAY
CHARDONNAY
750ml

WINE PRODUCT OF AUSTRALIA alc. 13.0% vol. PRODUCED AND BOTTLED BY
LINDEMANS WINES PTY LTD SYDNEY 2116, AUSTRALIA

Penfolds
VINTAGE 1990
PADTHAWAY
Chardonnay

13.0% vol WINE PRODUCE OF AUSTRALIA 75Cl

Heemskerk
Pipers Brook
Marions
Launceston
St Matthias
Tamar
1570 ▲ (5151)
TASMANIA
1615 ▲ (5298)
TASMANIA
Meadowbank
Moorilla
Hobart

CANBERRA

0   50   100 kms
0   50 miles

BELOW AND FAR LEFT:
The diverse styles of
Chardonnays reflect
their far-flung
geographical spread.
These have
production bases in
the Hunter Valley
(Wyndham), Barossa
Valley (Wolf Blass),
Adelaide Hills (Hill-
Smith), Riverlands
(Renmano) and
Padthaway
(Lindemans and
Penfolds).

WYNDHAM ESTATE
1988 OAK CASK
CHARDONNAY
SOUTH-EASTERN AUSTRALIA
PRODUCED AND ESTATE BOTTLED BY
WYNDHAM ESTATE WINES LIMITED,
BRANXTON, HUNTER VALLEY, AUSTRALIA
750ML PRODUCT OF AUSTRALIA

WOLF BLASS
BILYARA
CELLARS
SOUTH AUSTRALIAN
CHARDONNAY
AUSTRALIA'S MASTER WINEMAKERS
BARREL FERMENTED
IMPORTED BY THE GEORGE MORTON COMPANY.
HARTFIELD ROAD, LONDON SW19 3SE UK
PRODUCED BY WOLF BLASS WINES INTERNATIONAL, STURT HIGHWAY, NURIOOTPA, S.A. 5355
PRODUCE OF AUSTRALIA • 75cl • 12.0% VOL

Renmano
Chairman's Selection
South Australia
Chardonnay
1988
PRODUCE OF AUSTRALIA
PRODUCED AND BOTTLED BY
RENMANO WINES PTY. LTD.
RENMARK, SOUTH AUSTRALIA F53
13.5% Vol.   75cl
IMPORTED BY BERRI RENMANO WINES (EXPORT) LTD.
PLUMTREE COURT, LONDON EC4A 4HT.

H i l l - S m i t h E s t a t e
Air-Strip Block   Adelaide Hills
CHARDONNAY
1990
PRODUCE OF
AUSTRALIA
750ml
12.5% VOL

RIGHT: Rhine Riesling can be distinguished (Petaluma) or humble (Angove's) but is consistent both in terms of its overall style— crisp, clean and dry — and its value for money.

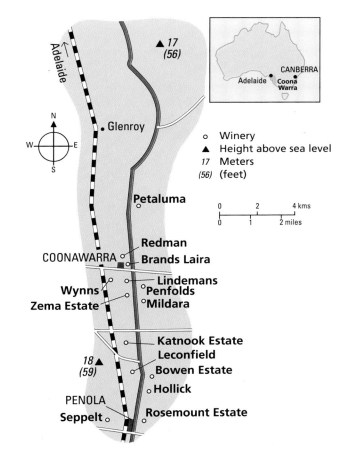

BELOW: Labels from three top producers of Semillon, Australia's richest and longest-lived white wine. Lindemans now blend Semillon with Chardonnay, which gives zest to the wine when young; Lehmann's wood-aged Semillon is an opulent wine at an affordable price while Mount Pleasant has for decades been the premier Hunter Valley vineyard of the McWilliams Wine Company.

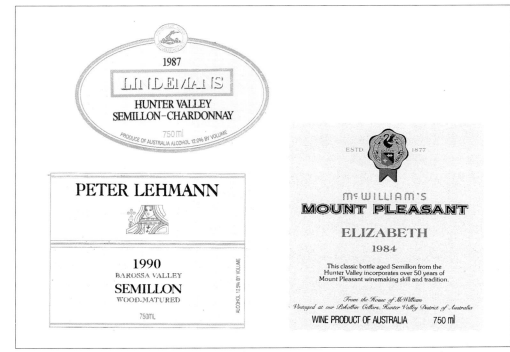

importance. The range of styles and prices will increase even further as winemakers and financial controllers experiment with its many possibilities.

Until the peremptory challenge of Chardonnay, Riesling ruled supreme, its throne straddling the Clare and Eden valleys of South Australia. The style is uniquely Australian: crisp, non-phenolic and dry, unlike the Rieslings of Germany or Alsace. They have a largely unrecognized capacity to age superbly in bottle, as anyone who drank a 1973 or 1975 Leo Buring Reserve Bin or a 1980 Petaluma Rhine Riesling in 1991 would readily attest.

The greatest of these wines do not acquire the kerosene or petrol aroma which is often described as the character of aged Riesling from Germany, but a delightful blend of lime juice and lightly browned toast. In more recent years, the Lower Great Southern region has emerged as a particularly distinguished producer of Riesling, with Alkoomi, Castle Rock, Forest Hill, Goundrey and Plantagenet among the best, all virtually guaranteed of a long and refined life, although commerical reality will ensure that only a relatively few bottles will survive to tell the tale. For Australians, the curiosity is that their style of Riesling is so little appreciated in overseas markets when Chardonnay is so popular.

The third classic Australian white wine is Semillon: in the unlikely environment of the very warm and humid Hunter Valley (Region V on the Winkler scale [see Appendix]), compared to Region I for the Yarra Valley), the grape produces one of Australia's unique table wines, the great Lindeman Semillons of yore (1970 was the last superb vintage, still a symphony in 1991) are a dying race, but Rothbury, McWilliams and Tyrrells are carrying the flame of the traditional unoaked style, while smaller makers such as Allanmere and Brokenwood are trying newer styles, using either oak or a variety such as Sauvignon Blanc to give the young wine the lift it needs.

The same solution is being used in the Margaret River region, which is emerging as another producer of quality Semillon, curiously with a much more herbal cast than the relatively soft — and certainly not cold — climate of the area would suggest. For young Semillon, left to its own devices, tends to be a pale and insipid thing, needing a minimum of five and more probably ten years to develop the honeyed, nutty, buttery aroma and flavor which so enchants those who encounter it for the first time

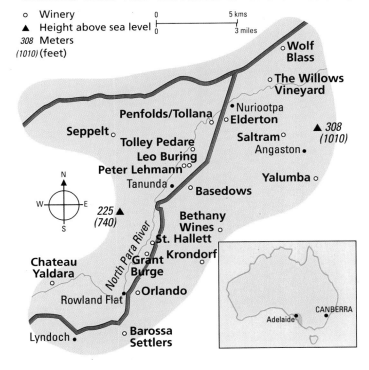

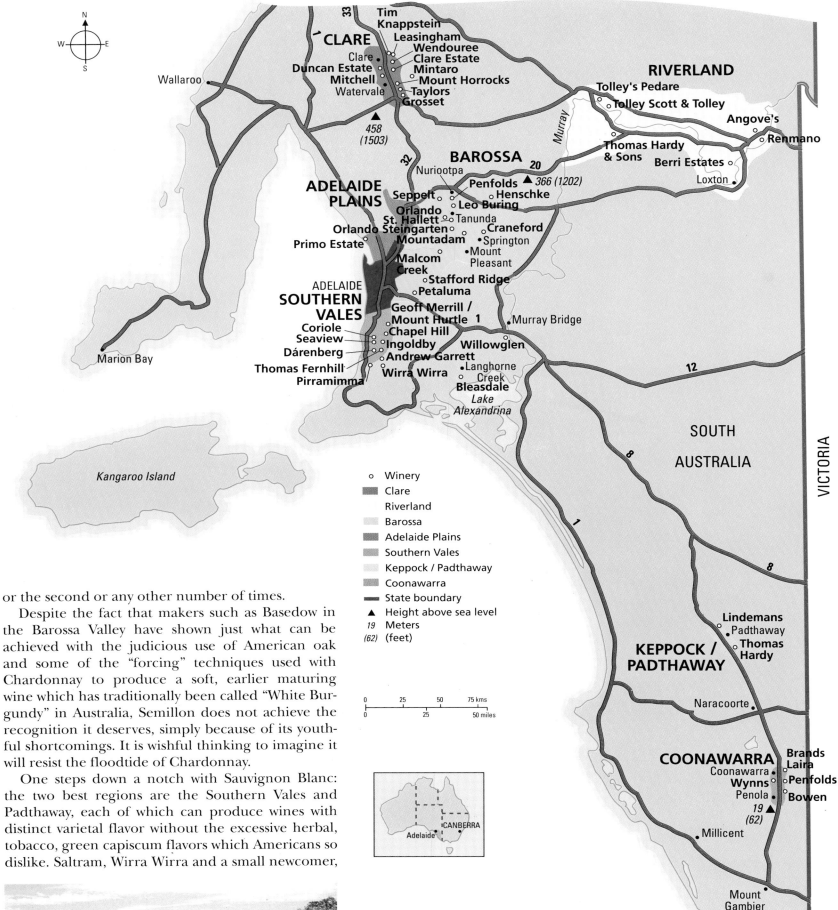

N
W — E
S

Wallaroo

33
CLARE
Tim
Knappstein
Leasingham
Wendouree
Clare
Clare Estate
Duncan Estate
Mintaro
Mitchell
Mount Horrocks
Watervale
Taylors
Grosset

RIVERLAND
Tolley's Pedare
Tolley Scott & Tolley
Angove's
Renmano

458
(1503)

32

Murray

BAROSSA 20
Nuriootpa
Penfolds
Henschke
366 (1202)

Thomas Hardy
& Sons
Berri Estates
Loxton

ADELAIDE
PLAINS
Seppelt
Orlando
Leo Buring
St. Hallett
Tanunda
Orlando Steingarten
Craneford
Mountadam
Springton
Primo Estate
Mount
Pleasant
Malcom
Creek
Stafford Ridge
ADELAIDE
Petaluma
SOUTHERN
VALES
Geoff Merrill /
Mount Hurtle 1
Murray Bridge
Coriole
Chapel Hill
Seaview
Willowglen
Ingoldby
Dárenberg
Andrew Garrett
Thomas Fernhill
Wirra Wirra
Langhorne
Creek
Pirramimma
Bleasdale
Lake
Alexandrina

Marion Bay

SOUTH
AUSTRALIA

12

VICTORIA

Kangaroo Island

8

○ Winery
Clare
Riverland
Barossa
Adelaide Plains
Southern Vales
Keppock / Padthaway
Coonawarra
State boundary
▲ Height above sea level
19 Meters
(62) (feet)

8

Lindemans
Padthaway
Thomas
Hardy
KEPPOCK /
PADTHAWAY

Naracoorte

0   25   50   75 kms
0   25   50 miles

COONAWARRA
Brands
Laira
Coonawarra
Wynns
Penfolds
Penola
Bowen
19
(62) ▲

CANBERRA

Adelaide

Millicent

Mount
Gambier

or the second or any other number of times.

Despite the fact that makers such as Basedow in the Barossa Valley have shown just what can be achieved with the judicious use of American oak and some of the "forcing" techniques used with Chardonnay to produce a soft, earlier maturing wine which has traditionally been called "White Burgundy" in Australia, Semillon does not achieve the recognition it deserves, simply because of its youthful shortcomings. It is wishful thinking to imagine it will resist the floodtide of Chardonnay.

One steps down a notch with Sauvignon Blanc: the two best regions are the Southern Vales and Padthaway, each of which can produce wines with distinct varietal flavor without the excessive herbal, tobacco, green capiscum flavors which Americans so dislike. Saltram, Wirra Wirra and a small newcomer,

Shaw and Smith, do particularly well with gooseberry, passionfruit accented wines from the Southern Vales, while Lindemans has made some wonderful wines in Padthaway. The Margaret River cannot be ignored, but the wines do tend to be rather leafy and herbal, and are usually blended with Semillon.

The remaining white varieties constitute a Joseph's coat of many colors: Chenin Blanc, Gewürztraminer, Muscat of Alexandria, Frontignac, Muscat Gordo Blanco, Verdelho, Marsanne, Trebbiano, Chasselas ... the list goes on and on, augmented in recent years by more *outré* varieties such as Viognier and Roussanne from the Rhône Valley, Verduzzo

LEFT: Padthaway is unique in Australia, as virtually all the plantings were established and are owned by the major companies — which in other districts rely on small, independent contract growers to supply much of their grape requirements.

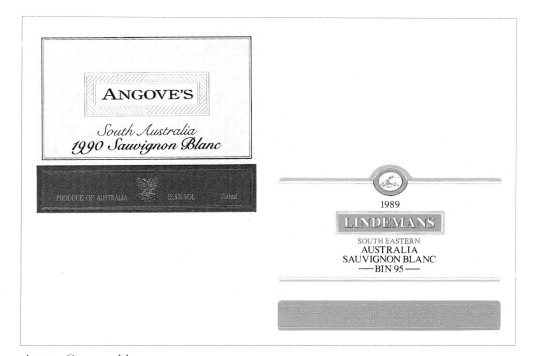

ABOVE: One would need to be very parochial to suggest that Australia's commercial brands of rather soft and bland Sauvignon Blanc pose any threat to those of New Zealand.

RIGHT: Storm clouds first gathered over Wynns Coonawarra Estate after the death of founder John Riddoch in 1901, presaging fifty years of struggle until David Wynn purchased the estate in 1951.

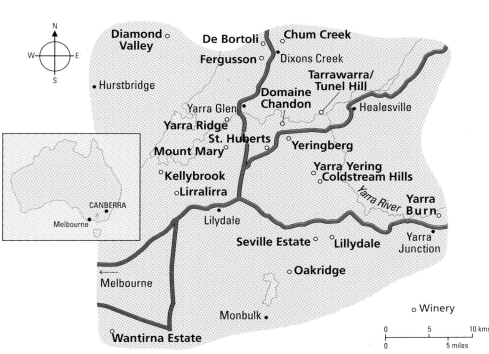

from Italy and who knows what else.

It will come as no surprise to find that Cabernet Sauvignon dominates the premium end of the red wine industry, or that it is almost as ubiquitous as Chardonnay in terms of its geographic spread. But it may come as a surprise to hear that as recently as 1979 the three Rhône varieties of Syrah (known as Shiraz in Australia), Grenache and Mourvèdre (or Mataro, as it is called in Australia) accounted for 77 percent of all red grape plantings. Great has been the fall of the latter two, for now the combined share has declined to 61 percent (with Shiraz accounting for 37 percent), a pattern putting Australia on a diametrically opposed course to California, where the Rhône Rangers are infinitely fashionable.

Cabernet Sauvignon may be ubiquitous, but few would argue with the proposition that Coonawarra produces the greatest examples. Some participants suggest that Coonawarra succeeds despite the best efforts of financial controllers who have been instrumental in fostering "advanced" viticultural techniques including mechanical pruning, minimal pruning (a euphemism for no pruning) and mechanical harvesting, all of which reduce the cost of production but by no means increase — or even maintain—quality.

The opposing view would say this is a case of sour grapes, pointing to the dominance of Coonawarra Cabernets in the all-important Australian wine show system, and their equally-marked dominance of the middle to upper sectors of the bottled wine market. The big names are Lindemans (which unleashed a major price war in the latter part of 1991) and its *sous-marque* Rouge Homme, Mildara (thanks to its volume-brand Jamiesons Run) and Wynns; the smaller producers are headed by Petaluma and Bowen Estate.

At its best Coonawarra produces Cabernet with an almost lush core of dark berry fruit (ranging from blackcurrant to mulberry) tempered by a hint

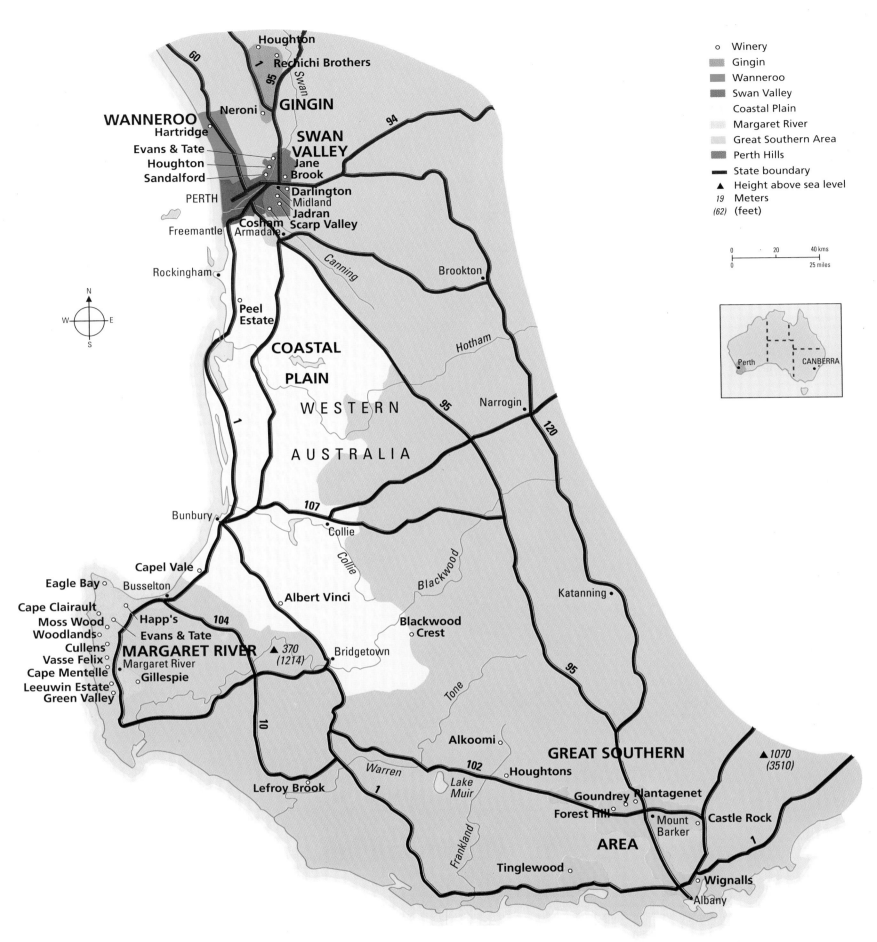

of herbaceous austerity; it is capable of absorbing a great deal of new oak which adds complexity and structure. The grape tannins are always soft, and the new oak is accordingly very useful.

The southern parts of Victoria also produce fine Cabernets, a little less opulent than those of Coonawarra, but with similar structure. The Southern Vales (Thomas Hardy, Ingoldby, Woodstock), make richer and stronger wines, often with a dash of dark chocolate, and as one moves north of Adelaide to the Barossa and Clare valleys, the same trend continues. Those of the Clare Valley have an uncanny ability to combine strength with finesse and age with grace for a decade or more: this district consis-

tently belies its technically warm to very warm climate with the elegance of its wines, with Mitchell, Tim Knappstein and Wendouree to the fore.

In Western Australia the Margaret River has achieved international acclaim: Moss Wood and Cape Mentelle with 100 percent varietal Cabernets, Cullen with Cabernet/Merlot blends. The style is quite unique: an inner core of perfumed, fragrant berry fruit surrounded by a rather tougher shell with a slightly gravelly edge which softens with age. Those of the Lower Great Southern region sit neatly alongside the Rieslings of that area, finely strung, reserved but very powerful and extremely long-lived.

Cabernet has become a significant variety in the

Hunter Valley: as it ages varietal character slowly yields to regional character with a gently earthy aroma and taste which some greatly admire, and some greatly dislike. Mudgee produces inky black, tremendously fruity wines which seem to retain more varietal character as they age.

Only in Tasmania does the grape struggle: the Tamar Valley gives wines with good color, flavor, extract and depth, but the other sub-districts struggle to avoid excessively leafy or herbal flavors.

The only areas in which Cabernet Sauvignon and Shiraz (the latter by far the most widely planted red grape, its 5,100 hectares/12,597 acres representing 27 percent of the red grape total) are not dominant are the Riverland regions. Shiraz in particular does not enjoy the high crop levels which are part and parcel of viticultural life there, and the wines are unacceptably low in color, flavor and body. (Cabernet Sauvignon, it must be said, does somewhat better in some spots, but still makes a humble wine.)

In almost all other regions, Shiraz is a very important grape: for half a century, indeed, it was the most important premium variety, keeping the flickering flame of Coonawarra alight (ironic given the present dominance there of Cabernet Sauvignon) and being wholly responsible for the best wines of the Barossa and Hunter valleys.

There are three quite different styles of Shiraz. The Hunter Valley is arguably the most distinctive: often raw, concentrated and tannic when young, it slowly evolves and softens into a silky, velvety wine with an aroma and taste which were once described as akin to that of a sweaty saddle after a hard day's ride. In small quantities this character is a gently earthy, faintly leathery (soft leather) backdrop to marvelously sweet fruit; in excess, it is bitter and tough. The very best wines live for forty years or more, rivaling those of Coonawarra.

The second is the super-fruity, lush style epito-

mized by Penfolds Grange and centered in and around the Barossa Valley. The secret here is sixty-to one-hundred year old vines bush-pruned in the European fashion close to the ground, often without trellises, and yielding around 15 hectoliters per hectare/0.8 tons per acre. These grapes provide a wine of exceptional concentration of flavor and extract which lends itself admirably to final fermentation and maturation in new American oak. The result is a wine which now has a worldwide reputation.

There are other wines made from similarly precious resources: St. Hallett Old Block Shiraz (Barossa Valley), Henschke Hill of Grace (Eden Valley), Brands Original Vineyard Shiraz (from the 1893 plantings at the birth of Coonawarra) and Château Tahbilk 1860 Shiraz (Central Goulburn), all made from ungrafted vines — with the 131-year-old vines of Tahbilk taking pride of place.

The third style is that of the cool regions of Victoria, South Australia and Western Australia, in which a pronounced Rhône-like pepper or spice appears. Mount Langi Ghiran at Ararat, near Great Western in central Victoria, is a leading name here, producing a wine with all the texture of a tapestry, the spice and pepper woven through deep red berry fruit and soft, mouthfilling tannins.

Necessity being the mother of invention, the extreme shortage of Cabernet Sauvignon in the 1960s led to the blending of Cabernet Sauvignon and Shiraz. Winemakers and commentators alike convinced themselves that this was a wholly synergistic union, as well as being distinctively Australian. The problem was, however, that with the honorable exception of Penfolds Bin 389 Cabernet Shiraz, winemakers tended to use the leftovers — pressings, culls and so forth — in the blend. What is more, the wisdom of hindsight suggests that while the structure of the blend may make sense, the flavor of

---

GROWER'S VIEW

Most of the vineyard at Château Tahbilk lies within or borders on a branch of the Goulburn River. The distributary provides water for supplementary irrigation and the red gums which line its banks provide some shelter from prevailing west and southwesterly winds. The area is only slightly undulating and lies between 130 and 140 meters/426 and 459 feet above sea level.

Our soils are all alluvial but vary from hard-setting clays and complex types to light, sandy loams. Most of these soils are naturally low in phosphorus and, despite regular cover cropping, low in organic matter. They are generally fairly acidic with a pH (calcium chloride) range from about 4.4 to 5.6. We have made a concerted effort to overcome soil acidity. We slake with applications of lime, we have lupin and cereal cover crops and we practice minimal cultivation. Excessively dense canopies resulting from high vigor and low single-wire trellises have been managed with conversion to a vertical shoot positioned system.

About half an hectare/1.2 acres of pre-phylloxera Shiraz planted in 1860 remains in production. Other plantings include about 5 hectares/12.4 acres planted before 1935. The most recent plantings of this variety date from 1969. Yields from the

older plantings are generally about 10 tonnes per hectare. A 5 hectare/12.4 acre planting of Cabernet Sauvignon completed in 1951 remains in production producing yields of about 8 tonnes per hectare. All plantings since 1985 have been of grafted material with clonally selected scion wood on *phylloxera* – and *nematode*-resistant rootstock.

We purchased a mechanical harvester for use in the 1992 vintage. Up to this point only very small quantities of fruit have been mechanically harvested. The harvest generally starts with Chardonnay or Sauvignon Blanc on about March 10 and usually ends with Cabernet Sauvignon being picked in the last week of April or early May.

The red wines are vinified using traditional Bordeaux techniques, which involve fermentation on the skins in 5 tonne/4.9 ton open vats for six to nine days followed by completion of fermentation and maturation in century-old oak cases.

The red wines of Château Tahbilk are renowned the world over for flavor, structure and long-term cellaring potential — in excess of forty years in the great years.

Alister Purbrick
CHATEAU TAHBILK

Shiraz is less compatible than that of Merlot and Cabernet Franc, and it is in this direction that the red blends of the 1990s are firmly headed.

Pinot Noir has been in existence since the earliest days, but like so many of the other premium varieties, it virtually disappeared around the turn of the century, with tiny pockets remaining in the Hunter Valley and elsewhere. In the red wine boom of the 1960s it followed the Californian pattern, being extensively planted in areas which were far too warm

---

GROWER'S VIEW

Our Hill of Grace vineyard has some of the oldest Shiraz grapes in South Australia, material that came over from France between 1860 and 1870. The vineyard comes from my grandmother's side, Polish people. The name "Hill of Grace" is a translation of the German *Genatenberg*, which was a church opposite a vineyard in the village where my German ancestors on my father's side came from.

I do not believe in long macerations for Shiraz. I follow a system developed by my father in the 1940s. The wines are fermented on the skins in open vats for just a week. The grapes are static, there's no physical maceration and the extract of the skins is allowed to seep slowly into the wines. The skins are still fermenting when we draw off the wine. What is different with our technique, compared with classic vinification in the Rhône and even in California, is that we avoid long twenty-one-day macerations. Why? Because we believe that Shiraz has lovely soft tannins, which would become needlessly harsh if we used too long a skin contact during fermentation. Our shorter macerations in no way impair the structure of our Shiraz, quite the reverse we feel. Some Californians would disagree, no doubt.

As for our Rhine Rieslings, we follow fairly Germanic principles of winemaking: clarified juice, clean steady fermentations at relatively cool temperatures of 10°-15°C/50°-59°F. At the end of fermentation, we chill everything down and keep the wines cold until bottling.

Stephen Henschke

HENSCHKE

---

for it to produce a wine with any character or recognizable varietal style. The inevitable consequence was a loss of confidence in the variety by winemakers and public alike, and continuing confusion (and disagreement) about how a Pinot should look and taste.

But with the resurgence of viticulture in the dress circle around Melbourne — the Yarra Valley, Mornington Peninsula, Geelong and South Gippsland — Pinot Noir has come back into its own as a table wine. All of these districts, and most conspicuously the Yarra Valley, can produce Pinot Noir with an at times startling resemblance to Burgundy: Coldstream Hills and Diamond Valley are two leading producers in the Yarra, Bannockburn leads Geelong, Dromana Estate the Mornington Peninsula, and Bass Phillip leads South Gippsland.

Other regions with obvious potential include Pipers Brook in Northern Tasmania (watch

Heemskerk since 1990), the Adelaide Hills around Mount Lofty and the Albany subdistrict of the Lower Great Southern, with Wignalls setting the pace.

Most of the early plantings of Pinot Noir are now diverted to sparkling winemaking, as are some of the newest in areas such as Tumbarumba in the Snowy Mountains of southern New South Wales.

ABOVE: Whether by choice (domestic) or of necessity (export), Australia's best wines are identified by brand and variety rather than the old generic labels such as claret or burgundy.

231

ABOVE: The very high sugar levels (over 20 baume) of raisined Brown Muscat grapes from Rutherglen attract a myriad of predators including birds, bees and wasps.

BELOW: The quality of sparkling wine improved dramatically over the latter part of the 1980s as classic varieties (Chardonnay and Pinot Noir) replaced inferior stand-bys, and exports soared.

Led by Seppelt (which is now in the same ownership as Seaview and Penfolds, the other biggest sparkling wine makers) the quality of Australian sparkling wine has been transformed over the past decade. Reflecting this, bottle-fermented sparkling wine sales rose from less than 5 million liters/1,320,000 U.S. gallons in 1980-81 to 26 million liters/6,864,000 U.S. gallons in 1989-90, making it the best performing sector of the market.

Pinot Noir and Chardonnay (with a little Pinot Meunier) have replaced Semillon, Colombard, Trebbiano, Muscat Gordo Blanco and Chenin Blanc as the base wines for the middle to upper priced brands. At the top end, newer producers such as Domaine Chandon and Croser have joined wines like Seppelt Salinger and gone one step further by sourcing their grapes from purpose-designed cool-climate vineyards, rather than settling for second best with warm-grown Pinot Noir and Chardonnay. The style remains distinctively Australian: fresh, crisp and clean, with fruit flavor kept under tight control but still driving the wine.

The performance of the fortified wine market — encompassing Sherry styles, tawny and vintage Port styles, Muscat and Tokay — has been the opposite, with a longer term decline. In 1960 sales of fortified wine constituted 70 percent of the total market; in 1991 the figure was 10 percent, and it continues its slow but inexorable fall. Which is a great pity: Australia makes superb *fino*, *oloroso* and *amoroso* Sherry style wines (and still vast quantities of cream Sherry styles of lesser station in life), very rich tawny Port styles which never fail to surprise and impress the Portuguese, idiosyncratic vintage Port styles and world class Muscat and Tokay.

The latter two, at least, are holding their ground, and indeed have recovered from their nadir in the sixties and seventies. Prices have risen, still providing only a derisory return on the massive investments in maturing stocks, but providing some encouragement. Years ago, I wrote this of Muscat: "Like Narcissus drowning in his reflection, one can lose oneself in the aroma of a great old Muscat. All this, and one has not yet felt the necessity of actually tasting the wine. That moment destroys the calm which preceded it; an old Muscat has an explosive intensity of luscious flavor, combined with high acid and a twist of wood-derived volatility, which strips the saliva from the sides of the taster's mouth, leaving the flavor in undiminished magnificence for minutes after the last milliliter has been swallowed." Small wonder that some see it as Australia's greatest wine.

GROWER'S VIEW

The "mesoclimate" of our vineyard is a rare combination of volcanic hill, alluvial creek flat and southeasterly aspect.

We have planted Cabernet on the volcanic hillside and Chardonnay on lower-lying alluvial soil. The climate is "Mediterranean" but since the vineyard is in the southern hemisphere, its southeast aspect minimizes the effect of heat and sunlight intensity.

People think Australia is hot and sunny, but in the lower Hunter Valley we have high humidity and the possibility of summer rainfall, which can lead to disease problems like downy and powdery mildew — and grey rot.

At harvest time, the grapes are picked cool, by hand, and early in the day; they certainly do not have to go far to their destiny.

In the winery, our approach is traditional but based on common sense. The Cabernet is fermented on its skins in open vats for several days and the "cap" is plunged by hand day and night. Our main concession to technology is a back-up of efficient cooling control. The Chardonnay ferments slowly in steel tanks for two weeks, then it finishes fermentation in French oak *barriques* and stays there for six months before filtering and bottling.

We do not filter our Cabernet. To achieve maximum character and complexity, the wine should be treated as little as possible, but of course an unfiltered red wine needs time to mature. In terms of cask maturation of our Cabernet, we age it partly in French oak *barriques* and partly in large old oak vats for fifteen months.

Stephen Lake
LAKE'S FOLLY VINEYARD

NEW ZEALAND

by Bob Campbell, M.W.

New Zealand wine has suddenly become very fashionable. Crisp, aromatic Sauvignon Blanc from Marlborough, full-flavored Chardonnay from Hawke's Bay and luscious, botrytized Riesling are just three examples of New Zealand wine now appearing on the retail shelves of fine wine stores in Europe, America and Australia.

The curious thing about this overnight popularity is that New Zealand has no history of fine wine production. While winemakers in Australia, California and South Africa were growing classical European grape varieties earlier this century, their New Zealand counterparts were making thin and often rather nasty table wines from American hybrid grapes.

Winemaking in New Zealand dates back to 1819 when the first vineyard was established at Kerikeri by the English missionary Samuel Marsden. New Zealand's first settlers were mostly of English working-class background. They craved the fruit of the barley rather than the grape, and beer rapidly became the national drink. Even today beer consumption is over 100 liters/24.4 U.S. gallons per capita while wine manages only 15.6 liters/4.1 U.S. gallons. The few European immigrants from Yugoslavia, Lebanon and France planted small vineyards to put wine on the family table. By the early 1900s several families had established their own wineries, mostly near Auckland. The outbreak of phylloxera, a strong prohibition movement and a population unaccustomed to wine, all severely handicapped the growth of New Zealand's early wine industry.

Winemakers reacted to *phylloxera* not by grafting their European vines on to American hybrid rootstock, but by growing the hybrid vines for grapes. Until the sixties most New Zealand wine was fortified. The small amount of table wine was thin and acidic with the "foxy" character of hybrid grapes.

When change came, it happened very fast. Winemakers had no idea just how good New Zealand wine could be. There was also little incentive to improve wine quality because the market for fine wine appeared to be so small. It was as though they were scratching a living by mining copper when a little further below the surface was a motherlode of gold.

The first glimmer of gold appeared when McWilliams released their 1965 Cabernet Sauvignon. By the early seventies wine enthusiasts queued

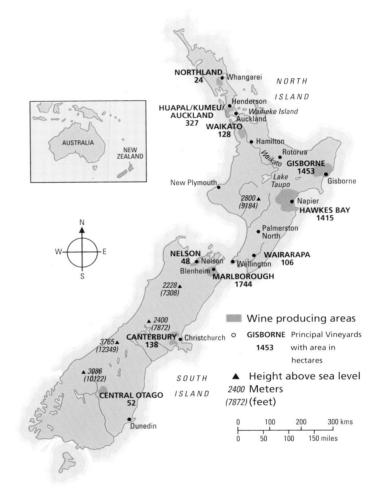

to collect their allocated bottles of this precious wine. Soon the gold rush was on. Every winemaker dreamed of making a wine that would bring prestige and profits.

Two key factors allowed New Zealand wine quality to progress at an enormously rapid rate. The first, and most important, was the land's potential to make top-quality wine. New Zealand has the approximate land area of Great Britain but the two islands of the former span an even greater latitude giving a wider variation in climate types. There are a large number of different soil types which, when matched with a wide range of mesoclimates, offer an enormous variety of growing conditions. Most of the country is not too far from the sea, giving a strong maritime influence which moderates diurnal and seasonal swings in temperature. The exception is the high altitude, inland area of Central Otago which offers a more continental climate.

By 1970 Auckland, Gisborne and Hawke's Bay had become established viticultural regions, and each

has since discovered new areas with exciting quality potential within their own boundaries. Beyond these big three grape-growing regions were small pockets of largely experimental vineyards, although very small scale winemaking often made it difficult to determine their real potential. Martinborough, Marlborough, Nelson, Canterbury and Central Otago are all fine wine regions which have only really been "discovered" in the last twenty years and it is very clear, judging by the successful prospecting for new vineyard sites in recent years, that New Zealand has yet to exploit its full viticultural potential.

The second factor that favored a rapid evolution in wine quality was the lack of viticultural and winemaking restrictions such as those imposed in traditional wine regions. There was no established way of doing things; no rule book written by wine authorities to preserve traditional quality and wine styles. All of the obvious grape varieties, viticultural practices and winemaking techniques have been tested by winemakers in an effort to coax the best results from the land. Government-funded research organizations have assisted vineyard development and the flow of information between winemakers.

In 1992 the Wine Institute of New Zealand hopes to introduce legislation which will offer wine buyers a guarantee of label authenticity without placing a straightjacket on winemaking or viticulture. Called the Regional Denomination scheme, it will insist that every wine must be made from 85 percent of the grape variety or varieties shown on the label, 85 percent of the vintage shown and 85 percent of the region, district and vineyard declared.

New Zealand has over 6,000 hectares/14,820 acres of vineyards which in 1991 produced around 5,500,000 cases of wine. Just over 11 percent of that was exported in that year, nearly double the percentage sold overseas in the previous year. In 1991 Marlborough had the largest area of bearing vineyards although Gisborne, a more productive region with higher-cropping grape varieties, produced more wine. Hawke's Bay is a close third both in vineyard

BELOW: New Zealand wine labels emphasize the grape variety, the strongest clue to wine style. The region is also named and this too can be a useful style indicator. Marlborough Sauvignon Blanc is different to Sauvignon Blanc from other regions. Where two varieties are shown, the first must comprise at least 50 percent of the blend.

area and wine production. Müller-Thurgau is the most commonly planted vine with around one-third of the national production. It produces a pleasant, light and often slightly sweet white wine that is mostly packaged into wine casks. Wine casks now account for nearly two-thirds of domestic wine sales. Chardonnay provides 10 percent of the national production, up from 5 percent in only five years. New Zealand Chardonnay is grown in every wine region. Regional differences and winemaker input make it very hard to generalize about New Zealand Chardonnay, which can vary from strong tropical fruit ripeness to fine, fruity, non-oaked, melony styles or even more herbaceous, steely and obviously cool-climate wines.

Sauvignon Blanc provides New Zealand with its highest profile wine internationally, thanks to the success of Cloudy Bay. Marlborough Sauvignon Blanc can be very aromatic with a strong red capsicum and herbaceous influence, while riper North Island wines can show melon, honeysuckle flavors. Many are fermented and/or aged in oak for extra complexity. Botrytis-affected dessert wines are a recent arrival. Riesling is the most popular variety and Marlborough the favorite region for the production of these very luscious and intense wines. Champagne-method wines are also newcomers. Marlborough is, once again, the most popular region. Most rely on the traditional blend of Chardonnay and Pinot Noir.

Cabernet Sauvignon is New Zealand's favorite red grape variety. It is now mostly blended with Merlot to add complexity, early drinkability and to tone

LEFT: The wide Marlborough Valley is now New Zealand's largest wine region. Free–draining stony soils, abundant sunshine and heat-retaining river boulders provide the ideal conditions for the development of strong-flavored Sauvignon Blanc, Riesling and Chardonnay.

down the often herbaceous character of New Zealand's cool-climate Cabernet. Pinot Noir is rapidly catching up to Cabernet Sauvignon in vineyard acreage if not in popularity, with a dramatic boost in plantings over recent years. Most is used in Champagne-method sparkling wine production although Martinborough Pinot Noir has proven that the variety can make excellent full-bodied red.

New Zealand has been a rapidly rising star on the international wine scene and yet wine quality has not begun to approach its zenith. Vine maturity and the growing experience of winemakers and viticulturists will continue to refine and improve New Zealand wine styles. The discovery of even more exciting vineyard sites promises to make an even greater contribution to overall quality growth.

GROWER'S VIEW

Kumeu River is a small, family-owned winery in the fertile Kumeu region northwest of Auckland. The majority of New Zealand winemakers truck grapes from several regions. I prefer to use only Kumeu grapes. Long-distance can be undesirable. I use gentle harvesting and juice extraction techniques to preserve the integrity of the fruit.

Auckland has a moderately high rainfall and water-retaining clay soils which together promote vigorous vine growth during the summer months. I try to reduce vine vigor with low-density planting (1,588 vines per hectare/643 vines per acre), and by using an open lyre-type trellising system for maximum light penetration. Vineyard workers hand pick vine leaves to reduce density. All grapes are hand-harvested.

Kumeu River produces around 18,000 cases of wine a year. We make Chardonnay, Sauvignon Blanc, Cabernet Sauvignon, Merlot and Cabernet Franc.

All of the whites are whole bunch-pressed before cold-settling the juice which is then racked into barrels where it is fermented using natural yeast. Fermentation temperatures are allowed to reach a maximum of 23°C/73°F although most New Zealand wineries tend to restrict this maximum to 15°C/59°F. The wines are encouraged to undergo a malolactic fermentation in barrel and remain on the yeast lees for three to four months. Reds are fermented in stainless steel before being racked into barrels where the length of maturation varies according to the vintage and required style.

Kumeu River wines are a product of New World technology, traditional techniques and meticulous attention.

Michael Brajkovich M.W.

KUMEU RIVER

SOUTH AFRICA

by Patrick Grubb M.W.

ABOVE: An aerial veiw of the lush Constantia Valley vineyards with Table Mountain in the background.

Over the last 300 years the vineyards of South Africa have both contracted and expanded. At the moment they exceed 93,000 hectares/230,000 acres, and stretch between Table Mountain in the West to recent plantings at Mossel Bay on the Garden Route in the Eastern Cape, and north through Malmesbury and Tulbagh towards the border with Namibia. In addition, separated by mountain ranges and the forbidding Karoo Desert, are the vineyards of the Orange River, 563 kilometers/350 miles northeast of Cape Town.

The story of the grape begins in 1656, with Jan Van Riebeeck, the first commander of the Cape Colony and tentative planting of vine cuttings at the foot of Table Mountain.

The arrival, nearly thirty years later, of French Hugenots fleeing persecution at home, brought to the Cape another level of expertise. Descendants of some of those families, the Jouberts, Malans, Nels, Rousseaus, de Villiers and others are still making wine in the area of Paarl and Stellenbosch.

Although the initiative of establishing vineyards on Table Mountain was Van Riebeeck's, the reputation of the Cape's wines was founded by Simon van der Stel with the planting and construction of Constantia in 1686. In subsequent years visits by Europeans to the cellar at Constantia increased the worldwide reputation of the wines in Europe.

Aristocrats and princes, including Frederick the Great, Louis Philippe of France and Napoleon, were among the purchasers of this legendary wine. But by 1859, when oidium arrived, followed by phylloxera seven years later, the decline in the fortunes of both Constantia, and Cape wine in general, was almost complete.

By 1904 the seemingly insurmountable crisis of phylloxera had given way to a massive glut of wine. Vineyard plantings were three times what they had been before the louse had struck. Over-production went unchecked, and there was little incentive to improve quality. It was 1918 before the message got through to the farmers.

The cooperative and protectionist system that they were forced to accept then has existed ever since. At first the powers of the all-embracing K.W.V. (Kooperatiewe Wijnbouwers Vereniging van Zuid-Afrika) were limited to the disposal of its members' produce, hammering the merchants to pay a higher price. Over the next two decades legislation was passed giving the K.W.V. the power to fix minimum prices for distilling wine, and to force growers to deliver to the K.W.V. a proportion of their surplus crop. Licences were required for any vineyard planted on a quota basis. These restraints on over-production were admirable in theory but in practice they have become generally counter-productive. Today the K.W.V. having saved the wine industry, must allow progress.

The winemakers of the Cape have a lot on their side. Climatically the Cape is ideally suited to the cultivation of the vine, with cool, wet winters and hot, dry summers. Cool maritime breezes offset the extreme heat of some almost desert regions. Irrigation is generally accepted as an essential, but does not so cosset the vine that the roots do not reach deep into the soil for nutriment. More farmers are aware of the importance of soil, aspect, climate and of planting the correct clone for their particular farm. The days when a large spread of grape varieties were planted on every farm are disappearing.

The most widely planted grape is Chenin Blanc (locally known as Steen) which since 1960 has more than doubled in planting and now accounts for about one-third of total production. The wine it produces varies in style and flavor according to the soil, microclimate and the extent of irrigation, from dry, fruity, still or sparkling to the generously sweet. Of the other white grapes, the Chardonnay, which

has received enormous publicity of late, accounts for less than 0.5 percent of all plantings. Colombard and Palomino comprise about 8 percent each, but the latter is declining as the demand for fortified wines has diminished. Other white varieties, in order of importance, are Muscat d'Alexandrie (known locally as Hanepoot), Cape Riesling (alias Cruchen Blanc), Clairette Blanche for the cheaper sparkling wines, the popular, though relative newcomers Sauvignon Blanc, Semillon, Weisser or Rhine Riesling, Gewürztraminer and Ugni Blanc. Plantings of red grapes declined in the 1970s as demand fell and account for about 14 percent of the total. About half of this total is Cinsault (known as Hermitage locally), which makes an ideal blending wine. Then follow Cabernet Sauvignon, Pinotage and Shiraz with minute plantings of Pinot Noir, Cabernet Franc, Merlot, Malbec, Gamay and Grenache. The oddly titled Pinotage is a variety peculiar to the Cape, originating in 1925 from a cross of Cinsault and Pinot Noir. As a wine it needs a minimum of three years in bottle, developing marvellous plum pudding aromas, but styles vary, with some having a marked acetone nose.

The vineyards lie in three main regions: Coastal, Breede River Valley and Boberg, with seven secondary districts of Overberg, near Hermanus on the coast, Olifants River, Piketberg, Klein-Karoo, Benede Oranje, Douglas and Andalusia. These last three, which are the furthest inland, require considerable irrigation in the extremely arid conditions. The Coastal Region includes the oldest farms at Constantia, Durbanville, Paarl, Stellenbosch, Swartland and Tulbagh. Further east over the Franschhoek and Du Toits mountains is the Breede River Valley, with the towns of Robertson and Worcester, where most of the fortified wines have been produced. Now many of the wineries are making excellent dry white and red table wines.

There are about seventy private wine estates in all and the number is increasing. Many are small, producing two or three thousand cases a year or less. But the idea of improved quality has spread rapidly, and efforts are now being directed at producing wines with more individuality.

Ten times larger in investment terms are the seventy cooperatives, spread throughout the wine regions, to which about five thousand farmers bring their grapes for crushing, vinification, bottling and sale. Here much depends upon the quality of the grapes that are delivered, and it is variable. A good deal of the production ends up being distilled or added to good blends held in reserve at K.W.V.'s headquarters in Paarl.

There are, though, several cooperatives with young winemakers who are out to break with the dull image of the past. Already they are making themselves felt. Among the best are Bolandse Koop. (Paarl), Botha (Breede River), Bottelary (Stellenbosch), Franschhoek (Paarl), Nuy (Worcester), Robertson, Simonslvei (Paarl), Rooiberg (Robertson), Velmoed (Stellenbosch), Vredendal (Olifants River) and Vlottenberg (Stellenbosch).

Then there are the equivalent of the *négociants* of France. Grapes are bought from estates or cooperatives, fermented, matured and bottled at a central winery and then marketed under a brand name. Acting in this way are Bertrams and Gilbey's; Bellingham and Union Wines; Douglas Green of

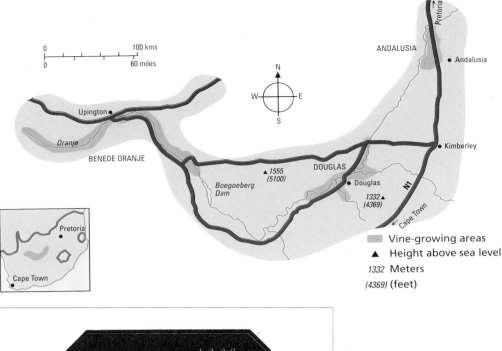

LEFT: Several South African wineries such as Delheim produce a "Bordeaux blend" of Cabernet and Merlot. The Vin de Constance label is a replica of the famed 18th century Constantia.

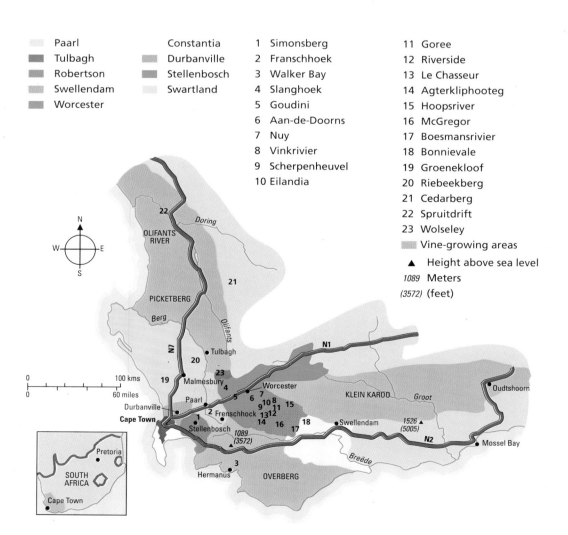

Paarl	Constantia
Tulbagh	Durbanville
Robertson	Stellenbosch
Swellendam	Swartland
Worcester	

1 Simonsberg
2 Franschhoek
3 Walker Bay
4 Slanghoek
5 Goudini
6 Aan-de-Doorns
7 Nuy
8 Vinkrivier
9 Scherpenheuvel
10 Eilandia

11 Goree
12 Riverside
13 Le Chasseur
14 Agterklipphooteg
15 Hoopsriver
16 McGregor
17 Boesmansrivier
18 Bonnievale
19 Groenekloof
20 Riebeekberg
21 Cedarberg
22 Spruitdrift
23 Wolseley

Vine-growing areas
▲ Height above sea level
1089 Meters
(3572) (feet)

237

ABOVE: This veiw of Stellenbosch Farmer's Winery shows the snow-covered mountains with the vineyards in the valley below.

Paarl; La Rochelle; K.W.V. at Paarl, which is by far the largest; the Oude Meester Group, Stellenbosch Farmers' Winery and Southern Cape Cellars. Next in size to the K.W.V. is the Oude Meester Group, selling under the Fleur du Cap label and at Western Province Cellars. It also controls several estates through its Bergkelder operation, which has contracts to provide all the expertise from grape to market place. The estates grow the grapes, harvest and make the wine, which is collected by tanker truck for central bottling and held for maturation. Some estates under the Bergkelder umbrella have a greater degree of autonomy. The best are Jacobsdal, La Motte, Le Bonheur, L'Ormarins, Meerlust and Middelvlei.

The other giant is Stellenbosch Farmers' Winery or "Farmers", as it is known locally. It led the way in producing table wine in the 1920s, when all other producers concentrated on sweet, fortified wine. Public demand grew rapidly and forty years later one brand alone, Lieberstein, was selling over 31 million liters/9,184,000 U.S. gallons per annum. In 1966 the group acquired the Nederburg estates, but before that, in the 1940s, Farmers had launched what became their flagship brand, Zonnebloom. These companies are encouraging the growers to provide the highest quality grapes and are paying a premium to boot.

Many of the most innovative strides in the vineyard, the winery and in marketing have come from research by these last two groups. However, earlier and continuing experimental work of sometimes greater significance has been carried out at Stellenbosch University and at the headquarters of the Research Institute of the Department of Agriculture. In the 1920s cold-fermentation was being developed and put into practice, before most people in Europe had even heard of the idea. The isolation of the *flor* yeast, which produces the *finos* of Jerez took place in the 1930s, as a result of experimentation by Professors Niehaus and Theron. There is a continuing, international cross-fertilization of ideas and practice.

So what of the future? Greater specialization seems likely, with certain areas making a reputation for certain grape varieties. There are already several wineries making excellent "Bordeaux blends" from Cabernet Sauvignon, Merlot and Cabernet Franc and this trend will certainly develop. A lot depends on political change. If this is without acrimony and at the right pace, the wine industry of South Africa will have a great future.

GROWER'S VIEW

Cabernet Franc seems to like this farm. My original intention, when I first started making wine in 1984, was to use it in our red wine blends. But in 1988 we started producing it as a varietal on the suggestion of a British Master of Wine who liked its precocious charm and good structure. And we have continued to do so ever since. I honestly cannot tell you why Cabernet Franc works so well for us, the soil seems too rich and the yields are naturally a bit high. But as the vines get older, the wine gets more character and we constantly fight to restrict the yield.

I watch Bordeaux closely for the best winemaking aids. For example our little stainless steel vats are designed to our specification from a model of ones I have seen used in Bordeaux. They have cooling jackets to control the temperature of fermentation. The beauty is that you can ferment in them and you can also store the wine in them. I still use the old fashioned Vaslin press I bought in 1984. It produces excellent results and I do not see the need of an expensive new membrane press.

We press the grapes hard, we give a lot of skin maceration, sometimes for as long as three weeks. It gives a character to the wine that I like. Contrary to what you might think, the tannins in the wine taste softer but also riper. We age our red wines in small oak *barriques*, usually for twelve to fifteen months. I buy my casks from an excellent cooper in Ludon in the Médoc. The wood is thinner-staved to allow for quicker maturation, and the casks are beautifully finished, there is almost never any seepage - unlike the casks which are assembled her in South Africa.

Norma Ratcliffe

WARWICK FARM

RIGHT: For many years KWV was the main export label for the bulk of Cape wines.

NORTH AFRICA

by Paul Richardson

BELOW: Morocco's French colonial past lingers on its labeling and appellation regulatins. Sidi Brahiam is a varietal Cinsault, Saharl an A.O.C. rose-but A.O.C. here dose not mean precisely the same as it does in France.

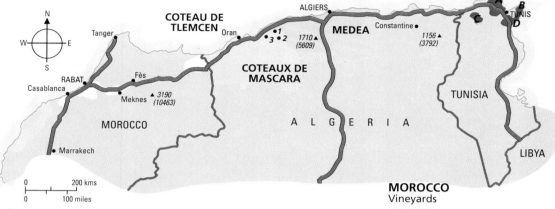

MOROCCO
Vineyards

ALGERIA
Oran
Alger
1 Ain Marane
2 Taughrite
3 Mazouna

TUNISIA
Vineyards
A Bizette-Mateur-Tebourba
B Kélibi-Cap Bon
C Thibar
D Grombalia
▲ Height above sea level
1710 Meters
(5609) (feet)

While the rest of the world's wine countries are buzzing with technical innovation and creative energy, not to mention marketing skill, the three major winemaking countries of North Africa have severe problems. The governments of Algeria, Morocco and Tunisia have all attempted to encourage better quality, but they are faced with the growing forces of Islamic Fundamentalism. Morale among wine growers, makers and exporters is low, so much so that a headline in Algeria's national paper *El Watan* proclaimed, in the summer of 1991: "The vine: threatened with extinction".

During the 1950s, when the French presided over the region, its wine exports accounted for a third of the total world wine trade. Much of that mighty flood naturally flowed north towards France, and was often used to beef up the wines of Burgundy. Since then Algeria's production, by far the biggest of the Maghreb countries, has fallen from over 1 million hectoliters/26,418,000 U.S. gallons in 1958 to a mere 1,800 hectoliters/47,552 U.S. gallons in 1989. Since 1986 the area under vine has shrunk from 33,276 of the 181,000 hectares/82,192 of the 447,070 acres of available agricultural land to only 14,775 hectares/36,494 acres.

Algeria's vineyards are to be found in the green northern rim of this vast desert country. Principal vine-growing areas are the western region round Oran, and the hilly countryside round Algiers where some of the more acceptable Algerian wines are made.

By 1962 when the French departed with the best of the region's winemakers (these ex-colonists headed for Corsica to make wine) twelve *crus* of V.D.Q.S. status had been created. Seven survive as present-day "quality zones", the best arguably being Coteaux de Tlemcen, close to the Moroccan border; Coteaux de Mascara, with its full-bodied red, and the three villages of Renault, Rabelais and Paul Robert, since renamed Mazouna, Ain Marane and Taughrite.

Perhaps the most successful North African style is rosé, which in Algeria is generally dry, clean, strong and fruity, like Provençal rosé. In Morocco too, rosé is the Western wine-lover's best bet, particularly the famous onionskin-colored Gris de Boulaouane. Its clean, refreshing, smoky fruit makes a good foil for the spicy local couscous.

Morocco has about 22,000 hectares/54,340 acres under vine. There is an *Appellation d'Origine Garantie*

(A.O.G.) designation for quality wines. The Fèz/Meknes region makes reds that are often better than those of the coastal plain around Rabat.

Tunisia's specialty is Muscat, which may be sweet or dry, and surprisingly delicate. The better reds are from Château Feriani and Domaine Karim. The appellation system has four levels: *Vins de Consommation Courant; Vins Supérieurs; Vins de Qualité Supérieuré and Appellation d'Origine Contrôlée.*

The most troublesome aspect of North African wine is its variable quality. In Tunisia and Morocco, it often seems that no two bottles with the same label contain the same wine. Vintage dates and terminology such as *Cuvée Réserve* and *Grand Vin* should not be taken seriously. The better wines can be surprisingly good.

GROWER'S VIEW

I have a small parcel of land in the beautiful countryside outside Medea, right at the center of one of our seven "quality zones", southwest of Algiers. Of my 5 hectares/12 acres, about a quarter is given over to Carignan, Cinsaut and Alicante Bouschet. I take all my grapes to the local *cave* of the O.N.C.V. (the state wine organization) for vinification.

Rising prices and our struggling economy are making production costs unrealistic: the price of copper sulfate, for instance, has risen by 400 percent in the last year. I have some very old vines — half are over forty years old — and they give disappointingly low yields.

I am contemplating uprooting my entire vineyard and planting cereals instead. Many thousands of my fellow *vignerons* have already done this.

Ahmed Bendjeloud

239

THE FAR EAST

by Michael Edwards

ABOVE: Suntory's Château Lion makes a fine dessert wine from Sémillon and Sauvignon grapes that have been affected by noble rot.

Oriental people traditionally are not great wine drinkers. Yet there is an old wine-making tradition in the Far East which has been revived in recent years.

The state of Maharashtra, northwest of Bombay, provides the wine success story of modern India. In 1982 a Champenois oenologist, Jean Brisbois, built a modern winery in the foothills of the Sahyadri mountains to produce Omar Khayyam, a *méthode champenoise* sparkling wine. It has fine, small bubbles and a dry clean delicate taste.

It was not until 1900 that a primitive wine industry was established by French and German settlers on the Shantung Peninsula. In the 1970s, the Remy-Martin group in collaboration with the Chinese government developed a wine at Tientsin called Dynasty, made from Muscat de Hambourg table grapes. It is a wine of little character, as is the well known Great Wall wine.

The best and most consistent wines of China come from the Shandong vineyards near Quindao on the Yellow Sea Coast where the Hua Dong Winery is a three-part investment of British, Hong Kong and Chinese interests. Several Rosemont Estate winemakers from Australia have supervised vinification. China's wine development is now very closely linked to the uncertain political future of the country.

In Japan the rigors of the climate, its diversity, and the largely inappropriate nature of the terrain of the three main islands, Kyushu, Honshu and Hokkaido, make the cultivation of the vine difficult. Japan can produce no more than 25 percent of the wine made in the French province of Alsace. The main wine-growing areas of Japan are the Yamanashi and Osaka districts, with the subordinate zones of Yamagata, Nagano and Okayama. All of these are situated on the central island of Honshu.

Torrential September rains and the acid soils can make grape growing extremely hazardous. Sémillon, Chardonnay and Riesling are increasingly used for white wines; Cabernet Sauvignon with Merlot, for red wines. Because of the humidity, these varieties are vulnerable to diseases like oidium and mildew and gray rot is a constant problem. Nonetheless, with the help of modern technology, the big three wine companies — Mann's, Mercian and Suntory — nowadays make good wines, both from the indigenous Koshu grape and from blends of European varieties.

GROWER'S VIEW

As Qingdao lies on the latitude 36° North, the climate is very favorable for *Vitis vinifera* grapes. The aspect of our vineyards, on sunny slopes, and the nature of the soil — a mix of sandy clay loam and limestone — promote good drainage. This is necessary in the rainy season in China, which falls between June and August.

In Qingdao, Riesling and Chardonnay are outstanding. Harvesting takes place during early- to mid- September, and is all done by hand.

For Riesling, we look for the dominant fruit and varietal character. We like to bottle this wine fairly young, after about eight months.

For Chardonnay we look for a more complex style with oak maturity with a majority of the wine maturing on its lees in new wood for nine to eleven months.

Wu Li Zhu

HUA DONG WINERY

Grape growing areas
Grape growing countries
▲ Height above sea level
741 Meters
(2430) (feet)

DIRECTORY

A

A.V.A.
See Approved Viticultural Area.

Abboccato
Italian term meaning between sweet and dry.

Acetic acid
A naturally occurring volatile acid in wine. An excess of acetic acid makes a wine faulty; it is then said to be suffering from volatile acidity. It will taste sour and vinegary. This can be caused by careless bottling or by fermenting out at too high a temperature.

Acidity
An essential element in wine, acidity gives wine its bite and freshness and enables certain white wines like Riesling to age. White wine, in particular, needs sufficient acidity or it will taste dry and lifeless. Lack of acidity is the most common fault in wines from hot climates. Equally, too much acidity, making wine taste green and harsh, is a problem at the climatic limits of vinegrowing. Acidity may be volatile (*see* Acetic acid), fixed (tartaric, malic, citric acids make up fixed acidity) or total, which is the combination of all acids in a wine.

Acquit
All French wines and spirits for export must be accompanied by an official French document called an *acquit-à-caution.*

Actual alcohol
The amount of alcohol present after fermentation has finished. It is usually measured as a percentage by volume and indicated on the label.

Adega
Portuguese term for a wine cellar or warehouse. Similar to the French *chai* or Spanish *bodega.*

Aftertaste
The impression left in the mouth after swallowing wine. A long aftertaste is a sign of quality.

Agiorgitiko
A red-wine grape variety native to Greece and grown primarily at Nemea in the Peloponnese. The quality and style of its wine varies with the altitude at which the vines are planted.

Aglianico
The Hellenic origin of this red grape is implicit in its name. It ripens late, and near Avellino in Campania,

Italy; makes the extraordinary Taurasi, a dark, powerful, tannic wine with structure and great potential to age. In Basilicata the grape makes robust Aglianico del Vulture.

Airén
A very widely planted Spanish variety, and the principal white grape of La Mancha. The white Lairén or Manchega, as it is also known, is capable of enduring climatic extremes and is relatively prolific by Spanish standards. Traditionally the Airén makes coarse, alcoholic wine, and is chiefly used for blending; with Cencibel, for example, to make the agreeable *claretes* of Valdepeñas. The quality of its product has improved with the introduction of modern methods of winemaking.

Albalonga
A Silvaner hybrid vine planted only sparingly in Germany. It makes lively and pleasantly fruity white wines.

Albana
Albana is the white grape of the D.O.C.G. Albana di Romagna rarely found elsewhere in Italy. Usually dry, it can come in varying degrees of sweetness, and even as a *spumante*, but is otherwise undistinguished in flavor.

Albariño
A white grape found on both sides of the Minho River. On the Portuguese side it is known as Alvarinho and makes Vinho Verde; on the Spanish it makes the most highly regarded of Galician varietal wines with high acidity and an aromatic, peachy character.

Albariza
The type of soil that marks the best areas within the Sherry region of southern Spain. *Albariza* has a very high chalk content of between 60 and 80 percent and is startlingly white. The other soil types in the region are *barros*, with up to 30 per cent chalk, and *arenas*, which are sandy, with only 10 percent chalk.

Alberello
A system of pruning used in parts of Italy. The vine is trained as a low bush.

Alcohol
Fermentation converts sugars into alcohol. Alcohol is produced until fermentation stops because all the sugar has been converted to alcohol, or because the alcohol level has reached 15 percent and killed off the remaining yeasts, or because it is too cold, or through the addition of sulfur. (*See* Actual and Potential alcohol.)

Aldehyde
An important chemical component of aromas, aldehydes are formed by the oxidation of alcohol and are an intermediate stage between alcohol and acid.

Aleatico

A grape variety related to the Muscat: around Bari in Apulia, Italy, it makes highly alcoholic red dessert wines in styles ranging from medium sweet to rich, the latter made from grapes dried before vinification to concentrate their natural sugar. Similar wines are made from the Aleatico on the island of Elba, and this ancient, once prized variety is still to be found in Latium. Vines grown on the volcanic soil above the crater lake of Bolsena produce a purplish, aromatic dessert wine, high in alcohol, which may be sweet or *liquoroso*, made with *passito* grapes.

Alicante Bouschet

Alicante Bouschet is a hybrid Teinturier grape used in the south of France to boost the color of wines made from more anemic varieties, notably Aramon. It was developed by Henri Bouschet in 1886, a crossing between Petit Bouschet (itself a crossing of Aramon and Teinturier du Cher) and Grenache. It is prolific, colorful and characterless and is grown mainly for *vins de table*, but happily as the European wine lake dries up and the demand for insipid red wine declines, vineyards of Alicante-Bouschet are gradually being pulled up. There is also a little in California's Central Valley for anonymous jug wines.

Aligoté

Aligoté is a white Burgundian grape, but is considered something of a poor relation to Chardonnay, especially as in the Côte d'Or it is grown on less favorable sites and consequently can produce rather thin, acidic wine. The relevant appellation is Bourgogne Aligoté, without any precise indication of provenance, apart from the grower's address on the label, with the one exception of the appellation of Bourgogne Aligoté de Bouzeron, from the Côte Chalonnaise village. Here, in the hands of a talented grower, Aligoté can show its firm, slaty character. Farther north in the Yonne around St. Bris-le-Vineux and Chitry-le-Fort, where it is not in such competition with Chardonnay, there are some fruitier examples of Aligoté. A little is also grown in Bugey, and outside France in eastern Europe, Bulgaria, Romania and the countries of the old Soviet Union.

Allegrini, Valpolicella

Valpolicella is one of Italy's most popular red wines, amd this 50 hectare/123.5 acre estate makes one of the best. Walter, Marilisa and Franco Allegrini make the first-rate single-vineyard Valpolicella La Grola, the 1985 intensely flavored yet finely wrought. Their 1990 Valpolicella Classico is a keenly priced introduction to the red wines of Verona with its vibrant, bitter cherry flavor.

Alois Lageder, Bolzano

Leading wine growers and merchants of the Alto Adige, the house of Alois Lageder was founded in 1855. From a fine range of single-vineyard wines, Pinot Bianco Haberlehof, Pinot Grigio Benefizium and Chardonnay Erlerhof are particularly good. Alois Lageder, great-grandson of the founder, is also a partner in the Portico dei Leoni *négociant* business, which makes an exceptional barrel-fermented Chardonnay.

Aloxe-Corton, Domaine Bonneau du Martray

The reputation of this famous domain's Corton-Charlemagne and Corton is so impressive that it is doubtful whether many wine enthusiasts realize it also cultivates some 5 hectares/12.4 acres of excellent Aloxe-Corton. Aloxe-Corton has never enjoyed a high reputation as a Burgundy of distinction, but a great winemaker's skill is not lost on his lesser wines. So proud of his wines is the owner, Comte Jean le Bault de la Morinière, that he is said to restrict the sale in France of his two *grands crus* to restaurants with three Michelin stars.

Gilbert Alquier et Fils, Faugères

Long-established family concern of 28 hectres/69 acres based in the village of Faugères in France. The best wine is aged in *barrique* and, while less robust than other wines of the appellation, has considerable finesse with a more international style.

Elio Altare, Barolo

Elio Altare cultivates a small vineyard of 5 hectares/12 acres at Cascina Nuova, in Piedmont, Italy. Altare believes that low yields in the vineyard make great wine and his Barolo and Barbera prove his point. His yields of Nebbiolo are commonly a minuscule 15 hectoliters per hectare/0.9 tons per acre. The results are some of the most concentrated wines in Barolo; but his genius as a winemaker ensures a purity of fruit that makes those wines always attractive and impeccably balanced. Look for his 1985 Barolo Vigna Arborina, one of the greatest wines of a great Barolo vintage. More modestly priced, his 1990 Dolcetto La Pria is a delightful bottle with all the abundant fruit of this variety but with a sleekness of texture and a concentration of flavor that are the hallmark of an Altare wine.

Altesino, Brunello di Montalcino

This 20 hectare/49 acre estate in Tuscany produces some of the best wines of Brunello, rich, tarry and very long-lived. The 1982, 1983, 1985 and 1988 are all blue-chip vintages here. The more affordably priced 1988 Rosso di Montalcino is a delightful, fleshy wine for relatively early drinking.

Altesse

A white grape native to the Savoie district in eastern France, although possibly of Cypriot origin, which makes full, scented, highly individual wines, both still and sparkling, from vineyards that stretch along both banks of the Rhône. The variety is also known locally as Roussette.

Altitude

Altitude is important for its effect on temperature: the higher you are the lower the temperature. In California and Australia high-altitude sites are much sought after for cooler mean temperatures and therefore a longer ripening period.

Alvarinho

See Albariño.

Amabile

Italian term for medium sweet.

Ampelography

The study of vine varieties.

Anbaugebeit

German term for a specified wine region. There are eleven such regions, each further divided into *Bereich* (district), *Grosslage* (general area) and *Einzellage* (individual vineyard).

Château L'Angélus, St. Emilion

L'Angélus has made great progress in the past decade, following the disappointments of the sixties and seventies. At that time the wines generally flattered in

their youth, but failed to live up to their early promise. Since 1980 there have been many changes: Professor Ribéreau-Gayon was brought in to advise on quality and technique, and at his suggestion aging in wood, previously unknown here, was adopted, the proportion of new oak varying according to the nature of the vintage. The style of the wines too has altered; typically they remain scented, fruity, well adapted to early drinking, but with more structure than formerly, and greater potential to develop. Perhaps the best of the recent vintages are those of 1983, 1984, 1985 and a powerfully tannic 1986. These seem to hold out clear hope for the future. The vineyard of this Bordeaux estate is on the slopes to the west of St. Emilion and is unusual in that the Cabernet Franc is the predominant grape variety.

Château d'Angludet, Margaux

An excellent Bordeaux vineyard; in the relatively distant past this *cru bourgeois* suffered greatly from the complexity of the French laws of inheritance. By the end of the Second World War the property was in a pitiful state, but in 1961 it was acquired by the Sichel family, which still occupies it, and the vineyard has been replanted and its reputation restored. The quality of the wine has improved as the vines have matured, and it shows complexity and depth of flavor, its fullness allied to finesse and breed. Notable recent vintages include 1978, 1980, a splendid 1983, 1985, 1986 and 1989.

Weingut Oknomierat August E. Anheuser, Nahe

This is a large German family estate producing a high proportion of sweeter wines for export markets. Most of the wines on its 52 hectares/129 acres of vineyards are Riesling; fermentation is cool, and maturation is in oak casks. The Anheuser family, who established this estate in 1869, also established Weingut Paul Anheuser, also in the Nahe, and wine merchants Anheuser & Fehrs.

Anselmi, Soave

Roberto Anselmi makes a fine range of exceptional Soaves. His single-vineyard Capitel Foscarino has been widely praised, but his standard Soave Classico is an immaculate wine at a reasonable price.

Ansonica

A delicate vine native to Sicily, where it is also known as Inzolia, it makes dry white wines in the central uplands of the island. Blended with Catarratto and Sauvignon the grape produces the excellent Regaleali, and it plays a part in the complex elaboration of Marsala. Along the coast, as far north as Tuscany, and on the islands it makes white table wines such as Ansonica del Giglio.

Anthocyanins

A type of polyphenol (tannins are another type) that help to give red wine its color. Anthocyanins, which are purple in color, are responsible for the purplish tinge of young red wine; they precipitate during the aging process, so that the tannins, which are reddish or yellowish in color, supply the color of mature red wine.

Piero Antinori, Tuscany

Chianti is probably the best-known wine of Italy, but in the 1970s its reputation was at a low ebb. It took an independent-minded aristocrat to show the world that Tuscany could produce great red wine by ignoring the stultifying restrictions of the Chianti D.O.C. laws. Marchese Piero Antinori, scion of a family firm of Tuscan landowners and winemakers dating back to 1385, introduced an innovative *vino da tavola* called Tignanello. This wine was made with 80 percent Sangiovese, but instead of adding the 10 percent of white grapes required by the Chianti legislation, he adds 20 percent of Cabernet Sauvignon. The resulting wine was aged in new oak *barriques* and showed excellent color, spice and beautifully defined fruit, enough to make it a serious alternative to good red Bordeaux. The even more intense Solaia followed, the 1982 in particular rivalling the concentration of a great St. Emilion.

LEFT Marchese Piero Antinori.

Where Antinori led, other producers in Chianti Classico followed, and by the end of the eighties almost every estate was making a "super-Tuscan" *vino da tavola*. In the 1990s Antinori has focussed his firm's red-wine ambitions on making model Chianti, notably his excellent Chianti Classico Peppolì, which is vinified and bottled at a modern winery at San Casciano near Florence. Antinori's enologist and winemaker Giacomo Tachis has masterminded the consistent quality of the company's wines since before the Tignanello initiative.

The Antinori estate of Castello della Sala in Umbria produces an exciting range of innovative white wines. These include the *barrique*-fermented Cervaro della Sala which is made from Chardonnay and Grechetto, and an intriguing dessert wine called Muffato della Sala made from botrytized Sauvignon and indigenous Italian varieties. Trials with Pinot Noir are planned. In a more traditional vein, the Orvieto Classico Campogrande is worth seeking out.

Appellation d'Origine Contrôlée (A.O.C.)

The top category for French wines, it is a guarantee that a particular wine comes from a defined area and has met a rigorous set of conditions, covering, among other considerations, pruning, yield and vinification. The formative idea for the present A.O.C. system dates from 1923 when Baron Le Roy of Château Fortia drew up a list of regulations to combat fraudulent Châteauneuf-du-Pape. The *Comité National des Appellations d'Origine* was established in 1935, and after 1945 it became an *institut*. It is the governing body of French wine.

Approved Viticultural Area (A.V.A.)

The American approximation of France's *appellation contrôlée* system used particularly in California. Areas are defined by their climate, soil and geography.

Château d'Aquéria, Tavel

This 45.5 hectare/112.3 acre domain in the Rhône produces outstanding Tavel Rosé. The 1990 is

exceptionally ripe and mouthfilling, a strongly flavored wine of the South.

Aramon

A red-wine variety still widely, though decreasingly, used in the French Midi. This grape was planted very heavily after the ravages of *phylloxera* in the second half of the nineteenth century, but is disdained nowadays as efforts are made to improve quality and to restore the traditional varieties of the Languedoc.

Arbois

A late-ripening grape native to the middle Loire, the Arbois or Menu Pineau is a variant of the Chenin Blanc, itself known as Pineau de la Loire, and makes wines of similar style. Increasingly the Arbois is being displaced by the Sauvignon. Arbois is also the name of an A.O.C. in France's Jura.

Arinto

This white Portuguese grape variety, supposedly if improbably akin to the Riesling, makes the wine of Bucelas, which enjoyed a considerable vogue in England after the Peninsular War. The grape has the virtue of retaining its acidity in hot conditions, and has the innate quality to make wine of some distinction. This makes it the more regrettable that for many years its potential has been ignored.

Château d'Arlay, Côtes du Jura

The property dates from the twelfth century, and the château is a classified national monument in France. The cellars, from the seventeenth century, are a little more recent. The estate has around 30 hectares/74 acres of vines, and grape varieties planted include Pinot Noir, Chardonnay and Savagnin. Only the local variety, Savagnin, can be used to make the regional specialty, Vin Jaune. Château d'Arlay makes a range of red, white and rosé as well as some Vin Jaune and the rare Vin de Paille.

Arneis

A long-established Piedmontese variety, traditionally little regarded and blended with Nebbiolo, but with modern methods now producing fruity, dry white D.O.C. wines of some individuality from the Roero hills.

Aroma

The smell of a young wine (mature wines have bouquet). "Primary aromas" are usually fruity and simple; the bouquet that develops later is more complex.

Château L'Arrosée, St. Emilion

A feature of this long-established Bordeaux vineyard is the variation in altitude and soil of its different sections. Its wine is rich, powerful, with finesse and flavor and considerable complexity; in many ways it may be considered a model of its rather unusual type. Despite its merit L'Arrosée remains a *cru* that is hard to find and consequently little recognized.

Ascorbic acid

Used as an antioxidant it may be added to wine before bottling. Its common name is Vitamin C.

Aspect

The slope of a vineyard's ground and the direction it faces are vital factors in the quality of grapes produced. Most northern hemisphere vineyards face south (north in the southern hemisphere) to gain maximum benefit from the sun. However, in hot climates a north-facing slope is often favored for white wines. The steeper the slope the more concentrated the sun's rays. This is particularly important for areas on the limit of vinegrowing, like parts of Germany.

Assemblage

Literally means "assembling". The careful blending of wine from different vats of different grape varieties and/or different vineyards or parts of a vineyard.

Assenovgrad, Bulgaria

Assenograd, 150 kilometers/96 miles southeast of Sofia, Assenovgrad is an important winery specializing in the production of Mavrud, a southern Bulgarian grape variety. Many believe that Mavrud produces Bulgaria's most distinguished and longest-lived red wine: a 1965 Assenovgrad Mavrud tasted at the winery in 1990 had a rich, figlike bouquet and sweet, full fruit. The winery is also known for good Plovdiv Cabernet Sauvignon made in a powerful, tannic style.

Assyrtiko

An acidic white grape native to the volcanic island of Santorini, and the main constituent of the wine of the same name. A *vin santo* is made with its *passito* grapes, and the variety is often blended with the Savatiano of Attica to lend definition to its wine.

Astringent

Usually associated with young, acidic red wines like young Chianti, this is a dry, acidic, mouth-puckering sensation. Should be balanced with fruit.

Atmosphere

A measure of the pressure inside a bottle of sparkling wine. Normally this is between five and six atmospheres at a temperature of 20°C/68°F.

Conte Douglas Attems, Lucinico

Conte Douglas Attems makes good Collio and Isonzo D.O.C. wines near Gorizia in northern Italy. He is a prominent local figure and the president of the Collio producers' consortium.

Aurora

This Franco-American hybrid vine (Aurora/Seibel 5279) is widely distributed in the eastern United States. Its wine is white, bland and unremarkable.

Ausbruch

Austrian term to describe a sweet wine between Beerenauslese and Trockenbeerenauslese.

Auslese

Literally "selected harvest." Selectively picked bunches, some of whose grapes will normally be affected by noble rot. Used for German and Austrian wines. Grapes thus picked must also meet a minimum level of ripeness, measured in degrees Oechsle, to qualify for the category.

Château Ausone, St. Emilion

This celebrated *premier grand cru classé* is usually ranked as one of the best of the St. Emilion district of Bordeaux.

The vineyard faces south and is sheltered and protected even in years of frost. Its soil is sand and clay over limestone, and the vines, Merlot and Cabernet Franc in equal proportion are venerable, their yield meager, so that the production of this Bordelais château is modest. Since the Revolution the property has changed hands only through inheritance, and its reputation at the end of the nineteenth century and the beginning of the twentieth outstripped that of any growth within the appellation. Many of its older vintages survive in sound condition today.

The great years persisted almost to World War II; then came a period of thirty years which, judged by Ausone's renown and past performance, must be accounted for as a failure. With the appointment of a young *régisseur,* (manager) only recently qualified, and very careful consultation with the winemaker of Pétrus, there came a significant revival. This period brought a long sequence of impressive, opulent wines almost unbroken from 1976 to 1988.

The complexity, power and many-faceted character of Ausone are remarkable and illustrate why ordinarily sober commentators declare it the only wine of Bordeaux that can stand comparison with Lafite at its best.

Austere
A tough, ungiving wine without generous fruit. The wine may just be immature. A fine young claret can be austere.

Autolysis
see Yeast autolysis.

Auxerrois Blanc
A white variety native to Lorraine, but widely planted in the Haut-Rhin of Alsace, where it makes acidic wines of little consequence, most of them destined for the production of Edelzwicker.

The grape is often confused with the much more distinguished Pinot Blanc and Pinot Gris, although it is related to neither. The Pinot Gris, for no clear reason, is often referred to as the Auxerrois, and curiously the Côt, the principal variety of the black wine of Cahors, is also known as Auxerrois in the far southwest of France.

Avignonesi, Vino Nobile dì Montepulciano
The Falvo brothers are the driving force behind this excellent wine firm based in the Avignonesi Palace in Montepulciano, Italy. The beautiful design of the labels is as striking as the splendid quality of the wines. The 1985 Vino Nobile dì Montepulciano is faultlessly made, its rich, deep fruit made more complex by exactly the right touch of toasty oak. The firm also makes an impressive Chardonnay called Il Marzocco.

Union de Champagne, Avize
The Union de Champagne is the outstanding cooperative-comglomerate of the Champagne region with a reputation for wines of very high quality. Avize takes in grapes from nine cooperatives whose members own excellently-sited vineyards mainly on the Montagne de Reims and the Côte des Blancs (all classed between 95 and 100 per cent). Avize's vinification plant is probably the most modern in Champagne, and the Union has developed a special winemaking technique which avoids the malolactic fermentation.

Avize works well within the industry on several levels. It supplies juice (rather than grapes) which contribute to the *assemblage* of such *cuvées* as Moët et Chandon's Dom Pérignon, Laurent Perrier's Grand Siècle and Taittinger's Comtes de Champagne.

It sells Champagne *sur lattes* to Rheims and Epernay houses, and it markets a lot of its own Champagnes, of which 40 per cent are now exported. Avize labels to look for are St. Gall and Pierre Vaudon. The top-of-the-range vintage Orpale *blanc de blancs* is a splendid wine of real vinous character.

Ayala, Champagne
Based in Aÿ, this traditional house was founded in 1860 by Edmond de Ayala. In 1937 it was bought by Jean-Michel Ducellier, the owner of Château La Lagune in the Médoc. Today the house produces around seventy-five thousand cases of Champagne.

B

Château de Bachen, Tursan
A recent vineyard venture in southwest France by chef Michel Guérard. The impressively equipped underground *chai* and well tended vineyards are beginning to produce impressive wines. A change in the V.D.Q.S. regulations allows Guérard to add a proportion of Sémillon and Sauvignon to Baroque, the local white-wine variety.

Backsberg, Paarl
Twice crowned Champion Winemaker at the Cape Championship Wine Show in South Africa and with numerous other awards, Sydney Back has a place in the history of Cape wine. His 160 hectare/395 acre estate was bought by his father, Charles, who arrived in 1916 from Lithuania with no knowledge of winemaking. Even before World War II, their wines were being exported to Britain. Michael, Sydney's son, is now running the viticultural side and consistency of quality is assured. The greatest successes have been Chardonnay, oak-fermented Sauvignon Blanc, a red Bordeaux-style blend and Shiraz.

Baco
Baco Noir is an early hybrid grape (Baco 1) derived from the Folle Blanche of Cognac. The vine is popular in the eastern United States, where its hardiness and early ripening are appropriate to the conditions, and it makes an acceptable red wine with some potential to age. Baco Blanc, also developed almost a century ago, is that rarity, a hybrid vine recommended in France. It makes thin white wine that is high in acid and low in alcohol, ideal for distillation, and speedily became the most important Armagnac grape. More recently it has lost ground to the traditional Ugni Blanc.

Badia a Coltibuono
Badia is a historic Chianti Classico estate whose centerpiece is the eleventh-century Abbey of Coltibuono. The estate's main vineyards are nearly 16 kilometers/10 miles away at Monti. Here, on steep limestone hillsides, the vines yield powerful, very tannic wines needing seven to ten years to reach maturity. In recent years, Badia Chianti Classicos have become a little lighter in style, but they remain very rich and full-bodied wines, exemplified in the 1985 and 1982 *riserva* vintages. The latter now tastes almost overripe and may well be eclipsed by the more classic 1983. The estate also makes a dense, muscular *vino da tavola* produced entirely from the Sangioveto grape. The 1982 will improve until the end of the century.

Baga
A prolific and heavily planted Portuguese red-wine grape variety, especially prominent in the Bairrada vineyards and the Dão region farther inland. The Baga makes deeply colored, fiercely tannic wines of moderate quality, and its increasing prevalence has meant the decline of a number of traditional varieties.

Baileys, Glenrowan, Victoria
One of the principal Australian fortified wine firms of northeast Victoria, the Baileys vineyards include 45 hectares/111 acres of red granite soil, which is ideal for the production of rich, viscous, dessert Muscats and

Tokays. The widely available 1984 Founders Muscat is lighter and more digestible with its floral aromas and gentle yet opulent flavors; good value, too. Baileys also produces a full range of table wines, the most interesting of which are its old-fashioned, monumentally built Shiraz-based wines.

Baked
A characteristic of some wines produced in very hot climates where the fruit has ripened too rapidly and the resulting wine is high in alcohol. The wine will taste hot.

Balance
Harmonious balance between a wine's fruit, tannins, sugars and acidity.

The Balgownie Estate, Maiden Gully, Victoria
The reputation of Australia's smaller "boutique" wineries owes a lot to the early example of Stuart Anderson, a former pharmacist, who planted a 10 hectare/25 acre vineyard near Bendigo in 1969. His first vintage was in 1973. Anderson is a Francophile who taught himself to make wine and participated in several vintages at Château Cissac in the Médoc. Throughout the late seventies and all through the eighties, Anderson's Cabernet Sauvignons especially showed excellent color and fruit, but also a welcome complexity of flavor that is distinctly French in style. His 1980 Cabernet Sauvignon is a wonderfully preserved wine. He has also produced delightful Shiraz and first-rate Chardonnay; look out for the 1984, which is as good an example of this grape as can be found outside Burgundy and better than much within it. His Pinot Noirs have been more mixed, lacking the verve and subtlety of the Burgundian model. Anderson sold his vineyard to the Mildara wine group in 1989. He continues as winemaker for the wines made from grapes grown on the estate, but Mildara has introduced a range of second division bought-in wines, called, confusingly, the Balgownie Première Cuvée Range. These are less interesting.

Joseph Balland-Chapuis, Sancerre
Although Joseph Balland-Chapuis makes fine Sancerre from vineyards around the picturesque village of Bué, it is his excellent Coteaux du Giennois from 5.5 hectares/13.6 acres of vines at Bonny-sur-Loire that is particularly important. The quality of this, made from Sauvignon Blanc, is waking rather a dormant V.D.Q.S. appellation to its potential. Some of the Sancerre *cuvées* are fermented in new oak *barriques,* and there are also experiments with late-picked *cuvées* from both appellations.

Ban de vendange
The official declaration, made each autumn in each winegrowing region of France, that picking may commence. The date is agreed each year between the growers and I.N.A.O. and announced by the prefect of the *département..*

Banfi Castello, Brunello di Montalcino
Banfi Castello is a new arrival in Montalcino but has made a positive impact. Originally it was looking for a white equivalent of its money-spinning Lambrusco and thought there was hope with Moscadello di Montalcino. It bought land in 1977 and 1978 and now has 3,000 hectares/7,410 acres, including 850 hectares/2,099 acres of vineyards, incorporating the old estate of Poggio alle Mura. This land has been landscaped and planted with a diverse mixture of grape varieties, not just Brunello and Moscadello but also Cabernet Sauvignon, Pinot Noir, Syrah, Pinot Gris, Chardonnay and Sauvignon Blanc. It makes not only traditional Brunello di Montalcino but also a range of innovative table wines. Methods are streamlined and modern, with cellars filled with stainless-steel vats and oak casks. Ezio Rivella masterminds the operation for the Mariani brothers.

Barbera
A red grape variety; robust, prolific, acidic and very widely distributed. The vine thrives almost anywhere and in consequence is often grown in poor and unfavorable conditions. This is reflected in the variable quality of the wine made from it. Where growers are prepared to accept lower yields of better grapes and to take pains with their vinification, Barbera can produce acceptable wines, round and fruity, pleasant young and capable of aging. At the same time, specialists are making wines of remarkable quality, sometimes D.O.C., sometimes *vino da tavolà*, sometimes from single vineyards. Often these are aged in cask, and usually they command exceptional prices. In Piedmont, Lombardy and Emilia-Romagna the grape makes varietal wines; elsewhere it is grown chiefly for blending. Barbera Sarda is a strain found on the island of Sardinia; Barbera Bianca is a white variant. The grape has spread to the New World with some success.

Barca Velha, Ferreira, Douro
Ferreira is the famous Port house; Barca Velha perhaps Portugal's most prized red wine, evolved through long experiment. The grapes employed in the blend are Portuguese and traditional, Tinta Roriz predominating, with lesser proportions of Tinta Barroca and Touriga Nacional, the techniques of vinification and maturation are those of Bordeaux. Fermentation takes place in stainless-steel vats, aging in new Portuguese oak. The resulting wine is complex, powerful and individual, slow to mature and capable of long life. It is sold as Barca Velha only in the best years, and production is modest, so the wine is both expensive and difficult to obtain. The effort made to find it, however, will be rewarded handsomely.

Gilles and Pierre Barge, Côte Rôtie
Located in the Rhône, Gilles and Pierre Barge make excellent Côte Rôtie. The 1985 is sensitively oaked and shows intense concentration of fruit and ripe tannins. The 1986 is more austere and tannic but will be drinking well in 1995.

Baroque
A white grape native to the Basque country and the Béarn. In the V.D.Q.S. appellation of Tursan it makes a highly individual *vin de terroir:* dry, perfumed, and with the potential to age. Also spelled Barroque.

Masil Barril, Priorato
This 15 hectare/37 acre private estate in the hills behind Tarragona, southwest of Barcelona, Spain, produces dark, strong, pungent red wines of up to 18 percent alcohol from the Garnacha grape.

Barrique
French word meaning "barrel" used in particular in Bordeaux, where the standard *barrique* is of 225 liters/59 U.S. gallons and is normally made from oak but can also be made from chestnut or acacia. There is now a worldwide fashion for aging red and white wines in new oak *barriques* to give the wine extra complexity. *Barrique* aging undoubtedly adds complexity, and many of the world's best wines spend a period in wood, but this is a labor-intensive process and is easy to overdo.

Marco De Bartoli, Marsala
At the head of his own 15 hectare/37 acre Vecchio Samperi vineyard since 1978, de Bartoli has transformed the outside world's perception of Marsala. Vecchio Samperi, his best-known product, is a dry, unfortified Marsala of refinement and balance. His Bukkuram is a lovely dessert Moscato that is grapy yet intensely rich; the grapes come from the remote island of Pantelleria between Sicily and North Africa.

Dr. von Bassermann-Jordan, Rheinpfalz
This estate can be traced back to 1250, but the Jordan family bought it in 1816. The direct descendant of that original buyer now owns it and practices traditional winemaking methods. Practically all the vines are Riesling, from 40 hectares/99 acres of vineyards. The style of the wines is delicate, often more delicate than many in the Rheinpfalz, but they have staying power as well and age successfully. They are matured in wood.

Château Bastor-Lamontagne, Sauternes
Through the caprice of its owner, this substantial Bordeaux property next door to Suduiraut was excluded from the 1855 classification. It makes excellent wines; in qualitative terms certainly at least the equal of many of the classed growths, and with their humbler status they represent exceptional value. Recent successes have been the vintages of 1975, 1976, 1982, 1983, 1985, 1986, 1987, 1988 and 1989. Since 1989 a second wine has been offered under the label Les Remparts de Bastor.

Bâtard-Montrachet, Domaine Ramonet
Domaine Ramonet in Chassagne-Montrachet stands out among even the best of the makers of white Burgundy.

The Ramonets own two parcels in the Bâtard-Montrachet vineyard from which, in the best years, they can make little more than 200 cases of wine. The wine is spectacular; Restaurant Taillevent in Paris may have a few bottles. Beyond that you are on your own.

Bâtonnage
French term used for the act of stirring up the fine lees in a barrel of maturing white wine at regular intervals to give an increased richness. Done with a piece of wood thin enough to fit through the bung hole of a barrel.

Jean Baumard, Coteaux du Layon
This family concern has vineyards in several appellations in the Loire, most notably 15 hectares/37 acres in Savennières and 6 hectares/14.8 acres in Quarts de Chaume. Its holdings in Savennières includes the famous 4 hectare/9.9 acre Clos de Papillon (butterfly shaped) vineyard, and it also owns the Clos Ste.-Catherine in the Coteaux du Layon. Some Anjou Rouge is made. Baumard's high reputation is well deserved.

Baumé
The French system of measuring must weight, or the amount of sugar in the grape juice. The American term is Brix, and the German term is *Oeschle*.

Domaine de la Baume, Béziers
New winery venture in France owned by Hardys of Australia. A state-of-the-art winery has been built to make *vin de pays* from bought-in grapes. The year 1990 was the first vintage released under the Chai Baumière label. Initially the wines will all be classic varietals, such as Chardonnay and Cabernet Sauvignon.

Château de Beaucastel, Châteauneuf-du-Pape
François and Jean-Pierre Perrin run their 130 hectare/321 acre domain in the Rhône with perfectionist care and a sleepless urge to make great wine. They are entirely successful, for Beaucastel is probably Châteauneuf's best red wine, if consistency, complex power and longevity are the yardsticks. The 1985 is extremely ripe, soft and full; the 1986 is tannic and withdrawn but it is likely to outshine the 1985 after ten years in bottle. The 1978 is massively structured. Of recent vintages, the 1989 will be a sumptuous bottle. The Perrins do not filter their wines.

LEFT: Georges de Latour, founder of Beaulieu Vineyards

Beaulieu Vineyards Georges de Latour Private Reserve Cabernet Sauvignon, Napa Valley
The first Beaulieu Private Reserve was made in the late 1930s. The name of de Latour, the winery's French-born founder, was not added until after his death in 1940. B.V. Private Reserve has been the benchmark California Cabernet Sauvignon almost since its first vintage. The few surviving bottles from the 1950s, which sold for less than US.$2 each when released, are worth US.$500 or more now. B.V. Private Reserve is a rich, intense wine but soft enough to be drinkable after a few years. But what a pity to drink it young: it's one of best of California's Cabernets to lay down.

Château Beaumont, Haut-Médoc

A substantial Bordeaux property, and one prominent throughout the nineteenth century, Beaumont has had to endure vicissitudes in the twentieth. By 1966, 2 hectares/5 acres only remained under vines, and in 1977 the replanted vineyard was all but destroyed by frost. The estate now belongs to a pension fund, but it owes its survival to Bernard Soulas, who bought it in 1979. He improved the drainage of the vineyard, replanted it and installed modern equipment. The vines are still young, and necessarily the wines of Beaumont are light in style, but the vintages of 1984, 1985 and 1986 show progress towards a more complete wine, with more richness and substance. As the vines mature this progress seems certain to be maintained. There is a second wine, Les Tours de Beaumont, while Château Moulin d'Arvigny is made for immediate drinking from the youngest vines.

Beaune Clos des Mouches, Joseph Drouhin

Maison Drouhin is a major owner of the Clos des Mouches, a *premier cru* vineyard in Burgundy and one of the best known of all the Beaune *crus*. Drouhin makes both a white version, from Chardonnay planted on the upper slope, and a red, from Pinot Noir grown at the base of the vineyard, in heavier soil. Many Burgundy enthusiasts prefer the white, which has both depth and liveliness. It is also harder to find. Both wines are always beautifully balanced and elegant and have considerable staying power. Most good vintages of Clos des Mouches can benefit from two additional years of cellaring, both in red and white.

Beaune Clos des Ursules, Maison Louis Jadot

The Burgundian house of Jadot is owned by the American importing firm Kobrand & Co., but André Gagey, the long-time director, closely oversees what is recognizably one of the most reliable and prestigious of the Beaune *négociant* houses. Jadot owns the Clos des Ursules vineyard, which is actually a sub-plot within the *premier cru* vineyard called Les Vignes Franches, southwest of the center of the town. The wines are fermented in traditional open vats and aged in oak for up to two years. Jadot red Burgundies are fleshy, concentrated, delicious wines. The Clos des Ursules, named after the Ursuline order of nuns who once owned it, is a wine that can be drunk young as, alas, most of it is, but will also age splendidly.

Château Beauregard, Pomerol

Beauregard remains a leading growth, although perhaps not quite in the front rank of any unofficial classification. For seventy years it was the property of the Clauzel family, before being taken over in 1991 by the Crédit Foncier de France, a bank that has owned vineyards in the Bordelais for more than a hundred years. This vineyard is well placed on the southern edge of the gravelly plateau and is planted with an unusually high proportion of Cabernet Franc, which gives a certain individuality to a rich, well-flavored wine that can be drunk young. The best recent vintages have been those of 1982, 1983 and 1985.

Bedell Cellars Long Island Merlot, Long Island

A surprising wine from America's newest fine wine-producing region, the North Fork of Long Island, 97 kilometers/80 miles east of New York City. Several years ago a delegation of Bordeaux winemakers, including several from the St. Emilion region, paid a working visit to the North Fork vineyards and professed to be astonished at what they found. While they were impressed with most of these New York State wines, they predicted great things from the local Merlot. This particular version displays much of the depth and balance one might expect from a decent St. Emilion or Pomerol, and yet it comes from relatively new vines. One

suspects that future vintages may produce something truly exceptional in the Bordeaux style.

Beerenauslese

Individually selected and extremely ripe grapes that will normally be affected by noble rot. These are some of the finest wines from Germany and Austria. Grapes so picked must meet minimum levels of ripeness, measured in degrees *Oechsle*, to qualify for the designation.

Beeswing

A very fine crust, resembling its namesake, that sometimes forms in old Port aged in bottle.

Château de Belcier, Côtes de Castillon

This is one of the outstanding properties of the appellation of Côtes de Castillon in Bordeaux. Belcier makes pleasingly robust, fruity wines that offer good value and are best drunk relatively young, although the excellent 1988 has the power and substance to develop over a longer period.

Bellavista, Erbusco

This 50 hectare/123 acre estate, in the Franciacorta D.O.C. region of northern Italy, produces excellent *méthode champenoise* wines. Look out for these wines: Cuvée Bellavista (100 percent Chardonnay), Gran Cuvée Brut Millesimato and Gran Cuvée Rosé Millesimato (both wines made from a mix of Chardonnay and Pinot Nero). Of Bellavista's still wines, Solsine (Cabernet Sauvignon and Merlot) is a stylish red of excellent, balanced flavors.

Domaine de Bellegarde, Jurançon

Pascal Labasse is one of a number of exciting young winemakers who are reviving interest in the French region of Jurançon and taking the wine to new heights. Others include Henri Ramonteau of Domaine de Cauhapé and Charles Hours of Clos Uroulat. Labasse uses skin contact in the vinification, and fermentation and aging in new oak has accentuated the aromas and tastes of apricot achievable from the Gros and, in particular, the Petit Manseng. His Jurançon *moelleux*, Cuvée Thibault, is superb.

Château Bellerive, Quarts de Chaume

With 17 hectares/42 acres of Quarts de Chaume, Jacques Lalanne owns about 37 percent of the appellation and produces very carefully crafted wine, designed to age. The château, *chai* and the surrounding vineyards are situated on the lower slopes of the appellation and are very well sited to maximize the sun's heat and the possible development of noble rot from morning mists rising from the Layon River. Yields are limited to 22 to 25 hectoliters per hectare/1.3 to 1.5 tons per acre through rigorous pruning and a green (early) harvest in July. Vinification is in wood, either in oak *barriques* or a mixture of oak and chestnut *foudres*. Old barrels are also used, many of them around twenty-five years old. His 1989 is among the best Loire sweet wines of that vintage.

Bellone

A grape long established in Latium. At Capena to the north of Rome, in the Castelli Romani, and in the Colli Albani, Colli Lanuvini and Velletri to the south, it forms part of the blends of pleasant white wines of primarily local interest.

Benmarl Vineyard Baco Noir, Hudson Valley

Mark Miller, an Oklahoma farmboy who became a highly successful magazine illustrator, went back to his roots twenty years ago when he founded Benmarl high on a slope overlooking the Hudson River in New York State, about 145 kilometers/90 miles north of New York City. Miller has remained a champion of the French-American hybrid despite the American public's overwhelming

preference for vinifera. The hybrids are crosses between sturdy native–American vines and the more elegant European viniferas. Time and again, Miller's wines have made his case for him. His Baco Noir is far superior; his Cuvée du Vigneron is truly extraordinary.

Bodegas Berberana, Rioja
One of the largest *bodegas*, Berberana makes Rioja in a full, lush fruity style, with many of the wines suitable for relatively early drinking. The three-year-old Carta de Plata is a bestseller. Of the older wines, Carta de Oro in great years like 1982 is a rich wine brimming with fruit. Reserva wines (an excellent 1985) show an added dimension of depth and spice.

Weingut Bercher, Baden
The origins of this German estate reach back to the fifteenth century. Most of its wines are fully fermented, with the Burgunder (Pinot) family playing a leading role. The top wines are produced from a much reduced yield, and some are aged in *barriques* and are remarkable examples of what is being produced in Baden nowadays.

Bereich
A legally-defined wine district in Germany. Each of the thirteen *Anbaugebiete* of what was West Germany is divided into *Bereiche*. There are two *Anbaugebiete* in the former East Germany. Covering such large areas, wines labeled *Bereich* inevitably vary in quality; the best wines are always more precisely named.

Bergsträsser Gebiets Winzergenossenschaft, Hessische Bergstrasse
A cooperative cellar handling 70 percent of the output of this small region of Germany. Standards are high and the members are given incentives to improve further the quality of their fruit. There are some 634 members, owning nearly 300 hectares/740 acres between them, over half planted with Riesling. Very little is exported.

Leon Beyer, Eguisheim
A family firm established in 1857, now headed by Leon Beyer and his son Marc in Alsace. The company specializes in firm, dry Alsace wines. The Beyers own 20 hectares/49.5 acres of vineyards and also buy in grapes, which, in the main, are vinified completely dry with no residual sugar. The best of the firm's wines, for example Riesling Cuvée Les Echaillers or Gewürztraminer Cuvée des Comtes d'Eguisheim, can in great vintages age for up to 20 years.

Bianchetta Genovese
A Ligurian white grape formerly widely planted around Genoa, but now in decline.

Winzergenossenschaft Bickensohl, Baden
Baden has some excellent village cooperative cellars, and this is one. Its members' vines include some top sites in Kaiserstuhl. This German cooperative started the revival of the Ruländer grape, sold as a dry crisp wine under its alternative name of Grau- or Grauer Burgunder.

Bodegas Bilbainas, Rioja
For those in search of a rich, old-fashioned Rioja with plenty of character that comes from a judicious use of oak, Bodegas Bilbainas is a consistently excellent source. The Viña Real 1982 is a full, rich complete wine; the *Reserva* from the same great year has an elegance and balance that should show at its peak between 1995 and 1998.

Billecart-Salmon, Mareuil-sur-Ay, Champagne
This small independent Champagne house with a justly high reputation, was founded in 1818 by Nicolas-François Billecart who had married a Mademoiselle Salmon. The firm remains in the family's control and is run by Jean-Roland-Billecart and his sons. Billecart looks for finesse and purity of fruit, and it uses a special fermentation technique to achieve this. After the first clarification process, a second *débourage* is provoked by chilling the must down to about 5°C/41°F, which acts as an additional filtration and eliminates most of the natural yeasts. The temperature of fermentation is then raised to about 12°-15°C/54°-59°F and proceeds slowly for about 21 days. The vintage *blanc de blancs* (excellent 1985) is made of prime Chardonnay fruit from Crémant, Avize and Le Mesnil-sur-Oger and is especially fine and delicate. Delicacy is also the keynote of the rosé *brut,* whose subtle salmon color is explained by the addition of a smaller amount of red wine is normally the case with other Champagne houses.

Biondi Santi, Brunello di Montalcino
Biondi Santi is the name of the family that made Brunello di Montalcino the wine that it is today. Federico Biondi Santi isolated the Brunello clone of Sangiovese in the middle of the last century and vinified it as a single grape variety, at a time when the wine of Montalcino was not dissimilar to Chianti. His son Tancredi continued his work, and the present incumbent of the estate is Franco. The Biondi Santi estate of Il Greppo consists of 11 hectares/27 acres. Methods are traditional with two styles of Brunello; the *annata* from ten- to twenty-five-year-old vines and the *riserva* from vines that are more than twenty-five years old, while Rosso di Montalcino is made from the young vines. The estate has a reputation for wines of immense longevity and boasts the oldest existing bottle of Brunello di Montalcino, from the 1888 vintage.

Blaauwklippen, Stellenbosch
Mining industrialist turned dairy farmer and *vigneron*, Graham Boonzaier bought this South African estate, then depressingly run-down, in 1971. With a huge investment, a lot of love and the enthusiasm and expertise of Walter Finlayson and latterly Jacques Kruger as winemakers, Graham has produced several award-winning wines. There have been a few inconsistencies in the past, but generally the best wines are Pinot Noir and Cabernet Sauvignon, which both age extremely well; steadily improving Chardonnays and, unusually for the Cape, a light-style Zinfandel. Current production is 40,000 cases.

Black Currant
Flavor and smell particularly associated with Cabernet Sauvignon.

Black Malvoisie
A black variant of the European Malvasia, which in California is planted sparingly as a constituent of blended wines.

Black Rot
Fungal disease that occurs in wet conditions. It attacks both grapes and vine leaves.

Blanc de Blancs
A white wine made solely from white grapes. Only really has meaning in reference to Champagne or other sparkling wines that may be made with the addition of black grapes, for almost all still white wine is made from white grapes only.

Blanc de Noirs
White wine, particularly sparkling, made from black grapes. It is most commonly used for Champagnes made from Pinot Noir and Pinot Meunier only.

Blandy's 10 Year Old Reserve Malmsey, Madeira
Founded in 1741, Blandy's is a leading shipper in the Madeira Wine Association. The company is perhaps best

known for its Malmsey wines, which are made from Malvasia Candida and Malvasia Babosa grapes grown in the warmest vineyards along the south coast of the island around Camara de Lobos. Its 10 Year Old Reserve Malmsey is sweet, full-bodied yet harmonious, the wine showing ripe fruit flavors and full, soft textures.

Weingut Blankenhorn, Baden
An old established German *weingut* and one of the best known in Markgräflerland, producing concentrated Burgunder and Gutedel (Chasselas) — the specialty of the district. "Pleasant and wholesome" is the usual description of Gutedel. Its role is similar to that of good basic Beaujolais.

Blauer Portugieser
Blauer Portugieser is an undistinguished red grape variety that is grown particularly in Austria and Germany. In Germany's Palatinate it makes off-dry pink Weissherbst and in Austria, south of Vienna, some rather dull red wine. It can also be found in Hungary, where it is called Oporto, and in France, where it is called Portugais Bleu.

Blaufränkisch
Blaufrankisch is a red, middle European grape variety, grown in Austria's Burgenland, where it is also called Limberger, and in the Württemberg region of Germany. In Hungary it is called Kékfrankos and features in Bull's Blood and other red wines. The flavor can be a little jammy, but with relatively high acidity.

Blending
The art of mixing together different wines, often several separate grape varieties, to make a harmonious whole. Red Bordeaux, Chianti and Champagne are among the most famous blends. Blending is also important in the Sherry, Cognac, Port and Whisky industries.

Blowsy
Overblown and obvious; the opposite of finesse. The term can refer to over-pungent Gewürztraminers.

Blush wine
Often from California, blush is a more marketable name than rosé. Juice is either free-run or from lightly pressed grapes. Zinfandel is often used in California and frequently labeled White Zinfandel; it is generally pink.

Boal
See Bual.

Bobal
A black grape that in the hills behind Valencia makes excellent rosé wines, among the best in Spain.

Bocksbeutel
The traditional flagon-shaped bottle of Franconia in Germany. "Goat's scrotum" is the direct translation. This shape is also used in Portugal and Chile.

Bodega
A Spanish winery.

Body
The weight of a wine, produced by alcohol and extract.

Wines from warm climates tend to have more body than those from cool climates.

Bogazkere
An indigenous Turkish red vine found chiefly in southern and eastern Anatolia.

Bollinger, Champagne
Champagne Bollinger is undoubtedly one of the great names of Champagne with a particularly proud tradition. It was founded in 1829 by Joseph Bollinger from Württemberg in Germany and Paul Renaudin, a Champenois. The firm has the great advantage of owning extensive vineyards totalling 140 hectares/346 acres, mainly in prime sites on the Montagne de Reims, and these supply 70 percent of its needs. The wines are traditionally made; the majority are vinified in small oak vats. The style of the wines is uncompromising, very full-bodied, austere when young but developing great character with age, epitomized in the magnificent R.D.

(Récemment Dégorgé) at the top of the range. Typically, Bollinger still uses traditional corks to age the wines in its Ay cellar, since it believes that these offer a better protection against oxidation than the now commonly used crown corks.

Bonarda
A red-wine variety formerly widely planted in Piedmont and elsewere in northern Italy, and nowadays often blended with Nebbiolo to make D.O.C. wines like Ghemme and Gattinara. Alone, it makes deep-red table wines that may be still or sparkling. What in the Oltrepò Pavese is often called Bonarda is in fact the Croatina grape.

Adega Cooperativa de Borba, Borba
This well run Portuguese cooperative makes good red wine, fresh, fruity and inexpensive, under the Borba and Convento da Vila labels. The white wines of Borba are improving.

Boschendal, Paarl
Originally established by a Huguenot refugee to South Africa in the late seventeenth century in the lovely Groot Drakenstein Valley, this estate was purchased in 1715 by another Huguenot family, the de Villiers. They continued to farm there until 1875, but a few years later, blighted by phylloxera, this vineyard along with many others in the district was turned over to fruit orchards under the ownership of Cecil Rhodes. The superb manor house, completed in 1812, has since been completely restored and is well worth a visit, as too is the highly-rated restaurant. The first winemaker, Achim von Arnim, in the late 1970s took on the task of replanting the vineyards and constructing a new winery, where he made outstanding sparkling wines. As the vineyards become more established watch for Chardonnay, Rhine Riesling, Gewürztraminer and Pinot Noir.

Boscò
A prolific grape found in eastern Liguria where it is the

dominant variety of the dry white D.O.C. wine of Cinqueterre, and, with *passito* grapes, makes the much rarer sweet Sciacchetrà.

Bosquet des Papes, Châteauneuf-du-Pape
Maurice Poiron makes first-rate Châteauneuf-du-Pape, vigorous, peppery but with fine, elegant fruit. Like most top growers of the Rhône he rates his 1986 more highly than his 1985. The former retains a deep purplish color, gives off the southern aromas of soft fruits and herbs and is extremely rich, velvety yet firmly structured and long on the palate. It is a superb bottle to be drunk from 1994 onwards.

Botrytis cinerea
Botrytis cinerea is the scientific name for a grape disease in which a mold (or "rot") forms on the skins of ripe grapes. This so-called noble rot (*pourriture noble* in France, *Edelfäule* in Germany, *Muffa nobilis* in Italy) is beneficial because it concentrates the sugars by feeding on the grapes' moisture, allowing wonderful sweet wine to be made. Noble rot imparts its own taste to the wine, a taste difficult to describe but easy to recognize. Encouraged by autumnal mists rising from rivers, followed by warm sunny days, Sauternes, Coteaux du Layon, Vouvray, Rheingau, Mosel and Tokay (in Hungary) are some of the areas most susceptible to noble rot. It is now possible to recreate the effect by spraying grapes with spores.

Bottle age
Both the time a wine spends being aged in bottle and the characteristic taste and smell of maturity it acquires from such aging are called bottle age. In a tasting note, it is usually a term of approbation.

Bottle sickness
After bottling wine goes into "shock," and its smell and taste are diminished. It needs a month or two to recover. Being transported over long distances has a similar effect.

Georges Boulon, Chiroubles
An outstanding Beaujolais grower, Georges Boulon produces first-rate Chiroubles and very good Fleurie and Beaujolais Villages at his Burgundian domain of some 17 hectares/42 acres. His Chiroubles Domaine de Clos Verdy is his best wine; aged in oak *foudres* for six months, it shows delicate aromas, racy fruit of great panache, plenty of substance but not too much alcohol. The wine ages well for two to three years. The 1989 is especially concentrated. His Fleurie Domaine des Côtes de Fontabon is a relatively uncomplicated wine for early drinking.

Bouquet
The smell of a mature wine, made complex by the process of aging.

Bourboulenc
A white grape of Languedoc/Roussillon and of Lirac and Châteauneuf-du-Pape in the southern Rhône. It makes a rustic, golden wine; fresh, supple and strongly alcoholic. The vine is seen to advantage on the limestone outcrop of La Clape to the south of Narbonne, where, confusingly, it is sometimes known as Malvoisie.

Henri Bourgeois, Sancerre
This long-established family firm, in the goats' cheese village of Chavignol in the Loire, is now run by Jean-Marie Bourgeois. The majority of its consistently good range of Sancerre is made in very modern stainless-steel vats and includes a very fine single-vineyard wine from the precipitous slopes of Les Monts Damnés. However, its prestige *cuvée* Etienne Henri is fermented and aged in new oak. A remarkable sweet late-harvest *cuvée* was made in 1989. Laporte is an associated producer whose vineyards are predominantly in Pouilly.

Bourgogne d'Auvenay, Domaine Leroy
The closest Burgundy lovers of moderate means are ever to come to a wine from Lalou Bize-Leroy was either the white or red generic Burgundy she bottles under the name of Bourgogne d'Auvenay. Bize-Leroy was half-owner of the renowned Domaine de la Romanée-Conti and, since 1988, of Domaine Leroy. This enterprise encompasses some of her earlier, non-D.R.C. holdings with the 14 hectare/34.6 acre Domaine Charles Noëllat, which she bought in that year. Thanks to Bize-Leroy's reputation for excellence, the Domaine Leroy began life with almost the prestige of the D.R.C., and its first wines have lived up to that advance billing. Its holdings are in many of the great vineyards of the Côte d'Or, but the same quality shows through in the (relatively) affordable generic wine.

Bourgogne Rouge, Domaine Mongeard-Mugneret
This Burgundy producer is based in Vosne-Romanée and has holdings that extend up and down the Côtes de Nuits. Jean Mongeard's best wines are most certainly his Grands Echezeaux, Echezeaux and Richebourg. But, happily for consumers who can only dream of these astronomically-priced wines, he makes lesser appellations as well. In the hands of a master, even an unpretentious Bourgogne Rouge becomes transformed into something superior. The wine lacks breed, but displays some of the qualities of old-time Burgundy, with good color, a chewy finish and the unmistakeable Burgundian *goût de terroir*.

Bouvet-Ladubay, Saumur
Established in 1851, Bouvet-Ladubay is the second-oldest sparkling wine producer in Saumur in the Loire. It is now owned by Taittinger. Cuvée Saphir is its best-known wine, although it has recently launched an oak-aged Cuvée Trésor, both white and rosé, and easily the most expensive Saumur sparkler. The house style is to use quite a high *dosage*.

Bouvier
An Austrian variety, a table grape that in the Burgenland and Styria makes unremarkable white wine used chiefly for blending. In Yugoslavia, as Ranina, it is grown to make Tiger's Milk.

Bovale
A Sardinian grape of Spanish origin chiefly grown for blending. It makes a dry red wine of little substance. The variety is also known as Nieddera.

Château Branaire-Ducru, St. Julien
For almost two hundred years, up to World War I, this fourth-growth Bordeaux property, formerly part of the Beychevelle estate, remained in the possession of related families. Its wines were highly regarded during the latter part of the nineteenth century, fetching prices consistently above their classification. In the twentieth century, Branaire's story was the familiar one of neglect and decline until in 1952 it was bought by Jean Tapie, who had owned vineyards in the French colony of Algeria. Branaire's fortunes revived, and in the fifties and sixties wines of distinction were made once again. Jean-Louis Tapie and his sister, Nicole Tari of Giscours, retained absolute control until 1987, when Tapie sold his half share to a French company of sugar refiners that has contributed handsomely to the continuation and expansion of the work of modernization.

Over the past two decades the wines of Branaire have been consistently successful, most recently with a splendid 1982, an impressively rich and powerful 1985 and a promising 1988.

Braquet

A vine of delicate constitution that, in the little appellation of Bellet, near Nice, makes red wine of great elegance and finesse. The Braquet is blended with much smaller percentages of Folle Noire and Grenache to make the red wine of the Château de Crémat, and with Folle Noire and Cinsaut it makes the rosé. In Piedmont, where it is known as Brachetto, the grape reflects the tradition of *frizzante* sweet red wines and, seems now to be enjoying something of a revival.

Breaky Bottom, England

Although this is a small vineyard of just over 2 hectares/4.9 acres, Peter Hall makes some of England's best dry white wine at Breaky Bottom, near the village of Rodmell to the south of Lewes. He has planted a number of different varieties, including Seyval Blanc.

British Made Wine

Not wine at all, in the legal sense, but "made wine" produced from imported grape concentrate. Poor in quality and cheap, British Made Wine only harms the reputation of English wine.

Brown Brothers, Milawa, Victoria

Established by John Francis Brown in 1889, the Brown Brothers vineyards now total some 160 hectares/395 acres. This family business offers an impressive range of varietal wines: its "limited production" range, for example, comprises some fourteen different varietals, and its "classic vintage" releases, which are at least five years old, include a Noble Riesling. The company's best red wine is the single-vineyard Koombahla Cabernet Sauvignon; the 1985 shows marked mint and eucalyptus flavors.

Weingut Bründlmayer, Langenlois

This 45 hectare/111 acre estate in Kamptal-Donauland north of Vienna makes wines that add style to many fine Austrian restaurants. In the volcanic soil of the Heiligenstein and the neighboring sites, the annual rainfall is low and yields are small. Wilhelm Bründlmayer, with little formal training in winemaking but using the experience he has gained abroad and from his father, now produces beautifully crafted wines, of which the steely Rieslings are particularly good. No chemicals are used in the vineyards.

Brut

The driest category of French sparkling wine, which can have up to 2 per cent residual sugar. *Brut zéro* or *Brut ultra* will have no added *dosage*.

Bual

The Portuguese Boal (Bual is the Anglicized form) is traditionally a grape best known for the rich, full style of Madeira that it makes. The vine is rare on the island nowadays, but it remains an approved variety in mainland Portugal and is still found in the blend that makes the idiosyncratic fortified wines of Carcavelos.

Bung

Stopper for a wooden barrel, now often made of plastic. The bung should be easily removable to facilitate tasting or topping up the contents.

Burger

This is the name in California for the little known Monbadon of the Midi, a white variety that makes dull wines chiefly useful for blending. The Burger was once the most heavily planted vinifera vine in California.

Burgunder

A generalized name in countries where German is spoken for varieties of the Burgundian Pinot: Frühburgunder, Spätburgunder, Blauer Burgunder, Blauer Spätburgunder, Weissburgunder. The Grauerburgunder, the Pinot Gris, is more familiar as the Ruländer, and sometimes as Tokaier. *See also* Pinot Blanc, Pinot Noir, Pinot Gris.

Leo Buring, Tanunda, South Australia

Now part of the Lindemans group, Leo Buring owns a 36 hectare/89 acre vineyard at Tanunda in the Barossa Valley of Australia with plantings of Chardonnay, Cabernet Sauvignon and Rhine Riesling. The firm also buys in grapes. Very good 1985 Cabernet Sauvignon Bin DR 488 made from Coonawarra and Barossa fruit. Magnificent Show Release Rhine Rieslings.

Ernest Burn, Gueberswihr

Leading Alsace grower of Gueberswihr and proprietor of Clos St. Imer, a limestone-based vineyard producing exceptional, complex Gewürztraminer and Muscat. Fine exponent of *vendange tardive* wines.

Guy Burrier, Pouilly-Fuissé

A respected wine broker in the Mâconnais and mayor of Fuissé, Guy Burrier owns 7 hectares/17.3 acres in the Pouilly-Fuissé appellation in Burgundy. He also buys in top-quality grapes from his neighbors, which he vinifies and markets under his own label. His best *cuvées*, notably Les Champs, are fermented and matured in oak.

Buttery

Term often used for Chardonnay's soft, buttery flavor.

C

C.V.N.E., Rioja

Founded in the nineteenth century, the Compañia Vinícola del Norte d'Espana is one of Rioja's finest *bodegas*, medium sized with an intelligent mix of traditional and modern methods. The winery is ultra-modern, but vinification is classical. The inexpensive Tinto (also known as Rioja Clarete) is excellent value, light, elegant but with well defined fruit. The Viña Real (excellent 1985) is more concentrated and solid, though the fruit is not masked by oak. At the top of the range, the Imperial Gran Reservas are wines of outstanding quality, full yet supple with clear fruit made more complex with just the right amount of oak. Of recent great vintages, the 1982 looks likely to be a quite exceptional bottle toward the end of the century, while for current drinking the 1976 exudes great class.

Ca' del Bosco, Erbusco

Located in the Franciacorta D.O.C. region of northern Italy, the ebullient Maurizio Zanella produces what is generally reckoned to be the finest range of *méthode champenoise* wines in Italy. He properly ages his sparkling wines in impressive underground cellars at his 60 hectare/148 acre Erbusco estate. His *Brut Zéro* is exceptionally fine. Zanella also produces Franciacorta D.O.C. Rosso and Bianco, but his *vini da tavola* are his most interesting still wines. These are intended to rival fine Bordeaux and Burgundy and are very expensive. The 1985 Pinero, made from Burgundian clones of Pinot Noir, is certainly as fine as some famous wines from the Côte d'Or; while the 1988 barrel-fermented Chardonnay is rich and complex, though priced at the same level as a Chassagne or Puligny.

Cabernet Franc

Cabernet Franc produces its most exciting wines in the red Loire appellations of Chinon, Bourgueil, St. Nicolas de Bourgueil and Saumur-Champigny. Simple Anjou, Saumur and Touraine Rouge are lighter versions. In the best years these wines have a sturdy concentration of flavor that enables them to age; in lighter years they have ripe cherry fruit that makes them ideal for drinking.

Cabernet Franc also features in some of the pink appellations of the Loire, notably Cabernet d'Anjou.

In Bordeaux, it is an important part of the blend, especially in St. Emilion, where it is more important than Cabernet Sauvignon; also a vital ingredient of other appellations of southwest France. In northern Italy it is planted alongside Cabernet Sauvignon, with little distinction between the two, especially if the wine is labeled simply Cabernet. In the New World, its impact has been very much less than that of Cabernet Sauvignon.

Cabernet Sauvignon

Cabernet Sauvignon is the grape variety that above all others has adapted from the Old World to the New World with unerring ease. Most of the great red wines of Bordeaux and some of the finest wines of the New World are based on Cabernet Sauvignon. It is the dominant grape variety in a blend of Cabernet Franc and Merlot and maybe Malbec and Petit Verdot, for wines from the Médoc and Graves, where the flavor is reminiscent of blackcurrants or cedarwood. It demands aging in small oak barrels, and the best wines also require several years of bottle age to reach their best. It is an easy variety to grow, as it buds and ripens late and is resistant to frost and disease, hence its easy adaptability to other countries and continents.

Elsewhere in France it plays an important part in the other appellations of the southwest, and in the Midi it is seen as an improving variety to enliven otherwise indifferent *vins de pays*. Mas de Daumas Gassac is a supreme example of just what can be achieved in the Midi, while in Provence, notably on estates such as Trévallon and Vignelaure, it is successfully blended with Syrah.

Across the Pyrenees it has been planted in Penedès by innovative producers such as Miguel Torres and Jean Léon, and features in Vega Sicilia and in Raimat. J. M. da Fonseca has some in Portugal. In Tuscany Sassicaia set the trend for Cabernet Sauvignon, closely followed by countless other Tuscan estates. The D.O.C. of Carmignano specifically allows for 6 to 10 percent of Cabernet Sauvignon to distinguish it from adjoining Chianti. Cabernet Sauvignon also grows in northeast Italy, where it is often blended with Cabernet Franc.

Eastern Europe too has espoused Cabernet Sauvignon, notably Bulgaria, but Hungary and Yugoslavia have also followed suit. There is Château Carras in Greece, experiments in Cyprus and Château Musar in the Lebanon, as well as examples in Israel.

Methods in California and Austrlia follow those of Bordeaux, with aging in new French oak barrels. In California Merlot is sometimes used for blending, while Australians often favor Shiraz. Cabernet Sauvignon is being produced with increasing success in New Zealand's Hawke's Bay; South Africa has good examples from the cooler areas of Stellenbosch and Paarl, while Chile is the most competent South American producer. There is some in Argentina and Brazil too. In fact there is hardly anywhere this versatile grape does not grow and produce exciting wine. The danger is that intrinsic regional characteristics and flavors are lost in the love affair with Cabernet Sauvignon.

Pascal Cailleau, Domaine de Sauveroy, Anjou

One of the young *vignerons* who are transforming Anjou Blanc Sec's reputation for dull wine. This 25 hectare/61.8 acre estate in the Loire produces, in an increasingly well-equipped winery, the customary range of Anjou wines: dry whites, rosés, reds and some very fine Coteaux du Layon. Cailleau is a great enthusiast and experimenter. His wines from 1989 and 1990 are particularly fine.

Calabrese

Although its name indicates a mainland Italian origin, the Calabrese, with more than 25,000 hectares/61,750 acres, is the most widely planted and most prized of Sicilian red-wine varieties. The grape makes powerful, deeply colored wine and shows to advantage in certain wines of Corvo and Regaleali. It is also valuable for blending. Also known as Nero d'Avola.

Calem Port, Vila Nova de Gala

A Portuguese house established in Oporto in 1859. Calem is still a family business and a Port player to watch. Under the direction of Joachim Calem, who is also the Oporto agent for General Motors and Ferrari cars, the company is constantly expanding — but always with an uncompromising eye for quality. Jeremy Bull, Calem's chief blender (*see* Blender's view) is one of the Port trade's most knowledgeable professionals — a man who carries his learning with a light touch. Calem's specializes in fine *colheitas* (tawny Ports from a single year). Look out for the 1962 *colheitas*, a wine of great refinement. There are good vintage Ports too, especially the 1970, made largely from fruit from the firm's Quinta da Fox. In 1990, Calem acquired the superbly sited Quinta da Ferradosa in the Douro Superior, which has the potential to make vintage Ports of the highest quality.

Calera Vineyard Pinot Noir, Jensen Vineyard, Monterey County

Josh Jensen, like many romantics before him, wanted to recreate Burgundy in California. Unlike most of them, however, he was willing to gamble time, money and hard work; and Calera, high up on the same lonely mountain range as Chalone Vineyards, is the realization of that dream. Or at least the beginning of it. Calera Pinot Noirs at their best come as close as any American wines ever have to emulating the elusive quality of fine Burgundy. Jensen makes different wines from small but separate vineyards. Whether the Jensen Vineyard is consistently the best, as some critics say, is problematical. It is one of Calera's best, and Calera is itself a source of some exceptional Pinot Noirs.

Calitor

A banal red-wine variety found in limited quantity in the eastern part of the south of France.

Campbell's Early

This American hybrid vine makes wholly unremarkable red wines. It is prominent in Japan, where with the Delaware it has roughly half the land under vines. The variety does well enough in difficult conditions, but its wines are not among Japan's best.

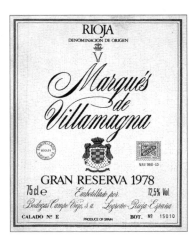

Bodegas Campo Viejo, Rioja

This Logroño *bodega*, founded in 1959, is the largest in Rioja and part of the giant beverage company Bodegas e Bebidas. Campo Viejo's inexpensive wines are sound and well made, but the *Gran Reservas* — sensuous, spicy, with a fine touch of oak and vanilla — are the wines to seek out. The Gran Reserva Marqués de Villamanga can be a splendid long-lived wine, especially in vintages like 1975, 1978 and 1982.

Canaiolo

A grape, both white and black, that formerly was well

regarded but is now of declining importance. The *bianco* is nowadays uncommon outside Umbria, where it still plays a subordinate role in the making of Orvieto and lesser blended wines. In the eighteenth century the Canaiolo Nero was the principal variety of Chianti, but its relative softness and low yield made it inevitable that it should lose ground to the more vigorous Sangiovese. It is still found in modest percentages throughout the Chianti and Chianti Classico vineyards, where it is considered particularly sutable for the *governo* method, and in Montepulciano.

Canard-Duchêne, Champagne

Now part of Veuve Clicquot, Canard Duchêne was founded in 1868 in the village of Ludes on the northern slopes of the Montagne de Reims. Its 17 hectares/42 acres of vines in the Montagne de Reims can supply only a small fraction of the grapes required for its annual production of around 250,000 cases. Most of its Champagne is drunk in France. Its top wine is the prestige Cuvée Charles VII.

Cannonau

A Sardinian variant of the ubiquitous Grenache. It occupies 20 percent of the land under vine on that island, makes powerful red D.O.C. wines that may be dry or sweet and contributes to the rosé wines.

Château Canon, Canon-Fronsac

This appellation covers a developing and highly promising area, and the tiny Château Canon represents the first venture into it of the Moueix family, best known for its association with their other Bordeaux property, Pétrus. The vineyard covers little over 1 hectare/2.47 acres and is planted 80 percent with Merlot. It can produce rich wine, fruity, tannic and powerful, reflecting both the excellence of its site and the careful vinification of its owners. Recent vintages of merit are those of 1982, 1983 and 1985.

Château Canon, St. Emilion

The vineyard of this Bordeaux property was assembled from smaller properties, and the château was built, by the former naval officer Jacques Kanon, between 1760 and 1770. More recently it has belonged to the Fournier family, and their ownership has been reflected in the many great vintages of the period between the wars and after the Second World War. The wine of 1929 is generally cited as the best of its year from the right bank of the river, and wines of similar splendor were made in 1947, 1953, 1955 and 1962.

Eric Fournier assumed control from his grandmother in 1972, and his great successes include 1978, 1979, 1981, 1982, 1983, 1985, 1986, 1987 and 1988.

Château Canon-de-Brem, Canon-Fronsac

Bordeaux property belonging to the Moueix family in this area of high potential. Canon-de-Brem extends to 20 hectares/49 acres of limestone soil and makes robust, tannic, concentrated wines. In general they need a minimum of five years aging, and in exceptional vintages like 1962 can show to great advantage after more than twenty years in bottle. Of more recent vintages, 1981, 1982, 1983 and 1985 are rich and powerful wines, capable of further improvement as they mature.

Château Cantemerle, Haut-Médoc

Problems of inheritance caused this highly regarded Bordeaux property to suffer badly from neglect during the sixties and seventies, and this was reflected in the deteriorating quality of its wine. In 1980 a syndicate of which the Cordier family was part acquired Cantemerle and spent heavily on replanting and the modernization of *cuvier* and *chai*. A revival was signalled by an excellent 1982, a yet better 1983, and an admirable 1985. Nineteen eighty-six was spoiled by hail, but wines of this quality suggest that it will not be long before Cantemerle justifies once again its considerable reputation.

Cap

The layer of grape skins and pips that forms on the top of fermenting wine. The cap should be regularly broken up so that more flavor, color, aromas and tannin can be extracted and also to prevent the cap being attacked by bacteria. *See also* Pigeage.

Caparzo, Brunello di Montalcino

The Brunellos of Caparzo are among the best, particularly those from the estate's top vineyard of La Casa. A long run of first-rate vintages — 1979, 1981, 1982, 1985, 1988, 1990 — speaks volumes for the consistent excellence of winemaking here.

Cape Mentelle, Margaret River

David Hohnen is a spectacularly successful Australian winemaker, widely traveled with an international outlook. He studied viticulture in California, did a stint with Dominique Portet at Taltarni in Victoria, then in 1976 with his brother Mark he bought the Margaret River vineyard of Cape Mentelle in Western Australia. He has won the coveted Jimmy Watson Trophy twice for his superb 1982 and 1983 Cabernet Sauvignon. Not a man to rest on his laurels, he bought the 40 hectare/99 acre Cloudy Bay vineyard in New Zealand, which by the late eighties had set new standards of excellence for Sauvignon Blanc. Of the Cape Mentelle wines, the 1984 Zinfandel is a spicy, beautifully textured wine.

Capsule congé

Stamped capsule on French bottle of wine, proving that tax has been paid on it.

Carbon dioxide

A by-product of fermentation. The bubbles in sparkling wine are trapped CO_2. Still white wine sometimes has some residual (or added) carbon dioxide to give freshness and bite. (*see* Spritz and Pétillant.)

Carignan

The red Carignan grape is Cariñena in Aragón, where it was first recognized and is the prime ingredient of the eponymous D.O. In Rioja and Penedès it is known as Mazuelo, as Carignan in Italy and Carignane in California and is most widely grown along the French Mediterranean for wines like Côtes du Roussillon, Coteaux du Languedoc, Minervois, Côtes de Provence and countless Vins de Pays. The technique of *maceration carbonique* has improved its flavor enormously, bringing out the fruit, but normally it is blended with Grenache and Cinsaut to make sturdy, and sometimes astringent wine. Its importance is declining in the Midi, especially in the Côtes de Provence, where its contribution to the appellation has been reduced from 70 to 40 percent. In California it is used for jug wine.

Carnelian

This relatively recent hybrid derived from the Cabernet Sauvignon, Carignan and Grenache is the result of efforts at the University of California, Davis to develop a hot-weather grape of distinction. The Carnelian has proved prolific, but its wine has tended to lack definition, and it rarely makes a varietal.

Carpenè Malvolti, Conegliano

This family firm makes excellent Prosecco di Conegliano, the elegant gently sparkling wine of the Treviso province in northern Italy. Annual production is about 25,000 cases.

Carr Taylor, England

A well-established vineyard set up in 1971 close to the

Sussex coastal resort of Hastings. David and Linda Carr Taylor run their 9 hectare/22.2 acre vineyard with style, even exporting their wines to Paris shops. Reichensteiner, Kerner, Schönburger and Pinot Noir are among the varieties planted. As well as their still wines, the Carr Taylors make both non vintage and vintage bottle-fermented sparkling wines.

Domaine Carras, Greece

In the late 1960s shipowner John Carras established the vineyards of Domaine Carras in the Halkidiki area of northern Greece. With the assistance of Professor Peynaud of Bordeaux, the estate planted French grape varieties to supplement indigenous Greek ones. The estate's flagship wine is the internationally praised Château Carras, a very good red wine made from Limnio, Cabernet Sauvignon and Cabernet Franc grapes with a dash of Merlot. Also worth seeking out are the red Meliton wine, a full-bodied Cabernet Sauvignon wine that has been aged for five years, and the Réserve Blanc, which is made from Sauvignon and Assyrtiko grapes. The majority of wines produced at Domaine Carras are governed by the Appellation of Origin "Côtes de Meliton."

Carricante

The chief variety of the D.O.C. white wines of Etna, on the island of Sicily. The vineyards lie high on the slopes of the volcano, and the Carricante makes fruity, dry white wines. Also known as Catanese.

Casa de la Viña, Valdepeñas

Well-regarded Valdepeñas estate owned by Bodegas e Bebidas, also owners of Campo Viejo Rioja.

Casse

A chemical disorder of wine. There are four kinds: iron, copper, protein and oxidasic. All cause haziness.

De Castelfort, Nogaro-en-Armagnac

De Castelfort is the premium label of the Caves des Producteurs de Nogaro, a leading Armagnac cooperative. This group of growers came together in 1963, initially selling all its brandies in bulk to the merchants of Condom. Since 1989, however, the cooperative has bottled its entire production and is now developing its own brands seen under the De Castelfort and Lafontan labels.

This is a quality-conscious operation. Only the traditional continuous still is used at Nogaro, and the *eaux-de-vie* spend six months in new oak barrels before further aging in older casks. The De Castelfort twelve-year-old Bas Armagnac is mellow and well balanced with a natural sweet fruitiness. Of the single-vintage Armagnacs, the 1965 is elegant, firm and long-flavored, while the 1942 has a vanillin richness and a marked touch of *rancio*, that slightly maderized characteristic — highly prized in a fine brandy — which is the beneficial effect of oxidation on the *eaux-de-vie* through the staves of the cask.

Castell'in Villa, Chianti Classico

There are at least half a dozen top Classico estates producing world-class wines. At Castell'in Villa the wines are a mirror image of the personality of the winemaker.

Coralia Pignatelli is a graceful, hardworking widow in her fifties. She was born in Greece but spent much of her early life in Switzerland, where she met and married Principe Riccardo Pignatelli della Leonessa, an Italian diplomat. The Pignatellis bought Castell'in Villa in 1968, a hilltop property near Castelnuovo Berardenga, with magnificent views of Siena 14 kilometers/8.7 miles to the west.

Princess Pignatelli now cultivates 54 hectares/133 acres of Chianti Classico D.O.C.G. vines. Her Chiantis are much admired in Tuscany for their consistent elegance allied to an inner strength of flavor that is a true expression of the Sangiovese grape grown on the warm soils of the southern part of the Classico zone. She is respected for her skill in making stylish Chianti in difficult years like 1987, 1984 and 1972. In good years her *riservas* are among the best four or five wines of the vintage: the 1983 *riserva* shows tremendous character due in part to long but judicious cask aging; and the 1986 is a masterpiece of lingering subtlety whose style has something in common with great red Burgundy.

Pignatelli also makes an impressive *vino da tavola* Santa Croce, which is made essentially from Sangiovese and a little Cabernet Sauvignon from her excellently sited Balsastrada vineyard. If that were not enough, the princess produces an exceptional extra-virgin olive oil.

Castello di Ama, Chianti Classico

A large amphitheater of superbly sited hillside vineyards enfold this model winery in the heart of Chianti Classico. The winemaker, Dr. Marco Pallanti, separately vinifies and bottles three different single-vineyard Chiantis — Bellavista, La Casuccia and San Lorenzo. In the 1985 vintage, all three showed excellent deep fruit made more complex by the use of new oak barrels. Pallanti, a frequent visitor to Bordeaux and Burgundy, also makes a seriously good Sauvignon Blanc and a very creditable Pinot Noir. He is a winemaker to watch, a man who has shown a new face of Chianti Classico while at the same time looking beyond Italy for inspiration.

Castello di Volpaia, Chianti Classico

The high-altitude vineyards of this 37 hectare/91 acre estate at Radda produce Chiantis that develop a lovely aroma and refinement after seven or eight years in bottle. The 1980 Volpaia Chianti Classico Riserva is a stylish star of an unsung vintage. The owner, Giovanella Stianti Mascheroni, is rightly proud of her 1983 Coltassala, a Sangiovese-based wine, rich, lithe and elegantly formed.

Fürstlich Castell'sches Domänenamt, Franken

Largest estate on the edge of Franken in Germany with many "solely owned" sites. The owner, Fürst zu Castell-Castell, comes from a family of bankers, foresters and farmers as well as vinegrowers, and the estate includes a good deal of woodland as well as vineyards. It dates back to the thirteenth century and grows no Riesling: the Silvaners are the stars of the estate, although Müller-Thurgau are grown in greater quantity in the 58 hectares/144 acres of vineyard. Silvaner is the classic grape of Franconia, and here it is shown at its best: earthy, spicy and well-structured.

Catarratto

A white grape widely planted in Sicily. It is the principal if not the most distinguished constituent of Marsala. Its yield is modest, but the variety occupies some 40 percent of the vineyard, makes the neutral dry white D.O.C. wines of Alcamo, and plays a part in both Corvo whites and Regaleali whites.

Catawba

A prolific North American grape derived from *Vitis labrusca* and for years very widely planted in the eastern states. It was the mainstay of nineteenth-century American sparkling wine production. It retains some

popularity, but is in decline as growers look for higher quality.

Joseph Cattin, Voegtlinshoffen

Excellent Alsace grower with important holdings in *grand cru* Hatschbourg. The family's Gewürztraminers grown on this site are sensuous, intense wines, full-bodied, fleshy and with a very marked spiciness — model examples of the grape from southern Alsace.

Cave

French term for wine cellar.

Caves Aliança, Bairrada

An important firm based in the Bairrada, but with wide and varied interests throughout Portugal, Caves Aliança makes Bairrada wines both white and red, the latter increasingly in a style that departs from tradition. Current commercial realities outside Portugal seem to dictate the production of a wine that may be drunk younger. Caves Aliança is prominent among those now making softer, fruity, more accessible wines that still retain Bairrada's characteristic richness and charm.

Caves São João, Bairrada

This well-known and well-regarded firm in the Bairrada in Portugal markets good red Dão wines under the label Porta dos Cavaleiros. Those of *reserva* quality exemplify the conservative tradition of Dão winemaking, and can be immensely long lived. From Bairrada itself it produces Frei João Reserva, an outstanding traditional Baga wine, typically rich and structured, with great potential to develop. It needs a minimum of ten years aging.

Caviste

French term for cellarman.

Caymus Vineyards Special Selection Cabernet Sauvignon, Napa Valley

Caymus has emerged in recent years as one of Napa Valley's finest producers of Cabernet Sauvignon. Beginning with a remarkably good 1984 vintage, this California winery has progressed from strength to strength. The 1987, the most recent release of the Special Selection Cabernet proved that the wines of the preceding four vintages were not aberrations. The 1987 is a magnificent wine, one that will improve and can be enjoyed well into the next century. The wine is complex, with prune, plum, cherry, coffee, cedar and anise flavors, and it has an extremely long finish.

Cayuga

A relatively recent hybrid developed in New York State, this is a robust and productive vine that makes a pleasantly firm dry white wine of some quality.

Charles de Cazanove, Champagne

Champagne house founded in 1811 by Charles Gabriel de Cazanove. The firm remained in family hands until 1958, when it was bought by Martini, who sold it to Moët-Hennessy. Charles de Cazanove recently returned to private ownership under the Lombard family. Annual production is around 15,000 cases a year. Champagne Stradivarius is the prestige *cuvée*.

Bernard Cazes, Languedoc-Roussillon

Bernard Cazes is the quieter half of a remarkable fraternal duo. His elder brother André is responsible for marketing, while Bernard is the winemaker. Many winemakers are responsible for two or three wines, usually from a limited range of varieties. Not so Bernard, for the firm's range of at least twelve different wines runs from dry Muscat and easy-drinking *vin de pays* through Côtes du Roussillon-Villages to finish with some remarkable *vins doux naturels*. All of these wines are among the best of their type in the Midi.

Bernard is modest about his achievements, and it is difficult to persuade him to talk in detail about his wines. Visiting their large 155 hectare/383 acre estate gives glimpses of Bernard's technique as he explains briefly the various pruning systems they use, the different methods for pressing the grapes and the various ways of stopping the fermentation in *vins doux naturel*, by adding alcohol.

The Cazes brothers are keen to produce wines for today's way of life; lighter wines that can be drunk, for example, at lunchtime without inducing a lengthy siesta. So although their Côtes de Roussillon–Villages and Aimé Cazes 1973, a remarkable *vin doux naturel*, are their flagship wines, equal care is taken when making their easy-drinking and refreshing Canon-du-Maréchal *vin de pays*.

Bernard and André Cazes have done much to show that it is possible to produce consistently high quality wines in Languedoc-Roussillon.

Cellier des Templiers, Banyuls

This is a leading cooperative and the largest producer of both *vin doux naturel* from Banyuls and table wine from Collioure, both in Roussillon. It is a large operation, which welcomes 400,000 visitors a year. Most impressive are the long ranks of *foudres*, each holding 500 or 1,000 hectoliters/13,210 or 26,420 U.S. gallons of maturing wine. The *foudres* are all old as slow oxygenation is the intention, not the tastes of new wood. Some wines, intended for early drinking, are stored outdoors in 600 liter/160 U.S. gallon wooden *demi-muids* in order to accelerate the maturing process, which is thus speeded up by a factor of three. Banyuls Grand Cru, the generally better Banyuls, is never given this harsh treatment.

Cencibel

See Tempranillo.

Central Valley, Chile

The long, thin Central Valley of Chile is more of a plateau than a valley, flanked as it is by mountain ranges, with the high Andes to the east and the much lower coastal range on the west. The valley itself measures no more than 72 kilometers/45 miles at its widest point and lies some 600 meters/1,970 feet above sea level. It is crossed by several rivers, which provide vital water for irrigation from the melted snows of the Andes. The Aconcagua River, with one winery, Errázuriz Panquehue, is to the north of Santiago, while the principal valleys to the south are the Maipo, Cachapoal, Lontué and Maule. The soil of the valley is volcanic.

All the wine producers of Chile are situated in the Central Valley, usually near Santiago, for historical reasons. However, recently there has been a move south. Miguel Torres bought land in Curicó, some 200 kilometers/124 miles south of Santiago and is introducing European techniques to Chile.

Cépage

French term for variety of grapevine.

Bruno Ceretto, Barolo/Barbaresco

Bruno Ceretto is one of the most forward-looking and quality-conscious producers in Piedmont. This merchant house is now a specialist in single-vineyard wines with two state-of-the-art wineries in Barolo and Barbaresco. Mario Ceretto, Bruno's brother, is chief winemaker. In the outstanding 1985 vintage, the Barolo Bricco Rocche Prapo is a dense, spicy wine needing another ten years to reach maturity, while the Barbaresco Bricco Asili shows fine aromas and is more open on the palate, with a fine long finish. The Ceretto brothers latest venture is the 85 hectare/210 acre La Bernardina estate near Gallo d'Alba, where they have planted Cabernet, Merlot and Chardonnay.

Château Certan-de-May, Pomerol
The oldest domain in the Pomerol district, de May bears the name of the Scottish family who held this Bordeaux property for more than three hundred years up to 1925. The vineyard is on the best part of the high ground between Château Pétrus and Vieux–Château–Certan, its soil gravel with a little clay. Formerly little of the wine was bottled at the property, but modernization and the installation of new *cuves* took place in 1976, and since then the wine has been transformed. It is vinified in stainless-steel and matured in new oak, watched over by Madame Barreau-Badar and her son, a graduate of La Tour Blanche. The wine is very deeply colored, immensely rich and concentrated, fruity and powerfully tannic, needing at least ten years aging. Great successes in this style have been the 1978, 1979, 1981, 1982, 1985, 1986, 1987 and 1988; the 1982 is quite outstanding.

Chablis Les Clos, Domaine Raveneau
François Raveneau and his son Jean-Marie produce some of the most expensive wines in Chablis. The Raveneaus, like many growers in the currently prosperous Chablis region of Burgundy, age their wines in wood, and they eschew that symbol of the parvenu winemaker, new oak. Consequently, their wines display a judicious blend of wood and the unique flinty qualities of the grapes grown in Chablis' famous Kimmeridgian limestone soil. The Raveneaus own vines in three of the seven *grand cru* vineyards and five of the twelve important *premier crus*. Their steely, powerful Les Clos is all that a Chablis should be.

Chablis Grenouilles, Cave Coopérative, La Chablisienne
Of the thirty Burgundy producers singled out in this list, this is the only cooperative. But La Chablisienne is no ordinary cooperative. Founded in 1923, it produces close to a quarter of the entire production of the Chablis appellation. It blends the wine of small producers, as all co-ops do, but its members include some thirty-five owners of holdings in all of the seven *grand cru* vineyards except Valmur. Most of these wines are bottled under the vineyard owners' names, but some are bottled under the name of the cooperative itself. Look out for their Grenouilles: at about 10 hectares/24.7 acres, Grenouilles is the smallest of the *grand cru* vineyards and often produces the most pungent and forward wines among the seven. Some 7.5 hectares/18.5 acres of Grenouilles are handled by La Chablisienne.

Chablis Les Preuses, Domaine René Dauvissat
René Dauvissat has holdings of about 3 hectares/7.4 acres in Les Clos and Les Preuses among the Chablis *grands crus,* and another 7 hectares/17.3 acres in some of the best *premiers crus* in this part of Burgundy. His wines keep for an astonishingly long time — fifteen or twenty years. Dauvissat is sparing with new oak, allowing the natural flavors of great Chablis to predominate. His *grand cru* wines age in wood for about twelve months, with one barrel in five being new Allier oak. The *premier cru* wines all age in old barrels.

Chai
Strictly speaking, a French term for a building for housing barrels of maturing wine, especially common in Bordeaux. Sometimes loosely applied to any Bordelais winemaking buildings.

Chalone Vineyards Reserve Pinot Noir, Monterey County
The history of Chalone Vineyards, high in The Pinnacles mountain range of Monterey County in California, goes back to the 1940s. But it only came into prominence in the 1960s under the management of Richard Graff. Graff, who is still one of the owners, learned early on that the vineyard's soil was perfect for the difficult Pinot Noir. He has produced superior, Burgundy-style Pinot Noirs at

Chalone for more than twenty years. The Chalone Pinot Noir, at its best, displays an unmistakable *goût de terroir*. The Reserves often have that extra bit of concentration that signifies a great wine.

Chambolle-Musigny Les Amoureuses, Domaine Comte Georges de Vogüé
Chambolle is a famous winemaking village in the Côte de Nuits a district of Burgundy's Côte d'Or. As often happens in Burgundy, its name is joined to that of its best-known vineyard, Musigny. Among the village's most celebrated vineyards — almost all making red wine — is Les Amoureuses, a *premier cru,* just below the *premier cru* Musigny. But it is an entirely different wine; less powerful, perhaps, and less structured, but in good years more elegant, more delicate, with a unique, spicy bouquet. Roumier and Clair-Daü produce beautiful Les Amoureuses, but the de Vogüé version can be incomparable. De Vogüé also produces a small quantity of white Musigny that is very rare and consequently overpriced.

Chambourcin
A successful and relatively recent French hybrid, the Chambourcin is planted in the Loire-Atlantique and in the United States. The vine is robust and prolific, and it makes well-colored, well-flavored red wines.

Chambrer
French term meaning to bring a red wine to the right temperature for drinking. This used to be room temperature, but today central heating often puts current room temperatures above the ideal.

Didier Champalou, Vouvray
Champalou is a rising star of Vouvray, a gifted young winemaker who created a domain at Le Portail from several smaller ones in 1985. The Champalou style emphasizes purity of fruit and elegance; there is nothing cloying about his wines. The 1990 vintage was a great success here, Champalou's *deuxième cuvée* a rich full wine of great persistence of flavor yet of exceptional finesse. A 1989 *moulleux* has the unctuous character of that year but it has excellent acidity too. Champalou also makes a fine Vouvray *mousseux*.

Chancellor
A hybrid vine (Seibel 7053) that formerly was widely planted, but is now outlawed in France. It is well established in the eastern United States and makes a bland if fruity red wine. It also plays a part in Port-style wines.

Chapoutier, Tain l'Hermitage
A leading northern Rhône *négociant* and grower with important holdings in Hermitage, the quality of its wines from Côte Rôtie, Hermitage, Crozes-Hermitage and St. Joseph have always been sound.

Chaptalization
The addition of sugar to grape juice before fermentation, so as to increase a wine's alcoholic strength. (Named after Napoleon's minister of agriculture, Auguste Chaptal.) Fermentation converts sugar to alcohol; adding sugar improves wine from not fully ripe grapes. The use of sugar is normally regulated by a country's wine laws. In France it is strictly regulated and not permitted in all areas; it is forbidden in Italy, where concentrated must is used, and is permitted only for some Q.b.A. wines in Germany.

Charbaut, Champagne
Epernay family Champagne firm established in 1948 by André Charbaut. Annual production is now 140,000 cases with an important percentage sold as own-label to supermarkets and merchants. It owns 56 hectares/138 acres of vineyard at Mareuil-sur-Ay.

Charbono

This red variety is the rarely found French Charbonneau and is planted in very limited quantities in California, where it makes a pleasant enough rustic red wine.

Chardonnay

Chardonnay is the fashionable white grape variety of the moment, for like its red counterpart, Cabernet Sauvignon, it has adapted to conditions all over the world, with hardly a wine-producing country that does not have some Chardonnay somewhere in its vineyards. It is a vigorous variety and very easy to grow, with good resistance to low winter temperatures. Its early budbreak makes it susceptible to spring frosts, but it also ripens early with a short growing season, which makes it suitable for cooler climates. For the winemaker it allows enormous versatility, responding well both to barrel fermentation and aging as well as to vinification in stainless-steel vats.

A village in the Mâconnais may have given Chardonnay its name. It is Chardonnay that makes white Burgundy, one of the great white wines of the world, with the most exciting examples to be found among the fine wines of the Côte de Beaune, in Corton-Charlemagne, Meursault, Puligny-Montrachet and so on. Chablis produces rather more steely wines, while those of the Côte Chalonnaise are not quite as fine, and those of the Mâconnais are softer. Chardonnay is a vital ingredient of Champagne and in a *blanc de blancs* Champagne is the only grape variety. It is grown elsewhere in eastern France, in the Jura, Bugey and Savoie, in the Ardèche and with growing success for *vin de pays* in the Midi. There is a little in Provence and in Corsica, and also in Haut-Poitou in western France.

Across the Alps, it features in the D.O.C.s of northeastern Italy and in numerous *vini da tavola* all over the country, notably in the Predicato del Muschio wines of Tuscany. In Spain it has been planted by Jean Léon and Miguel Torres among others and also in eastern Europe, especially in Bulgaria.

Almost all of the forty-three grape-growing states of North America produce Chardonnay, but there is little doubt that the most exciting examples come from California, where they aspire to emulate fine white Burgundy. The cooler regions of Australia, such as Victoria's Yarra Valley and Mount Barker in Western Australia, as well as Tasmania produce wines with good varietal character. New Zealand too is now making world-class Chardonnay. Interest in Chardonnay is growing in both Chile and Argentina. Even China, Canada and England have Chardonnay.

Charm

Imprecise term used to describe a harmonious wine that is attractive to drink.

Charmat process

A cheap way of producing sparkling wine by carrying out the second fermentation in a large, sealed tank instead of in individual bottles. Inevitably the results are not as good as bottle fermentation; bubbles are noticeably less fine and less persistent. The process is known as *cuve close* in France. Almost all German Sekt is made this way, as well as most Italian sparkling wines.

Domaine de la Charmoise, Touraine

One of the most easterly of Touraine domains, this is on the edge of the Sologne, best known for its flat, sandy land, its lakes and its hunting. Unusually for Touraine, the 50 hectare/124 acre Loire estate grows only Sauvignon and Gamay. The vines are trained high, and Henry Marionnet is continually experimenting with vinification techniques, trying to produce as natural a product as possible. The Gamay, made by *macération carbonique*, is elegantly fruity while the Sauvignon has weight without the excessive vegetal aromas of some Touraine Sauvignons. His special late picked Cuvée M is particularly impressive.

Fernand Charvet, Chénas

Fernand Charvet is the mayor of Chénas in Beaujolais, and his wine is among the finest and most naturally made of that commune with round, frank fruit and a lovely silky texture. Charvet also produces fine Moulin-à-Vent. His 1989s are splendid wines in an oustanding year, the extra richness perfectly balanced with good acidity.

Château Chasse-Spleen, Moulis

For many years the leading growth of Moulis, and in 1932 one of only six in the entire Médoc to be dignified as *exceptionnel* in the classification of the *crus bourgeois,* this Bordeaux property changed hands in 1976. Since that date, under the enlightened management of Bernadette Villars, there has been heavy investment in new equipment; experimentation with oak of different types and ages, and its use in differing proportions; even the computerization of certain aspects of vineyard management. The alliance of modern thinking and traditional methods, egg fining rather than filtration, for example, and minutely scrupulous winemaking, results in wine of strong individuality, with a pronounced bouquet, deep color, richness and breed. Recent vintages amply confirm Chasse-Spleen's preeminence in its district; with 1976, 1978, 1979 and 1980 all very fine, 1981 exceptional; 1983 powerful, slower to develop, 1985 and 1986 both rich and concentrated, promising much for the future.

Chasselas

Chasselas is of viticultural significance in Switzerland, where it is known as Fendant in the Valais, Dorin in the Vaud and Perlan around Geneva. On the other side of Lake Geneva in Savoie, it makes Crépy and features in a handful of *crus* of Vin de Savoie, such as Ripaille. In Germany it is cultivated almost exclusively in Baden. The taste is soft and lightly fruity, but fairly neutral. More used to be grown in France, and it is still grown especially in Alsace and for Pouilly-sur-Loire.

Gérard Chave, Mauves

To many people, Gérard Chave is Hermitage's best grower. He is certainly the sort of *vigneron* that one does not forget. A strikingly handsome man, with that serenity of demeanor that one often observes in the greatest winemakers, Chave is the living embodiment of the richness of the French provincial way of life. His family boasts a remarkable winegrowing tradition in the Rhône, having owned vineyards in Hermitage since 1481. Wine is a consuming passion, but Chave is also a considerable gourmet, a lover of dogs and good conversation, and is traditionally-minded and contemplative by nature.

Chave's Hermitage wines are extremely rich and well-balanced with tremendous depth of flavor, and they live very long, distinguished lives. Fortunately Chave keeps a remarkable cellar of older vintages. The 1961 still shows extraordinary vigor, flavor and aftertaste and, if well cellared, will live until the year 2020. The 1978 is a superbly constituted wine, an amalgam of rich, deep fruit and gloriously ripe tannins. For current drinking throughout the nineties, the unsung 1980 is a delicious bottle, aromatic with a lovely clear expression of mature Syrah fruit. The 1986 is a very underrated wine, which is likely to develop extremely well in bottle until 1998. The 1989 is spectacular; velvety with an animal character and perfect balance, it is the sort of ripe vintage that will taste good for many years to come.

Chelois

A hybrid (Seibel 10-878) formerly planted in France, but now found mainly in the eastern United States. It endures cool conditions, ripens early, and makes a satisfactory red wine that can benefit from aging.

Chenin Blanc

Chenin Blanc is a remarkably versatile white grape, ranging in taste from the searingly acidic to the lusciously sweet, with every shade of flavor in between. It can be still, *pétillant* or sparkling, and can be drunk when very young or will age for many years. It originates in Anjou, where it is also known as Pineau de la Loire, and is responsible for all the fine white wines of the Loire, from dry grassy Savennières to rich, honeyed Bonnezeaux and Quarts de Chaume, when it is affected by noble rot. Less exciting are basic Anjou and Saumur Blanc.

Outside the Loire Valley it is most successful as Steen, a dry white wine from South Africa, where it is also grown for dessert wine, notably Nederberg's Edelkeur. In California it produces soft fruity table wine, sometimes with a little residual sugar, and has a similar lack of prestige in Australia and New Zealand. Undoubtedly Chenin Blanc is at its best in a mature dessert wine, for it never loses the underlying acidity that ensures it immense longevity.

Château de Chenonceau, Touraine

Thomas Bohier, the builder of the beautiful château across the Cher River in the Loire, planted Chenin Blanc here at the beginning of the sixteenth century. Modern winemaking equipment has been cleverly incorporated into the old buildings. This is one of the best estates in the Touraine appellation, making fine still and sparkling Chenin, as well as red wine.

Bernard Chéreau-Carré, Château de Chasseloir, Muscadet

Proprietor of 120 hectares/296 acres of vines around the commune of St. Fiacre and a merchant selling a range of wines from the Loire. The various estate-bottled Muscadets are well made, and the top *cuvées* age well. Of particular interest are Comte de Loup de Chasseloir, made from vines of up to a hundred years old, and Château Coing de Saint-Fiacre. Some skin contact is used, and there is also a *cuvée* aged in new oak.

Château Cheval Blanc, St. Emilion

By tradition as well as official classification, Cheval Blanc has always occupied with Château Ausone a privileged position within the St. Emilion district of Bordeaux. Their soils, though, are different, as are the proportions of grape varieties used. Cheval Blanc has a tiny percentage of Malbec, a *cépage* disdained by Ausone. Again, while Ausone's fortunes endured a long decline, Cheval Blanc has always retained its eminence.

This Bordeaux property is far to the northwest of St. Emilion, and stands on the fringe of Pomerol, with gravel predominating in its soil. It has not changed hands other than by inheritance since its creation in the 1830s.

The wine of Cheval Blanc is deeply colored, perfumed, rich and intense without a trace of coarseness, full and vigorous. A part of the vineyard formerly belonged to Figeac, and when, inevitably, the two are compared it is almost invariably to the advantage of Cheval Blanc with its characteristically greater substance. In an observation made more than thirty years ago it was noted that, "in a good year, indeed, Cheval Blanc is an incomparable wine, and good vintages fall frequently." Their longevity too is remarkable. In relatively recent times the wines made during the administration of Jacques Hébrard have benefited from a new *cuvier* and modernized *chai* and have shown extraordinary distinction in such years as 1975, 1978, 1982, 1983, 1985, 1986, 1987 and 1988.

Domaine de Chevalier, Graves

A small Bordeaux property isolated by woodland to the southwest of Léognan, Domaine de Chevalier for many years now has produced red and white wines of consistent excellence, invariably in either color among the very best of the appellation. The red wine predominates, with 15 hectares/37 acres planted with Cabernet Sauvignon, Merlot and Cabernet Franc, as against just 3 hectares/7 acres under Sauvignon and Sémillon vines. Traditionally the red shows great delicacy and a subtly lighter style than many Graves of comparable quality, but latterly richer, more tannic and more substantial wines have been made. Legendary successes of the first half of the century may perhaps be disregarded; since 1945, when the vineyard was badly damaged by frost, there have been many notable vintages — 1953, 1955, 1959, 1961, 1962, 1964 and 1966 — more recently 1978, 1980, 1981, 1982, 1983, 1985 and 1986, some of them needing time to develop. The white Chevalier shows individuality, its richness and power balanced by finesse. With Laville Haut-Brion it is consistently among the best of the white Graves. The wine is fermented in cask and aged for 18 months before it is bottled. It then needs several years to approach maturity. Of recent vintages, 1982, 1983, 1985 and 1986 stand out. Whether red or white, Domaine de Chevalier is always expensive; the inevitable consequence of its limited production and great reputation.

Chewy

Big and robust wine with plenty of extract.

Chlorosis

Vine disease caused by a lack of chlorophyll that makes the leaves turn yellow.

Chocolaty

The aroma and flavor of chocolate are sometimes found in the range of wines, usually fairly mature, such as Pinot Noir, Italian reds like Barolo and *vins doux naturels*, in particular Banyuls.

Chorey-lès-Beaune, Domaine Tollot-Beaut

A very old Burgundian domain by current standards — it has been estate bottling since the turn of the century — Tollot-Beaut is in Chorey-lès-Beaune, the only serious wine commune between Beaune and Dijon to be located on the east side of the highway. Tollot-Beaut has holdings in Corton-Charlemagne, Corton, Corton Les Bressandes and some of the better Beaune vineyards. But its Chorey-lès-Beaune is a delightful wine still to be found at reasonable prices. It presents one of the dwindling number of opportunities to purchase appellation Burgundy from a prominent shipper at an affordable price.

Le Cigare Volant, Bonny Doon Vineyard, Santa Cruz County

The odd name of this wine derives from an ordinance passed in the 1950s by the town council of Châteauneuf-du-Pape in France, banning the landing of flying saucers, or, as they called them, flying cigars (*cigare volante*). Randall Grahm, the maverick owner and winemaker, chose Le Cigare Volante as the name for his interpretation of the famous wine of Châteauneuf-du-Pape. It was the first — and still is — of the best examples of how well California can produce Rhône-style wines. Rich, but never coarse, it set a pattern for some of America's newest and most exciting wines. After all, California's climate is much closer to that of the Rhône Valley than it is to that of Bordeaux or Burgundy.

Ciliegiolo

A red grape native to Tuscany and still used there as a subordinate variety. It is grown elsewhere to the south, but is of decreasing consequence nowadays.

Paul Cinquin, Régnié

An excellent producer of Régnié in Beaujolais, Paul Cinquin makes a very vibrant wine full of primary fruit that is not masked by the firm, often aggressive acidity

259

found in many Régniés.

Cinsaut

Cinsaut, sometimes spelt Cinsault, is a red grape variety, planted widely in the Midi and usually blended with Carignan and Grenache in appellations like Coteaux du Languedoc, Corbières and countless *vins de pays*. It also grows in Provence, Corsica, features among the thirteen varieties of Châteauneuf-du-Pape and is found in North Africa. In South Africa it is occasionally produced as a varietal wine and is one of the parents of Pinotage.

Château Cissac, Haut-Médoc

Much has been going on in recent years at this considerable Bordeaux property, which the Vialard family has owned for more than a century. Cissac was classed as a *grand bourgeois* in 1966, and upgraded to *exceptionnel* in 1978. Investment in technical equipment has been accompanied by experimentation, changes in grape mix and methods of vinification, and corresponding changes in the style of the wines made. Modern Cissac tends to be dark, tannic, slow developing, with the ability to age and develop over fifteen years or more. Recent successes have been 1981, 1982, a reserved 1983, 1985 and a very substantial 1986.

Château Citran, Haut-Médoc

A Bordeaux property of historic reputation, Citran, like a good many other châteaux in the Médoc, was in a lamentable state at the end of the war. Happily it was bought and painstakingly restored by the Miailhe family, who kept it until 1986. In the later seventies and in the eighties there was a clear decline in quality, probably attributable to overproduction. The vineyard was trading on its past reputation. Citran's future is uncertain; but the wines of 1988 and 1989, made under the new Japanese ownership, show undeniable promise.

Citric acid

Acid present in citrus fruit like lemons, limes and oranges. Citric is often used as a tasting note for white wines with a refreshing tang.

Citrus

Tasting term for lemon or lime flavors found in white wines with refreshing acidity.

Clairette

A white grape widely established in southern France. It contributes to Clairette de Die, and makes Clairette de Bellegarde, from near Nîmes to the west, and Clairette du Languedoc, which is made in two distinct styles. The first is a dry wine; the second, higher in alcohol, is made from overripe grapes and must have the characteristic maderized taste known as *rancio*, a designation it bears on its labels. The limited production of white Bandol is based on the Clairette, and the variety is found also in Israel in the vineyards endowed by Baron Edmond de Rothschild.

Auguste Clape, Cornas

Unquestionably the greatest grower in Cornas, Clape makes one of the best red wines not only of the Rhône but of France as well. His essential achievement is to combine the elegance of Syrah aromas with extraordinary power and persistence on the palate. Recent fine vintages include a ripe, voluptuous 1985, a tannic, brooding but inherently excellent 1986 and a round yet fine and very ripe 1989.

Claret

From the phrase *vin claret* ("clear wine"), this word is used in Great Britain to indicate red Bordeaux. Elsewhere, it is used for any red table wine.

Clarete

Spanish term for any wine that is light in color and body.

Classico

Italian term to denote core winegrowing zones within a particular area, like Orvieto or Soave. Thus often denotes the area where the best wines are produced. Chianti Classico is a special case as there are other designated quality zones, such as Chianti Putto.

Classification of 1855

Long-lived classification of the top estates of the Médoc into five categories, carried out for the Great Exhibition of 1855 in Paris. It remains unchanged today apart from the promotion of Mouton-Rothschild to *premier cru* status in 1973.

Michael Clavien Chardonnay, Valais

This Swiss wine from the Valais is matured in new oak and has the flavour to prove it. It is a gentle wine, with relatively low acidity, without being flabby. It has good Chardonnay character but is less heavy than many California examples.

Clean

Description applied to wine, often white, that is well made with clear flavors and no faults.

Château Clerc-Milon, Pauillac

Classed as a fifth growth in 1855, this Bordeaux property has belonged to the interests of the late Baron Philippe de Rothschild since 1970. After the purchase, a great deal of work was carried out in the vineyard, and the results of the reconstitution and replanting became clearly perceptible with the wine of 1981. Its deep color, fruit and harmony set the pattern for the yet more impressive successes of 1985, 1986, 1987 and 1988. The wines are likely to continue to improve.

Domenico Clerico, Barolo

At the head of his own 7 hectare/17 acre vineyard at Monforte d'Alba since 1976, Domenico Clerico is a rising star of Barolo, one of the leading wines of northern Italy. His wines are exceptionally elegant yet are faithful examples of the strength and nobility of the Nebbiolo grape. His 1986 Barolo Ciabot Mentin Ginestra combines superb aromas with great definition of flavor. Look for his 1988 Arte, a wine made from Nebbiolo grapes grown outside the Barolo zone and aged in new oak *barriques*. His lithe, graceful 1990 Dolcetto is full of primary fruit and is an ideal, less costly introduction to the wines of Alba.

Climat

This French word means "climate', but in reference to wine, particularly Burgundy, it means a named individual vineyard.

Climate

One of the crucial factors in determining the quality and style of a wine. Vines produce the finest wine where they have to struggle; regions where the weather gives the vines an easy ride year after year may produce good, reliable, clean wine, but are unlikely to reach the pinnacle of quality.

Warm, dry summers and cool, wet winters are the ideal; too much rain in the summer can cause rot. Enough sunshine is vital if the grapes are to ripen, but too much heat can result in a baked taste in the wine. In cooler areas, a long growing season is important, and a cold spring or a wet autumn may determine the quality of a vintage. Hail and wind are other problems: localized, short hailstorms are dreaded in most wine regions and can damage the wood of the vine as well as wiping out the crop. Wind can also do damage, and in parts of the world subject to strong winds, like the south of France, training systems and windbreaks have been developed to combat this. Frost late in the year may wipe out a large part of a crop.

Château Climens, Barsac

With Château Coutet, this is one of the two great wines of Barsac. This *premier cru* is often regarded as second only to Yquem among the wines of the Sauternes and Barsac. Typically it is less rich and powerful than Yquem, but Climens has astonishing flavor and elegance, more lusciousness than its fellow Barsacs, and a particularly brilliant golden color. The wine is perfectly harmonious, and so capable of very long life. This Bordeaux vineyard occupies a prime site in the best part of the southern district, and its red marl and gravel over a calcareous base is planted almost exclusively with Sémillon. The wine is fermented in cask and matured for twenty-four months before it is bottled.

Since 1971 Climens has belonged to Lucien Lurton of Doisy Dubroca, Brane Cantenac and other estates in the Bordelais. Outstanding under his regime have been 1971, 1975, 1976, 1978, 1980 and 1981. The 1983 Climens was among the greatest wines of a great vintage, while 1985, 1986, 1988 and 1989 were all exceptional in a decade of astonishing achievement. Climens has always been noted for its consistent excellence, and its successes have been many. During the past half-century there have been extraordinary years, such as 1943, 1947, 1949, 1952, 1955, 1961, 1962 and 1970.

Château Clinet, Pomerol

Vines have been grown here for more than two hundred years, and the Audy family has owned this Bordeaux vineyard for almost a century, but Clinet's history has been unremarkable in recent decades. Serious efforts to improve the quality of the wine began in the later seventies, with changes in the pattern of planting, the proportion of Merlot being increased significantly at the expense of the two Cabernets. In the mid-eighties much more rigorous standards of winemaking were imposed, and a policy of maturing the wine in a varying proportion of new oak was introduced, along with the decision to downgrade to the second wine, Domaine Ducasse, any *cuves* that might be judged less than outstanding. The 1986 vintage showed real distinction, a promise that was confirmed by the grace and quality of the 1987.

Clone

A vine or group of vines propagated asexually from a single parent vine. Clones are bred to have specific characteristics, such as resistance to rot or the ability to produce high yields. Clonal selection can be used to produce greater standardization in the vineyard and thus the bottle; using a variety of clones in a vineyard can, conversely, be used to increase complexity in a wine. There are good and bad clones, and growers are becoming more selective.

Clos

Vineyard that is enclosed, usually by a wall. Well-known examples include Clos de Vougeot (Burgundy) and Clos Cristal (Saumur–Champigny).

Cloudy

A fault in wine, suggesting that it has not been racked or fined sufficiently or that it has started to referment. Changes in temperature can also cause temporary cloudiness.

Cloudy Bay Sauvignon Blanc, Marlborough

New Zealand's cult wine in both export and domestic markets. Started by Australian entrepreneur David Hohnen, Cloudy Bay is now controlled by the Champagne house Veuve Clicquot, although Hohnen remains managing director. Twenty percent Semillon and a touch of barrel fermentation add complexity and style to this sensationally rich wine. The first Cloudy Bay vintage was in 1985; the best since then was 1991.

Cochylis

A moth, the larvae of which eat grapes.

Cococciola

A white variety, traditional to the Abruzzi in central Adriatic Italy. The grape is in decline, but still forms a part of the dull D.O.C. Trebbiano d'Abruzzo wines.

Coda di Volpe

The Foxtail of the elder Pliny and today still the principal grape of the D.O.C. white wines of Vesuvio and Lacryma Christi del Vesuvio. In percentage terms it makes a modest contribution to the more distinguished Greco di Tufo and Fiano di Avellino. A vine of the same name, but seemingly of different origin, is found in the Colli Piacentini, where it makes the sweet Vin Santo di Vigoleno.

Cogno-Marcarini, Barolo

In Piedmont, Italy, Elvio Cogno produces good traditional Barolo, with bottlings of separate parcels of Brunate, La Serra and Canun. The Brunate is usually the fullest and most structured, La Serra is softer and more aromatic. His 1982s are approaching maturity. Cogno also makes the Dolcetto Boschi de Berri from old pre-phylloxera vines. A visit to his picturesque low-ceilinged cellar in La Morra is always a pleasure as Cogno is an engaging man and his brother's excellent restaurant is close at hand.

Cold or cool fermentation

The importance of fermenting white wines at a low temperature has only recently been fully appreciated, and it is even more recent that the necessary cooling equipment has been widely available. Cool fermentation preserves freshness, flavors and aromas. Most white wine is fermented around 18°C/64°F. Fermentation at lower temperatures than this tends to produce uniform wines; some growers are now trying 21° to 22°C/70° to 72°F.

Cold Stabilization

Chilling wine in order to inhibit bacterial infection and spoilage, stop fermentation and precipitate tartrates.

Coldstream Hills, Coldstream, Victoria

James Halliday, a Melbourne lawyer and Australia's leading wine writer, bought this property in 1985 and planted a 15 hectare/37 acre vineyard on hillside sites of excellent aspect. The new winery was completed in 1988. Halliday specializes in Pinot Noir and Chardonnay, but he also grows Cabernet Sauvignon, Cabernet Franc and Merlot.

Halliday relished the challenge of making fine Pinot Noir, the most difficult wine in the world to produce consistently well. He has been very successful, winning more awards for this variety in 1988 and 1989 than any other Australian winemaker. The Four Vineyards site seems especially suitable for both Pinot Noir and Chardonnay. In the 1988 vintage, the Pinot Noir was impressive for its clear fruit and lingering persistence of varietal flavors, while the Chardonnay was elegant, firm and equally long. Halliday's Cabernet Sauvignons are excellently balanced with a touch of Cabernet Franc and Merlot.

Colheita

The Portuguese term for vintage or harvest.

Collage

See Fining.

Collard Brothers Hawke's Bay Chardonnay, Henderson

Collards is a small Auckland-based winery that has won great acclaim for its four Chardonnays from each of New Zealand's major wine regions: Auckland, Gisborne, Hawke's Bay and Marlborough. Collards has steadfastly produced wines that emphasize fruit flavor rather than oak, yeast or malolactic character. It has led other New Zealand winemakers away from clumsy, oaky styles to

wines of elegance and finesse. The lush, ripe fruit flavors of this Hawke's Bay wine are an eloquent example of the Collard's style.

André Collonge, Fleurie
A traditionally-minded Beaujolais grower André Collonge makes powerfully constituted Fleurie and Beaujolais-Villages of real staying power capable of aging well for up to three years. He formerly supplied his wines in cask to the Beaune négociant Louis Latour.

Colombard
In France Colombard is grown extensively in the departments of the Charente and the Gers for distillation into Cognac and Armagnac. However, with the fall in the consumption of spirits, it is increasingly made into fragrant, dry white wine, notably as Vin de Pays des Côtes de Gascogne and Vin de Pays Charentais. In California it has been extensively planted for everyday jug wine and enjoys a similar appeal in South Africa.

Columbia Chardonnay, Sagemoor Vineyards, Columbia Valley
This is a single-vineyard wine from Washington State that has quietly begun to make a name for itself, particularly in white wine. The Columbia Valley, defined by the Columbia River in the south-central part of the state, is known for lighter Chardonnays with good flavors, and that is just what this wine turns out to be. It has considerable intensity; so much so that one wonders why, so much praise is lavished on over-blown California Chardonnays that are too heavy in body and too high in alcohol. This wine would go well with just about any light meat or shellfish, but could easily stand on its own as a pleasant sipping wine.

Commune
France's smallest administrative unit, a commune consists of a village and its surrounding land. Each commune normally has its own elected mayor.

Concord
A heavy-cropping North American vine, a nineteenth, century derivative of *Vitis labrusca*. It produces excellent grapes and is still widely planted despite the pronouncedly "foxy" character of the dull wines made from them and the increasing prevalence of superior Franco-American hybrids.

Confrérie
Literally an association of colleagues. Used by some cooperatives in France, but its main use is for regional wine associations, such as the Jurade de St. Emilion or Confrérie du Franc Pineau, both set up to promote the wines and to serve as an opportunity to enjoy good food, drink and company.

Château La Conseillante, Pomerol
This was one of relatively few estates in Pomerol to emerge in the first half of the eighteenth century. Since 1871, this Bordeaux estate has belonged to the Nicolas family, and the present generation is dedicated to the improvement of its property and the retention of its habitual place among the three or four best wines of the appellation. Stainless-steel vats and the use of new oak have been adopted in recent years, and meticulous standards are maintained in vineyard and *cuvier*.

On the eastern fringe of the plateau, adjoining St. Emilion, the estate incorporates land acquired from Figeac early in the last century. The soil is gravel with an element of clay and carries a high proportion of Cabernet Franc as well as 10 percent Malbec.

The wines are individual in style, concentrated, rich and complex, and there have been many successful vintages during the past thirty years. Notable among them are the wines of 1961, 1962, 1964, 1966, 1970, 1973, 1978 and 1979.

A good wine in the difficult year of 1980 preceded the outstanding 1981, 1982 and 1985, the first vintage made with 100 percent new wood, and a rich and tannic 1986.

Consorzio
In Italy, voluntary consortium of regional growers to set minimum standards and to promote their wines. Most were set up before the D.O.C. legislation in order to bring such legislation about. Chianti Classico is the most famous.

Conte Tasca d'Almerita, Sicily
Giuseppe Tasca d'Almerita cultivates nearly 300 hectares/741 acres of vines on his historic Regaleali estate. His best-known white, Nozze d'Oro, is a blend of Sauvignon Blanc and Inzolia. This wine has plenty of substance but remains fresh and clean. His reds are very full flavored wines; the 1982 Rosso del Conte is still very tannic and will age for another five years.

Conte Zandotti — Tenimento, San Paolo
Enrico Massimo Zandotti makes exemplary dry Frascati *Superiore* from a 25 hectare/62 acre vineyard attached to his villa at San Paolo on the outskirts of Rome.

Aldo Conterno, Barolo
One of the most respected producers in the Langhe region of Piedmont, Aldo Conterno combines receptiveness to modern advances in winemaking with a real attachment to the best of tradition. His estate now extends to 25 hectares/62 acres of which 9 hectares/22 acres are planted in superb Barolo sites, notably the Bussia vineyard near Monforte d'Alba. His finest *crus* are Vigna Cicala and Vigna Colonella. In great years, the best vats of these *crus* form the base of a blend for his greatest wine, Barolo Gran Bussia. The 1985 Gran Bussia is a magnificent wine with a capacity to age for twenty, thirty, even forty years.

Aldo Conterno also makes excellent Barbera Tre Pile, and a fine *barrique*-aged *vino da tavola* called Il Favot, which is a blend of Barbera and Nebbiolo. Also worth seeking out is his Freisa La Bussianella, a delicious and deep fruity red wine with a slight sparkle.

Giovanni Conterno, Barolo
Giovanni Conterno, brother of Aldo, is a fierce defender of uncompromisingly traditional Barolo. But he is too intelligent a winemaker not to take advantage of such modern advances as temperature-controlled vinification. His monumental 1982 Barolo Monfortino was made in this way and shows every sign of being as great as the outstanding 1971. Giovanni's son Roberto is now closely involved in the winemaking.

Contino, Rioja
This single-vineyard Rioja by the Ebro River is owned by the directors of C.V.N.E. The wine is made from 70 percent Tempranillo, the balance coming from Viura, Garnacha, Mazuelo and Graciano grapes. Quality is outstanding, the style of the wine impressively combining

deep color, delicacy of aroma and mouthfilling generosity of flavor. Since the wine was first launched in the 1970s, there has been a long run of successful vintages: 1975, 1978, 1980 (underrated), 1981, 1982 (superb) and 1985.

Cooperage

The workshop where a cooper makes wooden barrels. Can also refer to the total storage capacity of a winery; an echo of the days when all wine was stored in wood. After a period of decline coopers are again in great demand owing to the worldwide fashion for aging wine in new oak barrels.

Cooperative

A group of growers banding together to produce and market their wines on a cooperative basis. (*Coopérative* in French, *cantina sociale* in Italian, *Winzergenossenschaft* in German.) Cooperatives are especially popular in southern France and many areas of Germany such as Baden. About 50 percent of all France's wines is produced by cooperatives. Just as with independent growers, standards vary from top quality to the barely drinkable. The oldest wine cooperative in the world is the Mayschoss-Altenahr in Germany's Ahr Valley, that country's most northerly vine areas. It was founded in 1860.

Copper sulfate

Widely used vineyard spray against fungal diseases.

Corbans Noble Rhine Riesling, Henderson

New Zealand is beginning to produce some very exciting botrytis affected dessert wines. The dry ripening conditions in Marlborough make the region an obvious choice for botrytis styles, for which Riesling is the most favored grape variety. This tight and stylish wine has enough botrytis influence to give lusciousness and intensity without dominating the varietal character.

Cordon

The trellis system for training vines along wires. *Guyot* is the best-known pruning system using wires.

Cordorníu, Spain

In the 1870s, José Raventos brought Champagne-method sparkling wine to his hometown of San Sadurní de Noya in Catalonia. Cava was born and Cordorníu, Raventos' firm, has since become one of the biggest sparkling-wine producers in the world. The Chardonnay-based Anna de Cordorníu is excellent. Other well-known *cuvées* include the Gran Cordorníu Brut, Rosé Brut and Grand Crémant.

Corked wine

Wine that has been spoilt by a faulty cork. The fault lies either in a diseased or poor quality cork or in the chemical solution used to prepare the cork. The wine may appear lifeless, often with a greyish tinge, and will smell and taste musty. Poor corks, the bane of winemaker and drinker alike, appear to be more common, probably because of the huge increase in demand. Corkiness in wine has nothing to do with harmless fragments of cork in a glass of wine. Also called corky.

Cortese

A vine long established in Piedmont, where it flourishes on clay and volcanic soil in the hills around Gavi and enjoys a climate tempered by the Mediterranean. Traditionally the grape was grown for the *spumante* wines of Asti, but since the war, and especially in the past twenty-five years, its role has been transformed. The Cortese is now the source of modish white wine that is scented, acidic, of extreme dryness, generally lacking in fruit and substance and usually overpriced. The Cortese still makes sparkling wines; latterly the best of these have been produced by the *méthode champenoise*.

Corton-Charlemagne, Louis Latour

If there is one producer of this superb *grand cru* wine who is *primus inter pares* it is Louis Latour. Corton-Charlemagne is certainly, along with le Montrachet and some Bâtard-Montrachet, the finest of all white Burgundies. For intensity and aging potential, it often surpasses them. It comes from a sun-drenched vineyard on the slope of the Corton hill where alcohol levels of 13.5 and 14 percent are not uncommon. The tragedy of Corton-Charlemagne is not that it costs so much, which it does, but that it is invariably drunk too young. Latour points this out vividly by opening twenty-year-old bottles for guests. They display a range of flavors and an unmatchable bouquet that few other white Burgundies will ever emulate.

Corton Clos du Roi, Domaine Daniel Senard

Philippe Senard, the fourth generation of his family to make wine at Aloxe-Corton in Burgundy, produces fewer than 4,000 bottles of Corton Clos du Roi each year but, along with his Clos des Meix, it is consistently one of his best. Because they are not over-oaked, Senard Cortons do not appear to be massive wines. But they are closed in and tannic when young and seem to add mass as they age in the bottle. They often need three to five years to come around. When they do, they are voluptuous and harmonious. A little more subtle than other Cortons, perhaps, but beautiful wines.

Corvina

A red-wine variety native to the Verona region of the Veneto and the dominant force in the blends that make Bardolino and Valpolicella as well as rosé wines. In good years selected Corvina semi-dried grapes (*see* Passito), are blended in careful proportion with Molinara and Rondinella to make the sweet Recioto della Valpolicella and the powerful, complex Amarone. The Corvina, susceptible to noble rot, gives richness, aroma and flavor to the wine, while the Rondinella contributes color and tannin.

Château Cos d'Estournel, St. Estèphe

The pagodas of the splendid *chai* of this celebrated second growth are a prominent landmark in the Médoc, and no less familiar from the label. This very considerable Bordeaux property takes its name from that Monsieur d'Estournel who bought back the estate in 1821, his family having sold it in the year of the comet, enlarged the vineyard to something like its present 54 hectares/133 acres, and built the famous *chai*. A century later it was bought by Fernand Ginestet of the well-known *négociant* family, to whose descendants it still belongs.

In its great vintages, and they are many, Cos d'Estournel is perhaps the best of all its appellation; since the Second World War there have been memorable wines in 1947, 1948, 1952, 1953, 1955, 1959, 1961, 1962, 1966 and 1967. Under Bruno Prats, himself a Ginestet on his mother's side, these successes have continued with the 1979, and then the splendid decade of the eighties, with 1982, 1983, 1985, 1986, 1987 and 1988 all outstanding.

The vineyard is notable for the high proportion of Merlot, which makes an obvious contribution to the color, richness, fruit and substance of the wine. Château de Marbuzet is the second wine of Cos, and a vineyard under its own name, while Maître d'Estournel is a wine of more modest appellation.

Château Cos Labory, St. Estèphe

At the time of the 1855 classification this Cos was in the same, incidentally British, ownership as the larger and better known Cos d'Estournel. It may have been this happy chance that determined fifth-growth status for a Bordeaux property that for very many years has made wines unworthy of that assessment and uncharacteristic of their appellation. Rich and concentrated wines were

made in 1986, 1988 and 1989, and it may be that following its feeble showing earlier in a decade successful almost everywhere else in the Médoc, the Audoy family is making serious efforts to improve the standing of their estate.

Cosecha
The Spanish term for vintage or harvest.

Cossart Gordon 5 Year Old Reserve Bual, Madeira
Now part of the Madeira Wine Association, Cossart Gordon, founded in 1745, has long been famous for its reserves of old wines. The 5 Year Old Bual is a rich and powerful wine, sweeter than a Sercial, with a velvety texture. Its cask aging is reflected in its delicate nuttiness and soft nuances of fruit.

Cossart Gordon 10 Year Old Reserve Verdelho, Madeira
Of lovely amber gold color, this Madeira has a fragrance and finesse on the nose. Although fuller than a Sercial, its flavor combines delicate fruit with a refreshing tanginess. The finish is clean and dry with a long aftertaste. Traditionally served with soup.

Côte
Slope of a hill or ridge. Burgundy's Côte d'Or, running from Dijon to Santenay, is the most famous example.

Coteaux
Hillsides, often a series of hillsides or ridges, as in the Coteaux du Languedoc.

Coteaux du Rieu-Berlou, St. Chinian
This is one of the best and most far-sighted *caves coopératives* in France's Languedoc region. A detailed study of its members' land and the different soil types has been carried out recently. It was Georges Gardet, director of Berlou from 1965 until his death in 1990, who really made the cooperative's reputation. Wines of all colors, in a range of qualities, are made. The best wines are sold under the Domaine de Schisteil label, with the top reds spending time in *barrique*.

Coulure
When vine flowers fail to set. Often caused by cold weather during flowering.

Counoise
A long-established but always subordinate red grape of the southern Rhône and Languedoc-Roussillon. It is of decreasing consequence nowadays as efforts are made to improve the blends of which traditionally it has been a part.

Courbu
A variety that with the Gros and Petit Manseng makes the fine and underrated wines of Jurançon in southwest France. It is found also elsewhere in the Pyrenean region.

Court noué
See Infectious degeneration.

Courtier
In France, a wine broker whose role is to find buyers for a grower's wine. Can act as an intermediary between growers and *négociants*. It is unusual for a *courtier* to hold stocks.

Château Coutet, Barsac
With Château Climens, Coutet is one of the two outstanding *crus* of Barsac has a similar record of consistent excellence. The wines differ. One expert observed: "generally Climens is bigger, rounder, fleshier, inclining more to lusciousness; Coutet is a smooth wine, fruitier, with more finesse, greater delicacy of flavor and fragrance." These are views expressed more than thirty

years ago, but in the main they still hold true.

A Bordeaux property much bigger than Climens, Coutet occupies a similar site in the southern part of Barsac, and it carries a larger proportion of Sauvignon. Since 1977 the vineyard has belonged to Monsieur Baly, but its restoration after the war was the work of the Rolland-Guy family. Following 1943, the best wartime vintage, under their management came the great successes of 1947, 1949, better than at Climens, and 1950, perhaps the preeminent wine of a difficult year; 1955, 1959 and 1962 made excellent wines, with 1971, 1975 and especially 1976 all outstanding. Under the present owner, several relatively lean years preceded an exceptionally rich and complex 1983, with further successes in 1988, and a 1989 that shows enormous promise for the future. The château also makes a pleasant dry white wine, and in certain vintages a tiny quantity of the dramatically rich, concentrated and unctuous Cuvée Madame from its oldest vines. In commercial terms this wine must be regarded as an extreme rarity.

Creamy
Term used to describe round, fat flavors on the palate from a range of white wines. Often used for good sparkling wines.

Crémant
High-quality French sparkling wine (with *appellation contrôlée*) made in a number of French regions. Best-known are those from Alsace, Burgundy (Bourgogne), Limoux and the Loire. Also means a Champagne made slightly less sparkling than usual.

Crianza
Spanish term for aging — literally, "nursing." Normally a *crianza* will have been aged for two years, often with a period in barrel.

Criolla
See Pais.

Crisp
Termed used to describe a cidic young white wine.

Croatina
A red-wine grape widely planted in northern Italy. The Croatina makes pleasant wines of little definition and is chiefly valuable for blending. In the Oltrepò Pavese of southern Lombardy the grape, there called Bonarda, combines with Barbera, Ughetta and Uva Rara, the true Bonarda Novarese, to produce excellent red wines; it also makes varietals. In the Colli di Parma and Colli Piacentini of Emilia the Croatina contributes to the blends of the D.O.C. wines of the same names, while in Piedmont, in the hills of Novara and Vercelli, the grape again is blended with Nebbiolo and Bonarda.

Château La Croix de Gay, Pomerol
For five generations this Bordeaux property has belonged to the Ardurat-Raynaud family, who can trace their origins in Pomerol as far back as 1477. The vineyard is made up of a number of small detached parcels, so that its soil, predominantly gravel, contains both sand and clay. During the eighties, under the direction of Professor Ribéreau-Gayon, significant efforts were made to improve the quality of the wine. A new horizontal press was put in, and both fermentations and *assemblages* were minutely controlled. Aging now takes place in wood, the proportion of new oak varying with the nature of the year, and casks and wine benefit from storage underground. Corresponding changes in the wine have been apparent, with additional richness, concentration and substance distinguishing the 1985, 1986, 1987 and 1988. These recent vintages should show to advantage within about five years of their bottling.

Brian Croser, Petaluma

Intellectual and man of action, Brian Croser is a seminal force in the modern Australian wine industry. Brilliant winemaker, influential consultant, formidable administrator, tireless international ambassador, Croser has done much for the good name of Australian wine in recent years; the only man who can challenge Croser's track record is Len Evans, his mentor, friend and collaborator.

Still in his early forties, Croser's rise to the top of his profession has been meteoric. Born and raised in South Australia, he gained a degree in Agricultural Science at Adelaide University in 1969. The Thomas Hardy Company had financed his studies, and after a stint with them, Croser pursued postgraduate studies in enology at the University of California, Davis. Marked as a high flier, he soon became chief winemaker at Hardy. In 1976, he went to New South Wales to establish the much admired Riverina College of Advanced Education's course in Wine Science and Viticulture.

Returning to the Adelaide Hills in 1978, Brian Croser, with help from Len Evans and Peter Fox, established what is now the Petaluma Wine Complex with its vineyards at Clare, Coonawarra and the Adelaide Hills. A winery was built at Piccadilly in the Adelaide Hills.

From the beginning Petaluma produced outstanding Rhine Rieslings, but it is the developing style of the Chardonnays that vividly illustrates Croser's rigorous, self-questioning approach to winemaking. Over the years, his Chardonnays have become increasingly more elegant, subtle and complex, reaching their peak at five to seven years. Most of his rivals' wines show at their best much younger, but often lose their character and fruit just at a time when Petaluma Chardonnays begin to blossom. It is a measure of Croser's integrity that he has refused to make a more precocious style of wine that might gain him favorable press reviews or a string of show awards.

By the reckoning of most critics, Petaluma now makes Australia's finest sparkling wine, which is simply called Croser. He saw the great potential of the cool vineyards of the Piccadilly Hills as an ideal site in which to grow Chardonnay and Pinot Noir for quality sparkling-wine production. In 1985, he went into partnership with Bollinger, which leaves him and his team of winemakers to make 15,000 cases a year of exceptional *méthode champenoise* wines. The Bollinger investment has also resulted in a first-rate new range of wines from Petaluma under the Bridgewater Mill label. For quality and value, look out for the Bridgewater Mill Sauvignon Blanc, the vital gooseberryish flavors of which give the lie to the myth that Australia cannot make invigorating wines from this grape to rival those of New Zealand and the Loire.

Cru

French word meaning "growth"; usually used to refer to a vineyard worthy of individual note. Wines of superior quality may be called *grans crus* or *premiers crus*.

Cru bourgeois

Member of the Syndicat des Crus Bourgeois, a voluntary organization for Médoc properties just below *cru classé* status in Bordeaux. Quality is uneven; some are the equal of classed growths, some are well below.

Cru classé

French term for classed growth; a property that has been classified. The term's use is largely confined to Bordeaux, in particular the classifications of the Graves, Médoc, St. Emilion and Sauternes. It is also used in Provence, but has little meaning there.

Crushing

In the traditional method of making red wine, all grapes are crushed, their skins broken, before fermentation. For carbonic maceration grapes must be kept whole.

Crusius, Nahe

A fine family estate regarded in Germany as being among the best on the Nahe. There are 11.5 hectares/28 acres of vines, all excellently sited, and planted principally with Riesling. The winemaking is traditional, and the wines have tremendous character, with each vineyard imprinting itself on its wines. From the Felsenberg and Roseberg vineyards the wines have great delicacy, a quality which is attributed to the melaphyr soil found here. Rotenfels is firm and racy, Bastei pungent and Norheimer Kirschheck very fragrant.

Crust

Heavy deposit thrown by Port. Crusted Port is high-quality Port from several vintages, matured for four years in barrel and then aged in bottle before being drunk. It throws a heavy deposit — hence the name — and should be decanted.

Cuvaison

French term to denote the length of time the grape skins are in contact with the fermenting must, adding color and tannins. Refers to red wine only.

Cuve

French term for vat.

Cuvée

Rather imprecise French term referring to a particular batch of wine or a blend. The tendency among French winemakers is to market an increasing number of individual *cuvées* rather than lump all their wine together in one blend, as was the general practice in the past. Often these *cuvées* are from young or old vines. A selection of the very best vats in a particular year is often labelled as a *tête de cuvée*. *See also* Second wine.

D

D.O.

See Denominacion de Origen.

D.O.C.

See Denominazione di Origine Controllata.

D.O.C.G.

See Denominazione di Origine Controllata e Garantita.

Didier Dagueneau, Pouilly-Fumé

Rather the *enfant terrible* of Pouilly in the Loire, Didier Dagueneau of Saint-Andelain is known for his experiments with skin contact, barrel fermentation and aging for his Pouilly-Fumé. Dagueneau's success comes from his restless perfectionism. The range of Pouilly includes Buisson Menard (unoaked) and Pur Sang (30 percent aged in large barrels). The 100 percent barrel-fermented and oak-aged Cuvée Silex is now one of the appellation's most renowned, impressive and expensive wines. A remarkable late harvest wine was made in 1990.

André Daguin, Auch

Chef-proprietor of the Hôtel de France in Auch and a leading gastronomic figure in Gascony, André Daguin also trades in small lots of old Armagnacs, which he buys from selected growers. His twenty-year-old Ténarèze is a fine floral and pleasingly dry Armagnac.

Francis Daroze, Roquefort

Francis Daroze is a specialist merchant dealing in single-domain Armagnacs. His standards of selection are exacting; every Armagnac he sells is distilled in a continuous still and is aged in casks from the huge local forest of Montlezun. The range of Daroze's brandies is

remarkable, and he has kept the individuality of Armagnac alive by financing the cost of distillation and storage for the many growers with whom he deals.

Château Dassault, St. Emilion

This Bordeaux property was renamed in 1955 by its owner, the aviation magnate whose name it bears, but its origins are much older. Predictably Monsieur Dassault gave much money, time and energy to the restoration, modernization and technical equipment of the vineyard and *cuvier*. Temperature-controlled vats were put in, and the decision taken to introduce new wood in varying proportions for the *élèvage* of the wine. The soil incorporates both sand and clay, and the wines are stylish, harmonious and admirably consistent. Recent successes have been the vintages of 1978, 1979, 1981, 1982, 1983, 1985 and 1986.

Daviau Frères, Domaine de Bablut, Château de Brissac, Anjou

This long-established family firm at Brissac-Quincié in the Loire produces a wide range of wines: *vin du pays* from Chardonnay and Sauvignon, various rosés, Anjou Rouge, Anjou Villages and the sweet Coteaux de l'Aubance. It owns Domaine de Bablut and rents the vineyards of Château de Brissac — over a 100 hectares/247 acres in total. Christophe Daviau, who studied enology at Bordeaux University and then spent time in Australia, is typical of France's younger generation of winemakers.

De Bortoli, Bilbul, New South Wales

Founded in 1928, this Riverina estate of 100 hectares/247 acres is one of the leading exponents of botrytized Semillon wines in Australia. The winemaker is Darren de Bortoli, grandson of the owner. Vintages of its botrytized wines have been consistently good during the last decade; look out for the 1982 in particular. The firm also markets a range of competently vinified table wines. These account for an increasing percentage of its turnover.

Débourbage

French term for letting the grape juice settle before fermentation; solid matter sinks to the bottom of the vat. Cold accelerates this process.

Decant

To pour wine from a bottle into decanter or carafe in order to leave sediment behind, in the case of old wines, or make young wines seem more mature through brief oxygenation — allowing them to breathe.

Dégorgement

French term for the process of getting rid of the sediment that forms in a bottle of sparkling wine after the second fermentation. The neck of the bottle is frozen, sediment ejected, *liqueur de expédition* (a mixture of cane sugar, the same wine in the bottle and, sometimes, grape juice) added and the final cork fitted.

Weingut Dr. Deinhard, Rheinpfalz

A German estate sharing the same buildings and administrator (Heinz Bauer) as Weingut Wegeler-Deinhard, but with separate vineyard holdings. It is known for elegant, characterful wines, from Riesling, Müller-Thurgau, Scheurebe, Gewürztraminer, Ehrenfelser and several others. Drier wines (*trocken* and *halbtrocken*) are a speciality, particularly at Kabinett level.

Marcel Deiss, Bergheim

A family domain of 20 hectares/49.4 acres with fine holdings in the Alsace *grand cru* vineyards of Altenberg de Bergheim and Schoenenbourg. Since the energetic and self-promoting Jean-Michel Deiss took over the winemaking, this domain has received glowing reviews in the American and British press. Deiss believes that each of his wines should reflect the *terroir* of its respective vineyard, and each *cru* or *lieu-dit* is vinified and bottled separately. Some tasters believe that the eight different Rieslings usually made each vintage are more remarkable for range than for consistent quality, and some of these wines can be diffuse and disappointing. Deiss's Gewürztraminers are more successful. The 1986 Gewürztraminer St. Hippolyte is an exotic star of the vintage.

Delamain, Jarnac

Established in Jarnac in 1762, Delamain is the Rolls Royce of Cognac houses, whose international reputation for pale, delicate Cognacs of great breed is entirely justified. The firm, still family owned, employs just twenty people and produces a modest 50,000 cases a year. Alain Braastad, whose mother was a Delamain, is the head of the company, and he is a man totally committed to quality. Delamain owns no vineyards but buys Cognacs that are at least fifteen years old from growers in Grande Fine Champagne. Delamain Pale & Dry is the company's best-known brand, a twenty-five-year-old Cognac, which, as its name implies, is a pale, elegant brandy of real refinement. The wood element is very discreet because only old casks are used to mature the *eau-de-vie*. The top of the range, Delamain Réserve de la Famille, is a magnificent fifty-year-old Cognac that comes from a single domain in the heart of Grande Fine Champagne.

Delas Frères, Tournon

Established in 1835, Delas Frères is a leading firm of *négociants* and growers in the northern Rhône. Since the Champagne house Deutz bought the company in 1977, a major investment program has pushed Delas to the front rank of producers. The firm owns 17 hectares/42 acres in Côte Rôtie, Hermitage, Condrieu and Cornas. The 1985 Cornas Chante Perdrix is a superb, dense wine.

Delatite, Mansfield, Victoria

Delatite means "Devil's River" in Aboriginal, taking its name from the stream that runs down from the Great Dividing Range of Central Victoria. The winemaker of this excellent 24 hectare/59 acre Australian estate is the talented Rosalind Ritchie. Her Rhine Riesling is particularly delicate with a zesty character, a consistently delightful wine in every vintage since 1986. The 1988 Cabernet Blend Devil's River is a lively mouthful with finely crafted fruit touched with the mint and eucalyptus flavors typical of Central Victoria.

Delaware

An early American hybrid that makes still and sparkling wines of some delicacy, less pronouncedly "foxy" than those of the Catawba and the Concord, and provides good table grapes. The vine is planted in the eastern United States, Brazil and in Japan, where it has an important share of the vineyard.

Delheim, Stellenbosch

An enormous estate in South Africa, drawing grapes from two farms, run with great verve and charisma by

Michael "Spatz" Sperling. In the past some inconsistencies in the quality have been noticeable, but probably because consumers have demanded too wide a range of wine styles. A new winemaker, Philip Constandius, will bring in some changes and may even reduce the present 65,000 case total production. Among the best wines are an excellent Reserve made from Cabernet Sauvignon and Merlot; outstanding Chardonnay; Gewürztraminer; botrytized Chenin Blanc/Sauvignon Blanc and, to be watched in future vintages, Pinot Noir.

Demi-muid
See Muid.

Demi-sec
French for medium sweet. Used for sparkling wines throughout France and medium sweet still wines from the Loire Valley, especially those of Montlouis and Vouvray.

Denbies Estate, England
This 100 hectare/247 acre estate planted in a dry downland valley just to the north of Dorking in Surrey is now easily England's largest vineyard. It is owned by Patrick White of Biwater, a local construction company. Planting began in 1986, and the first, small vintage was in 1989, which was not put on sale until 1991 along with the 1990 vintage. A large number of different varieties have been planted, including Champagne's three classic vines: Chardonnay, Pinot Noir and Pinot Meunier. Denbies intends to make 20 to 25 percent of its estimated 500,000 bottle production as sparkling wine.

Denominacion de Origen (D.O.)
Spain's system of demarcated wine areas. At the moment there are 36 D.O. regions.

Denominazione di Origine Controllata (D.O.C.)
Italian wine laws, somewhat similar to France's *Appellation Contrôlée* laws. The laws involve geographical limits of each zone, the permissible grape varieties, alcohol levels, maximum yield per hectare/acre and other quality controls.

Denominazione di Origine Controllata e Garantita (D.O.C.G.)
A more recent category to which certain D.O.C. wines have been promoted. *"Garantita"* is supposed to guarantee quality, whereas D.O.C. merely guarantees origin and method of production.

Département
Administrative unit in France (there are 95).

Deposit
Some fine red wines, particularly vintage Port, naturally throw a deposit as they mature. Decanting separates the deposit from the wine.

Jean Descombes, Morgon
The outstanding grower of Morgon and one of that Beaujolais commune's most extrovert *vignerons,* Jean Descombes is a man who understands that to make exceptional wine one needs exceptional grapes. His cellar has a specially designed reception bay for the incoming harvested grapes so that they may be treated as gently as possible prior to vinification. It shows in his wines, which display beautifully clear fruit, young or old, and marked tones of wild cherry and apricot. The 1989 is exceptional, and the 1990 very elegant. Jean Descombes' wines are exclusively distributed by Georges Duboeuf.

Deutscher Tafelwein
German table wine. Most wines in this lowest category are simple everyday wines. However, a few top-class

producers use this category for their experimental wines, which do not meet the Q.b.A regulations, perhaps because they use *barriques* or grape varieties not provided for in the regulations.

Deutz, Champagne
Champagne house founded in 1838 by William Deutz and Pierre Geldman, both natives of Aix-la-Chapelle, now Aachen in Germany. The firm is now run by the Lallier family, descendants of William Deutz. It owns 40 hectares/99 acres of vineyard, which supply around 40 percent of its grape needs. Annual production is in the region of 65,000 cases. The wines are traditionally made and of high quality throughout, culminating in the prestige Cuvée William Deutz. Their recent sparkling-wine enterprises in New Zealand and California have been highly successful, making quality wines that really challenge Champagne.

Diamond Creek Vineyards Cabernet Sauvignon, Volcanic Hill, Napa Valley
Al Braunstein sold his pharmaceutical business in Los Angeles in 1972 and moved north to fulfil a lifelong dream of becoming a winemaker. He became one of the best. His Diamond Creek Vineyards, on the slopes of Diamond Mountain, just outside Calistoga, produces some of the most sought-after Cabernets in California. After twenty years as a vintner, Braunstein is in the enviable position of knowing that whatever he produces, even in relatively lean years economically, will be snapped up by his fans. Experts argue over the relative merits of his three vineyards, all contiguous and all on different soils. Volcanic Hill might just be the first among equals — a bit more intense, a bit more structured, a bit more long lasting. For a less gifted enthusiast, any Diamond Creek Cabernet — Braunstein makes only Cabernet Sauvignon — is a rare treat.

Schlossgut Diel, Nahe
A mainly Riesling estate devoted to dry wines except in great vintages. As a matter of policy, no *Kabinett* wines are made, since the estate considers them to be too lightweight. The wines are particularly popular in leading German restaurants. There are 9.7 hectares/24 acres of vines.

Jean-Pierre Dirler, Bergholtz
A perfectionist and quiet-spoken man who looks more like a schoolmaster than a winegrower, Dirler cultivates a small 7 hectare/17 acre domain in Alsace, with prime sites in the *grand cru* vineyards of Saering and Spiegel above his home village of Bergholtz. He makes an exceptional Sylvaner from thirty- to sixty-old-year vines and arguably one of the finest Muscats in Alsace, exquisitely aromatic yet with an elegant firm acidity. He also produces a rare and wonderful Marc de Muscat, a powerful *eau-de-vie* that retains a strong flavor of the grape.

Distillation
The method used to a concentrate alcohol through evaporation and then condensation. All spirits are made by distillation.

Château Doisy-Daëne, Sauternes
This Bordeaux property, with its curious corruption of an English name, occupies a privileged position between Châteaux Climens and Coutet. The present owner, Pierre Dubourdieu, is an enthusiast and innovator who allies modern thinking with respect for tradition. His highly individual techniques of vinification and aging produce remarkable wines from the Sémillon alone. Fresh and light in style, these are balanced, complex and elegant wines capable of long life. Notable among recent vintages have been those of 1981, 1982, 1983, 1986, 1988 and 1989. A fine dry wine is also made, improbably from

a blend that includes Riesling, Chardonnay and Muscadelle as well as higher proportions of Sauvignon and Sémillon.

Château Doisy-Védrines, Sauternes
The largest of the three parts into which the former Château Doisy in Bordeaux was divided, Doisy-Védrines retains the original château and *chai*. It makes rich, fat, traditional wines quite unlike those of Doisy-Daëne and Doisy-Dubroca. Although production is relatively small, the wine is consistently successful, with excellent results in 1975, 1976, 1981, 1982, 1983, 1986, 1988 and 1989. In La Tour Védrines the property makes a good red wine.

Dolce
Sweet in Italian.

Dolcetto
A red wine grape established for several centuries in Piedmont, where it was formerly a source of *amabile* wines. Its current production is exclusively dry. The variety is planted in Acqui, Alba, the Langhe, Asti, the Alto Monferrato and Ovada, and its wines show considerable variation, attributable to differences of soil and climate. It is seen at its best in Ovada, where the deeply colored D.O.C. Dolcetto is robust, tannic and acidic, relatively high in alcohol and capable of aging. In Liguria, on the other side of the Apennines, the Dolcetto is known as Ormeasco and makes sound D.O.C. wines of that name on the hills inland from Imperia on the western Riviera.

Pedro Domecq, Jerez
The sherry, Spanish brandy and table wine house that is now Pedro Domecq was actually founded by Patrick Murphy, an Irishman, in 1730. It was not until 1816, after the Napoleonic Wars, that Pedro Domecq Lembeye joined the firm. By 1822 he had taken over and changed the firm's name to his own. The company now owns a little over 1,000 hectares/12,470 acres of vineyards in Jerez, as well as holdings in Rioja and 800 hectare/2,000 acres of vineyards in Mexico. But it is for Sherry that Domecq is best known. Its range includes La Ina Fino, Botaina Amontillado and Rio Viejo Dry Oloroso. There are also some exquisite old solera sherries, such as Sibarita.

Château La Dominique, St. Emilion
La Dominique stands next to Cheval Blanc, and if its soil is predominantly sandy, it shares some element of its famous neighbor's *gravel* and limestone. Since 1969 this Bordeaux property has belonged to Monsieur Fayat, who has spent heavily on modernization and technical equipment in *cuvier* and *chai*, and the use of new wood has been adopted. Under this regime the wines have been consistently impressive over the past twenty years. Typically they show fruit and richness, with a tannic structure that indicates their potential to develop. Outstanding in this period have been the wines of 1978, 1979, 1982, 1983, 1985 and 1986, the last three especially fat and concentrated and likely to need considerable time.

Dominus, Napa Valley
Californian wine law says that a wine must contain 75 percent of a particular grape to bear that grape's name. Winemakers who choose to make wines that might contain less than 75 percent Cabernet Sauvignon give these wines proprietary names that they hope will be even more prestigious than Cabernet Sauvignon's name. One of the most famous, and only five years or so on the market, is Dominus, a wine made by Christian Moueix, the manager and part owner of Château Pétrus. Moueix started in California by acquiring shares in one of the best Napa vineyards, the old John Daniel estate that once made Inglenook wines so famous. Daniel was a Cabernet man while Moueix is a Merlot man, which may explain why he prefers a free hand in blending. The results speak for themselves; Dominus is a supremely elegant wine, balanced, harmonious and, even after only a few years, a wine of great breed.

Donnafugata, Sicily
Gabriella Anca Rallo makes the excellent Donnafugata Bianco and Rosso at her vineyards south of Palermo. These are dry wines of considerable style. Signora Rallo also produces some Chardonnay and a very good rosé.

Weingut Hermann Dönnhof, Nahe
A 9 hectare/22 acre family estate whose wines have shot it to fame in Germany. Impeccable cellar procedure produces beautifully made, elegant wines in which the flavor of the grape variety and the soil are prominent.

Dopff au Moulin, Riquewihr
A family business founded in the seventeenth century, with a justified reputation for Alsace wines of the highest quality. The firm's vineyard holdings extend to some 77 hectares/190 acres with prime sites in the Eichberg at Turckheim for Gewürztraminer and in the Schoenenbourg at Riquewihr for Riesling. These Dopff *crus* are consistently superb. The company is also a leading producer of Crémant d'Alsace, the *méthode champenoise* sparkling wines pioneered by Julien Dopff in the early 1900s.

A.E. Dor, Jarnac
A small Cognac house based in Jarnac, A.E. Dor is still selling Cognacs from the nineteenth century. They are kept in demijohns. The 1889 Grande Fine Champagne, tasted in 1990, had 35 percent alcohol by volume and was extremely concentrated, with great richness of aromas and hints of liquorice on the palate.

From the range of blended Cognacs, the A.E. Dor Cuvée Number Eight is an exceptional forty-year-old brandy, a masterpiece of the blender's art. Its strength of 47 percent alcohol is not at all apparent, and it remains remarkably fresh with beautiful floral scents and clear, well defined fruit.

Dosage
Liquid sugar added to sparkling wine after *dégorgement* to give required degree of sweetness.

Doux
French word for sweet. Sweet Champagnes are labeled *doux*, as are some Loire sweet wines from great vintages, such as 1947.

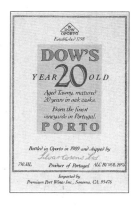

Dow, Vila Nova de Gala
Established in 1798 and now part of the Symington group, Dow makes dryish, penetrating vintage Port of high quality, based on fruit from Quinta do Bomfim at Pinhão. Top vintages: 1983, 1977, 1970, 1966. Quinto do Bonfir is regularly one of the best single-quinta Ports from second-level vintage years. Dow also make good crusting Port.

Downy mildew
A fungal disease, related to oidium, also called

Peronospera. An American export, it first appeared in French vineyards in the 1880s. Downy mildew can be controlled by spraying vines with copper sulfate or powdered sulfate.

Dromana Estate, Mornington Peninsula, Victoria
Gary Crittenden makes excellent Chardonnay, Cabernet and Pinot Noir on the 4 hectare/9.9 acre Dromana Estate in Australia. Crittenden insists on the most natural methods possible, both in the vineyard and in the winery: pesticides and chemical treatments are kept to a minimum, as is sulfur dioxide in the winemaking process. He also uses a second label, Schinus Molle, the wines of which may come from vineyards outside the Mornington Peninsula. The 1988 Schinus Molle Chardonnay is an exciting bottle at a very fair price; the wine shows a fine balance of ripe fruit and great length of flavor, made more complex by just the right amount of oak.

Domaine Drouhin Pinot Noir, Willamette Valley
Nothing did more to put Oregon wine on the map than the arrival in 1987 of Robert Drouhin in the Willamette Valley. Drouhin, one of the best-known Burgundy wine growers and shippers, had been scouting Oregon quietly for many years. But his announcement that he was buying vineyards and would build a winery came just at a time when the region had experienced a succession of bad vintages. Many winemakers were depressed, and his bold move inspired them all. His first release only served to support his original judgment. The second release was richer than the first; from 1991 onward the wines have been made with grapes from Drouhin's own vineyards. The first vintage was 1988, and as the Drouhin vineyards mature, the wine can only improve.

Robert Drouhin
Robert Drouhin is one of the most respected spokesmen for the Burgundy wine trade. Ever since he took charge of the Beaune merchant house of Joseph Drouhin in 1957, he has shown a single-minded commitment to authentic Burgundy and, unusually for a large *négociant*, he has never produced French wines from regions other than Burgundy and Beaujolais. When Drouhin turned his eyes to the New World in the eighties, he took a typically far-sighted decision in purchasing some 40 hectares/99 acres of vines in Oregon's Willamette Valley, where he planted Pinot Noir, the grape of red Burgundy. Under the direction of his talented daughter Véronique, Drouhin's 1989 Oregon Pinot Noir is a great success, showing elegant Pinot Noir fruit and vinosity. This wine may come to be seen as a model for less experienced Oregon winemakers to follow.

Yet Drouhin's reputation is rightly based on this firm's classic white wines from the Côte d'Or. The 1985 vintage, which Drouhin has always preferred to 1986, vividly demonstrates the house style of breed and finesse allied to great richness of flavor. The firm's plot in Beaune, Clos des Mouches, produced an exceptional wine in 1985; opulent and creamy with the hazelnut aromas of top-flight Chardonnay in a hot summer; and his Montrachet Marquis de Laguiche is a spectacular bottle exhibiting all the power and complexity one may hope for.

Drouhin's top-of-the-range red wines from the Côte de Nuits are some of the most exquisite in Burgundy. Thanks to his extension of the family domain between Gevrey and Nuits in the sixties and seventies, Drouhin owns holdings in the best *grand cru* and *premier cru* vineyards. Usually among his best wines — particularly in the trio of vintages 1988, 1989 and 1990 — are Griottes Chambertin, Echezeaux and Vosne Romanée Les Suchots.

Pierre-Jacques Druet, Bourgueil
Pierre-Jacques Druet is an enologist by training, and

unlike many other *vignerons* he did not have the advantage of taking over the family vineyards. Starting from nothing in 1980, his achievements have been impressive: no one in Bourgueil in the Loire has a better reputation. Druet uses traditional methods to make deeply concentrated wine, often very tannic when young, accentuating the commune of Benais' reputation for producing the most tannic wine in Bourgueil. His top *cuvée* is Le Grand Mont, a single vineyard. Druet also makes some Chinon.

Dry
Occasionally used on Champagne labels; between *brut* and *demi-sec*.

Dry Creek Vineyards Sauvignon Blanc, Sonoma County
David S. Stare founded Dry Creek Vineyards in Sonoma County in 1972 and quickly made a reputation as one of the foremost makers of top-quality Sauvignon Blanc in California. Dry Creek Sauvignon Blancs usually lean toward the Loire Valley style, but with somewhat less sharpness than would be found in a Sauvignon de Touraine. Even so, Stare's version has a nice bite to it and attractive freshness.

Georges Duboeuf, Romanèche-Thorins
Georges Duboeuf is often called the King of Beaujolais. As a young physical education student in Paris in the fifties, he became disenchanted with commuting to the gym on the *Métro* and returned to his family's estate in Pouilly. From small beginnings, he gradually built up a serious restaurant clientele for his wine, gleaned from the pages of the Michelin guide. In the early 1960s he went into partnership with Alexis Lichine, Paul Bocuse and Paul Blanc in a venture called L'Ecran Mâconnais-Beaujolais, which promoted the wines of its member growers and offered them the services of a mobile bottling plant. The growers started to bicker, so Duboeuf set up his own company, Les Vins Georges Duboeuf, at Chanes in 1964.

In thirty years, Duboeuf has revolutionized the Beaujolais wine region. His essential achievement has been to make the developed world appreciate the balanced, fruity charms of true Beaujolais. His success has been based on realistic prices, superb presentation and a clear-sighted commitment to the best modern methods of vinification, which emphasize the fresh, sprightly character of the wine. From September to November each year, the workaholic Georges Duboeuf and his son Franck taste more than seven thousand wines from three hundred Beaujolais growers, retaining only those wines that they actually like. It may be accurately stated that each of the domain wines selected is a very good example of its village and appellation.

The company's turnover now accounts for nearly 15 percent of Beaujolais sales worldwide. Georges Duboeuf is best known for his Beaujolais Nouveau, annual production exceeding 4 million bottles, but he has been quick to see that this market has now peaked. Duboeuf's main energies nowadays are directed to finding good-value alternative Gamay wines from the neighboring Coteaux du Lyonnais and from the Ardèche bordering the Rhône Valley. He has also bought a vineyard in Côte Rôtie. Nonetheless, Duboeuf's best wines remain his scrupulously chosen Beaujolais *crus* from individual domains. It is a mark of his undiminished critical standards that he is vocally critical of the general standard of indifferent wine currently being made in Régnié, Beaujolais's tenth *cru*.

Duca di Salaparuta, Sicily
This quality Sicilian wine house, founded in 1824, is admired for the consistent excellence of its Corvo wines; nearly half of the production is exported. The firm's great success in recent years has been a red wine called Duca Enrico. This is made from the indigenous Nero

d'Avola grape, is aged in small *barriques* and develops real complexity with aging.

Château Ducru Beaucaillou, St. Julien

Like nearby Beychevelle, Beaucaillou is splendidly sited, with sweeping views over the vast Gironde, and its 49 hectares/121 acres of gravelly soil are on the slopes of the best part of the vineyards along the river. The Bordeaux estate belongs to Jean-Eugène Borie, whose father acquired it during the Second World War at a time when the fortunes of this second growth were in relative decline. Borie is that rarity, a resident proprietor, and a considerable figure in the Médoc, while the revival of Beaucaillou is a testament to his energy and his dedication to quality.

Characteristically Beaucaillou is distinguished by a wonderful bouquet, balance and great elegance, with less richness and substance than is typical of the vineyards farther from the river. At its best it shows very great grace, something reflected in the high prices it commands, and its excellence is consistent. Notable wines were made in 1961, 1962, 1966, a remarkable 1970, 1971, 1975, and 1976, with a magnificent 1978. The past decade too has been one of almost uninterrupted success; following a light and rather shallow 1980 came the great vintages of 1981, 1982, 1983, 1985, 1986, 1987 and 1988. Of these perhaps the most remarkable was the astonishing 1982. These wines will need a minimum of ten or fifteen years to approach their full splendor.

Dulce
Sweet in Spanish.

Pierre Dumazet, Condrieu
Based in Limony, Condrieu's most southerly village, Pierre Dumazet makes exquisite white wines in a tiny vineyard. His 1989 Côtes-du-Rhône Viognier is a lovely aromatic and spicy wine for early drinking while his 1989 Condrieu Côte Fournet is intense, deep-flavored and made from old vines in the eye of this Rhône vineyard.

Dumb
Little aroma or flavor; sometimes a sign of youth. Many fine wines go through dumb phases and emerge again.

Duras
A black grape traditional to Gaillac, in southwestern France, where it does well on gravelly soil and makes substantial, rustic wines.

Durif
See Petite Sirah

E

E.V.A.
See English Vineyards Association

Earthy
Slightly rustic flavor, can be enjoyable but not usually found in the finest wines.

Eau-de-vie
Literally, "water" of life. Broadly can refer to any spirit but more usually used for French spirits made from or flavored with fruits other than grapes. A specialty of Alsace.

Ebullioscope
Machine for measuring the alcoholic content of wines and spirits.

Eclaircissage
See Green harvest.

Edelfäule
German name for noble rot.

Edge
Impression of tannins and/or acidity. Often a youthful characteristic suggesting that this harsh edge will round out with age.

Edna Valley Chardonnay, San Luis Obispo County
The Edna Valley, just inland from California's south central coast, with its hot days and cool nights, can be — in the right hands — an ideal setting for growing good Chardonnay and Pinot Noir. The Edna Valley Vineyard is a joint venture between a big management firm and Chalone Vineyards, which runs the property and makes the wines. The wines, while not quite up to Chalone levels, are top quality year after year. Chardonnay in this part of the country can be thin, bland and eminently forgettable if care is not taken. Not at Edna Valley Vineyards. Its Chardonnays are crisp and fresh, medium to light-bodied and full of intense Chardonnay flavors. Here, too, one finds that Burgundian touch that says the wine is influenced by the Chalone style of winemaking.

Egrappage
French term for destalking or separating grapes from their stems. Normally a destalking machine (*égrappoir*) is used.

Einzellage
Single vineyard site in Germany; for example, Bernkasteler Doctor or Schloss Johannisberg.

Eiswein
Literally, "ice wine" this German or Austrian wine is made from grapes picked while frozen on cold mornings or as late as December or January. The grape juice is concentrated because the water content has frozen so does not emerge from the press. Such wines are usually labelled "Beerenauslese Eiswein" because the speed of picking does not permit closer selection than bunch by bunch.

Elbling
A prolific German grape of ancient origin, but otherwise unremarkable, the Elbling, also known as the Kleinberger, is grown to make the sparkling Sekt, although its role is less important now than formerly. The variety is found also in Lorraine, Luxembourg and Liechtenstein.

Elegant
Imprecise term akin to finesse; well-balanced wine.

Elèvage
French term meaning the maturation of a wine; "Bringing up" is a literal translation. Generally refers to the process of aging wine in barrels and implies careful nurturing.

Elvira
A nineteenth-century American hybrid that is robust, prolific and adapted to the cool conditions of the eastern United States. Its wines are used chiefly for blending.

Emerald Riesling
A hot-weather hybrid developed just after the war at the University of California, Davis, the Emerald Riesling makes aromatic if slightly bland white wines of some acidity. The vine is productive, but curiously has never found wide acceptance.

L'En de l'El
One of six varieties which in the Gaillac region of southwestern France may be used for making white wines. The grape is often blended with Mauzac to make Gaillac Perlé.

English or Welsh wine
Wine made from grapes grown in vineyards in England and Wales. *See* British Made Wine.

English Vineyards Association (E.V.A.)
Almost all English and Welsh vineyards belong to this organization.

Enology
The science of winemaking. An enologist is a trained winemaker. Also spelled oenology.

Enzyme
Secreted by a yeast cell in order to convert grape sugar into alcohol. In addition, the enzyme pectinase can be added to newly crushed grapes to break down the slimy pectins and so make pressing easier.

Erbaluce
A long-established but uncommon grape grown to the north of Turin, Italy, to make dry white wines both still and sparkling, sweet wines and the rare and striking Caluso Passito. Much of the production of dry Caluso is dull and acidic and is sold in bulk, but in enlightened hands the Erbaluce can make dry wines of real distinction, the sparkling made by the *méthode champenoise*. The production of these, as of the *passito*, is very limited as yet.

Erinose
A vine disease caused by the unwanted attentions of small mites. Finely ground sulfur combats it.

Errázuriz Panquehue, Chile
Errázuriz Panquehue is the only winery in the warmer Aconcagua Valley, with 18 hectares/44 acres of vineyards there and another 150 hectares/370 acres in the cooler Mataquito Valley, farther south in Maule. Errázuriz was the name of the original owner of the estate, in the village of Panquehue. Today it belongs to the Chadwick family, who in a joint venture with Franciscan Vineyards of Napa Valley also sell wine under the name of Caliterra. Methods are innovative, with some sound Sauvignon, oak-aged Chardonnay, a recently introduced Merlot and some flavorsome Cabernet Sauvignon. Best of all is Don Maximiano, named after the founder of the estate, which spends two and a half years in French oak.

Erzeugerabfüllung
German term meaning bottled by the producer: estate bottled.

Estancia Cabernet Sauvignon, Alexander Valley, Sonoma County
Estancia is part of the Franciscan Vineyards family. It is less expensive than Franciscan wines, but it is a separate entity, not a second wine. It is, in fact, a lovely, relatively soft Cabernet with good body, a modicum of tannin for structure and a variety of delicious aromas that appear as it develops in the glass. Made from grapes from some of the best areas of the hot Alexander Valley in California, it develops fairly rapidly and needs little bottle age. It is widely available, and while still not too well known is the equal in quality to many wines at twice its price.

Château des Estanilles, Faugères
Michel Louison, originally from Touraine, bought this 25 hectare/62 acre property in Languedoc-Roussillon, France, in 1975. A charismatic extrovert, Louison loves to experiment and take chances. His 1991 plans included making a *vin de paille*. He has recently planted Syrah and Mourvèdre on a spectacularly well exposed hillside. His white Coteaux du Languedoc has a complexity not often found in the area's white wines, and his powerful *barrique*-aged reds need time to show their best.

Estate bottling
To bottle wine on the estate where the grapes come from is increasingly normal practice. This trend of the last thirty years helps to guarantee authenticity.

Esters
These aroma compounds are formed by the reaction between acids and alcohol during fermentation and aging of wine. Esters considerably contribute to the wine's bouquet.

Estufa
Tank used for heating Madeira to around 45°C/113°F to simulate the heat of the long sea voyage to the Americas that Madeira used to undergo.

Château Etang des Colombes, Corbières
Large 80 hectare/198 acre estate near Lézignan-Corbières in France owned by Henri Gualco, who is the president of the Fédération National des Caves Particulières, the association of independent growers, and a champion of the new quality wines from Languedoc-Roussillon. His wines reflect this drive for quality, and his whites, including the wood-aged Bois des Dames, are particularly impressive.

Etiquette
French word for bottle label.

Eutypiose
A fatal fungal vine disease whose spread is causing considerable concern, especially in Bordeaux and the Loire. The fungus spreads in wet conditions. Pruning is a

271

particularly dangerous time. Prunings needs to be burnt, and the wood cuts painted with a fungicide, a labor-intensive process.

Château l'Evangile, Pomerol

This Bordeaux property has belonged to the Ducasse family since 1862, although recently Domaines Rothschild have acquired shares.

The vineyard is enviably placed on the high plateau close to St. Emilion, and roughly 30 percent of it is the prized clay that so distinguishes Pétrus. It may be that in Ducasse's later years l'Evangile failed to make wines as notable as its advantages of site might suggest, although there were exceptional successes in years like 1966, 1970 and 1971.

Since Madame Ducasse assumed control there has been a clear improvement, with splendid wines made in 1985, 1988 and 1989.

Evans Family, Pokolbin, New South Wales

This is the label for Len Evans' unforgettably rich and intense Chardonnay made at Rothbury, his beautiful estate in the Hunter Valley. The wine is fermented in 100 percent new oak. The 1986 has everything: fresh floral aromas, a buttery roundness that is indubitably Australian, but "grip," acidity and huge character too.

Len Evans and the Rothbury Estate, Pokolbin, New South Wales

Len Evans is the Great Communicator of the Australian wine industry. This silver-tongued Welshman emigrated to Australia in 1953 and after various stints as a welder, ring barker and scriptwriter, he became food and beverage manager of the Chevron Hilton in Sydney in 1960.

The rest, as they say, is history. "For the best part of thirty years, it has been his face, his voice and his pen which has brought wine into the minds and houses of countless Australians who, were it not for Len, might never have raised a glass to their lips." One cannot improve on James Halliday's description.

The Rothbury Estate is likely to be Len's enduring achievement. In partnership with a group of Sydney businessmen and wine lovers, he bought this Pokolbin property in the Lower Hunter Valley in 1968. The handsome winery was completed in 1971 and immediately produced some outstanding wines: the 1972 Semillon White Label still showed beautifully preserved fruit and fine acidity in 1990.

But Rothbury was soon in financial trouble. As Len candidly admits: "We planted too much Shiraz, not foreseeing the end to the demand for it ... and we planted too many vines on soils that could not sustain an appropriate yield." Evans has fought to save Rothbury, and its much improved financial position is due to increased plantings of Chardonnay.

The Rothbury Chardonnay Reserve is the estate's most individual wine. The grapes are picked very ripe, and the wine is fermented in 100 percent new Vosges barrels; it then stays on its lees for over six months. The finished wine has huge strength of flavor, the 1987 a memorable and indubitably Australian bottle that has blown other Chardonnays right off the table at international competitive tastings.

Eventail de Vignerons Producteurs, Corcelles-en-Beaujolais

An association of quality-minded smaller growers in the Beaujolais and southern Mâconnais, the Eventail members cultivate their own vineyards, make their own wines but bottle and market them in an impressive central cellar in Corcelles-en-Beaujolais. Among members making excellent wines are André Large of Brouilly, André Pelletier of Juliénas and the Château de Chénas.

Excise

Tax levied on alcoholic drinks and other commodities.

Extra-sec

Intermediate degree of dryness found on sparkling wine labels, between *brut* and *sec.*

Extract

Soluble solids in wine that contribute to its body and substance. It is common for the regulations of a wine region to specify minimum levels of extract.

F

Elisabetta Fagiuoli, San Gimignano

The loquacious, extrovert Elisabetta Fagiuoli makes a first-rate Vernaccia di San Gimignano and an enjoyable, unpretentious, non-oaked Chianti at her 6 hectare/15 acre Montenidoli estate.

François Faiveley

The Nuits St. Georges house of J.H. Faiveley, established in 1825, has always been known as the provider of sturdy, consistently well-made red Burgundies. But since the studious-looking François Faiveley took charge of the winemaking in 1978, the quality of the wine has gone from strength to strength.

François has one overwhelming advantage: his family owns one of the largest domains in Burgundy. Of the total 112 hectares/277 acres of vineyards, 42 hectares/104 acres are in prime Côte d'Or sites, and there is a substantial estate of 70 hectares/173 acres in Mercurey. These provide about 85 percent of the firm's wine needs, the remainder coming from bought-in quality grapes that are vinified at Nuits St. Georges. Faiveley looks for the maximum development of the aromatic constituents of Pinot Noir in his red wines, which is why he macerates the grapes at a low temperature before fermentation. The fermenting wines can spend up to twenty days or so on the skins, and in big-volume vintages, about a fifth of the free-run juice is drawn off to increase concentration. The results are some of the most aromatic yet ageworthy red wines in Burgundy.

Faiveley uses new wood very carefully: only some *grands crus* see 100 percent new oak. And he does not like to filter his wines. Faiveley had a great success in the dilute 1986 vintage, a difficult year for red wines. The 1986 Nuits St. Georges Clos de la Maréchale has beautiful clear fruit and an ironlike firmness typical of Nuits. The 1988 Mercureys from Faiveley are marvellous yet reasonably priced examples of Pinot Noir. Faiveley is less well known for his white wines though they are immaculately made. The 1989 Corton-Charlemagne is one of the greatest wines of a great white Burgundy vintage.

Weingut Famile Umathum, Frauenkirchen, Burgenland

Estate near the Neusiedlersee in Austria with a fascinating range of characterful red and white wines, some of which are aged in *barriques*, others in large old casks. The blends from Chardonnay, Pinots Gris and Blanc (to quote the French nomenclature used by the estate) are remarkable, but look out for the 1989 Beerenauslese, a blend of Pinot Gris and Welschriesling. The wine was fermented and matured in *barrique* and, backed by 14 percent alcohol and a considerable amount of unfermented sugar, plus a good level of acidity, it is a stunner. A powerfully flavored wine, much influenced by noble rot.

Fan leaf

See Infectious degeneration.

Bodegas Fariña, Toro

The red wines of the arid Toro region near Zamora are among the strongest in Spain. This family *bodega* makes an excellent example from the Tinta de Toro grape, also known as Tempranillo.

Fat

Term for wine that feels round in the mouth, with plenty of extract.

Faustino Martinez, Rioja

Faustino is a sizeable quality-conscious independent *bodega* and the third largest exporter of Rioja. The firm specializes in light, perfumed and well-flavored reservas under the Faustino V label. The company's flagship wine is the profound, spicy Faustino I Gran Reserva.

Favorita

A variety grown chiefly in Alba, in Piedmont, where it makes slight, unremarkable white wines.

Livio Felluga, Brazano di Cormons

Livio Felluga is a prominent winemaker in Collio Goriziano and Colli Orientali. Two of his best wines are the Sauvignon di Rollat and the *vino da tavola* Terre Alte, which is a blend of Tocai, Pinot Bianco and Sauvignon.

Felsina Berardenga, Chianti Classico

Giuseppe Mazzocolin, a former teacher of Dante, manages this 50 hectare/124 acre estate at Castelnuovo Berardenga. Enologist Franco Bernabei has a strong influence on the winemaking; the resulting style of the wines, perhaps affected by Bernabei's attachment to a modified form of *governo,* is soft, forward and elegant. While there has been some inconsistency in the Chianti Classicos made here in the eighties — the 1983 Riserva is a much better, more complex wine than the over-soft 1985 — Berardenga does produce some memorable bottles. The 1985 *vino da tavola* Fontalloro, made from 100 percent Sangiovese, is a red wine of real breed, and the 1986 Chardonnay I Sistri shows a mastery of barrel fermentation, the oak flavors melding beautifully with fine varietal fruit.

Feminine

A wine of charm with round fruit and without aggressive tannins. St. Emilion is feminine in comparison to Haut-Médoc, as Chinon is in comparison to Bourgueil. Such comparisions, of course, smack of days gone by.

Fer Servadou

A traditional variety of the southwest of France, where it is known also as Fer, Braucol and Mansois in the Aveyron. It makes red and rosé wines, and has a subordinate role in the Madiran blend, but is losing ground with the introduction of more fashionable vines like the Cabernets and Merlot.

Fermentation

There are two fermentation processes: alcoholic and malolactic. In alcoholic fermentation grape sugars are changed to alcohol by yeasts. All wine undergoes alcoholic fermentation. The secondary, or malolactic fermentation, generally occurs after the alcoholic fermentation, has finished and changes the sharp malic acid to the softer, creamy, lactic acid. All red wines undergo the malolactic fermentation, but it is prevented in many white wines in order to keep the refreshing acidity.

Fernandez Cervera, Rias Baixas

Close to the mouth of the River Minho on the Atlantic coast of Galicia, this 20 hectare/49 acre estate is the home of a fine red wine called Lagar de Cervera made from the Albariño grape. The estate is owned by Bodegas La Rioja Alta.

Pierre Ferrand, Segonzac

Pierre Ferrand directs a 27 hectare/67 acre estate at Segonzac in the heart of Grande Fine Champagne. As one of the first Cognac growers to sell his brandies in the export market, he has been very successful in the United States. It is not difficult to see why, for his range of Grande Fine Champagne Cognacs displays a superb velvety texture and a smooth, almost molasses-like richness matched by few of his rivals. His Sélection des Anges (twenty-five -years-old) and his Réserve Ancestrale (fifty years old) are magnificent *eaux-de-vie,* whose warm flavors stay in the mouth for hours after one has put down one's glass.

Ferrari, Trento

Franco, Gino and Mauro Lunelli manage this leading Trento producer of *méthode champenoise* wines with an annual production of about 900,000 bottles. The firm is best known for its range of brut *cuvées,* including Brut (100 percent Chardonnay) and the first-rate Giulio Ferrari Riserva di Fondatore.

Pierre Ferraud et Fils, Belleville-sur-Saône

This family firm of Beaujolais *négociants* has a justified reputation for wines of the highest quality. Pierre Ferraud specializes in Beaujolais *crus* that he markets unblended from top-quality domains. He ages his wines in large oak *foudres* for five to six months before bottling, a practice rarely used by Beaujolais *négociants* today. Ferraud's bottlings of Chénas in particular are exceptionally fine, and he is the largest buyer of this underrated *cru.* The Ferraud family also make an outstanding Fleurie, the Clos des Garands, which is aged in *barriques.* This wine needs to be kept for at least two years before drinking, when it shows a powerful complexity not normally associated with Beaujolais.

Château de Fesles, Bonnezeaux

Jacques Boivin is the most respected vigneron of this appellation in the Loire. His wines regularly have a power and concentration rarely matched in other Bonnezeaux. His secret is low yields, selective picking and attentive winemaking. The 33 hectare/82 acre estate was recently sold to Gaston Lenôtre, the Parisian chef, although Boivin will continue to make the wine. The 1989 is particularly impressive.

Sylvain Fessy, Belleville-sur-Saône

Also seen under the label Vins Dessalle, the Beaujolais wines of the young *négociant* Sylvain Fessy can be very fine and stylish. Established in 1978, this Burgundian firm was immediately successful on the United States market. Fessy produces a seductive style of Beaujolais, rich yet lithe and not too alcoholic. Look out for these *cuvées:* Juliénas Cuvée Michel Tête, Fleurie Cuvée Métrat and Moulin-à-Vent Cuvée Ernest Lafond.

Maria Feyles e Figlia, Barolo/Barbaresco

Maria Feyles is a small, high-quality producer based in Alba. Robust, substantial Barolo Ginestra (excellent in 1988) and Barbaresco are her leading wines.

Fiano

A grape variety of ancient origin that in Campania makes Fiano di Avellino, a dry white wine of complexity and subtle flavor, with the capacity to age.

Château de Fieuzal, Graves
A Bordeaux property just outside Léognan, Fieuzal makes both red and white wines from its 23 hectares/57 acres. The red is classified; the white, a relatively recent venture, is not, despite its undoubted merit. Both red and white wines benefit from skillful winemaking and modern equipment in *cuvier* and *chai*.

During the eighties the red wines gained in concentration and structure without losing their characteristic elegance; new oak is used in their maturation, and the wines are capable of aging. Recent successes include 1982, 1983, 1985 and 1986. The white Fieuzal, made from 60 percent Sauvignon and 40 percent Sémillon, is fermented in new wood and emerges fragrant, crisp and fruity, but its production is sadly limited.

Château Figeac, St. Emilion
At some 40 hectares/99 acres Figeac today represents only a fifth of its size in the eighteenth century, but it is still a considerable Bordeaux property. The story of its decline is the familiar one of problems of inheritance allied to mismanagement, in this instance during and after the wars of Napoleon. By the 1820s large parts of the estate were being sold off, and ten years later more than 30 hectares/74 acres of the best soil of Figeac were sold to make what is now Cheval Blanc.

Inevitably this link prompts comparison of the wines of the two great vineyards, which, with that of Ausone, in almost any year are ranked at the top of their appellation. The elegant Figeac as a rule is marginally lighter than Cheval Blanc with its great substance, but it is still a rich and powerful wine, complex and concentrated. Commonly this minute variation is attributed to the fact that the soil of Figeac is planted with both Cabernets in equal proportion, while those of Cheval Blanc are planted with Cabernet Franc alone. In 1947 Thierry Manoncourt took over the management of the estate, which an ancestor of his had acquired in 1892.

The great vintages have been many, especially notable since the war being those of 1945, 1949, 1950, 1953, 1955, 1961, 1964 and 1966. These successes have continued into the seventies and eighties. Outstanding in that period have been the wines of 1970, 1971, 1978, 1981, 1982, 1983, 1985, 1986 and 1988.

Paul Filliatreau, Saumur-Champigny
Paul Filliatreau is unusual among Saumur-Champigny growers in the Loire in that he makes and sells two *cuvées*: one from young vines that is ready to drink soon after release and a *vieilles vignes*, which, depending on the year, is aged in oak *barriques* and is best kept a year or so. His example has now been followed by other growers with various special *cuvées*. Filliatreau's vineyard plots are very scattered. The wines have a deservedly good reputation.

Finesse
Imprecise term for high quality, but finest wines all have finesse. Harmony is all-important.

Fining
Various unwanted particles may be suspended in wine stored in barrels or vats, and fining (*collage* in French) is the process of clarifying wine by removing these particles. Egg whites are a traditional and still much used agent. As the whites gradually sink to the bottom of a barrel or vat, they take unwanted debris as well. Gelatine, bentonite clay and dried blood are also used.

Finish
The length of time a wine's flavor persists in the mouth. A long finish is a mark of quality.

Firm
Good structure; i.e. the opposite of flabby.

Fixed acidity
The malic, tartaric and citric acids found in grapes are fixed because they cannot be removed by distillation.

Flinty
See Gunflint.

Flor
White yeast cap that forms on the top of some Sherry vats, essential for the making of a *fino* and *manzanilla*. The *flor* cap protects the wine against oxygen, and the chemical interaction with the wine produces *fino's* distinctive taste.

Flora
A white hybrid derived from the Gewürztraminer and Sémillon, the Flora is another of Dr. Olmo's creations at the University of California, Davis. Its wines are aromatic but tend to lack definition and are rarely offered as varietals. The best of them are made in relatively cool conditions.

Floraison
French term for flowering of the vines.

Emile Florentin, St. Joseph
Dr. Emile Florentin practices organic viticulture at the Clos de l'Arbalestrier within the St. Joseph appellation in the Rhône. He produces both white and red St. Joseph of strikingly old-fashioned character. The 1985 St. Joseph Blanc is an uncompromising, sinewy wine aged in old barrels; the 1983 Rouge shows magnificent depths of fruit, great complexities of flavor and should still be drinking well in the year 2000.

Florio, Marsala
Founded in 1833 by Vincenzo Florio, this is the largest producer of Marsala with a production of 3.5 million bottles. From the wide range offered, the dry Riserva Egadi is worth seeking out.

Flute
Ideal glass for sparkling wine, showing the bubbles to best advantage.

Folle Blanche
No longer the principal grape of the Charentais wines destined for distillation into Cognac, the Folle Blanche still flourishes in the sandy soil of the Bas-Armagnac, where it makes white wines of low alcohol and high acidity, ideal for the production of *eaux-de-vie*. It is widely planted in the Pays Nantais, where it is known as and makes the lively V.D.Q.S. Gros Plant and may be bottled *sur lie*.

Folle Noire
A variety quite unrelated to the Folle Blanche. It makes full, tannic, well-colored wines capable of aging, and in the little appellation of Bellet makes red and rosé wines when blended with the Braquet, Grenache and Cinsaut. Also known as Fuella.

Fonseca Villa Nova de Gaia
Founded in 1622 and now part of the Taylor group, Fonseca is famous for vintage Ports of massive power, with huge fruit and flesh (1980 excepted). Top Fonseca vintages: 1985, 1977, 1963, 1948. The Fonseca-Guimaraens from lesser vintage years is first-rate (excellent 1987 and 1976). This firm has few rivals for the consistent excellence of its Ports across the range, with "Bin 27" one of the best branded Ports and good white "Siroco" Port. Fonseca's pre-eminence owes everything to Bruce Guimaraens, one of Port trade's best tasters. Bruce is now ably assisted in the vineyards by his son David, who studied viticulture at Roseworthy College in South Australia. Fonseca owns three superbly sited

estates in the Douro: Quinta do Panascal, Quinta do Cruzeiro and Quinta de Santo Antonio. These account for 60 per cent of the firm's requirements.

Domaine Font de Michelle, Châteauneuf-du-Pape
This Rhône property is run with immaculate care by the Gonnet brothers. Font de Michelle consistently produces the finest white Châteauneuf-du-Pape. The 1990 is a brilliant, limpid wine with toasty aromas and a faultless balance of fruit and oak on the palate. The 1989 red wine is a classic Châteauneuf, with admirable spice, ripe tannins and a complex vinosity that will develop superbly in bottle for ten years.

Fontanafredda, Barolo
This famous firm of merchants and growers at Serralunga d'Alba was founded in 1878 by Conte Emanuele Guerrieri, son of King Victor Emmanuel II. The Fontanafredda style of Barolo is strong-flavored and markedly tannic, characteristics that are typical of Barolo wines from the Serralunga zone. Since the 1982 vintage, Fontanafredda has produced six different Barolo *crus:* San Pietro, Gallaretto, Bianca, Gattinera, La Rosa and Garil. The 1982 Barolo La Rosa is particularly ripe and long, with at least another ten years of development in the bottle ahead of it.

Forastera
The dominant variety of the dry white D.O.C. wines of Ischia, where it flourishes on the volcanic soil of the island.

Philippe Foreau, Clos Naudin, Vouvray
With 12 hectares/29.6 acres of some of the best situated land in Vouvray the Foreau family has been making fine wine in the Loire for three generations. Philippe took over from his father, André, in 1983 and has since been reaching new heights. As in all the best Vouvray estates, traditional methods are married with modern winemaking knowledge. Foreau's wines tend to be softer, less austere than those of Gaston Huet. Some spectacularly rich *cuvées* of *moelleux* were made in 1989 and 1990.

Fortana
A red-wine variety native to the northwest of Emilia-Romagna between Parma and Piacenza. Near the Adriatic coast north of Ravenna the grape makes the tannic D.O.C. Bosco Eliceo, which may be dry or sweet, still or sparkling. There the Fortana may be known as Uva d'Oro. Another synonym is Fruttana.

Château Fortia, Châteauneuf-du-Pape
Château Fortia is one of the best-known estates of Châteauneuf-du-Pape in the Rhône and the home of the Le Roy de Boiseaumariée family. The red wines of Fortia are still among the finest of the commune, deep colored, peppery, with very rich fruit. The 1988 is one of the best vintages produced here, with better structure than the a typically soft 1985.

Fortified wine
Wine to which grape brandy has been added. Before the advent of bottles and corks, this was done to enable wine to keep longer. Port, Sherry, Madeira and *vine doux naturel* are all examples.

Les Forts de Latour, Pauillac
While this unclassified wine is commonly thought to be among the ever-swelling ranks of the second wines of prominent châteaux in Bordeaux, it is more properly described as a *vin de marque.* This is because its production is based on three parcels of vineyard that do not appear on the 1759 map of the Latour domain, with the admixture of the yield from vines deemed too young to contribute to the *grand vin.* More important than this distinction is the fact that since its first vintage, in 1966, Les Forts has made wines very like that of Latour proper, but lighter and ready to drink earlier. They have consistently commanded prices equivalent to those of the second growths of the Médoc. Notable vintages have been frequent, as in 1966, 1967, 1970, 1975, 1978, 1979, 1981, 1982, 1983, 1985, 1986, 1987 and 1988.

Foudre
French term for a large wooden wine cask.

Foulage
French term for crushing, as in breaking grape skins in a crusher (*fouloir*).

Bernard Fouquet, Domaine des Aubuisières, Vouvray
A rising young producer making some of the best wines of this Loire appellation from 20 hectares/49.4 acres of vines. His *sec* is fermented in cement while the *demi-sec* and *moelleux* are always fermented in the traditional style in old oak *barriques* and *demi-muids.* His best *cuvées,* such as Les Marigny (*moelleux*) and Les Perruches (*sec*), come from individual vineyard parcels.

Château Fourcas-Hosten, Listrac
Traditionally the best Listrac, Fourcas-Hosten changed hands in 1971 after having belonged to the same family in Bordeaux since 1810. Since then considerable improvements have taken place in vineyard and *cuvier* and in the attitude to winemaking, something clearly reflected in the quality of the product. Characteristically the wine now is full, deep and fruity, with richness and structure. It is no longer aggressively tannic, but still capable of development over fifteen or twenty years. Recent successes include 1981, 1982, 1983, a notable 1985, and a splendid 1986 of immense promise.

Foxy
Flavor associated with America's native varieties, such as *Vitis labrusca,* though the taste in fact resembles foxes less than it does boiled sweets or hawthorn blossom.

Château de Francs, Bordeaux Côtes de Francs
A watchtower dating in part from the twelfth century, the Château de Francs dominates the hilly vineyards of the appellation of the same name northeast of St. Emilion. This small area of Bordeaux enjoys the advantages of low rainfall and exceptionally long hours of sunshine. Recent successes include 1988 and 1989, both rich, powerful and structured wines. Les Douves de Francs is a light and perfumed second wine of agreeable quality, while a little dry white wine is also made.

Frapin, Segonzac
Based at Segonzac, this traditional Cognac firm is owned by Max Cointreau and his wife, their huge estate extending to 350 hectares/865 acres in Grande Fine Champagne. Frapin Cognacs have a full chestnut color and an intense concentration of flavor, this style owing a lot to the high percentage of new Limousin oak casks in which the brandies are stored. Their best Cognac is the single-vineyard Château de Fontpinot with its marked fruitiness acting as a counterbalance to the powerful wood flavors.

Frappato di Vittoria
A black Sicilian grape, planted around Vittoria in the south of the island, where it makes pale, long-lived, highly alcoholic wines. The variety is important to the D.O.C. blend of Cerasuolo di Vittoria.

Fratelli Bischi, Verdicchio
Verdicchio — the Italian white wine as famous for its green amphora bottle as for its agreeability with fish — comes from the Marches, and the Bischi brothers

produce exceptional Verdicchio in their well-placed vineyards near Matelica.

Free-run juice

Juice extracted from grapes simply by pressure of their own weight. Except for wines made by *macération carbonique*, this is always the best-quality juice because the more pressure exerted when pressing grapes, the more bitter flavors the juice will have.

Freisa

A prolific but delicate and unpredictable vine much affected by varying conditions and seen to best advantage in the Basso Monferrato of Piedmont. It makes wines of variable color that may be still, sparkling, sweet or dry. Freisa is not among the most prized of Piedmontese wines, but its dry *frizzante* style is appealing, and the variety now seems on the ascendant after a prolonged decline prompted by faltering demand for its *amabile* production.

Freixenet, Spain

Freixenet is the main rival to Cordorníu as a producer of sparkling wines, with a very strong presence in the United States. Freixenet was the first Cava producer to introduce automatic *girasols*, or *gyropalettes*, in place of *pupitres* for *remuage*. Freixenet's best-known wines are the Cordon Negro and the Brut Nature and the increasingly popular and keenly priced Carta Nevada. At the top of the range, Freixenet offers some fine vintage wines.

Frescobaldi, Chianti

Frescobaldi is one of the old, established families and merchants of Chianti, and its association with wine goes back to the fourteenth century. They have little land in Chianti Classico but concentrate on Rufina, Pomino and the Colli Fiorentini, as well as managing an estate in Montalcino, Castelgiocondo. The Castello di Nipozzano in Rufina includes 124 hectares/306 acres of vines, with the *cru* of Montesodi and a substantial planting of Cabernet Sauvignon. Frescobaldi was also a prime mover in the development of Galestro and Predicato wines.

Frizzante

Semi-sparkling Italian wine, often quite low in alcohol.

Frost

During winter vines are well adapted to withstand severe cold. However, spring frosts are an ever-present danger in the vineyards of much of France, Germany and Britain. Frosts destroy the young tender shoots.

Fruit or fruity

The quality of the fruit is the central determining factor in wine. Good wines will impress with their concentration of fruit, while poor ones will be thin and meager because the vines have been allowed to produce too many dilute grapes.

Fumé Blanc

See Sauvignon Blanc.

Furmint

This is the principal variety of the legendary Tokay, and so is inseparably associated with Hungary. The grape is planted fairly widely and makes powerful, alcoholic, varietal wines. With Hárslevelŭ, and sometimes a little Yellow Muscat, it is blended to make the princely Tokay. The vine is readily susceptible to noble rot, and the *Aszú* berries of the Furmint are an essential element of the process that makes Tokay, a process thought to have evolved during the seventeenth century. It is the proportion of *Aszú* grapes that determines the concentration of the wine, its nature and quality.

Weingut Rudolf Fürst, Franken

Excellent German estate in south Franken producing red and white wine in almost equal proportions, to the highest standards. The reds are aged in cask, the whites in stainless steel.

Gaglioppo

A vine of ancient and obscure origin and many designations. In Calabria it makes the red D.O.C. Cirò, and is widely used for blending to produce red and rosé wines. Also known as Montonico Nero.

Angelo Gaja, Barbaresco

Angelo Gaja is Italy's most discussed winemaker. In just thirty years he has transformed a traditional family wine business in Barbaresco into Piedmont's most prestigious estate. A single-vineyard Barbaresco from Gaja now commands the price of a first-growth claret, which says as much about the man's remarkable flair for marketing as it does about his exceptional skills as a winemaker.

Behind the showmanship, Gaja has always shown a sleepless curiosity about wine and a perfectionist's passion to improve his own. Gaja's quest to make great wine began in the vineyards. In the mid-sixties he introduced a pruning system that radically reduced the yields of Nebbiolo by restricting growth to ten buds per vine. Improvements in vinification followed in the seventies, with the arrival of Guido Rivella, Angelo's enologist. Cleanness of flavor, purity of fruit and elimination of harsh tannins were all achieved by a logical sequence of innovations in the cellar. Among the most interesting was the use of nitrogen during vinification to eliminate oxidation and volatile acidity in the wines, a bedevilling fault of the old style Barbarescos.

Barbaresco is Gaja's chief priority, enormous care going into the making of his three single-vineyard *crus*. The Sori San Lorenzo (3.9 hectares/10 acres) tends to produce deep-flavored, well balanced wine; the Costa Russi (4.4 hectares/8.4 acres) yields one with sensuous aromas and a velvety texture; while the Sori Tildin (3.4 hectares/8.4 acres) usually has the deepest color, the most intense flavor, and the greatest capacity for aging. In 1988, Gaja turned his attention to Barolo with his purchase of the 28 hectare/69 acre Marenca-Rivette

vineyard at Serralunga. There he eventually intends to produce 5,000 cases of Barolo a year; but there are also substantial plantings of the French varieties Cabernet Sauvignon and Chardonnay. Gaja's vinifications of these varieties prior to 1988 have produced good results, though respected tasters might argue that his Chardonnays from his Gaja & Rey vineyard have been more successful than his Cabernet Sauvignons. The latter nonetheless remain interesting wines of considerable potential, but it is difficult to justify their very high prices.

Gaja's company, Gaja Distribution, is the Italian agent for a string of top-flight Bordeaux, Burgundy and California wine estates.

Gamay

Gamay means red Beaujolais, for it is the sole grape variety used for everything from Beaujolais Nouveau to the longer-lasting *crus* like Moulin à Vent and Morgon. Its full name is Gamay Noir à Jus Blanc, to distinguish it from other Teinturier versions. It also grows in other nearby appellations, such as Côtes Roannaises, Côtes du Forez, St. Pourçain and Coteaux du Lyonnais, as well as spreading along the Loire Valley for Gamay de Touraine and Anjou Gamay, and can be found in the Ardèche and Savoie. Elsewhere in Burgundy, Gamay is a constituent of Passe-Tout-Grains. It has not traveled to the New World, but in California a grape called Gamay Beaujolais has been identified as a clone of Pinot Noir, while Napa Gamay is the Valdiguié of the Midi. Contrary to popular belief Gamay is not the Kékfrankos of Hungary.

Gamay Beaujolais

See Pinot Noir.

Gamy

Aroma and flavor developed by some mature wines; typically they smell of well-hung game such as pheasant. Pinot Noir and Cabernet Franc are among varieties that develop these characteristics.

Gamza

This is the Bulgarian name for the Hungarian Kadarka, the Skadarska of Yugoslavia and the Cadarca of Romania. In Bulgaria the variety is the third most widely planted of the native vines, and it makes characteristically robust, aromatic red wines with the substance to improve with aging.

Gan Eden Chardonnay Alexander Valley, Sonoma County

Gan Eden means Garden of Eden in Hebrew, and the winery, located near Sebastopol in Sonoma County, is one of a small group of wineries in California dedicated to producing only Kosher wines for an increasingly sophisticated clientele of observant Jews no longer attracted by the traditionally heavy, sweet Kosher wines made from Concord grapes. Gan Eden Chardonnays are characterized by their soft, approachable style and their intense fruit. Owner winemaker Craig Winchell has produced some excellent Kosher Gewürztraminers, also from Alexander Valley fruit.

Garganega

A widely cultivated but low-yielding variety, seen at its best in the Veneto, to the east of Verona, where it is the principal constituent of Soave. The intrinsic merits of the grape seem likely to become more widely recognized as growers nowadays aim to produce wines of quality rather than mass-market appeal. With Trebbiano and Tocai the Garganega makes Bianco di Custoza.

Garnacha

See Grenache.

Garrafeira

Portuguese term for wine that has been aged for a minimum of two years followed by at least a year in bottle for red wines, and six months aging before bottling and six months afterward for white wines. Many of Portugal's finest wines come into this category.

Garvey, Jerez

Founded by the Irishman William Garvey, who settled in Jerez in southern Spain in the 1790s. William Garvey's son Patrick was the first to develop the production of *fino* successfully. Taken over by Rumasa in 1978, the firm is now owned by a German cooperative. It has vineyard holdings of 600 hectares/1,480 acres. The Garvey's range includes San Patricio Fino, Tio Guillermo Dry Amontillado and Ochavico Dry Oloroso.

Rolly Gassmann, Rorschwihr

Louis Gassmann is generally reckoned to be one of the best three or four winemakers in Alsace, a master of long, slow fermentations giving wines of structure and staying power. Gassmann's misfortune is that his vineyards are not particularly well sited and he owns no *grand cru* holdings. His Rieslings tend to show an aggressive *goût de pétrole* (*see* Petrolly) affected by the heavy soils of Rorschwihr. His Tokays, by contrast, are a triumph of the winemaker's art, with rich roasted-coffee aromas and a mouthfilling presence on the palate. His Pinot Auxerrois is fine, vinous and long, while his Gewürztraminer Cuvée Anné 1983 is a great concentrated wine of voluptuous richness framed by a sinewy acidity that should ensure that the wine will still be drinking well for many years to come.

Gazela, Vinho Verde

A Vinho Verde of some quality, made at Barcelos in Portugal by the huge Sogrape concern.

Château Gazin, Pomerol

This Bordeaux property is still large despite the loss of 5 hectares/12 acres to Pétrus twenty years ago. That fact gives an indication of the quality of the soil, all of it on the high plateau of Pomerol. The vineyard has belonged to the family of Bailliencourt since the end of the First World War, but despite this continuity Gazin has performed erratically in recent decades, and its reputation has declined in spite of the excellence of the wines made in 1970, 1975, 1976 and 1978. Efforts now are being made to improve quality, with a new *régisseur (manager)*, and in the eighties there has been a string of successes, with the wines of 1982, 1983, 1985, 1986 and 1987 outstanding, though likely to require time to mature.

Gebiet

A German term for a region or district. Not an official European Community term.

Gélas, Vic-Fezensac

A family firm founded in 1865, Gélas makes a range of uncompromisingly traditional and altogether excellent Armagnacs. The *eaux-de-vie* are distilled to a strength of 52 percent alcohol by volume in a continuous still; they are then aged in new Montlezun oak. Outstanding twenty- to twenty-five-year-old Hors d'Age and a very fine range of single-domain vintage Armagnacs are among their products.

Marius Gentaz, Côte Rôtie

A top grower of Côte Rôtie in the Rhône, Gentaz made a magnificent 1985: deepest ruby in color, intense bouquet redolent of violets and truffles and a huge flavor at once velvety and ripely tannic.

Gewürztraminer

A spicy, highly individual variant of the Traminer (*gewürz* means "spicy"). It is difficult to cultivate, prone to frost damage and *coulure*, but a fine autumn allows the

Gewürztraminer's pinkish grapes to produce fat, unctuous wine; aromatic, structured and intensely flavored. The wine is grown in Germany, Italy, central Europe, California and the Antipodes, but is seen at its incomparable best in Alsace, where it occupies 20 percent of the vineyards. In exceptional years, which include 1983, 1986 and 1989, *vendange tardive* and *sélection de grains nobles* wines are made.

Bruno Giacosa, Barolo/Barbaresco

Bruno Giacosa owns no vines but buys in the finest grapes from the best estates of Barolo and Barbaresco. The results are some of the most complex and long-lived wines in Piedmont. The 1978 Barolo Rionda from Serralunga is a legendary wine of awesome power, while the 1982 Barbaresco Santo Stefano is an exquisite amalgam of lovely aromas and graceful, finely wrought flavors.

Joël Gigou, Jasnières

The Gigous are the leading champions in the gradual renaissance of this small appellation on the south-facing hillside overlooking the Loir River (a tributary of the Loire). The characteristics of individual vineyards such as Clos St. Jacques are stressed. *Moelleux* wines are made in exceptional years, such as 1989 and 1990. They also make Coteaux du Loir white from Chenin Blanc and red from Pineau d'Aunis and Gamay.

Giró

An ancient Sardinian grape variety of Spanish origin. The vine is unproductive, and its popularity is declining, but it still makes red D.O.C. wines in the south of the island.

Château Gloria, St. Julien

This *cru bourgeois* vineyard in Bordeaux, which currently extends to some 48 hectares/118 acres, was the creation over half a century of the late Henri Martin, a former mayor of St. Julien and a notable figure in the Médoc. It represents the patient accumulation of small parcels of land in the best part of the appellation, and the high prices obtained by its wine over many years attest to Martin's judgment and skill. Typically, Gloria makes rich wines of substance and bouquet, tannic yet balanced, and its good vintages are many, as in 1962, 1964, 1966, 1970, 1971, 1973, 1975, 1976, 1978 and 1979. During the eighties, with the exception of 1980 and a rather lightweight 1981, there has been an unbroken run of successes up to 1988. Here, as at Château St. Pierre, Martin's other property, his work and his tradition are being carried on by his son-in-law, Jean-Louis Triaud.

Gobelet

Pruning system that trains the vine into a bush shape. Much used in Languedoc-Roussillon as protection against the heat of the summer and high winds like the Mistral. It is also used in Beaujolais.

Gonzalez Byass, Jerez

One of the most important Jerez houses, founded by Manuel Maria Gonzalez Angel around 1835. The name Byass comes from Robert Byass, who became a partner in 1863. Since 1988 the company has been entirely owned by the Gonzalez family. Gonzalez Byass owns 2,000 hectares/4,940 acres of vines. Its famous Tio Pepe is the world's top selling *fino* brand; Tio Pepe retains its quality despite huge production. Other famous Gonzalez Byass Sherries include Amontillado del Duque, the superb Apostoles Dry Oloroso and Matusalem Sweet Oloroso.

Gosset, Champagne

Very old, small independent house in Ay founded in 1584. Its characterful, full-bodied but delicate Champagnes are always given plenty of bottle age before sale. Its small annual production of around 30,000 cases ensures that it is not very well known, but its reputation as one of the best Champagne houses is well deserved. The vintage Grand Millésime is particularly impressive. The Gosset family also owns Château de la Grille in Chinon.

Léopold Gourmel, Cognac

Pierre Voisin of Léopold Gourmel is one of the most original merchants working in Cognac today. A former mechanical engineer and the local Volvo agent in the Charente for many years, he decided to establish his own Cognac business in the mid-1970s. He is a specialist in the light, fruity and early maturing Cognacs from the Fins Bois, and he also buys some Cognacs from the best part of the Petite Champagne around Archiac. Gourmel Cognacs are the palest shade of gold and show an exquisite, elegant fruit that one associates more with a fine wine than with a powerful spirit. They have not a trace of caramel and come unblended from one provenance and from a single year, though no mention of the vintage appears on the label, as this practice has been largely banned in Cognac since 1946.

Two Gourmel Cognacs should not be missed. The Age des Epices (thirteen years old) has a herbal, spicy bouquet and very fine fruit, while the Quintessence (twenty years old) shows red tints among the gold on account of its long years in Tronçais oak casks; the time in wood also imparts the *rancio* nose, that highly prized characteristic, an almost Madeira-like vinosity that comes from the beneficial effect of long, slow oxidation. Gourmel Cognacs are increasingly available in many Michelin three-star restaurants in France.

Goût Anglais

"To the English taste." In particular refers to the English taste for *brut*, mature Champagne.

Goût de terroir

The flavor of some wines is marked by the character of the soil in which the grapes were grown. For instance, flinty soils often give wine mineral flavors.

Governo

The once-widespread practice in Chianti of adding a small proportion of must from semidried grapes to wine that had finished fermenting. This addition induced a slight refermentation, giving more color and body. It is now mostly used only by producers wanting to make an early-drinking style of Chianti.

Graciano

A grape variety traditional to the Rioja, but increasingly rare. Its wine is well colored, scented and long lived, but the vine is both delicate and low yielding, and consequently unfashionable. In France it is known as Morrastel, and there too its share of the vineyard has declined dramatically.

Grafting

In terms of winemaking, grafting means attaching the scion (part of the vine that produces grapes) to a rootstock. The *phylloxera* epidemic was resolved by grafting European vinifera scions to *phylloxera*-resistant American rootstocks.

Graham, Vila Nova de Gaia

This Port firm was founded in 1808, though it initially traded in textiles only. Graham makes sweet, rich, multi-dimensional vintage Port, based on fruit from Quinta dos Malvedos below Tua and other nearby quintas. Top vintages: 1985, 1983, 1970, 1963. Also rich fruitcakey tawnies.

Giorgio Grai, Bolzano

Giorgio Grai is an eminent Italian enologist, whose wines are revered but hard to obtain largely because he does not have the time to distribute them widely. Visitors wishing to taste some of the best wines of the Alto Adige should go to the Edy bar on Bolzano's Walther Platz, where a range of Grai's wines is served. Both his 1986 Pinot Bianco and his 1986 Gewürztraminer are excellent, profound expressions of their respective grapes, but they should be allowed to breathe for a while in the glass to show their full character.

Alain Graillot, Crozes-Hermitage

Alain Graillot bought his Crozes vineyard in the Côtes-du-Rhône, now some 18 hectares/44.5 acres, in 1985. He has quickly established himself as one of the best growers of the appellation. His best *cuvée* is La Guirade, a powerful *vin de garde* aged in new oak. The 1989 is especially fine, with blackcurrant aromas and a latent spicy richness, needing four to five years to blossom. Graillot also makes a red Crozes-Hermitage for early drinking, which is partially stored in stainless steel, and an attractive, relatively straightforward white Crozes.

Grand Duchess Brut Sparkling Wine, Ukraine

Grand Duchess is a sparkling wine produced at Odessa on the Black Sea from a mix of Aligoté, Sauvignon and Traminer grapes. The Odessa Wine Company, which makes the wine, was founded in the 1890s by a Monsieur Roederer from Rheims, France.

Château Grand-Puy-Lacoste, Pauillac

This vineyard was created early in the eighteenth century and in the nineteenth was classed as a fifth growth. Since 1978 the Borie family of Ducru Beaucaillou have controlled this estate in Bordeaux, and Xavier Borie's modernization of the *cuvier,* with the installation of new vats, has been reflected in greatly improved wines. The 1981 was successful in a difficult year, the 1982 spectacular in a great one. Since then very notable wines of power and richness have been made in 1983, 1985, 1986 and 1988, so that there can be little doubt that the new team has revitalized Grand-Puy-Lacoste. Typically, its wines are powerful, rich and intense, with a pronounced bouquet and a tannic austerity in youth somewhat akin to that of Lynch-Bages, Grand-Puy-Lacoste's neighbor on the plateau. In Lacoste-Borie the property makes a second wine in a lighter style.

Château Grand Traverse Johannisberg Riesling, northern Michigan

This 30,000-case winery near Traverse City in northern Michigan is committed to vinifera grapes in a climate meant for native varieties or hybrids. The risk is high, but the results have been worth it over the years. The best wines are the Rieslings, especially the late-harvest naturally sweet wines, reflecting owner Edward O'Keefe's studies at the wine school at Geisenheim in Germany. He has even managed to produce some first-rate *Eisweine* when his late-harvest grapes have been hit by sudden frosts in late fall. These wines have the kind of sugar-acid balance that even the best California Rieslings can't always achieve.

Grande Escolha Quinta do Cotto, Douro

The restrictions on the production of Port, Portugal's most famous fortified wine, imposed by the vineyard classification system have prompted a number of growers, Miguel de Champalimaud of Quinta do Cotto prominent among them, to improve the quality of their red wines. His magnificent Grande Escolha, sold under the label only in its best years, is a blend of the traditional varieties of the Douro, Tinta Roriz, Tinto Cão, Touriga Nacional and Touriga Francesa, aged in new Portuguese oak. The wine is powerful, highly individual and demands long aging.

Grande Marque

In Champagne, a member of the Syndicat de Grandes Marques de Champagne. Not in itself a guarantee of quality: the reputation of the house is a better guide.

Bodegas La Granja Remelluri, Rioja

This boutique *bodega* is the home of an outstanding single-estate Rioja situated in one of the highest points of the region at Labastida. The grapes are harvested late so that the tannins are fully ripe, and the acidity is balanced by alcohol. The aim is that the wines should become silky and smooth with age — "essential, in my opinion, for a Reserva Rioja," says owner Telmo Rodriguez. Tempranillo is the backbone of Remelluri Riojas, and everything is done to preserve the primary character of this great grape, which has certain affinities with Pinot Noir. The *reservas* are called La Bastida de Alava, the 1985 a model of opulent fruit and silky textures.

Grape variety

There are many hundreds of grape varieties used for making wine. The "noble" wine grapes of Europe are of the *Vitis vinifera* family; other families, such as *Vitis rupestris,* are native to other parts of the world, notably North America. The grape variety is one of the major factors in determining the taste of a wine.

Grapy

Curiously few wines smell of grapes. Some German white wines and Muscats do smell grapy.

Estates Grassa, Côtes de Gascogne

Yves Grassa and his family have several estates dotted

around the Armagnac region of France, totalling 160 hectares/395 acres. Their base is just to the east of the small town of Eauze. Half of their production is Armagnac and half wine, mostly sold as Vin de Pays de Côtes de Gascogne. They use a varying blend of Ugni Blanc, Colombard and Gros Manseng, with their best *cuvée* being aged in oak for five to six months. They also produce a 100 percent Gros Manseng Cuvée Tardive. The wines are generally best drunk young before the fresh fruit flavors tire.

Alfred Gratien, Champagne

A small family owned and run house that fully deserves its high reputation. Alfred Gratien is the only Champagne firm to have been founded by a Saumur house. Alfred Gratien founded his Saumur business in 1864 and opened his Champagne concern six months later. Gratien, Meyer, Seydoux & Cie is now run by Alain Seydoux. Alfred Gratien's yearly production is around 17,000 cases of traditionally made Champagne, and it is given plenty of bottle age before being released.

Gratien et Meyer, Saumur Mousseux

This Loire firm was founded in 1864 shortly before its Champagne sister firm, Alfred Gratien. The two firms are run by the charmingly ebullient Alain Seydoux, who understandably prefers to live in the Loire's gentle climate rather than in chillier Champagne. Gratien et Meyer's sparkling wines are consistently reliable. The red *demi-sec* Cuvée Cardinal, made from Cabernet Franc, is fun and excellent with soft fruits.

Gray Riesling

An unremarkable, but in California widely planted, gray variant of the black Trousseau of the Jura, this grape has no connection with the Riesling proper. Its agreeable varietal wines are well received despite, or perhaps because of, their hint of sweetness. The variety is also known as Chaucé Gris.

Gray rot

The same fungus as noble rot, but on the wrong grapes at the wrong time. Wet weather causes the rot to destroy the grapes.

Great Western Blanc de Blancs New York State sparkling wine, Finger Lakes

If this dry, delicate, deep-flavored sparkling wine is an example of what can be done in New York State's Finger Lakes wine district, the region has a bright future. Long a source of indifferent wines made from odd-flavored, native labrusca grapes, the Finger Lakes region has been making a tortuous and not always successful transition to European vinifera grape varieties. This sparkling wine is made entirely from Chardonnay. It makes sense because New York's State's climate is much closer to that of Champagne's than to California's. Great Western has made a surprisingly good attempt to rival Champagne.

Grecanico

A variety of Hellenic origin that is decreasingly planted nowadays, but still makes pleasing dry white table wines in western Sicily.

Grechetto

A variety established in Umbria, where it makes dry white D.O.C. wines and forms a part of the blends of others, such as Torgiano, Colli Perugini and Colli del Trasimeno. The grape is also found as a subordinate variety in Latium.

Greco

A white variety brought to Italy by the ancient Greeks. On the volcanic soil of Campania it makes the distinctive, dry, fragrant Greco di Tufo. In Calabria semidried Greco (Greco di Bianco) grapes produce the scented Greco di Gerace, one of Italy's outstanding dessert wines.

Greco Nero

A variety of ancient Hellenic origin widely used in Calabria for blending, generally with Gaglioppo. The grape is found also as a subordinate variety in Sicily and Sardinia.

Green

Term used for a wine that tastes unripe and acidic.

Green harvest

To thin out the bunches of grapes in July or August to reduce the yield and increase quality. Known in France as *Vendange verte/Eclaircissage*.

Green Hungarian

A white variety of uncertain origin that in California makes fruity, substantial, decidedly bland wines of varying degrees of sweetness.

Grenache

Grenache can be white or gray, but is best known as a red grape of Spanish origin, where it is called Garnacha and is widely planted all over the country, particularly in Rioja, Navarre, Catalonia and Ribera del Duero. It produces heavy, alcoholic wines, which tend to age quickly and consequently benefit from blending with other varieties.

In France it is one of the more important of the thirteen varieties of Châteauneuf-du-Pape and features in all the red appellations of the southern Rhône, as well as those of the Midi, along the Mediterranean from Nice to Perpignan. It is also grown in Corsica, North Africa and in Sardinia, where it is called Cannonau.

It has spread to California, Australia and South Africa, mainly for dessert wines and Port-style wines, rather than table wine.

Grignolino

An unusual Piedmontese red variety indigenous to Monferrato to the northeast of Asti. It makes pale, dry wines that show individuality and a youthful freshness and elegance. Traditionally the better wines have been produced from small parcels of favorable soil and exposition, but there are signs that cultivation on a larger scale may be contemplated. The grape is sometimes blended with Barbera and Freisa to make the limited production of Rubino di Cantavenna.

Grillo

By tradition this is the noblest grape of Marsala, but in percentage terms the Grillo is subordinate to the Catarratto Bianco.

Grip

Refers to the hold that tannins or acidity have on the palate. For long life wines need grip.

Bernard Gripa, St. Joseph

Currently making one of the best wines of St. Joseph in the Rhône, Bernard Gripa cultivates a vineyard of 3.5 hectares/8.6 acres at Mauves. His 1989 St. Joseph is spectacular, a red wine of poised elegance, which at the same time is opulent and mouthfilling.

Jean-Louis Grippat, St. Joseph

A very good grower based at La Sauva near Tournon in the Rhône, Grippat makes textbook St. Joseph, fleshy, round, with flavors of raspberries and wild cherries. Excellent 1986 and a first-rate 1989. Grippat also makes forward, pleasurable Hermitage.

Domaine Jean Grivot, Vosne-Romanée

The Grivots own about 10 hectares/24.7 acres of vines spread out over fifteen of the best Burgundy appellations. Their biggest holding is about 4 hectares/9.9 acres in their own village, but even that is

divided among three or four separate vineyards. They are said to own about 0.33 hectares/0.8 acres in Richebourg, which would produce, at most, about 125 cases a year. The Grivots are among those who follow the precepts of enologist Guy Accard, which means maceration to extract color and flavor and high-temperature fermentation to extract color and flavor. It seems to work. They make about 900 cases of their Clos Vougeot each year. It is a wine to seek out and cherish.

Grk
A native Yugoslav variety, found chiefly on the island of Korčula, this grape makes yellowish and highly individual dry white varietal wines.

Groot Constantia, Constantia
This, the most famous wine estate outside Europe in the eighteenth century, was sold in 1885 to the then colonial government of South Africa in the wake of phylloxera. It has remained a government research institute and national monument ever since. Following some rather uninspiring years in the 1970s, the quality of the wines has rapidly improved since the mid-1980s. The 100 hectares/247 acres of vines are not irrigated. The most successful products are the Shiraz, which has always maintained its quality, a blend of Cabernets Sauvignon and Franc and now a good and improving Chardonnay, Weisser Riesling and Gewürztraminer. The old star is again in the ascendant.

Groppello
A traditional variety grown chiefly around Lake Garda in eastern Lombardy. On its own it makes unremarkable table wines, but the grape forms part of the blends of superior D.O.C. wines, both red and rosé.

Grosslage
A grouping of individual, neighboring vineyard sites (*eEinzellagen*) in Germany. *Grosslagen* vary from very small to very large.

Grossvernatsch
See Schiava.

Château Gruaud-Larose, St. Julien
This large Bordeaux estate consistently makes wines that whatever the year must be considered among the finest of the Médoc. The property was created from smaller holdings in 1757, and its quality was soon recognized, with the early classifications, as well as that of 1855, invariably assessing Gruaud-Larose as a second growth. The estate was divided in 1867, although its great reputation remained intact, and was not reunited until 1934, when Monsieur Cordier of the *négociant* house was able to buy the second part of the vineyard, having acquired the first just after the war.

The wine of Gruaud-Larose is usually perfumed, deeply colored, with richness, evident fruit and a persistent flavor. It has greater substance than the more austerely elegant wines made nearer to the river, like Léoville-Lascases and Ducru-Beaucaillou, the two growths with which habitually Gruaud-Larose disputes supremacy in St. Julien.

Very notable wines were made in 1953, 1955, 1959, 1961, 1962, 1964, 1966, 1970, 1975, 1978 and 1979. The eighties have seen a similar tale, with a charmingly fruity 1980, and a 1981 that was a notable success in a difficult year, followed by a stupendously rich, concentrated and tannic 1982. Further successes came in 1983 and, especially, 1985 and 1986, both wines of exceptional potential, 1987, 1988 and 1989, the two last again impressively rich, concentrated and structured. These wines will need upward of ten years to approach maturity, with years like 1980 and 1987 accessible rather sooner.

The second wine, Sarget de Gruaud-Larose, is soft, rich and deeply colored, with some of the quality of the *grand vin,* and can be drunk much earlier.

Grüner Veltliner
A white wine grape widely planted in Lower Austria and inseparably associated with Vienna. The wine is dry, fruity, slightly *spritzig*, with a style that evokes Alsace. The variety is also found in the Wachau and in Moravia, where, obscurely, it is known as Riesling.

Guerrieri-Rizzardi, Bardolino
The Guerrieri-Rizzardi family estate extends to 130 hectares/321 acres in Bardolino, Soave and Valpolicella. Search out the excellent Bardolino Tacchetto and from a range of whites, the grapy, off-dry Moscato Dògoli.

Etienne Guigal, Ampuis
Etienne Guigal is probably the greatest Rhône name in the English-speaking world, an Ampuis-based merchant and grower founded by Guigal, a former cellarmaster with Vidal Fleury, in 1946. Etienne Guigal's son, the meticulous Marcel, now runs the company. One feels that he regards all the press attention focussed on himself in the 1980s as a distraction from his main goal of making great, long-lived Rhône wines. Guigal has not been deflected from his mission, for his wines from Côte Rôtie, the firm's specialty, are some of the most complex and fascinating in the world. The downside is that they are now stratospherically priced.

Guigal owns major holdings in Côte Rôtie with prime sites in the Côtes Brune et Blonde, and it also buys in grapes from forty growers. Fermentation can take up to three weeks, and the wines are aged in cask for three years. The finished wines have monumental structure, and the 1985 vintage is a model of the Guigal style. In that year, the Brune et Blonde did not attract the hyperbolic praise heaped on the single-vineyard wines, but it is altogether excellent, round with beautifully clear Syrah fruit. Of the single *crus,* La Mouline (100 percent Côte Blonde) is a sensuous, perfumed wine, extremely rich with a lingering aftertaste. The La Landonne is burlier, hugely structured with an awesome concentration of flavor.

The Guigal star of 1985 is La Turque, the first vintage of this *cru,* which combines the sensuous allure of La Mouline with the devastating power of La Landonne. La Turque now commands prices comparable to first-growth clarets. On a more earthbound level, Guigal produces one of the most satisfying Côtes-du-Rhône wines available, as well as fine examples of Condrieu, Hermitage and Gigondas.

Château Guiraud, Sauternes
This very substantial Bordeaux estate is the Château Bayle of the 1855 classification, and, with Yquem, one of only two *premiers crus* within the commune of Sauternes itself. Guiraud was rescued from a seemingly irreversible decline at the beginning of the eighties, when the Canadian Narby family acquired it. Very heavy investment has been made in vineyard, *chai* and château; this was first reflected in the admirable wine of 1983, with the splendid vintages of 1985 and 1986 amply confirming the revival of Guiraud. The proportion of Sauvignon is as high as 45 percent, so that the wine tends to be less luscious than others of the appellation. The dry wine, G, is a Bordeaux Sec made from 100 percent Sauvignon, and La Dauphine du Château Guiraud a red Bordeaux Supérieur that is produced in considerable quantity.

Gunflint
Some wines, such as Pouilly-Fumé, are said to have a taste of gunflint; the taste is clean and hard, somehow reminiscent of flint struck with steel. Also called simply flinty. To the French it is *pierre-à-fusil.*

Guntrum, Rheinhessen
Both a wine estate and a merchant house, the latter with many wines from elsewhere as well as such commercial basics as Liebfraumilch. The estate, though, is much

more notable for lovers of German wine. Each grape variety and vineyard site from the 67 hectares/166 acres is made separately, and the grape varieties include Riesling (about 30 per cent of the total), Müller-Thurgau, Silvaner, Scheurebe, Kerner, Rulander, Gewürztraminer and Bacchus, as well as various new crossings being grown for experimental purposes. Winemaking is modern, and the premises are right next to the Rhine.

Château La Gurgue, Margaux

A small *cru bourgeois* vineyard very close to Château Margaux in Bordeaux, La Gurgue has been revitalized since its acquisition in 1978 by the owner of Chasse-Spleen, whose daughter, Bernadette Villars, now makes the wine. Heavy investment, allied to talent, has transformed the property and its product. The excellent 1981, 1982 and 1983 vintages make it hard to believe that as recently as 1975 the wine was refused the appellation. The wine is rich, powerful and tannic, and the 1985 and 1986 will need time to illustrate their impressive promise.

Gutedel

See Chasselas.

Guyot

A pruning system widely used in France and elsewhere: The vines are trained on wires. A single *guyot* system produces vines with a trunk and one arm, a double *guyot*, a trunk and two arms.

Gyropalette

A *gyropalette* is a large metal container that can hold up to 500 bottles of sparkling wine. The bottles in the *gyropalette* can be manipulated all at once, thus simplifying the process of riddling (*rémuage* in France), in which the bottles are manipulated one at a time. This method (where the container is called a *girasol*) was invented in Spain, and adopted in Champagne and other sparkling-wine districts.

H

Weingut Fritz Haag, Mosel-Saar-Ruwer

Owner Wilhelm Haag, considered by many the best winemaker on the Mosel in Germany, is known for wines of exquisite delicacy with a clear, well-focussed flavor. No *süssreserve* is used, and the wines can be lean in youth, needing bottle age to come round, but they are worth the wait. Nearly all are Riesling, from just 4.5 hectares/11 acres of vineyards.

Halbstück

A German barrel of about 610 liters/161 U.S. gallons.

Halbtrocken

Half-dry in German: sweeter than *trocken*, or dry.

Hamilton Russell Vineyards, Overberg-Walker Bay

The tireless efforts of Tim Hamilton Russell and former winemaker Peter Finlayson since 1975, often against enormous bureaucratic interference, have definitely established this vineyard as among the best in South Africa. A precedent was set by planting vines in a coastal valley near the fishing port of Hermanus, where no vines had been grown before. The cooler climate is ideal for producing top-flight Pinot Noir, Chardonnay and Sauvignon Blanc.

Hard

Very tannic wine. Usually applied to red wines that need further aging.

Thomas Hardy & Sons, Reynella, South Australia

Thomas Hardy & Sons, founded by a Devon immigrant in the middle of the last century, is now the third largest wine producer in Australia. Hardy produces small amounts of Australia's best vintage and tawny Port-style wines, sourced from McLaren Vale Shiraz fruit. White wines are the company's strong suit. The 1988 Padthaway Chardonnay (Collection Series) has alluring exotic fruit and a hint of oak. There are impressive late-harvest Rieslings. Anticipating the free market in the E.E.C. beginning in 1992, Hardy acquired Ricasoli, the important Tuscan wine producer, in 1990, and it now also owns the La Baume vineyard in the Languedoc.

Hárslevelü

A grape variety found in Hungary and to a very limited extent in Czechoslovakia, the Hárslevelü makes varietal wines of some reputation, but its chief distinction is its contribution to the legendary Tokay.

Hartenberg Estate, Stellenbosch

This 110 hectare/270 acre South African estate is a future star. The previous owners were Gilbeys, and some excellent aged reds were sold under the Montagne label. Now in private hands, winemaker Danie Truter has made some exciting reds, notably Shiraz and Cabernet Sauvignon. There is also a superb blend of Chenin Blanc (botrytized), Morio Muscat, Gewürztraminer and others. Watch out for the delicious L'Estreux.

Gérard Hartmann, Voegtlinshoffen

Very good grower in Alsace producing exceptional Muscat. His Gewürztraminer and Tokay-Pinot Gris from *grand cru* Hatschbourg are concentrated, full-flavored wines that keep well for seven to eight years.

John Harvey, Jerez

Although this Bristol shipping firm was founded in 1796, it was not called John Harvey until after 1822, when John Harvey joined his uncle's firm. Following the Rumasa debacle, Harvey's bought the Jerez firms of Palomino and Vergara and de Terry from the Spanish government. They now own some 1,700 hectares/4,200 acres of vines. Harvey's Bristol Cream is the world's best-selling brand of Sherry. Other Harvey's Sherries include 1796 Fine Old Amontillado and 1796 Palo Cortado.

Château Haut-Batailley, Pauillac

This fifth growth is the smaller part of the old Batailley estate in Bordeaux, which was divided at the time of its acquisition by the Borie family, who still retain Haut-Batailley but are better known for their Ducru-Beaucaillou and Grand-Puy-Lacoste. At the same time the vineyard was entirely replanted, and with its young vines for years made wines with less than the characteristic depth and power of the better wines of Pauillac. As the vines matured, so did the wines improve, with successful vintages in 1961, 1962, 1966, 1970, 1978 and 1979. In the past decade the wines have shown more richness and structure and seem now more typical of the appellation. The best examples of this new, more concentrated style

have been the 1982, 1983, 1986 and 1987. These wines still illustrate Haut-Batailley's tradition of making wines that are ready for drinking rather earlier than other classed growths of Pauillac.

Château Haut Bertinerie, Premières Côtes de Blaye

This small and extensively renovated Bordeaux property makes outstanding dry white wines in the modern manner, certainly among the best of their appellation. Both the 1989 vintage and the 1990, vinified in new wood, provide elegant expressions of the Sauvignon grape. Under the same label Monsieur Bantegnies makes a fruity, scented rosé from the Cabernet Franc; it too is aged in cask.

Château Haut-Marbuzet, St. Estèphe

The success of this *cru bourgeois* and the acclaim given its wines are the justification of the vision and industry over forty years of Hervé Duboscq and his son Henri, who now manages this Bordeaux vineyard. This is composed of parcels of land acquired piecemeal during that period; an accumulation that now amounts to some 45 hectares/111 acres. Duboscq is an enthusiast and an innovator; he favors high-temperature fermentation to obtain maximum extraction, long maturation and aging in new oak only. According to his perception of the power and vigor of the year he will choose between wood from the Allier or the milder oak of the Nivernais, and all his bottling is done by gravity, without the use of pumps. Typically his wines are deeply colored, with fruit, spice, tannin and a pronounced bouquet. Outstanding over the past twenty years have been the vintages of 1970, 1975, 1978, 1979, 1981, 1982, 1983, 1985, 1986, 1987 and 1988, from which it may be seen that however modern the thinking and the techniques employed at Haut-Marbuzet, their result is one of consistent excellence.

Hautes Côtes de Beaune, Les Alouettes, Domaine Moillard

Hautes Côtes de Beaune is an old Burgundian appellation that virtually disappeared in the years between the wars. Those were hard times in Burgundy: even the most famous wines went begging, and lesser appellations were ignored or pulled up to make way for more profitable crops. Now everyone wants Burgundy, and the Hautes Côtes de Beaune vineyards, which mostly run along the top of the Burgundian slope, have been revived. The wines are usually light and relatively short-lived. But the best of them, usually including those from the Moillard firm, are true Burgundies at still reasonable prices.

Heat summation

System of classifying vinegrowing areas by annual average temperatures devised by the University of California, Davis.

Heavy

Term to denote too much alcohol and extract in a wine. Not necessarily a fault: it can apply to a perfectly good wine drunk at an inappropriate time, like an Australian Shiraz on a hot summer's day.

Hectare

Standard metric European measurement of surface area euqal to 10,000 square meters. One hectare = 2.47 acres.

Hectoliter

A hundred liters.

Charles Heidsieck, Champagne

The beginnings of the three Rheims firms using the name Heidsieck all stem from Florens-Ludwig Heidsieck, a wool trader who set up a Champagne firm in 1785. Charles Heidsieck was founded by his great nephew Charles-Camille in 1851. Henriot took control in 1976 until Rémy Martin bought the firm in 1985. Annual production is nearly 300,000 cases, all from bought-in grapes, as the firm has no vineyard holdings. Champagne Charlie is its prestige wine.

Heidsieck Monopole, Champagne

This Champagne house was established by Florens-Ludwig in 1785. Monopole was added in 1923 because of the success of its biggest-selling brand, Dry Monopole, which had been launched in 1860. The house was bought by Mumm in 1972, so it is now part of Seagram. One hundred and fifty thousand cases is its average production and it has 110 hectares/272 acres of vines. The top *cuvée* is Diamant Bleu, a blend of equal proportions of Pinot Noir and Chardonnay.

LEFT: Joe Heitz, winemaker at Heitz Cellars, as a student in the Beaulieu Vineyards lab in the 1950s with the legendary oeonlogist, André Tchelistcheff.

Heitz Cellars Martha's Vineyard Cabernet Sauvignon, Napa Valley

When winemaker Joe Heitz announces that he is about to release another vintage of his famed Martha's Vineyard Cabernet, fans begin lining up at his retail shop in the Napa Valley in California at 4:00 a.m. So eagerly do his followers await each new release that Heitz has had to work out a complicated system of allocations that angers more people than it pleases because so many must be turned away. The wine is made from grapes of a single vineyard named after the owner's wife. The wine is extraordinarily concentrated and almost opaque, with a unique taste of mint and eucalyptus that, once experienced, is never forgotten.

Henriot, Champagne

Since 1985 Henriot has been part of Veuve Clicquot. This Champagne house was set up in1808 by Appoline Henriot to market the wines from her father's vineyard. Now it is in the fortunate position of owning 103 hectares/254 acres of vines that supply it with around 80 percent of its needs. Annual production is about 125,000 cases, and it has two prestige *cuvées*: Cuvée Baccarat (mainly Chardonnay) and Réserve Baron Philippe de Rothschild.

Henriques and Henriques 10 Year Old Malmsey, Madeira

Established in 1850, this independent firm is the largest in the Madeira wine trade in terms of capital. The firm owns several prime vineyards, the largest being the 6 hectare/15 acre Ribeira da Cacha; the company is

planting a further 7 hectares/17 acres at Ribeira do Escrivão. Its 10 Year Old Malmsey, translucent and deep caramel in color, is very rich in fruit with a balancing note of acidity.

Henriques and Henriques 10 Year Old Sercial, Madeira

Russet brown in color, this wine is strong and dry, its mellow richness coming from long cask aging that tones down the marked acidity of the Sercial grape. Sercial ripens with difficulty in the coolest vineyards on the north side of the island of Madeira. It is sometimes wrongly thought to be the same grape as the Rhine Riesling. In Portuguese Sercial is called Esgana Cão, which means "dog strangler."

Henschke, Keyneton, South Australia

The Henschke family, which is of German and Polish origin, produces a superb repertoire of both white and red wines. Its vineyards are farther east than those of the hot Barossa Valley, and at a higher altitude of 400 meters/1,312 feet. Stephen Henschke is indisputably one of Australia's finest winemakers, highly intelligent, incisive, but thoughtful and open-minded. Most commentators agree that his greatest wine is the Hill of Grace Shiraz, which has some of the oldest vinestock in South Australia, brought over from France in the 1860s. It is said that his Shiraz vinification is traditional, but he in fact avoids the classic Rhône method, that is to say long maceration of the wine on the skins. At Keyneton, the cap is submerged for about seven days, and the wine is then drawn off while the skins are still fermenting; in this way, the lovely soft Shiraz tannins are preserved, the wine deriving its vinosity and length of flavor from the great age of the vines. The 1986 Hill of Grace is outstanding. Modern, mainly Germanic methods of vinification characterize the Henschke white wines (lovely Rhine Rieslings), which are beautifully clean, pure flavored and show a masterly light touch. The 1988 Semillon is at once deep flavored and extremely elegant.

Heredade de Esporão, Alentejo

This substantial estate in Portugal holds enormous promise for the future. Noble grapes and indigenous varieties are among the fifty or so planted on its 2,000 hectares/4,900 acres, and a splendid, modern *adega* has been built.

Weingut Freiherr Heyl zu Herrnsheim, Rheinhessen

This is probably the best estate in the whole of the Rheinhessen in Germany. There are 28.1 hectares/69 acres of vines, mostly Riesling, Müller-Thurgau and Silvaner, from the best sites in Nierstein, like Olberg and Pettenthal. The estate also owns the whole of the Niersteiner Brudersberg vineyard, some 1.3 hectares/3.2 acres in size. The wines are matured in oak. There are so many cheap, commercial wines of dubious quality from the larger area of the Bereich Nierstein that the name Nierstein has been devalued, but these are the real thing, and a reminder of how good Nierstein can be.

Vinicola Hidalgo, Sanlúcar de Barrameda

A small *bodega* founded in 1792 in Sanlúcar de Barrameda, this is still run by the Hidalgo family. It owns some 220 hectares/540 acres of vines. Its range includes the well-known La Gitana Manzanilla, Napoleon Amontillado, Jerez Cortado Palo Cortado and Oloroso Especial Dry Oloroso.

Hine, Jarnac

Hine is one of the most famous names in Cognac, with strong English associations. The firm was established in Jarnac in 1782 by Thomas Hine, a Dorset man. Now part of the powerful Moët-Hennessy group, the company is still run by the cousins Jacques and Bernard Hine, who continue to produce Cognacs of elegant definition marked with a discreet but definite oak presence. Bernard Hine is one of the most knowledgeable and communicative tasters in the Charente, and his outstanding ability as a blender is seen in the firm's best-known brand, Hine Antique, with its bright chestnut color, warm, kind flavor and just the right amount of oak. Hine is also the specialist in early-landed vintage Cognacs. Specially selected Grande Fine Champagne Cognacs of a single year are first aged in Jarnac for three years, after which they are shipped in cask to England, where they mature in a damp, cool cellar for about fifteen years before bottling. The dampness of the English climate allows the alcoholic content of the brandy to reduce quite naturally from an opening landed strength of around 60 percent to an eventual saleable strength of 40 percent. There is little need of artificial reduction. The resultant brandy is very aromatic with an unadulterated, natural flavor. The 1972 Hine Grande Fine Champagne is especially attractive.

Hock

English word for wine from the Rhine, a corruption of Hochheim, a village in the Rheingau.

Reichsgraf und Marquis zu Hoensbroech, Baden

Fifteen hectare/37 acre German estate founded some twenty-five years ago producing a range of interesting wines. The whites up to *Auslese* level are all dry, with *Kabinett* wines forming the backbone of the business. The estate aims for wines that are relatively high in alcohol. The balance of vines is 30 percent Weissburgunder, 20 percent Silvaner, 15 percent Riesling and 15 percent Spätburgunder, and the estate is the sole owner of the Michelfelder Himmelberg site.

Weingut von Hövel, Mosel-Saar-Ruwer

A 200-year-old German estate with Romanesque cellars. Eberhard von Kunow makes superb, concentrated Saar wines with good acidity and discusses them with enthusiasm. The estate is sole owner of the Hütte site in Obermmel, and nearly all the vines are Riesling.

Hua Dong Winery, Quindao, China

The Hua Dong Winery near Quindao on the Yellow Sea coast makes China's best wines. Charles Wish from Australia was the first winemaker here, and the Quindao Riesling has been consistently well made under his care, with good varietal character. Further varietals such as

Cabernet Sauvignon, Cabernet Franc and Chardonnay are planned.

S.A. Huet, Vouvray
This family firm in the Loire has been made famous by Gaston Huet, still active in his eighties. The traditionally made wines tend to be very austere, needing many years to soften and evolve, although some of the 1989s and 1990s are spectacularly rich. Noël Pinguet, Gaston Huet's son-in-law, has been the winemaker since 1974. In the Clos de Bourg, Le Haut Lieu and Le Mont it has some of the finest vineyards in Vouvray, which are now cultivated biodynamically. Gaston Huet was mayor of Vouvray from 1947 to 1989, president of the Comité des Vins de Touraine for many years and remains a great ambassador for the wines of Touraine.

Johnny Hugel
Jean Hugel is probably the best known Alsace wine merchant in the English-speaking world. Voluble, extrovert, trilingual, "Monsieur Johnny" is as much at home in a New York penthouse as he is on the vineyard slopes of his beloved Riquewihr. He has spent most of his working life spreading the word about the neglected beauty of the wines of Alsace.

By precept and example, he has made his fellow wine producers more fully aware of Alsace's extraordinarily rich viticultural heritage, and thanks largely to him Alsace is now seen as the home of great dessert wines to rival those of Bordeaux, Germany and the Loire.

Hugel et Fils has been a winegrower and merchant in Riquewihr since 1637. The family owns some 26 hectares/64 acres in the prime vineyards around the town, notably in the Sporen and Schoenenbourg *Grands Crus*.

Hugel wines are an excellent introduction to the wines of Alsace with a clean, aromatic style allied to a rich, round, hedonistic flavor. They are, in a word, charming. It is a style that consumers worldwide obviously like: Hugel now exports wines to 120 countries.

The Hugel family has specialized in late-harvest wines for at least 130 years. In exceptional autumns, favorable to the development of noble rot, tiny amounts of *vendange tardive* and *sélection de grains nobles* wines are made and stashed away for many years, to be opened for some special occasion.

Hugel recalls that at the silver wedding celebration of his parents, an 1861 Gewürztraminer Vendange Tardive was served. Hugel pioneered the marketing of these special wines on a commercial basis. In 1984, he was asked by the authorities to draft the legislation governing the making of *Alsace vendange tardive* and *sélection de grains nobles* wines. That the requirements are the most stringent of any fine wine in France is a measure of Johnny Hugel's vision.

Humagne du Valais, Albert Biollaz, Valais
The Humagne vine is indigenous to the Valais in Switzerland. From a yield of 60 hectoliters/3.5 tons per acre in vineyards 500 metres/1,640 feet above sea level, this wine tastes fresher through having been fermented at a low temperature. With less than 11 percent alcohol it is light, well structured and rustic in style.

Hungerford Hill, Pokolbin, New South Wales
This Pokolbin winery produced a good range of varietals from both Hunter Valley and Coonawarra fruit in the early eighties in Australia. Quality has slipped in recent years. Hungerford Hill was acquired by Seppelt in 1990, so a revival of good vintages may be expected in the future.

Huntington Estate, Mudgee, New South Wales
Huntington Estate in Australia produces the best wines of Mudgee and is the brainchild of Bob Roberts, a man of wide culture and an essentially self-taught winemaker. His red wines have great fruit, ripe tannins, a touch of gaminess, and they live a long time, being aged in large American oak vats. Look out for the rich blackcurrant-cassis flavored 1988 Cabernet and the peppery 1984 Shiraz/Cabernet. The annual music concerts at the Huntington Estate attract the best artists from Sydney.

Huxelrebe
A heavy-cropping German hybrid vine derived from the Chasselas. In favorable sites in its native land it is able to make Auslese wines. In England, where the Huxelrebe is quite widely planted, its quality is lower, but it remains capable of producing acceptable if rather neutral wines.

Hybrid
The result of crossing *Vitis vinifera* with another species of vine, often the American family of *Vitis labrusca*. The idea is to have both the quality of *Vitis vinifera* and resistance to cold or disease of the other species. In the past hybrids were invariably of poor quality. However, recently quality crosses like Seyval Blanc have been produced that give excellent results in cold climates like England.

I

Impigno
A rare Apulian grape grown between Bari and Brindisi and found nowhere else. It is the principal variety of the D.O.C. Ostuni Bianco.

Incrocio Manzoni
The generalized name given to strains of hybrid (*incrocio*, in Italian) vines developed by Professor Luigi Manzoni at the research institute at Conegliano in the Veneto. Incrocio Manzoni 6/0/13, derived from Pinot Bianco and Riesling Renano, makes successful dry white wines, while Incrocio Manzoni 2/15, Prosecco crossed with Cabernet Sauvignon, is a prolific red producer. (The numbers refer to the vine row and the number of the grafted vine.)

Infectious degeneration
An untreatable virus disease that follows a phylloxera attack. The vine's leaves turn yellow, hence the disease's other name of fan leaf, and the plant mutates. The disease remains in the soil, killing replacement vines ever more rapidly.

Inky
Used to describe the purple blackness of some young red wines and likely to indicate high levels of tannin.

Inniskillin Riesling, Ontario
Canada has about 14,160 hectares/35,000 acres of grapes, about 85 percent of which can be found on the Niagara Peninsula that connects southwestern Ontario, Canada, to Niagara County, New York. The vineyards stretch westward from Niagara Falls to about 64 kilometers/40 miles west of Hamilton, Ontario. There are vineyards along the shore of Lake Erie and another 2430 hectares/6,000 acres in the Okanagan Valley of British Columbia. Inniskillin, in Ontario, pioneered the production of wine from vinifera — European — grapes. Gewürztraminer and Chardonnay are made, too, but the Riesling seems to do particularly well in this northerly clime. In 1988 Inniskillin purchased the Hughes Vineyard in Napa Valley, California.

Inzolia
A delicate vine native to Sicily, where it makes dry white wines in the central uplands of the island. Blended with Sauvignon, the grape produces the excellent Regaleali, and it plays a part in the complex production of Marsala.

Iron Horse Blanc de Noirs Wedding Cuvée, Sonoma County

Iron Horse, in Sonoma County's Green Valley appellation, near Sebastopol, makes a variety of quality wines, but its major interest has always been sparkling wines. Wedding Cuvée has always been one of its top bottlings. Sparkling wine became somewhat of an obsession with California wineries in the 1980s, but Iron Horse never had any problem staying ahead of most of the competition; its sparkling wines are consistently among America's best. The Wedding Cuvée is a full-bodied wine, with elegant small bubbles, rich flavor and a delightful bouquet.

Irrigation

While usually illegal in European Community demarcated areas, irrigation is essential in hot areas like parts of Australia. Best done by a drip system, by means of a pipe along each row of vines, rather than by using a sprinkler.

Isole e Olena, Chianti Classico

Piedmont-born Dr. Paolo de Marchi is the enlightened viticulturist at the head of this improving estate at Barberino Val d'Elsa. He produces just one Chianti Classico, a fruity, approachable wine for relatively early drinking; the soft appeal of this wine is due in part to a good proportion of Canaiolo in the grape mix. His excellent Vino da Tavola Cepparello is made entirely from Sangiovese; the 1988 is firm and tannic, a wine that will age well until the late nineties. Among new plantings de Marchi has had most success with Syrah. The 1988 was the first vintage for this variety; the wine is round and succulent with a gamy character.

J

Paul Jaboulet Aîné, Tain l'Hermitage

Founded in 1834, this famous *négociant* and grower once enjoyed a justified reputation for producing the most consistently high-class wines from the Côtes-du-Rhône. However, Jaboulet's preeminent position has been challenged in recent years by such firms as Guigal and the revitalized Delas Frères. Nonetheless, Jaboulet remains a very fine if erratic source of northern Rhône wines. The family owns 25 hectares/62 acres of Hermitage, which encompasses the little Chapelle de St. Christophe at the top of the Hermitage hill. Hermitage La Chapelle can be a magnificent bottle, developing a warm velvety texture after twenty years. The 1961 is a legendary wine, and of recent years 1978, 1983 and 1988 are outstanding. However, some tasters have complained of inconsistent bottlings.

By contrast, the Jaboulet Crozes-Hermitage Domaine de Thalabert is a model of consistency, concentrated fruit and great length of flavor. The 1985 is a memorable bottle, voluptuous yet elegant, and the 1989 is also exceptional, intensely perfumed with an impressive extraction of red fruit flavors and soft tannins. Jaboulet's red wines from the southern Rhône — a Côtes-du-Rhône from Séguret and Châteauneuf-du-Pape Les Cèdres — seem less concentrated over the last decade when compared with their splendid counterparts from the 1960s.

Jacquère

Jacquère is a white-wine grape grown in the Bugey and in parts of Savoie, notably the *crus* of Abymes and Apremont, for making dry, rather stony wine.

Jacquesson, Champagne

Founded in 1798, Jacquesson is proud to be both the fifth oldest Champagne house and to have had Napoleon Bonaparte as a devoted admirer. This Epernay firm remains independent and is now run by the Chiquet family. It makes around 30,000 cases, and its 22 hectares/54 acres of vines supply 60 percent of its requirements. The wines are of consistently high quality. The range includes the vintage Perfection and Signature, a prestige *cuvée*.

Joseph Jamet et Fils, Côte Rôtie

Joseph Jamet's sons, Jean-Paul and Jean-Luc, now manage this leading Côte Rôtie estate in the Rhône. The brothers have introduced modern fermentation techniques that emphasize elegant Syrah fruit. The 1985, perhaps the last vintage in the old style, is dense and tannic. The 1986 is finely balanced and already delicious to drink, as is the 1987, a soft, forward wine and a star of this vintage.

Jammy

Slightly derogatory note for red wines, suggesting rather boiled, perhaps even synthetic-tasting fruit. However, some young reds, particularly those made by carbonic maceration, have a certain jamminess that contributes to their charm.

Janneau, Condom

Probably the best-known Armagnac name in the English-speaking world, this large firm was founded by a Cognaçais, Pierre Etienne Janneau, in 1852. The giant Cognac house of Martell bought a third of the shares in Janneau in 1946. The Janneau style of Armagnac, particularly in its less expensive brands, is light and fruity, reflecting a high percentage of early-maturing *eaux-de-vie* made by the double-distillation method. The company does, however, have excellent stocks of traditionally made older Armagnacs that are important elements in its top blends. Janneau employs a cooper, Monsieur Videau, who makes just two oak barrels a day. These are reserved for the Armagnacs of the Domaine de Mouchac, the company's own estate.

Jacky Janodet, Romanèche-Thorins

Directing an outstanding Beaujolais domain of 7.2 hectares/17.8 acres based at Romanèche-Thorins, Jacky Janodet makes dense, rich, satiny Moulin-à-Vent and Morgon from very old vines. These wines are aged in large oak *foudres* for up to a year before bottling. The Morgon is perhaps his best wine, with a marvellous minerally character framing the opulent fruit. A little Beaujolais Blanc is also made at the domain, as is a well-constituted Beaujolais-Villages.

Robert Jasmin, Côte Rôtie

One of the best growers of Côte Rôtie, Jasmin's winemaking style is incomparably subtle yet substantial, exuding class and refinement year after year. The solidly built 1985 retains a feminine floral aroma, which is repeated in the dense tannic 1988. The 1989 is a wine of ripe, friendly charm, full flavored but with that exquisite elegance that is Jasmin's signature.

Domaine Jau, Roussillon

A substantial estate in the Algy Valley in Roussillon, France, owned by the Daure family, who used to be sizeable vermouth producers. The winery is very well equipped, and much replanting of quality varieties has been done on the well-exposed, infertile hillsides. The Daures make Côtes du Roussillon red, white and rosé, and Muscat de Rivesaltes. They also own the Domaine de Valcros in the dual appellation of Banyuls/Collioure.

Château la Jaubertie

Nicholas Ryman is an Englishman who, having sold his very successful stationery business, moved to Bergerac in southwest France and bought a vineyard, Château la Jaubertie, in 1973. Using Australian techniques the wines

have continually improved. Now the wines of la Jaubertie are among the best of the appellation. Wines of all colors are made, with the Sauvignon being particularly successful.

Jermann, Villanova di Farra

Silvio Jermann is the lone wolf of Collio. As a young man, he turned his back on D.O.C. wines and created Vintage Tunina, a rich white *vino da tavola* made from very ripe Sauvignon and Chardonnay grapes as well as other varieties, including Picolit and Malvasia. His latest wine is a barrel-aged blend of Chardonnays of the 1986 and 1987 vintages called Where the Dreams Have No End.

João Pires, Setúbal Peninsula

Somewhat improbably, this modern and highly equipped *adega* on the Setúbal peninsula in Portugal has an Australian winemaker in Peter Bright. French as well as native Portuguese varieties are used, and the wines include the predominantly Cabernet Quinta de Bacalhoa, a hugely popular dry Muscat and the ripe-flavored Tinto da Anfora made at Moura near the Spanish border from Periquita, Trincadeira, Moreto and Aragones grapes. This *tinto* is aged in wood and with its softness and nuances of vanilla is reminiscent of Rioja.

Charles Joguet, Chinon

Unusually for a highly successful *vigneron*, winemaking is not Charles Joguet's first career, for he is a sculptor. He commutes regularly to Paris, from the Loire, where he has his studio. His wines have a great concentration of fruit and with age develop remarkable gamy aromas. Clos de la Diotterie, with its very old vines, is currently his best vineyard, although the Chêne Vert, with its younger but maturing vines, shows dramatic promise.

Weingut Karl Heinz Johner, Baden

All the wines on this new German estate are aged in *barriques*. The climate in Kaiserstuhl allows the Spätburgunder to be produced convincingly in the French manner with an alcoholic fermentation on the skins for up to fourteen days and a malolactic fermentation to soften the acidity. To avoid difficulties with the control authorities, who would rightly say that the wines are not typical of the district, all are sold as table wine.

Juliusspital-Weingut, Franken

Large and historic German estate of 180 hectares/395 acres spread throughout many of the best-known villages of Franken. The holdings include 21 hectares/52 acres in the Stein vineyards, overlooking Würzburg. The vines are principally Silvaner, Müller-Thurgau and Riesling, with a spread of other varieties including Gewürztraminer, Muskateller and Spätburgunder. All are matured in oak, some of the casks being over a century old. The estate is a charitable foundation, run for the benefit of the Julius hospital in Würzburg. The third-largest wine estate in Germany, it can outdo even the Hospices de Beaune in scale.

Juve y Camps, Spain

Excellent Penedès Cava producer whose Brut Natural Reserva de la Familia is drunk by the Spanish royal family.

K

Kabinett

Lowest ripeness category of the *Qualitätswein mit Prädikat* classification. Often lower in alcohol than others.

Kadarka

A red-wine variety of Balkan origin that is now widely planted in eastern Europe and especially in Hungary, where it is the principal variety. Throughout its range it makes good robust dry wines, occasionally *Aszú* wines in Hungary, and sweeter styles in Macedonia and the Austrian Burgenland.

Kanonkop, Stellenbosch

Until 1930 the vineyard was part of the great South African Uitkyk (pronounced ate-cake) property. It was then bought by the Hon. Paul Sauer and run as a separate estate with winemaker Danie Rossouw. Beginning in 1975 a young and very dedicated Stellenbosch graduate and Springbok rugby player called Jan Coetzee began to concentrate on Cabernet Sauvignon and Pinotage. His skill in the vineyard and the cellar produced some outstanding wines. He then moved on to establish his own winery, and since 1980 Beyers Truter has consolidated Kanonkop's supremacy in the red wine market. The Paul Sauer label goes on the top blended wine, 70 percent Cabernet Sauvignon, 15 percent Cabernet Franc and 10 percent Merlot, with the balance being Malbec and Souzão.

Rauienstrauch'sche Weingutsverwaltung Karthauserhof, Mosel-Saar-Ruwer

This estate was established in the fourteenth century by Carthusian monks, and acquired by the family of the current owner when Napoleon sold off church land. The Karthauserhofberg (hill) is divided into Orthsberg and Stirn. The wines tend to be higher in acidity than many on the Ruwer, which is to the benefit in the best vintages. There are 19 hectares/47 acres of vineyard. The estate also breeds Prussian Trakehner horses.

Kerner

Kerner is a new German grape variety, developed in 1969 from a crossing of red Trollinger and white Riesling. Of all the new German grape varieties, it has the greatest similarity to Riesling in flavor, as well as having good resistance to frost and giving high yields. It is now extensively planted, especially in the Rheinhessen and Palatinate. It is also grown in South Africa and England.

Weingut Reichsgraf von Kesselstatt, Mosel-Saar-Ruwer

One of the largest estates in the Mosel-Saar-Rüwer in Germany with a well-equipped, recently-built, above-ground cellar. In all, it owns 96 hectares/237 acres of vineyards, which are all planted with Riesling. Standards are very high. The von Kesselstatt estate in fact includes four different estates, all under the same ownership. Some of the best sites in the Mosel-Saar-Ruwer are included: vineyards like Graacher Josephshöfer, of which it is the sole owner, Graacher Himmelreich and Brauneberger Juffer. The Reh family, which owns von Kesselstatt, also owns a number of other estates in Germany, including Faber, the Trier-based largest producer of Sekt.

Khan Krum, Bulgaria

Close to Varna in eastern Bulgaria, Khan Krum is a very modern cooperative specializing in the production of white wines, especially from Chardonnay. Ugni Blanc and Aligoté, and a fresh clean Sauvignon Blanc are vinified in temperature-controlled stainless-steel vats. Some barrel fermentation (in 225 liter/60 U.S. gallon *barriques*) is used for Chardonnay. The 1989 Varna Chardonnay tasted at Khan Krum in 1990 showed a healthy pale color, good steely acidity, a fine definition of Chardonnay flavors and a respectable length on the palate.

Klein Constantia, Constantia

Once a part of Simon van der Stel's great South African

wine farm and estate, it was split from the main farm and most of the vineyards in 1766. A little white wine was made, but it was less expensive and of slightly inferior quality than the renowned sweet red wine of "High" Constantia. After various vicissitudes "Little," or as it was sometimes known, "Hoop-Op," was bought in 1982 by Dougie Jooste. Today it is a model wine farm. The scrubland has been replaced by row upon row of Cabernet Sauvignon, Merlot, Shiraz, Sauvignon Blanc, Weisser Riesling, Chardonnay and, for their newly launched Vin de Constance, Muscat de Frontignan. The wine that made Constantia a legend in Europe has come full circle. The whites are very good and, with time, the currently rather austere reds will progress.

Weingut Klören, Nahe
A small German estate producing mainly dry or medium-dry wines from a wide range of vine varieties.

Klostergut St. Lamprecht, Rheinpfalz
A German estate acquired by the Bergdolt family in 1754. Rainer Bergdolt produces stunning wines, some with 16 percent alcohol, and uses a lot of *barrique* aging. Most of the vines are Riesling (30 per cent), Kerner (15 per cent) and Müller-Thurgau (12 per cent), and there is an emphasis on dry wines with a fresh, flowery style.

Tim Knappstein, Clare, South Australia
A graduate of Roseworthy College, Tim Knappstein is the outstanding winemaker of the Clare Valley. Since his first vintage in 1977, he has established Clare as one of Australia's best wine regions with a long run of beautifully made wines, notably Rhine Riesling, Cabernet Sauvignon and Cabernet/Merlot. Wolf Blass became the majority shareholder in his firm in 1986, but Knappstein remains the winemaker, and his family still owns the vineyards in Clare. He is a particularly fine exponent of Fumé Blanc, and he has had good success with Gewürztraminer, which are further achievements to add to his mastery of Rhine Riesling, Cabernet and Merlot. Knappstein is an unsentimental wine technologist; he refrigerates all his wine from the point of pressing right through the maturation process until it is bottled. A mixture of French and American oak is used for cask aging, and the Knappstein Cabernet Sauvignons follow the Bordeaux tradition of classic *assemblage:* 80 percent Cabernet Sauvignon, 10 percent Cabernet Franc and 10 percent Merlot. The proportion of the grape mix is sometimes varied according to the character of the vintage. The result is a rich, multi-flavored wine, sometimes with a hint of licorice. Excellent Cabernet Sauvignon vintages include 1988 and 1986. By contrast, his straight Cabernet/Merlot blend can sometimes taste leaner, more angular.

Knudsen-Erath Oregon Pinot Noir, Yamhill County
Oregon burst on the wine scene in the early 1980s as the great hope of Pinot Noir enthusiasts. They were beginning to feel the pinch of Burgundy prices, and at that time only a couple of California wineries had been able to make even an acceptable Pinot Noir. With its milder climate, Oregon appeared to be the ideal location for growing the recalcitrant Pinot Noir grape. A couple of good vintages seemed to indicate that Oregon's cottage industry was capable of great things. Then several bad years disillusioned some people, but now the Oregonians seem to be back on track. Dick Erath is one of the more skilled Pinot Noir makers. From most recent vintages his wines have been light but concentrated in the true Burgundy style.

Kodru, Moldavia
Kodru, a red wine that ages well, is made from a traditional Bordeaux blend of 70 percent Cabernet Sauvignon and 30 percent Merlot. The grapes come from vineyards 8.7 kilometers/12 miles from Kishinev, the capital city of Moldavia. The Kodru 1987 was aged in oak for three years and is a wine of deep ruby color with a good fruit-acidity balance.

Charles and Christian Koehly, Rodern
This small domain of 8 hectares/19.8 acres enjoys an increasing reputation for Alsace wines of the highest quality. Charles Koehly's son Christian is a very talented winemaker and a feisty dynamic character who at 34 was the youngest-ever president of the Comité Interprofessionnel des Vins d'Alsace. Avoiding the twin pitfalls of excessive oxidation and oversulfuring, Koehly imbues his wines with a fine acidity, purity of fruit and the complex individuality of his *terroirs*. Rieslings are his forte, supremely elegant yet vigorous wines exemplified by his floral and forward 1990 Riesling St. Hippolyte. His 1986 Riesling Grand Cru Altenberg de Bergheim is poised and profoundly flavored.

Koshu
A native-Japanese grape with a documented history that dates back to the twelfth century. A vinifera variety, it provides table grapes and makes a white wine suitable for blending. With its proven adaptability to the difficult conditions of Japan the Koshu has been used in the development of experimental vines.

Kotsifali
A red variety native to Crete, where it makes substantial, alcoholic wines and is used for blending.

Kozhusny Winery, Moldavia
Kozhusny is a leading Moldavian winery, and the Director's Reserve 1986 is one of its most remarkable wines. Made from a blend of Cabernet Sauvignon, Merlot and Pinot Noir, the 1986 was a small vintage, vinified and matured in oak casks — a deep-colored, rich wine of great finesse. It should age well for at least 10 years.

Marc Kreydenweiss, Alsace
Promising 10 hectare/24.7 acre estate at Andlau in the Bas-Rhin, formerly known as the Domaine Fernand Gresser. Gresser's grandson Marc Kreydenweiss now works the vineyards and makes the wine. He is lucky to have holdings in three *grand cru* sites — Moenchberg, Wiebelsberg and Kastelberg — all situated on the schistous outcrop around Andlau. In the past, the quality of the wines was erratic, but thanks to Kreydenweiss's friendship with Léonard Humbrecht, Alsace's greatest winemaker, vintages have been much more successful since 1986. Kreydenweiss is not afraid to experiment: his late-picked Pinot Auxerrois, for example, is an attractive peach-flavored wine, though his *barrique*–aged Sylvaner is disappointing, the wood dominating the fruit. His Riesling Grand Cru Kastelberg is consistently his best *cuvée*, a steely wine that ages exceptionally well for up to ten years.

Henri and Rémi Krug, Champagne
Everyone has his or her own favorite Champagne. More often than not, among Champagne lovers that favorite will be Krug. It would be almost impossible to find

anyone who did not have the highest respect for both the wine and the company.

Krug was founded in 1843 by Johann Joseph Krug, who came from Mainz in Germany. Krug, which is based in Rheims, owns 16 hectares/40 acres of top-quality vines in Ay, growing Pinot Noir, and in Le Mesnil, growing Chardonnay. Its holdings supply some 20 percent of its needs. The remaining 80 percent, which includes some Pinot Meunier, comes from various parcels around Ay, Mareuil-sur-Ay, Oger and Avize among other places. Henri and Rémi Krug, the fifth generation, now run the house, although the Cognac firm Rémy Martin has been the majority shareholder since 1977. The wines continue to be made by traditional methods. The base wine is always vinified in 205 liter/54 U.S. gallon wooden casks. The malolactic fermentation is not permitted. The blend is made from many different lots of wine: there may be up to fifty different wines in the nonvintage Grande Cuvée, which represents 80 percent of Krug's production. The finished Champagne is given an extremely long time in bottle before it is released for sale.

Grande Cuvée, which replaced the highly regarded, full-bodied Private Cuvée, is a Champagne of great finesse and length. The Krug Grand Cuvée one drinks now contains a percentage of wines — 35 per cent to 50 per cent — dating from the early 1980s back to the early 1970s. The rare and expensive single vineyard Clos du Mesnil, made solely from Chardonnay grapes grown in that 1.9 hectare/4.6 acre walled vineyard, is a superlative Champagne.

Kuentz-Bas, Alsace
This tight-knit family business of Alsace *négociants* and growers is based in Husseren-les-Châteaux. The family domain is relatively small — 12.5 hectares/30.9 acres — in Eguisheim, Husseren and Voegtlinshoffen and accounts for 30 percent of their grape requirements; the remainder is bought as grapes or made wine from smaller growers. Kuentz-Bas wines are generally well balanced, understated and elegant. They make impressively harmonious yet intense *Vendange Tardive* Gewürztraminers.

Kumeu River Chardonnay, Kumeu
Innovative New Zealand winemaker Michael Brajkovich who studied at Roseworthy and worked both in Californian and for the Moueix family of Château Pétrus in Bordeaux, combines New World technology and Old World tradition to produce wines with quality and character. His soft, broad Chardonnay shows strong malolactic influence giving the wine a buttery, creamy texture and almost nutty flavor. A controversial Chardonnay, it stands apart from other mainstream wines.

L

L.B.V.
Late bottled vintage — a Port term for port of a single vintage, bottled after four to six years in cask. Seldom anywhere near vintage Port in quality.

Château Labégorce-Zédé, Margaux
A *cru bourgeois* vineyard of ancient origin in Bordeaux, Labégorce-Zédé is managed by the owners of Vieux Château Certan. It produces attractively fruity wines of some substance, and their quality has improved over the past dozen years.

Laberdolive, Labastide d'Armagnac
Pierre Laberdolive is the fourth generation of a family of growers that produces what many consider are the finest vintage brandies of Bas Armagnac. These Armagnacs need long aging but can be magnificent. The 1979 Domaine de Jaurrey is still powerful and rugged, an adolescent *eau-de-vie* in which the alcohol has not yet assimilated the tannin. The 1970 Domaine de Pillon, by contrast, is splendidly ripe and fruity, a perfect expression of *les sables fauves,* the yellowish sandy soils of the western Bas Armagnac. The 1946 Domaine de Jaurrey is made exclusively from the Folle Blanche grape and is wonderfully aromatic and tautly structured, with great persistence on the palate.

Château Lafaurie-Peyraguey, Sauternes
This is the larger part of the divided Peyraguey domain in Bordeaux, which was classed as a *premier cru* in 1855, and it retains the spectacularly improbable château, which dates in part from the thirteenth century. Since before the First World War the property has belonged to the prominent house of Cordier, curiously without achieving the recognition accorded their red wines like Gruaud-Larose and Talbot in St. Julien. Certainly an ill-judged technical decision, which led to a series of thin indifferent wines, was made in the middle sixties, and not until its reversal did quality improve with a fine and elegant 1981. The proportion of Sémillon has been increased greatly, and the modern wines are vinified and matured in wood, 30 percent of it new. The immediate result of these changes has been the notable successes of 1983, 1985, an extraordinary 1986, 1988 and 1989. There is obvious promise for the future here.

LEFT:
Château Lafite in Pauillac.

Château Lafite-Rothschild, Pauillac
Just as Latour stands at the extreme south of Pauillac, so Lafite dominates the northern border, and indeed a part of the vineyard stretches into St. Estèphe. A perceptible faltering in quality from the end of the Second World War until the mid-seventies can be attributed in part to the neglect of absentee owners, in part to the practice of bottling over an extended period, so that bottles of the same vintage often differed markedly in character. Eric de Rothschild assumed control of the Bordeaux estate in 1974, and with the advice of Professor Peynaud and the appointment as *régisseur* of Monsieur Crété, set about improving the situation. The new regime found early success with the 1975, the best Lafite since 1959, and confirmed the achievement with the wines of 1976, 1978, 1979 and 1981. There were startlingly powerful, tannic wines in 1982 and 1983, wines quite atypical of a vineyard customarily distinguished by its finesse and elegance.

The benign decade of the eighties continued with a slighter, unremarkable 1984; then came a more characteristic 1985, perfumed and harmonious, followed by another intense, improbably powerful wine in 1986. A backward 1987 and an initially more accessible 1988 of great distinction show huge promise for the future. In great years Lafite is immensely long lived. Maurice Healy, who attended the dinner at the château in 1926 wrote that the 1811 Lafite was opened on that occasion to tumultuous applause. That was a wine then 115 years old; a wine made in the year of the comet, the year before Napoleon's Russian campaign.

Lafite's second wine, variably called Carruades or Moulin des Carruades and made from the yield of vines not yet twelve years old, commonly shows delicacy and finesse.

Château Lagrange, St. Julien

Lagrange was bought in 1983 by the Japanese company Suntory, whose declared aim is to restore it to prominence. Vast sums have been expended on the renovation and replanting of this vineyard in Bordeaux, with a significant reduction in what had been an excessive proportion of Merlot. The existing *cuvier* and *chai* have been handsomely restored, and two new *chais* constructed; air conditioning and temperature controlled stainless-steel vats have been put in, new wood employed, and appropriate works carried out on the château and its park.

Similarly meticulous attention has been given to administration, viticulture and winemaking, and progress is already apparent. The first wine made wholly under the new regime was that of 1984. This was a good wine in a difficult year, but one far surpassed by the rich and fruity 1985 and a more powerful and concentrated 1986, which will need time, as will the 1987. The 1988 vintage promises well, the wine is fleshy, rich and deeply colored.

Château La Lagune, Ludon

A Bordeaux vineyard on soil akin to that of Margaux and first planted early in the eighteenth century, La Lagune enjoyed considerable fame in the nineteenth century. By 1954, however, a mere 4 hectares/10 acres remained under vines, and even this pitiful residue was blighted by the frosts of 1956. Since 1958, under successive owners, a sustained program of investment, replanting and modernization has been carried out, and the property is now a model of its kind. The quality of the wine has shown a corresponding improvement certain to continue as the vines reach maturity. Outstanding wines were made in 1976, 1978, 1982, 1983, 1985 and 1986. La Lagune has great appeal, and it remains remarkable value for money.

Lairén

See Airén.

Lake's Folly, Pokolbin, New South Wales

Lake's Folly was one of the first and perhaps the most famous of Australia's "boutique" wineries, founded by Max Lake, a Sydney surgeon, in 1963. Despite local scorn, Lake first planted Cabernet Sauvignon, a variety that had not been produced in the Hunter Valley since the 1940s. His choice of a hillside volcanic site for Cabernet proved good, for he has produced ageworthy elegant red wines from this grape since 1964. His Cabernets are unfiltered. Best vintages are 1969, 1972, 1978, 1981 and 1987. Chardonnay was first planted on the lower-lying alluvial creek land in 1969. The Lake's Folly Chardonnay style is spicy and shows the influence of new French oak. The 1986 and 1987 show an increasing elegance. Stephen Lake, Max's son, is now the winemaker.

Lamberhurst, England

Owned by Kenneth McAlpine, for fifteen years this was England's largest productive vineyard, with around 23 hectares/57 acres. Planting began in 1969 and by 1975 had reached 12.5 hectares/31 acres. Stephen Skelton, who founded Tenterden Vineyard, is now the winemaker. The winery's capacity is now 500,000 bottles, and some grapes are bought in. Lamberhurst has a variety of vines, including Huxelrebe, Müller-Thurgau and Seyval Blanc. Schönburger is the most interesting of its range. Some bottle-fermented sparkling wine is also made.

Lambrusco

A vine heavily planted in the predominantly clay soil of the Po valley around Modena and Sorbara. Traditionally the grape produces a purplish, foaming wine of fruit and flavor, either dry or *amabile,* the latter generally destined for export. Modern thinking tends towards a paler wine of notable freshness. There is also sparkling white Lambrusco. The variety's origins are Apennine, but its strains are found in areas as remote from each other as the Alto Adigé, Apulia and Sicily.

Château Lamothe, Premières Côtes de Bordeaux

The 35 hectares/86 acres of this Bordeaux property are sited high above the Garonne, and its traditional vines do well on the limestone base. Lamothe makes only red wines, and they show consistent merit, as in 1979, 1982, 1983, 1985, 1986 and 1988. They are powerful, structured and deeply colored, with a pronounced bouquet and considerable elegance.

Château Lamothe-Guignard, Sauternes

This is the larger part of the old Lamothe, which was classed as a second growth in 1855 and since 1981 has belonged to the Guignard family of Château de Rolland in Barsac. This Bordeaux vineyard is admirably placed on an outcrop above the little river Ciron, which plays so important a part in the microclimate of Sauternes. Lengthy fermentations, maturation in cask and early bottling produce elegant, well-structured wines with fruit and bouquet. Notable under the new owners have been the vintages of 1983, 1985, 1986, 1987 and 1988.

Landwein

German equivalent of a French *vin de pays. Landwein* may not be sweeter than *Halbtrocken.*

Château Lanessan, Haut-Médoc

Although omitted from the 1855 classification of Bordeaux, Lanessan was well known and well regarded in the nineteenth century, and throughout the twentieth it has produced vintages of unusual merit. In good years the wine has a pronounced bouquet, great fruit, richness and finessse. Of recent vintages, 1975, 1978, 1981, 1982, 1983, 1986, 1988 and 1989 were successful; consistency is among the virtues of Lanessan.

Lar de Barros, Tierra de Barros

The Tierra de Barros in the province of Badajoz produces the cheapest wines in Spain, but this vineyard of 250 hectares/617 acres near the Portuguese border makes a ripe, substantial red wine that is well regarded.

Château Larmande, St. Emilion

Although this Bordeaux vineyard has belonged to the Méneret-Capdemourlin family for almost a century, only in the last two decades has any serious effort been made to improve quality. A new *cuvier* was built and equipped with stainless-steel vats, the use of new wood was adopted and the property as a whole was revitalized by Jean-François Meneret and his sons. The vineyard itself has

been extended, and the proportion of Merlot built up at the expense of the Cabernet Sauvignon. This level of energy and investment was first rewarded by an excellent 1979, a wine scented and fat yet balanced and with the substance to develop. Further successes in the same style followed in 1981, 1982 and 1983; then came 1985, a splendid, impressively promising 1986 and a highly appealing 1988. It seems likely that these fine wines will need a minimum of five years' aging.

Domaine Laroche, Chablis
The nearly 100 hectare/247 acre Domaine Laroche, with prime sites in *Grands Crus* Blanchots and Bougros and Les Clos and in *Premier Cru* Fourchaumes, is the foundation of one of the most dynamic and quality-conscious houses in Chablis. Headed by Michel Laroche, who studied enology in Dijon, the operation includes a major *négociant* business which accounts for nearly 10 percent of the region's Chablis production, marketed under the Henri Laroche label. The domain wines are excellent examples of steely-dry Chablis of great verve. Sensitive barrel fermentation and oak-aging add extra complexity. The 1989 Chablis Grand Cru Blanchots Vieilles Vignes is a masterpiece of lingering subtlety, which will age well until the year 2000.

Larresingle, Condom
This Armagnac firm founded in 1837 takes its name from the imposing thirteenth-century Château de Larresingle, a walled village that is owned by Maurice Papelorey, the president of the company. Papelorey and his son Arnaud are tireless ambassadors for Armagnac in Japan, Britain and the United States. The Larresingle style is subtle and understated, which may explain Maurice Papelorey's preference for the violet-scented, drier Armagnacs of the Ténarèze.

Château Larrivet-Haut-Brion, Graves
This small vineyard in Bordeaux produces unclassified wines, both white and red, the latter predominating. Customarily, the red wines have shown fruit, breed and the capacity to age. More rigorous standards have been applied over the past five years, with new wood now being used for 40 percent of production. A very little white wine is made, from 60 percent Sauvignon, 40 percent Sémillon, fermented in new oak. Great efforts are being made to improve quality, and the vineyard has obvious potential.

Laski Rizling
See Welschriesling.

Château de Lastours, Corbières
Leading Corbières estate of 150 hectares/370 acres in northeast Corbières in France, based around a rehabilitation home for handicapped people who help run the estate. The oak aged Cuvée Simone Deschamps is its powerful top wine and has gained a high reputation both in France and abroad.

Late harvest
Late-picked grapes. Usually particularly ripe and may be affected by noble rot. *Spätlese* in German.

Château Latour, Pauillac
The vineyard is at the extreme south of the appellation, separated from Léoville-Lascases only by the shallow valley of a small stream. The soil too is shallow, pebbly and inhospitable, well adapted to the vine.

It is a curiosity that from 1670 for nearly three hundred years Latour passed by inheritance or marriage to related families; that era that came to an end in 1963 when British interests assumed control. A further reshuffling of shareholdings took place in 1968, and since then Allied Lyons has been the owner of this Bordeaux property.

LEFT: Château Latour in Pauillac.

The events of 1963 allowed the beginning of very considerable works of modernization and enlargement in *cuvier* and *chai*. Temperature-controlled stainless steel replaced the old oak vats, and an underground cellar was excavated to provide additional space for cask storage. The decision was taken to introduce a *vin de marque* under the name Les Forts de Latour.

The *grand vin* itself has always been massive, deeply colored, formidably tannic and intense, with a pronounced and individual bouquet. Traditionally it has needed many years to evolve into the marvel of richness and intensity that is Latour at its best. In this style the great vintages have been many, and they are long lived. Examples, to go back only half a century, are those of 1937, 1943, 1945, 1947, 1949, 1955, 1959, 1961, 1962, 1964, which illustrated Latour's ability to make sound wine in problematic years, 1966, 1970, 1975 and 1978. When properly kept a Latour of a good year will drink well after fifty years and more. The characteristically slow maturing of the wine has been a problem in the conditions of the past thirty years, and perhaps the aim now is to make a wine that will be ready earlier, an important commercial consideration. Vintages like those of 1981, 1982, 1985, 1986 and 1988 suggest that in the past decade this plan has been undone by the weather, and certainly traditionalists will hope so.

Lattes, sur
French term for Champagne that has undergone the second fermentation but that has not yet been degorged. A certain amount of Champagne is traded between companies at this stage. The only way the purchaser can influence the style is by the *dosage*, but even so the wine is sold under the purchaser's label.

Laurent-Perrier, Champagne
Founded in 1812, this company was bought, resuscitated and expanded by the de Nonancourt family in 1936. Laurent-Perrier remains independent and today is one of the largest Champagne groups, producing over 600,000 cases a year. The range includes two prestige *cuvées*, Grand Siècle and the vintage Millésime Rare. It also has a significant range of still Coteaux Champenois. Champagne de Castellane is one of its brands.

Lean
Usually refers to a wine, such as Riesling, that is strongly marked by acidity in its youth; may suggest the potential to age and soften.

Lees
Yeasts and other debris that gradually precipitate out of wine after fermentation.

Bernard Léger-Plumet, Pouilly-Fuissé
A former general practitioner turned *vigneron,* Léger-Plumet makes splendidly racy, taut Pouilly-Fuissé and Saint-Véran at his 4.5 hectare/11 acre vineyards near Solutré in Burgundy.

Legs
See Tears.

Peter Lehmann, Tanunda, South Australia
Peter Lehmann founded this Australian company in 1980, and by the end of the last decade he and his team of winemakers had earned the deep respect of professional buyers and critics for immaculately vinified white wines from Barossa, particularly Semillon and Rhine Riesling. His Botrytis Semillon was outstanding in 1985 and 1988 and provided the consumer with sharply priced alternatives to the great dessert wines of Bordeaux. The Lehmann red wines, Shiraz and Shiraz/Cabernet Sauvignon, are well made.

Jean Léon, Penedès
This single estate in the Penedès hills belongs to a Californian restaurateur. One hundred hectares/247 acres are planted with Cabernet Sauvignon, the wines showing highly extracted color, fruit and tannins sufficient to ensure a very long life. As a rough rule of thumb, a Jean Léon Cabernet from a good year needs to be kept for ten years before drawing the cork. The 1978 and 1989 vintages are approaching maturity. A smaller amount of Chardonnay is also made.

Château Léoville Barton, St. Julien
Like Château Leoville Poyferré, its fellow second growth, Léoville Barton was formerly a part of the great domain of the *émigré* Marquis de Las Cases. In 1826 it was acquired by Hugh Barton, an Irishman whose forebears had come to Bordeaux in 1725 and whose descendant, Anthony Barton, still owns the property as well as the neighboring Langoa, which his ancestor bought in 1821. There is neither château nor *chai* at Léoville Barton, so Barton lives at Langoa and makes and matures the wines of both his estates there. His uncle and predecessor ran the two properties for more than half a century, and it may have been an innate conservatism, or a simple reluctance to adapt to changing circumstances, that in his later years led to a slight faltering in the generally admirable standards maintained here. The new owner has rectified the omissions, introducing modern temperature-controlled equipment and imposing more rigorous standards of selection, and there has been perceptible improvement in the quality of the wine.

Notable successes in the past decade have been the 1980, 1981, a remarkable 1982, and 1983, with 1985 and 1986 showing great promise for the future. The vineyard is planted with a very modest proportion of Merlot, and the wine derives much of its individuality from the more austere and tannic Cabernet Sauvignon and Petit Verdot. The finer vintages need upward of ten years to approach maturity.

Château Léoville-Las-Cases, St. Julien
This is the largest remaining part of the great Bordeaux estate of the *émigré* marquis whose name it bears and to whose descendants it belonged into the present century. It makes extraordinary wine which, year in, year out, is invariably the finest of its appellation and among the very best of the Médoc as a whole. The greater part of the vineyard, more than 40 hectares/100 acres, is walled, and the gate with its arch and lion is familiar from the label.

Very little seems to have changed in 150 years, and the great reputation of the wine remains unaltered. Wines of very great merit were made in 1961, 1962, 1966, 1970, 1975, 1978, 1981, 1982, 1985, 1986, 1987 and 1988. Even in problematic years like 1964, 1967, 1973, 1977 and 1984, wines of unusual quality were produced.

In its great vintages Las-Cases consistently makes wines comparable with those of the first growths of the Médoc. Indeed, were there to be a revision of the classification, Las-Cases would be a likely candidate for promotion. In style its wines are deeper, darker, more tannic and structured than those of its few rivals within the appellation; they are rich, concentrated and complex, with great power allied to finesse and bouquet. Typically these wines will need around fifteen years to begin to fulfill their potential. They are the product of the exacting standards of viticulture, selection and winemaking of Michel Delon, whose generation is the fourth of his family to manage the property. The modern Las-Cases is a monument to his passionate dedication.

The second wine, Clos du Marquis, has been made since before World War I and traditionally has offered quality and value. Latterly it has become yet better with the introduction of a third wine, Domaine de Bigarnon, which is made with the harvest of the youngest vines.

Château Léoville Poyferré, St. Julien
A portion of the original Léoville estate, this second growth enjoyed a great reputation during the second half of the last century, when it was managed together with Lascases. For more than seventy years it has belonged to the Cuvelier family, but despite this continuity of ownership there can be no doubt Poyferré declined after World War II. Since 1979, there have been changes in the administration of this Bordeaux property, and heavy investment and modernization have taken place. Quality has improved greatly in the past decade, with a sound 1980 followed by notable wines in 1981, 1982 and 1983, the two last especially outstanding. Wines of similar distinction were made in 1986, 1987 and 1988.

Lieu-dit
French for "place name"; used for a vineyard site.

Limberger
See Blaufrankisch.

Limnio
An ancient and obscure grape variety that is native to Greece and found nowhere else.

Lindemans, Coonawarra, South Australia
Lindemans is now part of the giant Penfolds empire, with very important holdings in the major wine regions of Australia. The company's Coonawarra red wines are first-rate: the 1985 Cabernet Sauvignon St. George's Vineyard is a majestic wine with mouthfilling cassislike fruit, tremendous depth of flavor and life-giving acidity that should ensure further development in bottle until the end of the century. The 1986 Pyrus — a blend of Cabernet Sauvignon/Merlot and Cabernet Franc — is more expensive but lacks the excellent balance and definition of flavor of the St. George.

Weingut K & H Lingenfelder, Rheinpfalz
Rainer Lingenfelder makes wonderful dry Scheurebe and Riesling wines, top-quality rich but not too sweet dessert wines and much sought-after red wines from this German estate. The *barrique*–aged Spätburgunder is undoubtedly among the best in Germany, and it is probably this, more than any other single wine, that has made the name of the estate. The white wines, though, with high extract and lots of character, should not be overlooked. There are some 10 hectares/25 acres of vineyards.

Liquoroso
Italian term for a wine that is relatively high in alcohol; usually used for sweet dessert wines.

Listel, Vin de Pays des Sables du Golfe du Lion
The wine arm of La Compagnie des Salins du Midi, which was founded in 1856, this is an enormous enterprise with around 1,800 hectares/4450 acres in the south of France; 1,400 hectares/3460 acres are in Languedoc, principally along the sandy coast, and are classified as Vin de Pays des Sables du Golfe de Lion. The rest is in Provence, except for a vineyard in the Côtes-du-Rhône. Along the Languedoc coast the company is able to grow ungrafted vines as the phylloxera aphid is unable to penetrate sand. The company, which has long made good-value everyday wines, is now also producing some more upmarket Chardonnay and Cabernet Sauvignon varietals.

Llano Estacado Chardonnay, West Texas
Texas is bigger than France, and since its wineries are all over the state, it's impossible to generalize on the wine they make. Llano Estacado is in the flat, desertlike country near Lubbock, in the Panhandle part of the state. The winery was founded in 1976, and its 6 hectares/15 acres originally encompassed seventy-five different varieties of grapes. Experimentation eventually bought that down to a manageable dozen or so, with a particular emphasis on Chardonnay. Llano Estacado Chardonnays regularly turn out to be crisp, clean, nicely balanced and long-lasting in the mouth. Whether it's the soil, the climate or the winemaker's skill, these wines seem to have a particularly intense varietal, or Chardonnay, character.

Bodegas Los Llanos, Valdepeñas
This is a modern winery with a heavy investment in new wooden casks. The *gran reserva* is a ripe, soft, vanilla red wine that is popular in Britain.

Long
The flavor of a good wine should persist on the palate. The opposite is short.

Lopez de Heredia, Rioja
This Haro *bodega* founded in 1887 is steeped in tradition and is rightly famous for its old oak-aged wines. These are Riojas of the highest class with no concession made to modernity: the wines are still fermented in wooden vats and are never filtered. The best *reservas* of the *bodega* are the Viña Tondonia and Viña Bosconia, exceptionally long-lived red wines that are made from 50 percent Tempranillo, 30 percent Garnacha, 10 percent Mazuelo and 10 percent Graciano. Properly cellared, great old vintages of Viña Tondonia like the 1964 will still taste marvellous throughout the 1990s.

Gustave Lorentz, Bergheim
Important growers and merchants in Alsace, who with their sister firm Jérome Lorentz are a force to be reckoned with. Their own domain is some 25 hectares/62 acres,

specializing in discreet Gewürztraminers of considerable breed and finesse from the vineyards of Altenberg de Bergheim and Kanzlerberg. The Lorentz style of winemaking may lack obvious street appeal, but given bottle maturation of three to four years and plenty of air once the cork is drawn, the wines show real complexity and nuances of flavor.

Loureiro
A grape variety found mainly in the Lima region of the Portuguese Minho, where it makes supposedly laurel-scented Vinho Verde. The grape is found also in Spain.

Château La Louvière, Graves
Since 1965 this Bordeaux estate has been owned by André Lurton. La Louvière makes unclassified red and white wines from its 53 hectares/131 acres. Its record over the past twenty-five years has been one of constant progress; the vineyard has been replanted and the *cuvier* and *chai* rebuilt and equipped on modern lines. With its advantages of site, on largely gravelly soil between Châteaux Carbonnieux and Haut-Bailly, allied to meticulous winemaking, it is no surprise that La Louvière should have progressed and hold promise of further improvement. Outstanding white Graves has been made throughout the past two decades, with 1982, 1984, 1985 and 1986 notable among recent years. As the red varieties have matured, so the quality of the wine made from them has advanced. Wines of the past years have been rich and aromatic, with power, fruit and flavor. Especially successful were the vintages of 1978, 1979, 1982, 1983, 1985 and 1986. Red or white, the unclassified La Louvière is consistently better than much Graves officially rated its superior.

Lumassina
A grape, perhaps a variant of Trebbiano, planted around Savona, to the west of Genoa, where it makes lively white wines.

Château Lumière, Honshu, Japan
Some of Japan's best wines are made at Château Lumière. The style of the label and the contents of the bottle are both influenced by Bordeaux. The red wine is a classic mix of Cabernet Sauvignon, Cabernet Franc and Merlot. The white is akin to Sauternes and is made from botrytis-affected Semillon and Sauvignon grapes. Both wines age well for up to five years.

Emilio Lustau, Jerez
This high-quality, independent firm was established in 1896 and is now one of the top seven exporters of Sherry. Lustau exports Sherry under its own name as well as supplying quality Sherries for own-label ranges. The Lustau range includes an *amontillado*, a *palo cortado* and a dry *oloroso*. There is an East India cream, but finest of all is the Almacenista range. These are small parcels of rare Sherries bought from small stockholders, or *almacenistas*. They are some of the most interesting and complex Sherries available today and extraordinarily good value.

Château Lynch-Bages, Pauillac
This large property in Bordeaux, well placed on the plateau to the south of Pauillac, has been making wine of note at least since the early years of the eighteenth century.

Lynch-Bages was classed as a fifth growth in 1855, but always has been judged better, commanding prices comparable to those of the lesser second growths. Since 1937 the estate has belonged to the Cazes family, and today it is occupied and directed by Jean-Michel Cazes. The château has been meticulously restored, and the *cuvier* and *chai* modernized and enlarged.

Typically Lynch-Bages is dark and rich, with a pronounced bouquet of black currant, ripe tannins, concentration and substance. It is a robust wine of great

distinction. Notable successes have been the 1981, the extraordinary successive vintages of 1982 and 1983, 1985 and 1986, the last a wine of astonishing power and potential. These splendid years followed an uncharacteristically weak period in the seventies, when only the wine of 1970 itself seemed to exemplify the individuality of Lynch-Bages. In the earlier postwar years there were outstanding vintages in 1945, 1952, 1953, 1959, 1961, 1962 and 1966. Château Haut-Bages-Averous is regarded as the second wine of Lynch-Bages and is sold as such, but it is in fact a *cru bourgeois* in its own right. A novelty for a Médoc château is the Blanc de Lynch-Bages first offered in 1991; this is made from 40 percent Sauvignon, 40 percent Sémillon and 20 percent Muscadelle.

M

Macabeo

Macabeo or Maccabeo is a Spanish white grape variety. It is one of the ingredients of white Rioja, where it is called Viura, and is grown elsewhere in northern Spain, notably for Cava in Penedès, where it is usually blended with Xarello and Parellada. It has also crossed the Pyrenees and features in the white wines of the Midi, especially in the Pyrénées-Orientales for *vins de pays* and Côtes du Roussillon blanc. It tends to be short on taste, fairly high on acidity and needs blending with more flavorsome varieties.

Macération

The steeping of grapes in their own juice to extract color, flavor and tannins from the skins. All red wines are made in this way. Rosés are either made by a brief period of maceration, or by blending red and white wine. The latter method is illegal in the European Community, except for Champagne.

Macération carbonique

French term for carbonic maceration. This fermentation method was pioneered in the Beaujolais to produce light, fruity wine without much tannin. Grapes must be carefully hand picked and the grape skins kept intact as the fermentation initially takes place inside the grape itself. The grapes are placed in sealed vats, and carbon dioxide, either naturally produced or added, keeps out the oxygen. Widely used in the south of France and elsewhere.

Macération pelliculaire

See Skin contact.

Maculan, Breganze

Fausto Maculan is the outstanding winemaker of Breganze, a D.O.C. zone in Italy's Veneto region. Of his D.O.C. wines, his La Fratta vineyard produces an opulent red made from Cabernet Sauvignon and Cabernet Franc. Maculan's most distinctive offerings are his declassified dessert wines. The 1990 botrytis-affected Acininobili will develop into a great bottle by the year 2000.

Maderized

This term is applied to wines, particularly whites, that are past their prime and have become oxidized. Such wines often have aromas and tastes reminiscent of Madeira — but a maderized wine has most often been spoilt (by heat and exposure to air). Small quantities can add to a wine's complexity but too much destroys a wine.

Château Magdelaine, St. Emilion

Following its acquisition by Monsieur Moueix in 1953, this property in Bordeaux has been making consistently successful wines. The land under vines is divided between the limestone soil of the plateau and the clay of the slopes, and at 80 percent the proportion of Merlot is unusually high, a characteristic of Moueix wines. *Elèvage* is carried out in about 50 percent new wood. The wine is brightly colored, scented, with great elegance and an appealing delicacy. In recent times there have been outstanding wines in 1975, 1976, 1978, 1979, 1980, 1982, 1983, 1985, 1986, 1987 and 1988, more than a few of them among the most notable examples of the appellation as a whole.

Henri Maire, Arbois

Henri Maire is a French grower and *négociant* based in the town of Arbois. In France the firm is most widely known for the advertisements for Vin Fou, a branded sparkling wine. Its vineyard holdings total some 340 hectares/840 acres. Henri Maire produces a wide range of local wines from various properties, such as Domaine de Montfort (67 hectares/165 acres) and Domaine de Grange Grillard (55 hectares/136 acres). The range includes Vin Jaune as well as whites, rosés, *vins gris* and reds.

Maîtres Vignerons de la Presqu'ile de le Saint-Tropez, Côtes de Provence

A very successful grouping of twelve growers, producing a range of high-quality wines, in an area of France that is still best known for its rosés. Les Maîtres Vignerons maintain quality through careful selection.

Malbec

Malbec is one of the red grapes of Bordeaux, where it is sometimes called Pressac. It is unimportant in the Médoc and St. Emilion, but is still popular in Blaye and Bourg. It really comes into its element in Cahors, where as Auxerrois it must account for a minimum of 70 percent of the wine, with Tannat and Merlot. There is a little in Pécharmant, outside Bergerac, and some is grown in the Loire Valley, where it is called Côt and is sometimes blended with Gamay and Cabernet. It is generally less popular in France than it used to be as it suffers badly from *coulure,* however, it is planted extensively in Argentina, where it can produce a wide range of wine styles, from light to full bodied, depending on the method of vinification. There is a little in Chile too.

Malolactic fermentation

The process that changes sharp malic acid to softer lactic acid, making wines softer and rounder. Most red wines undergo a malolactic fermentation, but it is less common with whites, as winemakers want to guard the refreshing acidity. Malolactic fermentation normally takes place after the alcoholic fermentation, although at times the two fermentations occur simultaneously.

Malvasia

The Malvasia grape is thought to have come from Asia Minor. Widely traveled but now disappearing, it is still grown in Spain and Italy, and also to a much lesser extent in Portugal, Yugoslavia, France, Austria and Germany. To add to the confusion, Malvoisie is often a synonym for grapes that have nothing to do with Malvasia, namely for Pinot Gris in Switzerland and in the Loire Valley, for Macabeo in Limoux, for Bourboulenc in the Languedoc and for Vermentino in Corsica.

Malvasia is at its best in central Italy, where there are several different strains. As Malvasia Bianca di Candia it features in Frascati and Marino; as Malvasia del Chianti it is used in sharply diminishing quantities for Chianti, as well as for Galestro and Vin Santo. Malvasia Nera is grown in Apulia, while Malvasia delle Lipari and Malvasia di Sardegna are usually heady dessert wines. In Spain Malvasia features in Rioja and Navarre. In Madeira it gave its name to Malmsey and is also grown in Portugal for dry white table wine.

Malvasia delle Lipari, Sicily
The Greeks brought the Malvasia grape to the Lipari Islands. It makes a sweet wine of orange, rust-toned color with a splendid fruits-and-herbs bouquet. The grape was moribund on Lipari until revived by the Milanese designer Carl Hauner; his Malvasia *passito* is very fine. There are also *dolce naturale* and *liquoroso* versions of this D.O.C. wine.

Malvoisie Fletrie, Etat du Valais, Valav
A splendid Swiss Pinot Gris, harvested with 18.4 percent potential alcohol at Leytron in the Valais, the wine now has 14.5 percent actual alcohol and is noticeably sweet. The big Pinot Gris flavor is well developed, but the wine will not reach its peak until near the end of the century. Sweet Swiss wines are rare and have a similar weight and power to their counterparts in Alsace.

Mammolo
A traditional variety, long established in Tuscany and seldom seen elsewhere. It is still used for its aromatic qualities in the making of Chianti and Vino Nobile di Montepulciano.

Domaine Manciat-Poncet, Mâcon-Chamay
An outstanding family-owned domain in Burgundy with 6 well placed hectares/15 acres on the chalky soil of the southeast-facing slopes of Mâcon-Charnay. Chardonnay predominates, although a diminishing amount of Mâcon Rouge is also made. Claude Manciat has a further 5 hectares/12.4 acres of Pouilly-Fuissé at Vergisson. Roughly 10 percent of production is fermented in new wood, which adds a discreet complexity to the blend.

Manseng
Manseng is the grape for Jurançon and can either be Gros or Petit. Gros Manseng is generally used for Jurançon Sec, while Petit Manseng makes delicious Jurançon *moelleux* when the grapes are left on the vines in a process called *passerillage,* to dehydrate in the autumn winds of the Pyrenees. Manseng is one of the underrated grape varieties of southwest France. More interest is, however, being taken in it, with plantings in the Côtes de Gascogne, as well as Côtes de Saint-Mont, Pacherenc du Vic-Bilh and Blanc de Béarn.

Marc
The debris (grape pips and skins) left after fermentation and pressing. The English term is pomace. It is either used as a fertilizer or distilled to make the *eau de vie,* which is also called *marc.* Most *marcs* are pretty rough, although a few are remarkably fine. Examples include Marc de Bourgogne and *grappa,* the Italian version.

Marchesi di Gresy, Barbaresco
Alberto di Gresy runs this 12 hectare/30 acre estate with great panache. The di Gresy wines are especially elegant and subtle, characteristics that are shaped by modern winemaking techniques that include a fairly short maceration on the skins and a shortish spell in wood before bottling. The estate's best-known *cru* is Barbaresco Camp Gros. The 1985 is scented with generous, open fruit; already approachable, this wine will hold up well in bottle for another seven years. Marchesi di Gresy also produce an excellent, stylish Dolcetto and have made new plantings of Chardonnay, Sauvignon and Barbera.

Maréchal Foch
A crossing of Goldriesling with a native American vine, this hybrid (Kuhlmann 188-2) is planted sparingly in the United States and Canada and remains of purely local interest.

Château Margaux, Margaux
With Lafite, Latour and Haut-Brion, Margaux emerged at the beginning of the eighteenth century as a great wine of Bordeaux under its own name, and it has been accounted a first growth since 1855. Its wines epitomize the qualities ascribed to the appellation as a whole; elegance, generosity, finesse, subtlety, complexity and a beautiful color.

For a brief period after an admirable 1961 the quality of Margaux faltered, the consequence of lack of investment and indifferent administration. All this was changed in 1977, when, following a French government veto on American interest, the property was acquired by André Mentzelopoulos of the Felix Potin grocery chain. Vast sums were invested in vineyard, *chai* and château and Professor Peynaud was brought in to oversee the vinification of what became the harmonious, powerful vintage of 1978, a very great wine that will be drinking well into the next century. With sustained investment, astute management and scrupulous winemaking, Margaux has regained its eminence as a wine of astonishing elegance, richness and subtlety. Sadly Mentzelopoulos died before he could see the full result of his vision, drive and enthusiasm, but under the direction of his widow and daughter the château has produced a sequence of extraordinary wines: 1980, 1981, 1982, 1983, 1985, 1986, 1988 and 1989. Pavillon Rouge, its second wine, compares in quality with and commands the prices of Bordeaux second growths, while in Pavillon Blanc the property makes a small quantity of white wine of distinction and high price, derived from Sauvignon Blanc fermented in new oak.

Marne et Champagne, Champagne
This firm specializes in stockholding (it is the second largest) and Buyers' Own Brands. Its recent acquisition of Besserat de Bellefon and Lanson, without their vineyards, makes it the second largest player in Champagne, with an annual production of about 1,666,000 cases. Alfred Rothschild, often seen in French supermarkets, is one of its brands.

Marqués de Cáceres, Rioja
This modern *bodega* was established in the 1970s by Henri (or Enrique) Forner, owner of Château Camensac in Bordeaux. French winemaking techniques influence the Cáceres white Rioja, which sees no wood and is fresh and clean. The red wines are aged in newish oak *barriques* for no more than twenty-four months, the fruit flavors always dominating the oak but with a good background of tannin. Traditionalists say that these are atypical Riojas, but it is hard to deny that they are well-made wines giving a great deal of pleasure. Excellent *reserva* vintages for Cáceres include 1981, 1982 and 1985.

Marqués de Griñon, Toledo, Rueda (non D.O.)
Carlos Falco, Marqués de Griñon, studied enology at the University of California, Davis, and on his return to the family estate near Toledo, he planted Cabernet Sauvignon and Merlot with the aim of making a Bordeaux-style red wine. Matured in American oak, the wine has a lot of flavor and character and ages well in bottle for seven to ten years. The 1984 is an excellent effort in a minor year. Falco also makes a fresh crisp white wine from the Verdejo grape.

Marqués de Murrieta, Rioja
This is one of the most traditional *bodegas,* founded in 1872, now making wines exclusively from its own vineyards. Very long wood aging is the Murrieta style, and this applies even to the white wine, which is heavily oaked, with an old-fashioned honeyed character. The red wines show rich fruit, plenty of sweet mellow oak and a silky finish; the *reservas,* often aged in wood for ten years, are complex wines with marked notes of vanilla and red soft fruits. Look out for the Gran Reserva Castillo de Ygay, which is made only in exceptional years: the 1968 is the currently available vintage in Britain and the United States.

Marsanne
Marsanne is the principal white grape variety of the northern Rhône, grown alongside Roussanne for the white versions of appellations such as Hermitage, Crozes-Hermitage, and St. Joseph, as well as St. Péray. It can be found in the Swiss canton of the Valais, where it is called Ermitage. It has also traveled to Australia, where it is concentrated in Victoria, on estates such as Château Tahbilk and Mitchelton.

Martell, Cognac
One of the oldest Cognac firms, Martell was founded by Jean Martell, a Jerseyman, in the early eighteenth century. A giant of the industry, and now part of the Seagram empire, Martell as a company still produces Cognacs of good quality and marked character. The firm owns important estates in the Borderies, which produces particularly nutty, round brandies. The *maître de chai* believes in strong distillations achieving a relatively neutral spirit, which is then aged in close-grained Tronçais oak, assuring long, slow maturation. Martell believes passionately in blending, and even in its top *cuvées,* containing a higher proportion of Fine Champagne brandies, there always remains a percentage of *eau-de-vie* from the Borderies. The twenty- to thirty-year-old Martell Cordon Bleu is excellent, rich and round.

Martinborough Vineyards Pinot Noir, Wairarapa
Martinborough Vineyards bears the name of a region at the southern end of New Zealand's North Island that produces the country's finest Pinot Noir. Winemaker Larry McKenna is obsessed with the desire to make truly great Pinot Noir. He has worked a vintage in Burgundy and travels to Pinot Noir conferences all over the world in an effort to unlock the secret of this most challenging grape variety. McKenna's reward so far has been a trophy for the country's top Pinot Noir in 1988, 1989 and 1990. His is a big, plummy wine with complexity, warmth and a soft texture.

Marzemino
A grape known for several centuries under various names in northern Italy. In Trentino it makes flavorful, aristocratic wines; elsewhere in the northeast, and in Lombardy and Emilia, it is grown chiefly for blending.

Mas Amiel, Maury
This 130 hectare/320 acre estate in Languedoc-Roussillon in France is dedicated exclusively to making Maury, a *vin doux naturel,* from Grenache Noir. There is both a vintage, bottled young, and a reserve, aged in wooden vats. Mas Amiel has an extraordinary outside park of 3,000 glass carboys in which the wine ages throughout all weathers.

Mas de Daumas Gassac, Vin de Pays de l'Hérault
The most expensive French *vin de pays.* Mas de Daumas Gassac comes from a 25 hectare/62 acre vineyard with a privileged position in the hills of Languedoc. The red, first released in 1978, contains a high proportion of Cabernet Sauvignon as well as Syrah and other grapes, although it is definitely a wine of the south and not an imitation Bordeaux. Mas de Daumas Gassac has been an inspiration to many other *vignerons* from the Midi and demonstrates the area's potential.

Mauro Mascarello, Barolo
Mauro Mascarello is a fine exponent of traditionally made Barolo. Turning full circle, he has essentially returned to the old ways after experimenting with new winemaking techniques in the early 1970s. His best Barolo is a wine from the Monprivato vineyard in Castiglione Falletto. Outstanding vintages for Monprivato are 1978, 1982 and 1985.

Mastroberardino, Atripalda
This is a family firm of great winemakers of southern Italy, with a virtual monopoly of quality wines from Campania. Following a disastrous earthquake in 1980, the cellars at Atripalda were rebuilt and stainless-steel fermenters installed. At this time the company bought 100 hectares/247 acres of vines in the Avellino hills. The yields of the predominant Greco and Aglianico grape varieties have been reduced to about 40 hectoliters per hectare/2.3 tons per acre. Mastroberardino has breathed new life into Lacryma Christi; the 1985 is a well-made light red wine. But the firm's best red is Taurasi from their Radici vineyard. Both the 1983 *normale* and the 1977 *riserva* are very good.

Mataro
See Mourvèdre.

Mathier-Kuchler Pinot Noir, Valais
A Swiss wine from the German-speaking part of the Valais, where much of Pinot Noir is destined to be blended with Gamay to be sold as Dôle. It has a strong, full Pinot Noir flavor, and although the acidity is too low for the wine to be sold in the European Community, there is sufficient body to compensate. A good example of a Swiss Pinot Noir is from the Marriafeld clone.

Matua Valley Merlot, Auckland
Merlot responds well to New Zealand's cool climate. Used mostly in tandem with Cabernet Sauvignon, this is one of the few examples where the grape flies solo. A fairly intense wine with strong gamy, berry fruit flavors that show no hint of herbaceousness, a feature of many New Zealand reds.

Mauzac
A white grape that must make up at least 70 percent of Blanquette de Limoux. The Mauzac endows its wine with fragrance, fruit and acidity. It is found farther to the southwest, notably at Gaillac, where the limestone base suits it, and produces aromatic but short-lived dry wines of character. It contributes to the sparkling wine of Gaillac too, which may be made by the *méthode gallaçoise* or by the *méthode champenoise.*

Mavron
The principal variety of Cyprus, accounting for three quarters of the land under vines, the Mavron produces great quantities of generally coarse and alcoholic red wines of varying degrees of sweetness. It is blended with the white Xynisteri to make the ancient, long-lived and sometimes distinguished Commandaria, the traditional dessert wine of the island, made from *passito* grapes.

Mavrud
A southern Bulgarian grape variety that makes fruity, mild red wines, pleasant in their maturity but relatively short lived.

Mechanical harvesters
These machines are increasingly used instead of picking by hand because they are much quicker, easier to

organize and allow growers to pick at night — especially attractive in hot climates. In some circumstances they may damage the vines. Machines cannot be used for selective picking for sweet wines, for wines to be made by carbonic maceration or for quality sparkling wines.

Melnik
A red-wine variety native to Bulgaria that makes some of that country's best wines. These are wines of individual character, deeply colored and intense, with the tannic structure to repay aging. Sadly the admirable Melnik accounts for only a tenth of the land occupied by the much inferior Pamid.

Mencia
A fine but relatively rare Spanish variety found chiefly in Galicia. Its origins are obscure, but its pale red wines have bouquet and finesse. The grape is also used for blending, commonly with the Tempranillo.

Mendoza, Argentina
The province of Mendoza represents the heart of the Argentinian wine industry, with many of the most important wineries situated on the plains around the city of Mendoza, or, some 37 kilometers/60 miles farther south, around the town of San Rafael. There are about 180,000 hectares/444,600 acres of vineyards, all depending upon irrigation for survival. Criolla is still the most common grape variety, but it is beginning to decline in favor of more interesting varieties, such as Cabernet Sauvignon, Chardonnay, Merlot, Syrah, Sauvignon, Semillon, Riesling and Chenin Blanc. However, quantities of these are still very small. There is phylloxera, but it has little effect in the sandy soil.

Mercier, Champagne
Epernay house founded by Eugène Mercier in 1858 and for many years administered from Paris. Mercier was bought by Moët et Chandon in 1970. Its cellars are the second most extensive in Champagne (no surprise that Moët's are the largest) and visitors are driven around on an electric train. The majority of Mercier's production is sold in France, and it rather lacks the cachet of other Champagne houses.

Mercurey Clos des Myglands, Maison J. Faiveley
There are six *premier cru* vineyards in Mercurey, the best-known of the wine communes of the Côte Chalonnaise in Burgundy. The Clos des Myglands is not one of them. Why this should be so is not clear. The vineyard is entirely owned by Faiveley, and its wine is always among the best from the appellation. Mercurey is only 20 kilometers/12 miles south of Beaune, but its wines were largely ignored until twenty years ago, when Côte d'Or prices began to soar. Faiveley's most famous vineyard is the Clos de la Maréchale in Nuits-St.-Georges, but the Clos des Myglands is a less expensive way to learn what good wines this house can make. Faiveley also makes some excellent white Mercurey, from Clos Rochette.

Merlot
Merlot takes second place to Cabernet Sauvignon in many parts of the world, not least in Bordeaux, where it is blended with Cabernet Sauvignon and Cabernet Franc. However, it comes into its own in St. Emilion and Pomerol, as the dominant part of the blend, and in the case of Château Pétrus is almost the sole constituent of the wine. It buds and ripens early, but is susceptible to spring frost and also to *coulure* at flowering. As well as being a vital ingredient of claret, it features in most of the red appellations of the southwest and has spread to the Midi as a *cépage améliorateur* (a grape variety not common to the Midi, but used to improve the traditional blends) with some success in enlivening the coarser varieties of the South.

Merlot is also popular in northeast Italy, where it produces easy to drink red wines in such D.O.C.s as Grave del Friuli, Collio, Colli Orientali and so on, and in the Veneto's Colli Euganei and Colli Berici. Merlot has also reached Tuscany, notably at Ornellaia, an Antinori estate, where they use it for blending with Cabernet Sauvignon. There is a tiny amount of Merlot in Spain, in Ribera del Duero and Penedès, and more in eastern Europe, especially Yugoslavia, Hungary and Bulgaria.

In the New World there are many examples of pure Merlot. In California it is used for blending with Cabernet Sauvignon, though Cuvaison makes an excellent varietal version, while Australians tend to favor Shiraz. There is a small amount in New Zealand, such as at Esk Valley; in South Africa, for Meerlust's Rubicon and in Chile and Argentina. The true potential of Merlot outside Europe has yet to be realized.

Geoff Merrill, Reynella, South Australia
A former chief winemaker with Thomas Hardy, Geoff Merrill sports a luxuriant handlebar moustache. There is nothing flashy about his wines, though, which show a quiet elegance and considerable class. Merrill likes to harvest early to maintain a decent level of acidity. He makes just two wines each year — a Semillon/Chardonnay and a Cabernet Sauvignon with a little Cabernet Franc in the blend. The 1986 and 1987 Cabernet Sauvignons are both excellent wines — spicy, stylish and racy.

Louis Métaireau et ses Vignerons d'Art, Muscadet
Louis Métaireau makes some of the best and most expensive Muscadet in the Loire. He is the leader of a cooperative venture of nine *vignerons* who make and bottle their wine separately and then sell under a common label. Their particular strengths are the very rigorous wine selection and the insistence of a genuine *sur lie* bottling. Cuvée Number One is their top wine, while the Grand Mouton is from a jointly owned vineyard.

Méthode champenoise
Bottle fermentation — the way to make the best sparkling wine. After the first fermentation, the wine is bottled and yeast and sugar added to induce a second fermentation. The sediment that results is removed by the processes of *remuage* and *dégorgement*. The carbon dioxide produced remains dissolved in the wine under pressure, to be released when the cork is removed. From 1994 the term *méthode champenoise* will be limited to sparkling wine produced in Champagne.

Meursault Les Genevriéres, Francis Jobard
Anyone wanting to visit cellars in Meursault in Burgundy would do well to start with the shy, somewhat diffident Jobard. It is a way to establish a benchmark by which to judge everything that comes after. Few, if any, will match his standards. He has vines in Les Charmes, Les Genevrières and Les Poruzots, among the *premier cru* vineyards, and only a skilled taster could say which is his best. Traditionally, Genevrières is the best of the three vineyards, just below Les Perrières in reputation, but in Jobard's hands differences tend to even out. The wines are intense and elegant. He also makes some red wine from the Blagny appellation at the southern tip of Meursault.

Jos Meyer, Wintzenheim
Excellent firm of Alsace growers and *négociants* founded in Wintzenheim in 1857. The present head of the company, Jean Meyer, looks coldly on current fashions for *vendange tardive* wines or those made from Pinot Noir. Instead, buying grapes mainly from Wintzenheim and Turckheim, Meyer makes first-rate dry, complex and profound wines. His Pinot Blanc Les Lutins is arguably the finest example of the grape in Alsace, coming from vineyards close to the Hengst.

Meyer-Näkel, Ahr

This innovative German estate produces serious red wine from Spät and Frühburgunder — the latter also a variety of Pinot. Yields are low. Some wines are partly aged in *barriques*, and most are softened by malolactic fermentation. All the red wines are dry.

Alain Michaud, Brouilly

Alain Michaud makes an exceptionally concentrated Brouilly in the *lieu-dit* of Beauvoir, a 1.5 hectare/3.7 acre Beaujolais vineyard established by his grandfather in 1910. The yields are tiny, the flavors of the wine a superb amalgam of rich fruit, powerful tannins and a hint of vanilla. The 1989 is splendidly ripe, the 1990 more austere and needing two to three years in bottle before the cork is drawn.

Robert Michel, Cornas

For great black Cornas made in an uncompromising, tough style, Michel's wine is one to look out for. His 1985 Cornas La Geynale is still shut-in and unyielding, but it is likely to be a superb multiflavored wine around the year 2000, when the tannins have softened.

Microclimate

Microclimate refers to the combination of factors —type of soil, altitude, drainage, orientation to the sun — that affect the quality of wine. Because of geographical differences, every locality has its own microclimate; some favor grape growing, some do not. Neighboring vineyards may have substantially different microclimates.

Millerandage

French term for the failure of embryonic grapes to swell and develop. It is caused by difficult conditions during flowering. Also known as shot berries.

Mission

See Pais

Mistelle

Drink made by the addition of grape brandy to unfermented grape juice. The proportion is generally three quarters juice to one quarter alcohol. Pineau des Charentes, Floc de Gascogne, Cartagène (from Languedoc) and Ratafia (from Champagne and Burgundy) are some of the best-known examples.

Mitchelton, Mitchellstown, Victoria

A large Australian winery in the Goulburn Valley, Mitchelton has three ranges of wine: the Thomas Mitchell keenly-priced varietals; the Mitchelton Label Series; and the Classic Release wines. Search out the 1986 Rhine Riesling Wine Maker's Selection (*Beerenauslese* in style) and the 1987 wood-aged Chardonnay, which shows a good balance of oak and orchard fruit flavors.

Moelleux

French for sweet. Dessert style wines from areas such as the Loire, Gaillac and Jurançon are often labelled thus.

Moët et Chandon, Champagne

Much the biggest Champagne house, especially with the recent acquisition of Pommery, it was founded in Epernay by Charles Moët in 1743 and now produces around 1.5 cases or 18 million bottles a year. With this scale of production and Moët's promotional success in persuading victorious Grand Prix drivers to spray the crowds with Champagne froth, standards of the N.V. are felt to be variable. However, the well-known prestige *cuvée* Dom Pérignon is among the greatest Champagnes.

Domaine aux Moines, Savennières Roche aux Moines

Madame Laroche bought this 13 hectare/32 acre Loire property, classified as a national monument, from the state in 1982. The estate was founded by the monks of St. Nicolas of Angers in 1130 and was confiscated during the Revolution. Although the vines are now only seven years old she made one of the best Savennières in both 1989 and 1990. Her wines are complex with an interesting combination of mineral and fruit flavors.

El Molino Pinot Noir, Napa Valley

This little winery near St. Helena in the Napa Valley in California is destined for great things in the years to come. It burst on the wine scene in the late 1980s with one of the most remarkable Pinot Noirs yet seen in America. What made the wine so unusual was that it was grown in areas where Pinot Noir is not thought to thrive, and it was made by a winery with absolutely no track record of producing good wine of any kind. The El Molino Pinots are big and earthy and, it would seem, not meant to be long-lasting. But they are very much in the style of old-fashioned red Burgundies — dark in color, full of flavor and even a bit rough around the edges. Modern Burgundies try for less body and more delicacy, as do most of their American counterparts. But many Burgundy lovers yearn for the traditional style, and it is to them that El Molino will appeal the most.

Monastrell

A very widely planted Spanish red-wine variety that is found in Catalonia, Aragón, the Rioja Baja and the Levante. It makes a relatively dry red wine, pale yet substantial, and capable of aging, and is much used for blending in varying styles.

Château Monbrison, Margaux

A little *cru bourgeois* of some 14 hectares/34.5 acres Monbrison was acquired by the American Davis family in 1921 and remains in their possession. Currently this Bordeaux property is making outstanding wines with the breed and finesse typical of the appellation. Recent successes include 1979, 1981, 1982, 1985, 1986 and 1989. In Château Cordet the property makes a light and stylish second wine from its young vines.

Robert Mondavi

Robert Mondavi's contribution to the California wine industry has been immense. He is still a tirelessly innovative winemaker, and he communicates the pleasure of drinking good wine to a large audience like nobody else. Above all, he has been a great defender of the wine industry against the antialcohol lobby and the new prohibitionists in the United States. Mondavi has sedulously cultivated the image of a small winery, but his wine operation is very large. His futuristic winery near Oakville has been conceived for large-volume production, but the attention to detail and the commitment to quality is as great as in the most highly regarded "boutique" vineyard.

Mondavi's most highly rated wines are probably his Cabernet Sauvignons. His Reserve Cabernet was spectacular in 1974 and excellent in 1978, 1984, 1985 and 1986. Mondavi's most talked-about wine project was his joint venture with Baron Philippe de Rothschild called Opus One. Since the first vintage in 1979, the aim was to produce a Cabernet Sauvignon-based wine that was midway in style between a Napa Valley wine and a great Médoc. Early vintages seemed over oaked, but since 1985 the wine has started to show a finesse allied to power that looks like achieving the goals of Mondavi and the late Baron Philippe. The 1987 is the best vintage to date.

Mondavi deserves praise for his continual experiments with Pinot Noir. Both the 1984 and 1985 reserves are rich, spicy yet elegant wines. Other varietals are impeccably vinified — lush, early maturing Chardonnays, full Fumé Blancs, delicious Chenin Blancs, and the charming, light Moscato d'Oro.

For the future, Mondavi's purchase of 182 hectares/450 acres of vineyard land in Carneros in 1988 may result in some exciting new Chardonnays and Pinot Noirs from this stable toward the end of the 1990s.

Robert Mondavi Reserve Cabernet Sauvignon, Napa Valley

This is the wine on which America's best-known vintner and the best-known premium winery have based their reputation. A tireless experimenter, Mondavi has taken his Cabernet through many mutations since the first vintage, 1965, appeared a quarter of a century ago. It began as a big muscular wine, went on to become a muted, so-called food wine, and is now back to a somewhat more elegant variation on the original Mondavi theme. Through it all Mondavi Cabernet has remained one of the most honored, most wanted of all California wines, not only in this country but in the growing market for American wines around the world. Current versions of the wine are medium bodied with intense fruit, deep color and a taste that seems to last forever in the mouth.

Mondeuse

Mondeuse is a red grape variety that makes quite sturdy, fruity red wine in the Bugey and in Savoie. Arbin, a *cru* of Vin de Savoie, has a particular reputation for Mondeuse. In Italy Mondeuse is called Refosco and is grown in Friuli as a varietal wine in the D.O.C.s of Grave del Friuli, Colli Orientali and Latisana. The best clone is Refosco del Peduncolo Rosso, so called because the stalks turn slightly red when the grapes ripen.

Monemvasia

An ancient and justly celebrated Greek variety native to the Cyclades, and the vine from which the various strains of Malvasia or Malvoisie are derived.

Monica

A red-wine grape of Spanish origin and decreasing popularity. In Sardinia it makes D.O.C. wines that may be dry or, unusually, sweet.

Monmousseau, Touraine

The house was founded in 1886 by Alcide Monmousseau. In 1933 the firm bought the Saumur house of Bouvet-Ladubay. In 1974 it merged with Taittinger, but has recently become independent again. Armand Monmousseau, the present director, became the president of the Comité Interprofessionel des Vins de Loire in 1990. Monmousseau carries a range of well-made still wines from the Loire, but its specialty is Touraine and Vouvray sparkling wines.

Monsanto Il Poggio, Chianti Classico

Fabrizio Bianchi, a Milanese textile manufacturer, makes great Chianti in a 5 hectare/12 acre vineyard called Il Poggio, which is the finest plot of his 45 hectare/111 acre Monsanto estate. The grapes from Il Poggio are harvested a fortnight later than the main crop, usually achieving an extra degree of alcohol. The resulting wines may well be the richest, densest Chiantis of all; certainly throughout the seventies they showed sensuous, extremely complex bouquets, enormous power and depth of flavor and an extraordinary capacity to age well for up to twenty years. The Il Poggio vintages in the 1980s are just as impressive, with a monumental, highly extracted 1982 and a wonderfully harmonious 1988 (the best wine ever produced here?).

Les Caves du Mont-Tauch, Fitou

The Fitou appellation consists of two enclaves within Corbières in France: one on the Mediterranean coast and the other, larger part, accounting for 60 percent of the appellation inland in the hills of the Haut Corbières. The Caves du Mont-Tauch, founded in 1913 at Tuchan, is its largest and most important cooperative. It makes a wide range of wines, including the stylish single-vineyard Château de Ségure.

Montana Sauvignon Blanc, Marlborough

Although its head office is in Auckland, Montana pioneered the Marlborough region and introduced the world to New Zealand Sauvignon Blanc. The company boldly planted 20 hectares/50 acres of an unknown (to New Zealand) grape variety in an unproven region. Its courage was rewarded with a wine style that spearheaded a very successful export drive to the U.K. and won much acclaim at home. Strong gooseberry and capsicum flavors make it easy to identify the grapes used in this wine.

Château de Montauriol, Fronton

The largest estate in Fronton, in southwest France, is Château Bellevue-la-Forêt with 105 hectares/260 acres, and its easy-drinking, fruity Cuvée Tradition is deservedly popular. However, it was the arrival of Richard Mayor, a Swiss entrepreneur, at Château Montauriol in 1987 that showed that it was possible to make complex, structured wines from the Négrette grape. Carte Noire is the top wine. It has a high proportion of Négrette and is aged in new oak for around a year. Low yields of around 30 hectoliters per hectare/1.8 tons per acre — the poor soil of Montauriol keeps yields down — gives concentrated fruit that marries well with the oak.

Monte Vertine, Raddain Chianti

Sergio Manetti was the pioneer of *barrique*-aged Sangiovese wines in Chianti. Since 1977 he has not used the Chianti Classico designation for his wines, preferring to label them under the estate name of Monte Vertine. His best-known wine is Le Pergole Torte, a pure Sangioveto. The 1985 could be his best effort to date, a superbly expansive wine of great depth of flavor. Manetti also produces an exceptional *vin santo*.

Montecello, Rioja

Acquired by the Sherry firm Osborne in the early seventies, this is now a thoroughly modern-minded *bodega:* cool fermentations and bottle maturation rather than cask aging are the general rule. Attractive citrussy Viña Cumbrero Blanco and fine *gran reservas*.

Château Montelena Chardonnay, Napa Valley

When Mike Grgich ruled Château Montelena in the 1970s, he astonished the wine world with the intensity and power of his Chardonnays. Mike has his own winery now, Grgich Hills, and wine styles have changed, but Montelena continues to turn out some of the best white wines in the country. Some of the muscularity of the Grgich epoch may have moderated, but the intensity of

flavor is still there and, if anything, the wines are more harmonious than ever. Comparisons are inevitable, and the best American Chardonnays are always put up against the best white Burgundies. Château Montelena can hold its own in that sort of face-off, but it tends to compare more with the wines of the northern portion of the Côte d'Or, with Corton-Charlemagne, than it does with the racier wines of Meursault and Puligny to the south.

Montepulciano
A red variety widely planted in the central provinces of Italy. It is perhaps best known for the D.O.C. Montepulciano d'Abruzzo, a mellow, tannic wine of some substance, and the rosé Cerasuolo. In the Marches the grape contributes to the D.O.C. Rosso Piceno and makes the pleasing table wine Vellutato. The vine has no relation to Vino Nobile di Montepulciano.

Montonico Bianco
An ancient variety still grown near Bianco in the extreme southeast of Calabria, where it makes dry and sweet white wines of the same name.

Château Montrose, St. Estèphe
With Calon Ségur and Cos d'Estournel, this second growth is consistently one of the outstanding wines of its appellation in Bordeaux in any year. The large vineyard has belonged to the Charmolüe family for almost a century, and traditionally Montrose has made old-fashioned, dark, dense, powerfully tannic wines that are slow to mature and immensely long-lived. Its great vintages have been many, exemplified by 1920, 1929, 1952, 1953, 1960, 1962, 1964, 1966. In the past twenty years or so, under Jean-Louis Charmolüe, the style of the wine has altered subtly, perhaps to adapt to a changing world. The proportion of Merlot has been increased significantly, and a modern *chai* was built to supplement the existing one with its handsome wooden vats. Over this recent period the most notable wines have been those of 1970, 1975, 1976, 1978, 1979, 1983 and the five successive years from 1985. The vintages of 1985 and especially 1986 were hugely powerful and tannic, certain to develop only slowly, but those of 1988 and 1989 show more immediate promise.

Montù
A variety native to Emilia-Romagna. Between Modena and Bologna it makes the lively white Castelfranco, which may be sweet or dry. The grape itself is sometimes known as Montuni or Bianchino.

Morey-St.-Denis Clos de la Roche, Domaine Ponsot
This vineyard in Burgundy is shared by some illustrious growers. Ponsot makes several different wines from its various holdings within this famous vineyard in Morey-Saint-Denis. Its *vieilles vignes* bottling is made in impossibly small quantities, and collectors vie for it at any price. The Ponsot wines are perhaps more restrained than some others from the Clos, but they develop beautifully as the years pass. Devotees talk of wild cherries and truffles and a certain chewy sensation in the mouth. In other words they are very big wines. They need years to develop but are well worth the wait.

Morey-St.-Denis Clos de St. Denis, Domaine Dujac
It is difficult to believe that Jacques Seysses has been making wine in Burgundy since 1968. As an innovator and an uncompromising advocate of quality, he has inspired a whole generation of younger winemakers in Burgundy. His own wines have gone from strength to strength over the years. To choose among the Dujac Clos de la Roche, the Clos de St. Denis, the Echezeaux and the Bonnes Mares is close to impossible; they are all wines of elegance, concentration, and wonderful aroma. The *grand cru* wines can be oaky when young but these

wines age well and the woodiness soon blends in. Seysses makes some Meursault from purchased grapes under the Druid label.

Morio-Muscat
A Sylvaner x Pinot Blanc crossing widely grown in the Rheinhessen and Rheinpfalz areas of Germany. It makes white wines with an aroma reminiscent of potpourri.

Morrastel
See Graciano.

Morris, Rutherglen, Victoria
One of the greatest producers of fortified Muscats and Tokays, Morris makes exceptional dessert wines in a classic, complex style in Australia. The Old Praemium Liqueur Tokay and The Old Praemium Liqueur Muscat can be recommended unreservedly. The twenty-five- to thirty-year-old Show Muscat is magnificent, a stunning amalgam of raisiny intensity and a marked *rancio* flavor, an oxidizing trait that comes from many years of cask aging.

Morton Estate Black Label Chardonnay, Hawke's Bay
One of Hawke's Bay's and indeed New Zealand's consistently top Chardonnays. A big, bold wine with an appealing peachy/tropical fruit lusciousness that will develop complexity with age. Very serious Chardonnay.

Moscadello
This traditional grape, a variant of Moscato formerly used in Tuscany to make dessert wines, has all but died out and has been supplanted by the small-berried Moscato Bianco, best-known for Asti Spumante in Piedmont. Where the Moscadello still exists in Montalcino it is no longer an approved variety, but its sweet *frizzante* wine remains agreeable. Also known as Moscadelleto.

Moscatello or Moscatellone
See Muscat.

Moss Wood, Willyabrup, Western Australia
A small Margaret River winery, Moss Wood has an exceptional reputation, out of all proportion to its size and modest annual production of 4,000 cases. Keith Mugford is both owner and winemaker, his Pinot Noirs showing a new dimension of taste for this variety grown in a hot climate. The 1987 Moss Wood Pinot Noir is an original and fascinating wine with its woodsmoke aromas and great generosity of flavor; yet it keeps that elusive balance of fruit, smoothness, elegance and spice so prized by lovers of great Pinot Noir. The 1987 Moss Wood Cabernet Sauvignon shows marvelous depth of fruit and a distinctive character of blackcurrant leaves on the nose. Lovely wood-aged Semillons, too.

Mostosa
A white-wine variety grown primarily for blending in the Marches, Latium and Apulia.

Mourvèdre
Mourvèdre is at its best in the appellation of Bandol, where it accounts for at least 50 percent, and usually much more, of the blend and produces wines of considerable character and stature. It can be a difficult grape to ripen and is generally at its best in vineyards close to the sea, but with fairly moist clay soil. It likes long hours of sunshine. Mourvèdre also features in Châteauneuf-du-Pape, Côtes de Provence, Côtes-du-Rhône and other appellations of the southern Rhône. It is sometimes grown as a *cépage améliorateur* elsewhere in the Midi.

In Spain it is called Murviedro or Mataro and grown in insignificant quantity. In Australia, where it is known as Mataro, it is more popular, but of undistinguished quality.

Mousseux
French for sparkling.

Château Mouton-Rothschild, Pauillac
The soil of this Bordeaux estate is largely gravel and flint, and Cabernet Sauvignon represents 85 percent of the vines, a much higher proportion than at the adjoining Lafite, with which Mouton habitually is compared. The modern Mouton is the creation of Baron Philippe de Rothschild. As a young man he took control in 1923, ending his family's tradition of absentee ownership, and ran the vineyard for more than sixty years with panache, commercial acumen and an astute understanding of publicity. While his wine museum is fascinating, and the estate with its great *chai* and underground cellars a showpiece of the Médoc, perhaps a more important achievement was his introduction of château bottling. This was an innovation seventy years ago, and has been obligatory since 1972 for classed growths.

Although it is at the opposite end of the appellation from Latour, Mouton is closer in style to Latour than to its neighbor Lafite, and with its pronounced note of cassis has more than a little in common with Lynch-Bages. Typically the wine of Mouton is dark, rich and concentrated, with a powerful and persistent bouquet; it is high in alcohol, but perfectly balanced. Mouton is slow to mature, but less so than Latour, and it is as long-lived as its fellow first growths of Pauillac.

At its best Mouton is a wine of astonishing power and grace, and its great years are many. Notable since the war have been 1945, 1947, 1949, 1952, 1953, 1955, 1959, 1961, 1962, 1966, 1970, 1975, 1978, 1982, 1984, 1985, 1986, 1987 and 1988. The admirable consistency of the eighties serves to counterbalance a period in the sixties and seventies when too many indifferent wines were made.

Mouton was elevated to the ranks of the *premiers crus* by government decree in 1973. It has no second wine.

Mouton Baronne Philippe is the former Mouton d'Armailhac. While it is the same ownership as Mouton, and indeed in the eighteenth century was a part of it, the two vineyards are run quite separately. Mouton-Cadet, introduced in the thirties, is a reputable brand of blended red and white Bordeaux.

Muga, Rioja
This medium-sized *bodega* is run by the Muga brothers, who are sticklers for tradition. The wines are fermented in wooden casks, and treatments are kept to a minimum. Muga's standard red Rioja is a delight: quite light in color, this wine has a delicate aroma and a surprising richness that is distinctly Burgundian in style. The Muga *reservas*, named Prado Enea, are excellent, velvety wines. Excellent *reservas* were made at Muga in 1981, 1982 and 1985.

Muid
Somewhat antiquated and vague French word for a small wine cask, the size of which varies from district to district. A *demi-muid* is half of this far from specific quantity.

Weingut Müller-Catoir, Rheinpfalz
Cellarmaster Hans-Günter Schwarz, undoubtedly one of Germany's leading winemakers, has a clear philosophy. Each wine is looked after individually to reach its full potential of quality.

Müller-Thurgau
The white Müller-Thurgau is the most established of the German crossings. It was created in the 1880s by a Dr. Hermann Müller, from the Swiss canton of Thurgau, who crossed Riesling with Sylvaner. Today it is Germany's most popular grape variety, producing light, flowery wine in prolific quantity, having replaced Sylvaner and Riesling on less favorable sites. It fares well in other cool-climate vineyards, such as England, Luxembourg and the high-altitude vineyards of the South Tyrol, and also in Austria. In the New World it is little favored, except in New Zealand, where it is popular for boxed wine.

Mumm, Champagne
Champagne firm founded in 1827 by two Germans, P.A. Mumm from Rüdesheim in the Rheingau and a Herr Giesler. Having bought Perrier-Jouët in 1969, Mumm, in turn, was bought by the multinational Seagram in 1973. While its eye-catching and best-selling Cordon Rouge N.V. can be variable in quality, the prestige René Lalou is consistently superb.

Mumm'sches Weingut, Rheingau
Large (70 hectares/173 acres) very professionally run German estate under the same ownership as Schloss Johannisberg. Nearly all the vines are Riesling, and the wines have good balance and fruit. All are aged in cask. Most are Riesling in the classic Rheingau style of good fruit and racy acidity. The estate is sole owner of two sites, Hansenberg (3.8 hectares/9 acres) and Schwarzenstein (4 hectares/10 acres). It also owns a restaurant at Burg Schwarzenstein, above Schloss Johannisberg, where there is a splendid view of the Rheingau; all the estate's wines are on offer here. The estate was founded, in fact, on the profits from the sale of the 1811 vintage of Schloss Johannisberg, the famous Comet vintage. A banker, Peter Mumm, bought the whole harvest of Schloss Johannisberg (which was controlled, at the time, by one of Napoleon's marshalls) and on the proceeds bought land in the neighborhood.

Château Musar, Lebanon
The leading winemaker of Lebanon, and certainly the most tenacious, is Serge Hochar of Château Musar. The estate was founded in 1930 by Gaston Hochar, Serge's father, who planted vines in the Bekáa Valley, northeast of Beirut. Serge Hochar, who studied wine in Bordeaux, became winemaker in 1959. His red wines are very much in the Bordeaux mold, matured in *barriques* and capable of long life. The grape mix is Cabernet Sauvignon, Syrah and Cinsault, the last two varieties giving a spicy richness and hearty flavor to the wines. The white wine of Château Musar is made from 90 percent Chardonnay and 10 percent Sauvignon, giving the wine a mouthfilling

flavor. The Chardonnay rootstock is very old and is known locally as Oibadeh. Despite constant fighting in the Bekaa Valley, Hochar has produced wine in every vintage except 1984.

Muscadelle

Muscadelle is grown in Bordeaux, as a small but important part, 5 per cent at the most, of the blend for Sauternes; the rest is comprised of Sauvignon and Sémillon. It is also found in the other sweet appellations of the Gironde and in Monbazillac. It has some of the grapy character of the Muscat grape.

In Australia it has transpired that the grape known as Tokay is in fact Muscadelle. It is used for some delicious Liqueur Tokay, a dessert wine not unlike Liqueur Muscat.

In California it is often called Sauvignon Vert and makes varietal wines of lesser character.

Muscadet

The Muscadet, or Melon de Bourgogne, a white variant of the Gamay, was brought to the Pays Nantais on the Atlantic coast of France in the first half of the seventeenth century, and after the great freeze of 1709, which destroyed the existing vines, it was planted throughout the valleys of the Sèvre and the Maine. Today the vineyard extends to some 10,500 hectares/25,900 acres. The name of Muscadet is shared by the refreshing, uncomplicated wine it makes. The Muscadet has no connection with the Muscat and Muscadelle vines, while the Melon d'Arbois is in fact the Chardonnay. The Melon de Bourgogne has all but vanished from its native Burgundy. Also known as Pinot Blanc in California, and as Weisserburgunder in Germany.

Muscat

The Muscat grape variety comes in three forms, Muscat d'Alexandrie, Muscat Blanc à Petits Grains and Muscat Ottonel. The best is Muscat Blanc à Petits Grains, which is used in France for the better *vins doux naturels* of the Midi and for Muscat de Beaumes-de-Venise. It is also grown in the Rhône Valley for Clairette de Die Tradition and across the Alps accounts for the fresh grapiness of Asti Spumante. The Goldenmuskateller and Rosenmuskateller of the South Tyrol are variations of the same variety. In California it is called Moscato di Canelli and in Australia makes wonderful Liqueur Muscat. Surprisingly it is Muscat Ottonel, a newer variety developed in the last century, that accounts for Muscat d'Alsace, where it has largely replaced Muscato Blanc à Petits Grains. Some is also grown in Austria for dessert wines.

Muscat d'Alexandrie, although the oldest variety of Muscat, is now deemed to produce better table grapes than wine, for it does not have the flavor and perfume of Muscat Blanc à Petits Grains. However, it is still grown in the south of France, especially for Muscat de Rivesaltes, and in Spain, in Alicante, Valencia and Málaga, where it is called Moscatel. In Portugal it makes Moscatel de Setúbal and in Italy Moscato di Pantelleria, where it is known as Zibibbo. In Italy it may also be called Moscatello or Moscatellone. In South Africa it is called Hanepoot and makes sweet fortified wines, while Australians call it Gordo Blanc and use it for wines resembling cream Sherry.

Must

Grape juice before it begins to ferment.

Must weight

Grape juice's natural sugar content before fermentation. The higher the must weight the higher the potential degree of alcohol.

Mustimeter

Portable gadget for measuring a grape's ripeness.

Mutage

French term for the process of artificially stopping fermentation. This may be done by adding sulfur dioxide and then filtering, or it may be done by adding grape brandy. The latter method is used for *vins doux naturels* or Port. The intention is always to leave residual sugar in the wine.

N

Nasco

An antique variety native to Sardinia, which in the south of the island makes the white D.O.C. wine Nasco di Cagliari, which may be dry, semisweet or sweet. The sweet fortified styles hold the most interest.

Nebbiolo

Until recently Nebbiolo had never travelled outside northeast Italy, where it is grown, in Piedmont for wines like Barolo and Barbaresco, as well as for most or all of the blend for Gattinara, Ghemme, Lessona, Sizzano and others. In parts of Piedmont it is known as Spanna. In the Valtellina on the Swiss border in Lombardy it makes Sassella, Grumello, Valgella and Inferno and is also found in the Valle d'Aosta, as well as near Brescia, where it is an ingredient of Franciacorta.

The name is said to originate from the *nebbia,* or fog, that often covers the vineyards of Piedmont. Tannin is its chief characteristic, so that it tends to produce tough, solid wines that require several years of aging, in cask or bottle or both, to show their true potential. However, there is a current trend toward slightly softer, more accessible wines. Nebbiolo has attracted little attention in the New World. However, one or two California growers are now trying to redress the balance.

Neethlingshof, Stellenbosch

This is now a 160,000 case giant, but make no mistake, with Günter Brözel at the winemaking helm, this estate will win blue ribands for top-quality South African wines. Already showing impressive results from heavy investment in vineyards and cellar, Hans Schreiber, the owner since 1985, is determined to make his wines and his excellent restaurant second to none. At present the leading wines are the Cabernet Sauvignon, the Lord Neethling, named after a previous owner, which is a blend of Cabernet and Tinta Barocca, the Sauvignon Blanc, Gewürztraminer and several late-harvest wines touched by botrytis.

Négociant

French term for wine shipper and merchant. Négociants traditionally used to buy wine in bulk and bottle it. Since the war many *négociants* have gone out of business. As the demand for individual quality wines grows, those surviving are having to reassess their role. They remain important in Bordeaux and Burgundy.

Négociant-éleveur

French wine merchant who matures wines.

Negoska

A Greek red vine that plays a subordinate role in blended wines.

Negroamaro

A heavy-cropping black grape grown on the Salento plain of Apulia. It makes powerful, alcoholic red wines and dry rosé wines under denominations such as Salice Salentino, Leverano, Copertino and the recently created Nardò.

Nerello

A very widely planted Sicilian variety that makes red

D.O.C. wines of some distinction, as well as table and blended wines.

Niagara
An American hybrid derived from the Concord, the Niagara is well established in the eastern states and makes white wines, both still and sparkling, in varying styles. These are marked by a pronounced "foxy" character, but despite this the vine has been planted as far afield as New Zealand and Brazil.

Nicolas Feuillatte, Champagne
Brand name used by the large cooperative Centre Vinicole de la Champagne at Chouilly. Nonvintage and vintage *cuvées* are produced.

Nielluccio
A red wine variety that is native to Corsica and resembles the Sangiovese. It flourishes especially on the limestone of Patrimonio, where it makes powerful, tannic and long-lived A.O.C. reds and fresh, frank rosé wines. Elsewhere on the island the grape lends distinction to the lesser appellations.

Niepoort, Vila Nova de Gaia
Founded in 1842, this tiny independent Port house produces high-quality Ports across the range. Vintage Ports are sweet and rich with delicious fruit concealing very firm tannins. Top vintages: 1987, 1985, 1970, 1955. Fine tawnies, especially colheitas (those of a single year); excellent L.B.V.; and a very good range of white Ports of a fine Moscatel.

Nitrogen
A vital constituent of soil, encouraging flowering and the growth of new wood. In excess it can cause problems. In the winery, nitrogen is used as an inert gas to protect wine from contact with oxygen.

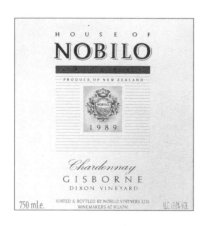

Nobilo Vintners Dixon Vineyard Chardonnay, West Auckland
Big, oaky Chardonnay from a very good vintage. The 1985 Dixon Chardonnay won the *Decanter* magazine trophy for New Zealand's top export wine. Nobilo has continued to make the same very robust style, which now has a proven cellaring record.

Nobling
A German hybrid vine based on the Silvaner and of no great consequence. It is planted only modestly and seems to have been superseded by more recent experimental crossings.

Nocera
A red-wine variety grown for blending in Calabria and Sicily. Its role is always minor.

Nosiola
A variety native to Trentino and rarely seen elsewhere. To the north of Trento itself the Nosiola makes fruity, perfumed dry white D.O.C. wines, and its *passito* grapes produce a sumptuous *vin santo*.

Nuits-St.-Georges Clos de l'Arlot, Domaine de l'Arlot
This is a relatively new property in Burgundy, carved from vineyards in Prémeaux previously owned by a local grower and now by Axa, the Paris insurance group that owns Château Pichon-Baron in Bordeaux. The winemaker is Jean-Pierre de Smet, who used to work for Jacques Seysses in Morey-St.-Denis. De Smet brought Seysses' philosophy with him: long maceration on the stems, no filtering and bottling after eighteen months in 50 percent new oak. The results so far: big wines, with lots of fruit and deep Burgundy flavors. De Smet's track record is brief, but Burgundy specialists, never unduly generous, predict fine things for him. Domaine de l'Arlot produces a small amount of Nuits-St.-Georges white.

Nuragus
A heavy-cropping Sardinian variety of obscure, possibly Phoenician, origin. It takes its name from the ancient dry stone towers that dot the island, and near Cagliari in the south makes a slight D.O.C. white wine of little individuality.

Nuy Cooperative, Worcester
One of the best-run cooperatives in South Africa, with twenty-one members and a very experienced winemaker, Wilhelm Linde, who has won national trophies for the wines. Its fortified Red and White Muscadel, in particular, stand high on the list of the Cape's top wines. It has also produced some very attractive dry white wines from the rather lowly Colombard grape.

Oak
The Romans liked the taste of honey and spices in their wine; modern drinkers like oak. The oaky taste comes from keeping wine in oak barrels, and the smaller and the newer the barrel the stronger the oaky flavor. French oak is particularly popular, especially from the forests of Tronçais, Allier, Nevers, Limousin and the Vosges. Others used include American, Spanish and Yugoslav oaks. Oak chips are a legal and cheap alternative in some countries.

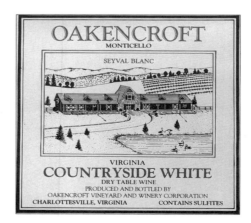

Oakencroft Vineyard Seyval Blanc, Virginia
One of the few things at which Thomas Jefferson failed was growing grapes and making wine. A connoisseur with a magnificent cellar of French wines, Jefferson tried everything to get fine grapes to grow at Monticello and elsewhere in Virginia. He even hired an Italian viticulturalist. Alas, nothing worked. He was two centuries too early.

Today, there is a small but flourishing wine business in the horse country south and west of Washington, D.C. Felicia Warburg Rogan's Oakencroft has been one of the most consistently good producers of Chardonnay. The wines are clean, with good fruit and a pleasant, tangy finish.

Bodegas Ochoa, Navarre
This well-known *bodega* in the Ribera Alta produces excellent, strong-flavored red wines from Tempranillo and Cabernet Sauvignon.

Vincent Ogereau, Anjou
Ogereau is typical of a number of open-minded, dedicated young winemakers who are producing stunning wines in Anjou, where standards, in the past, were decidedly patchy.

Ogereau's attention to detail has paid off, in particular with the *moelleux* Chenin Blancs he produced in 1989 and 1990. The Coteaux du Layon Saint Lambert Cuvée Capus 1989 is certainly one of the finest Loire wines made in that year. This wine was vinified and aged in new oak. The oak has married perfectly with the rich, opulent fruit, giving great depth and complexity. Undoubtedly a wine that will last for a century or more.

Ogereau has worked closely with Didier Coutenceau, the well-known local enologist who specializes in Chenin Blanc. They have experimented both in the 20 hectare/49 acre vineyard and in the cellar, with different vinification techniques.

Although it is with Chenin Blanc that Ogereau excels, his Anjou Blanc Sec, Anjou Rouge and Anjou Villages are all extremely well made.

Oidium tuckeri
Powdery mildew — a fungal disease was the first of the three great afflictions to hit the vineyards of France in the second half of the nineteenth century. Oidium which first appeared in Bordeaux in 1851 can be controlled by spraying vines with copper sulfate or powdered sulfur.

Okuzgozu
An indigenous Turkish red variety found chiefly in southern and eastern Anatolia.

Olarra, Rioja
Established by a group of Spanish businessmen in the 1970s, Olarra quickly became successful on account of the rich-full character of the first wines and their reasonable price. Today the style of the wines is soft and attractive with hints of toasty oak. The company's best wine is the Rioja Cerro Añon Reserva.

Olasz Rizling
See Welschriesling

Olivella
A black grape grown in Campania, where it is prominent in the red D.O.C. wines of Vesuvio, as well as Solopaca and Taburno to the North. It is found also in Latium, as a subordinate variety used for blending. Also known as Sciacianoso and Palombina.

Côtes d'Olt, Cahors
This cooperative at Parnac is the leading producer of Cahors, vinifying 45 percent of the appellation's wine. It makes a wide range of *cuvées* as well as marketing the wine of a number of important French estates, such as Châteaux Caix, Lagrezette and Les Bouysses. Caix belongs to the queen and prince of Denmark and the magnificently restored Lagrezette to Antoine-Dominque Perrin, the director of Cartier.

Omar Khayyam, Narayangoan, India
In 1982 Jean Brisbois, a Champenois enologist from Piper Heidsieck, started building a modern winery near Poona, financed by the Indage hotel group, to produce *méthode champenoise* wines. In 1985, the Chardonnay-based Omar Khayyam was released. It is a sparkling wine of excellent quality with fine, small bubbles and a dry, clean, delicate taste. The company now plans to

add still wines made from Chardonnay and Cabernet Sauvignon to its portfolio.

Optima
One of a good many relatively recently evolved German white-wine hybrids. It is grown primarily to add weight to blended wines.

Opus One, Napa Valley
The label of this expensive and relatively rare Cabernet Sauvignon bears the likenesses of Robert Mondavi and the late Baron Philippe de Rothschild, the owner of Château Mouton-Rothschild. Back in the 1970s, the two men conceived the idea of a wine that would combine California's richness with Bordeaux's elegance. More than a decade later, the result is an exceptionally good Californian wine. The French contribution would have to be described as restraint and a touch of subtlety for the grapes, the soil, the climate and even the winery are all from the Napa Valley. Opus One is more Bordeaux in style than Robert Mondavi's signature wines.

Organic viticulture
Vine growers are increasingly concerned about ecology and the environment, and there is a general move to reduce the use of herbicides, insecticides and other chemical sprays in the vineyard. Natural methods of controlling weeds and insects are now more widely used. While there is no agreed definition for organic viticulture or wine, there are a number of organizations, such as Nature et Progrès, U.N.I.A. and Terre et Vie, that define and promote organic methods.

Orlando, Rowland Flat, South Australia
Orlando is one of the three largest wine companies in Australia, a majority shareholder being Pernod-Ricard of France. Grapes for Orlando wines come from all the principal wine regions of South Australia. The company's famous Jacob's Creek is made from Shiraz, Cabernet and Malbec. It is an extremely reliable wine and is excellent value for the money. Look out too for the very affordably priced Orlando R.F. Chardonnay.

Château Les Ormes de Pez, St. Estèphe
A *cru grand bourgeois* that still offers very good value, Les Ormes de Pez came into existence at the time of the Revolution, when the Château de Pez was confiscated from its aristrocratic owners. In more recent times, since 1930 this property in Bordeaux has belonged to the Cazes family of Lynch-Bages; indeed, for many years the wine of Les Ormes was made there, a short distance away in Pauillac. This is no longer the case, and the property has its own highly modern *cuvier* and *chai*, with temperature-controlled stainless-steel vats. The wines are matured for upward of a year before bottling takes place. Typically they are dark, rich and concentrated, with evident fruit and less tannic austerity than many of this appellation, so that they can be enjoyed young. Over the past decade there has been a string of successes; 1978, 1979, 1981, 1982, 1983, 1985, 1986, 1988 and 1989 were all very fine, with 1982 especially notable. Even in the difficult year of 1984 Les Ormes de Pez contrived to make a creditable wine.

Ortega
This white variety is a cross between Müller-Thurgau and

Siegerrebe (Madeleine Angevine x Gerwürztraminer). The Ortega is grown mainly in the Rheinhessen and the Rheinpfalz in Germany and is regarded as being among the most successful of the newly established German varieties.

Ortrugo
A grape that makes lively, dry, varietal white wines, *frizzante* and *spumante*, in the Colli Piacentini in the extreme northwest of Emilia-Romagna.

André Ostertag, Epfig
A prominent grower in the Bas–Rhin in Alsace, Ostertag attracted favorable publicity for his wines on the release of his outstanding 1983 vintage. Ostertag wines are rather arbitrarily divided into *vins de fruit* and *vins de terroir*. The former are intended for early drinking and show the fruity aromas of their respective grape varieties; the *vins de terroir* are wines for the long haul, more complex and reflective of the soil types on which the grapes are grown. Ostertag's best vineyard site is the *Grand Cru* Muenchberg, where the red sandstone soil yields particularly elegant Riesling.

Domaines Ott, Côtes de Provence
Famous 150 hectare/370 acre estate in the south of France using organic methods to produce some of Provence's most expensive wines. The estate was founded in 1896 and now extends to three properties: Clos Mireille, Château Romasson and Château de Selle. Perhaps best known for its whites and rosés.

Ottavianello
An Apulian variant of the Cinsaut, which on the coast between Bari and Brindisi makes the bright red Ostuni D.O.C.

Ouillage
French term for topping up barrels to make up the loss from evaporation. It is essential that barrels are kept full, for otherwise the wine will oxidize.

Oxidation
The effect of too much oxygen on most wines is to spoil them. However, slow oxidation is an essential part of maturation. All wines aged in cask undergo slow oxidation, usually to their benefit. For a few wines, like *oloroso* Sherry, oxidation is essential to the character of the wine.

Oyster Bay Sauvignon Blanc, Marlborough
An almost exclusively export wine from this mid-sized New Zealand family company. Only two wines are made under the Oyster Bay label, a Chardonnay and a Sauvignon Blanc, both from Marlborough grapes.

P

pH
The standard measure of a wine's acidity or alkalinity. The lower the pH, the higher the acidity. Malolactic fermentation has the effect of raising the pH. The pH is often used to judge the ripeness of grapes: white grapes are normally picked with a pH of between 3.1 and 3.4, red grapes between 3.4 and 3.6.

Pagadebit
The name of this white grape variety grown in Italy means "pay debt," which can be taken as a measure of its reliability. Under the new denomination Pagadebit di Romagna it makes fruity white wines that may be dry or *amabile,* and *frizzante* in either style. The grape exists elsewhere along the Adriatic coast, and in Apulia, where

once it was widely planted, it is known as Bombino Bianco.

Bruno Paillard, Champagne
The youngest of the Champagne houses was founded in 1981 and attained the coveted *négociant-manipulant* status in 1984. Bruno Paillard's N.V. and vintage are well made, quite full-bodied wines with very attractive bready aromas. Production is now in the region of 20,000 cases a year.

Pais
Despite the significant increase in plantings of better grape varieties in Chile, Pais, which was probably brought to the country by Spanish Jesuits in the sixteenth century, still accounts for a large proportion of the vineyards, producing very ordinary wine in prolific quantities for the domestic market. Pais is thought to be the same variety as the Criolla of Argentina, and to be closely related to the Mission of California. While Mission is disappearing from California, Criolla is still important for domestic consumption in Argentina, making pale red wine in generous quantity from the irrigated vineyards of Mendoza.

Palacio de Brejoeira, Vinho Verde
This resoundingly named estate near Monção in the extreme north of Portugal, separated from Galicia only by the Minho river, makes a highly regarded and highly priced Vinho Verde from the Alvarinho grape. Characteristically, this uncommon variety endows its wines with an acidity, a higher degree of alcohol, and a subtle complexity of flavor denied those made from the Trajadura and the Loureiro.

Il Palazzino, Chianti Classico
Il Palazzino is a small 6 hectare/14.9 acre estate at Monti producing excellent, full-bodied Chiantis. The 1988 *riserva* is splendid with ripe tannins, not too much alcohol, mouth-enveloping fruit and a velvety texture. It deserves keeping until 1996.

Château Palmer, Margaux
A third growth of 1855, Palmer ranks second only to Chateau Margaux among the wines of this commune in Bordeaux. In its great years, which are many — 1961, 1966, 1967, 1970, 1971, 1975, 1979, 1983, 1985, 1986, 1988 and 1989 — Palmer can rival or surpass any of the first growths. Its characteristics are depth of color, a pronounced bouquet, perfumed and persistent, with concentrated fruit and richness allied to that feminine delicacy attributed to great Margaux. Unusually, the wine is made with a proportion of Merlot as high as 40 percent. Its vinification and *élèvage* are carried out in a traditional, even an old-fashioned, manner which is handsomely justified by its results.

Palmer Vineyards, Long Island Cabernet Franc, Long Island
Long Island's North Fork, where almost all of its vineyards are located, has a maritime climate, heavily influenced by Long Island Sound, in most cases less than 1.6 kilometers/1 mile away, and by the Atlantic Ocean, never more than 32 kilometers/20 miles to the south. It makes sense that Bordeaux varieties should prosper in these New York State vineyards because Bordeaux's vineyards are in a similar setting. Cabernet Sauvignon and Merlot are grown, but this wine shows that Long Island may have more to offer than anyone had guessed. The wine has good fruit, is a bit harder than a local Merlot but gives promise of a long life and, possibly, an interesting future for an underrated grape.

Palomino
Palomino is the principal grape variety of Jerez. When made into a table wine, even in Jerez, it is rather dull, but when allowed to grow *flor* and aged in a solera

system, it makes one of the world's finest wines. It has traveled to South Africa, California and Australia, where it is used for Sherry-style wines and also makes unexciting table wines. As Listan in the Midi it makes indifferent *vin ordinaire* and is disappearing from the region.

Pamid

A red wine variety native to Bulgaria and still widely planted, although heavily outnumbered by such interlopers as the Cabernet Sauvignon and Merlot. The Pamid makes sweetish, commonplace red wines of little distinction. A white Pamid also exists.

Château Pape-Clément, Graves

This Bordeaux vineyard, first planted in 1300 for the future Pope Clement V, remained the property of the Church until the Revolution. Since 1939 it has belonged to the Montagne family, who acquired the vineyard two years after its devastation by hail. Not until 1959 was a wine produced in keeping with Pape-Clément's former reputation. Further successes were the vintages of 1961, 1962, 1964 and 1966; then followed a series of relatively poor wines, light, lacking in substance, some of them the inevitable consequence of overproduction. Not for ten years did the wines improve; then came the spectacular 1985, and with a new administrator and new equipment the improvement has been sustained. Splendid wines, deeply colored, concentrated and powerful, were made in 1986, 1988 and 1989. These are wines reminiscent of the great vintages of the past, and the future of Pape-Clément seems assured. For a number of years the château has made a tiny amount of fine white wine, unusually from Sauvignon, Sémillon and Muscadelle in equal proportion.

Parellada

Parellada is a white grape variety found mainly in Catalonia for Cava, for which it is usually blended with Macabeo and Xarello. It is at its best for table wine in Torres' Viña Sol, for which it is grown in the cooler vineyards of the upper Penedès.

Passerillage

Long hot autumns and the seasonal retraction of a vine's sap shrivel grapes that are left on the vine, turning them into raisins and concentrating the grape sugars. The resulting wine will be sweet. The term is French.

Passito

Can be the Italian equivalent of *passerillage*, but usually refers to an Italian wine made from grapes that have been partially dried.

Pasteurization

Method of sterilizing wines through heat, killing off bacteria. Named after Louis Pasteur. Flash pasteurization is most commonly used — the wine's temperature is raised to 80°C/176°F for between thirty seconds and one minute. While it is suitable treatment for everyday wines that will be drunk quickly, pasteurization should not be used on wines that need to be aged, as the process greatly affects a wine's maturing potential.

Weingut Dr. Pauly-Bergweiler, Mosel-Saar-Ruwer

This German cellar, probably the most modern of any private estate on the Mosel, is known for Rieslings with a very clear, direct flavor. No *Süssreserve* is used. It owns 11.3 hectares/28 acres of vineyards, half of which are on the steepest slopes, and which include some of the most famous sites in the Mosel: vineyards like Graacher Himmelreich, Wehlener Sonnenuhr and Brauneberger Juffer Sonnenuhr. Half the firm's production is exported.

Château Pavie, St. Emilion

This is a very large vineyard in Bordeaux on the slopes to the southeast of St. Emilion itself, and its wines are aged in cellars cut out of the limestone. Toward the end of the last century the vineyard and its proprietor played a notable part in the long struggle against the menace of the phylloxera. More recently and for thirty-five years it has been owned by the Valette family. If its reputation generally has been one of inconsistency, perhaps a reflection of its varied soil, over the past

dozen years Pavie has improved greatly. The wine shows more depth and richness than formerly, but has lost nothing of its habitual charm and breed. Impressive wines were made in 1978 and 1979, and in the past decade those of 1981, 1982, 1983, 1985, 1986 and 1988 were all successful, the 1982, 1985 and 1986 perhaps outstandingly so.

Château Pavie-Decesse, St. Emilion

The 9 hectares/22 acres of this vineyard in Bordeaux on the limestone plateau at the top of its hill were lost from Pavie proper toward the end of the last century. In 1970 they were bought back by the Valette family, owners of the larger property, but the two have been kept entirely separate. The fermentations are carried out in stainless-steel vats, and new oak, one third replaced each year, is used for the aging of the wine. The grape mix is not identical to that at Pavie, and the wine is generally more tannic, with compensating fruit and flavor. Of recent years, excellent examples have been 1980, 1981, 1982, 1983 and especially 1985, and their quality is such that there can be no doubt that Pavie-Decesse is wholly capable of maintaining its individual identity.

Pecorello

A Calabrian red-wine variety that is blended with Gaglioppo, Greco Nero and others to make the upland red Savuto near Rogliano. This is a wine of sadly limited production.

Pecorino

A grape formerly more highly regarded. It is capable of making fruity white wines of some acidity, but nowadays plays only a minor part in the unremarkable Falerio dei Colli Ascolani of the Marches. The variety is still found in Umbria, Latium and the Abruzzi.

Pedro Ximénez

After the Palomino the second Sherry grape, although it is planted only sparsely at Jerez, where it is difficult to grow. There it makes sweet wines for blending, but at Montilla, to the south of Córdoba, it makes dry wines, together with the sweet destined for the sweetening of commercial Oloroso. Farther south still it plays a part in Málaga, where with the Moscatel it is one of the two remaining varieties authorized to be replanted. The Pedro Ximénez is found in Catalonia as well as throughout the south of Spain, and it makes huge amounts of alcoholic but otherwise unremarkable white wines, much of it used for blending. The variety is found also in California, Australia, New Zealand, South Africa and Argentina.

Henri Pellé, Menetou-Salon

This Loire estate, founded in 1935, now has 25 hectares/61.8 acres at Morogues in the appellation of Menetou-Salon and 5 hectares/12.4 acres in Sancerre. All the wines, whether whites from Sauvignon Blanc or reds and rosés from Pinot Noir, are very well made with good varietal character. Pellé's very reasonably priced Menetou-Salons are a rebuke to the many poorly made and more expensive wines that are labeled Sancerre. The top *cuvée* from Menetou-Salon Blanc comes from the Clos Blanchais.

Penfolds, Nuriootpa, South Australia

Founded by a doctor in the 1840s, Penfolds is the biggest wine firm in Australia, producing an estimated 1.8 million cases (including bulk sales) annually. The company enjoys a thoroughly justified reputation as a specialist red winemaker of the highest class. Penfolds' Grange Hermitage a magnificent expression of the Shiraz grape, leads the field and is often called Australia's best red wine. It comes fom Nuriootpa in the Barossa Valley. But such wines as that produced at the Magill Estate are also outstanding in their category. Penfolds has made some superb Show Release wines in limited quantities over the years. These are labeled by bin number and are collectors' items. The 1980 Bin 80 A and the 1982 Bin 820 are both superb. White wines have not been Penfolds' strong suit in the past, but the company's Chardonnays are increasingly well made.

Peppery

Characteristic of Grenache Noir, especially in the wines of the southern Rhône.

Bodegas Pérez Pascuas, Ribero del Duero

Immaculate small *bodega* run by two brothers making elegant, aromatic Tinto Joven and a more substantial oak-dominated *crianza*.

Pernand-Vergelesses Les Vergelesses, Domaine Rapet

The Rapet family owns some excellent parcels in both Corton-Charlemagne and Corton, but it also makes good wines from its holdings both in the Savigny-lès-Beaune and Pernand-Vergelesses vineyards. According to Burgundian lore, Pernand-Vergelesses has a less than favorable location for making fine wine because of its exposure to the northeast. The soil is said to make up the difference, provided the winemakers are skillful enough to extract the best from their grapes. The wines are tough when young and need time to develop. But develop they do, into earthy wines with long staying power. They are also relatively good bargains for fine Burgundy.

Peronospéra

See Downy mildew.

Perricone

A Sicilian red-wine grape, grown chiefly in the center and west of the island, where it produces robust, deep-colored wines widely used for blending. Under its alternative name of Pignatello the grape makes varietal wines.

Perrier-Jouët, Champagne

Best-known for its Art Nouveau-decorated Belle Epoque bottles, this prestige *cuvée* comes in both white and rosé. This Champagne house was founded by Pierre-Nicholas-Marie Perrier in 1811. Jouët, his wife's maiden name, was added to avoid confusion with the firm his nephew set up, Joseph Perrier. It was bought by Mumm in 1959 and has been in the Seagram group since 1969. Perrier-Jouët has 108 hectares/267 acres of vines, some in the Côte des Blancs and the rest in the Marne Valley. Production is around 240,000 cases.

Bodegas Pesquera, Ribera del Duero

Owner Alejandro Fernandez makes some of the finest

red wines of Spain from his 60 hectare/148 acre vineyard. Reflecting Fernandez's superstar status as a winemaker, prices for Pesquera doubled during the 1980s. These red wines are made from Tempranillo and are aged in oak for twenty-four to thirty months; they have a remarkable concentration of flavor. The 1986 Pesquera is rated one of Fernandez's best wines to date.

Pétillant

Generally refers to wines with a slight prickle or spritz from residual carbon dioxide. This is particularly common in young wines. *Perlé* is the term used in Gaillac, France. A more specific use is for the half-sparkling wines produced in Vouvray and Montlouis, whose maximum pressure should not exceed two atmospheres at 20°C/68°F.

Petit château

Lesser château in Bordeaux, below *cru classé* and *cru bourgeois* standing, and also applied to châteaux from outlying versions of Bordeaux, such as Côtes de Bourg or Côtes de Francs. Such wines can often be good value.

Petit Verdot

A traditional Bordeaux red variety, the Petit Verdot is now found only in the Médoc, and there only rarely. In a good year it can contribute alcohol, acidity and substance, thus balancing perhaps an excess of Merlot, but the vine is hard to grow, susceptible to disease and yields only a small crop, which invariably is very late to ripen. These factors have hastened its decline.

Château Petit-Village, Pomerol

A Bordeaux estate well placed on high ground and traditionally the best growth of the gravelly part of Pomerol, Petit-Village is now the property of the insurance group Axa, and is managed by Jean-Michel Cazes of Lynch-Bages. The vineyard was almost entirely destroyed by the frosts of 1956, and the replanting was ill-judged in that too small a proportion of Merlot was put in. This error has been rectified, and since investment and modernization took place during the period when Bruno Prats of Cos d'Estournel was in charge, the wines of Petit-Village have been notably successful in recent vintages. They have a pronounced and persistent bouquet, great depth of color and flavor and tannic power allied to finesse. Very fine wines have been made in the past fifteen years, with 1978, 1979, 1982, 1983, 1985, 1986 and 1987 especially outstanding.

Petite Arvine, Alphonse Orsat, Valais

The Arvine, or Petite Arvine — they are the same vine — produces big wines in the Valais in Switzerland from a yield of 30 to 40 hectoliters per hectare/1.8 to 2.4 tons per acre. They develop well in bottle over many years. This example, with more than 14 percent natural alcohol, has enormous flavor and considerable style. An excellent wine to be served after meals or as an aperitif.

Petite Sirah

This is the Durif, developed in France more than a century ago, but rarely seen there now. It has no connection with the Syrah of the Rhône valley. In California the grape is widely grown and makes robust, well-colored tannic wines that may be sold as varietals, or, more commonly, used for blending.

Petrolly

The classic aroma of mature Rieslings. The aroma often shades toward diesel or paraffin and is sometimes found in old dry Chenins and mature Muscadets.

Château Pétrus, Pomerol

Pétrus is a phenomenon. It is preeminent in its appellation, and in terms of price it can outstrip the first growths of the Médoc. If the huge success in the world market of this small Bordeaux property must be attributed to the enthusiasm, skill and judgment of Jean-Pierre Moueix, the beauty of the wine is to the credit of Madame Loubat and her niece and successor Madame Lacoste.

The vineyard is planted almost exclusively with Merlot, and its soil on the high plateau is largely clay. The wine is distinguished by its color, richness, flavor and substance, all of these found in Pétrus to a more intense degree than among its neighboring Pomerols.

Outstanding vintages were those of 1945, 1947, 1949, 1950, 1953, 1961, 1962, 1964, 1966, 1967 and 1971, with a further sequence of astonishing successes in the seventies and eighties. Increasingly the style of these later wines seems hugely substantial, alcoholic and slow maturing, with the vintages of 1982, 1983 and 1986 especially marked in this respect with their concentration, tannins and dense richness.

Château de Pez, St. Estèphe

De Pez can be shown to have been making a *grand vin* since at least the seventeenth century. The vineyard has an ideal exposure, and the vines, with an unusually high proportion of Cabernet Sauvignon, do well on its gravelly soil. Robert Dousson has managed what was formerly his aunt's estate for more than forty years with enthusiasm and scrupulous care. His wines are typical of the appellation at its best; they are deeply colored, rich, structured and long-lived. Usually they need ten years or so to show their full potential. Outstanding wines were made in 1959, 1964, 1966, 1970, 1971, 1975 and 1976, and during the past decade the most successful have been 1980, 1982, 1985 and 1986. While it is designated officially a *cru bourgeois* de Pez is much better than that, certainly the equal of many of the leading classified growths.

André Pfister, Dahlenheim

A rising star of the Bas-Rhin in Alsace, André Pfister runs an immaculate domain of 7 hectares/17 acres at Dahlenheim, due west of Strasbourg. Pfister believes in the most natural winemaking methods and a minimum use of sulfur dioxide. His wines are especially clean and pure flavored. From a recent tasting of the 1989 and 1990 vintages mention should be made of a crisp Silvaner 1990, an exceptionally well balanced Tokay-Pinot Gris 1989 and a steely long-flavored Riesling Grand Cru Engelberg 1989. The Engelberg vineyard is remarkable in that the soil is based on a stratum of pure chalk to a depth of 20 meters/65 feet.

Château Phélan-Ségur, St. Estèphe

Well-placed on gravel close to Montrose, this *cru bourgeois* has had a rough passage over the past decade, during which the quality of the wine has been uneven in the extreme. For more than sixty years this Bordeaux property belonged to the Delon family, and fine vintages such as 1934, 1937, 1945, 1947, 1949, 1952, 1955 and 1964 attest to its potential, but in 1986

Phélan-Ségur was sold to Xavier Gardinier of Champagne Pommery. There have been differing views about the 1983 vintage, and the new owner refused to release the wines of 1984 and 1985, declaring that they had been affected by a chemical treatment used under the former regime. A legal action then took place, but the terms of its conclusion have not been disclosed. Clearly it will be necessary for Gardinier to reestablish the good name of Phélan-Ségur and to restore faith in its product.

The early signs seem promising, with a notable 1986, a more than adequate 1987, and a splendid 1988 of richness and power offering hope for the future. There is a new and pleasing second wine, Frank Phélan, named in tribute to a figure from the estate's history.

Philipponnat, Champagne

This small Champagne firm is based at Mareuil-sur-Ay. A relatively young house, it was founded in 1912 by the Philipponat family. Since 1987 it has been controlled by the Marie-Brizard Group. The Clos des Goisses, from a single vineyard of 5.5 hectares/13.6 acres, is their finest wine. Annual production is around 40,000 cases.

Phylloxera vastratrix

This is the Latin name of the tiny louse that nearly wiped out most of Europe's vineyards during the latter part of the nineteenth century. The minute insect attacks vine roots. Many of today's vines are grafted onto American rootstock, which is resistant to the louse. Vines planted in sand appear to be immune from attack: the insect is unable to negotiate sand. Today a new strain of *phylloxera,* to which some commonly used American rootstocks are less resistant, is threatening the world's vineyards, especially in California.

Château Pibran, Pauillac

This is a small *cru bourgeois* close to Mouton. In 1987 it was acquired by the insurance group Axa, which numbers among its Bordeaux properties the nearby Pichon Longueville Baron, Cantenac-Brown in Margaux and Petit-Village in Pomerol, and like them it is managed by Jean-Michel Cazes of Lynch-Bages. Under the new regime the wines of 1987 and 1988 have been pleasingly fruity and tannic, with an appealing bouquet, and it seems highly probable that future vintages will show the improvement already demonstrated at other estates directed by Cazes.

Picardan

One of the lesser of the thirteen varieties permitted under the Châteauneuf-du-Pape appellation.

Château Pichon-Longueville Baron, Pauillac

The reputation of this Bordeaux vineyard was established in the first half of the nineteenth century. It was classified as a second growth in 1855, and its 1928, 1947, 1949 and 1953 were excellent. More recently, in the sixties and seventies, Pichon Baron made wines both inconsistent and, given its advantages of site and soil, quite unsatisfactory. The vintages of 1981, 1982, 1985 and 1986 showed rather better, but still inadequately when viewed against the Médoc as a whole in those years. In 1987 the vineyard was sold to the insurance group Axa, and its administration entrusted to Jean-Michel Cazes of Lynch-Bages. Given his

RIGHT: Phylloxera attacks a vine root.

performance elsewhere, and the level of investment, it seems certain that the early promise of the wines of 1987 and 1988 will be fulfilled in future years. In Les Tourelles de Longueville the château makes a pleasant if insubstantial second wine.

Château Pichon-Longueville Comtesse de Lalande, Pauillac

This large and handsome Bordeaux estate is the second and, in terms of current quality, the more important part of the divided Pichon domain. Roughly a third of the vineyard lies in St. Julien, although today all the wine bears the Pauillac appellation, and it is planted with an unusually high proportion of Merlot.

Since 1926 it has belonged to the Miailhe family, prominent in Bordeaux since before the Revolution, and since 1978, following the resolution of a less than elegant family dispute, it has been owned and managed by Madame de Lencquesaing. Under her direction the works of construction and modernization that her brother had begun in the late sixties have continued, so the property is now a model of its kind.

Pichon-Longueville had always been capable of making very remarkable wines, and now that problems of inconsistency have been overcome, Pichon Lalande is in the forefront of the second growths of the Médoc. It is able generally to rival, and on occasion to surpass, the first growths. Characteristically the wine is deeply colored, with an intense and persistent bouquet, depth, richness and structure. It is softer than other great *crus* of the appellation, a reflection perhaps of its Merlot content and its debt to St. Julien. Among the splendid vintages of recent years have been those of 1961, 1962, 1964, 1966, 1970, 1975, 1978, 1979, 1981, 1982, 1983, 1985, 1986, 1987 and 1988.

Picolit

A Friulian variety, formerly widely grown in the Colli Orientali to make good dessert wines. The vine is difficult to grow and susceptible to disease, and little Picolit of distinction is made nowadays.

Picpoul

See Folle Blanche.

Pigato

A vine of Hellenic origin, long established in western Liguria, where it makes fruity, substantial, dry white wines under various denominations.

Pigeage and remontage

French terms for methods of breaking up the cap of pips and grapeskins formed during fermentation, so as to extract flavor and tannins. *Pigeage* involves the use of a plunger to force the cap down into the fermenting juice below; it may also be done by jumping into the vat and using the legs. *Remontage* includes pumping juice over the cap, breaking it up by releasing air or inert gas into the juice.

Pignoletto

A grape variety apparently native to Emilia, Italy, although some claim that it is derived from the Riesling. In the Colli Bolognesi it makes light, white varietal wines that may be still or *frizzante*.

Pignolo

An ancient and indigenous red-wine variety of Friuli's Colli Orientali, Italy, the Pignolo has found new favor in a *vino da tavola* of great individuality.

Pinot Beurot

See Pinot Gris.

Pinot Bianco

See Pinot Blanc.

Pinot Blanc

Pinot Blanc is the white version of Pinot Noir, and the two are indeed related. Pinot Blanc is well established in Alsace, for soft, grassy Pinot Blanc d'Alsace, or it may be used as an ingredient of Crémant d'Alsace and Edelzwicker. Insignificant amounts are also grown on the Côte d'Or, but otherwise it does not feature much in French viticulture.

In Germany and Austria it is called Weissburgunder. It is grown in Baden and the Palatinate and is sometimes aged in oak. It is given similar treatment in Austria, where it is grown near the Yugoslav border and around Vienna. It is also popular across the frontier, in Slovenia and Slavonia, as Belic Pinot.

In Italy there has been some confusion between Pinot Bianco and Chardonnay. Most Pinot Bianco is found in Friuli, the Veneto, Trentino and the Alto Adige, although it has spread farther south. Its high acidity and fairly neutral character make it particularly good for sparkling wine.

There is confusion in the New World too. Most Australian Pinot Blanc is really Chardonnay, while most South African Chardonnay is probably Pinot Blanc. In California Pinot Blanc has been paid little attention, with the notable exception of an oak-aged wine from Chalone Vineyards.

Pinot Grigio

See Pinot Gris.

Pinot Gris

Pinot Gris is neither red nor white, with a skin color that can vary considerably, sometimes looking almost black and sometimes nearer white. It performs best in the cooler, more northern vineyards of Alsace and Germany, which allow for the development of its aromatic character.

The most exciting examples of Pinot Gris come from Alsace, where it is called Tokay-Pinot Gris. Here it makes a spicy aromatic wine, which in the best years may have noble rot and be vinified as *vendange tardive* or *sélection de grains nobles,* with considerable aging potential.

In Germany, particularly in the Palatinate and Baden, as Ruländer, it produces flavorsome wines that are fuller and heavier than Riesling, and deeper in color. As Pinot Grigio it grows all over northeast Italy and should not be confused with the similar Tocai. It tends to have a rather neutral flavor.

In Hungary it is called Szürkebarat and is grown successfully near Lake Balaton. In Switzerland it is called Malvoisie, and it is also to be found in Luxembourg, Austria, Yugoslavia and Romania. It has made little impact in the vineyards of the New World. Other synonyms include Grauerburgunder and Pinot Beurot.

Pinot Meunier

The least regarded, but with 48 percent of the vineyard the most heavily planted, of the three Champagne grapes, the robust Pinot Meunier is grown for its dependability and heavy yield. The variety is excluded from the *grands* and *premiers crus,* but its soft roundness makes it invaluable for blending with the finer, more complex Pinot Noir and the elegant Chardonnay. The vine is grown also in the Loire valley to make rosé wines.

Pinot Noir

Pinot Noir is a sulky, temperamental grape variety. It is difficult to grow, is particularly susceptible to rot and benefits from a long, cool ripening season, so that it performs badly in the hotter conditions of some New World vineyards. It certainly does not have the easy adaptability of Cabernet Sauvignon.

Pinot Noir is the grape variety of red Burgundy,

where it can produce wines that are simply outstanding. Aged in oak, it should have a sweetness reminiscent of raspberries, with undertones of vegetation and chocolate. The color will never be very deep, but this does not prevent it from aging for several years. With such an elusive character it can often disappoint. Pinot Noir grows throughout Burgundy, from Irancy outside Chablis right down into the Mâconnais. It is also an important part of the Champagne blend, and is at its best in the villages of the Montagne de Reims. It features in other appellations of eastern France, such as Sancerre Rouge, Pinot Noir d'Alsace, Côtes du Jura and a little in Savoie.

Across the Rhine it is called Spätburgunder and makes some of the better red wines of Germany, notably in the Ahr, Baden and Württemberg. The same *Prädikat* categories apply as for white wines, although the best reds are fermented dry and aged in barrel. Pinot Noir has also crossed the English Channel.

South of the Alps it grows in the cool Alto Adige and in northeast Italy, where it is known as Pinot Nero. There are a few examples in Tuscany too. In the Oltrepò Pavese it is used for sparkling wine, and there is some in the Valle d'Aosta.

Pinot Noir also grows in central and eastern Europe. In Austria it is called Spätburgunder, Burgundac Crni in Yugoslavia, and Nagyburgundi in Hungary. In California it has presented a considerable challenge, which Californians are just beginning to master, most successfully in the temperate region of Carneros. In California it is also sometimes — and mistakenly — known as Gamay Beaujolais. Cool Oregon also produces some good examples of Pinot Noir. Success has been limited in Australia, but with better examples beginning to come from cooler regions, such as the Yarra Valley outside Adelaide. The cool climate vineyards of New Zealand may well offer more potential, particularly from Martinborough and the South Island.

Pinotage
The black Pinotage is a peculiarly South African grape variety, a cross between Pinot Noir and Cinsaut that was developed in 1925 by Professor Perold. If prevented from overproduction, it makes warm spicy wine, with a distinctive flavor. The occasional planting is found in New Zealand.

Pipe
Large wooden cask used for Port. Pipes vary in size during the maturation process. A Douro pipe, used for blending and storing 440 liters/116 U.S. gallons of wine with 110 liters/29 U.S., gallons of brandy, holds 550 liters/145 U.S. gallons; lodge pipes, used for maturing the wine, hold between 580 liters/153 U.S. gallons and 620 liters/164 U.S. gallons; shipping pipes hold 534.24 liters/141 U.S. gallons.

Piper-Heidsieck, Champagne
This house was founded by one of Florens-Ludwig Heidsieck's nephews in 1834. He died almost immediately, and when his widow married Henri-Guillaume Piper in 1837, Heidsieck became prefaced by Piper. It was the first Champagne house to change over to mechanical *rémuage* using *gyropalettes*, a technique developed in Spain. The house owns no vineyards, so must buy in all its grapes for its production of around 400,000 cases. Florens-Louis and Rare are its two prestige *cuvées*.

Piper's Brook, Tasmania
Viticulturalist Dr. Andrew Pirie planted vines near Launceston in 1974 with the aim of making wines in the European tradition. The cool climate of Tasmania and his own talent have resulted in a finely crafted 1988 Pinot Noir, elegant, delicately scented and with poised flavors

of plum and cherry. He was no less successful with his 1987 Chardonnay, another wine in an understated Burgundian style, fine-drawn, subtly fruity, and of excellent definition of flavor.

Bodegas Piqueras, Almansa
Leading *bodega* near the castellated Valencian town of Almansa, producing a red wine called Marius.

Château de Pitray, Côtes de Castillon
This is the best wine of its appellation, which covers an area in Bordeaux in which production has increased greatly over the past fifteen years. Pitray consistently makes fruity, balanced, well-colored wines for relatively early drinking, within half a dozen years or so, and they represent excellent value. Improvement can be looked for as the regulations impose stricter standards on the region as a whole.

Plavac
The best native Yugoslav variety is the Plavac Mali. It makes robust, tannic red wines with the capacity to age, as well as pleasant rosé wines, the finest being those called Opol. Like its white and yellow counterparts, the Plavac Mali does well on sandy soil and is planted along the Dalmatian coast and on the offshore islands.

Plummy
Can refer to both the plummy color and flavor found in some reds. Merlot often tastes plummy.

Pol Roger, Champagne
One of the few undisputed great names of Champagne and well known as the favorite Champagne of Winston Churchill. Its prestige Cuvée Sir Winston Churchill repays his devotion as does the black border around the label of its Extra Dry White Foil *cuvée*. Still in family control, this Epernay house was founded in 1849 by Pol Roger. It owns 70 hectares/173 acres of vines in the Vallée de la Marne and Côte des Blancs, which supply about 40 percent of its grapes. The firm is now run by Christian de Billy and Christian Pol-Roger.

Pollera Nera
A red wine grape long established in Liguria. On the eastern Riviera it is blended with a higher proportion of Sangiovese to make the newly recognized D.O.C. wines of the Colli di Luni. The Pollera is an approved variety in neighboring Tuscany, but always a subordinate one.

Polyphenols
Chemical term for phenolic compounds, the coloring matter in red wine. Polyphenols are composed of anthocyanins and tannins.

Pommery & Greno, Champagne
Founded in 1836 by Louis Pommery and Narcisse Greno. Pommery Champagne enjoyed great success in the later decades of Queen Victoria's Britain. The house was bought by Lanson in 1979 and then became part of the large B.S.N. Group, which sold it to Moët-Hennessy at the end of 1990. Pommery has 300 hectares/741 acres of vines, and the house produces a little over 400,000 cases a year. Louise Pommery is its prestige *cuvée*. Pommery

owns the Château de Crayères, now a Michelin three-star restaurant and hotel run by Gérard Boyer, in the center of Rheims.

Ponzi Vineyards
One of the best producers of Pinot Noir in Oregon's Willamette Valley, Ponzi, in the village of Beaverton, about 15 miles from Portland. This is a small family operation with a total production of less than 10,000 cases a year. Originally the Ponzis, Dick and Nancy, planned to make Alsace-style wines, like Riesling, Silvaner and Gewürztraminer. It was the unexpected success of Pinot Noir in the Willamette region that changed their minds. They still produce Riesling and some Chardonnay but, like most Oregon winemakers, they lavish most of their attention on Pinot Noir.

Oregon Pinot Noirs went through some indifferent vintages in the mid- to late 1980s but got back on track as the decade closed. Ponsi's 1988s were wines of considerable depth and intensity. They held up well against some of the best Burgundian competition. There is a regular Pinot Noir and a reserve; the reserve spends more time in French oak.

Porte-greffe
French term for rootstock, on to which a vine is grafted.

Potential alcohol
Degree of alcohol grape must would reach if all the grape sugars were converted to alcohol.

Château Poujeaux, Moulis
Poujeaux has belonged to the Theil family since 1920. Currently it is classed as a *cru grand bourgeois exceptionnel*. This Bordeaux vineyard is close to Chasse-Spleen, the leading growth of the district, and shares its well-drained gravelly soil. In general its wine is deeply colored, with a pronounced bouquet; rich, powerful and tannic. It matures slowly and is capable of long development. All four of the traditional vines are planted, and the proportion of Petit Verdot is high, at over 10 percent. The wine is made in an old-fashioned manner, with long maceration and fermentation, while filtering is disdained. Successful recent years have been 1978, 1981, 1982, 1983, 1985 and a powerful, potentially long-lived 1986.

Poulsard
A vine native to the lower slopes of the Jura and to Bugey, producing perfumed, fine-skinned black grapes with little tannin or color; well adapted to the making of rosé wines.

Pourriture grise
See Gray rot.

Predicato
Unofficial category of *vini de tavola* in Tuscany that use unauthorized grape varieties. *Predicato* wines were pioneered by several leading producers, and the regulations governing their production are self-imposed.

There are four categories of *Predicato*: Predicato di Cardisco, red wine based on Sangiovese, but with up to 10 percent other grapes (not Merlot or Cabernet) allowed; Predicato di Biturica, red made from 30 percent or more Cabernet, plus Sangiovese and up to 10 percent other grapes; Predicato del Muschio, white from Chardonnay or Pinot Bianco with, in the latter case, up to 20 percent Italico or Rhine Reisling, Pinot Grigio or Müller-Thurgau; Predicato del Selvante, white from Sauvignon, with up to 20 percent other grapes.

Premier cru
See Cru.

Press wine
Always refers to red wine. Wine that is pressed from the skins and pips after fermentation has finished, and thus is more tannic and coarse. May be kept apart and sold as cheap table wine, be distilled into alcohol or be added in whole or in part to the rest of the wine to give more tannin and backbone. Conversely in carbonic maceration the press wine is the best quality.

Château Prieuré-Lichine
Russian-born, French-bred and American-trained, Alexis Lichine was already a prominent wine merchant when he purchased the dilapidated Château Cantenac-Prieuré in 1951. After changing the name to include his own, he spent the next thirty-five years restoring the old Benedictine priory and expanding its vineyards. Through trades and more than sixty judicious purchases he increased his vineyard holdings from 11 hectares/27 acres to 62 hectares/155 acres.

Ever the merchant, he scandalized his conservative Médocain neighbors by erecting billboards along the roadways, encouraging visitors to stop at his château. It was, he promised them, open every day of the year for a tour of the cellars. Now other château owners vie with each other to lure tourists but thirty years ago it was considered unseemly.

As his holdings grew, Mr. Lichine become more severe in his selection of *cuvées* for his blend, and quality improved steadily over the years. Most professionals today rate Prieuré-Lichine as one of the best of the fourth-growth properties in the 1855 classification. Lesser *cuvées* go into the second label, Château de Clairfont. Production is about 25,000 cases a year.

Since Alexis Lichine's death in 1988, his son Sacha has been in charge at Prieuré-Lichine.

Primitivo
An early-maturing variety, possibly related to the Californian Zinfandel. It is grown in Apulia, between Taranto and Brindisi, to make powerful, purplish wines with the potential to age. In style they range from dry to the fortified *liquoroso dolce naturale*. Much of the Primitivo's production is blended.

Producteurs Aimery Limoux, Blanquette de Limoux
This large and well-equipped cooperative produces 80 percent of all sparkling wine from Limoux in France, both Blanquette and the newer appellation of Crémant. It also has well-made Chardonnay, one without oak and the other oak aged. Two years ago it instituted the promotional auction *Torques et Clochers* to sell individual *vignerons'* barrel-fermented and aged Chardonnay.

Produttori di Barbaresco, Barbaresco
This Piedmont cooperative is rightly regarded as the best in Italy. A measure of its total commitment to quality is that 40 percent of its wine production is in single-vineyard Barbarescos of the highest class. Look out for the 1982 Barbaresco Asili, a magnificent wine offered at a reasonable price.

Prohibition
America's experiment (the Volstead Act) in forbidding the sale and distribution of alcoholic beverages started in 1920 and was ignored by many, offering opportunities to gangsters and increasing the rate of deaths from efforts at home distillation of "moonshine."

The effect on the California wine industry was catastrophic. Those wineries that survived did so by supplying grapes to home winemakers, for making wine at home remained legal. The Act was repealed in 1933. Recently prohibition has come back on the American political agenda, and new laws in France have severely limited advertisements for alcohol.

Prosecco
A white variety now found chiefly in the eastern Veneto

around Treviso, although its origins lie in Friuli. The grape makes D.O.C. wines, *frizzante* and *spumante,* which may be dry or sweet. Bottle or tank fermentation are employed in preference to the *méthode champenoise.*

Pruning
Like many fruit plants, vines need to be pruned every year if they are to give their best. Pruning encourages new growth and is a big factor in deciding how many bunches of grapes will be produced. Hard pruning will limit the yield, the key to quality wine. However, the importance of pruning is now being reassessed, and some properties in Australia prune little or not at all.

Puiatti, Collio
Vittorio Puiatti is a grumpy bear of a man, but he is unquestionably one of Friuli's best winemakers. With his son Giovanni, he buys in the best grapes of Collio and vinifies excellent Sauvignon, Pinot Bianco and Chardonnay. As chief winemaker at Eno Friulia, he is a practitioner of the *metodo friulano,* a white-wine process designed to achieve bright, fruity wines.

Puligny-Montrachet Les Combettes, Domaine Etienne Sauzet
Gérard Boudot, Etienne Sauzet's son-in-law, makes the wine now, but there has been no diminution of quality since Sauzet established his considerable reputation in the 1960s and 1970s. All the Sauzet wines are classic white Burgundies, but the Les Combettes may be slightly easier to find, simply because the Sauzet holdings in that vineyard are somewhat larger than they are in Bâtard and Bienvenue-Montrachet, and in Puligny Les Perrières and Puligny La Truffière. Sauzet wines should be drunk at between five and ten years of age.

Puttonyos
Puttonyos are the baskets used in the harvest of *Aszú* (nobly rotten grapes) used in making Hungarian Tokay. The more *puttonyos,* the sweeter the wine. Two, three, four, five or six are the normal amounts, with eight *puttonyos* going into Aszú Essencia.

Château Puygueraud, Bordeaux Côtes de Francs
This Bordeaux property enjoyed prosperity at the end of the last century and the beginning of this one, but its decline was such that all its vines were uprooted at the end of the Second World War. Replanting was not undertaken until the end of the seventies, with the first vintage from the new vines that of 1983. Since then, despite the immaturity of the vineyard, results have been remarkable, with the 1988 especially promising. Today, Puygueraud rightly is regarded as a rising star and the inspiration of its small appellation. The vineyard is planted with 40 percent Merlot, the remainder split equally between Cabernets Franc and Sauvignon. While it benefits from the site and microclimate of the Côtes de Francs, much of its success must be attributed to the expertise and enthusiasm of the Thienpont family, best-known for their Vieux Château Certan.

Q

Quaffable
Easy-drinking, casual wine with little tannin; wine to be quaffed, not sipped. *Gouleyant* is the French equivalent.

Qualitätswein bestimmter Anbaugebiete (Q.b.A.)
In Germany, as in all European Community countries, wine is divided into table wine and quality wine. *Qualitätswein,* "quality wine," comes from thirteen specified regions, or *Anbaugebiete;* the region will be stated on the label. In addition to complying with restrictions on grape varieties and yields, the wine must undergo chemical analysis and pass a tasting panel.

Qualitätswein mit Prädikat (Q.m.P.)
Literally, "quality wine with special attributes." In German wine law the category above Q.b.A. The special attributes or *Prädikat,* are *Kabinett, Spätlese, Auslese, Beerenauslese, Eiswein* and *Trockenbeerenaulese.*

Quinta da Aveleda, Vinho Verde
A well-known and well-made Vinho Verde that, although it is not a single-vineyard wine, takes its name from a property near Oporto in Portugal belonging to the Guedes family of Sogrape. The estate also makes the typically dry Casal Garcia.

Quinta de Pedralvites, Bairrada
A product of the huge Portuguese-based Sogrape concern, this is a single-vineyard white wine, very fresh and fragrant, made in a dry modern style from the Maria Gomes grape.

Quinta do Carmo, Borba
This old-family property in Portugal's Borba D.O. makes traditionally big, deeply colored red wines, and recently has attracted Rothschild investment on the winemaking side, so that progress may be anticipated.

Quintarelli, Valpolicella
Giuseppe Quintarelli is perhaps the most individualistic winemaker of the Veneto. His 10 hectare/24.7 acre Valpolicella Classico vineyard is situated on the slopes above Negrar. His single-vineyard Cà del Merlo is made in a very traditional way; maceration on the skins is as long as twenty days, and bottling is still done by hand — the 1985 is a Valpolicella of unsurpassed richness. Quintarelli is also a fine white winemaker. His 1990 Bianco Secco is a skilfully blended wine dominated by Tocai; it has broad flavors of great character yet finishes fresh and crisp.

R

Rabigato
A prolific white grape variety widely planted throughout Portugal, where it is also known as Rabo de Ovelha (Ewe's Tail.) It makes alcoholic wines of no great distinction and is an important contributor to white Port.

Rafanelli Winery
For almost two decades, this modest family winery in Sonoma's Dry Creek Valley has been producing some of California finest Zinfandels. The Rafanelli's secrets, which they readily divulge to anyone who asks, include very old vines that produce wines with remarkably intense flavors, and what one writer described as old-fashioned, hands-on, low-tech winemaking.

The winery was founded by Americo Rafanelli, who started as a grape-grower, eventually managed vineyards for absentee owners, then made bulk wine. Fine wines came along in 1974 and he made them until his death in 1987. His son Dave carries on in his father's old-world tradition.

Madame Raymond Ragnaud, Cognac
Madame Raymond Ragnaud farms 18 hectares/45 acres of vines, all situated on the best slopes of Grande Fine Champagne around Ambleville. She is unquestionably one of the finest producers of Cognac, her brandies showing exuberant fruit and great depth of flavor. The Château d'Ambleville Réserve Extra is just a little over five years old, but its mellow warmth is striking proof that a Cognac need not be old to be beautiful. The daily

management of the domain is now in the hands of Ragnaud's daughter and son-in-law.

Raimat, Costers del Segre

Belonging to the Raventos family of Cordorníu, Raimat comprises a 900 hectare/2,223 acre irrigated vineyard situated in a semidesert near Lérida, Spain. The Raimat range of wines includes Abadia (a Bordeaux blend), Cabernet, Merlot, Pinot Noir and Tempranillo.

Rancio

An oxidized flavor found in certain fortified wines and acquired after long aging. Typical of *vins doux naturels*.

Domaine Raspail-Ay, Gigondas

Dominique Ay makes outstanding Gigondas at his 18 hectare/44.5 acre domain in the Côtes-du-Rhône. The 1985 has rich fruit, the 1986 more obviously tannic, leaner but with the capacity to age extremely well for up to ten years. The 1988 may yet prove the best of the trio, showing all the wild herb aromas and the complex animal and fruit flavors one associates with great Gigondas; the balance of fruit and tannin is faultless. This is a wine for keeping until 1995.

Weingut Jochen Ratzenberger, Mittelrhein

This estate produces a modern style of Riesling wine that is much appreciated by German wine buffs. Very clean, ripe acidity results in elegance and length of flavor. The style is more refined than is often the case with Mittelrhein wines and is well-balanced.

Château Rausan-Ségla, Margaux

Classified as a second growth in 1855, and in that category regarded as inferior only to Mouton, Rausan-Ségla for many years failed to justify its reputation. Since 1960 this Bordeaux property has been in varying British hands, but while the vineyard benefited from investment and replanting, it was not until the excellent 1982 vintage that clear signs of recovery became apparent, something confirmed by the success of the lighter 1983 and the concentrated, stylish 1985. Given the relative youth of its vines, Rausan-Ségla shows obvious promise for the future now that the native virtues of the vineyard are matched by modern equipment and scrupulous winemaking.

Ravat

Ravat Blanc (Ravat 6) is an early ripening hybrid derived from the Chardonnay, but the difficulties of growing the vine and its susceptibility to disease have inhibited its prospects of commercial success. Ravat 51, a Pinot Noir hybrid, is more familiarly known as Vignoles.

Ravenswood Zinfandel, Sonoma County

The resurgence of red Zinfandel over the past five years or so has been a heartening development for American wines. The so-called white Zinfandel, which is more of an aperitif than a wine, coupled with the craze for Cabernet Sauvignon, threatened for a time to drive genuine Zinfandel into oblivion. Happily, thanks to such California wineries as Ravenswood and Ridge, it is thriving once again. Ravenswood produces several superior Zinfandels, including some blockbuster single-vineyard wines. This bottling — Sonoma County — can include grapes from the Alexander Valley, Dry Creek and the Sonoma Valley, depending upon the vintage and the winemaker's judgment. It is a full-bodied, garnet-colored wine with the characteristic rough edges of a classic Zinfandel.

Château Rayas, Châteauneuf-du-Pape

Rayas vies with Beaucastel as the best wine of Châteauneuf. The haphazard state of the Rayas cellar and the reclusive nature of the owner, Jacques Reynaud, may be discouraging to the modern-minded, but the red wines of this estate — made largely from Grenache grapes — can be the most exciting of the appellation. Old vines, low yields and a lengthy time in oak (up to four years) give wines of extraordinary intensity and character. Best years are 1978, 1981, 1986 and 1988. Jacques Reynaud's second wine, Pignan, is also a great Châteauneuf, fleshier and more forward than Rayas.

Château Raymond-Lafon, Sauternes

A *cru bourgeois*, Raymond-Lafon adjoins Yquem and Sigalas-Ribaud in Bordeaux, and it makes wines worthy of its illustrious neighbors. This distinction can be ascribed to the benign influence of Pierre Meslier, for more than a quarter of a century the *régisseur* of Yquem. Meslier acquired the neglected vineyard in 1972 and at once began to apply similarly rigorous standards of viticulture, selection and vinification. The wine is matured in cask, with around a third of the limited production in new wood. The new owner's sure touch was soon displayed, with notable successes in 1975, 1976, 1978, 1980, 1982, 1983, 1984 and 1985. Raymond-Lafon still offers exceptional value but is hard to find.

Château Rayne-Vigneau, Sauternes

Although this *premier cru* has belonged to a syndicate since 1971, the Vicomte de Roton still lives in the château, as did his de Pontac ancestor at the time of the 1855 classification. Rayne-Vigneau is a considerable Bordeaux property, and in the relatively recent past it has been overproductive, with a consequent drop in the quality of the wine. Latterly the vintages of 1983, 1985 and a rich and concentrated 1986 have suggested that the estate may yet regain its ancient splendor. A dry wine called Rayne–Vigneau sec accounts for roughly 20 percent of production. Rayne-Vigneau acquired a certain notoriety in 1925 when the then vicomte disclosed to a wondering public large numbers of precious and semiprecious stones from deposits on his property. No satisfactory scientific explanation of this phenomenon has yet been published.

Recioto

Italian wine made by half-drying grapes to concentrate their sweetness, then allowing them to ferment. If the resulting wine has high residual sugar the wine is called Recioto; if it is fermented dry it is called Amarone. Examples are Recioto di Soave and Recioto della Valpolicella.

Reduction

The opposite of oxidation. In the absence of air, wines are said to be reductive. Examples are Champagne or Beaujolais Nouveau; the smell of bottle-aged wine is also reductive. At the other extreme is oloroso Sherry, matured in cask and thus oxidative; or fresh young wine with little bottle age.

Refosco

See Moudeuse.

Reichensteiner

Reichensteiner is a white grape variety, developed at Geisenheim in Germany in 1978 from a crossing of German Müller-Thurgau, French Madeleine Angevine and Italian Early Calabrese. It is named after a castle in the Mittelrhein and produces fairly neutral wine in generous quantity in Germany and occasionally wines of a little more character in England.

Schloss Reinhartshausen, Rheingau

A fine German estate with holdings in top sites, including Erbacher Marcobrunn. It is the sole owner of the climatically privileged Erbacher Rheinhell vineyard on an island in the Rhine where vines are organically grown. Facing that island is a luxury hotel which forms part of the estate and belongs, as all of it does, to the Prussian royal family. The current generation of von Preussens are the great-grandchildren of Kaiser Wilhelm II. Most of the vines are Riesling, full-bodied and rich; there are also some cheaper commercial lines.

Remontage

See Pigeage.

Remuage

The process of gradually turning and tilting bottles of sparkling wine made by the Champagne method, so that the deposit formed during the second fermentation rests on the cork. It can then be extracted by *dégorgement*. Used always to be done by hand using special wooden racks. Now increasingly done by computer-controlled machines (*gyropalettes*). The English term is "riddling."

Remy Martin, Cognac

Remy Martin dates from 1724, but its current position as one of the three most important Cognac firms, along with Martell and Hennessy, is a post-1945 achievement. After the Second World War, Remy Martin put all its efforts into the sale and promotion of its V.S.O.P., which was made from a blend of brandies coming exclusively from Grande and Petite Champagne. Nearly all its Cognacs are sold outside France. The quality of the range is impressively high, the Remy touch being a clean, fruity style with a very attractive note of vanillin oakiness. Its better Cognacs are models of their kind. The Napoléon has an average age of sixteen years. Amber in color, it shows a fine balance of delicacy, spice and concentration, while the X.O., with an average age of twenty-five years, has a subtler, more ethereal character. The top of the range Louis XIII is a magnificent brandy. No *eau-de-vie* in the blend is less than forty years old.

Reserva

Spanish wine that has been aged for a minimum time before being sold; some of this time in wooden barrels. *Gran rreserva* wines have been aged even longer. An indication of quality.

Réserve de la Comtesse, Pauillac

This is the second wine of Pichon Longueville Comtesse de Lalande, itself one of the outstanding second growths of the Médoc in Bordeaux. Up to a third of the harvest may be used for Réserve de la Comtesse.

Weingut Balthasar Ress, Rheingau

A German estate with holdings from one end of the Rheingau to the other, from Assmannshausen to Hochheim. The Riesling wines are characterized by firm, refreshing acidity. The estate is a member of the Chanta group of producers, who commit themselves to producing *halbtrocken* wines to higher standards than the legal minimum. The estate is also the leaseholder of Schloss Reichhartshausen, the *schloss* of which is used as a business school. The owner of the Ress estate, Stefan Ress, commissions an artist each year to design a label for a top *auslese*.

Domaine du Révérend, Corbières

This started as a brave new venture by a young couple, Eric and Agnès Français, and a friend, Jean-Pierre Lenthéric, who built a winery in Cucugan in the Haut Corbières in France. Unfortunately, despite a very positive reaction to their wines, they ran into a financial crisis. However, they have had the good fortune to be rescued by Bordeaux's Peter Sichel.

Ribolla

After years of decline, the Ribolla is enjoying something of a revival in Collio and the Colli Orientali of Friuli. The Ribolla Gialla makes appropriately yellow *vini da tavola* of high acidity, with the capacity to age and soften. The Ribolla Nera, better known as Schioppettino, produces highly individual red varietals. Both grapes are also used for blending.

Domaine de Ribonnet, Vin de Pays Haute-Garonne

Very individual and interesting estate in southwest France, run by the Swiss Christian Gerber. He took over the rundown estate with its magnificent fifteenth-century château in 1974. He has planted a wide range of grape varieties, including Chardonnay, Cabernets Sauvignon and Franc, Syrah, Gamay and Chasselas. Most of the wines are sold as varietals, except for Cuvée Clément Ader — a blend of Merlot and Cabernets Franc and Sauvignon. Ader was a pioneer of aviation and owned the château at the beginning of this century.

Rich

Refers to a wine high in extract and alcohol that is round and full on the palate. It is particularly used for sweet wines.

Domaine Richeaume, Côtes de Provence

Organically run vineyard in the south of France producing some impressive, robustly well-structured reds from Grenache, Cinsaut and Carignan as well as Cabernet Sauvignon. A white and rosé are also made. The 25 hectare/62 acre estate at the base of Montagne Sainte-Victoire is owned by Hoening Hoesch, a well-traveled German who was educated at Yale and then settled in France. The Cabernet Sauvignon is aged in *barriques* for five to ten months.

Domaine Richou, Anjou

The Richou family have been *vignerons* in the Loire for many generations and can date their involvement in wine back to 1550 to a Maurice Richou, who was a *viticulteur* or vinegrower, as well as a doctor. Didier Richou, who is now the winemaker, produces the usual gamut of Anjou wines. Of particular note are his Anjou Gamay, Anjou Blanc Sec and the sweet Coteaux d'Aubance, especially from such fine years as 1947, 1959, 1989 and 1990.

Weingut Max Ferd. Richter, Mosel-Saar-Ruwer

Outstanding German estate, producing well differentiated, cask-matured Riesling wines from Brauneberg, Mülheim, Graach, Wehlen and other

districts. The top wines are matured in cask. *Eisweine* are also a specialty.

Ridge Vineyards Montebello Cabernet Sauvignon, Santa Clara County

Ridge Vineyards made its name as a producer of fine Zinfandels, but its greatest wine is this Cabernet Sauvignon made from the vines in its home vineyard high in the mountains near Santa Cruz. At its best, the Ridge Montebello is a wine of great depth and complexity. The color is dark and the flavors are highly concentrated. It is a California wine that can compete with the best in the world. And it is priced accordingly. Annual production is small, and competition for it among Cabernet fans can be keen.

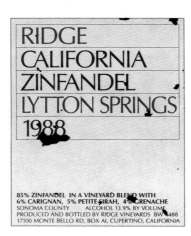

Ridge Zinfandel, Santa Clara County

Ridge makes a variety of Zinfandels from grapes hauled in from all over California, and only a dedicated Ridge watcher can keep track of them all. Two worth noting, however, are the Geyserville and Lytton Springs Zinfandels, both from Sonoma County areas. The wines may vary in taste and bouquet, but the essential Ridge style is rarely absent. The wines are intense, rich and deep-colored. The best display levels of complexity that many Cabernet producers would envy. There are a number of wineries currently producing intensely flavored Zinfandels, but they all owe something to Ridge, which proved these wines had great potential and stayed with them when they were out of fashion.

Domaine Joseph Rieflé, Pffafenheim

Traditional Alsace family estate of 17 hectares/42 acres, now given a new lease of life by Jean-Claude Rieflé, who has installed temperature-controlled fermentation systems in the cellar. Owing to mainly clay-limestone soils and a very dry microclimate at Pfaffenheim, the Rieflé wines show great power and persistence of flavor. Especially successful *vendange tardive* and *sélection de grains nobles* wines from the Pinot Gris in 1988 and 1989.

Riesling

Several different grape varieties include Riesling in their name. The true Riesling is Rhine Riesling, which is usually simply called Riesling but may be described as Johannisberg or White Riesling, especially in California. It should not be confused with Emerald, Welsch or Gray Riesling are not related.

Riesling is the grape variety responsible for nearly all the great wines of Germany, especially the lusciously sweet *Beerenauslese* and *Trockenbeerenauslese,* from grapes affected with noble rot, in the very best vintages, not to mention stylish *Kabinett* and *Spätlese* as well as elegantly honeyed *Auslese.* These are wines that in the best years develop even finer flavors with bottle age. Across the Rhine in Alsace, Riesling is usually fermented dry, with a more steely character than German Riesling, except in the ripest years, when richer *vendange tardive* and *sélection de grains nobles* wines are made.

In northeast Italy there is a little Riesling Renano, but the unrelated Welschriesling tends to be more common here, as well as in Austria and eastern Europe, where it is often called Olasz Rizling or Laski Rizling.

Riesling has traveled to the New World with some success. In California and Oregon there are late-harvest Rieslings, but they tend to be just a little heavier and more alcoholic than their German counterparts. The Barossa Valley produces some of Australia's most successful Rieslings, both sweet and dry, while there are some delicious late-harvest Rieslings from the cooler vineyards of New Zealand. In South Africa Riesling is called Weisser Riesling to distinguish it from the inferior South African or Cape Riesling. These wines tend to be off dry.

Riesling Italico
See Welschriesling.

Château Rieussec, Sauternes

Since 1984 this *premier cru* has belonged to Domaines Rothschild of Lafite. The Bordeaux vineyard profits from an exceptional hilltop site, but during the earlier postwar period, under two separate proprietors, Rieussec made strangely inconsistent wines of widely divergent styles, some nevertheless excellent, like the 1971, 1975, 1976 and 1983. Under the new owners, and with a new *régisseur* in Charles Chevallier, there have been notable successes in 1985 and 1986, while the vintages of 1988 and 1989 show great promise for the future. Rieussec seems destined to become another star among Rothschild possessions.

Rio Negro, Argentina

The Rio Negro, some 965 kilometers/600 miles south of Mendoza in northern Patagonia, is the coolest vineyard area of Argentina. Although the main activity here is sheep farming, there are also about 8,000 hectares/19,760 acres of vines, planted with French grape varieties. The climate is significantly cooler than in Mendoza, with a shorter ripening season.

The principal producer is Humberto Canale, a family company that was founded in 1906, with vineyards in the valley of the Negro, planted with Cabernet, Merlot, Pinot Noir, Malbec, Semillon, Sauvignon Blanc, Chardonnay and Riesling. It is working hard to improve its wines.

La Rioja Alta, Rioja

This outstanding *bodega* celebrated its centenary in 1990. Methods are traditional, the wines spend a long time in cask and half the production is of *reserva* and *gran reserva* wines. The Viña Arana Reserva, made from 70 percent Tempranillo, is subtle and stylish, the 1982 ripe and sweet, the 1973 still a sprightly old wine, garnet-colored with lingering Tempranillo fruit. The fuller, richer, spicier Viña Ardanza is made from 60 percent Tempranillo with 25 percent Garnacha. The 1981 Viña Ardanza is a muscular, well-constituted wine for long aging. In a different class are the Gran Reservas 890 and 904, which are released only in exceptional years after a minimum of six years in cask and three to four in bottle. The 1973 Reserva 904 is a magical wine whose ethereal scent might be mistaken for that of a great Bordeaux or Burgundy.

Bodegas Riojanas, Rioja

This important *bodega* is still family run, and winemaking methods are a mix of the old and the new. Monte Réal Bianco shows a good balance of fruit and oak. There are two *reserva* styles: Viña Albina is elegant and fine-drawn, the Monte Réal more intense and concentrated.

Ripasso

A technique used by some producers in the making of Valpolicella to produce wines with greater depth. It involves pumping the young wine into vats containing the lees left over from the fermentation of an Amarone.

Riserva
Italian wine that has been aged for a minimum time before being sold. The term indicates quality.

Rkatziteli
A very heavily planted Russian variety, still predominant in its native Georgia, where it can make very acceptable white wines that with their aroma, acidity and spice evoke Alsace. The grape is also the base for a great number of less appealing dessert wines and Port and Sherry imitations. In Bulgaria the Rkatziteli is cultivated on an industrial scale to make both still and sparkling wines, and it is found elsewhere in eastern Europe, as well as in the eastern United States, California and China.

Domaine de Roally, Mâcon-Viré
First-rate small 3.08 hectare/7.6 acre estate in Mâcon-Viré owned by Henri Goyard. The wines, exclusively Chardonnay, are fermented in tanks and show crisp lively fruit with a touch of silky richness. These are wines to be drunk within three years of the vintage.

Louis Roederer, Champagne
This is another of that select band of undisputedly great Champagne houses. Its high-quality range starts with the consistent nonvintage Brut Premier and culminates in its prestige Cuvée Cristal, both white and rosé and, unusually, bottled in clear glass. It owns 185 hectares/457 acres of vines in various parcels in the Côte des Blancs, Montagne de Reims and the Vallée de la Marne. This gives Roederer 80 percent of its needs for its annual production of about 140,000 cases. The house was founded in 1776, although the eponymous Louis Roederer did not join the firm until 1827.

Rolet Frères et Fils, Arbois
One of the largest and most important estates, some 55 hectares/136 acres in the Jura in France. The estate was founded in 1968. It grows a wide variety of grapes, some, like Trousseau and Poulsard, being native to the region, while others, like Chardonnay and Pinot Noir, are international. The wines are sold under their varietal names and include a *vin jaune* and a sparkling wine made from Chardonnay. There are tasting premises in Arbois.

Rolle
See Vermentino.

Weingut Römerhof, Grosshöflein, Burgenland
In the Neusiedlersee-Hügelland Anton Kollwentz has a reputation for producing Welschrieslings that have the acidity of Rieslings, high-quality Cabernet Sauvignon, Pinot Blanc and Chardonnay, as well as the traditional Austrian vine varieties, such as Blaufränkisch. Yields are low, and the alcohol content is appropriately high. His reds, in particular, keep well. Some wines are aged in small casks.

Romorantin
Traditionally the variety that produces the pale yellow, characteristically floral wine of Cheverny (V.D.Q.S. since 1973), the Romorantin is steadily losing ground to grapes of wider reputation, like Sauvignon and Chardonnay.

Rondinella
A heavy-cropping red-wine grape native to the country round Verona, and with Corvina an essential element of the blends that make Bardolino and Valpolicella. The Rondinella lends color and substance to the concentrated and complex Amarone and Recioto della Valpolicella.

Rooiberg Cooperative, Robertson
Impressive banks of switches that control the flow of wines all over the winery belie the dedication and drive to make top-class South African wines from grapes drawn from forty farms. Dassie Smith won the coveted General Smuts Trophy for the best winemaker in 1982, a joint award with Sydney Back of Backsberg. The selected Dry Reds are impressive, as are Pinot Noir, Shiraz, Chenin Blanc, fortified Muscadel and a superb Edel Latoes made from grapes with noble rot, mainly Chenin Blanc and Rhine Riesling.

Rootstock
Rootstock is a vine's root, or piece of root, used for grafting. Since *phylloxera* most vines are grafted onto American rootstock which is resistant to the louse's ravages.

Rosemount Estate, Denman, New South Wales
Rosemount Estate, from small beginnings in 1970, is now one of the most powerful wineries in Australia, with 400 hectares/988 acres of vineyards in the Upper Hunter Valley and the Coonawarra district of South Australia. Expert winemaking, adroit marketing and an unapologetic commitment to profit are the reasons for the spectacular success of an ever-expanding operation. Rosemount is best known for its Chardonnays: in the mid eighties the Show Reserve Chardonnay was the taste of Australia for many British consumers, and this wine catalyzed the massive expansion of Australian wine sales in the United Kingdom from 1985 to 1988. The Roxburgh Chardonnay is rated Rosemount's best wine; the 1987 is hugely flavored with butter-rich fruit and toasty oak. In future years, it will be interesting to see if it holds its position at the top of the Rosemount range, for it may be challenged by the company's new Giant's Creek Chardonnay, which, though less extrovert a wine, already shows much complexity in the 1990 vintage. Rosemount's affordably priced 1988 Diamond Reserve Red (Cabernet Sauvignon and Shiraz based) is soft, delightful drinking.

Rossese
A vine of modest yield, but traditionally the principal red-wine variety of western Liguria. It makes the leading D.O.C. Dolceacqua and other more recently elevated wines of the Riviera di Ponente.

Rossignola
A red-wine grape native to the Veneto and still included in the blends that make Valpolicella and Bardolino, although its use is no longer mandatory.

Rossola Nera
A traditional variety from which the Austrian Roter Veltliner is derived. It is native to the terraced vineyards of the Valtellina in the extreme north of Lombardy, but over many years has been losing its territory to the superior Nebbiolo, there known as Chiavennasca. Also known as Rossara.

R. Rostaing, Côte Rôtie
Rostaing established himself as a superstar of Côte Rôtie in the Rhône in the 1980s, and his wines are now on strict allocation and hard to find. His 1984 Côte Blonde is a spectacular wine in a patchy vintage, perfumed, sleek textured and extraordinarily rich. His 1985 La Landonne is magnificent with many layers of flavor and a brooding power. Keep until at least 1995.

Rouge Homme, Coonawarra, South Australia
Rouge Homme derives its name from Bill Redman, who planted vines in Coonawarra in the early 1900s. Lindemans acquired the firm in 1965, maintaining the vineyards and the Rouge Homme label. Greg Clayfield is one of Australia's most promising red winemakers, his 1988 Pinot Noir a wine of considerable style. Rouge Homme is best known for Cabernet Sauvignon, the 1978 Classic Wine Release a rich sumptuous Coonawarra Cabernet of great staying power. Clayfield is also making excellent Chardonnay.

Round
A wine that is harmonious on the palate. One that is ready to drink and is without sharp acidity and harsh tannins.

Roussanne
Roussanne is one of the white grape varieties of the northern Rhône and can be used with Marsanne for white Hermitage and the other white appellations of the region. Its flavor is more delicate than Marsanne, and it has better aging potential. It can also feature in Châteauneuf-du-Pape and in the Côtes-du-Rhône and is even found in Montecarlo, a white wine of Tuscany, and as Bergeron in the Savoie village of Chignin.

Multier, Château du Rozay, Condrieu
Château du Rozay is one of the best-known estates of Condrieu. The Viognier grape is barrel fermented, yielding luscious, intense wines marked by apricot and peach aromas. Both the 1989 and 1990 vintages are vivid, very ripe expressions of Viognier fruit.

Rubicon, Napa Valley
Film producer and director Francis Ford Coppola comes by his love of wine through his Italian heritage. This may be why Rubicon, from his vineyard estate in the Napa Valley, in California, is so delightful to drink with hearty Italian meals. However, Rubicon is not a simplistic one-dimensional red wine but a highly sophisticated wine with a fascinating range of tastes and aromas. Coppola insists that his wine remains in cask and bottle for seven years before he will release it.

Ruby Cabernet
Another hot-weather hybrid developed just after the war at the University of California, Davis, this is a crossing of Carignan with Cabernet Sauvignon. The vine is well distributed in California and in Australia, but its wines, for all their color and bouquet, lack substance and individuality. They lack distinction, but may be offered as varietals or used for blending.

Ruché
A rare and obscure Piedmontese variety grown to the northeast of Asti. The grape makes a limited quantity of highly individual, purplish red wine that is dry, full, scented in youth, and capable of aging. The name appears as Ruché, Roché, and Rouchét.

Ruinart, Champagne
Rheims Champagne house founded by Nicolas Ruinart in 1727 and acquired by Moët et Chandon in 1963. Although now part of a multinational company, Ruinart has retained an individual image of quality. The Dom Ruinart vintage *blanc de blancs* is particularly fine.

Ruländer
See Pinot Gris.

Russe, Bulgaria
On the banks of the Danube in northern Bulgaria, Russe is an important wine-production area with a modern cooperative and a wine school — the only one on the Balkan Peninsula. White wines are Russe's strength, producing respectable Aligoté, Chardonnay and Italian Riesling. An interesting wine is the Riesling/Misket blend. Misket, a local grape, gives an attractive floral note to this wine.

Rustenberg Wines, Stellenbosch
This South African estate is surely one of the most beautiful wine farms in the world. The well-maintained homestead, Schoongezicht, built in the eighteenth century, was enhanced by the addition of a Cape Dutch frontage in about 1815. Since 1892 there have been four winemakers. Alfred Nicholson, an English immigrant, was the first, who through marriage became owner of the property. He was bought out in 1945 by Peter Barlow, who also owned the farm next door, Rustenberg. Alfred's son Reg Nicholson then took up the reins until 1975, advancing the renown at home and overseas of Rustenberg and Schoongezicht. The current winemaker is Etienne le Riche. The best wines are the Rustenberg Reserves, a Bordeaux blend requiring maturation like any great Bordeaux, a Pinot Noir, Sauvignon Blanc and a supreme Chardonnay.

S

Domaine Roger Sabon, Châteauneuf-du-Pape
An underrated Côtes-du-Rhône domain, Sabon makes peppery, spicy Châteauneuf for relatively early drinking. The 1985 is now soft textured with extrovert red fruit flavors. The 1990 is aromatic, vibrant and surprisingly long on the palate. The domain also makes an excellent red Lirac; the 1979 has well evolved fruit but a touch of tannin to ensure a decent life.

Sack
From the Spanish *sacar,* a word used for export wine, this is an old English word for a sweet, fortified wine, usually Sherry.

Sacy
Sacy was grown extensively in the Yonne, until Chardonnay was established as the one and only grape variety of Chablis. It tends to make somewhat thin, acidic white wine, but can provide a suitable base for Crémant de Bourgogne. It is also used for white Bourgogne Grand Ordinaire and grows in St. Pourçain, where it is called Tressallier.

Guy Saget, Pouilly-sur-Loire
A grower and *négociant* firm now run by Jean-Louis Saget. Guy Saget himself is moving away from traditional *négociant* activities. In addition to the 30 hectare/74 acre estate in Pouilly it has recently bought a number of individual properties throughout the Loire. These include the 70 hectare/173 acre Château Chupin in Anjou, Domaine des Hauts Boulay with 6 hectares/14.8 acres in Montlouis and the 30 hectare/74 acre Domaine d'Artois in Touraine-Mesland. A substantial program of new investment is now underway in these properties.

Sagrantino
A low-yielding red vine long established in Umbria, but until recently in disfavor. Under the Perugian denomination of Montefalco it makes powerful wines of individual style; nowadays often dry, but traditionally sweet and made from *passito* grapes.

Saignée
French term for a method of making rosé. The literal translation is "bleeding," which describes the process: juice is run off red-wine vats early in the fermentation process. The juice that is run off is pink; that which is left is a deeper red than it would otherwise be.

Clos Sainte-Magdelaine, Cassis

Cassis is a small coastal appellation in Provence, France, squeezed in by building development. Although reds and rosés are made, Cassis is best known for its whites. Clos Sainte-Magdelaine is the appellation's leading estate. From the cliffs above Cassis, it produces a white blended from Marsanne, Ugni Blanc, Clairette and a small amount of Sauvignon, and a rosé made from Cinsaut, Grenache and Mourvèdre.

Salon, Champagne

Salon is a small, prestige house founded in 1914, a decidedly awkward time on the eve of the World War I, by Eugène-Aimé Salon in Le Mesnil-sur-Oger. Often referred to as Salon Le Mesnil, it rapidly gained a very high reputation and in 1928 became Maxim's house Champagne. Production is tiny: around five thousand cases of traditionally made Champagne in those vintages deemed worthy of carrying the Salon name. In 1976 it was bought by Besserat de Bellefon, part of the Pernod-Ricard group, and was subsequently sold to Laurent-Perrier in 1988.

Salta, Argentina

Salta is the most northern wine region of Argentina, nearly 1,126 kilometers/700 miles north of Mendoza, but the vineyards are among the most temperate in the country, for they lie at 1,700 meters/5,577 feet or more above sea level in the foothills of the Andes. This is a small area, planted mainly with white grape varieties, in particular Torrontes, which is the most individual variety of Argentina. It is said to be a mutation of Malvoisie, brought from the Canaries in the 1550s. Presumably it has some relationship with the Terrantez of Madeira.

Michel Torino and Bodegas Etchart are two of the best producers, making wines with a gentle aroma, with some of the pithy orange flavor of Muscat and just a touch of sweetness.

Samalens, Laujuzan, Armagnac

An ultra-traditional firm established in 1887. Samalens makes Armagnacs in the old style, with rich, prunelike flavors. The V.S.O.P. is aged for eight to ten years and is a full-blooded brandy with rich, sweet oak. The fifteen- to twenty-year-old Vieille Relique belies its name and is a virile and forceful Armagnac of great character.

San Felice, Chianti Classico/Brunello

San Felice is a major force in Chianti, its estate near Siena extending to 190 hectares/469 acres. The company also has an experimental vineyard on the estate, and in 1990 they opened a luxury hotel a couple of minutes' walk from the winery. The quality of winemaking here is very high, with the poised, pure-flavored Il Grigio and the weightier, more complex Poggio Rosso (a fine 1986) the stars of the Chianti Riserva range. San Felice also produces an outstanding Brunello di Montalcino; the 1985 is a classic wine that deserves keeping until 1995.

San Martin Petite Sirah, Baja California, Mexico

Wine has been produced in Mexico since the friars arrived with the first Conquistadores. It has been made, on and off, ever since in the mountains north of Mexico City, but it was never a serious industry, and the wine, in modern times at least, was never particularly good. On several occasions in this century, the Mexican government has made half-hearted attempts to create a wine industry in Baja California, and some of the wines have been quite drinkable. This Petite Sirah, imported by the San Martin Winery and available mostly in California, is proof that Mexico has a wine future should it choose to pursue it. The wine is unsubtle, but it has good body and color and could serve as anyone's simple table wine.

Luciano Sandrone, Barolo

Luciano Sandrone produces minuscule amounts of exceptional Barolo. His yields are low, and he uses French *barriques* to bring his wines to a relatively early maturity. His 1985 Barolo Cannubi Boschis, a wonderfully rich and perfumed wine, may well be the greatest star of a great vintage. Sandrone also makes grapy, intensely flavored Dolcetto.

Sangiovese

The red Sangiovese grape is grown all over central Italy. There are numerous different clones and variations, divided broadly into Sangiovese Grosso and Sangiovese Piccolo, with a considerable range in quality. Pure Sangiovese is at its best in the D.O.C.G. of Brunello di Montalcino, made from the Brunello clone of Sangiovese Grosso, which was identified and isolated by the Biondi Santi family in the last century.

Sangiovese is the principal grape variety of Chianti, where it is blended with other grapes, principally Canaiolo and a smattering of white Trebbiano and Malvasia. Sangiovese is also produced as a varietal wine, a *vino da tavola,* by numerous of the more innovative Tuscan estates eager to prove the neglected quality of this grape. These wines may be called Predicato del Cardisco, but usually have a fantasy name like Cepparello or Fontalloro.

There is no doubt that the quality of Sangiovese is improving enormously as its characteristics are better understood. In the D.O.C.G. of Carmignano it benefits from blending with a small percentage of Cabernet Sauvignon and in other wines such as Tignanello, the combination of Cabernet and Sangiovese is particularly appealing. In Vino Nobile di Montepulciano the blend is very similar to Chianti; the grape used in a clone of Sangiovese called Prugnolo Gentile, Morellino di Scansano, from around Grosseto, is the only classified Tuscan red besides Brunello that may be made entirely of Sangiovese.

Sangiovese Piccolo is the inferior variety commonly planted in Emilia-Romagna for prolific and usually undistinguished quantities of Sangiovese di Romagna. Unfortunately some has crept into the vineyards of Chianti, but this error is gradually being remedied, with work on clonal selection and the replanting of vineyards. Just about all the other red D.O.C.s of central Italy include Sangiovese.

Until recently Sangiovese was not deemed worthy of consideration outside central Italy, but as its quality is proven in Tuscany, it has excited interest in California, with some as yet experimental plantings.

Santa Rita, Chile

Santa Rita in the Maipo Valley is one of Chile's leading wineries. It was founded in 1880 and is now owned by a wealthy business tycoon, who also has a second winery, Viña Carmen. No expense has been spared for new equipment in the cellars. There are gentle pneumatic presses, stainless-steel vats for white wine and enormous redwood vats for red wine, as well as large vaulted cellars and an insulated warehouse filled with new French and American oak barrels. Experimentation with ferment-

ation techniques and types of oak continues, especially for Chardonnay and Cabernet Sauvignon. Its best Cabernet Medalla Real spends twelve months in French oak.

Sassicaia, Bolgheri
Sassicaia, Italy's most famous *barrique*-aged Cabernet Sauvignon, is made on the Marchesi Incisa della Rocchetta estate in western Tuscany. The first vintage was in 1968. Sassicaia became a cult wine in the United States in the eighties, and it now commands high prices in international markets. The quality of the wine remains outstanding, and great wines were produced in 1982 and 1985. The gloriously ripe flavors of the latter are a memorable tasting experience, but it also has an impressive harmony not always found in red wines from that hot Tuscan summer; but then the Sassicaia estate is very close to the Mediterranean and benefits from the maritime influence. The current grape mix is 75 percent Cabernet Sauvignon and 25 percent Cabernet Franc.

Sauvignon Blanc
Sauvignon Blanc produces crisp white wine with a strong varietal character and an aroma reminiscent of gooseberries, asparagus, flint and even cats. It rarely ages well and can lack subtlety.

It is at its best in the Loire Valley, in the appellations of Sancerre and Pouilly-Fumé, as well as lesser Ménétou-Salon, Reuilly and Quincy, Sauvignon de Touraine and some of the *vins de pays* of the Loire. There is a small quantity of Sauvignon around the Burgundian village of St. Bris-le-Vineux, for the V.D.Q.S. of Sauvignon de St. Bris.

Farther south it features in Haut-Poitou and is one of the grapes of the white wines of Bordeaux, both dry and sweet. Here it can benefit from blending with Sémillon to fill out the flavor and also from aging in oak barrels. Several of the white wines of the southwest, such as Bergerac and Côtes de Duras, and so on, depend upon Sauvignon. A little is planted by adventurous growers in the Midi, and in Provence it is one of the permitted varieties of Coteaux d'Aix-en-Provence, Côtes de Provence and Cassis.

A little Sauvignon is grown in Penedès, and it has crossed the Alps to northeast Italy to feature in the D.O.C.s of Friuli and Trentino. There is some in eastern Europe too.

Otherwise the most exciting examples come from New Zealand, notably from the Marlborough vineyards of the South Island. Here the wines may be aged in oak and have a fuller, riper flavor, or alternatively they see no oak and have a crisp, fresh pungency. In California Sauvignon is often aged and termed Fumé Blanc, notably by Robert Mondavi. In Australia it is generally less exciting than Chardonnay or Semillon. It is becoming important in South Africa, and it is also grown in Chile with some success but suffers from a confusion of identity.

Sauvignon Vert
See Muscadelle.

Sauvion et Fils, Muscadet
Important Loire family firm of growers and *négociants*. Its 23 hectare/57 acre property, Château du Cléray, and the series of Découvertes are among the best Muscadets available. The Découvertes are a number of individual growers' wines (always *sur lie*) selected annually by the Sauvions for their quality.

Savagnin
A white grape derived from the Traminer of Alsace. Cultivated on the poorest soil of the Jura, it makes, after five or six years maturation in cask, Vin Jaune. The Savagnin is often blended with a much higher proportion of Chardonnay to make A.O.C. Côtes du Jura.

Savatiano
A white grape, the most heavily planted in Greece, especially in Attica. It makes a little varietal wine, but the bulk of its great yield is destined for the production of Retsina.

Schaumwein
German term for sparkling wine. *Qualitätschaumwein,* the better product, is called *Sekt*.

Scheurebe
Scheurebe is a German grape variety, developed by Georg Scheu in 1916, as a cross between Riesling and Silvaner. It is considered to be one of the more successful German crossings, giving good yields as well as a distinctive flavor and aroma, not unlike grapefruit pith. It ripens well and is susceptible to noble rot.

Schiava
Schiava is a red grape that is found in Württemberg as Trollinger; in the Alto Adige as Vernatsch or Schiava and in England as Black Hamburg, where it is preferred as a table grape. It is the most prolific grape of the Trentino-Alto Adige and at its most distinctive in the soft, easy to drink St. Magdalener. Variations of it include Grossvernatcsh or Schiava Grossa, Kleinvernatsch or Schiava Piccola or Gentile and Grauvernatsch or Schiava Grigia.

Schleinitz'sche Weingutsverwaltung, Mosel-Saar-Ruwer
This German estate has been in family ownership since 1650, and its owner, Konrad Hähn, believes in ecological viticulture. All the vines are Riesling, and styles vary from wines with steely acidity to those with greater softness and fruit.

Charles Schleret, Turckheim
Little known outside his home commune of Turckheim, Charles Schleret, an elderly bachelor, is one of the best winemakers in Alsace. His wines are a model of consistency in difficult years like 1984 as well as in great ones like 1983, 1985 and 1989. His 1986 Tokay-Pinot Gris Cuvée Exceptionnelle is a splendid amalgam of toasty aromas, broad almost botrytized flavors and, withal, an elegant, well-defined finish.

Schlosskellerei Esterhazy'sche, Eisenstadt, Burgenland
Large estate with cellars in Austria under the Schloss where Joseph Haydn was *kapellmeister*, with vineyards around the famous wine town of Rust, as well as in other villages like St. Georgen, Gross höflein and Eisenstadt itself. The princely family of Esterhazy have been making fine wine in the Burgenland since the seventeenth century: today their dessert wines and dry Rieslings are exceptional.

Domaines Schlumberger, Guebwiller
The largest domain in Alsace and still family owned, the Schlumberger vineyards around Guebwiller extend to 140

hectares/346 acres of which 70 hectares/173 acres are in *grands crus* Kitterlé, Saering, Kessler and Spiegel. The scale of the operation is huge, and while there have been some administrative problems at Schlumberger in recent years, there has also been an honest attempt to restrict yields to 50 hectoliters per hectare/2.9 tons per acre. The style of Schlumberger wines is very rich and unctuous, exemplified in the intense late-harvest Gewürztraminer Cuvée Christine and the more rarely seen Cuvée Anne. Generally good but not outstanding quality.

René Schmidt, Riquewihr
Respected Alsace producer with an outstanding Gewürztraminer Cuvée Particulière, subtle, delicately spicy, with superb definition of flavor.

Domänenweingut Schloss Schönborn, Rheingau
This German estate is undoubtedly among the finest in the Rheingau; it is certainly the largest privately-owned estate in the Rheingau. The von Schön born family, a dynasty of great political power, bought it in 1349. It produces superb, beautifully made Rieslings of great class and serious Spätburgunder (Pinot Noir). Some, though, have criticized the wines for being too heavy. *Eiswein* can hit the top notes in indifferent vintages. Eighty-six per cent of the vineyards are planted with Riesling.

Schönburger
An early ripening Pinot Noir hybrid that is widely planted in Germany and to some extent in England. Its wine is white, aromatic and of some quality.

Sciacarello
After Nielluccio the second of the two red *cépages nobles* of Corsica. The grape is grown in granitic soil in small and fragmented holdings on the hills around Ajaccio, where it makes full, perfumed, long-lasting A.O.C. wines. The Sciacarello also makes rosé wines of some distinction.

Sec
French word for dry, as in Vouvray Sec or Jurançon Sec. In sparkling wines, less dry than *brut* but drier than *demi-sec.*

Second wine
A recent term, popular in Bordeaux, for wine that is not good enough to go under the château's name and that is bottled and sold by the château under another label. Often includes wine made from young vines. This practice of selection has improved the quality of Bordeaux's top wines while providing bargains for wine drinkers. Examples include Les Forts de Latour, La Grange Neuve de Figeac and Carruades de Lafite Rothschild.

Sekt
German term for sparkling wine. *Deutscher Sekt,* or "German sparkling wine," may be made by the tank method or by the transfer method of bottle fermentation. The Champagne method is seldom used in Germany.

Sélection de Grains Nobles
In Alsace, a very high-quality sweet wine made from nobly-rotten grapes. Such wines are rigorously controlled: the grower must inform the authorities in advance of his intention to make an S.G.N., and the grapes must reach high minimum levels of ripeness. S.G.N. wines must be from a single vineyard; chaptalization is forbidden.

Sella & Mosca, Sardinia
This important 400 hectare/988 acre wine estate is the leading quality producer in Sardinia. Look out for the still and sparkling wine of Torbato di Alghero and the unusual and delicious Anghelu Ruju, a sweet Port-like red wine made from partially dried grapes.

Selvapiana, Chianti Rufina
This 27 hectare/66.7 acre Rufina estate is run with immaculate care by the hospitable Francesco Guintini. Yields are low, and in great vintages Selvapiana *riservas* can easily live for twenty years: the 1968 was vigorous and alive when tasted in 1990. The estate also produces very good wines in difficult years. The 1987 is a case in point; positive, firm and fruity, it is a real bargain.

Sémillon
Sémillon is the principal grape for Sauternes and the other sweet wines of Bordeaux, as well as Monbazillac. The classic blend is 80 percent Sémillon to 20 percent Sauvignon with perhaps a drop of Muscadelle. It has thin skin and is therefore particularly susceptible to noble rot. In the Graves and Pessac-Léognan it is the base of many of the dry white wines, but is always blended with Sauvignon, and benefits from aging in oak barrels. It also features in other dry white appellations of southwest France.

In the New World Semillon loses its accent. You have to go to Australia to find pure dry Semillon. In Australia's Hunter Valley Semillon assumes a character not found elsewhere, making a full-bodied wine that develops considerable depth of flavor with barrel and bottle age. Some Semillon is grown in both New Zealand and California, but mainly for blending with Sauvignon.

Seppelt Great Western, Great Western, Victoria
The vastly improved quality of Australian *méthode champenoise* wines in the 1980s is largely due to Seppelt. This large sparkling-wine firm, part of the larger Seppelt empire, leads the shift toward Chardonnay and Pinot Noir as the key ingredients in quality blends. Look out for such labels as Salinger, Great Western Vintage Brut and Fleur de Lys: these are consistently excellent wines produced in commercially important quantities at fair prices.

Sercial
This grape variety, which has given its name to the driest style of Madeira, is late ripening and difficult to grow and has been hard to find since the *phylloxera* ravages of the last century. Its grapes are aromatic, and their wine makes certainly the subtlest of the four traditional styles of Madeira. In Portugal itself the Sercial is found in the vineyards of the Dão and the adjacent Bairrada region, where it makes good white wines.

20 Year Old Setúbal, José Maria da Fonseca, Setúbal
Setúbal has been one of Portugal's demarcated areas since the early years of the century, and the old, established firm of José Maria da Fonseca of Azeitão has had a virtual monopoly of the limited production of its pronouncedly aromatic Muscat wine. Native Portuguese varieties make up about 30 percent of the blend, but the Muscat d'Alexandrie predominates. The fermentation is halted by the additon of grape spirit, and the wine is aged in wood. Traditionally there have been two styles of Setúbal; the fresh, youthful six-year-old, and the intesely

rich, sometimes slightly faded twenty-year-old in which the characteristic fragrance of the Muscat grape is transmuted to a complex caramel. It seems probable that in the future vintages will be declared, and that the younger wines will be marketed earlier than has been the case. The family firm of Fonseca also makes well-regarded red wines in Periquita, from the grape of the same name, and the blended Quinta de Camarate and Pasmados.

Jacques Seysses, Domaine Dujac

After nearly twenty-five years on the Côte d'Or, Jacques Seysses is the "master" at whose feet sit many of the younger generation of Burgundy winemakers. Seysses abandoned an early banking career in the sixties for the life of a *vigneron* in Morey-St.-Denis. He bought a fine old Burgundy house, now lovingly restored, and replanted the vineyard with low-yielding Pinot Noir vines from Henri Gouges in Nuits-St.-Georges. His first vintage at the re-named Domaine Dujac was in 1968. The Domaine is now some 11 hectares/27 acres with important plots in the Grands Crus Clos de la Roche (1.8 hectare/4.4 acres) and Clos St.-Denis (1.6 hectares/4 acres). Among smaller holdings there are parcels in Bonnes Mares, Echezeaux, Gevrey-Chambertin Les Combottes and Charmes-Chambertin.

Seysses strongly believes in a noninterventionist approach both in the vineyard and in the cellar. He avoids pesticides and chemical treatments and uses organic manure to dress his vines. His fermentations are long and slow; he does not filter his wines, and although he uses new wood for aging his *grands crus* he also favors relatively early bottling no longer than fifteen months after the vintage.

The attraction of great Burgundy is its inimitable scent, and Dujac's wines are especially aromatic. The Clos St.-Denis is a lovely, spicy, gracefully perfumed wine: the 1972 (an underrated year) drunk in 1988 was a stunning amalgam of gamy richness restrained by a velvety texture and subtle lingering fruit. The Clos de la Roche tends to be burlier, more tannic: the 1985 is a splendidly structured wine, a wine for drinking in the year 2000, in marked contrast to some '85 wines from other growers, which are beginning to taste too soft. Look out too for Dujac's lovely *vin gris*, a delicate rosé made in high-volume vintages.

Seyval Blanc

A robust, early maturing Franco-American hybrid (Seyve-Villard 5276) derived from the Chardonnay; it produces attractively fruity white wine. As a hybrid, it is not permitted for "quality wines" — A.O.C. or the equivalent — in the European Community, but is found increasingly in areas with difficult climates, like the United Kingdom and the eastern United States.

Sherry-like

The smell of oxidation. Should only be found in Sherries or wines of that style, like Vin Jaune. Otherwise the wine is faulty.

Shiraz

See Syrah.

Short

A wine whose flavor fades rapidly.

Weingut Thomas Siegrist, Rheinpfalz

A family estate, rapidly rising in fame in Germany, producing outstanding dry red and white wines. Pinot wines are often matured in *barriques* and Rieslings in large, old casks.

Château Sigalas-Rabaud, Sauternes

This portion of the divided Rabaud estate has been in the same ownership since 1864. The considerable reputation of this Bordeaux property has been sustained over the past twenty-five years by a sequence of perfumed and liquorous wines of great distinction. The grapes are very carefully selected, with several *tris,* and yields are consequently low. Vinification is unusually carried out in stainless-steel, and maturation too is in *cuve.* In general the wines are light and fruity and can be enjoyed in their youth, but they are capable of long life. Notable recently have been the 1976, 1981, 1982, 1983, 1986 and 1988.

Silvaner

Silvaner was at one time widely planted in Germany but has in recent years given way to Müller-Thurgau. It is still the principal grape variety of Franconia, where it makes some distinctive, dry, flinty wines. It is grown in Austria and in Alsace, as Sylvaner, to provide a base for Edelzwicker, but now tends to be replaced by Pinot Blanc. A little is grown in the Alto Adige, and also Switzerland, but it has found little flavor in the New World.

Silver Oak Cellars, Napa Valley

This all-Cabernet Sauvignon winery in the Napa Valley was started in the early 1970s by Justin Meyer and Raymond Duncan as a upscale affiliate to their main interest, Franciscan Vineyards. The first Cabernets came exclusively from the Alexander Valley. Later, after selling Franciscan Vineyards, two Napa Cabernets were added to the Silver Oaks line. One is designated Napa Valley, the other, Bonny's Vineyard, came from vines grown adjacent to the winery in Oakville and named for Mr. Meyer's wife.

Typically, Silver Oak Cabernets spend two years in barrels, usually American oak, another two years in the bottle before they are released. Consistently high in quality, they are eagerly sought by collectors and can be difficult to find in the open market.

Château Simone, Palette

Owned by René Rougier, the 15 hectare/37 acre Château Simone is undoubtedly the leading estate in this small appellation just to the southeast of Aix-en-Provence in France. Indeed for many years it was the only commercial Palette estate. Wines of all colors are made here, although the red, made from Grenache, Mourvèdre and Cinsaut and capable of aging, is the best known.

Château Siran, Margaux

A *cru bourgeois* at Labarde on the southern fringe of the appellation, Siran is owned by Monsieur Miailhe, whose ancestor bought the Bordeaux property in 1848.

The vineyard makes wine of consistent quality, a reflection of the long continuity of ownership. It may be that since 1970 the wines have lost something of the perfumed delicacy that characterized the great vintages of the fifties and sixties, showing more concentration and structure, vigor, fruit and flavor. Notable recent years have been 1970, 1975, 1978, 1981, 1982 and 1985. This is a vineyard of great potential, clearly deserving of a higher classification, and its wines still offer very good value.

Robert Skalli, Languedoc-Roussillon

Skalli is an important *négociant* who buys in grape must from contracted growers and makes the wine at his extensive and very modern premises in Sète in the south of France. He believes that the future in the Midi belongs to varietal wines. His wines, particularly the Chardonnay and Cabernet Sauvignon, have been very successful in Britain. The wines are sold under various labels such as Fortant de France, and are available in several levels of quality. There are also vineyards in California (St. Supéry) and Corsica (Coteaux de Diana).

Skin contact

Technique used in white-wine making. After pressing,

the grape juice is left to macerate on the skins at low temperature for up to twelve hours. It can make the wine more aromatic and give greater extraction and usually deeper color, but it can also result in heavier wines with less finesse. Skin contact is often used for just a portion of a particular *cuvée*. (The French term is *macération pelliculaire*.)

Smoky

Aroma and flavor that can come from various sources. It is a characteristic of some varieties like Sauvignon Blanc and Cabernet Franc. It is also a characteristic imparted by oak barrels with a high toast.

Château Sociando-Mallet, Haut-Médoc

Little more than twenty years ago this old Bordeaux property was in disrepair, with no more than 5 hectares/12 acres in production. Since then Jean Gautreau has replanted and enlarged the vineyard; there are now 30 hectares/74 acres under vines and an entirely new *chai*. His aim is to make old-fashioned *vins de garde*, capable of development over fifteen or twenty years. This policy could not hope to succeed fully while the vines were very young, but a sequence of lean years has been followed by the vintages of 1978, 1980, 1982, 1983, 1985 and 1988. These are rich and concentrated wines, capable of improvement as they mature. These impressive results seem certain to be maintained as the vines themselves approach full maturity. This *cru bourgeois* is undoubtedly one to watch.

Soft

Round fruit with no aggressive tannins and acids.

Soil

Vines produce the best wine grapes in poor, well-drained soil. On rich soil vines will produce a lot of poorer quality fruit. The type of soil in a vineyard is a crucial consideration in the choice of vine.

Solar das Bouças, Vinho Verde

A good single-vineyard Vinho Verde made with a high proportion of the aromatic, notionally laurel-scented Loureiro grape. The estate, near Braga in Portugal, is the property of the well-known Port house Quinta do Noval.

Solera

Maturation method especially associated with Sherry. A system of fractional blending is used, in which only the final stage, from which mature wine is drawn off for bottling, is, strictly speaking, the *solera*. Previous stages — the barrels that replenish each other and, eventually the *solera*—are called *criaderas*, or nurseries. Barrels of the youngest wine replenish the next youngest, which replenish the slightly older, and so on, with usually a third of the volume being withdrawn at a time. When the younger wine is added to the older it both refreshes it and takes on its character. A *fino solera* may have up to seven stages, or scales; a *manzanilla* may have up to fourteen.

Sonoma-Cutrer Les Pierres, Sonoma County

Several Californian wineries have devoted themselves exclusively to one grape, usually Chardonnay. Sonoma-Cutrer was one of the first, and it is still the most successful purely Chardonnay winery. It makes a blend and several single-vineyard wines, one of which is Les Pierres — the stones. Les Pierres Chardonnays are consistently rich and intense and avoid the heaviness and oily characteristics that plague so many California Chardonnays. Winemaker Bill Bonetti styles this wine after some of the best white Burgundies, such as Chassagne-Montrachet. Several prominent Burgundian winemakers consider Les Pierres one of the California Chardonnays that come closest to their style of winemaking.

Domaine La Soumade, Rasteau

André Romaro makes one of the most concentrated and altogether excellent wines in the Côtes-du-Rhône-Villages appellation. His domain of 6 hectares/15 acres is at Rasteau, the secret of the intense flavor of his red wine being very low yields. Both his 1986 and his 1989 are complete wines with every quality one may hope for: tremendous fruit, mouth-enveloping flavor, a real taste of the *terroir* and a long, beautifully defined finish. Exceptional quality-price ratio.

Spätlese

One of the six categories of *Qualitätswein mit Prädikat*. It signifies German or Austrian wine made from late-picked grapes, that must reach minimum levels of ripeness.

Spicy

A characteristic of varieties like Pinot Gris, Gewürztraminer and mature Syrah. Usually said of a wine with a pronounced aroma.

Spritz

Carbon dioxide left in (or added) to a wine gives it a slight prickle on the tongue and an impression of freshness. Known as *spritzig* in German, *frizzante* in Italian and *pétillant* in French.

Château St. Jean Pinot Blanc, Robert Young, Alexander Valley Vineyards, Sonoma County

A lengthy name for a modest wine, but Robert Young grapes are such a mark of quality that no wine producer could afford to leave them off his label. Pinot Blanc might well be called the unknown wine of California. Only a few wineries make it, but it invariably turns out to be an interesting wine, far superior to Sauvignon Blanc, with which it competes for bored Chardonnay drinkers. Pinot Blanc is dry, full-flavored and devoid of idiosyncratic flavors and aromas like so many Sauvignon Blancs. This version has plenty of fruit, a good acid balance and just enough backbone not to be obtrusively flabby. Chardonnay may be riding high at the moment, but then whatever happened to Chenin Blanc?

St. Macaire

A red-wine variety of Girondin origin, but one seldom seen in the Bordelais today. In California the vine is planted in modest quantity, but, as in France, makes wines of very limited interest.

Château St. Pierre, St. Julien

This fourth-growth Bordeaux property has a documented history from the seventeenth century. From 1767 until after the Second World War it remained in the family of the Monsieur Saint Pierre whose name it bears, although the estate was divided and subdivided before eventually being reunited. Some portions of the original vineyard have been incorporated into neighboring properties, notably the recent creations Châteaux Gloria and du Glana. In 1982 St. Pierre was acquired by the late Henri Martin of Gloria and his son-in-law, who now controls both vineyards. This change of ownership was at once reflected in an improvement in the wine, beginning

with a substantial, concentrated 1982, 1983 and 1985 showed finesse allied to richness and structure, with 1986 more powerful, while the vintages of 1987 and especially the harmonious 1988 exemplify those qualities of breed, finesse and bouquet commonly attributed to the appellation.

Verwaltung der Staatlichen Weinbaudomänen Niederhausen-Schlossböckelheim, Nahe

The Naha State Domain is widely considered to·be one of the leading estates in Germany. It was established by the king of Prussia in 1902 and was the first to plant Riesling on the now famous Kupfergrübe site. More land was added, and in 1946 the State of Rheinland-Pfalz took over the estate. Nowadays any cellar without a few bottles from this estate is undernourished. Its wines from a number of German villages throughout this German region are always well differentiated and true to type. The vines are mostly Riesling, with some Müller-Thurgau and Kerner, and have great subtlety and finesse.

Stag's Leap Wine Cellars Cask 23, Napa Valley

This is the wine that won international acclaim in 1976 when it bested a group of first growth Bordeaux châteaux in a blind tasting in Paris, thus convincing Europe that California was making world-class wines. Warren Winiarski, owner and winemaker at Stag's Leap, has gone to great lengths over the years to ensure that Cask 23 has kept its reputation. Made from grapes from what may be the best site in Napa Valley's Stag's Leap appellation, Cask 23 is coddled like a Bordeaux first growth. The result is an elegant red wine of great intensity and breed. Winiarski is a master at producing fine Cabernets and this is, regularly, his best.

Weingut Stallmann-Hiestand, Rheinhessen

As often happens in the Rheinhessen in Germany, this 16 hectare/39.5 acre estate has a wide range of vine varieties among which the Weissburgunder (Pinot Blanc) is particularly successful.

Stambolova, Bulgaria

A quality-controlled wine area of central southern Bulgaria, Stambolovo is best known for Merlot wine, which is characterized by its brilliant ruby color and lush, full berrylike fruit. A 1983 Stambolovo Merlot Reserve, matured in new oak showed no sign of age when tasted in 1990 — a wine of ripe tannins and full concentrated flavors.

Stanley Wine Company, Clare, South Australia

The Stanley Wine Company, one of the great names of the Clare Valley, was bought by Thomas Hardy in 1987. The Stanley Wine Company's strength is its Rhine Rieslings, notably the excellent Bin 7 Riesling.

Staatsweingut Steinberg-Hattenheim, Rheingau

One of the estates owned by the state of Hesse in Germany. The 30 hectare/74 acre Steinberg vineyard — the best-known vineyard on the Rhine — is enclosed by a stone wall and produces intensely flavored wines for long-term keeping.

Weingut Georg Stiegelmar, Gols, Burgenland

Leading Austrian estate near the Neusiedlersee, producing a wide range of wine, most bottled separately according to the variety. Its elegant Pinot Noir, from thirty-year-old vines, has sufficient acidity, character, and a long flavor: an unusually good Austrian example of this difficult grape. But the wines are expensive: Stiegelmar is fashionable in Austria and demand is great.

Still

Nonsparkling wine. Also means distillation equipment.

Stony Hill Chardonnay, Napa Valley

The first vintage at Stony Hill, which is located in the hills just north of St. Helena in the Napa Valley, was in 1950. James Laube, who has written extensively on Napa Valley wines, says that the 1964 Stony Hill Chardonnay is the greatest California Chardonnay he has ever tasted. In fact few wine lovers ever get to taste these exceptional wines because so little is made — rarely more than 3,500 cases a year. Fred and Eleanor McCrea started the vineyard in 1946 and expanded it slowly over the years. The wines are noted for their exceptional longevity. Stony Hill Chardonnays from the 1950s and 1960s, when they turn up, display an astonishing freshness and complexity. These old wines, which sold for U.S. $3 or $4 a bottle when released, often bring $500 at auctions today.

Rodney Strong Vineyards Reserve, Sonoma County

For more than twenty years, Rodney Strong Vineyards was known as Sonoma Vineyards in California. And for most of that time, the winery's top-of-the-line offering was its Alexander's Crown Cabernet Sauvignon, made from grapes grown on a rise looking north over the Alexander Valley; the rise where, incidentally, Strong lives. More recently he has come out with a reserve wine that he says is the best wine he's ever made. It is a bit more restrained than the Alexander's Crown, perhaps, but it has a liveliness all its own. The Reserve is 100 percent Cabernet. It is quite soft and approachable, but there is no lack of concentration and power. No respectable winery in California wants to be caught without its super-, or ultra-premium wine. It's still a pretty exclusive club, but with this wine Strong has made himself eligible for a life-membership.

Stylish

An imprecise term that refers to a wine that has a harmonious balance of fruit, tannin and acidity.

Château Suduiraut, Sauternes

This splendid Bordeaux estate, which adjoins Yquem, was in pitiful decline when it was acquired during the Second World War by Monsieur Fonquernie, whose descendants still own the huge property. His careful restoration of the vineyard and scrupulous winemaking were reflected in a series of remarkable wines during the fifties and sixties, before a period of uneven results. These were doubly disappointing in that Suduiraut in its best years is among the greatest of all Sauternes. An outstanding 1976 signalled a revival confirmed by the vintages of 1978, 1979, 1982, 1983 and 1988. Perfumed, powerful, rich, unctuous and deeply colored, Suduiraut tends to need a minimum of ten years to be seen at its best and can last for half a century or more.

Suhindol, Bulgaria

Suhindol is Bulgaria's oldest winery, founded in 1909 near the northern wine commune of Pavlikeni. The winery is famous for its red wine made from the Gamza grape. Souhindol Gamza is an elegant and delicious wine, aromatic, with well-defined fruit, not

unlike Pinot Noir. The cooperative also produces good Cabernet Sauvignon from the Suhindol, Sakar Mountain and Svichtov vineyards. The 1985 Svichtov Cabernet Sauvignon is excellent with its full ruby color, intense to the rim of the glass, and its rich tarry fruit flavors.

Sulfur dioxide
The essential antiseptic in winemaking, widely used to prevent oxidation and kill unwanted wild yeasts and harmful bacteria. It may be added to fermenting must to arrest fermentation if residual sugar is required in the final wine; it may be also added to wine to prevent oxidation. There are legal maximum levels for sulfur in wine, and these are in many cases lower than they used to be. It is far less common now to find a wine that smells of sulfur.

Suntory, Honshu, Japan
Suntory is a leading player in the Japanese wine industry. These are wines of good quality and are made both from the indigenous Koshu grape and from blends of European varieties. The company's flagship wine is the sweet Bordeaux-style Château Lion, which commands a high price.

Supérieur
A French term that generally denotes no more than an extra half percent or so of alcohol, and in some cases a smaller yield. Bordeaux Supérieur has a minimum of 10.5 percent alcohol by volume, instead of plain Bordeaux's 10 percent, and a maximum basic yield of 40 hectoliters per hectare/2.3 tons per acre as opposed to 50 hectoliters per hectare/2.9 tons per acre.

Sur lie
French term for wine that is bottled straight off its lees in order to preserve its freshness. Muscadet *sur lie* is probably the best-known example.

Süssreserve
Unfermented grape juice added to wine to increase its sweetness. Used in Germany for Q.b.A. wines and Q.m.P. wines up to *Spätlese* level; also in England and Wales.

Sussumariello
A variety brought across the Adriatic to Apulia from Dalmatia. It contributes color and acidity to the blended red and rosé wines of Ostuni and Brindisi.

Sutter Home Amador Reserve Zinfandel, Napa Valley
Thanks to its enormous success with White Zinfandel, and its ubiquitous presence on the airlines, Sutter Home has become one of America's best-known California wineries. Among winelovers it is known for what some consider is the "real" Zinfandel, the solid good-value-for-the-money red wine that few wineries make better. Sutter Home is in the Napa Valley, but its best Zinfandel grapes come from Amador County, some 161 kilometers/100 miles to the east in the foothills of the Sierra Madre Mountains. There, the hotter climate and higher elevation produce intensely rich, full-flavored fruit. The best go into the reserve wine. The result is not subtle or nuanced, but straightforward, thoroughly satisfying wine. Not for refined gourmet meals, perhaps, but a great steak wine and most reasonably priced.

Malcolm Swan, Domaine des Anges, Ventoux
A refugee from a London advertising agency, Malcolm Swan bought the 8 hectare/20 acre Domaine des Anges near Mormoiron in 1973 in the Côtes-du-Rhône. The grape mix is Grenache, Syrah, Carignan and Cinsaut. He aims to produce an early maturing red wine of primary fruit flavors, and part of the crop is made by carbonic maceration. The 1990 is decadently ripe and fruity.

Sylvaner
See Silvaner.

Syrah
Syrah is a red grape of Middle Eastern origin. It produces wines of the northern Rhône, Hermitage, Cornas and Côte Rôtie, as well as Crozes-Hermitage and St. Joseph, with a peppery, blackcurrant taste. It has the ability to age for several years. Syrah is also one of the thirteen varieties of Châteauneuf-du-Pape, is included in the Côtes-du-Rhône and is planted throughout the Midi, as well as in Provence, as a *cépage améliorateur*, where it is increasingly important in both appellations and *vins de pays*.

As Shiraz it is widely grown in Australia and makes some distinctive spicy wines; it is at its very best in Grange. More interest is being taken in Syrah in California, where it is no relation to Petite Sirah. There is also a little in Argentina and a considerable amount in South Africa, as well as an isolated example in Tuscany.

T

T-budding
A method developed in California and Australia that permits the rapid conversion of a vineyard from one grape variety to another. Instead of uprooting and replanting, with the inevitable loss of a crop over several years, the vines are cut off above ground level and a bud of the new variety inserted into the trunk. Only one year's production is lost. The technique allows growers to keep up with rapid swings in fashion.

Tafelwein
German term for table wine. Table wine that comes from Germany is called *Deutscher Tafelwein*.

Chateau Tahbilk, Tahbilk, Victoria
Founded in 1860, Chateau Tahbilk is the oldest wine estate in Victoria. Alister Purbrick, great-grandson of the founder, makes the wines, which show a continuity of style rarely found in Australia. The red wines are made in much the same way as they were fifty years ago, with very high extraction of color and tannins; aging in large old vats rather than new *barriques* is the invariable rule. Purbrick rates Cabernet Sauvignon his best wine — the 1981 is excellent — though many think as highly of the Shiraz, which is made in part from low-yielding ungrafted vines dating from the 1860s. In any event, both these wines, almost regardless of vintage, are extremely long-lived and need at the very least ten years' bottle age. Marsanne, Chateau Tahbilk's best-known white wine, sees no wood, as delicacy and pure fruit are the intended style. Nonetheless this wine ages well, developing a waxy fullness when it is about five years old.

Taittinger, Champagne
Although Taittinger is one of the Champagne region's most respected names, the firm did not acquire the Taittinger name until 1932. After World War I Pierre Taittinger bought Château de la Marquetterie near Epernay, where he had been billeted as a young cavalry officer. He soon took over the ancient firm of Fourneaux Forest et Successeurs, which was founded in 1734. Annual production is about 330,000 cases, and its 250 hectares/618 acres of vines supplies half its needs. The range includes two prestige *cuvées*, the 100 percent Chardonnay Comtes de Champagne and the Taittinger Collection. For every vintage of Collection a leading modern artist is commissioned to design the bottle. Taittinger owns the Saumur house of Bouvet-Ladubay.

Taltarni, Moonambel, Victoria
Taltarni is the leading wine estate of the Pyrenees region of Central Victoria in Australia, with a substantial vineyard of 120 hectares/296 acres. French-born winemaker Dominique Portet is the son of a former *régisseur* of Château Lafite, his red wines very much in the Bordeaux mold. Strongly flavored Cabernet and Shiraz is the specialty here; 1978, 1982, 1986 and 1990 all excellent vintages. Very good wood-aged Sauvignon Blanc and a fine range of *méthode champenoise* wines; look out for Taltarni *Brut Taché*.

Tannat
The main red wine variety of Madiran and the Béarn in the southwestern corner of France. the grape is picked late and in a good year produces a dark, powerful, appropriately tannic wine, high in alcohol and acidity, which needs several years to develop. In consequence it is often blended with the Cabernet Franc or Cabernet Sauvignon. In what remains of the ancient Basque vineyards the Tannat makes Irouléguy. Under the name Harriague it is a mainstay of the Uruguayan wine industry.

Tannic
An essential characteristic of red wines destined for long aging. The taste is harsh in the mouth, like tannin in strong tea.

Tannin
Substance present in grape skins, pips and stalks. An essential element of good red wine, as it provides the backbone to allow wine to mature. Very tannic red wines often taste harsh in youth and mellow only with age.

Tardy et Ange, Crozes-Hermitage
Consistently reliable producers of Crozes-Hermitage, Tardy et Ange emphasize sprightly fruit rather than extract or complexity in their red wines of the Rhône region. The 1989 and 1990 vintages are attractive.

Château du Tariquet, Eauze
Yves Grassa is the fifth generation to manage this impressive 225 hectare/555 acre estate, of which 50 hectares/124 acres are reserved for the distillation of excellent Bas Armagnac, which is made in a traditional continuous still, heated by a natural log fire. Excellent mellow XO Armagnac and a rich, deep amber single vintage 1972. Grassa also makes a nonappellation *eau-de-vie* from Folle Blanche. The major part of the estate's production is in immaculately vinified Vin de Pays des Côtes de Gascogne.

Tart
Acidic.

Tartrates
Harmless and flavorless precipitation of tartaric acid in white wine. Some winemakers reduce their wine to below -5°c/23°F in order to precipitate these salts before bottling. Tartaric acid is an important element of acidity in wine.

Taylor, Nova Villa Nova de Gaia
Celebratng its tercentenary in 1992, Taylor is the Rolls-Royce of Port houses. The firm's vintage Ports — severe, imposing, very long-lived — command the highest prices. Vintage Ports based on the harvest from Quinta de Vargellas are sold as fine single-quinta wine from second-level vintage years. These unblended wines have a marked violet aroma. Quinta de Vargellas, high in the Douro Superieur, is a famous "open house' for wine merchants and journalists from around the world; its warmth of character owes everything to Gillyanne Robertson, wife of Taylor's managing director. Top Taylor vintages: 1977, 1970, 1963, 1948.

Tazzelenghe
An ancient and obscure grape variety native to Friuli and seen to advantage in the Colli Orientali, where it makes red *vini da tavola* wines of individuality and high acidity. The grape is also used in modern blends.

Tears
Swill wine round the inside of a glass and let it settle: it will run back down the sides in "tears." Alternative terms are "legs" or "gothic windows." Tears are indicative of high levels of alcohol.

Cave de Técou, Gaillac
Although this is the smallest of the three cooperatives in the Gaillac region of southwest France, it makes the most interesting wine from its 700 hectares/1,730 acres of vines. Wines of all colors are made, as well as some sparkling wine. Its most impressive wines are two oak-aged reds intriguingly called Passion and Séduction.

Teinturier
French name for red grapes with red juice. Most noble red varieties have white juice and pulp. Examples of *teinturier* grapes include Dornfelder, Alicante Bouschet and some types of Gamay.

Domaine Tempier, Bandol
Lucien Peyraud and his family have done much to assist the revival of Bandol wines. They use traditional, organic methods on their 28 hectare/69 acre domain in the south of France. Although they make rosés, it is their robust, long-lived reds for which they are best known. The red is made from some 60 percent Mourvèdre, the rest being mainly Cinsaut and Grenache. The wine is aged in wood for around two years.

Tempranillo
Tempranillo is the best red variety of Rioja, accounting for about 40 percent of the area and planted mainly in Rioja Alta and Rioja Alavesa. It has thick skins, giving deep-colored wine without too much alcohol, and it blends well with Garnacha, Mazuelo and Graciano. It is also grown to a limited extent in Penedès and Navarra, more so in Valdepeñas, where it is called Cencibel, and in the Alentejo and Douro districts of Portugal, as Aragonez and Tinta Roriz respectively. In California, it is related to the Valdepeñas of the San Joaquin Valley. Other synonyms are Ojo de Liebre, Ull de Llebre, and Tinto Fino.

Tenterden, England
Established in 1977 by Stephen Skelton, who then became Lamberhurst's winemaker. The 7 hectare/17 acre estate has recently changed hands and is now owned by Malcolm Kay. It is fast establishing itself as one of England's premier vineyards. Its Seyval Blanc is particularly well regarded, and there have been some interesting experiments with fermenting and aging in new oak.

Tenuta di Capezzana, Carmignano
This excellent estate, in the Montalbano hills northwest of Florence, typifies the flair and imagination that the best Tuscan winemakers now bring to their craft. In 1968 Conte Ugo Contini Bonacossi brought some Cabernet cuttings back from Château Lafite and planted them in his vineyards. Once they had come into production, he experimented by adding a small amount to his best-known red wine, Carmignano, which was granted its own D.O.C. in 1975. The 1985 Carmignano Riserva is a delicious wine of crimson color with a lean, racy yet flavory character. But perhaps his greatest wine is the Bordeaux-style Ghiaie della Furba, which is made from Cabernet and Merlot. Deep ruby in color, strongly fruity and herbaceous on the nose, the 1985 has a fullness in the mouth, balanced by an elegant vinosity,

that recalls a first-rate St. Emilion. Count Ugo's son Vittorio now makes the wines, which include a stylish oak-free Chardonnay.

Teroldego

A red-wine variety long established in Trentino, where it flourishes on the gravel of the Rotaliano plain. It makes substantial, deeply colored D.O.C. wines capable of aging; these are the best wines of Trentino. The Teroldego also makes rosé and is blended into lesser D.O.C. red wines.

Terre Rosse, Zola Predosa

In the sixties the late Enrico Vallania pioneered the production of excellent, nationally known red and white wines in the hills above Bologna. The estate takes its name from the limestone *terra rossa* soil, which has proved so suitable for Cabernet Sauvignon. The Vallania family now make a special Cabernet in great years, called Cuvée Enrico Vallania. The estate also makes good Sauvignon, Chardonnay, Pinot Bianco, Pinot Grigio and Malvasia.

Terroir

French word meaning "soil" or "earth". The phrase *goût du terroir* ("taste of the soil") indicates a wine with a characteristic earthy taste — a *vin de terroir*

Château du Tertre, Margaux

This fifth growth, the only one of the commune of Arsac to be classified, after years of decline was bought in 1961 by Monsieur Capbern Gasqueton, the owner of Calon Ségur. Under his expert control the château has been restored, the vineyard replanted and production brought back to its former level. His winemaking is traditional, with a lengthy fermentation followed by two years in cask. Unusually for the appellation, du Tertre has a proportion of Cabernet Sauvignon as high as 80 percent. The wine is scented, elegant, rich and concentrated, characteristically well-colored, and it represents good value, commonly surpassing more than a few better known and more expensive Margaux. This Bordeaux vineyard is still improving. Outstanding recent vintages are those of 1978, 1979, 1980, 1982, 1983 and 1985.

Château Tertre Rôteboeuf, St. Emilion

This small Bordeaux vineyard occupies the southeastern outcrop of the limestone plateau above the Côte de Pavie, and is planted with 80 percent Merlot and 20 percent Cabernet Franc. The owner, Francois Mitjavile, assumed control in 1978 and reversed the practice of making the wine alongside that of Bellefont-Belcier. Nowadays it is made with scrupulous care from grapes selected for their ripeness, with long maceration to accentuate their color, extract and richness, with an unusually high percentage of new oak used in the maturing of the wines. Their style is individual; rich and structured, high in alcohol and acidity. Remarkable examples were made in both 1985 and 1986, which may well need upward of ten years to reach their potential.

Dominique Tessier, Domaine les Hauts Sanziers, Saumur

The Saumur appellation in the Loire can often be undistinguished, particularly for red wines. The attractively fruity reds of Saumur-Champigny are often preferable. However, many of the best wines come from the south of the appellation from around Le Puy Nôtre Dame, and Domaine les Hauts Sanziers is perhaps the best estate. This large family property is now run by Dominique Tessier. An extraordinary number of grape varieties are grown — all those permitted for the A.O.C. plus some not often seen, such as Pinot Blanc and Chazan, which is related to Chardonnay. The Saumur Blanc *sec* made from 100 percent Chenin is particularly successful.

Thames Valley, England

This 7 hectare/17 acre vineyard has a rapidly growing reputation. Some thirty grape varieties, a staggering number, have been planted, including known varieties like Chardonnay, Scheurebe and Seyval Blanc and little-known varieties like Würzer and Ehrenfelser. As well as making impressive dry white wines, Thames Valley made some very fine late-picked wines in 1989.

Jean Thévenet, Mâcon-Clessé

A leading grower of Clessé-Quintaine, Thévenet farms some 7.5 hectares/18.5 acres of vines at Domaine de la Bon Gran in Burgundy. He now also manages the neighboring Domaine Emilian Gillet. Thevenet's wines are concentrated yet fruity and aromatic, a style achieved by his insistence on restricting the yield of his Chardonnay vines to 40 hectoliters per hectare/2.4 tons per acre. Because his vineyards are close to the Saône River, Thévenet is able to make a sweet Mâcon Clessé in warm humid autumns like 1989 when the grapes have been affected by noble rot. He is considered one of the finest winemakers in the Mâconnais. He favors long, slow fermentations, followed by nine to twelve months in oak before bottling.

Thin

A wine that lacks fruit and is meager in the mouth.

Thompson Seedless

This is the familiar Sultana of Asia Minor, which in California bears the name of the grower who more than a century ago first planted it on a commercial scale. The vine relishes hot, dry conditions and is both prolific and very heavily planted. It produces vast quantities of sweet and seedless grapes, primarily for drying to make raisins, but also for the table and to make bland wines that may be still or sparkling as well as indifferent American Sherry-style wines. The Thompson is widely used for blending, and while its vocation is not that of wine grape, its production is so enormous that statistically the variety is important. It has been planted in Australia and South Africa, but again is not regarded as primarily a wine grape.

Three Choirs, England

These 19 hectares/47 acres of vines in Gloucestershire are now well established and run by Tom Day. The Three Choirs name arises from the vineyard's nearness to the cathedrals of Gloucester, Hereford and Worcester, which host the Three Choirs music festival. The estate's well made range of wines includes a bottle-fermented sparkler and some intriguing late-harvest wines, when the weather permits.

J. Tiefenbrunner-Schloss Turmhof, Bolzano

The Tiefenbrunners make some of the most highly regarded wines of the Alto Adige, both from their Schloss Turmhof vineyard and from selected growers. Their Feldmarschall comes from Müller-Thurgau grapes grown in the Fennberg vineyard at an altitude of over 914 meters/3,000 feet. Not surprisingly, this wine shows extraordinary freshness and aromas.

Tinta Barroca

This is a robust and widely planted vine that can support cool conditions and gives a generous yield. It is classed as good rather than very good, but with its large production makes an important contribution to the making of Port. The variety is found in California and South Africa, where it makes substantial varietal wines.

Tinta Cão

A variety of considerable antiquity and one classified as very good for Port, the Tinta Cão resists both damp and fungal attack and produces very deeply colored grapes, typically in small bunches. Its yield too is small, and in consequence the vine has fallen into obscurity, although there are hopes to revive it and to achieve better yields. The grape remains a recommended variety in the Dão region.

Tinta Madeira

A black grape of Portuguese origin that makes varietal dessert wines in California and contributes to the best American Port-style wines.

Tinta Negra Mole

Tinta Negra Mole, or Negramole, is the most extensively planted grape of Madeira, constituting a large proportion of wines called after the grape varieties Malmsey, Bual, Verdelho and Sercial. Such wines are easily distinguished on the palate from those really made from the four noble varieties. It is thought to be a cross between Grenache and Pinot Noir, although neither of those grow on the island. Some Tinta Negra Mole is also produced on the Portuguese mainland for table wine.

Tinta Roriz

See Tempranillo.

Tinto Fino

See Tempranillo.

Tinto Velho, José de Sousa Rosado Fernandes, Alentejo

This is a substantial, traditionally made Portuguese red wine, fermented in clay vessels, derived from the indigenous Trincadeira, Periquita, Moreto and Aragones grapes. The wine is the epitome of old-style Portuguese practice, and it ages well.

Jacques Tissot, Arbois

Tissot was perhaps destined for winemaking, as he was born within 200 meters/219 yards of the vines that belonged to Louis Pasteur, the great chemist who invented pasteurization in the nineteenth century. From his 14 hectares/35 acres in France's Arbois, Jacques makes Vin Jaune and *vin de paille* as well as wines from Chardonnay and Trousseau, the local red variety.

Tobacco

An aroma found in some mature red wines.

Philip Togni Cabernet Sauvignon, Napa Valley

Togni started life as a petroleum engineer but ended up making wine in Algeria, Chile and Bordeaux, where he worked for Alexis Lichine at Château Lascombes before coming to the Napa Valley in California in the early 1960s. Over the years, he worked for many if not most of the pioneer fine winemakers in the area. A perfectionist, he developed a reputation as an obdurate fellow not always eager to compromise. Now he has his own small spread high up on the side of Spring Mountain where he answers to no one but himself. True to his European training, his Cabernets are compact and precise rather than big and brawny, which does not mean they lack finesse. They are beautifully crafted wines that achieve elegance without losing any of the rich tastes one expects from good California wines.

Tokay

See Pinot Gris.

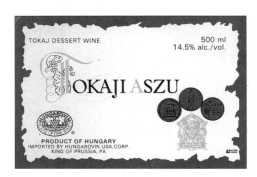

Tokay, Hungary

Tokay is the great white wine of Hungary made predominantly from the Furmint grape around the town of Tokaj. There are three styles of Tokay wine. The basic wine is called Tokay Szamorodni; "Szamorodni" means "as it was grown" or "as it comes." The wine may be sweet or dry according to the weather during the vintage. Tokay Szamorodni is a wine of strength; the dry version tastes like Sherry, though it is actually unfortified. Tokay Aszú is a sweet dessert wine made from grapes affected by *Botrytis cinerea*, or noble rot. The quality of Tokay Aszú is measured by *puttonyos* — baskets containing 30 liters/8 U.S. gallons of botrytis-affected grape must that are added to casks of base wine with a volume capacity not exceeding 130 liters/34.3 U.S. gallons. The sugar content and the resulting quality and concentration of flavor is determined by the number of *puttonyos* — 3 *puttonyos*, 4 *puttonyos*, 6 *puttonyos* — added to the base wine. The more Aszú botrytis-affected grapes added, the more intense and luscious the wine.

Tokay Esszencia is made entirely from botrytis-affected grapes, shriveled to the point that they resemble raisins. The natural weight of the berries in the vat forces a syruplike nectar from the grapes. Extremely rich and concentrated, this liquid is allowed to ferment for years in barrels known as *gônci*. Many consider it the greatest dessert wine in the world. The Hungarians feel it has magical powers.

Torbato

An uncommon if traditional variety grown in northwestern Sardinia, where it makes the best white wines of the island. The vine is related to the Tourbat of Roussillon.

Miguel Torres, Penedès

The Torres family has been making wine near Barcelona for more than 300 years, but it was the late Miguel Torres (he died in 1990) who made this company the most prominent wine firm in the Penedès after the Second World War.

His son, Miguel Torres Jr., is a well-known figure on the international wine scene. Torres studied enology in France at the University of Dijon, and on his return to Penedès introduced French varieties into the vineyards alongside indigenous Spanish ones. Torres has had

particular success with such varietals as Gewürztraminer, Riesling, Chardonnay and Sauvignon, which he planted in the cooler hills of the hinterland. But he is also a champion of white Spanish grapes like Parellada, which produces excellent, crisp white wine in the cool mountain climate. In the winery, Torres pioneered the use of cold fermentation for his whites, but as he says, "I also believe that a wine should reflect its local environment. In some cases we are returning to traditional methods, fermenting in new oak casks and leaving the wine on its lees until May the following harvest."

For his red wines, Torres uses traditional grapes like Garnacha and Ull de Llebre (the Catalan name for Tempranillo) as well as classic varieties from abroad; Cabernet, Merlot and Pinot Noir grow well in the warm vineyards of Medio Penedès. Torres's greatest achievements have been with Cabernet, best seen in the top-of-the-range Gran Coronas Black Label. This is a world-class red wine, rich and intense, with floral violetlike aromas, a succulent black-fruits flavor and a persistent finish. The 1983 is an excellent example of its kind, following the somewhat controversial 1982.

Much of Miguel's energy today is devoted to his Chilean winery. Touring the Americas in the 1970s, he finally chose Chile because of its superb viticultural potential and in 1979 bought a run-down estate near Curicó. The technical expertise of the Penedès operation was quickly replicated in Chile. Stainless-steel fermenters were imported from Spain and oak barrels ordered from America. Torres's Chilean Cabernets can taste quite austere when young but develop an admirable complexity after two to three years in bottle. The Sauvignons and Chardonnays show an increasing mastery of oak, vintage by vintage.

Château La Tour Blanche, Sauternes

In 1855 this *cru*, named after the tower that still adorns its label, was classed second only to Yquem, but its great reputation has not persisted into recent times. This is usually attributed to the fact that since 1910, when the enigmatically named Monsieur Osiris gave it to the state as a viticultural and enological school, this Bordeaux property has been managed erratically, with no consistent policy. This has been reflected in the uneven quality of the wines, although results improved during the kindly decade of the eighties. There were reasonably successful vintages in 1979, 1981, 1982, 1983, 1985, 1986 and in 1988, when cask fermentation was tried with pleasing results. The dedication of Monsieur Jausserand, its current administrator, may yet restore the estate.

Château La Tour-Haut-Caussan, Blaignan

For more than a century this small *cru bourgeois* has belonged to the Courrian family in Bordeaux, whose methods are traditional. No weedkiller is employed in the vineyard, and the grapes are picked by hand and vinified with scrupulous care. The wine is matured in casks, 25 percent of them new each year. The results are very satisfactory, but the wine is hard to find, with little available for export.

Château La Tour Martillac, Graves

Four generations of the Kressmann family have been associated with this Bordeaux property, which they have owned since 1929. There is a respect for tradition here; with old vines, fermentation in wooden vats, and the use only of manure from cattle kept to provide it. The red wines are characterized by elegance, fruit and flavor, and a certain lightness of body; those of 1981, 1982, 1983 and 1985 have shown to advantage. The white wines ally a charming freshness in youth with the ability to develop over many years.

Touriga Francesa

A Port variety officially classified as very good, this vine gives a heavier yield than the Touriga Nacional, and its wine, though marginally less deep and powerful, is more perfumed and so an important element of the blend.

Touriga Nacional

This is the most notable Port variety, officially classified as very good. The vine's yield is modest in the extreme, but it is largely impervious to disease and makes a massive, dark and powerful wine of great quality. In the Dão region this Touriga was formerly an important red-wine variety, but its share of the vineyard has diminished greatly. In compensation it has found recognition in Australia and California.

Trajadura

A Portuguese white grape, and one of the principal varieties used to make Vinho Verde. In Galicia, across the Spanish border, it is known as Treixadura.

Traminer

With a thousand years of recorded cultivation, this variety is widely distributed in Europe and the New World. Of its many forms, the Gewürztraminer of Alsace is the finest expression, as well as the best known. For many years the Savagnin of the Jura was thought to be a Traminer, but this view cannot be sustained.

Louis Trapet, Chambertin

Trapet's Chambertins, while hardly inexpensive, are realistically priced. They are superb wines — rich and intense with that indefinable combination of smoke and earthiness that is the hallmark of the best wines from the Côte d'Or in Burgundy. They are *vins de garde,* wines to lay down. They probably need six years after their release to reach maturity.

Trebbiano

Trebbiano is the world's most prolific grape variety, producing rather dull white wine in vast quantity, either for table wine or distillation. In France, where it is called Ugni Blanc, it is grown in the Charente and the Gers for distillation into Cognac and Armagnac respectively. It features in most of the white wines of Midi, but is usually blended with other grape varieties for flavor. It features in numerous Italian wines, particularly in central Italy, such as Orvieto, Frascati, Verdicchio, and also Soave in the Veneto. Trebbiano is allowed in Chianti, but in a decreasing amount, and provides the backbone of all the other Tuscan whites, as well as *vin santo.* It has been introduced into the New World, to Australia and California, but mainly for distillation.

Treixadura

See Trajadura.

Trenel et Fils, Charnay-lès-Mâcon

One of the best three or four *négociants* working in the Beaujolais and Mâconnais region, Trenel produces immaculately vinified wines across a broad range, from fresh, citrussy Mâcon-Villages and richly fruity Pouilly-Fuissé to tannic, deep-flavored Morgon le Py and a grandly structured Moulin-à-Vent La Rochelle. These are big, full wines, less elegant than the wines of Pierre Ferraud, for example, but no less rewarding. Trenel also produces the definitive Crème de Cassis, a regular sight behind the bar of many Michelin three-star restaurants in France.

Domaine des Tres Cantous, Gaillac

An individualistic and iconoclastic winemaker, Roger Plageoles loves to experiment. His particular specialty is using the Mauzac grape, local to this part of southwest France, in a wide variety of styles, from dry to very sweet and from still to sparkling. He is also fascinated by old

grape varieties, such as the Ondenc, that are on the point of extinction.

Château de Trévelin, Rolaz-Hammel, Valais

The vineyards of Château de Trévelin are entirely planted with Chasselas. They lie in La Côte, 19 kilometers/12 miles west of Lausanne, Switzerland, overlooking the Lake of Geneva. The yield is kept low and irrigation is allowed — particularly useful in hot summers, like that of 1989. Although the 1989 has a little over 12 percent alcohol, the flavor is surprisingly delicate, and the slight sparkle adds charm. A most attractive wine.

Triage

French for selective picking. A technique used especially in Sauternes: only the ripest grapes or those affected by noble rot are picked, leaving the rest to ripen further and be picked on a subsequent occasion. *Vendange par tri* is an equivalent term.

F.E. Trimbach, Ribeauvillé

Winemakers and merchants since 1636, Trimbach is a highly respected firm in Alsace and one of the best known in the English-speaking world. The style of the wines is elegant and understated with fine, delicate fruit and length of flavor.

The firm's best wines come from the family vineyards, notably the tiny 1.5 hectare/3.7 acre Clos St. Hune, where the Riesling grape grown on limestone soil yields a magnificent wine, austere when young but capable of very long life. The 1977 Clos St. Hune is a legendary wine in a difficult year. Other excellent Trimbach *cuvées* include Riesling Frédéric Emile and Gewürztraminer Seigneurs de Ribeauvillé. Winemaker Pierre Trimbach believes in relatively high fermentation temperatures of 20° to 25°C/68° to 77°F to ensure both maximum character and staying power in his wines.

Trocken

German term for dry wine. Trocken wines are very fashionable in Germany.

Trockenbeerenauslese

Very sweet wine made by special selection of individual grapes that are intensely concentrated (shriveled and raisinlike) through noble rot or overripeness. Used in Germany and Austria.

Trollinger

See Schiava.

Château Troplong-Mondot, St. Emilion

This domain in Bordeaux of 30 hectares/74 acres was formed from smaller parcels in the middle of the last century. The setting is splendid, with the château placed on the summit of a hill, but until very recently, and despite a number of outstanding years like 1928, 1949 and 1970, Troplong Mondot has failed to make wines of the quality that might reasonably be expected of it.

The new management, headed by the owner's daughter, who is also the niece of Monsieur Valette of Pavie, seems to be making serious efforts to improve standards. New oak, for example, is used increasingly, and the early results have been promising, with a successful 1985 followed by a notable 1986 and 1987. The 1988 wine is fleshy, powerful and deeply colored, with a pronounced bouquet and considerable complexity.

Château Trotanoy, Pomerol

It is fitting that this small Bordeaux estate should produce wines of such distinction, and command such high prices, since the Moueix family, best known for their involvement with Pétrus, has done more than anyone to advance the cause of Pomerol, and indeed may be considered to have established its market worldwide.

The vineyard is planted with 85 percent Merlot on soil that has a significant admixture of clay with its gravel. Characteristically the wine resembles that of Pétrus, with richness, color and bouquet, and the great vintages have been many, with 1970, 1971, 1975, 1976, 1978, 1979, 1981, 1982, 1983, 1985 and 1986 all memorable over the past twenty years, and the 1982 and 1986 perhaps especially remarkable.

Trousseau

A variety indigenous to the Jura. It yields an unexceptional crop of grapes, rich in color and tannin, to make the concentrated, long-lived A.O.C. wines of the region. Trousseau is often softened by the introduction of a small proportion of Pinot Noir.

Tyrrell's Pokolbin, New South Wales

Murray Tyrrell is the "voice of the Hunter," always ready with an acerbic remark about some new wine trend not to his liking. But he has been, and is, a highly intelligent and far-sighted *vigneron*. It was Murray who introduced Australians to Chardonnay in 1971, and of recent vintages the 1987 Vat 47 Chardonnay is an excellent wine, with its lush fruit, buttery flavor and toasty vanilla oakiness. More of an acquired taste are his Pinot Noirs; full-blooded and gutsy, they cannot be said to lack flavor, and the 1985 is his best effort to date. Tyrrell's Shiraz is his most striking red wine; a great tarry mouthful, the 1983 needs another ten years to reach maturity. At the bottom of the range, Tyrrell's Long Flat Red and Long Flat White (both blends) are some of the best-value wine drinking in Australia today.

U

Ugni Blanc

See Trebbiano.

Ull de Llebre

See Tempranillo.

Weingut Undhof, Stein, Lower Austria

Leading 14 hectare/34.6 acre estate at Krems. Refined, elegant wines of great depth made by traditional methods in spotlessly clean old wooden vats. Owner Erich Salomon has restored a seventeenth-century Capuchin monastery near his estate and uses it as a showcase for the wines of the whole of Austria; all the wines there can be tasted, and there are also exhibitions of vinous antiques on loan from Vienna. Of Salomon's own wines, the Riesling, Grüner Veltliner and Traminer are especially noteworthy.

Union des Producteurs de Plaimont, Côtes de Saint-Mont

This is one of the largest and best equipped cooperatives

in southwest France, producing a wide range of wines, in particular Madiran, the entire production of the V.D.Q.S. Côtes de St-Mont and the popular white Côtes de Gascogne from Colombard and Ugni Blanc. The main site is in the village of St.-Mont with subsidiary sites at Plaimont and St. Aignan.

Domaine Vacheron, Sancerre

The remarkable growth in the popularity of Sancerre since the end of the Second World War has tempted too many Sancerre winemakers to stretch their wines. Not so Domaine Vacheron which, with vineyards in Sancerre itself, continues to be driven by quality. From its nearly 20 hectares/49.4 acres of vines, two thirds of its production is white — a Sancerre with both power and finesse — and the rest is planted with Pinot Noir. Both its red and rosé Sancerres are undoubtedly among the best of this frequently abused appellation of the Loire.

Domaine Val Brun, Saumur-Champigny

The Charruau family have been *vignerons* since 1726 in the village of Parnay, a little to the east of Saumur. Jean-Pierre Charruau and his wife took over this early nineteenth-century Loire estate in the village of Parnay in 1966. He has now been joined by his son, Eric, and together they are making some impressively full-bodied Saumur-Champignys. Les Folies 1989, a *cuvée* made from old vines, is especially good and can be kept many years, although it is delicious now. Val Brun also made a little sweet white Coteaux de Saumur in 1989 and 1990.

Château Val-Joanis, Côtes du Lubéron

The promotion of the Côtes de Lubéron to full *Appellation Contrôlée* status in 1988 owes much to the effort of this estate, which showed what could be achieved in France's Lubéron. The Chancel family invested substantial sums in a brand-new winery and produced their first wine in 1982. All three colors are made.

Valdepeñas

See Tempranillo.

Valdespino, Jerez

The Valdespino family has been involved in growing grapes since the fourteenth century. The Sherry house was established in 1837 by Antonio Fernandez de Valdespino. The high-quality range, produced by using traditional methods, includes Inocente Fino, Coliseo Amontillado, Cardinal Palo Cortado and Don Gonzalez Dry Oloroso.

Miguel Valdespino

No Jerez house is more traditional and none has a higher reputation for quality. Miguel Valdespino, the present head of the firm, insists on the most rigorously old-fashioned methods in the *bodegas*. In a real sense, his are hand-made Sherries: all the wines are fermented in large wood casks, and racking is still done by hand.

The company's best-known product is the famous Innocente *fino* Sherry that comes unblended from the family vineyard of that name in the Macharnudo district. This is a classic *fino* with a remarkable complexity of flavor. Intense, lingering tastes are the hallmarks of the Valdespino style. Even the firm's Montana and Deliciosa *manzanillas* have vinous depths not normally associated with these salty-fresh Sherries from the seaside vineyards around Sanlúcar de Barrameda.

The Valdespino *amontillados* are remarkably vigorous wines, mostly in a very dry style. The Don Tomás Amontillado is a rare old wine: translucent, amber-gold in color, with lovely zesty bitter-fruits aromas; a mouth-puckering dryness on the palate at first, then a long, beautifully defined flavor. The viscous, intensely sweet Pedro Ximénez is a sensuous mix of raisiny flavors.

The Valdespinos have also been making good brandies since the fifteenth century. Their Bodega del Inocente, in the heart of Jerez, houses a grand 100-year-old copper still, though it has not been used since the last century.

Edoardo Valentini, Montepulciano d'Abruzzo

Edoardo Valentini is generally recognized as the greatest producer of Montepulciano d'Abruzzo. He makes very strict selections of grapes for the wines that appear under his own label, bottling about 5 percent of his crop. The remainder is sold off in bulk. His Montepulciano d'Abruzzo is a superb, rich, intense red wine needing ten years of aging (the 1982 is now excellent), while his Trebbiano is of the few great white wines made from this workhorse grape.

Valentino, Barolo

Valentino is a fine Barolo producer whose winemaking style stands midway between the traditionalists and the modernists. Yet his most distinctive wine is Bricco Manzoni, a blend of Nebbiolo and Barbera; the 1985 is a velvety mouthful with a mingling of fruit, spice and "animal" flavors.

Vallarom, Trento

This estate makes hand-crafted wines from French varieties in a cellar more reminiscent of the Côte de Beaune than Alpine Italy. The 1989 barrel-fermented Chardonnay is rich and complex.

Vanilla

The characteristic aroma and flavor imparted by new oak barrels, especially those made from American oak, is most often compared to vanilla.

Vasse Felix, Cowaramup, Western Australia

Established in the sixties and acquired by the Holmes-à-Court family in 1987, this estate produces the most stylish Cabernets on the Margaret River. In 1986, 1987 and 1989 the Cabernet Sauvignon consistently showed a lovely cassis and black fruits flavor, vibrant yet poised and elegant. The winery also makes good *méthode champenoise* wines.

Vega-Sicilia, Ribero del Duero

This estate of 150 hectares/370 acres under vine produces Spain's most prestigious and expensive red wines. From the range, the excellent Valbuena third and fifth year offer the best quality-price ratio. The vintage Vega-Sicilia Unico spends a lengthy time in cask and is not released until it is at least ten years old; it is an intense, complex red wine. The 1976 is first-rate. Top-of-the-range Unico Riserva Speciale is a blend of very old red wines, mostly from the 1950s, offered at stratospheric prices.

Vegetal

A wide category of tastes and odors found in certain wine, only rarely described as pleasing. Sauvignon Blanc wines from the Loire Valley are often described as "vegetal" when compared with their counterparts from Bordeaux or California. Green, herbaceous, and grassy are descriptions that convey similar taste and odor sensations in wine.

Vendange

French term for harvest.

Vendange tardive
French term for late-harvest , particularly applied to Alsace wines made from fruit picked toward the end of October. The wines are always rich and sometimes sweet.

Vendange verte
See Green harvest.

Venegazzù, Venegazzù del Montello
This historic estate of the Loredan Gasparini family is now owned by Giancarlo Palla. The winery's reputation is founded on its excellent Cabernet-based red wines. The 1982 Venegazzù Etichetta Nera was one of the finest reds produced in Italy during the last decade. Good Pinot Bianco, Pinot Grigio and an excellent grappa are also made here.

Venica Dolegnan del Collio
Adelchi and Giorgio Venica are two brothers whose *pensione* and 21 hectare/52 acre vineyard overlook the Yugoslav border. This is the best part of Collio, and the brothers are very fine white winemakers. Their 1990 Sauvignon Vigneto del Cerò has all the freshness of the Alpine atmosphere, but a rich complexity too.

Véraison
French term for the ripening stage when grape skins change color.

Verdelho
The most planted white grape of Madeira and one of the traditional varieties that gave their names to the wines made from them. In style it falls between the dry and aromatic Sercial and the opulent Bual. The vine is still recommended for white wines in the Dão region, and it is an important constituent of white Port. In Australia the Verdelho makes highly individual wines.

Verdicchio
The best-known grape of the Marches; with only a small proportion of the land under vines the Verdicchio produces the region's most prominent wines, and their quality is improving steadily. The still white wine has always an element of the *frizzante.* The production of sparkling Verdicchio is increasing; the wine may be made by the *méthode champenoise* or by tank fermentation.

Verduzzo Friulano
This antique white variety is grown throughtout the Friuli region of northern Italy as well as in the Piave district of neighbouring Veneto, but it is traditionally seen at its best in the far north of the Colli Orientali of Friuli, where the Verduzzo Giallo makes the D.O.C. Ramandolo, a dessert wine that may be *amabile* or *dolce.* Farther south near Collio, in the Isonzo district, and in the Grave del Friuli, the Verduzzo Verde makes dry white wines.

Vermentino
This Italian white-wine grape is the leading variety in Liguria, where it makes fine light wines. It also appears in several Sardinian wines, including the powerful Vermentino di Gallura. As Rolle it grows on the suburban slopes outside Nice and is blended with Chardonnay to make the delicately fragrant white wine of Bellet. There is some dispute over whether Vermentino is the same grape as Malvoisie.

Vernaccia
This name is borne by unrelated vines in various parts of Italy. Vernaccia di San Gimignano is a variety that for more than 700 years has made the dry acidic white wine of the celebrated medieval town. Some progress is being made in a drive to improve the quality of the still wine, but while the production of tank-fermented

spumante is increasing, the wine remains indifferent.
Vernaccia di Serrapetrona is a dark grape that makes a deeply colored purplish sparkling wine that survives in the hills of the western Marches. The wine is sweet, and the best of its modest production is made by the *méthode champenoise.*

The Vernaccia di Oristano is a grape native to the west coast of Sardinia. It makes a rustic, archaic wine high in alcohol that is vinified and matured over a long period. The development in its casks of a form of *flor* allows loose parallels with the production of Sherry and the Vin Jaune of the Jura. The wine may be fortified, but is better in its natural style.

Vespaiola
A vine indigenous to that part of the Veneto around Breganze to the north of Vicenza, where it makes the dry white Vespaiolo and contributes to the blended D.O.C. wines of Breganze. It shows to advantage in the rare and remarkable dessert wine Torcolato, made from *passito* grapes, and in Acininobili, made from berries concentrated by the action of *Botrytis cinerea.*

Vespolina
A Piedmontese variety grown in the region of Novara, the Vespolina is used chiefly for blending with the superior Nebbiolo to make such wines as the D.O.C. Ghemme, Fara and Sizzano. The grape is also grown in the Oltrepò Pavese of southern Lombardy, where it is known as Ughetta and is often blended with Barbera, Croatina and Uva Rara to make dry red and rosé wines that may be still or *frizzante.*

Veuve Clicquot Ponsardin, Champagne
Founded in 1772 by Philippe Clicquot Muiron, Veuve Clicquot was really developed by his son's widow, Nicole-Barbe Clicquot, who added her maiden name of Ponsardin. During her long reign production went from 50,000 bottles of Champagne to about 3 million when she died in 1866. Veuve Clicquot is now part of the Louis Vuitton-Moët-Hennessy combine with a production of about 550,000 cases a year. Its 280 hectares/492 acres of vines supply an important part of its needs. Grande Dame, named after the widow, is their prestige *cuvée.*

Vidal Blanc
A hybrid vine (Vidal 256) derived from the Trebbiano or Ugni Blanc. It is well adapted to the conditions of the eastern United States and is well established there. The Vidal makes a fresh and fruity white wine of some merit, and deserves a wider recognition.

Vieilles vignes
French term for old vines. Such vines yield fewer, but better-quality grapes. The term is not legally defined, but old vines are usually at least thirty years old and can occasionally be more than a hundred. Normally used in a property's top wine or for a special *cuvée.*

Vieux Château Certan, Pomerol
A growth that was greatly prized in both the eighteenth and the nineteenth centuries, Vieux Château Certan has retained its reputation into the late twentieth. This Bordeaux estate has belonged to the Belgian family Thienpont for almost seventy years. The vineyard adjoins that of Pétrus on the high plateau, and about 40 percent of it is the same clay. The wines have a certain individuality, with a pronounced bouquet, a paler color and less substance than many Pomerols, and their evident fruit is accompanied by great delicacy and a persistent flavor. Like others within the appellation, the vineyard was impaired by the frosts of 1956, but in the seventies and eighties many wines of distinction made, like 1971, 1978, 1979, 1981, 1982, 1983, 1985 and 1986. This last

was a wine of immense power, and with the almost equally successful 1985, one fit to mark the start of the stewardship of Alexandre Thienpont.

Domaine du Vieux Télégraphe, Châteauneuf-du-Pape
This property derives its name from a tower near Bédarigues where the eighteenth-century inventor Chappe conducted early experiments in the optical telegraph system. This Rhône estate, now the property of the Brunier family, extends to some 40 hectares/99 acres and produces some of the best wines of Châteauneuf-du-Pape.

Since the beginning of the 1980s, the winemaking style has accentuated rich, suave fruit rather than wood-influenced complexity. Indeed, no oak casks were evident on a visit to the domain in 1989. Nonetheless, vinification is immaculate with a pure, fruity 1981 and a very rich 1983. Critics disagree about the 1985: some find it exceptional with a Port-like concentration, others say it is too alcoholic and lacks definition. For lovers of a classic, tannic style reminiscent of the great 1978, both the 1986 and the 1988 may be the vintages to seek.

Château Vignelaure, Coteaux d'Aix
This 60 hectare/148 acre estate at Rians, in the northeast of this French appellation, was bought by Georges Brunet of Château La Lagune in the Médoc in the 1960s. He proceeded to prove that high-quality wines could be produced in Provence with the right equipment and grape varieties.

Brunet planted Cabernet Sauvignon as well as the traditional varieties. Brunet sold the estate in 1987; the current owner is Sonu Shivdasani. The red is a blend of around 60 percent Cabernet Sauvignon, 30 percent Syrah and 10 percent Grenache. The wine is aged in wood for two years or more. Some critics have felt that recent vintages have been below par. and the new owner has decided to declassify the bulk of the production of 1986, 1987 and 1988.

Vigneron
French word for a winegrower.

Vigneti Le Monde, Grave del Friuli
Piergiovanni Pistoni-Salice, a man totally committed to quality, makes delicious Pinot Grigio, Chardonnay and Pinot Bianco at this leading Grave del Friuli estate. The Grave del Friuli wines are akin to those of Collio, though they do not have quite the same refinement. Pistoni-Salice's best wine is probably his Cabernet Franc. The 1990 is a really delightful red wine, clean with very well defined fruit.

Vignoles
This is a successful Pinot Noir hybrid (Ravat 51) that in the eastern United States makes dry white wines reminiscent of Alsace, as well as sweeter styles from late-harvested grapes.

Villa Maria Reserve Cabernet Merlot, Auckland
Villa Maria has won more gold medals for its reds than any other New Zealand winery. This Reserve label is its flagship wine. Hawkes Bay Cabernet Sauvignon gives the wine intense berry flavors with a fine herbal influence, while the Hawkes Bay Merlot softens and adds a gamy complexity to the blend. Maturation in mainly Nevers *barriques* adds slightly more than a seasoning of oak influence. All the qualifications for a long and prosperous bottle development.

Weingut Villa Sachsen, Rheinhessen
A German estate of 25 hectares/62 acres known for spritzy, fresh, clean-tasting, cask-matured Rieslings. The estate is owned by the St. Ursula Weingut, well-known for the commercial Goldener Oktober range.

Château Villars, Fronsac
The 16 planted hectares/39 acres of this Bordeaux property at Saillans are split between the limestone flats and slopes. The vineyard makes consistently rich and fruity wines of substance, a proportion nowadays aged in new wood. Recent successes include 1979, 1983 and 1986.

Vin Delimité de Qualité Supérieure (V.D.Q.S.)
Somewhat of a halfway house between *vin de pays* and full *Appellation Contrôlée* status, both in quality and in the strictness of the regulations. It is likely that in time all current V.D.Q.S. wines will be promoted to A.O.C. and thus possible that this classification will be abolished.

Vin de Garde
French term for a wine worth aging.

Vin de Paille
French term for wine made from grapes that have been dried, traditionally on straw, after picking to concentrate their sugars. Another Jura specialty, occasionally made in other regions of France like the Rhône Valley — Gérard Chave of Hermitage is one famous practitioner.

Vin de Pays
The quality level above *vin de table* in French wine law. *Vins de pays* must come from a delimited geographical area. The quality should be above that of basic table wine.

Vin de Table
French for simple "table wines"; the lowest category of French wines.

Vin de terroir
See Terroir.

Vin Doux Naturel (V.D.N.)
Fortified sweet wines mainly from the Languedoc Roussillon region of France. They may be white, rosé or red. In time all can tend to turn tawny in color and take on a *rancio* character. In all cases the fermentation is stopped by the addition of alcohol, leaving the wine naturally sweet. Examples include Muscat de Rivesaltes, Banyuls, Maury, Muscat de Beaumes de Venise, Muscat de Frontignan.

Vin du Pays
French term for country wine; used for local wines. This term has no legal meaning and should not be confused with *vin de pays*.

Vin Jaune
An expensive specialty from the Jura in eastern France. Made from the Savignan grape, the wine is aged for at least six years in small oak barrels that are never topped up. The wine grows *flor*, like *fino* Sherry. Unlike Sherry, the wine is not fortified.

Jean-Jacques Vincent, Château de Fuissé
A dynamic and thoughtful grower and director of the 45 hectare/111 acre Château de Fuissé, Jean-Jacques Vincent is the most famous estate in the Pouilly-Fuissé appellation. Vincent's wines command a higher price than any of his rivals in this part of Burgundy. The price looks less daunting when one tastes the wine, which is extraordinarily rich, concentrated and often long-lived.

The 1961 Vieilles Vignes was vigorous and alive when drunk in 1989. Vincent also produces a model standard *cuvée* of Pouilly-Fuissé under the Château de Fuissé label, and one from young vines called Domaine de l'Arrillière. His Saint-Véran allies a steely structure

to rich fruit. Less well known is his excellent Beaujolais from the family's small holding in the Morgon Charmes vineyard.

Vinicola do Vale do Dão, Dão
This subsidiary of the enormous Portuguese Sogrape concern markets Dão wines of quality under the label Grão Vasco and has introduced to the region new standards of winemaking based on modern thinking and modern technical equipment.

Vinification
The process of turning grapes into wine.

Vino da Tavola
Italian table wine. Not just the cheapest wines, since many of Italy's finest winemakers use the label as a way of getting round over restrictive D.O.C. legislation.

Vintage
Either the grape harvest in general terms, or wine from a single harvest. Not in itself a sign of quality: many fine wines (non vintage Champagne, tawny Port) are blends of more than one year.

When a vintage is stated on a label, it may be important in a number of ways. In wines best drunk young (for example, Muscadet) it helps the buyer avoid old, stale wines. In wines requiring bottle age (for example, claret) it indicates the likely degree of maturity. In wines from regions where the weather, and thus the quality of the wine, varies greatly from year to year, it indicates likely style, quality and maturity.

Vintner
An old-fashioned English term for a wine merchant who, back in the Middle Ages, was a member of the Vintners Company. In England today there are still Free Vintners, who have the right to sell wine in a certain place and who need not apply for a licence to do so. "Vintner grown" is sometimes seen on American wine labels, indicating that the grower and the winemaker were the same person.

Viognier
Viognier is a white grape variety that makes the most distinctive, fragrant white wines of the northern Rhône, namely Condrieu and Château Grillet. It can also be included in white Côtes-du-Rhône and occasionally a pure Viognier Côtes-du-Rhône may be found. It may also be added to Côte Rôtie, to soften the sturdy flavor of Syrah. The perfume and flavor are reminiscent of dried apricots. Production is tiny as it is fragile and difficult to grow. Viognier is also providing a challenge to a handful of Californian growers with some increasingly exciting results.

Viticola Suavia, Soave
Giovanni Tessari produces excellent Soave Classico in his 10 hectare/24.7 acre hillside vineyard above Fitti. Tessari only uses the juice from a first light pressing of his grapes, and he likes cool temperature-controlled fermentations at 15°C/59°F. His 1990 Soave Classico Monte Carbonare is as good an example of a single-vineyard wine as it is possible to find.

Vitis vinifera
The species of vine that includes all the classic European varieties.

Viura
See Macabeo.

Volatile acidity
See Acetic acid.

Volnay Clos de la Bousse d'Or, Domaine de la Pousse d'Or
The names here derive from a local patois that has virtually disappeared. They are versions of the same geographical description of the local terrain and beyond that have no interest other than for the incomparable wines made by the domain from the Bousse d'Or vineyard.

This is the province of Gérard Potel, one of Burgundy's best-known winemakers. There are no *grands crus* in Volnay and, among the thirty-five *premier crus,* the Bousse d'Or is usually rated below some other properties, such as the Clos des Chênes and Champans. But its grapes in Potel's hands become something very special. The wines are deep in flavor and color, perfect examples of the delicacy and charm that characterize the best Volnays.

Volnay Clos des Chênes, Domaine Michel Lafarge
Traveling south along the Côte d'Or, Volnay is the last major red-wine-producing commune. Its wines have never been as robust as some of the more northerly vineyards of the Côte de Nuits, but they are often unmatched for silky elegance. One commentator has called them the most fragrant and seductively feminine expression of the Pinot Noir grape in Burgundy. They are relatively light-bodied, but even so can display surprising concentrations of flavor and bouquet. Clos des Chênes is considered one of the best vineyards and Michel Lafarge one of the best growers. An unbeatable combination.

Volnay Clos des Chênes, Château de Meursault
This great Burgundian vineyard like the Clos des Chênes is shared by several owners. The Château de Meursault is owned by André Boisseaux, whose principal wine business is the Patriarche shipping firm in Beaune. It's a bit confusing; one might reasonably expect to find Meursault under the Château de Meursault label, but in fact it is a proprietary name. If Les Caillerets is the grandest of all Volnays, as has been suggested, then Clos des Chênes, which is leaner and harder when young, is a close second, with its scent of violets and dark cherries.

Vosne-Romanée, Domaine Jean Gros
The Burgundian Domaine Jean Gros produces a variety of excellent wines from Vosne-Romanée, ranging from a delicious and very rare Richebourg to a substantial Hautes Côte de Nuits, much of which is sold under the Michel Gros name. While the domain has fine *grand cru* holdings, its best-known wine comes from the wholly-owned Clos de Réas, a *premier cru* vineyard just south of the tiny village of Vosne-Romanée. New oak barrels are used for both the *grand* and *premier cru* wines, and since all the wines are given at least eighteen months of wood aging, the oak taste can be pervasive in the young wines. It takes two to three years of extra bottle aging to bring about a proper balance, but then the wines are very fine.

Vosne-Romanée Les Charmes, Domaine Méo-Camuzet
Jean Méo owns vines in the Richebourg vineyard, in Corton, and 3.1 hectares/7.6 acres, or almost 6 percent, of the Clos de Vougeot. What's more, his vines at Clos de Vougeot are in one of the best locations in the vineyard. But it is in the Les Charmes vineyard, where he has about 2 hectares/4.9 acres, that the oldest vines are found — they average about thirty-three years — and that some of the best, albeit unheralded Méo-Camuzet wines are to be found. Henri Jayer, one of the finest winemakers in Vosne-Romanée in Burgundy, made the Camuzet wines for many years. When they were inherited by Méo, he bought Jayer along as consultant. After a few rocky vintages, the wines emerged in the true Jayer style: intense, powerful

and long-lasting. Jayer has retired from his own vineyards. Méo-Camuzet may become their avatar.

Vosne-Romanée Les Suchots, Domaine Confuron-Cotetidot

Jacky Confuron, a short, stocky grower shaped like one of his oak barrels, makes intensely rich Burgundies from his small holdings in Chambolle-Musigny, Clos Vougeot, Nuits St.-Georges and Vosne-Romanée. Confuron was an early disciple of the enologist Guy Accad and his insistence on long, cold maceration of the grape bunches before they are fermented. This process is said to extract intense color from the grape skins and to impart equally intense aromas to the finished wine. The technique has worked well for Confuron, who macerates his fruit for a week or more. He then adds to the power of his wines by neither fining nor filtering them. His Vosne-Romanée Les Suchots is especially good, displaying a richness of fruit underpinned by ripe tannins. This is one of the best wines made by the Accad method.

Vosne Romanée Romanée-Conti, Domaine de la Romanée-Conti

This is the apogee of Burgundian prestige. To be allowed to purchase a single bottle of Romanée-Conti, a wine merchant must agree to buy fifteen bottles of the domain's other stunningly expensive wine. The worldwide demand for the approximately 650 cases of Romanée-Conti made each year is nothing short of remarkable. But few are the critics who will deny the wine's quality, although there were vintages in the early 1970s that drew some complaints. Books have been written on the special merits of the D.R.C., as the domain is called, but late harvesting and severely restricted yields undoubtedly have much to do with the exceptional richness and intensity of the wines. The domain also owns the La Tâche vineyard and has holdings in Montrachet, Bâtard-Montrachet, Echezeaux, Grands Echezeaux, Richebourg, Romanée-St.-Vivant and Vosne-Romanée.

Château la Voulte-Gasparets, Corbières

Excellently managed 50 hectare/124 acre property in Boutenac in the northern Corbières in France, making some of the most stylish wine of the appellation. The property, with its stony limestone slopes, has a long tradition of fine wine. The Cuvée Réserve and Cuvée Romain Paric, which are aged in *barrique*, are particularly good.

Vranac

A red wine variety especially prominent in Montenegro, where it is the dominant grape; and in Macedonia, the Vranac makes strong, well-colored dry wines of some quality.

W

Richard Ward and David Graves, Saintsbury

Richard Ward and David Graves founded this Carneros winery in 1981, specializing in fine Chardonnays and exceptional Pinot Noirs. The justified acclaim that greeted their wines is due to the partners' clear idea of what California wine should be about. They sought elegance *and* fullness of flavor in their wines, and they have stuck consistently to this approach.

Ward and Graves own no vines but buy in grapes from Carneros, the cool southern area that straddles Napa and Sonoma. The wines have abundant fruit yet are impeccably well balanced and age well. The Chardonnays are completely fermented in new oak barrels which gives them a toasty vanilla style.

Somehow their regular bottling of Chardonnay seems as good as the more expensive Reserve wine. This was certainly the case in the 1986 vintage.

There are two styles of Saintsbury Pinot Noir. The Garnet is a light, fresh Pinot for early drinking, while the Carneros Pinot has greater spice and concentration and a more obvious touch of oak. The 1990 Garnet is extremely elegant yet tastes of ripe fruit, while the Carneros Pinot Noir in the same vintage is explosively fruity on the palate with fine smoky aromas and a rich spiciness; there is plenty of tannin to ensure a long life. The 1989 is a Saintsbury Pinot Noir vintage to avoid; it rained heavily at harvest time, and the wines are atypically dilute.

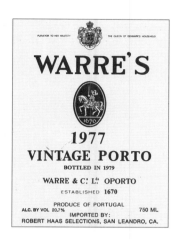

Warre, Vila Nova de Gaia

Founded about 1670, Warre makes opulent, subtle vintage Port, less powerful than some but with beautiful purity of fruit. Top vintages: 1985, 1977, 1966, 1963. Very good Quinta da Cavadinha single-quinta Port from second-level vintage years. The 'Traditional' LBV (requiring decanting) is perhaps the best of all; and there's a good tawny range.

Wegeler-Deinhard, Rheingau

One of a trinity of German estates owned by Deinhard. There are 55 hectares/136 acres here, planted 95 percent with Riesling, and the majority of the wines are dry or medium-dry. The other estates owned by Deinhard are in the Rheinpfalz, at Deidesheim, and at Bernkastel in the Mosel, where Deinhard has holdings in the Doctor site. Deinhard has recently started pursuing a policy of rationalizing the number of wines it produces by amalgamating the wines of some lesser sites; top wines like Bernkasteler Doctor are, however, still being kept separate.

Domaine Weinbach, Kientheim

An outstanding domain of 23 hectares/57 acres at Kientzheim, Weinbach is run by the perfectionist Colette Faller. Her top *cuvées* are exquisite wines. The Riesling Cuvée Ste. Catherine — complex, finely defined, extremely elegant — was particularly successful in 1986, 1988 and 1990. Colette Faller is perhaps the finest exponent of Gewürztraminer in Alsace, steering a perfect middle path between intense richness and restrained elegance. Her 1983 Gewürztraminer Sélection de Grains Nobles is unquestionably a very great dessert wine.

Wellow, England

With some 33 hectares/82 acres, entrepreneur Andy Vining's Hampshire vineyard is one of England's largest. Planting started in 1985, and now some fifteen different varieties have been planted, including Bacchus, Chardonnay, Pinot Noir and Seyval Blanc. A visitor center has been set up and a new winery is planned.

Welschriesling

Welschriesling, not to be confused with Rhine Riesling,

is grown mainly in eastern Europe for fairly undistinguished, but soft, drinkable white wines. It grows easily in a warm climate and is a prolific producer. It is probably at its best in Austria, where it can develop noble rot with some attractive results. It goes under a variety of names, including Wälchriesling, Olasz Rizling in Hungary, Laski Rizling in Yugoslavia and Riesling Italico, or Italian Riesling, in northeast Italy.

Domechant Werner'sches Weingut, Rheingau
The Werner Michel family, who own this estate, bought it in 1780 from the Duke of York; and the original Werner's son was the Domechant, or Dean, of Mainz, who saved the cathedral when the French would have destroyed it. There are now some 12.5 hectares/30 acres under vine, nearly all planted with Riesling. Winemaking is basically traditional, producing excellent, full-flavored Hochheimer. The estate overlooks the confluence of the Main and Rhine rivers.

Schloss Westerhaus, Rheinhessen
Fine German estate on high ground across the Rhine from Winkel in the Rheingau. The wines from the chalky soil have high acidity that does wonders for them in good years.

Williams & Humbert, Jerez
This house was founded in 1877 by Alexander Williams with £1,000 lent by his father-in-law, C. F. Humbert, with the proviso that his son Arthur become a partner. The firm had particular success with Dry Sack, launched in 1906. Williams & Humbert was bought by Rumasa in 1972 and, after its expropriation in 1983 by the Spanish government, was sold eventually to Antonio Barbadillo, who has since sold half to a consortium led by B.V. The range includes Pando Fino and Dos Cortados Palo Cortado as well as Dry Sack, a commercial *amontillado*.

Wine of Origin
In South African wine law, a wine from a demarcated area. There are seventeen such regions, some being further divided into wards.

Warren Winiarski, Stag's Leap
The scholarly and detached Warren Winiarski became famous when his Stag's Leap Vineyard Cabernet Sauvignon outshone some Bordeaux classed growths in a 1976 blind tasting in Paris. Winiarski made this wine into a model of sleekly textured, vibrantly fruity Cabernet Sauvignon in 1976, 1977 and 1988. His best wine is the Cabernet Sauvignon Cask 23, which is a selection of the ripest grapes from the Stag's Leap Vineyard. The 1985 Stag's Leap Cask 23 is a California Cabernet of sensual, smoky, "animal" aromas, gloriously ripe tannins and intensely rich fruit; it is unquestionably one of the best wines to have come out of the Golden State during the 1980s. It is also expensive. His 1987 Petite Sirah is a stylish, warm-flavored, spicy wine for much less cost.

There are signs that Winiarski is making great strides with the quality of his white wines, notably Chardonnay, which have always been less highly regarded than his reds. The 1987 Chardonnay Reserve shows a discernible note of toasty oak, but structure, length and subtly defined fruit too. The 1989 Sauvignon Blanc Rancho Chimiles has a good herbaceous nose and a minty, eucalyptus character about it.

A glimpse of the Winiarski winemaking touch can be seen in the excellent-value second range of wines called Hawk's Crest. Winiarski is one of the most gifted winemakers in California, whose special talent is to draw the last ounce of flavor and character from his Stag's Leap grapes.

Winzergenossenschaft
German word for cooperative.

Weingut Hans Wirsching, Franken
This 45 hectare/111 acre German estate in east Franken produces stunning wines, in particular from Silvaner, Müller-Thurgau and Riesling. Average yields run from 65 hectoliters per hectare/3.8 tons per acre for Müller-Thurgau to 40 hectoliters per hectare/2.4 tons per acre for Riesling. Picking is usually delayed, but acid levels do not seem to suffer.

Woody
If a wine spends too long in barrel its fruit may fade, leaving a faded, dry woody taste.

Wyndham Estate, Dalwood, New South Wales
Founded in 1829, the Wyndham Estate was acquired by Orlando in 1990. This is by far the largest of the Hunter Valley wineries and has seen huge expansion since 1970, masterminded by Brian McGuigan. Wyndham's success is due to a clear-sighted recognition of wine drinkers' preferences, so the Wyndham wines are made for easy, early drinking. Although Wyndham's is underrated in Australia, the firm has had great success on export markets. The wines are well-made. Look out for Bin 444 Cabernet Sauvignon and the fragrant Bin 222 Chardonnay-Semillon.

Adam Wynn, Mountadam
Adam Wynn is a loner. As a member of a prominent South Australian wine family, he might have been expected to attend the local, nationally prestigious Roseworthy Wine College. Instead, he pursued his wine studies in Bordeaux with great distinction. The traditional French way of making fine wine has been his model ever since, though like all modern winemakers, Adam sets great store by absolute cleanliness in the cellar.

When the family firm, Wynns, became a public company in 1970, he soon left to found the Mountadam Winery on the High Eden Ridge with help from his father, David Wynn. Of the 28 hectares/69 acres of vineyard planted at Mountadam, over 60 percent is Chardonnay. Since 1984, Adam has been in charge of winemaking. The 1987 Mountadam Chardonnay is an exceptional wine, extremely rich with a length and complexity of flavor that put it in the world class; and like many memorable bottles, it strongly reflects the personality of its maker. Adam Wynn also makes quite exceptional Pinot Noir and often excellent Cabernet Sauvignon. He does not filter his estate wines, which are aged in French Tronçais oak for twelve months before bottling. Annual production of the estate wines is some 7,000 cases, which includes some Rhine Riesling and a new Chardonnay/Pinot Noir sparkling wine. A second range of wines is made at Mountadam under the David Wynn label. These are sourced from bought-in Eden Valley grapes, notably Chardonnay and Shiraz.

X

Xarel-lo
An acidic Catalonian white grape, heavily planted around Barcelona and in the Penedès, where it is an important constituent of the sparkling wines of the region. The variety is also blended, with Parellada and Macabeo, to make unremarkable still wines.

Xynisteri
This is the most widely planted of the white grapes of

Cyprus, and it makes wines that generally are rather dull, although their character and quality vary with the altitude of the vineyard and the date of picking. Xynisteri makes the dessert wine Commandaria, on its own, or blended with the red Mavron.

Xynomavro
The best native Greek variety, and one widely planted in northern Greece. It makes tannic, acidic, deeply colored red wines with the capacity to age, and is also used for blending.

Y

Yarra Yering, Coldstream, Victoria
Established in 1969, this small winery in the Yarra Valley of Australia produces just 3,000 cases a year. Winemaker Dr. Bailey Carrodus makes exceptionally complex and concentrated red wines. The 1987 Yarra Yering Dry Red No 2 is a superb, multi-dimensional wine that will develop well in bottle until the end of this century.

Yeast
Yeasts occur naturally on grape skins and convert the grapes' sugar into alcohol. Nowadays cultured yeasts are often used as well as or instead of the natural yeasts, in order that winemakers can be more certain of the results. Yeasts cannot work at very low temperatures and are mostly killed off once the alcoholic strength reaches around 15 percent.

Yeast autolysis
The breakdown of dead yeast cells in the sediment of a wine, particularly in Champagne after the second fermentation and before *dégorgement*. It gives the wine a characteristic "bready" aroma. Many New World sparkling-wine makers try specifically to avoid this character.

Yeasty
Aroma and flavor often found in quality sparkling wines as a result of autolysis after the second fermentation. The Champenois, however, prefer to use the word "bready."

Yield
Amount of grapes harvested, usually expressed as hectoliters per hectare or tons per acre. The need to restrict yields is widely recognized: quality and quantity seldom go together in the matter of vineyard yield. The French term is *rendement*.

Z

Zevenwacht Wines, Stellenbosch-Kuilsrivier
Relative newcomers in South Africa, these wines have quickly established themselves thanks to the skills of Neil Ellis, now succeeded by Eric Saayman. Certainly an estate to watch in the future as it gets into top gear. Already its Cabernet Sauvignon, Pinot Noir, Rhine Riesling, Gewürztraminer and a blend of Sauvignon Blanc, Chenin Blanc and Riesling look good.

Zibibbo
See Muscat.

Zilavka
The admirable white grape of Bosnia-Herzegovina, which especially around Mostar makes a fine, full, aromatic and alcoholic wine when blended with about 30 percent of other native varieties.

Weingut Zilliken, Mosel-Saar-Ruwer
This is a traditional German cellar, where wines are matured in oak *fuder* and high standards are maintained. It was in fact the estate of the Master Forester of the king of Prussia, and is now owned by his descendent, Hans Joachim Zilliken.

Domaine Zind-Humbrecht, Turckheim
Léonard Humbrecht of Domaine Zind-Humbrecht is one of Alsace's greatest growers and winemakers. His family have been growers in Gueberswihr since 1652, but it was his marriage to Geneviève Zind of Wintzenheim in 1959 and the uniting of the two families' vineyards that created an important viticultural domain of 18 hectares/44.5 acres. Over the last thirty years, the domain has more than doubled in size and now offers a fascinating range of single-vineyard wines from some of the finest sites in Alsace.

Each *cru* at Zind-Humbrecht is separately vinified and separately bottled. The Brand vineyard at Turckheim is based on granite and produces especially elegant Riesling; the Clos Jebsal on complex upland soils within the same commune gives extremely concentrated Pinot Gris. The Herrenweg on rich alluvial soil at the bottom of the Wintzenheim Valley makes a freshly round Gewürztraminer, while the Hengst's example of the same grape is finer but with a powerful depth of flavor that owes much to the pebbly soil.

The Goldert at Gueberswihr, largely composed of limestone, is ideal for the lovely floral Muscat. The Clos St. Urban at Rangen is part of Alsace's most southerly *grand cru*. The soil is volcanic and pervades the flavor of the wine with a minerally ironlike strength, be it made from Gewürztraminer, Riesling or Pinot Gris, all of which are grown in the Humbrecht's Rangen vineyard.

The Clos Windsbuhl at Hunawihr is a recent acquisition. Here the Humbrechts have planted Chardonnay as well as Pinot Gris. Their long-term intention is to make a wine from a blend of both varieties, simply labeled Clos Windsbuhl. It will not be entitled to *appellation contrôlée* status, but it will probably rival a great white Burgundy. The first released vintage is likely to be the 1992.

Léonard Humbrecht's son Olivier, France's first Master of Wine, now makes the wines, while Léonard looks after the vineyards. The style of the wine has become notably more elegant since the 1989 vintage.

Zinfandel
Zinfandel is a peculiarly Californian grape variety. Its probable origin is the Primitivo grape of southern Italy. Zinfandel produces a wide variety of different styles of wine, ranging from heady, raisiny late harvest and Port-style wines, through robust berry-flavored table wines from wineries like Ridge to light red jug wines and even pale blush wines, which are often called White Zinfandel.

Vinification techniques vary from carbonic maceration for early consumption to serious oak aging for long-term drinking. Zinfandel prefers cooler growing conditions, but is also planted in the hot Central Valley for rather jammy jug wines. A little has been introduced into South Africa and also Western Australia, but otherwise it does not stray outside California.

Wine and Food

by David Ridgway

Matching food and wine is an art, but it is an art that should always be fun. It should never, therefore, be made too complicated; it should be treated as one of those games that it is almost impossible to lose. If all else fails, an eccentric match of wine and food can always be passed off as one's own personal taste.

A large part of the secret is to look at the meal as a whole, rather than tackling each dish as a separate entity. Just as each course should balance the one before and the one after, so that one doesn't end up with chicken in everything, so the wines should complement each other as well as the food. Food and wine should suit one's stomach and mood, as well: a combination that works well at dinner may not be welcome at lunch, and the sort of wine that appeals when it is snowing outside may not be so attractive in a heatwave, even if the food is the same.

As in all games, a few rules are a good starting point. "Guidelines", though, is perhaps a better word than "rules": these should not be thought of as unbreakable. As the French put it, "Tous les goûts sont dans la nature", or there is room for everybody's likes and dislikes.

These guidelines can be summarized as follows:
- Light wines before heavy wines
- Young wines before old wines
- Simple wines before complex wines
- Dry wines before sweet wines
- White wines before red wines
- White wine with fish and white meat; red wine with red meat
- Let the sauce decide the wine
- Local wines with local foods

Food and wine have an effect on each other, and that effect should be beneficial. When well matched, food will soften the tannin and lower the acidity of wine; wine will enhance the flavor of food and help both the digestion and the appetite. But, as in all marriages, one partner will dominate. The dominant partner may stimulate the other, but it will still dominate. In wine growing regions this is so well accepted that the traditional food is often simple and intended to show off the wine.

Adhering to this custom is one of the easiest ways of producing a good wine and food marriage. Escargots de Bourgogne, for example, with an Aligoté from the same region; gazpacho with a crisp Jerez *fino;* osso buco with Barolo. All these combinations

are tried and tested, and based on irrefutable logic: local flavors lend themselves to local wines, and even the seemingly unlikely marriage of wild boar with white wine is entirely natural if looked at in a regional context. A splendid German Riesling *Auslese* with local wild boar is a complex and fascinating combination: a classic.

Thinking of Riesling with wild boar can help to elucidate the white wine with fish, red wine with red meat rule. The color of the dish overall is perhaps a better guide to the color of the wine: white wine, then, with pale food, red with dark. Light reds are generally a happier match than white with dark fish like shark; any sort of red could be a mistake with sweetbreads in cream sauce. The reason could lie in the texture of the food: fish is generally less dense than meat so needs a less "dense" wine; as it approaches meat in its denseness so the wine changes, too. However, this should not be overstated: letting the sauce decide the wine is just as important. What this means is simply allowing the flavors of the dish as a whole, not just its staple constituent, to decide one's choice. The somewhat neutral flavor of chicken is an obvious example: with delicate, creamy flavors it will demand a white wine; with assertive, spicy tastes, a red.

The other guidelines are based on entirely practical considerations of what one's palate can cope with. Drinking light wines before heavier ones, and young wines before older ones is all part of allowing a meal to build to a climax; lighter or younger wines do not show to advantage after older or heavier ones, and the palate does not want them. To reverse the natural order would be like offering salmon mousse after roast partridge. Similar reasoning applies to drinking simple wines before complex ones: to do the opposite would make the simple wines look poor in comparison. Equally, a dry wine will taste unpleasantly raw after the palate has been swathed in the richness of a sweet wine.

However, there are times when the food demands that these guidelines be broken. Cheese and foie gras are two such occasions. Many cheeses go best with young wines that have plenty of acidity, yet cheese is usually served towards the end of a meal, necessitating a move back from old wine to young. Foie gras is superb with a sweet, generally botrytized white wine, yet is offered at the beginning of a meal. Very old wines, too, can pose a problem, as they may well have lost body as they have gained in age;

setting them against rich food may overpower them.

So the guidelines are not infallible, nor are they intended to cause anyone to lose sleep. Matching good wine with good food should be enjoyable. In the examples that follow, the choice of wine for each course of a meal should be taken as an indication only; if your local shop doesn't stock Hermitage Blanc, for example, then try something of similar weight and depth of flavor. The only unbreakable rule of matching food and wine is to relax about it.

Aperitif: A good aperitif should sharpen the appetite (if necessary) and relax the company; it should not dull the wits or the palate with excessive alcohol or cloying textures. This does not necessarily rule out sweet drinks, but they must have good balancing acidity; young Sauternes or young *moelleux* Vouvray can both be excellent. The trend towards serving a limited number of wines at a meal means that the same wine can be served as an aperitif and with the first course, whether this is a dry white wine, *fino* Sherry, Sercial Madeira or Champagne; and remember a full meal is still to come.
Manzanilla or *fino* Sherry; chilled young tawny Port (ten year old, for preference); dry sparkling wines and most dry white wines.

First courses
Soups: Soups do not really require wine, but if one is to be served then it is traditional to choose a dry fortified wine — which may even be an integral part of the soup. Since one does not really need extra liquid with soup, the greater concentration of a fortified wine or even a spirit can work well.
Fino Sherry; Sercial or Verdelho Madeira; dry Vermouth; whatever wine or spirit is in the soup.

Foie gras: This is probably the richest first course to serve. It may be in the form of pâté, or it may be fresh. If the latter, it may be served hot, in which case it has more affinities to meat in general and is best served with a red wine. In all other cases a sweet white wine should be chosen. Much will also depend on whether it is duck or goose liver, the former being much more pungent and requiring a more assertive wine. But both, being luscious in texture, need a wine that is rich and has good acidity and, therefore, fairly young.
Alsace *Sélection de Grains Nobles;* good young Sauternes or Monbazillac; California late harvest Gewürztraminer; Cabernet Franc, if served hot.

Smoked fish: The powerful, pungent flavor and oiliness of smoked salmon, trout or mackerel can be difficult to match with wine. Gewürztraminer is often recommended, but can be too cloying. If the fish is not too heavily smoked, then some whites are good; if the fish is very smoky then try dry Sherry or dry Madeira.
Napa Valley Sauvignon Blanc; Swiss whites from Valais; *fino* Sherry; Sercial Madeira.

Pâtés, terrines and forcemeats: This heading covers everything from vegetable terrine through salmon rillettes to classic pâtés and terrines and have one thing in common: they all need light, soft, young and fruity wines. The guideline on choosing local wine with local fare comes in useful here, with coarse pâtés needing rustic, fruity wines. Pâtés in general

lend themselves well to white wines, and in Burgundy, the home of many of France's finest pâtés, it is common to serve a crisp young wine like Aligoté or Mâcon Blanc to cut through the fattiness.
Sylvaner; Crépy from Savoie; Coulanges-la-Vineuse from Burgundy; Corbières.

Snails, frogs' legs: These are two dishes in which the sauce is more important than the main ingredient when choosing a wine. The most common way of preparing both is with garlic butter, which needs a crisp, dry white wine; in wine growing regions a red or white wine sauce is common, in which case simply drink the same wine as is used in the sauce.
Bourgogne Aligoté; Loire Valley or New Zealand Sauvignon Blanc.

Asparagus and artichokes: Both are difficult to match, and can bring out odd flavors in wine. Robust, fortified wines work well, as do fairly alcoholic, wood aged whites.
Vin Jaune; Sherry; Montilla; fat, oaky Chardonnay from California or Australia.

Melon: The combination of sugar and acidity can make the choice of wine difficult. The simplest and best answer is fortified wine. Young tawny Port; *vin doux naturel* from Banyuls or Maury.

Ham: Cured meats, sausages need light, fruity reds. Beaujolais, most reds made from Gamay; Dolcetto.

Wild mushrooms and truffles: These are more often used as part of a dish rather than as a dish in themselves. If used as a first course they adapt well to a good round red with some bottle age wine that is earthy and slightly vegetal to echo their flavor.
Pomerol; Washington State Merlot; Barolo.

Salads: Much depends on the salad ingredients. A plain green salad requires a simple dry white only; for crab salad, match the wine to the crab. Care should be taken over the amount of vinegar used in the dressing: lemon juice is better if there is good wine to be drunk. Or, if Sherry vinegar is used, light Sherry can work well as an accompaniment.
Sauvignon Blanc or Chardonnay from California or Australia; *fino* Sherry.

Pasta: Pasta is a neutral base for other tastes, and it is these others that decide the wine. Tagliatelle with shellfish needs a good dry white. Spaghetti bolognese cries out for young, fruity red.
With fish: Soave Classico; Sauvignon Blanc from the Loire Valley or New Zealand. With meat: Valpolicella; Chianti: With cream sauce, light Italian Chardonnay; dry German Riesling: With tomato sauce: earthy red like Barbera or southern Italian.

Eggs: Eggs can bring out the worst in a wine; choose soft reds without too much tannin. Even when eggs and wine do match, the combination does little to flatter the wine, so avoid uncorking anything too expensive.
Soft reds: young Chianti; Valpolicella; German or Austrian red.

All fish: Fish is easier than meat to match with wine because it usually is prepared more simply.

Shellfish: It is useful to make a distinction between molluscs and crustaceans here. Molluscs like oysters, clams or mussels are often served raw and need light young whites as their saltiness will spoil a weightier white. Crustaceans, whether hot or cold, are more wine friendly. and provide an opportunity to searve rich, buttery Chardonnays or dryish *Auslese* Rieslings. Lobster in a rich cream and butter sauce with a ten year old Corton Charlemagne is one of the greatest gastronomic treats in the world.
Molluscs: Muscadet, simple young Chablis, non-vintage Champagne. Crustaceans: if plain, non-vintage Champagne; good mature Chablis; Alsace Riesling; If with rich sauce: top Chardonnay from Burgundy or Australia; Hermitage Blanc.

Freshwater fish: Fish like pike or trout can have an earthy flavour which is best matched with a crispness in the wine, but these fish are also delicate in flavor and easily overpowered. Salmon is more robust and needs a richer wine; try a slightly chilled light red. Good German Riesling; *Grand Cru* Chablis; Savennières; Loire reds; Beaujolais.

White sea fish: Very easy to match. The texture, delicacy of white fish puts most white wines at their ease. Elegant whites and Champagne.

Fish stews: Often strongly flavored, so match them to a local wine or use the same wine that is used in the cooking. Pair bouillabaisse with the white wine of Cassis, (the Provence A.O.C., not the blackcurrant liqueur used in *kir*), or richer dishes like creole gumbo with something more substantial, like a reserve Chardonnay from Napa Valley. Eels or lamprey are often cooked in red wine sauces, in which case they will need good medium-bodied reds. Bear in mind that stews contain plenty of liquid and need less to wash them down than drier dishes.
Well—flavored dry whites with fairly high alcohol: Cassis, Bandol Blanc; white Rioja (not too oaky); young red Médoc or Graves with Lamproies à la Bordelaise.

Oily fish: Sardines and mackerel, espesially smoked mackeral, need something sharp and tangy, like Sancerre or Vinho Verde, Muscadet or Gros Plant. Shark and tuna are meatier fish and will go equally well with white or red; dry rosé can be good. The choice of wine for such fish will depend greatly on whether it is being eaten before or instead of meat. Manzanilla; Loire Valley Sauvignon Blanc; Vinho Verde; Rosé de Provence; Loire or Alsace red.

White meat

Pork: Much depends on how it is cooked. Roast pork, in many parts of Germany, is paired with dry Riesling to balance its richness; in Portugal, however, it may be cooked in Port and accompanied by a tannic red. Generally an easy meat to match with either white or red.
German or Alsace Riesling; Sylvaner; Douro red.

Chicken: Provides one of the most neutral backgrounds to wine. Choose the wine according to the sauce: fairly hefty reds with tomatoes and green peppers; assertive whites with a cream and mushroom sauce.

Pinot Gris; Chardonnay; red Médoc or Graves, Côtes de Provence; virtually anything.

Turkey: Like chicken, turkey will go with almost any wine. But since it is the festive dish *par excellence* , it seems logical to match it, on festive occasions, with the most festive of wines.
Champagne; Pauillac or St. Julien; Napa Cabernet Sauvignon.

Veal: In flavor and texture, veal is a lighter, softer version of beef. Red Bordeaux works well, but one could also choose an assertive white.
Red Bordeaux (preferably from St. Julien); Alsace Tokay-Pinot Gris; Chardonnay; Hermitage Blanc.

Red meat

Beef: This is one of the most red wine-friendly dishes, however it is cooked. Be it a simple roast or served with a rich truffle sauce, most reds stand up and show well.
Cabernet Sauvignon from anywhere; Syrah/Shiraz; Pinot Noir; Rioja Reserva; Barolo.

Lamb: Nearly as simple as beef to match with wine, but the extra fat means that wines with more acidity work best.
Red Bordeaux from Pauillac or Graves; Chinon; Portuguese reds; Chianti.

Feathered game: The longer game birds are hung the gamier they become—and the richer and gamier should be the wine. Mature Pomerol or Hermitage have that rich, earthy flavor required.
Pomerol; Syrah/Shiraz; mature red Burgundy.

Furred game: This covers hare (and, these days, rabbit) as well as venison and wild boar, and the flavors vary tremendously. Hare and rabbit are rank in flavor and need something mature and robust, like Burgundy from a good year, or Châteauneuf-du-Pape with ten years' bottle age. The same wines will go with wild boar or the beefier-tasting venison. It is common in Germany to serve a good mature Riesling with wild boar.
Côte de Nuits, Châteauneuf-du-Pape; Brunello di Montalcino.

Duck: Wild duck comes under the heading of game, but domestic duck is a very different bird. It should not be excessively fatty, but much depends on how it is reared. For reasonably lean birds, reds are preferable to whites, if they have good body, fair tannin, but no bitterness. Lovers of white could choose rich tastes with good acidity.
White Burgundy; Alsace Pinot Blanc; Rioja Reserva; medium bodied red Bordeaux from the Médoc or Graves; Pinot Noir.

Goose: Like turkey, this is a festive dish, but its fattiness makes whites with good acidity a good bet, or reds with reasonably high tannin.
Alsace Pinot Blanc; Aligoté; St. Emilion; Cabernet Franc.

Casseroles: A wide category, but all casseroles tend to be strongly flavored and so need assertive wines. Some wines, that one would normally consider too pronounced in taste to go with plain meat, often

work well with casseroles. Cassoulet with a good rustic Cahors is wonderful.
Cahors; Côtes de Provence; Zinfandel; Chianti Classico.

Hot meat pies: These are basically casseroles encased in pastry. The wines should therefore be similar to those which partner well with casseroles, though toned down a little because of the pastry.
Côtes du Ventoux; Gigondas; Hunter Valley Shiraz.

All offal: Wines with too much astringency tend to bring out the natural bitterness in offal.

Liver: This needs a fairly simple backdrop with obvious flavors.
Saumur Champigny; Bulls' Blood.

Kidneys: The noblest of offal, and the offal most associated with gastronomy, kidneys do however, present problems, with their bitterness and pungency. Choose wines with soft tannin and good body.
Pinot Noir; Zinfandel.

Tripe: Wines with plenty of acidity will balance the greasiness and help lighten the texture.
Crémant d'Alsace; Sylvaner; very tart cider.

Sweetbreads: These lend themselves to a great range of wines. In Bordeaux, where they are often cooked in Sauternes, a young Sauternes is the perfect accompaniment; alternatively, a Savigny-lès-Beaune will perfectly match the delicacy of pan-fried sweetbreads. No powerful, spicy reds here.
Late harvest Sémillon; Alsace Tokay-Pinot Gris; light Pinot Noir.

All cheeses: Cheese helps most wines; it will do little to make great wines greater, but it covers a multitude of sins in lesser ones.

Blue cheese: The saltiness of these means that they are often eaten with sweet wines; witness the classic marriage of roquefort and Sauternes, or stilton and vintage Port.
Sauternes; late harvest Gewürztraminer; vintage Port.

Soft cheese: Like game, soft cheeses change in flavor from youth to maturity. Generally speaking they need the assertiveness and fresh acidity of young Syrah or Pinot Noir. Alsace Gewürztraminer with münster is a classic combination.
Pinot Noir; Syrah/Shiraz; Grenache; Gewürztraminer.

Hard cheese: When the wine trade advocates buying on an apple and selling on cheese this is the cheese it means. A mouthful of mature cheddar or cantal will do wonders for many a wine. The milder English cheeses need medium weight reds like Bordeaux; hard Swiss cheeses need full bodied whites.
Cabernet Sauvignon; Nebbiolo; Hermitage; Alsace Tokay-Pinot Gris.

Goats cheese: Best with white wine. Chavignol and Sancerre is a classic combination, but all need either high acidity in a wine or sweetness (with balancing high acidity).
Sancerre; Alsace Tokay-Pinot Blanc; Sauternes, young Gamay.

All desserts: These are often thought to be very difficult to match with wine because of their sweetness, but the alternative of sticking to water is surely defeatist. Even if a sweet wine does not match the dish perfectly, it will still allow one to wallow in lusciousness, which is what one should be allowed to do at the end of a meal.

Cakes and pastries: These can be a wonderful backdrop to late harvest wines. An almost dry almond tart with Sauternes is divine.
Sauternes; Vouvray *moelleux;* sweet *oloroso* Sherry; late harvest, new world Semillons and Rieslings from the New World.

Puddings: Steamed puddings can be heavy, and benefit from sparkling wines like Asti Spumante; one of the few foods, in fact, that Asti will match. Light fortified Muscats are also good, and cream Sherry can match Christmas pudding very well, especially if it has some bottle age. If a sparkling wine is chosen, it should not be dry, as is the case all too often in France.
Muscat de Rivesaltes; Asti Spumante; Bual or Malmsey Madeira; cream Sherry.

Meringues: Only a fortified wine will stand up to all the sugar, but if they are served with fruit then the fruit should decide the wine.
Moscatel; Australian Liqueur Muscat.

Crème Brûlée, crème caramel: Eggs and sugar, which separately are among the greatest enemies of wine, here combine to make a most amenable backdrop for most wood aged fortified wines.
Tawny Port; cream Sherry; Bual or Malmsey Madeira; Marsala.

Chocolate: Can easily overpower wines. A light chocolate mousse can be excellent with a rich Sauternes, but otherwise choose a fortified wine.
Sauternes; tawny Port; *vin doux naturel* from Banyuls or Maury.

Ice cream: If served on its own, rather than as part of a dish, its coldness tends to dull the palate so a subtle wine will be completely lost. The best choice is very pungent fortified wines.
Australian Liqueur Muscat; Moscatel; Lagrima; *vin de paille.*

Soufflés: Let the flavoring decide. With a Grand Marnier soufflé, serve Grand Marnier; with raspberry soufflé, an *eau de vie framboise.*
Liqueur to match the flavor of the soufflé.

Fruits and nuts: Dried fruits are easy to match with all sorts of wine, fortified and unfortified, though Port and Madeira are the classics. Fresh fruit is trickier because of its acidity, though peaches go well with Sauternes or the lighter California late harvest wines. An alternative is to go for an aesthetic combination, like pink Champagne with strawberries.
Pink Champagne; Sauternes; light California late harvest wines, Port; Madeira; *vin santo* with dried fruit and nuts.

Digestif: After lunch drinks are generally lighter than after dinner drinks: offer young, light brandies

and *eaux de vie* as pick-me-ups after the lunch, and older Cognacs and Armagnacs after dinner, when there is the time to enjoy them. It might be appropriate to match the brandy to the wines that have gone before: a *grappa* to finish an Italian meal, for example, or an Alsace *eau de vie* after an Alsatian meal.

Serving Wine

Matching the right wine with the right food is a great part of the pleasure of drinking well, but serving a wine badly can spoil a lot of that pleasure. A great wine is unlikely to be ruined, if it is poorly served, but it could lose a lot of its complexity.

The easiest way to ruin a red wine is to serve it too warm. At too high a temperature red wine will lose its fruit, and the alcohol will become too volatile, and while a wine poured too cold will soon warm up in the glass, the reverse is unlikely to happen. The old adage that red wines should be served at room temperature is largely to blame; room temperature, when the rule was developed, was cooler than it is in many a centrally-heated modern house. The tannins found in modern reds are also often softer than those of generations ago.

The ideal temperature will however vary according to the time of year; in summer the wine should be a few degrees cooler than in winter, whatever the room temperature. Older wines should be served closer to cellar temperature than younger ones, and less tannic wines can be served cooler than more tannic ones. As a rule of thumb the best all round temperature is around 62°F/17°C; a wine at this temperature in a room at 75°F/24°C will gain about 10°F/5°C in half an hour. But red Bordeaux needs to be very slightly warmer than red Burgundy.

White wines suffer more from the opposite problem: chilling them too much dulls the aroma and flavor. A temperature of 50°F/10°C, or slightly below cellar temperature is right for most white wines and Champagne. Also remember that the colder the wine, the more people tend to drink.

The question that probably causes the most controversy is that of whether or not to decant. There are a number of reasons why one might decide to decant a wine. The original one was to separate a wine from its sediment; another is to allow a wine to breathe more rapidly, which may be a good or a bad thing depending on the age of the wine. Bordeaux has traditionally decanted its wines for both these reasons, but also partly because the great wines of Bordeaux have always been owned by the aristocracy and landed gentry who were more likely to possess expensive crystal decanters than the peasant farmers (as they tended to be in the past) of Burgundy. In Burgundy there is seldom any objection to drinking sediment with the wine. More practically, Burgundy has generally less tannin than Bordeaux, so the wine supports decanting less well; the fruit can fade rapidly in a decanter.

If the wine is too cold, decanting from a cold bottle to a warmer decanter is also a quick way of warming a young wine a few degrees without harming it; it also saves the time taken in warming up the cold bottle. Very old wines, though must be treated more gently; chilling the decanter slightly will avoid shock to such wines.

From about 1920 to about 1950 it was usual to decant Champagne as well as red wines; still white wines, too, were often decanted. The reason was simply that all wines look beautiful in a good decanter, and Champagne could show off its color and effervescence. Decanting Champagne has fortunately died out, but decanting an old Sauternes or Riesling is worth considering, particularly as white wines so rarely receive adequate breathing time. Alsace Riesling, in particular, can gain complexity from half an hour in a carafe, though Chardonnay seems to need this less. Most Champagnes benefit from being opened five to ten minutes before being served.

Vintage Port is traditionally decanted. Sediment is one reason; the necessity of letting the wine breathe another. Old vintages need five hours in a decanter to open properly; newer vintages, from the twenties, or the turn of the century, need three to four hours to allow the excess alcohol to disappear.

Perhaps, then, it is better to look at when not to decant. Burgundies are rarely decanted, for example, and with old wines (over twenty years old), great care should be taken to avoid losing their often fragile bouquet. The oldest, most delicate wines are best not decanted. Old wines are best decanted at cellar temperature, since the cooler the wine the less chance there is of oxidation. The wine should be poured into a decanter held almost horizontal. This way bubbling of the wine will be avoided. Older wines, too, should not be decanted more than half an hour before the meal, though younger wines need not be treated with such caution and may be decanted up to four hours in advance. If in doubt, though, remember that it is better for a wine to open out in the glass at the end of the meal, than too soon in the decanter.

The glasses themselves are also important. Wine glasses should be as thin as possible, and should be of the appropriate shape. A good all-purpose glass is tulip shaped and should not be filled to more than one third. The right shape will not only help to contain the bouquet, but will also direct the wine to the appropriate part of the tongue, so emphasizing or subduing the acidity; the right size will enable the wine to be swirled in the glass to release the bouquet, without spilling wine everywhere.

A Memorable Meal

There are two ways of planning a meal. The most usual way is to start with the food and then agonize over the wines to go with it; the second, and for me the more interesting way, is to start with the wine and choose the food to complement it. It is the more precise way of doing things, and it is also the most practical way for most people at home faced with a limited choice of wines.

Whenever possible, I like to serve wines in pairs. The contrast between them makes for the most interesting comparisons; but this is, it should be stressed, not a contest, either between the wines or between the drinkers. Instead it is a way of drawing more attention to the wines.

The starting point is the aperitif. This is as much a moment of détente and conviviality as of wetting of the appetite; it is also the only point in the meal at which the palate is completely fresh.

As this is the ideal meal, it must have the ideal

aperitif: Champagne, therefore, and preferably a Champagne containing a high proportion of Chardonnay. My first thought would be the finest of all Krug Champagnes, Clos du Mesnil, but since I enjoy old Champagne and find even the first vintage of Clos du Mesnil, the 1979, still rather young, I would stay in the same village, Le Mesnil-sur-Oger, and choose a wine from the excellent house of Salon. I would opt, in fact, for the first vintage of its *cuvée* S, the 1971, which is now reaching perfection.

So to the white wines. It would be interesting to choose two Chardonnays from the same vintage as the Champagne, and my favorites here are Corton-Charlemagnes, one from the house of Louis Latour, the other from Rapet. Drinking these two side by side can only enhance the individuality of each.

With two great white Burgundies with the fish, the contrast of a great red Bordeaux is called for. The vintage must change and I would put it back by a decade, to 1961. This year is only now beginning to show its true worth. It can also, conveniently, boast two arch rivals, Palmer and Latour; in their different ways these two wines are the epitome of this excellent vintage. Serving them together brings out the best in them and in the food.

Now, the question is whether to move to cheese before dessert or the other way round. Personally, being more gourmand than gourmet, and a lover of Port with cheese, I would put the dessert first; this not only changes the pace of the meal but also allows a greater choice of wines. For the dessert wines I would return to the 1971 vintage; one of my pair would be Schloss Vollrads *Beerenauslese* from the Rheingau, and the other, for greater contrast, the best Sauternes of that year, from Château Climens.

Then to the cheese, and the Port. Obviously this must be vintage, this being the ideal meal, and the vintage that is showing the best at the moment is 1963. For concentration, style and indescribable depth of flavor that 1963 must be Quinta do Noval Nacional, a rarity made from ungrafted vines.

With the difficult part of the fantasy behind, all that is left is the choice of food. Salon le Mesnil S 1971 needs little or nothing; perhaps just a few plain puff pastry strips to harmonize with the bakery flavors of the Champagne. With the Corton-Charlemagnes, though, I would be more ambitious. I would prepare two different fish dishes, and the first would be langouste in a girolles and cream sauce. Mushrooms are going to be the common denominator throughout this ideal meal, so the baked sea bass to follow the langouste would be stuffed with cèpes.

The main course, designed to enhance the Palmer and Latour 1961, would be a simple roast crown of lamb with, to make the wines work a little harder, a casserole of truffles and foie gras.

It is the dessert that poses the hardest problems for us gourmands. The desire for sugar has to be balanced against the enjoyment of the wine, and I would settle on a fig bourdaloue, where the vanilla cream and light caramel would blend perfectly with the light vanilla and caramel flavors of the wine.

Choosing the cheese is much easier, but few cheeses go better with vintage Port than stilton and mature cheddar.

But this is only an ideal meal so far: to become a memorable one it needs good company and good conversation. Fine wine and fine food only have meaning if they find a receptive audience.

The Sommelier

The profession of sommelier is probably the third oldest in the world; the first sommeliers, no doubt, were Dionysius' cup bearers on Mount Olympus. For many people, though, it has the same stigma as the oldest profession of all.

The term sommelier dates back to the Middle Ages and could be derived from the French term for beasts of burden — *bêtes de somme*. This is not to suggest that the poor sommelier was treated thus; rather, it was beasts of burden that brought wine and other provisions to the great houses of the time, and it was only the most noble of families that drank anything other than the local wine.

Another derivation is from the word *somme* which used to mean a duty or an office.

The duties of a sommelier have changed since those years. They cover, in fact, a host of different roles, from pouring everyday wine in inexpensive bistros to taking part in (and preferably winning) wine tasting contests. These extremes, however, are seldom found together in one person.

Leaving aside both extremes, to be an efficient and (one hopes) unpretentious sommelier requires knowledge of a broad range of subjects. Languages and basic enology, for example: any sommelier worth his salt should be able to pontificate in three or four languages on such amusing topics as the malolactic fermentation and the yeast strains best suited to a must with more than 7 percent alcohol in it. Such information is useful not only when dealing with winemakers, but can also come in handy should he or she want (God forbid) to be pompous with a client.

Geography, too, is important, not just in the sense of knowing the layout of the vineyards, but in knowing their soils. When he has finished on the topic of yeasts, a good sommelier should be able to extol the merits of Kimmeridgian or Portland soil for Chablis, for example. Then there is the history of wine: the family trees of the major wine producing families, together with the consequences of the likes of Prohibition in the United States; the battle of Castillon of 1453 or the Methuen Treaty of 1703.

A certain financial acumen is useful, too, as the wines in a restaurant cellar could easily be worth several millions of pounds or dollars, and the buying or selling of wine depends very largely on predicted inflation rates and bank borrowing rates. All this of course is in addition to the sommelier's more public role as somebody well versed in matching the best food to the best wines.

Perhaps the single most important attribute of a good sommelier, though, is an understanding of human nature. Not only must he be able to pacify the unruly, but he must also be able to interpret a client's needs: does a request for a light wine, for example, really mean something light in body and alcohol, or does it mean something light in price? In fact, it is probably only in the field of actually serving wine that the modern sommelier's duties coincide with those of this medieval counterpart. He must still know the order in which different ranks of nobility must be served, and he must have a good memory, for woe betide the sommelier who forgets what a customer drank last time — even if last time was five years ago.

Memorable Bottles

by Frank Prial

It had been tedious in Hungary — a week of bureaucrats and red tape, bad food and dull wine. The Malev jet from Budapest landed at Zurich at 11 a.m. and we were soon on the autoroute speeding towards Basel. Three hours after the greyness of what was then the Eastern Bloc, we were at the lovely old Drei Königin Hotel, on a terrace which juts out over the Rhine, toasting free enterprise with a bottle of Krug.

Was that the best bottle I've ever tasted? We said so then. But that was after a week of sensory and political deprivation — even the mild Hungarian version — and any wine would have seemed delicious. Besides, that particular bottle was more than great Champagne, it was, for us, a reaffirmation of Western values.

Is there such a thing as a great wine in the abstract? Can wine's pleasures be separated from time and place and people? Formal tastings fade from memory. Trying to recall the best bottle at one of them, an expert will say: "I'll have to consult my notes …"

I can remember the taste of an inexpensive Sauvignon de Touraine at a seaside restaurant in Martinique twenty years ago, but I can't for the life of me recall some First Growth Bordeaux tasted in the cellars where they were made.

In 1977, when Eric de Rothschild took over the management of Château Lafite-Rothschild from his uncle Baron Elie de Rothschild, he invited a few people to spend a weekend at the château and taste every good vintage made there since Baron James de Rothschild had bought the place in 1868.

Consulting my notes — as they say — I see that for dinner on September 30 we drank the 1949, 1929, 1900 and the 1888 Lafites. For lunch the next day, we were served the 1959, 1934 and 1873. With dinner that night, we drank 1953, 1945, 1918, 1893, 1869 and 1921.

The 1869 was superb — striking proof that fine wines can indeed live long and distinguished lives. But my recollection of those wines is not a visceral thing. That I reserve for the tasting itself, in that magnificent old country house, filled with flowers and memories. There were the walks in the gardens between tasting sessions, while the leaves drifted down; there was the Pol Roger before dinner, the talk of great wines and great meals, the company of wine connoisseurs who were modest about what they knew.

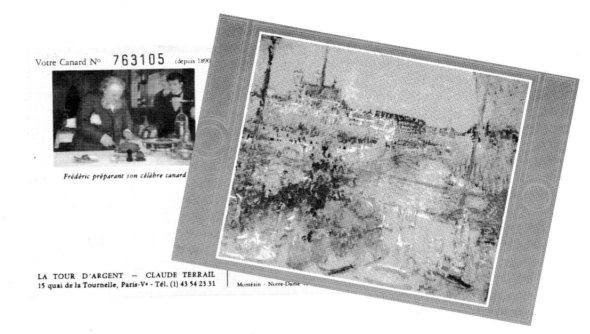

In short, the wines were extraordinary, but it was the event that made them memorable.

Good wines, like good times, cannot always be planned ahead. On an assignment in Pakistan some years ago, I had acclimatized myself to the strict Muslim rules against alcohol and was looking ahead glumly to several weeks of total abstinence in sweltering Karachi. Until an American diplomat, a teetotaller himself, recalled that there was some wine available at the consulate's mini-supermarket.

Sure enough, an entire shelf was given over to (mostly Californian) wines. I managed to find half a dozen Louis Martini Cabernets and an equal number of white wines bottled by Torres of Spain. Overjoyed, I lugged them back to my room at the Hotel Intercontinental and called up a couple of other journalists marooned there with me.

We — I think there were four of us — had dinner in the room and, with great facility, polished off the twelve bottles of wine. The Torres whites, cooled in the bathtub, were particularly delicious. Opening a Torres white now should, I know, conjure up images of bullfights and dark-eyed senoritas. I see — and smell — sunbaked Karachi where wine in any form was and still is forbidden.

Château Filhot is one of the best properties in Sauternes. It is not Yquem, of course, but then nothing else is, either. I was lunching one day at the Tour d'Argent with the late André Mentzelopoulous, the man who remade Château Margaux. It

ABOVE: Almost as thrilling as sipping wine at the three–star La Tour d'Argent restaurant in Paris is a visit to its legendary wine cellar.

was a delightful lunch and as it came to an end he suggested some Champagne as a fitting finale.

We decided to look at the wine card and there, almost unnoticed among the dessert wines, was a half bottle of 1911 Château Filhot for U.S.$20.

"I wouldn't recommend it," said the wine steward. "The label is almost all gone and the color is quite dark".

Yes, but a 1911 wine for U.S.$20. We ordered it. The color was dark but the taste, even after seventy-five years, was unforgettable; old, long past its prime, but still redolent of honey, almonds and all the spices of the Levant. In five minutes, the wine was dead. Exposure to the air. But what a fascinating five minutes. A great wine? No. A memorable wine? Oh, yes.

The Filhot had, at least, a pedigree. Not all memorable wines do. Swiss red wine is often made from the Pinot Noir grape. A hundred miles away, it produces the great wines of Burgundy. In Switzerland, it becomes harsh, often unpleasant wine that is best passed up for Beaujolais. Well, most of the time.

We had scrambled halfway down the long but safe path from the Gornergrat to Zermatt one clear August day and were probably fatigued as much by the stupendous scenery as the thin air and the occasional slippery slope. We came to a small heavy-timbered inn set in the center of a meadow. One could munch on a sausage, sip a beer or a glass of wine while gazing down the valley towards Zermatt and beyond.

The red wine came in liters. The top screwed off: the wine was drinkable — just. But as we poured a glass, young people waved from the cable cars high above and the first sky-divers of the day floated down into the wildflowers around us. The scene, the view, the day — were unforgettable. And, purely by association, so was that scruffy Pinot Noir.

Memorable bottles? There was that night in Beverly Hills ... We'd had a magnificent dinner at Jean Léon's La Scala, one of the last of the great restaurants in Los Angeles. Léon, who has his own vineyards and winery in Spain, knows the importance of a good bottle to a great meal. We had finished, said goodnight and were piling into our car for the trip back to Malibu. Jean appeared at the window. "For the trip out to the coast", he said, and passed us a magnum of Dom Perignon and two glasses — for the thirty minutes ride along the beach.

A great wine? Perhaps not. A memorable wine? Ask our driver; she had to watch the road while we worked on that magnum in the back seat.

Obviously, in this writer's opinion at least, memorable bottles often have little or nothing to do with the quality of the wine within. Which is not to say that quality never plays a role in determining what is memorable and what is not.

George Linton is a Hungarian and a veterinarian. He is also a wine collector's wine collector. Actually, that's not entirely true; George drinks his wines and enjoys them immensely — something most collectors rarely do. For them the pleasure is possession; drinking the wine is losing possession of it. They are like collectors of first editions who would never cut the leaves of one of their books.

George Linton, who lives in the San Francisco area, began collecting wine forty years ago. Once, he picked up an importer's license — not difficult in the U.S. — to make his collecting easier. Later, he

opened a retail shop — for two hours a week — for the same reason. It enabled him to buy wines he could not buy as a mere consumer. California wineries interested in completing their own wine libraries call George Linton. Invariably he has more of their wines than they do.

Dinner with Linton may begin with three different Champagnes, perhaps three examples of Roederer Cristal, followed by three Beaulieu Vineyards Private Reserve Cabernets from the 1960s, followed by three Bordeaux First Growths from 1945. Linton dinners are small and intimate, usually consisting of eight people. The food is excellent and the conversation, which he dominates, is sparkling — mostly scandalous tales about the wine trade. Once again, the ambience turns great wines into memorable wines.

It was during a visit to George Linton's only-open-two-hours-a-week retail shop that I first met Jeremiah Tower, the chef and creator of famous California restaurants such as the Santa Fé Grill and Stars. I was poking round in the profusion of bottles and cases when a young Englishman came in and greeted George with:

"I've just had the most extraordinary tasting in my life up at the Mondavi Winery. They set it up yesterday for some wine writer from New York".

I was the wine writer, as I explained to Jeremiah after we'd been introduced, and it was indeed an extraordinary tasting.

Bob Mondavi is an extraordinary winemaker and the most ardent of all advocates for California wine. I've had many a Mondavi tasting since then but they never fail to astonish. To make a point about his wines, Mondavi will pull out and open First Growths from three vintages and rare white Burgundies from six. The tasting that so impressed Jeremiah Tower included, as I recall, some thirty rare, or at least very expensive, French and California wines.

But the most memorable bottle I can recall sharing at the Mondavi winery was not a Mondavi wine at all. I had turned up at the winery for the first time ever, unknown and unannounced. I was immediately asked to lunch. At table were Mondavi, André Tchelistcheff, the doyen of California winemakers, Louis Martini, Brother Timothy, winemaker for the Christian Brothers, and Australian winemaker Len Evans. Len Evans had brought with him a bottle of Grange Hermitage, then as now Australia's most famous red wine.

It was a superb bottle. But what made it especially memorable for me was stumbling into a lunch with four of the legendary figures of the California wine business and sampling with them, for the first time, a truly great wine.

Hugh Johnson, who well may be the best known wine writer in the English language, lives in a magnificent old house in Essex. The foundations are all that remains of a building listed in the Domesday Book. In fact there are two separate foundations and consequently two separate wine cellars.

Johnson is of the opinion that no one should visit a wine cellar without a glass in one hand and, preferably, a bottle of Champagne in the other. The trick is to lead him on in the first cellar to the point where the bottle is empty. With luck, he will produce another for the second cellar. I don't rightly recall what Champagne we drank, but hearing Johnson expound on his wines and others

LEFT: Elizabeth-Lily Bollinger ran her family's Champagne house from the time of her husband Jacques' death in 1941 through the harsh occupation years until her own death at age 78 in 1977. She was a skilled taster and, even in later life, cycled regularly through the Bollinger vineyards.

in a cellar that predates the Norman Conquest is enough to qualify any bottle as memorable.

Even more memorable perhaps, is a bottle of the bubbly I shared once with Sacha Lichine. His father, the unforgettable Alexis Lichine, had died a few months earlier and by special dispensation from the French authorities had been buried among the vines at his beloved Château Prieuré-Lichine in the Médoc, north of Bordeaux.

Sacha had invited me to walk out in the vineyard with him to see the simple grave on a slight rise with a view of, besides the Prieuré, half a dozen world famous wine properties. It was a sad moment so we brought along a bottle of Champagne to lift our spirits. And, there, amid the vines Alexis had loved, we toasted his memory and each other. A great Champagne? I can't recall. A memorable Champagne? No need to ask.

Champagne must certainly be the most evocative of wines. How many moments — solemn, victorious, tender — became indelible in someone's mind because a glass of Champagne made them special? Christian Bizot, the president of Champagne

Bollinger, once served a 1914 Bollinger at his home in Ay, near Epernay.

The wine was almost amber in color and its effervescence was only a memory. But what a time it recalled. The Archduke Ferdinand had been assassinated on June 28 and by early September, German artillery was shelling Rheims cathedral. By the time the 1914 vintage had been picked, the vineyards were in enemy territory; Von Moltke's troops had smashed through the Champagne country and were at Meaux, not 40 kilometers/25 miles from Paris.

That fall, the Allies pushed the Germans north of Rheims in the great Battle of the Marne. When the wine was made the following year the invaders were gone. The slaughter would go on for another four years but not for another twenty-six years would the German conquerors once again rule in Champagne. What incredible times that bottle must have known.

Has anyone ever really had a good bottle of wine on an airplane? Perhaps on the old Boeing Clippers, when passengers actually left their seats and moved to a dining compartment to be served. And what

LEFT: The 1914 Bollinger was harvested behind enemy lines. The Germans had fought through the Champagne country that summer and were not pushed back until November. The wine was still drinkable over 60 years later.

ABOVE: A typical wine list on Air France's Concorde between New York and Paris. Not listed is the iced vodka that always accompanies the fresh caviar.

VINS BLANCS

Bourgogne

CHABLIS "Les Blanchots" 1984

*Ce Chablis d'un beau jaune aux reflets verts au délicat nez floral,
se caractérise par de subtiles et fougueuses sensations en bouche.*
This beautiful yellow Chablis with green highlights has a delicate
flower scent and exudes both a subtle and strong taste.

Bordeaux

SAUTERNES BARSAC CHATEAU CLIMENS 1979

*Ce premier cru de Sauternes, vous offre toutes les qualités d'un grand vin liquoreux.
Les vendanges tardives lui procurent une douceur et un parfum inimitables.*
Sauternes offers the palate all the qualities of a great, sweet white wine,
wich gets its unique smoothness and fragrance from the late harvest of its grapes

VINS ROUGES

Bordeaux

CHATEAU GRUAUD LAROSE 1980

*Ce Saint-Julien allie une belle couleur grenat
aux parfums de caramel, fruits rouges et a une belle souplesse.*
This Saint Julien, combines a rich garnet-red with an aroma
of caramel and red fruits and a marvellous lingering aftertaste.

Bourgogne

VOSNE ROMANÉE "Les Malconsorts" 1982

*Ce vin né en Bourgogne, d'un bon millésime,
vous offre un délicieux parfum de fruits rouges et une grande délicatesse.*
This red Burgundy of a good wintage exudes a delicate
and delicious bouquet of red fruits.

CHAMPAGNE

LAURENT PERRIER "Cuvée grand siècle"

---

about the dirigibles? The Hindenburg dining room seated twenty or thirty in front of huge windows that gave a panoramic view of the world below. I have seen an old wine list from the Graf Zeppelin: it listed some of the best Rhines and Moselles of the 1920s and 1930s. Certainly any wine sipped while cruising majestically over the ocean like that would have been unforgettable.

In the early days of the Boeing 747, first class passengers on American Airlines were invited up to the second deck lounge for cocktails while the first class compartment was transformed into a dining room. The chairs were turned so as to make tables for four. Some notes I kept from that epoch — the early 1970s — show that I enjoyed a good Charles Krug Cabernet on a New York to Los Angeles flight. That was truly a luxurious way to fly and, of course, was abandoned as soon as possible.

Concorde service, on Air France at least, is truly *de luxe* but can be too much of a good thing. Passengers arriving at the special Concorde Lounge at Charles De Gaulle airport are greeted by an astonishing array of food and wine. There were three Champagnes being poured the last time I made the trip. And, of course, it all begins again once the plane takes off.

On that particular flight, the Champagne, which never stopped flowing, was Laurent Perrier, Cuvée Grand Siècle; the white was a *grand Ccru* Chablis, Les Blanchots 1984, and the reds were Gruaud Larose 1980 and Vosne Romanée Les Malconsorts 1982. If that was not enough there was a good Sauternes, Château Climens 1979, and, of course, nearly-frozen vodka with the caviar.

The trouble with indulging oneself on the three-and-a-half hour, 11 a.m. flight is that one arrives in New York at 8.45 a.m., just in time for breakfast. Regular Concorde passengers tend to pass up most of the food and drink, settling for juice or a glass of Champagne. Indeed, a glass of Laurent Perrier at 18,288 meters/60,000 feet is very much a memorable occasion.

I have tried to establish the fact that memorable bottles of wine depend more on the occasion at which they're consumed than on what is in them. Even so, it would be wrong — and unfair — to deny that many bottles manage to stand on their own. They are, in other words, great wines, whenever and wherever they are drunk.

I've chosen a dozen all-time greats. There could be three dozen, or six dozen, but one has to draw the line somewhere and twelve is a traditional and manageable number.

Among the Burgundies, the 1978 Echezeaux of Henri Jayer, the 1959 Corton-Charlemagne of Louis Latour and the 1934 Le Musigny of the Comte de Vogüé stand out. In Bordeaux, the list would include the 1945 Château Mouton-Rothschild, the 1961 Lafite-Rothschild and the 1985 Château Lynch-Bages.

California would contribute the 1968 Beaulieu Vineyard Georges de Latour Private Reserve and Ridge Vineyards 1984 Monte Bello Cabernet. Champagne? Any vintage of Krug's Clos du Mesnil. From Châteauneuf-du-Pape, Château Rayas 1985, and from Alsace, Zind-Humbrecht's 1985 Gewürztraminer from the Hengst vineyard. Finally, Angelo Gaja's Barbaresco Sori Tilden 1985.

The Structure of the Wine Trade

by Bill Baker with Frank Prial, Ian Jamieson and Jay Hyams

We take it for granted, these days, that wines from the smallest and remotest of vineyards should be on sale in places as far–flung as Chicago and Tokyo. Such is the international wine trade. But it was not always so.

In the early Middle Ages, Venetian and Genoese merchant ships brought Greek and Sicilian wines to the ports of London and Bruges. This wine was soon supplanted by the light, red wine of Bordeaux, which the English took to calling claret. During the three centuries — from 1154 to 1453 — that Bordeaux and the surrounding country was English, the English wine fleet appeared each autumn at Libourne and then sailed up the Thames to London loaded with casks of wine only a few weeks old. It was usually available in London taverns by Christmas. This new wine was eagerly awaited, for by the time it arrived the previous year's vintage, left sitting in open casks, was only just palatable: no one then thought of seeking out older wines, and in fact the price of wine declined markedly with age. Nor did anyone bother about the names of individual winemakers or vineyard areas: the wine casks were anonymous.

Wine was then very much an agricultural commodity, a situation that changed only during the seventeenth century with the introduction of corks and cylindrical bottles, which made it possible for quality wines to mature and changed the marketing of Bordeaux. A leader in this movement was Arnaud de Pontac, owner of Château Haut-Brion, who used his wealth and influence to promote his wine, particularly in England. Thus it was no fluke of fate that Pepys tasted his Ho Bryon. There were other leading vineyards in Bordeaux, and their names grew in importance—the eventual classifications reflected the efforts put into these individual holdings—but Haut-Brion long held its special fascination.

The English stuck with their claret, which had changed from the frothy pinkish wine of the Middle Ages to something altogether different, and others inherited their taste. In 1787, just four years after the Treaty of Paris formally acknowledged American independence, Thomas Jefferson visited France and wrote home about "the very best Bordeaux wine. It is of the vineyard of Obrion, one of the four established as the very best, and it is of the vintage of 1784, the only very fine since the year 1779". Although its name was still problematic, the château's fame was spreading.

Britain has always led the world in the discovery and merchandising of wine. On the basis of simple arithmetic, Germany can claim to import more wine, but Britain comes a close second and, far more importantly, imports more quality wines, making Britain the center for Bordeaux, Burgundy – and wine connoisseurship. Britain leads the world in education about wine, with both journalistic and scholarly writers, and originated the qualification Master of Wine, the most respected title a wine writer or merchant can obtain. The British market has had an enormous impact on the styles of wine, and the British are intimately involved in the production of wine, particularly in France. This involvement ranges from the large — scale impact of the British market — Champagne tastes the way it does today primarily because of what British drinkers wanted in the 1860s — to the smallest details of individual producers — the venerable Haut-Brion changed its label due to complaints from a prominent British wine writer (Edmund Penning-Rowsell). The wine fleet no longer fills the Gironde each fall, but its place has been taken by crowds of merchants out of London who come to France to sample the year's wine. The judgments of those men and women are still determinant.

The ranks of the British retail wine trade were once filled by the sons of good families, upper-class men in a sedate "establishment" world who were complacent about their position and the position of the British wine trade worldwide. That insular world has recently been disturbed by the arrival of the so-called supermarket wine buyer. This new breed of wine merchant now controls a significant part of the British market. A few supermarkets, notably Sainsbury, Tesco and Waitrose have introduced some interesting, up-market products, but the proportion of sales of these wines is probably very small.

Those who graduate from Mateus and Liebfraumilch move on to the second part of the retail trade—a sector that is important and growing—which is characterized by such stores as Oddbins. These boast well-stocked shelves with carefully chosen wines of every level, even some expensive stock, although it probably does not move quickly. Oddbins has captured the imagination of several eminent wine writers, whose columns in national daily papers have considerable influence. The wine trade press seems to have moved its allegiance from traditional and specialized merchants toward the su-

permarket and wine warehouse sector of the market. The men in pinstripes are not amused by this, despite the fact that some of them, wearing the hats of agents, supply these outlets with wine. Here can be seen the breakdown of the structure of the British wine trade. Retailers are often wholesale agents, and businesses like Oddbins (owned by the world's second largest wine and spirits firm, Seagrams) not only buy through the traditional route of wholesalers but also send their buyers all over the globe to taste and negotiate direct deals with producers. The aim of such efforts is to cut out as many middlemen as possible.

The next section of the retail trade is the high-street multiples, such as Victoria Wine and Unwins. Most of these are fronts for larger operations.

These three sectors account for the vast proportion of retail wine sales to the general public. The remainder of the market is contested by smaller, more specialized businesses. In London there are such firms as Justerini & Brooks, also owned by I.D.V., Berry Bros. & Rudd and Corney and Barrow, and in the country there are the more traditional firms, such as Adnams, Lay and Wheeler, Tanners and Averys, some of which are still family owned and run. These have expensively produced lists brimming with wines from all over the globe. Important in their areas, they deal nationwide by way of mail order. Graduates of supermarkets and Oddbins, along with those buyers either too idle or too old-fashioned to use such outlets patronize these more traditional firms, which pride themselves on offering not only a good range of wines but also sound advice, personal service and sometimes even credit. These are the guardians of the traditional way of selling in the retail sector.

Another vital part of selling to the public is undertaken by the International Co-operative Exhibition Wine Society, better-known as the Wine Society. From their headquarters at Stevenage the society sends out a huge number of cases, many bearing their own labels but also other, finer wines from impeccable sources. The Wine Society is Britain's most important mail-order business, and few oganizations come anywhere near it in sales and quality.

Occupying a small niche in the overall scheme are the specialist merchants, each of which concentrates on a particular corner of the market. In some cases this is a wine-producing area: Robin Yapp for Rhône and Loire wines, Roger Harris for Beaujolais, Laymont and Shaw for Spanish wines. Others deal with a single aspect of the trade, such as Peter Wylie, Reid Wines and Farr Vintners, who deal with old and rare wines. Nicholas Davies of the Hungerford Wine Company makes the greater part of his sales in wines that are not yet even in bottle. Such *en primeur* sales have been of great importance in the 1980s. Since wine merchants have been increasingly unable to hold stocks until they are fully mature, they—and many journalists, both in Britain and the United States—have managed to shift the burden of holding expensive stock from merchants to the general public, who have been convinced that by buying early—wine futures—they get unrepeatable prices, which up to a point can be true.

The whole of this retail sector might seem orderly, something akin to a ladder formed by sales and determined by price, quality and size of business. In reality, however, it is very different, with many of the traditional retailers and specialist merchants acting themselves as agents of producers abroad. As such, they sell to one another, to wholesalers, to Oddbins and to supermarkets.

All the wines on an Oddbins shelf, in a Lay and Wheeler catalog or on a Wine Society list must be bought somewhere, almost always somewhere off the British Isles. Most merchants prefer to buy from as close to source as possible. The bigger enterprises ship most of their wines direct from the country of origin, in most cases direct from the grower or winery concerned. Many wine producers, however, want to have representation on the British market, and this can be done in three ways. Large and important houses, like big Champagne producers, usually have a subsidiary in Britain: Möet et Chandon, Laurent Perrier, Pol Roger and so on. Other wine producers also do this, for example, Louis Latour, Penfolds and so on. Other producers join together and take individual shares in a business to represent them all. A leading example of this is Maisons Marques et Domaines, which represents Roederer for Champagne, Bouchard Père et Fils for Burgundy, Marqués de Murrieta for Rioja, Schlumberger in Alsace. There are also producers that elect to sell most of their wine through an independent merchant with whom they have had a special relationship, often over a period of many years. Leflaive uses Corney and Barrow, many California producers use Geoffrey Roberts Associates, Hugel uses W. Loeb. Quite a few of the individual agents and even some primary producers try to have an even more localized "agent" system, with regional wine merchants acting as subagents. All the agents sell wine to all the retailers. Some of the larger retailers are given preferential terms, discounts, incentives in the form of tasting samples and even "listing allowances"—actual cash payments to ensure their products are prominently displayed. This is iniquitous and constitutes a form of bribery.

Wholesalers are the least scrupulous of the players in the sales-oriented section of the British wine trade. They may assure their traditional wine trade accounts that they will sell their wares only to them and not go directly to hotels and restaurants, corporate and private accounts. When it comes to the crunch, however, they—or at least most of them—sell to anyone with a large enough bankroll. This causes great confusion over prices and considerable antagonism among customers.

London is the center of the wine auction market. Auctions take place in Holland, Switzerland, the United States, Australia and even France, but Christie's and Sotheby's, the main contenders in this important sector of the market, trounce all opposition and have been crucial in maintaining London's supremacy in the wine world.

Auctions are actually clearing houses for unwanted wine. Such wine comes from several sources. Wine businesses often find themselves with overstocks of wine, fine or otherwise, that they wish to sell off to satisfy their accountants, tidy-up their lists or make room in warehouses. The occasional bankruptcy sale provides another source. There are also savvy private individuals who buy enough at the right time to meet their own needs and leave a portion to sell later to maintain their cellars. There are also firms in the wine trade that play the auction market in the way others play the stock market,

buying and selling blue chip wines and taking a turn each time. Yet other firms remorselessly dump poorly bought wine (of which every firm has at least some) onto unsuspecting bargain hunters. Finally — although the public at large often believes such sales come first—there are sales from the cellars of deceased individuals. This is the best source of all and one that second-hand wine merchants try to tap into before the auctioneers. Buying at auction is fraught with danger. While there are often good values to be had, there is also an enormous quantity of dross.

The biggest buyers at auction are a class of merchants best defined as brokers. Although these buy and sell their own stock, they also use the lists of other firms and broke the stock that is on offer for a small margin. There are several of these broking firms, including Richard Kihl, Octagon and Kurtz and Chan, but the most successful is Farr Vintners. These brokers send representatives to auctions to snap up any bargains that may be offered. They buy wherever they can at the lowest possible price and then sell their wares worldwide. Most of the businesses involved at this level are, in effect, commodity dealers. They are primarily interested in classed growth claret, fine Burgundy from top domains, old Port and premium Champagnes. Other wines float in and out of this ambit, including top-name Italians, Sauternes—especially d' Yquem—Madeira and Alsace. There is friendly rivalry among these brokers and such firms as Reid Wines and Peter Wylie Fine Wines, but the name of the game is spot the bargain, buy it up cheap and sell it fast. The brokers do not restrict their buying to the United Kingdom but in true commodity-broker style buy in Europe and the United States if they find bargains or if the exchange rate is favorable. This leads to parallel trading in such things as Champagne, which understandably annoys the agents and principals to the point of distraction. Wines that are in colossal demand—Leflaive white Burgundies, for example—can change hands many times, the price increasing with each exchange. Several years ago Vincent Leflaive was distressed that much of his wine was reaching the United States and angering his agents there. The explanation was that brokers in the United Kingdom were purchasing stock allocated to merchants in Europe at favorable exchange rates, marking it up and then selling it to merchants in the United States. Even now bottles of wine from the most famous of all Burgundy domains, Romanée-Conti, bear a legend on the label declaring export of the particular bottle to the United States.

No matter what measures are taken to prevent this sort of trade there will be those who manage to get around them. This is a pity for several reasons, not least that wine does not enjoy transatlantic flights in aircraft holds. International trading in fine wine does no end of harm to a wine and its reputation. Bottles that have been bought by American collectors and stored in less than perfect conditions in California or Florida tend to be prematurely aged. Bottles that crisscross the Atlantic with the change in exchange rates tend to differ markedly from those kept since purchase in cool European cellars. There is no way of knowing what you are getting from either auctions or brokers until the bottles arrive. If they have the compulsory United States slip label, which bears the name of a merchant there—beware. Sadly, it has been known for mer-

chants to soak these off when the wines return from abroad—there is no protecting against such activity.

The second-hand market is used by almost all merchants. Most would prefer their customers not know that this is where a high proportion of their stock comes from. It is also used by almost all merchants for disposing of inadequate stock.

Several multinational companies take part in the wine and spirits trade. Many provide lessons in how best to vertically integrate a business. International Distillers and Vintners Ltd., a subsidiary of Grand Metropolitan, owns businesses right across the spectrum of the market. For instance, they own a controlling interest in Croft Port and Gilbeys Gin. They then wholesale the products themselves through Morgan Furze a subsidiary, and then sell in the retail market through Justerini & Brooks. Imagine the number of costly internal transactions that could be involved in buying a case of Croft from J.&B. Such companies use standard business practices to market their own brands—for just like the tobacco trade, the brand is of prime importance.

The number of hands through which a bottle of wine may pass before reaching the hands of its final consumer can be legion. The hands may belong to independent companies or to subsidiaries of international concerns. Clearly, the simplest and cheapest route is when a chain like Oddbins sends a buyer to Australia, he discovers a new winery (increasingly difficult these days) that has no agent in the United Kingdom, agrees to buy the wine and ships it. Oddbins then sells it—a journey from grape to consumer in two transactions. Even if the buyer is forced to go through an agent in the United Kingdom or if the winery adds a little to the price to cover its commission to an agent, the number of middlemen is minimal. This relatively breezy transaction should be compared to the possible fate of a case of Château Giscours sold from the château through Gilbey (I.D.V.) to Morgan Furze. The wine sits in a Morgan Furze warehouse for a few years because no one is able to sell it. Then, in one of its regular turnouts of stock, Morgan Furze sells it at auction. The auctioneer takes a commission, and the box of wine passes to Farr Vintners, who mark it up modestly and sell it to Reid Wines, who mark it up and sell it to a top restaurateur, who marks it up outrageously and sells it to the final drinker. Well before reaching an export market, many French wines provide income to more than three businesses. The traditional example of how this happens is provided by the old, established Bordeaux trade.

Bordeaux is not just a market for top châteaux. At the bottom end of the Bordeaux production spectrum are cooperatives that make generic Bordeaux and sell it directly through export markets. This is precisely what happens to wines from California or Australia, Italy or Bulgaria, but it is not the part of Bordeaux that interests those of us fascinated by the role of the middleman.

As the Bordelais are fond of indicating on their labels, Bordeaux is a land of châteaux: individual, often majestic, buildings with attached vineyards. However, few of the top Bordeaux châteaux deal directly with foreign buyers. Buyers and proprietors often know one another well and become friends and colleagues, and proprietors may even lavishly entertain buyers at the property, but the buyers will almost certainly not buy the property's wine direct.

Instead, they buy it from a *négociant* in Bordeaux. Basically, this is for historical reasons. In the eighteenth century most châteaux were owned by absentee landlords whose employees on the spot were likely to be illiterate peasant farmers. The châteaux had neither the connections nor the ability to sell their product to the export market. Hence the rise of the *négociant* to the primary position in the Bordeaux marketplace. Many of the firms operating in the eighteenth century are still active today. Shröeder & Schyler even work from the same premises at 97 Quai des Chartrons where they began trade in 1739. Schyler was Dutch, and many other *négociants* were and are of non-French origin. Nathaniel Johnson was of English origin; Barton of Irish stock; Hanappier, Swedish; Mestrezatr Swiss. *Négociants* often own, through later prosperity, parts or entire châteaux. Palmer is the obvious example, one-third owned by Sichel, Mahler Besse and Miailhe. The three flags—British, Dutch, and French—that fly over the house represent those interests. The multi-branched Cruse family owns Pontet Canet and Issan, while across the river in Libourne the influential family firm of Jean-Pierre Moueix owns or part-owns Magdelaine, La Fleur-Pétrus, La Grave Trigant de Boisset and Lagrange Pomerol and manages Château Pétrus as well. Over and above these visible ties *négociants* often have special agency agreements with particular châteaux that they have represented for many years. They are thus under legal or moral contract to take a proportion of the crop each year, good or bad. This was not much of a burden in the 1980s, a decade in which nearly every vintage was good or very good. However things are changing.

The good years led to over ambitious prices, which during the recession of the late 1980's and early 1990's created a cycle of swelling stocks and declining demand. This glut of excellent wine forced *négociants* to sell off their stocks cheaply, bringing about the remarkable situation of finding bottles of d'Yquem and Cheval Blanc on supermarket shelves, sometimes at prices below those the *négociant* paid. At the same time, Bordeaux—and France in general—is facing other problems. Australia, Spain, South Africa, even eastern Europe and South America are making increasing inroads on the French market. Using aggressive export strategies, these wines are taking their places on French wine shelves. There are also changes in consumer tastes. Many quality French wines are complex reds, and the greatest worldwide demand is for white wines, simple and easy-drinking. Even the French themselves are changing their taste in wine, not just drinking less wine but turning away from the classic French wines to the easier wines of the South. And France, like all the world's winemaking nations, must face the international trend against alcohol.

As has occurred in other industries, this pressure is leading to a concentration of ownership, with the range of small producers giving way to a field dominated by a few large companies. Many lower-quality producers are being forced out of business, and the leading producers are strengthening their positions. One way to do so is by owning a *négociant*. Lafite, Latour and Mouton-Rothschild already own *négociants* that handle some of their distribution. For their part, *négociants* are increasing their investment in viticulture and employing more aggressive marketing strategies, such as brand development.

Négociants are not the only people standing between the châteaux and the export market. Most châteaux sell to the *négociants* through a further middleman, the *courtier*. *Courtiers* advise proprietors on what sort of price they are likely to be able to command for their wine each year. They watch the market conditions, the amount of unsold stock the *négociants* have and make a judgment. For this consultation *courtiers* are paid about 2 percent by way of commission, a fee that can amount to a substantial sum. These men are the pinstriped brigade of Bordeaux, and they wield enormous influence. Some are of foreign ancestry, the most significant being M. Lawton of the firm Tastet & Lawton.

Thus, the traditional route from château to export market involves two middlemen, or four transactions.

Burgundy could not be more different from Bordeaux, and its situation, too, reflects history. Thanks to the practice of giving vineyards to religious orders, by the time of the Revolution much of Burgundy's best wine land was owned by monasteries. In the wave of anticlericalism following the Revolution, the vineyards were taken from the church, divided into small parcels and sold. This system of small ownership still prevails in Burgundy, where there are few large estates. Most of the cultivation and much of the winemaking is in the hands of small growers, many of whom own a few vines in various villages and vineyards. Increasingly, the pattern that exists in Bordeaux, where grower sells to *négociant*, is disappearing in Burgundy. Because there are so many small growers, most were in the habit of selling their product (in cask, unlike in Bordeaux) to *négociants* who would keep the wine until they considered it ready to bottle and then blend several casks, often from more than one grower, to make their own house version of the wine in question. The growers were under moral or legal contract to the *négociants* and vice versa. Today many growers prefer to cut out the *négociant* and make their own wine and market it under their own label. The scene in Burgundy is far less disciplined than that of Bordeaux, and what pertains here is basically the same in the rest of France and indeed Europe. Most growers and all *négociants* have national agents in the United Kingdom and several local agents in the United States. These agents believe they have exclusive rights to the wines of the property concerned. However, they have only the proprietor's good word, and most proprietors will sell to anyone with the money. Many a merchant has found that firm reserves he thought he had placed with vignerons have vanished. This is most true in Burgundy, where demand consistently outstrips supply despite the Burgundians efforts to make their vines produce as many berries as possible.

Walk into any French restaurant in a wine-producing region and you will find the wines offered dominated by those produced in that area. Even in great restaurants—three stars in *Michelin*, 19.5 in *Gault-Millau*—the wines made in regions outside that of the restaurant are usually given scant attention. Some consider this sensible, others see it as a bizarre form of provincialism for a country that produces the majority of the fine wine available. This regional chauvinism is bolstered by the producers of the region, who encourage the view that at least one wine from the region is certain to admirably accompany any dish the chef might wish to prepare.

The regionalism displayed in the French restaurant market is clearly reflected in the wine available in retail outlets, with the exception of the very lowest levels—the chain supermarkets—where the standard Crozes-Hermitage and Beaujolais are always available. The only real exception to this oddly subjective market is Paris, where serious wine shops sell a proper range of French wine. But even with increased imports from abroad, it is still exceedingly difficult to obtain even fine wines from anywhere farther afield, than Italy or Spain. It seems unlikely that this will change in the future. It is also difficult to find older vintages in France except at enormous prices in the very best hostelries. This is because wine is looked at very differently in France. It is still an agricultural product, a commodity that the producer sells as soon as he can after it is in the bottle—and sometimes even before that. Most producers keep a few bottles back for tasting and entertaining in the future. Some châteaux in Bordeaux keep good stocks, and the greater ones exchange parcels of wine with one another, but this is only at the very highest level. It is not unknown for proprietors, especially in Bordeaux, to enter the market in the United Kingdom to obtain a few cases of older wines from their property. Will the single European market change this? Probably not, for it is an attitude built on centuries of regionalism.

Just as the internal market in France represents little choice compared to that of England, so the internal markets of the other important wine-producing countries reflect the same sort of regionalism. Wines from the Veneto do not often turn up in Palermo restaurants, just as wines from Penedés are scarce in Rioja. Only the top-class restaurants in Italy list wines from France or California. The only wine that transcends this is Champagne, which is available universally, despite the fact that most winemaking countries offer an adequate alternate.

The situation is entirely different in European countries that do not produce wine. Like their British counterparts, wine enthusiasts in Belgium and Holland have built up relationships with producers all over the world. The wine markets of nonproducing countries always offer greater breadth and depth of choice than those of producing countries. Many private houses in Belgium and Holland boast cellars of great importance and quality, so much so that London auction houses like Christie's and Sotheby's actively search for such jewels. Just as in the United Kingdom, the Belgian trade was famous for shipping wine in cask and bottling it at home. Much of the fine and rare wine in cellars there was bottled in Belgium. Understandably, markets free of local pressure thrive on all products available from outside. Even in Scandinavia, where the governments of Norway and Sweden operate state monopolies for the sale of alcohol, the range of wines available is more balanced and broader than in most Parisian wine shops.

In Germany, since only about 5 percent of growers own more than 5 hectares of vineyard, viticulture is mainly a part-time occupation, relying heavily on low-paid or even unpaid family labor. Many of these small growers with insufficient land to make winemaking and bottling worthwhile deliver their grapes to merchants or cooperative cellars (*Winzergenossenschaften*).

The cooperatives receive the crop from 37 percent of the total vineyard area, but their involvement varies greatly from region to region. They are proportionately strongest in the Ahr valley and the Hessische Bergstrasse, where they are supplied by 91 percent of the area under vine. In the much larger regions of Württemberg and Baden, where the average holding is less than one hectare, the cooperative share is 88 and 82 percent respectively. Some of the village cooperatives, particularly those of Baden, have a growing reputation for their wine. Of the total of 314 cooperatives, 144 have no winemaking facilities. They operate as pressing stations or depots for grapes that are then passed on to larger cellars. About 80 percent of cooperative wine is sold in the more profitable way in bottle, rather than on the chronically depressed bulk-wine market. Wholesalers and retail chains, including discount stores and supermarkets, account for 69 percent; 17 percent is bought directly by consumers; and restaurants account for a further 8 percent. About 5 percent of cooperative wine is exported.

During the last twenty years, producers' associations (*Erzeugergemeinschaften*) have been formed under a law that provides them with a wide choice of company structure. The most effective of these, such as the Erzeugergemeinschaft Deutsches Eck on the Mosel, have set themselves winemaking standards well beyond the legal minimum. This Mosel group has succeeded in producing better wine and has persuaded its customers to accept higher prices.

Merchants who buy wine in bulk and then bottle and sell it under well-known names account for a large share of German exports. Nearly half of all Rheinhessen wine is bottled outside the region, and much of it is sold as Liebfraumilch, which accounts for some 10 percent of German wine production. Liebfraumilch is hardly seen in Germany itself. Although exports declined steadily in the early 1990s, sales in eastern Germany, mainly under *Grosslage* names, will probably swallow any surplus. In this respect the balance between wine consumption and exports on the one hand, and production and imports on the other, is almost as even as it can be.

Apart from the offerings of the good cooperative cellars, the best German wines come from state, city or privately owned estates. Wine-merchandising businesses owned by Jews were destroyed in the Third Reich and have not been replaced. As a result, estate bottlers are often obliged to develop sales directly to the consumer. Perhaps to avoid the possibility of prices being undercut, most postwar wine merchants have concentrated more on imported wines, although outside vinegrowing regions, specialist merchants now offer a good range of German "producer bottlings".

As indicated by such independent critics as the *Michelin* guide, Germany is experiencing a remarkable flowering of fine restaurants. Many estates look on the elegant restaurant table as the proper environment for their elegant wines. This gastronomy has led to a growing preference for dry wines, although the volume of sales through restaurants is still relatively modest and that through less expensive cafés often nonexistent. The various estates make wines for varying types of customers, with sales to the export markets being strongest from the Mosel-Saar-Ruwer, Rheingau, Rheinhessen, Rheinpfalz and the Nahe. For the most part, the exciting wines of Baden and Franken remain in Germany.

Some producers have joined other producers to

promote their wines at home and abroad. Wine consumption in Germany remains at about 26 liters per capita, and there is a trend toward drinking better–quality wine. Although the trade is still dominated by those who sell inexpensive wine, the excellent vintages of 1988, 1989 and 1990 have helped strengthen the reputation of fine wine producers that are mostly state-owned or private estates.

The wine-trade situation is very different in the United States. The so-called Great Experiment of Prohibition — the banning of the manufacture, transportation, and sale of all alcoholic beverages in the United States — ended in 1933 with the ratification of the Twenty-first Amendment to the Constitution, but six decades later it continues to cast a long shadow over the country's wine and spirits industry.

To placate the "dries," who continued to be a factor in Congress and the nation, the proponents of Repeal wrote and had enacted a body of some of the most complicated liquor controls in the world.

Because Prohibition was originally a local option—Maine adopted it as early as 1829—he new laws were written so as to return that option to the states. Under the Twenty-first Amendment, each state was empowered to enact its own laws controlling the importation, distribution, sale and taxation of alcoholic beverages within its boundaries.

The Amendment also established a three-tiered system of suppliers, wholesalers or distributors and retailers. This was to eliminate, or at least impede, the chances for corruption inherent in the tied-house concept in which a producer or supplier owns the retail outlets or restaurants where his beverages are sold. The tied-house concept can be found in Britain, where large breweries traditionally have owned many of the pubs where their beers are sold.

At the time of Repeal, fine wine was a minor factor in America's beverage trade. As wine became more popular, however, producers all over the world had to learn the different laws applicable to the sale and consumption of alcoholic beverages.

In theory, an American winery or a foreign wine importer sells its wine to a distributor who, in turn, sells it to a retailer or a restaurant who then sells it to a customer. It is the producer's obligation to meet the Federal government's licensing and tax requirements. The distributor normally handles state and local tax and licensing requirements. This is the system originally envisioned by the framers of the Twenty-first Amendment. In practice, literally hundreds of exeptions to the system have come into being. There are modified three-tiered systems that permit the distributor to hold a retail license but not a restaurant license. There are states where taverns and restaurants can sell "off-premises", in other words, act as retailers, but only when normal retail outlets—wineshops—are closed. In some states where grapes are grown and wine is made wineries can sell directly to retailers within that state and to customers who actually visit the wineries. There are the so-called control states, such as Pennsylvania, where the state goverment owns and manages the distribution and retail sales of all alcholic beverages. The control states are monopolies , not unlike the alcholic beverage monopolies in Canada and the Scandinavian countries. Some states, like California, permit wine sales in supermarkets. Some, like New Jersey, permit supermarket sales if the wine and spirits section is separate from the food section and

can be closed off during the hours and days when alcoholic beverage sales are banned in that state. Other states, like New York, allow beer to be sold in food stores but not in liquor stores. Over time, wine producers have learned to live with the patchwork quilt of American laws affecting wine and spirits, including the often bizarre regulations set by the U.S. Treasury Department's Bureau of Alcohol, Tobacco and Firearms regarding wine labels. The B.A.T.F. can and does reject new labels for any of dozens of reasons ranging from the placement of certain letters to the alleged lack of taste in some illustrations.

In recent years, the principal marketing problem for many winemakers has been the shrinking number of distributors. In sections of the country where there were once dozens of small distributors there are now only one or two, usually large organizations handling many brands. These large distributors, are reluctant to take on new names. At the same time, wine producers are unhappy about having to sign up with distributors who are unlikely to be able to devote much attention or manpower to yet another line of wines.

But the three-tiered system is the law; there is no end-run around the distributor. To generate sales, many wine producers go on the road to supplement or, more likely, take the place of the distributor's salesman. Thus, people who gave up urban or suburban life to become winemakers or growers find themselves moving from airport to airport and hotel room to hotel room as they work to find a public for their wines.

The anti-alcohol lobby is still strong and wields increasing influence. The United States is thus a market fraught with problems, and yet some outstanding companies exist, with broad ranges of goods for sale. There are stores in Washington, New York, and California with truly impressive inventories that include all the world's greatest producers. Feeding from such outlets is a growing band of informed and for the most part wealthy consumers. There are many outstanding cellars in the hands of connoisseurs in the United States, but there is also a vast drift of consumers who, unsure of their own opinion or taste slavishly follow one or another of the wine newsletters. Of these, the two most influential are the *Wine Spectator* and the *Wine Advocate*, the latter written by the most influential man in the wine world today, Robert W. Parker Jr. In just over fifteen years, Parker has become the guru of the American wine consumer. If Parker rates a wine over 90/100 on his 50-100 scale, the wine is guaranteed to be a sell-out, and the price will rocket up so high that future wines from its producer will be almost impossible for merchants to sell.

Parker's immense influence can make life difficult for merchants trying to sell wines he has rated at less than 75. But the merchants themselves are partly to blame. They trumpet his high ratings in their advertising and, of course, they try not to stock any wines he has not praised. Mr. Parker has received his share of criticism from the wine trade but there is no gainsaying the fact that he provides a valuable service to wine drinkers. There are probably 800 American Chardonnays on the market at this writing. Who, other than a Robert Parker has the time, the interest and the dedication to taste them all and rate them? There are flaws in the Parker rating method but until someone provides something better, thousands of consumers are going to be grateful for his help.

Storing and Serving Wine

by Jon Thorn

The key to enjoying quality wines is proper storage. Inexpensive table wine is made for immediate consumption and easy drinking, but quality wine is actually made to mature and improve in the bottle, often for many years, before the wine shows its full beauty and range of flavors.

There was a time when most people either had a cellar of their own or bought wine from a merchant who sold it when the wine was ready to drink. But times have changed.

The most acute problem a wine lover faces today is not what wine to buy, but where and how to keep the wine until maturity. Happily, there are many solutions to suit the needs of any wine buyer faced with the need of a cellar.

It is generally true that many mid-priced to expensive wines are sold in an immature state. These wines will certainly benefit from some more bottle age, be it six months, or five or more years. As one progresses up the price scale this rule applies ever more strictly .

Those French wines which are often bought and drunk far too young are Champagne, Chablis, Bordeaux and Rhône. Additionally this is true of Australian Semillons, California Chardonnays, all quality German wines, Spanish and Italian Cabernets and vintage Port. All of these wines should certainly be stored for a good period before they are drunk.

The ideal domestic cellar is one that is both space efficient and easily accessible. That usually requires storing wine in three ways: in bins of small shelf sections for up to forty bottles; in the original wooden cases or as single bottles. A bin can be made of bricks and can be further sub-divided into two or four areas by using plywood planks to form internal diagonal walls.

All three means of storage can be used against a single wall, starting with bins on the floor, then wooden cases on top, and racks for bottles on top of the cases. One useful point to remember about wine racks, especially those in a domestic space, is that a double depth rack can often fit where a single depth rack can fit, doubling your storage in that same site.

The perfect cellar, however, is simply the one that best suits the wines to be stored. The budget and the available space, adapting as the cellar grows and changes. Without an underground cellar, wine can still certainly be stored at home. However it is necessary to be a little more creative when planning to keep wine at home in quantity.

LEFT: The *Schatzkammer or* "treasury room" at Kloster Eberbach in Hattenheim in the Rheingau contains one of the finest collections of German wine. It lies beneath a twelfth-century Cistercian monastery building. Only one person has the key. The oldest bottle is from 1857, and the most valuable probably 1893.

RIGHT: Part of the cellar of Lord McAlpine from West Green House in Hampshire, England, sold in May 1990 by Sotheby's. The jewel was probably the largest private collection of large-format Château Latour 1971. Unusual items were some very mature vintage Champagne, and Madeiras from 1862 to 1954, including Bastado 1870.

The best wine storage sites in the average home are the loft, the wardrobe bottom, the space under the stairs, the garden shed, the space under a bed, the garage or in a coal hole, bearing in mind that wine stored in these imperfect conditions must be protected from the heat. Major work can be done to build a customized cellar into a spare room. The storage system can be built horizontally or vertically to accomodate any space.

To convert a real cellar to wine storage requires first a thorough cleaning, and second, good organization of the space. There should be an electric light, any plant life should be killed. This can be done by using one part bleach to four parts water. Dig out any cracks in the cement or bricks and fill them in with a water resistant filler.

The question of the ideal temperature at which to store wine is usually a rather academic one. The simple answer for most people is, "as cold as possible". If the site feels cool, then it will certainly be a good temperature at which to keep wine. If it feels very cold, however, then one should think about raising the temperature a little.

The least expensive way to lower or raise the temperature of a cellar is to locate the sources of heat and cold and then to insulate accordingly. To take a reading, tape a thermometer to each surface and then isolate the thermometer by taping a newspaper over it. A more reliable, but, of course, more expen-sive way to achieve a lower temperature is to install an electric chiller or air conditioner.

Some wine merchants and bonded warehouses will also store wine, but before taking this option consider that pottering in a cellar is a major plea-sure. Another consideration is that wine companies can go bankrupt, so only store wine with reputable people.

If outside storage is the best route, then it is es-sential that your name and address be marked clearly on the case and that insurance be arranged to cover the replacement value of the wine, not the purchase value. There is a wide variety of companies which offer this service, from specialist clubs, to warehouses.

Many of these storage sites will be bonded, which means that wine stored in these storage facilities does not attract duty or tax on the purchase price until it is removed from the site. This option is only of interest if the wine is bought *en primeur* or at auction, where wine is often offered with an in-bond arrangement available.

Another solution is to buy a pre-fabricated cellar for installation in the home. There are two kinds. The Eurocave electric temperature–controlled cabinet, specifically designed for wine storage, is now only one of many such products available. These units come at various prices, sizes, and levels of so-phistication and provide great advantage for they

can be moved and plugged in anywhere. Installation is simple

Not so the Spiral Cellar, which consists of a series of units which together form a spiral stair with space in the walls to store bottles. The entire unit is fitted into a large hole in the ground at some cost and is fixed permanently in the space into which it is installed.

One of these methods will be suitable for most cellarers, but there is a measure which applies to them all: value for money. The way to calculate this and to allow the comparison of different systems is the cost per bottle stored; this figure is gained by dividing the cost of the solution by the number of bottles stored.

The cellarer's next step is to get organized, and to keep the cellar organized. Pre-printed cellar books are not of much use; far more flexible is a loose leaf binder filled with pages that make clear what one has, and also what one is going to need. Divide this up by the different styles of wine kept, say, Bordeaux, Burgundy, then by any sub-regions, say, Margaux, and by château. Add to each entry information about where the wine was purchased, the price, how many bottles are in storage, comments on the wine and the occasions on which the wine was drunk.

Finally, organize the bottles in the cellar according to some system. With single bottles it can help to place neck labels on the bottles with just "Margaux, '79" marked on them, for instance.

For anyone who enjoys wine it is definitely worth taking time and expense over storage. The litany of these needs is: dark, still, cool, flat, dry or moist.

Wine that is stored in the light may become tired, taste off, and if it is a white, or especially a sparkling wine, it can turn a nasty color and become unpleasant in no time at all.

Bottles that are moved around will also not develop to their best. Wine will recover from a journey and can be moved from one place to another, but a life of continual movement will tire a wine out. The exception to most of these rules is Madeira, which is virtually cooked and was used in the seventeenth and eighteenth centuries as ballast by ships to mature it.

The "right" temperature for maturing wine is around 10°C/50°F. The warmer a wine the faster it will mature, but also the less complex it will be when mature. The most important factor, however, is not the average temperature, which has been found to be acceptable for maturation between 7°C/45°F and 18°C/65°F, but the absence of large and frequent swings in temperature values. Incremental seasonal change is not a problem, partly because wine remains a natural product, even after its final fermentation.

Bottles must be kept flat so the wine stays in contact with the cork to keep it moist and airtight. Some people in the trade talk about a wine "breathing through the cork", but there is no evidence for this. What does happen is seepage; the wine finds its way under the capsule as a sticky paste, but it does not mean a wine is "off".

Bottle care is in reality cork care; the wine depends on the cork. A short or poor quality cork can lead to problems. Sadly for the future of some wines, the price of cork, most of which comes from Portugal, has been rising rapidly, and it seems likely that some producers will cut costs by using cheaper corks.

Dry or moist sounds like a contradiction in terms, but one does not want too much of either. If the storage site is too dry the corks will become brittle and if too moist, labels can fall off and molds develop.

The reason why one should be so concerned to mature fine wines is that they taste better if they mature properly before they are drunk. Young Bordeaux can have both roughness and finesse, but the most noticeable quality is tannin, a muscular astringency at the back of the mouth which comes from grape skins, pips and stalks. It can feel hard, sharp or soft on the palate, while in many young quality wines, the fruit should give the impression of being a tight kernel.

In white wine it is the acidity which gives structure and is the motor for maturity as tannin is in red wine, although acidity can also be very noticeable in some red wines. Maturity in both red and white wine means a balance between the different elements —tannin, acidity, fruit and alcohol — and an overall impression of elegance, complexity and completeness.

Plotting the maturity curves of different wines takes account of the fact that different grape varieties mature in different ways, to which is added the variable of vintage. The Cabernet Sauvignon can take a long time to mature, while the best grape of Germany, the Riesling, is unusual in that initially it is wonderfully refreshing and floral. Then, for two or three years it becomes more "dumb", only to come back with more structure and a more petrolly flavor. A good Riesling can carry on maturing for twenty years, and fully mature Riesling has astonishing power and penetration, as well as delicacy and finesse.

An example of a very mature Riesling comes from a tasting in 1991 at Kloster Eberbach; a Steinberger Kabinett from 1952. Tasting notes read: "Mid-gold color; very honeyed fruit on nose. Great depth of fruit on palate, great finesse, very full and rich, Madeirizing slightly. Amazingly, still lively acidity, still delicate, with light appley fruit and a very long finish."

The final maturity criterion is the most variable of all: personal taste. It is often said in the wine trade that the French drink their red Bordeaux too young and the British drink it too old. National tastes do seem to differ. These trends mask the really important point which is that different people like different things, and one of the major joys of keeping wine is exploring your own vinous likes and dislikes.

However you store your wine, it is with serving wine that the pleasure really begins. The most important things to be considered when serving wine are decanting, glasses, temperature, corkscrews and wine preservers.

There are two main reasons to decant the wine from the bottle. Primarily wine is decanted to separate the wine from any sediment which may have been thrown. Sediment is both harmless and tasteless, which brings one to the second reason to decant: wine looks beautiful in a fine decanter.

There is currently some concern that minute quantities of lead might contaminate wine while it is stored in a lead crystal decanter, particularly if an acidic wine is left in such a decanter for a long

period of time. Some crystal companies are now producing lead-free crystal decanters but are mainly doing so to reduce the exposure of their staff to lead.

Before decanting, the bottle should stand upright for a day and then slowly be poured into the decanter with a lighted candle behind it so the moving pile of sediment can be seen. Decanting starts the process of aeration which takes place most effectively in the glass, when the wine releases its full bouquet and flavor, often taking up to half an hour to do so fully. Main grape varieties which do develop in the glass are the Cabernet Sauvignon, Merlot, Pinot Noir and Chardonnay, while those that do not are the Sauvignon Blanc, Gewürztraminer, Riesling and Gamay.

The glass itself may help or hinder this development. There are two kinds of glass in general use for Champagne — the saucer and the flute. The flute concentrates the delicate bouquet of Champagne, or any wine, while the saucer does the opposite; again, the flute slows down oxidation of the wine and allows the visual appreciation of the bubbles, unlike the saucer.

One question often asked about Champagne is why there should be different strengths of bubbles in wine poured from the same bottle into (apparently) the same glasses. The cause is the minute surface imperfections inside the glass which precipitate carbon dioxide to form the gas bubbles. André Simon, the great wine and food writer, had small stars etched into the bottom of his Champagne glasses to get a better mousse.

The general rules for all wine glasses are that they should be simple, clean, and tulip-shaped. The Austrian company of Riedel produces two of the best ranges of wine glass; the Vinum, and the top-quality Sommelier, of which the Bordeaux and Burgundy glasses really do bring out the best in these wines.

There is no one ideal temperature for serving wine: different wines show their virtues at different temperatures. Generally speaking these tempera-

tures are: sparkling wine, 4°C/39°F; sweet wine, 6°C/11°F; Champagne, Sherry, dry white wine, 8°C/46°F; Beaujolais, 11°C/52°F; white Burgundy, 14°C/57°F; Rioja, 16°C/61°F; Bordeaux, red Burgundy, Chianti, 17°C/63°F. Bear in mind also that it may take a refrigerator up to two hours to chill a wine, but an ice bucket full of ice and cold water needs only twenty minutes.

To open the bottle, cut the capsule on or under the rim of the neck and wipe away any dirt or debris, then remove the cork. There are many instruments, ancient and modern, for this but the best is the Screwpull selfpulling corkscrew perfected in 1979 by Texan Herbert Allen, and much imitated.

When opening a Champagne bottle never point it at anything alive or breakable; also hold the cork firmly in case it pops out. To cut down on waste, pull the cork out gently, keeping the bottle at a 45 degree angle, and twist the bottle, not the cork.

If you find that you have some wine left over, it should keep for a day or two with the cork replaced, which is best done by cutting the dirty part of the thinner end of the cork off and replacing that end into the bottle.

Pouring the remaining wine into a clean half bottle is another method of storage and alternatively one can use the Vacu-vin pump and rubber stopper, which creates a vacuum between the stopper and the wine. This ingenious idea does not work with wines which contain a lot of carbon dioxide, which you can see if a froth forms on top of the wine. A similar solution, but different in effect, is the Wine Saver, a handy device which injects a layer of inert flavor-free gas on top of the wine to prevent oxidation. This solution is worth exploring for finer wines.

There is now nothing to stop you getting the most from your wines. Pleasure from wine is one of the most complete experiences humans can have, at once sensual and intellectual. Wine is made to be enjoyed.

RIGHT: Different wines have different styles of bouquet hence the need for different shapes of glass. This range, from Riedel, is designed for (left to right): Burgundy, Bordeaux, Champagne, Chardonnay, Riesling. The different shapes help to deliver the wine to the appropriate part of the tongue.

Appendices

Bordeaux Classifications Before 1855

The year of 1855 saw the classification of the vinyards of the Médoc that has become accepted as "official", but this was by no means the first classification. Brokers and merchants had long made, and published, their own classifications, two of which are reproduced here, by kind permission of *The Vine*.

The first is that of Thomas Jefferson who was Minister in France for the United States in the years before the French Revolution, and was a keen follower of the wines of Bordeaux and other places. His classification is as follows, *livres* being the unit of currency:

First Growths	*Second Growths*	*Third Growths*
(1,500 *livres* per *tonneau*)	(1,000 *livres*)	(800 - 900 *livres*)
Château Margaux	Château Rauzan	Château Calon-Ségur
Château La Tour	Château Léoville	Château Mouton (Rothschild)
Château Haut-Brion	Château Gruaud-Larose	Château Gorse (Brane-Cantenac)
Château Lafitte	Château Kirwan	Château d'Arboete (Lagrange)
	Château Durfort	Château Pontet-Canet
		Château de Terme
		Château de Candale (Issan)

The châteaux' current names, where different, are given in brackets.

The last important independent list before 1855 was that published in the second edition of *Traité sur les Vins du Médoc et les Autres Vins Rouges du Médoc et les Autres Vins Rouge du Département de la Gironde*, published in 1845. The author was Wilhelm Frank.

First Growths	*Third Growths*	*Fourth Growths*
Château Margaux	Château Desmirail	Château Talbot
Château Lafite	Château Dubignon-Talbot	Château Marquis d'Alesme
Château Latour	Château Ducru-Beaucaillou	Château Beychevelle
Château Haut-Brion	Château D'Issan	Château Calon-Ségur
	Château Brown	Château La Tour-Carnet
Second Growths	Château Lascases (later Cantenac-Brown and Boyd-Cantenac)	Château Duhart-Milon
	Château Poyferré	Château Dubignon, Margaux (since disappeared)
Château Brane-Cantenac	Château Barton Ganet, Cantenac (now part of Pouget)	Château Branaire
Château Cos d'Estournel	Château Giscours	Château Ferrière
Château Durfort-Vivens	Château Kirwan	Château Lafon-Rochet
Château Gruaud-Larose	Château Lagrange	Château La Lagune
Château Lascombes	Château Langoa	Château Clerc-Milon
Château Léoville:	Château Lanoire, Margaux (since disappeared)	Château Marquis de Terme
Château Mouton (Rothschild)	Château Montrose	Château Prieuré-Lichine
Château Pichon-Longueville	Château Pouget	Château Palmer
Château Rauzan	Château Malescot	Château St. Pierre Bontemps
		Château Dubarry

The 1855 Classification of Sauternes and Barsac

Château	Commune	Château	Commune
First Great Growth (Premier Grand Cru)		*Second Growths (Deuxièmes Crus)*	
Château d'Yquem	Sauternes	Château d'Arche	Sauternes
		Château Filhot	Sauternes
First Growths (Premiers Crus)		Château Lamothe	Sauternes
Château Guiraud	Sauternes	Château Myrat	Barsac
Château La Tour-Blanche	Bommes	Château Doisy-Védrines	Barsac
Château Lafaurie-Peyraguey	Bommes	Château Doisy-Daëne	Barsac
Château de Rayne-Vigneau	Bommes	Château Doisy-Dubroca	Barsac
Château Sigalas-Rabaud	Bommes	Château Suau	Barsac
Château Rabaud-Promis	Bommes	Château Broustet	Barsac
Clos Haut-Peyraguey	Bommes	Château Caillou	Barsac
Château Coutet	Barsac	Château Nairac	Barsac
Château Climens	Barsac	Château de Malle	Preignac
Château Suduiraut	Preignac	Château Romer	Preignac
Château Rieussec	Sauternes	Château Romer-du-Hayot	Preignac

The 1855 Classification of the Médoc

Château	Commune	Château	Commune
First Growths (Premiers Crus)		**Fifth Growths (Cinquièmes Crus)**	
Château Lafite	Pauillac	Château Pontet-Canet	Pauillac
Château Latour	Pauillac	Château Batailley	Pauillac
Château Mouton Rothschild	Pauillac	Château Grand-Puy-Lacoste	Pauillac
(declared a First Growth in 1973)		Château Grand-Puy-Ducasse	Pauillac
Château Margaux	Margaux	Château Haut-Batailley	Pauillac
Château Haut-Brion	Pessac	Château Lynch-Bages	Pauillac
	(Graves)	Château Lynch-Moussas	Pauillac
		Château Dauzac	Labarde-Margaux
Second Growths (Deuxièmes Crus)			
Château Rausan-Ségla	Margaux	Château Mouton-d'Armailhacq Pauillac	
Château Rauzan-Gassies	Margaux	(known as Mouton-Baron-Phillippe	
Château Léoville-Las Cases	Margaux	from 1956; as Mouton-	
Château Léoville-Barton	St.-Julien	Baronne-Philippe from 1975)	
Château Léoville-Poyferré	St.-Julien	Château du Tertre	Arsac-Margaux
Château Durfort-Vivens	Margaux		
Château Lascombes	Margaux	Château Haut-Bages-Libéral	Pauillac
Château Gruaud-Larose	St.-Julien	Château Pédesclaux	Pauillac
Château Brane-Cantenac	Cantenac-Margaux	Château Belgrave	St.-Laurent
		Château Camensac	St.-Laurent
Château Pichon-Longueville-Baron	Pauillac	Château Cos Labory	St.-Estèphe
Château Pichon Longueville	Pauillac	Château Clerc-Milon-Rothschild	Pauillac
Comtesse de Lalande		Château Croizet-Bages	Pauillac
Château Ducru-Beaucaillou	St.-Julien	Château Cantemerle	Macau
Château Cos d'Estournel	St.-Estèphe		
Château Montrose	St.-Estèphe		
Third Growths (Troisièmes Crus)			
Château Giscours	Labarde-Margaux	**Exceptional Growths (Crus Grands Bourgeois Exceptionnels)** *	
Château Kirwan	Cantenac-Margaux	Château Villegeorge	Avensan
		Château Angludet	Cantenac-Margaux
Château d'Issan	Cantenac-Margaux		
		Château Chasse-Spleen	Moulis
Château Lagrange	St.-Julien	Château Poujeaux-Theil	Moulis
Château Langoa	St.-Julien	Château La Couronne	Pauillac
Château Malescot-Saint-Exupéry	Margaux	Château Moulin-Riche	St.-Julien
Château Cantenac-Brown	Cantenac-Margaux	Château Bel-Air-Marquis d'Aligre	Soussans-Margaux
Château Palmer	Cantenac-Margaux		
Château La Lagune	Ludon	*It should be noted that Château Villegeorge was taken off the	
Château Desmirail	Margaux	list in 1973 when it was acquired by Lurton. The 1978	
Château Calon-Ségur	St.-Estèphe	Classification lists 18 properties as exceptional. These are	
Château Ferrière	Margaux		
Château Marquis-d'Alesme-Becker	Margaux	Château d'Agassac	Ludon
Château Boyd-Cantenac	Cantenac-Margaux	Château Andron-Blanquet	St-Estèphe
		Château Beausite	St-Estèphe
		Château Capbern	St-Estèphe
Fourth Growths (Quatrièmes Crus)		Château Caronne-Ste-Gemme	St-Laurent
Château Saint-Pierre-Bontemps	St.-Julien	Château Chasse-Spleen	Moulis
Saint-Pierre-Sevaistre		Château Cissac	Cissac
Château Branaire	St.-Julien	Château Citran	Avensan
Château Talbot	St.-Julien	Château Le Crock	St-Estèphe
Château Duhart-Milon-Rothschild	Pauillac	Château Dutruch-Grand-Poujeaux	Moulis
Château Pouget	Cantenac-Margaux	Château Fourcas-Dupré	Listrac
		Château Fourcas-Hosten	Listrac
Château La Tour-Carnet	St.-Laurent	Château du Glana	St.-Julien
Château Lafon-Rochet	St.-Estèphe	Château Haut-Marbuzet	St-Estèphe
Château Beychevelle	St.-Julien	Château Marbuzet	St-Estèphe
Château Prieuré-Lichine	Cantenac-Margaux	Château Meyney	St-Estèphe
		Château Phélan-Segur	St-Estèphe
Château Marquis-de-Terme	Margaux	Château Poujeaux	Moulis

The 1959 Classification of the Graves

Château	Commune	Château	Commune
Red Wines		**White Wines**	
Château Haut-Brion	Pessac	Château Bouscaut	Cadaujac
Château Bouscaut	Cadaujac	Château Carbonnieux	Léognan
Château Carbonnieux	Léognan	Domaine de Chevalier	Léognan
Domaine de Chevalier	Léognan	Château Couhins	Villenave-d'Ornon
Château de Fieuzal	Léognan		
Château Haut-Bailly	Léognan	Château La Tour-Martillac	Martillac
Château La Mission-Haut-Brion	Talence	Château Laville-Haut-Brion	Talence
Château Latour Haut-Brion	Talence	Château Malartic-Lagravière	Léognon
Château Latour-Martillac	Martillac	Château Olivier	Léognan
Château Malartic-Lagravière	Léognan	Château Haut-Brion	
Château Olivier	Léognan		
Château Pape-Clément	Pessac		
Château Smith-Haut-Lafitte	Martillac		

The 1985 Classification of St.-Emilion

First Great Growths (Premiers Grands Crus Classés)

Château Ausone
Château Cheval Blanc
Château Beauséjour-Duffau-Lagarosse
Château Belair
Château Canon
Château Figeac
Clos Fourtet
Château La Gaffelière
Château La Magdelaine
Château Pavie
Château Trottevieille

Great Growths (Grands Crus Classés)

Château l'Angélus
Château L'Arrosée
Château Balestard-La-Tonnelle
Château Beauséjour-Bécot (Demoted from being a
   Premier Grand Cru Classé in 1986)
Château Bellevue
Château Bergat
Château Berliquet
Château Cadet-Piola
Château Canon-la-Gaffelière
Château Cap-de-Mourlin
Château Chapelle Madeleine
Château-le-Châtelet
Château Chauvin
Château Corbin
Château Corbin-Michotte
Château Couvent-des-Jacobins
Château Croque-Michotte
Château Curé-Bon-La Madeleine
Château Dassault
Château Faurie-de-Souchard
Château Fonplégade
Château Fonroque
Château Franc-Mayne
Château Grand-Barrail-Lamarzelle-Figeac

Great Growths (Grands Crus Classés) continued

Château Grand-Corbin
Château Grand-Corbin-Despagne
Château Grand-Mayne
Château Grand-Pontet
Château Guadet-St.-Julien
Château Haut-Corbin
Clos des Jacobins
Château La Clotte
Château La Clusière
Château La Dominique
Clos La Madeleine
Château Lamarzelle
Château La Tour-Figeac
Château La Tour-du-Pin-Figeac
Château La Tour-du-Pin-Figeac-Moueix
Château Laniote
Château Larcis-Ducasse
Château Larmande
Château Laroze
Château La Serre
Château Le Prieuré
Château Matras
Château Mauvezin
Château Moulin du Cadet
Clos de l'Oratoire
Château Pavie-Decesse
Château Pavie-Macquin
Château Pavillon-Cadet
Château Petit-Faurie-de-Soutard
Château Ripeau
Château St.-Georges-Côte-Pavie
Clos St.-Martin
Château Sansonnet
Château Soutard
Château Tertre-Daugay
Château Trimoulet
Château Troplong-Mondot
Château Villemaurine
Château Yon-Figeac

The Grands Crus of Burgundy

Commune	Vineyard	Color	Commune	Vineyard	Color
Chablis	Blanchots	White	A.O.C. Corton Charlemagne	Le Rognet Corton	White
	Bougros	White	A.O.C. Corton	Le Rognet	Red
	Les Clos	White		Les Vergennes	Red
	Grenouilles	White	Aloxe-Corton	A.O.C. Corton	Red
	Les Preuses	White		A.O.C. Corton-Charlemagne	White
	Valmur	White		A.O.C. Corton Corton	
	Vaudésir	White		Les Carrières	Red
Gevrey Chambertin	Chambertin	Red		Le Corton	Red
	Chambertin Clos de Bèze	Red		Corton Clos des Meix	Red
	Chapelle-Chambertin	Red		Corton Clos du Roi	Red
	Charmes- Chambertin	Red		Corton La Vigne au Saint	Red
	Griotte-Chambertin	Red		Corton La Toppe au Vert	Red
	Latricières-Chambertin	Red		Corton Les Rénardes	Red
	Mazis-Chambertin	Red		Corton Le Rognet	Red
	Mazoyères-Chambertin	Red		Corton Les Bressandes	Red
	Ruchottes-Chambertin	Red		Corton Les Chaumes	Red
Morey St.-Denis	Bonnes Mares	Red		Corton Les Combes	Red
	Clos des Lambrays	Red		Corton Les Fiètres	Red
	Clos de la Roche	Red		Corton Les Grandes Lolières	Red
	Clos Saint.-Denis	Red		Corton Les Grèves	Red
	Clos de Tart	Red		Corton Les Languettes	Red
Chambolle-Musigny	Bonnes Mares	Red		Corton Les Maréchaudes	Red
	Musigny	Red		Corton Les Mourottes	Red
		and White		Corton Les Moutottes	Red
Vougeot	Clos de Vougeot	Red		Corton Les Pougets	Red
Flagey-Echezeaux	Echezeaux	Red		Corton Les Perrières	Red
	Grands Echezeaux	Red		Corton Les Paulands	Red
Vosne-Romanée	Richebourg	Red		Corton Les Vergennes	Red
	La Romanée	Red	Pernaund-Vergelesses	A.O.C. Corton Charlemagne	White
	Romanée-Conti	Red	Puligny-Montrachet	Bâtard-Montrachet	White
	Romanée-Saint-Vivant	Red		Bienvenues-Bâtard-	
	La Tâche	Red		Montrachet	White
Ladoix-Serrigny	A.O.C. Corton Charlemagne	White		Chevalier-Montrachet	White
	Les Basses Mourettes	White		Le Montrachet	White
	Les Hautes Mourettes	White	Chassagne-Montrachet	Bâtard-Montrachet	White
	Le Rognet-Corton	White		Criots-Bâtard-Montrachet	White
A.O.C. Corton Charlemagne	Les Basses Mourettes	White		Le Montrachet	White
	Les Hautes Mourettes	White			

The Grands Crus of Alsace

To gain the A.O.C. of Alsace *Grand Cru*, a wine must come from one of the vineyards listed below, and must have a minimum alcoholic content of 10 percent if Riesling or Muscat d'Alsace, or 11 percent if Gewürztraminer or Tokay Pinot Gris. The maximum yield is 70 hectoliters per hectare/4 tons per acre. Only the four grape varieties mentioned above are permitted.

*Some of the *Grand Cru* vineyards are awaiting final delimitation; these are marked in the following list with an asterisk.

Vineyard	Commune	Grapes
Steinklotz*	Marlenheim	All four
Engelberg*	Dahlenheim	All four
Altenberg de Bergbieten	Bergbieten	All four
Altenberg de Wolxheim*	Wolxheim	Riesling, Gewürztraminer
Bruderthal*	Molsheim	All four
Kirchberg de Barr	Barr	Gewürztraminer, Riesling, Tokay Pinot Gris
Zotzenberg*	Mittelberg-heim	Gewürztraminer, Riesling, Tokay Pinot Gris
Kastelberg	Andlau	Riesling
Wiebelsberg	Andlau	Riesling
Moenchberg*	Andlau and Eichhoffen	Riesling, Gewürztraminer
Muenchberg*	Nothalten	Riesling
Winzenberg*	Blienschwiller	Riesling, Gewürztraminer, Tokay Pinot Gris
Frankstein*	Dambach-la-Ville	Riesling, Gewürztraminer
Praelatenberg*	Orschwiller and Kintzheim	All four
Gloeckelberg	Rodern and Saint-Hippolyte	Tokay Pinot Gris, Gewürztraminer
Altenberg de Bergheim	Bergheim	Gewürztraminer, Riesling
Kanzlerberg	Bergheim	Tokay Pinot Gris, Riesling, Gewürztraminer
Geisberg	Ribeauvillé	Riesling
Kirchberg de Ribeauvillé	Ribeauvillé	All four
Osterberg*	Ribeauvillé	Riesling, Gewürztraminer, Tokay Pinot Gris
Rosacker	Hunawihr	Riesling, Gewürztraminer
Froehn*	Zellenberg	Gewürztraminer, Tokay Pinot Gris, Muscat
Schoenenbourg*	Riquewihr	Riesling, Muscat, Tokay Pinot Gris
Sporen*	Riquewihr	Gewürztraminer, Tokay Pinot Gris
Sonnenglanz	Beblenheim	Tokay Pinot Gris, Gewürztraminer
Mandelberg*	Mittelwihr	All four
Marckrain*	Bennwihr	Gewürztraminer, Tokay Pinot Gris
Mambourg*	Sigolsheim	All four
Furstentum*	Kientzheim and Sigolsheim	Riesling, Gewürztraminer, Tokay Pinot Gris
Schlossberg	Kaysersberg and Kientzheim	All four
Wineck-Schlossberg*	Katzenthal	Riesling, Gewürztraminer
Sommerberg	Niedermorschwihr and Katzenthal	All four
Florimont*	Ingersheim	All four
Brand	Turckheim	Riesling, Gewürztraminer, Tokay Pinot Gris
Hengst	Wintzenheim	Gewürztraminer, Tokay Pinot Gris, Riesling
Steingrubler*	Wettolsheim	Riesling, Gewürztraminer
Eichberg	Eguisheim	Riesling, Gewürztraminer, Tokay Pinot Gris
Pfersigberg*	Eguisheim	All four
Hatschbourg	Hattstatt and Voegtlinshoffen	All four
Goldert	Gueberschwihr	All four
Steinert*	Pfaffenheim	Gewürztraminer, Tokay Pinot Gris, Riesling
Vorbourg*	Rouffach and Westhalten	All four
Zinnkoepflé*	Soultzmatt and Westhalten	All four
Pfingstberg*	Orschwihr	All four
Spiegel	Bergholtz and Guebwiller	All four
Kessler	Guebwiller	Gewürztraminer, Tokay Pinot Gris, Riesling
Kitterlé	Guebwiller	Riesling Gewürztraminer Tokay Pinot Gris
Saering	Guebwiller	All four
Ollwiller	Wuenheim	Riesling, Gewürztraminer
Rangen	Thann and Vieux-Thann	Riesling, Tokay Pinot Gris, Gewürztraminer

The Denominazione di Origine Controllata e Garantita of Italy

D.O.C.G., Region	Color	Grapes
Albana di Romagna, Romagna	White	Albana
Barbaresco, Piedmont	Red	Nebbiolo
Barolo, Piedmont	Red	Nebbiolo
Brunello di Montalcino, Tuscany	Red	Sangiovese
Carmignano, Tuscany	Red	Sangiovese, Cabernet Sauvignon, Canaiolo Nero
Chianti Classico, Tuscany	Red	Sangiovese, Canaiolo Nero, Trebbiano Toscano and others
Chianti Colli Fiorentini, Tuscany	Red	Sangiovese, Canaiolo Nero, Trebbiano Toscano and others
Chianti Montalbano, Tuscany	Red	Sangiovese, Canaiolo Nero, Trebbiano Toscano and others
Chianti Rufina, Tuscany	Red	Sangiovese, Canaiolo Nero, Trebbiano Toscano and others
Chianti Colli Aretini, Tuscany	Red	Sangiovese, Canaiolo Nero, Trebbiano Toscano and others
Chianti Colli Senesi, Tuscany	Red	Sangiovese, Canaiolo Nero, Trebbiano Toscano and others
Chianti Colline Pisane, Tuscany	Red	Sangiovese, Canaiolo Nero, Trebbiano Toscano and others
Gattinara, Piedmont	Red	Nebbiolo, Bonarda
Torgiano, Umbria	Red	Sangiovese, Canaiolo Nero, Trebbiano Toscano and others
	White	Trebbiano Toscano, Grechetto, Malvasia and others
Vino Nobile di Montepulciano, Tuscany.	Red	Sangiovese, Canaiolo Nero, Malvasia and others.

The Approved Viticultural Areas of the U.S.A

A.V.A	State
Alexander Valley	California
Altus	Arkansas
Anderson Valley	California
Arkansas Mountain	Arkansas
Arroyo Grand Valley	California
Arroyo Seco	California
Atlas Peak	California
Augusta	Missouri
Bell Mountain	Texas
Ben Lomond Mountain	California
Benmore Valley	California
California Shenandoah Valley	California
Carmel Valley	California
Carneros	California
Catoctin	Maryland
Cayuga Lake	New York
Central Coast	California; includes A.V.A.s of Chalone, Santa Ynez Valley, Lime Kiln Valley, Carmel, Santa Maria, Livermore, Arroyo Seco, Edna Valley, York Mountain, Cienega Valley, Paso Robles, Paicines, Pacheco Pass and Monterey
Central Delaware Valley	Pennsylvania and New Jersey
Chalk Hill	California
Chalone	California
Cienega Valley	California
Clarksburg	California
Clear Lake	California
Cole Ranch	California
Columbia Valley	Washington and Oregon
Cumberland Valley	Maryland and Pennsylvania
Dry Creek Valley	California
Edna Valley	California
El Dorado	California
Escondido Valley	Texas
Fennville	Michigan
Fiddletown	California
Finger Lakes	New York; includes the A.V.A. of Cayuga Lake
Fredricksburg in the Texas Hill Country	Texas
Grand River Valley	Ohio
Grand Valley	Colorado
Guenoc Valley	California
The Hamptons, Long Island	New York
Hermann	Missouri
Howell Mountain	California
Hudson River Region	New York
Isle St. George	Ohio
Kanawha River Valley	Ohio and West Virginia
Knights Valley	California
Lake Erie	New York, Pennsylvania and Ohio; includes A.V.A.s of Grand River Valley and Isle St. George
Lake Michigan Shore	Michigan; includes A.V.A. of Fennville
Lancaster Valley	Pennsylvania
Leelanau Peninsula	Michigan
Lime Kiln Valley	California
Linganore	Maryland
Livermore Valley	California
Lodi	California
Loramie Creek	Ohio
Los Carneros	California
Madera	California
Martha's Vineyard	Massachusetts
McDowell Valley	California
Mendocino	California; includes A.V.A.s of Anderson Valley, Cole Ranch, McDowell Valley and Potter Valley
Merritt Island	California
Mesilla Valley	New Mexico and Texas
Middle Rio Grande Valley	New Mexico
Mimbres Valley	New Mexico
Mississippi Delta	Mississippi, Louisiana and Tennessee

A.V.A	State
Monterey	California
Monticello	Virginia
Mount Harlan	California
Mount Veeder	California
Napa Valley	California; includes A.V.A.s of Stag's Leap District and Howell Mountain
North Coast	California; includes A.V.A.s of Alexander Valley, Anderson Valley, Chalk Hill, Clear Lake, Cole Ranch, Dry Creek Valley, Guenoc Valley, Howell Mountain, Knights Valley, Carneros, McDowell Valley, Mendocino, Napa Valley, Northern Sonoma, Potter Valley, Russian River Valley, Solano-Green Valley, Sonoma-Green Valley, Sonoma Valley and Suisun Valley
North Fork of Long Island	New York
North Fork of Roanoke	Virginia
North Yuba	California
Northern Neck George Washington Birthplace	Virginia
Northern Sonoma	California; includes A.V.A.s of Alexander Valley, Chalk Hill, Dry Creek Valley, Knights Valley, Ohio River
Ohio River Valley	Indiana, Ohio, West Virginia and Kentucky
Old Mission Peninsula	Michigan
Ozark Highlands	Missouri
Ozark Mountain	Missouri, and Arkansas; includes A.V.A.s of Altus, Hermann and Ozark Highlands.
Pacheco Pass	California
Paicines	California
Paso Robles	California
Potter Valley	California
Rocky Knob	Virginia
Rogue Valley	Oregon
Russian River Valley	California; includes A.V.A. of Sonoma – Green Valley.
San Benito	California; includes A.V.A.s of Paicines, Cienega Valley and Lime Kiln Valley.
San Lucas	California
San Pasqual Valley	California
San Ysidro District	California
Santa Clara Valley	California
Santa Cruz Mountains	California
Santa Lucia Highlands	California
Santa Maria Valley	California
Santa Ynez Valley	California
Shenandoah Valley	Virginia and West Virginia
Sierra Foothills	California
Solano – Green Valley	California
Sonoita	Arizona
Sonoma Coast	California
Sonoma–Green Valley	California
Sonoma Mountain	California
Sonoma Valley	California; includes A.V.A.s of Temecula and San Pasqual Valley
South Coast	California
Southeastern New England	Connecticut, Rhode Island and Massachusetts
Stag's Leap District	California
Suisun Valley	California
Temecula	California
Texas Hill Country	Texas
Umpqua Valley	Oregon
Virginia's Eastern Shore	Virginia
Walla Walla Valley	Washington and Oregon
Warren Hills	New Jersey
Western Connecticut Highlands	Connecticut
Wild Horse Valley	California
Williamette Valley	Oregon
Willow Creek	California
Yakima Valley	Washington
York Mountain	California

The Minimum Oechsle Levels of Germany, Region by Region

Wine of all quality levels, from Tafelwein to Trockenbeerenauslese, can in theory be produced in all thirteen of Germany's wine regions. Each quality category requires minimum levels of ripeness, measured in degrees Oechsle, and these minimum Oechsle degrees vary according to the grape variety and the region. Minimum oechsle degrees for the three main white grape varieties of Germany, plus one red variety, are listed below.

Region	Grape Variety	Minimum Levels
Mosel-Saar-Ruwer, Ahr Mittelrhein	Riesling	Q.b.A: 51 Kabinett: 67 Spätlese: 76 Auslese: 83 Beerenauslese/Eiswein: 110 Trockenbeerenauslese: 150
	Müller-Thurgau, Silvaner, Spätburgunder	Q.b.A: 60 Kabinett: 73 Spätlese: 80 (Spätburgunder: 85) Auslese: 88 Beerenauslese/Eiswein: 110 Trockenbeerenauslese: 150
Rheinhessen, Rheinpfalz	Riesling	Q.b.A.: 60 Kabinett: 73 Spätlese: 85 Auslese: 92 Beerenauslese/Eiswein: 120 Trockenbeerenauslese: 150
	Müller-Thurgau, Silvaner	Q.b.A.: 62 Kabinett: 73 Spätlese: 85 Auslese: 95 Beerenauslese/Eiswein: 120 Trockenbeerenauslese: 150
	Spätburgunder	Q.b.A.: 62 Kabinett: 76 Spätlese: 90 Auslese: 95 Beerenauslese/Eiswein: 120 Trockenbeerenauslese: 150
Rheingau, Hessische Bergstrasse	Müller-Thurgau, Silvaner, Riesling	Q.b.A.: 57 Kabinett: 73 Spätlese: 85 Auslese: 100 (Riesling: 95) Beerenauslese/Eiswein: 125 Trockenbeerenauslese: 150
	Spätburgunder	Q.b.A.: 66 Kabinett: 80 Spätlese: 95 Auslese: 105 Beerenauslese/Eiswein: 125 Trockenbeerenauslese: 150
Württemberg (ex Bereiche Bayrischer Bodensee)	Riesling, Silvaner	Q.b.A.: 57 Kabinett: 72 Spätlese: 85 Auslese: 95 Beerenauslese/Eiswein: 124 Trockenbeerenauslese: 150
	Spätburgunder	Q.b.A.: 60 Kabinett: 75 Spätlese: 88 Auslese: 95 Beerenauslese/Eiswein: 124 Trockenbeerenauslese: 150
	Müller-Thurgau	Q.b.A.: 60 Kabinett: 78 Spätlese: 88 Auslese: 95 Beerenauslese/Eiswein: 124 Trockenbeerenauslese: 150
Franken	Riesling, Müller-Thurgau, Silvaner,	Q.b.A.: 60 Kabinett: 76 (Spätburgunder: 80) Spätlese: 85 (Spätburgunder: 90)
Franken	Spätburgunder	Auslese Beerenauslese/Eiswein: 125 Trockenbeerenauslese 150
Baden Bereiche Bodensee, Badisches Frankenland	Silvaner	Q.b.A: 63 Kabinett: 79 Spätlese: 88 Auslese: 101 Beerenauslese/Eiswein: 124 Trockenbeerenauslese: 150
	Müller-Thurgau	Q.b.A.: 63 Kabinett: 76 Spätlese: 85 Auslese: 98 Beerenauslese/Eiswein: 124 Trockenbeerenauslese: 150
	Riesling	Q.b.A.: 60 Kabinett: 76 Spätlese: 85 Auslese: 98 Beerenauslese/Eiswein: 124 Trockenbeerenauslese: 150
	Spätburgunder	Q.b.A.: 69 Kabinett: 82 Spätlese: 91 Auslese: 101 Beerenauslese/Eiswein: 124 Trockenbeerenauslese: 150
Other bereiche	Silvaner	Q.b.A: 66 Kabinett: 79 Spätlese: 92 Auslese: 105 Beerenauslese/Eiswein: 128 Trockenbeerenauslese: 154
	Müller-Thurgau	Q.b.A.: 66 Kabinett: 76 Spätlese: 89 Auslese: 102 Beerenauslese/Eiswein: 128 Trockenbeerenauslese: 154
	Riesling	Q.b.A.: 60 Kabinett: 76 Spätlese: 86 Auslese: 100 Beerenauslese/Eiswein: 128 Trockenbeerenauslese: 154
	Spätburgunder	Q.b.A.: 69 Kabinett: 85 Spätlese: 92 Auslese: 105 Beerenauslese/Eiswein: 128 Trockenbeerenauslese: 154
Saale-Unstrut and Sachsen/Elbe Valley	Riesling	Q.b.A.:57 Kabinett: 70 Spätlese: 76 Auslese: 88 Eiswein Beerenauslese: 110 Trockenbeerenauslese: 150
	Müller-Thurgau, Silvaner, Spätburgunder	Q.b.A.: 60 Kabinett: 73 Spätlese: 80 (Spätburgunder 85) Auslese: 95 Beerenauslese/Eiswein: 110 Trockenbeerenauslese: 150

The Winkler Scale of California

The Winkler Scale is a system of classifying wine growing regions according to their temperature. It was devised by Professors A.J. Winkler and Maynard Amerine at the University of California, Davis, in the 1930s; they used it to divide the winemaking map of California into five regions. It should be appreciated, however, that there are individual microclimates that may make a site an exception to the general rule.

The system is based on the concept of "heat summation". A vine is active above 10°C/50°F. The heat summation, measured in "degree days", for a particular spot is arrived at by taking the average temperature of each day between 1st April and 31st October (this being the vine's growing period), then subtracting 10°C/50°F for each day. For example, if the temperature from midnight to midnight varies between 6°C/61°F and 30°C/86°F, then the average temperature for that day is 23°C/73°F. Take away 10°C/50°F, and the heat summation for that day is 13 degree days if measuring in Centigrade, 23 degree days if measuring in Fahrenheit.

Region 1: 2,500 degree days or fewer. Includes Carneros, Santa Cruz Mountains, parts of Sonoma Valley, parts of Russian River Valley, parts of Anderson Valley, parts of Monterey. Recommended grape varieties include Riesling, Sauvignon Blanc, Chardonnay, Cabernet Sauvignon and Pinot Noir. Equivalent to France's Côte d'Or and Champagne, and to the vineyards of the Rhine in Germany.

Region 2: between 2,500 and 3,000 degree days. Includes parts of Alexander Valley, parts of Anderson Valley, Chalk Hill, parts of Edna Valley, parts of Mendocino, parts of Napa, parts of Sonoma. Recommended grape varieties include those recommended for Region 1. Equivalent to Bordeaux.

Region 3: between 3,000 and 3,500 degree days. Includes parts of Alexander Valley, parts of Monterey, the north of Napa Valley, Redwood Valley, San Benito, parts of Santa Clara. Equivalent to France's Rhône Valley. Recommended grapes include Carignan, Ruby Cabernet, Semillon, Sauvignon Blanc.

Region 4: between 3,500 and 4,000 degree days. Includes Lodi area of San Joaquin Valley. Recommended grapes: Barbera, Ruby Cabernet, Emerald Riesling, grapes for port-style wines. Equivalent to southern Spain.

Region 5: Over 4,000 degree days. Includes most of San Joaquin Valley. Recommended grapes include Verdelho, Souzão, Tinta Madera. Equivalent to North Africa.

Barrel Sizes

Cask or Barrel	Region Used	Capacity (liters/U.S. gallons)
Foudre	Alsace, France	No standard size, but large. Might be, for example, 1000/264.2
Pièce	Beaujolais, France	216/57.1
	Burgundy, France	228/60.2
	Loire, France	Around 220/58.1, but varies
	Vouvray, Loire, France	225/59.4
	Mâconnais, France	215/56.8
	Southern Rhône, France	225/59.4
	Champagne, France	205/54.2. Also known as Feuillette
Barrique	Bordeaux, France	225/59.4
Tonneau	Bordeaux, France	A figurative rather than an actual barrel.

Production figures are often quoted in tonneaux. One tonneau = four barriques or 900 liters/237.8 U.S. gallons

Queue	Burgundy, France	No barrels this size, but sales at the Hospices de Beaune auction are in queues; 456/120.5
Quartaut	Beaujolais, France	One-quarter Beaujolais pièce, or 54/14.3
	Bordeaux, France	One-quarter Bordeaux barrique, or 56/14.8
	Burgundy, France	One-quarter Burgundy pièce, or 57/15.1
Demi-barrique	Bordeaux, France	Half barrique, or 112/29.6
Feuillette	Beaujolais, France	Half Beaujolais pièce, or 108/28.5
	Burgundy, France	Half pièce, or 114/30.1
	Chablis, France	132/34.9
	Champagne, France	205/54.2 Also known as pièce
Demi-muid	Midi, France	Varies in size; could be 600/171.7
Fuder	Mosel, Germany	1,000/264.2
Stück	Rhine, Germany	1,200/317
Doppelstück	Rhine, Germany	2,400/634
Halbstück	Rhine, Germany	600/158.4
Viertelstück	Rhine, Germany	300/79.2
Hogshead	Australia and South Africa	295.3/78
	Madeira, Portugal	209/55.2 half Madeira *pipe,* or
	Marsala, Italy	209/55.2
	Port, Portugal	259/68.4
	Sherry, Spain	Half butt, or 245.4/64.8
	Tarragona, Spain	400/105.8
	Cognac, France	545.2/144
	Armagnac, France	272.6/72
Pipe	Madeira, Portugal	418/110.4
	Marsala, Italy	422.6/111.6
	Port, Portugal	Three different sizes: Douro *pipe* = 550/145.2 ; *lodge pipe* = around 600 / 158.4; shipping *pipe* = 534/141
Quarter cask	Port, Portugal	127.2/33.6
	Sherry, Spain	122.7/32.4
Butt	Sherry, Spain	490.7/129.6
Octave	Sherry, Spain	61.4/16.2
Aume	Alsace, France	114/30.1. Mainly for shipping
Ohm	Rhine, Germany	150/39.6. No longer used
Doppelohm	Rhine, Germany	300/79.2

Bottle Sizes

The standard bottle size is 75 centiliters/1 U.S. pint, 9 ounces. Other bottle sizes are listed below.

Region	Bottle	Capacity (liters/U.S. measurment
Jura, France	Clavelin	0.64/1 pint 6 ounces
Champagne, France	Split	Quarter bottle: .20/7 ounces
	Half bottle	.375/14 ounces
	Magnum	Two bottles: 1.5/3 pints 3 ounces
	Jeroboam	Four bottles: 3/6 pints 5 ounces
	Rehoboam	Six bottles: 4.5/1 gallon, 1 pint, 8 ounces
	Methuselah	Eight bottles: 6/1 gallon, 4 pints 11 ounces
	Salamanazar	Twelve bottles: 9/2 gallons, 3 pints
	Balthazar	Sixteen bottles: 12/3 gallons, 1 pint 6 ounces
	Nebuchadnezzar	Twenty bottles: 15/3 gallons, 7 pints 11 ounces
Bordeaux, France	Fillette	Half bottle: 0.375/12.68 ounces
	Magnum	Two bottles: 1.5/3 pints, 3 ounces
	Marie-Jeanne	Three bottles (no longer used): 2.25/4 pints 10 ounces
	Double magnum	Four bottles: 3/6 pints 5 ounces
	Jeroboam	Six bottles: 4.5/1 gallon, 1 pint 8 ounces
	Imperial	Eight bottles: 6/1 gallon 4 pints 11 ounces
Beaujolais, France	Pot	0.50/1 pint 1 ounce

Vintage Guide

Vintage guides are by their nature a rough rule of thumb. The well-tried system of Frank Prial, one of the co-editors of this book, has been adapted with this vintage guide. The system is twofold: a number rating for quality and a letter rating denoting drinkability.

The principal wine regions of the world have been covered, some of them with vintage details that have not appeared before in any comparable works of reference. Where records permit, the span of the chart reaches back to one of the great vintages of the century, 1945. Many of the contributors to the book have provided specialist advice on this chart and in this connection a few additional points about individual areas should be noted:

the **Champagne** and **Port** entries in the chart are based on the years in which a vintage was declared as is the practice in these two regions. Vintage information for wines of **Australia** should be seen in the light of the fact that in this country there are vast differences between wine regions and the broadly consistent weather conditions with less marked differences from year to year than is usual in Europe.

The **South Africa** vintage details go back to 1945 with the **proviso** that stocks of vintages prior to 1978 are virtually all in private hands and are thus rarely seen other than the odd bottle at auction. Until the 1970's noble white grape varieties which produce wines with staying power were unknown except Chenin

FRANCE/Red Wines	1990	1989	1988	1987	1986	1985	1984	1983	1982	1981	1980	1979	1978	1977	1976	1975	1974	1973	1972	1971	1970	1969	1968	1967	1966	1965
Bordeaux	9a	9a	8a	6c	8a	8b	4d	7c	8b	6c	4	7	9	4	6	6	3	6	2	6	8	3	1	6	9	1
Burgundy	9a	9a	9a	7c	6c	9c	4d	5c	6c	4c	5	7	8	4	7	1	2	6	7	9	6	9	3	7	6	1
Beaujolais	7c	7c	8c	6d	6d	8d	-	-	-	-	-	-	-	-	-	-	-	-	-	-	-	-	-	-	-	-
Rhône	9a	9a	9a	7c	7b	8b	6c	8b	6c	6c	4	7	10	4	7	6	3	6	6	9	7	9	-	8	7	1
FRANCE/White Wines																										
Alsace	9b	9b	8b	4c	7b	8c	5d	9c	5d	6c	5	7	3	-	9	7	-	5	-	9	8	9	-	7	9	-
Burgundy	8b	9b	7b	5c	7b	8b	6d	7c	6c	6c	-	7	8	-	7	4	3	5	3	8	6	7	-	5	5	-
Sauternes	9a	9a	9a	-	8b	6b	6c	8c	5d	7c	-	3	-	-	8	8	-	6	-	9	8	4	-	9	4	-
Vouvray/Anjou	9a	9a	9a	-	8b	7b	-	8c	5d	6c	-	-	-	-	8	8	-	6	-	9	-	-	-	8	-	-
Champagne	9a	9a	8a	5c	7b	8b	-	7c	9c	7c	-	7	6	-	7	7	-	8	-	8	7	7	-	-	8	-
ITALY																										
Piedmont	8a	10a	7a	6b	7b	10a	5a	6c	9b	5d	5d	6d	9c	5d	6d	-	8c	-	-	9c	8c	-	-	8c	-	-
Tuscany	10a	5b	10a	5c	8b	10b	3d	5b	8b	5d	5d	6d	7d	8	2	8	8	5	2	9	8	8	8	9	7	3
SPAIN																										
Rioja	7a	7b	6b	7c	6c	6c	4c	7c	10c	9c	6c	6c	5d	1d	6c	5d	4d	6c	1d	2d	10c	4d	8d	2d	6d	4d
Ribera del Duero	8a	6b	7b	7c	8c	8c	4c	6c	8c	9c	6c	-	-	-	-	-	-	-	-	-	-	-	-	-	-	-
Penedes	6b	6b	8c	4c	6c	4c	8c	6c	8c	8c	8c	-	-	-	-	-	-	-	-	-	-	-	-	-	-	-
PORTUGAL																										
Table Wine	7a	6b	9b	4c	5c	9c	5c	8c	9c	4c	10c	-	-	-	-	-	-	-	-	-	-	-	-	-	-	-
Vintage Port	-	-	-	8a	-	9a	-	9a	7a	-	8b	-	7b	10a	-	7c	7b	-	6c	-	9b	-	-	7c	9c	-
GERMANY																										
Mosel	7a	10a	8a	6c	7b	8b	5c	10c	6c	7c	5d	7d	5	4	10	9	4	8	-	9	7	7	-	6	4	-
Rhine	8a	9a	7a	6c	7b	9b	5a	9c	7c	7c	5a	8d	5	4	9	10	4	8	-	10	7	7	-	6	4	-
U.S.A.																										
California (Red)	7a	8a	7b	8b	7b	9b	7b	6c	5c	5c	7	5	7	6	6	7	8	6	7	6	9	7	8	-	8	-
California (White)	7a	7a	8b	9b	7c	9c	7b	7c	6c	6c	5	-	-	7	-	8	-	-	7	-	-	-	-	-	-	-
AUSTRALIA																										
Hunter Valley (Red)	8a	8a	7c	9a	8b	8b	4d	7c	8d	8b	7c	6	6	7	6	6	3	6	9	4	7	-	-	-	-	-
Hunter Valley (White)	6b	8b	7c	8c	9c	6c	8c	7c	7c	-	-	8	-	-	8	-	-	9	-	7	-	-	-	-	-	-
Barossa Valley (Red)	9a	8a	8a	7a	8b	7b	7c	7c	7c	6c	7c	6	5	7	7	6	-	-	-	9	8	-	-	-	-	-
Barossa Valley (White)	9a	8a	9a	9a	8b	7c	7c	-	9c	6c	6c	7	-	-	-	-	-	-	-	8	-	-	-	-	-	-
Margaret River (Red)	9a	8a	8b	8b	8c	7c	7c	6c	7c	7c	6c	8	7	3	7	6	4	8	1	-	-	-	-	-	-	-
Margaret River (White)	9a	8b	8b	8b	8c	7c	6c	6c	8c	7c	4c	-	-	-	-	-	-	-	-	-	-	-	-	-	-	-
NEW ZEALAND																										
Chardonnay	6b	9b	5c	7c	7c	6c	7c	8c	6d	6d	6d	5d	-	-	-	-	-	-	-	-	-	-	-	-	-	-
Sauvignon Blanc	4c	8c	7d	8d	8d	7d	8d	7d	7d	8d	6d	3d	-	-	-	-	-	-	-	-	-	-	-	-	-	-
Cabernet Sauvignon	6b	9b	5c	9b	7c	7c	6c	9c	7d	6d	7d	2d	-	-	-	-	-	-	-	-	-	-	-	-	-	-
SOUTH AFRICA																										
Cape Red Wines	8b	7b	7b	7c	7b	5d	8b	5c	6d	4d	6d	4d	7c	4d	3d	3d	8d	4	4	6	7	6	6	6	5	4
Cape White Wines	5b	5c	7c	5d	7c	6d	4d	4d	5	7	3	6	6	5	3	3	7	6	3	5	6	-	5	-	-	-

Blanc and a little Rhine Riesling. It should be noted that some of the "Natural Sweet" whites and botrytised whites will live longer than the chart indicates. In the past, too, the red varieties of Cabernet Sauvignon, Shiraz, Pinotage used to be blended together and in any case varied from micro-climate to micro-climate.

In the **United States** the wines rated are Californian ones of the North Coast viticultural regions in Napa, Sonoma, Mendocino and Lake Counties. This ignores some of the other fine wine-producing areas in the state but from year to year California's enormous variety of wine regions often produce wines that differ more in style than they do in quality.

Key to Ratings

Numbers: 1 (the worst) to 10 (the best). These numbers represent a wine's potential when fully mature.

Letters:
- A: Wine needs more bottle age
- B: Can be drunk now but would probably be better with more age
- C: Ready to drink
- D: May still be good but approach with caution
- –: You are unlikely to find this vintage/wine available

1964	1963	1962	1961	1960	1959	1958	1957	1956	1955	1954	1953	1952	1951	1950	1949	1948	1947	1946	1945	Exceptional Vintages pre 1945
6	1	7	10	5	9	–	3	–	8	–	9	7	–	4	9	7	8	–	10	1926 1928 1929 1934 1937 1943
4	1	7	7	–	9	–	4	–	5	–	5	7	–	–	9	5	8	–	9	1911 1915 1919 1923 1928
–	–	–	–	–	–	–	–	–	–	–	–	–	–	–	–	–	–	–	–	
9	–	7	7	4	9	–	6	–	7	–	7	7	–	–	7	–	7	–	7	1928 1929 1934
–	–	–	–	–	–	–	–	–	–	–	–	–	–	–	–	–	–	–	–	
4	–	7	7	–	8	–	–	–	–	–	–	–	–	–	–	–	–	–	–	1928 1929 1933 1934 1937 1942 1943
–	–	9	9	–	6	–	7	–	8	–	7	7	–	–	7	6	7	–	9	1919 1921 1928 1929 1934 1937 1942 1943
–	–	8	8	–	8	–	–	–	8	–	7	7	–	–	8	–	8	–	8	1921 1929 1934 1937
7	–	8	8	–	7	–	7	–	7	–	7	7	–	–	8	7	8	–	9	1914 1928 1937 1943
8c	–	–	9c	–	–	9d	–	–	–	–	–	–	–	–	–	–	10d	–	–	
9	2	8	8	2	7	9	6	2	9	7	2	6	9	2	9	8	9	2	8	
10d	–	–	–	–	–	–	–	–	–	–	–	–	–	–	–	–	–	–	–	
–	–	–	–	–	–	–	–	–	–	–	–	–	–	–	–	–	–	–	–	
–	–	–	–	–	–	–	–	–	–	–	–	–	–	–	–	–	–	–	–	
–	–	–	–	–	–	–	–	–	–	–	–	–	–	–	–	–	–	–	–	
–	10c	–	–	8c	–	8c	8c	–	9c	–	–	8c	–	8c	5d	10c	9c	5d	10c	1896 1900 1904 1912 1920 1924 1927 1934 1935
8	–	–	4	–	7	–	–	–	–	–	–	–	–	–	7	–	8	–	9	
8	–	–	3	–	8	–	–	–	–	–	–	–	–	–	7	–	8	–	9	
8	–	–	–	7	8	8	–	–	7	8	–	–	8	–	8	–	8	–	–	
–	–	–	–	–	–	–	–	–	–	–	–	–	–	–	–	–	–	–	–	
–	–	–	–	–	–	–	–	–	–	–	–	–	–	–	–	–	–	–	–	
–	–	–	–	–	–	–	–	–	–	–	–	–	–	–	–	–	–	–	–	
–	–	–	–	–	–	–	–	–	–	–	–	–	–	–	–	–	–	–	–	
–	–	–	–	–	–	–	–	–	–	–	–	–	–	–	–	–	–	–	–	
–	–	–	–	–	–	–	–	–	–	–	–	–	–	–	–	–	–	–	–	
–	–	–	–	–	–	–	–	–	–	–	–	–	–	–	–	–	–	–	–	
6	4	6	4	3	4	5	3	3	4	5	4	5	6	5	4	5	5	4	8	
–	–	–	–	–	–	–	–	–	–	–	–	–	–	–	–	–	–	–	–	

INDEX

W9-CHE-401